MAINSPRINGS OF
CIVILIZATION

ELLSWORTH HUNTINGTON, Yale University

New York — JOHN WILEY AND SONS, INC.

London — CHAPMAN AND HALL, LIMITED

To

E and G and C

Three Fellow Conspirators Who,
Each in a Special Way, Have
Done More than Their Bit
to Make This Book a Reality

PREFACE

This book is an attempt to analyze the role of biological inheritance and physical environment in influencing the course of history. It is part of a still larger plan which includes an interpretation of the main trends of history in the light of these two factors as well as of the cultural factor which is generally the main topic in histories of civilization. The book begins with the great unknown force which impels all kinds of evolution—physical, biological, cultural, spiritual. The objective of Part I is to gain an understanding of the continuity of the evolutionary process and of the way in which its earlier phases have prepared the way for the evolution of human culture and for its present flowering in civilization.

Part II deals with heredity. Its main thesis is that the truth lies between two common, but erroneous, viewpoints, namely, that of the "racists" who uphold the "Nordic myth" and the "Aryan" fallacy, and that of the many anthropologists who maintain that biological inheritance of mental traits has no cultural significance. A study of the selective action of migration, nomadism, religion, and other factors leads to one of the main features of the book—the concept of "kiths," or groups of people with a similar culture and language and with the custom of intermarriage. Their characteristics appear to depend on heredity as well as culture. Their effect on history seems to stand out conspicuously in such widely diverse types as the nomads of Arabia, the Parsis of India, the poetic people of Iceland, the New England Puritans, the Jews, Quakers, Junkers, Mongols, and many others. Careful study of the biological as well as cultural qualities of kiths would apparently illuminate almost all periods of history and might explain a surprising number of puzzling details.

Part III is devoted to a similar study of physical environment. The field is so immense that only a few major aspects can be treated at all fully. Climate, diet, and density of population, with all that they signify concerning disease, efficiency, mental alertness, and national character, receive most attention. Psychological reactions, as exemplified in religion, Indian nationalism, and Japanese belligerence, receive special attention. Physical factors, such as vegetation, seacoasts, and mountains, are also considered in their appropriate relationships, especially in a study of the geographic optima for outstanding periods of human progress. The stages selected for examination include the invention of agriculture, the great irrigation civilizations of Babylonia and Egypt, Greece in its prime, the Dark Ages when Ireland shone like an isolated light far on the western horizon, and the dawn of the Middle Ages.

Before these stages are discussed, there are several chapters on cycles, which comprise the most original portion of the book. If any parts excite controversy, it will probably be those devoted to the theory of kiths and this section about cycles. One hypothesis in this section seeks to explain an apparent association of atmospheric ozone with animal reproduction. Another is based on a seeming connection between business cycles and atmospheric electricity. The author is well aware that these new ideas need careful experimental testing. Even if they prove to be basically sound, they will inevitably have to be greatly modified. Nevertheless, even in their present preliminary form, they ought to stimulate wide discussion and investigation.

In a certain way this book is a résumé of the author's entire life-work, including what seem to him the most significant ideas in twenty-seven books and numerous articles. It is much more than that, however, for it attempts to summarize the best thought of many minds. In addition, it contains large sections which are entirely new.

Plans for this book were first laid almost a quarter of a century ago. Several times the writing was begun, but was interrupted and then taken up again *de novo*. One reason was that three times on a large scale and at other times on a small scale the material which was designed for a chapter proved so abundant and seemed so important that it was expanded beyond the limits allowable for a single topic in a book of this kind. Thus *The Character of Races, The Pulse of Progress, Season of Birth,* and, to a less degree, *After Three Centuries* are books which represent stages in the working out of the present volume. Each of these led to a recasting of the author's plan. Only a strong feeling that the long-projected work must be finished has prevented the writing of still another such preliminary book devoted to cycles.

In the writing of the present volume I have been peculiarly fortunate in the quality and enthusiasm of assistants, collaborators, and critics. Literally scores of persons are responsible for ideas which have so blended with mine that I cannot tell which is which, and may seem to claim the ideas of others as my own. If any such persons read this book, I hope they will be charitable. Certain others have helped so conspicuously that there is scarcely a page where some contribution from one or another of them fails to appear. Mr. Charles L. Ziegler worked for years, transcribing and interpreting literally millions of figures which form the basis of a large part of the statistical material on which many diagrams, tables, and verbal statements in this book are based. Mr. Edward R. Dewey of the Foundation for the Study of Cycles has freely given many days to criticising the chapters on cycles and preparing diagrams for them. Mr. Chapin Hoskins also gave to these chapters the benefit of his years of careful analysis of cycles in business.

The value of a great university as a place in which to carry on research needs no proof. One evidence of its worth is the many kindly colleagues who cheerfully answer difficult questions upon which the author himself might otherwise spend weeks of work. In so widely inclusive a book as this, such assistance has been of special importance and is hereby most gratefully acknowledged, although the names of the helpers are too numerous to mention. Similar gratitude is due to members of the library staff, whose unfailing readiness to help has been marked by a personal interest quite different from the perfunctory assistance which one sometimes gets elsewhere. It is no small convenience to be able to ask for some book which is to be found in only one American library, for example, and have it ferreted out and placed in your hands a few days later. Then, too, a great university has a remarkably fine group of hangers-on in the form of wives of graduate students who pay for their husbands' education by acting as secretaries. They do not stay long, unfortunately, but while they last they are the finest sort of assistants. Two of them have had much to do with this book. Mrs. Donald Muller has been a real collaborator. She brought to my attention many good points found in books which she read on her own initiative and in her own time in connection with chapters which I was writing. She and Mrs. William Hale both worked most assiduously in preparing the bibliography and diagrams of this book. They showed no sign of impatience even when they copied a chapter for the fifth time.

Other Yale contributions to this volume include statistics of stature furnished by Mr. William Deegan of the Gymnasium and estimates of the relative status of various religions by Professors Bainton, Latourette, Vieth, and Weigle. Professor Whitney Griswold has criticised the chapter on the Junkers, and Professor Theodore Crane has made valuable suggestions concerning several of the earlier chapters in the book.

Help in respect to specific problems or chapters has been received from many persons outside Yale University. These include, among others, Mr. George C. Simpson, Superintendent of Kew Observatory, Dr. A. J. Lotka of the Metropolitan Life Insurance Company and his associate, Mr. Paris R. Eastman; Professor Earnest Albert Hooton of Harvard University and his associates in anthropology; Mr. Walter G. Bowerman of the New York Life Insurance Company, and Dr. Irving Schell of the Blue Hill Observatory. My daughter, Anna S. Huntington, has been another helper, especially in the chapter on diet.

Finally, three friends have criticised the entire manuscript. My colleague, Professor Robert M. Yerkes, whose pioneer studies of the psychology of apes as well as of men are widely known, has read my "bird's-eye" view of civilization with what he calls a "worm's-eye" view—a view so penetrating and stimulating that it has entailed weeks of work upon the author. Professor Stephen S. Visher, who has been unexcelled as a persistent and friendly critic of my work, has dotted the pages of the manuscript with hundreds of small suggestions and a good many larger ones. The last of this trio is Professor Raymond H. Wheeler of the University of Kansas. His extraordinary knowledge of the details of history and his interest in the problem of climatic influences make him an unusually competent critic. To all of these and to all other helpers, known and unknown, including especially the three anonymous friends to whom the book is dedicated, I render hearty thanks.

E. H.

New Haven, January, 1945

ACKNOWLEDGMENTS

The author wishes to express his cordial thanks to the following for permission to reprint copyrighted material from the publications mentioned after their names:

American Association for the Advancement of Science: Articles by W. C. Allee and J. O. Perrine in *The Scientific Monthly*, vols. 56 and 58.

D. Appleton-Century Company: *I've Come a Long Way*, by Helene Kuo.

In Barbary, by E. A. Powell.

Ernest Benn Limited: *Denmark and Sweden, with Iceland and Finland*, preface by James Bryce.

H. H. Clayton: *Solar Relations to Weather*, by H. H. Clayton.

The John Day Company: *The Ageless Indies*, by Raymond Kennedy.

Dodd, Mead and Company: *In Search of Ireland*, by A. E. V. Morton.

Doubleday, Doran and Company: *Iceland*, by Vilhjalmur Stefansson.

Ecological Society of America: Article by V. E. Shelford and W. P. Flint in *Ecology*, vol. 24.

Encyclopædia Britannica: Brief quotations from several articles in the Fourteenth Edition of the Encyclopædia Britannica.

Harper and Brothers: *Dawn of a New Era*, by E. P. Cheyney, numerous quotations.

Harvard University Press: *New Types of Old Americans at Harvard*, by G. T. Bowles.

Paul B. Hoeber: *Nutrition and Physical Degeneration*, by W. A. Price.

Henry Holt and Company: *The Rise of Brandenburg-Prussia*, by S. B. Fay.

Geography of the Mediterranean Region, by Ellen S. Semple.

Houghton Mifflin Company: *Annals and Memoirs of the Court of Peking*, by E. Backhouse and J. O. P. Bland.

The Planters of the Commonwealth, by C. E. Banks.

Alfred A. Knopf: *The Racial Basis of Civilization*, by Frank S. Hankins.

The Macmillan Company: *Weather Influences,* by O. E. Dexter.

Jews in a Gentile World, ed. by I. Graeber and S. H. Britt (quotations from Coon and Jacobs).

The Chinese: Their History and Culture, by Kenneth Latourette.

Manchuria, Cradle of Conflict, by Owen Lattimore.

Nationalism, by Rabindranath Tagore.

The Royal Institute of International Affairs and the Oxford University Press: *A Study of History,* by A. J. Toynbee.

Princeton University Press: *Icelandic Poems and Stories,* ed. by Richard Beck.

Reynal and Hitchcock: *Man, Bread and Destiny,* by C. C. Furnas and Clifford Cook.

University of Pennsylvania: Privately printed thesis of A. H. Hobbs entitled *Differentials in Internal Migration.*

Yale University Press: *The Sealand of Ancient Arabia,* by R. P. Dougherty.

The Evolution of Earth and Man, article by Richard S. Lull.

CONTENTS

Part I

THE BACKGROUND OF CIVILIZATION

Part II

HEREDITY

Part III

PHYSICAL ENVIRONMENT AND HUMAN ACTIVITY

22. Diet and National Character 417
23. Agriculture, Disease, and Diet 432
24. Cycles, Rhythms, and Periodicities 453
25. Two Intriguing Cycles 477
26. Broader Aspects of Environmental Cycles . . . 508
27. Historic Phases of Climatic Cycles 529
28. Worldwide Climatic Cycles 548
29. Geographical Optima of Civilization 573
30. Ages of Darkness and Revival 591

      Bibliography 613
      Index 631

Note: *For a complete list of illustrations and tables see the following headings in the index: Diagrams, Maps, Tables.*

PART I

THE BACKGROUND OF CIVILIZATION

CHAPTER 1

THE SUPREME FACT

A. The Unity of Civilization

The course of history may be summed up in two main statements. First, for thousands of years civilization has been persistently advancing along certain definite lines. Second, the rate of march varies incessantly, both from time to time and place to place. As for the first statement, even the most backward people make some progress along lines like those followed by the most advanced. Tools tend to increase in number and complexity. There is a growing ability to utilize natural resources. Among primitive as well as advanced people, an increase in density of population leads to more complex forms of government and society. Everywhere new forms of speech develop in response to new ideas. Communication by means of pictures, signs, and finally letters tends to develop as people advance out of savagery.

Among diverse ethnic stocks and in widely separated regions the forward march takes place in much the same way, although at different rates. The general line of development in the Old World and the New has been essentially the same. Of course, fair comparisons are possible only between similar stages of progress and similar geographic regions. Such comparisons show that the main elements of culture are surprisingly similar among the savages of the Amazon Basin and of the lower forests of central Africa, among the Pueblo Indians and the villagers of Persia, among the advanced lowland cultures of the Mayas in Yucatan and of the Khmers in Indo-China. In like fashion the native civilizations on the plateaus of Peru and Mexico, on the one hand, and of Ethiopia, on the other, although seemingly unrelated, have much in common. The feudal systems of Japan and western Europe, although apparently of local origin, are curiously alike. Hundreds of comparisons of this same kind might be made.

Such similarities have aroused much controversy. Some anthropologists insist that they indicate transmission of ideas from region to region. Others feel sure that similar methods have sprung up independently in widely separate places. The majority maintain that after the original primitive migrations from Asia to America only an occasional cultural item was carried from the Old World to the New. Such more or less accidental transfers may explain why the signs of the zodiac are closely similar in Egypt and Yucatan. Nevertheless, there is little reason to think that the major features of civilization were thus carried. Man appears to be so constituted that, wherever the physical environment permits, he will in due time evolve such ideas as the raising of cereals, the taming of animals, irrigation, the construction of houses of mud, wood, or stone, the making of artificially smoothed paths, the smelting of metals, and the use of pictographs or letters.

A similar spontaneous development occurs along more abstract lines. As soon as families live in groups, a form of government is sure to arise. Its successive stages are similar all over the world. Practically everywhere, too, the mysteries of nature lead to a belief in unseen spirits, both good and bad, and in a life of some sort after death. Prayers and ceremonies to propitiate the spirits are almost universal. At certain cultural stages they tend to be associated with dances and sacrifices. In hundreds of other ways the general trend of progress seems to be similar in all continents and among all races. Quincy Wright [1],* expresses this well when he says that the biologist does not assume that resemblances in either the form or behavior of living things always indicate a common origin. The wing of the bird and the bat, the fin of the whale and the fish, the trapping behavior of the ant lion and worm lion are believed by zoologists to be independent developments. Such resemblances indicate a tendency for structures or traits of different origin to be similar because they are adapted to similar situations. The details, however, vary greatly, but such differences from place to place are of minor importance compared with the uniformity of the main tendencies. Today, more than

[1] p. 477.

* Footnotes such as this are used when a specific year, page, or additional name is needed to complete a reference. The rest of the reference, or the complete reference when no number accompanies a name, may be found in the bibliography at the end of this book.

ever, civilization tends toward control over nature, freedom of movement, and large social, economic, and political units.

It is difficult to give a precise definition of civilization, to fix the exact point at which human culture passes from barbarism to civilization. Nor is such definition necessary for the purposes of this book. Everyone recognizes that in some parts of the world the people are savages, whereas in others they have a low form of civilization. We ourselves claim to be highly civilized, but a thousand years hence our present methods of war, human exploitation, waste of precious resources, and lack of planned parenthood will doubtless be considered barbarous. In general it may be said that civilization begins when people learn to practice agriculture, live in permanent communities, establish a definite form of government, and acquire the art of writing. Civilization, however, is a process as well as a condition. It is the process of making people civilized. If civilization is a good thing, savages need the process so that they may possess the condition. We possess the condition, but need more of the process in order, for example, to get rid of war. In other words, although we live in a certain stage of civilization, there are innumerable stages below us and above us. It is hard to tell where they begin, and no man knows where they will end.

No adequate explanation of this supreme fact of history—this persistent forward march along a few main lines—is yet available. We cannot tell why civilization keeps forging ahead any more than we can tell why progressively higher types of animals evolved during the geological ages until man at last appeared. We can ascribe the development of civilization to the laws of God or to the immutable constitution of the universe, but this is little more than a confession of faith or of ignorance. We can say that it is part of the great process of evolution inherent in all nature but this is merely a fact and not an explanation. No one really understands why human tools, in the broader sense, have advanced from simple flints to elaborate ocean liners and why the social unit has expanded from the family to the International Labour Office.

B. Blind Alleys of Civilization

The inexorable forces which drive civilization forward seem to accomplish their full work only under special conditions. This is evident from the fact that many types of human culture fail to develop into true civilizations. They become blind alleys, as Toynbee has called them. The Eskimos, for example, show marvelous skill in maintaining themselves on cold, icy seacoasts. They seem, however, to have reached the limit of possible development unless they have help from outside their own physical environment. For centuries practically the only changes in their culture have arisen from contact with Europeans. The same condition is found among desert nomads. For thousands of years there has been little change in their habits except through such items as iron tools introduced from outside. They appear to have progressed as far as is possible without help from other types of culture. So, too, in pre-Columbian days the Haida Indians of the Queen Charlotte Islands off the coast of British Columbia developed a unique culture based on fishing in landlocked waters surrounded by forested, hilly land too cool for primitive agriculture. Their culture shows evidence of high inventiveness, but it apparently could make little additional advance without help from regions of broader opportunity.

Blind alleys of human culture usually occur in geographic environments which impose special difficulties. Some, to be sure, may be due to innate lack of mental ability, as perhaps was true of the extinct Tasmanians. In general, however, blind alleys are found in environments where only one highly specialized method of making a living is feasible except among people who bring an advanced civilization from some more favored region. If animals are the only available resource, especially if the animals must be followed from place to place, a large part of the activities which promote civilization are impossible. The Bedouins of the desert, because of the scarcity of water and grass, must follow their camels and sheep in frequent migrations. The Haidas used boats to follow the salmon. The inventions and discoveries made during the early stages of progress along a blind alley are quite as clever as those made by more advanced people in similar stages. They might serve as a foundation for further growth, if the physical environment were sufficiently rich in possibilities. Even if there are such possibilities, low mentality, inertia, disease, or the relative ease of life in a tropical climate may prevent people from having new ideas or putting them into execution. The lowlands of New Guinea appear to be such a region.

On the other hand, the Eskimos appear to be vigorous enough, but their cold home offers no incentive to agriculture. Wild berries and a few edible leaves or roots are not a sufficient basis for that art. Hence cultural evolution has little chance to deal with anything except animals. In similar fashion when desert nomads first began to

wander with camels and sheep, they made many clever inventions—
skin bags for milk, dried cheese that will keep for months, saddles,
woolen clothes and bags, tents that can be quickly struck and easily
carried, a patriarchal mode of government, and raids as a means of
overcoming the disasters of drought. These cultural items appear to
have reached practically their present form at least four thousand
years ago. Since then the desert nomads have been in frequent touch
with relatively high civilizations in the surrounding well-watered regions. Nevertheless, their type of culture has adopted only a few
minor items of civilized life. It cannot take more because outside
of the oases, or irrigated tracts, a poverty-stricken environment makes
it impossible to practice agriculture and unprofitable to erect great
buildings, develop industries, or live in cities. The Haidas, too, because of the impossibility of agriculture in their environment, could
not gain the cultural advantages which spring from ownership of
land, steady work in the fields, and forethought as to what shall be
done months hence about the ripening and storage of crops. All
these achievements are necessary, however, if industry, science, art,
literature, and government are to reach high levels.

Thus we see that cultural inventions which might lead to civilization make a promising start along many lines, but most of them
prove to be headed toward blind alleys. Only a few follow lines that
permit great progress. These few lead to civilizations such as those
of China, the Mayas, Persia, and western Europe, which at first sight
seem highly diverse. At equivalent stages, however, they are much
alike. Bishop seems to be right in saying that "the better known
civilizations, whether Babylonian, Egyptian, Assyrian, Indic, Homeric,
or Keltic, have all, without exception, like the Chinese civilization,
developed out of one and the same set of fundamental elements, discoveries, and inventions." As time goes on, these civilizations either
die out or converge still more toward a single standard type. This
type contains elements derived from many sources, but of late it has
taken most of its new characteristics from western Europe. Large cities all over the world are becoming more and more alike, and so are
the lives of the more intelligent people. To a less extent the life of
villages and farms also tends toward a standard type. Iron plows,
electric lights, buses, sewing machines, public schools, political parties,
newspapers, bath tubs, and gasoline engines are samples of the items
of modern civilization which are pushing out from the main centers.
A thousand years hence civilization will presumably be much closer
than now to a single standard type.

C. Growing Diversity of Human Culture

This does not mean that all parts of the world will become alike. Present tendencies point strongly in the opposite direction. In the future countries as diverse as Canada, France, Bulgaria, China, Venezuela, and Borneo will presumably all tend toward the same general type of civilization, but some will move rapidly, others slowly. Century by century the contrasts between one part of the world and another have been increasing. A thousand years ago even the most advanced people had no printed books. Today books can go everywhere, but Australian Blackfellows, remote Eskimos, half-naked Alacalufs in windy Tierra del Fuego, and wandering tribes in northeastern Siberia make practically no use of them. Printing has changed life enormously in the most advanced nations; it has scarcely touched the backward people of Sierra Leone; and it has had an intermediate effect upon countries such as India.

The same general principle applies to other inventions and discoveries. Consider the magnitude of the changes since 1900 in each of three countries. Let the United States stand for the most advanced type, Bulgaria for a fairly advanced middle type, and the Pygmies of central Africa for a very backward type. Since 1900 the number of motor vehicles in the United States has increased from practically none to one for every four or five people. In Bulgaria up to the outbreak of World War II the increase had been merely to one vehicle for more than a thousand people. Among the Pygmies there has been no increase at all. Intermediate people, such as the Chinese, occupy intermediate places with more cars than the Pygmies, less than the Bulgarians. Essentially the same situation prevails in respect to washing machines, radios, airplanes, tooth paste, shoes, strawberries, chocolate, or practically any other useful article or luxury.

Customs have likewise altered in similar fashion. For good or ill our marriage customs have changed so much that divorces are now several times as numerous as in 1900. Bulgaria has changed less in this respect, China still less, and the Pygmies not at all so far as we know. In dress the same thing appears. Our women's skirts have gone up to the knee; bathing suits have shrunk still more. Men often wear low-necked shirts and bright blue pants. Most of the Bulgarians still wear peasant costumes, although the rich and the city people follow our lead. The great mass of the Chinese have not altered their costumes, and at last reports the Pygmies wore as little as ever.

We aspire to universal equality of opportunity, a genuinely co-operative organization of all nations, and a type of education which will find out how each child can be psychologically adjusted to a changing world. A few Bulgarians are thinking about such things. So are some Chinese, but the proportion among the 450 million people of that country is smaller than among the 6 million of Bulgaria. Most of the Chinese and practically none of the Pygmies have ever heard of such ideas. Thus the most advanced nations change very rapidly; the moderately advanced, somewhat; the backward, only slightly; and the most backward, scarcely at all. As a result the different parts of the world are drawing farther and farther apart from decade to decade and century to century.

Many people fear that these rapid changes in the most advanced countries may lead to permanent decay. Sound judgment as to the future, however, must be based on the long past. The changes of thousands of years are far more significant than those of a century. Reasoning in this way, we may expect that for thousands of years civilization will continue to advance rapidly in some parts of the earth, less rapidly in others, and very slowly in still others. Thus the general contrast between one region and another will increase. We may also expect that in the most advanced countries civilization will ultimately involve an almost incredible control over nature and an improvement of economic, political, and social methods until they function as perfectly as the best motor car. We may reasonably hope that there will be less human suffering, more beauty and joy, and greater co-operation among nations as well as among men. Such a view is by no means blind optimism. It merely assumes that in the long run the evolution of civilization will follow the main trends of the past rather than the minor fluctuations of the present.

D. *Basic Factors in Variations of Civilization*

Let us turn now to the second of the main statements which sum up the course of history. In the future, as in the past, the march of civilization will doubtless vary constantly from period to period and from place to place. We know much more about the factors which control such variations than about the basic cause of the evolution of civilization.

These factors are the same for all forms of culture, even the most primitive. By culture we mean every object, habit, idea, institution, and mode of thought or action which man produces or creates and then passes on to others, especially to the next generation. When culture becomes so advanced that people practice agriculture, live in settled communities, have a definite form of government, and learn the rudiments of making records, the beginnings of civilization occur. The factors which cause variations in the rate at which culture and civilization advance include biological inheritance, physical environment, and cultural endowment. All three play a part in every human action. A primitive hunter, for example, teaches his boy to kill rabbits with small round stones. Biological inheritance gives both father and son good muscles and eyes and a brain which enables them to select the right stones and throw them hard and straight. If the boy inherits feeble-mindedness, badly shaped arms, or cross-eyes, he cannot hunt rabbits in this way no matter how well his father teaches him. Physical environment plays its part by providing stones of the right kind and grassy or bushy land where rabbits can find food and shelter. Cultural endowment is involved because the father teaches the boy how to choose stones, how to throw them, and how to approach the rabbit.

Among modern, sophisticated people, the interaction of biological inheritance, physical environment, and cultural endowment is more complex than among savages, but the principle is the same. A manager of a department store, for example, is dictating a difficult letter. The quality of the letter depends partly upon his inherited talents and his training. It depends also on his feelings. He may write a most unwise letter because of physical conditions, such as discomfort from his food or the heat in his room. Similar conditions may lead his stenographer to make stupid blunders. It is often said that civilization lessens the effect of physical environment. This statement needs modification. The effect is not so direct as among primitive people, but it is just as strong. The manager and his stenographer are working in a building where the walls, windows, and heating arrangements all show definite adaptations to local building materials and climate. They feel dull, work poorly, and perhaps go home early on a hot, muggy day but work splendidly when the air is cool and bracing. Their ability to work is influenced by food and recreation, which depend considerably upon climate, soil, and topography. A hurricane, heavy snow, or earthquake upsets their lives even more than it does those of savages. An insect pest or fungus in some far country may raise the prices which they pay for tires or chocolate candy. Thus physical environment has as great an effect upon them as upon the rabbit hunter. The difference is that they are affected by the environment in a wide range of places and through many indirect channels, such as transportation and the yield of crops in far countries, whereas the effect on the savages is direct.

Biological inheritance, physical environment, and cultural endowment have the same sort of relation to rabbit hunting or letter writing that food, drink, and air have to life. All are essential, and all play a part in every phase of activity. Any one of the three may acquire predominating importance under special circumstances, although it may not be of greater weight than the others in the long run. No matter whether a man is deprived of food, drink, or air, he dies. If the conditions of inheritance, environment, or endowment become bad enough, civilization will perish. History must, of course, devote more time to cultural matters than to biological inheritance or physical environment, just as the daily work of the world as a whole must be concerned especially with food. Nevertheless, the fact that cultural activities loom so large must not make us forget that they are dependent upon inheritance and environment. The main purpose of this book is to bring out the way in which variations in inheritance and physical environment are related to the growth of culture and the course of history.

E. Specific Events as Factors in Civilization

Historians disagree as to how far the growth of civilization depends upon a relentless law of evolution and how far upon the more or less accidental occurrence of specific events. One type of student magnifies the importance of relatively minor events, such as a battle, a famine, a treaty, or a meeting of kings. Another, such as Spengler, looks upon national cultures almost as living beings with distinct stages of birth, youth, maturity, old age, and death. The viewpoint advanced in this book may be illustrated by comparing the march of civilization to a great tide which moves steadily forward as a wide, flat wave. On top of the wave huge swells, due to a storm far out at sea, cause the water to rise and fall so much that the tide itself is not noticed until some time has elapsed. These swells correspond to the rise and fall of nations, and are due to the broad interplay of biological inheritance, physical environment, and cultural endowment. Smaller waves due to local winds may be so rough that away from the shore they cause the observer to overlook the long ground swell as well as the tide. Such waves correspond to specific historic events, such as wars, the achievements of great personalities, and financial crises. Upon these in turn are superposed small ripples which are analogous to minor events such as a congressional debate, a commercial treaty, a new machine, or a soul-stirring book.

Consider for a moment the degree of importance to be attached to specific historical events. A famine, a migration, the birth of a genius, a battle, the production of a new machine or a literary masterpiece—each of these alters the march of civilization to at least a slight degree. Each, to be sure, is only a minor incident in man's entire cultural development, but it does its part in advancing or retarding civilization or in changing its course. There can be no question as to the reality of this effect.

What we are concerned with, however, is the ultimate effect of thousands of such events. If certain historical events had never occurred, would others have taken place in such a way that today civilization in general would be essentially the same as it actually is? The emphatic no with which we first answer this question is modified when we consider long periods of time and remember that other, perhaps similar, events would have occurred if the actual events had never taken place. If Darwin had not developed the theory of evolution, Wallace or others would doubtless have done so because of the general progress of science. If Richard the Lionhearted had never lived, the king who replaced him might not have taxed his people for a ransom, but would the world wars of our century have been different? Or suppose there had been no Lincoln. America would certainly be different today. Some unwise, selfish leader might have arisen; the South might have won the war; there might be two nations instead of a single United States of America. Thousands of Americans might be a little more selfish and harsh if they had never stood reverently in the Lincoln Memorial at Washington and read those grand words: "With malice toward none; with charity for all; with firmness in the right as God gives us to see the right, let us strive on to finish the work we are in; . . . to do all which may achieve and cherish a just and lasting peace among ourselves and with all nations." But in spite of all this, would slavery still persist in America? The chances are strongly against it. Economic pressure and the general progress of moral judgment would probably have ended it. Would there be two nations instead of one? Perhaps, but we may feel reasonably confident that strong forces would be tending toward unity.

The Crusades illustrate the same point more clearly. Their consequences are rightly said to be still with us. The Crusades introduced the West to the learning of the East and paved the way for the Renaissance. They had strong repercussions upon the political and economic life of both western Europe and the Occident. We might talk profitably about their effect for page after page. But suppose they had never occurred. Would other conditions have brought East and West together a little later? Would there have been a renaissance for other reasons? Would the progress of civilization have been accelerated if the waste of life and treasure involved in the Crusades had not occurred? No one can answer those questions with certainty, nor can anyone say how far our present civilization would be different if there had been no Crusades. This does not minimize the importance of the Crusades, but it suggests that in the long evolution of civilization they were no more than a great storm wave upon the back of a tide.

World War I and the Russian Revolution of 1917 form another wave of the same kind. Their repercussions still reverberate, as they will for a long time. Nevertheless, some phases of their effect have already disappeared; others are fading out or being neutralized in such ways as are illustrated in Figure 1. The heavier dashed line shows what happened to American meat. During the war exports rose to nearly ten times their previous level. Then a gradual decline brought them down to the prewar level about 1930. Thereafter they diminished still more until the level was practically what would have been expected on the basis of what was happening before the war began. The essential point is that the general trend of exports from the United States is controlled by forces more durable than world wars. It depends on the number of people and cattle in the United States and elsewhere, upon standards of living and general prosperity, upon changes in transportation, and many other factors. A world war alters many of these conditions temporarily, but when it is over, exports of various kinds ultimately became stabilized at approximately the level determined by pre-existing causes.

The curve for Russian coal in Figure 1 teaches the same lesson as the one for American meat. When World War I broke out, the Russians were rapidly increasing their consumption of coal because they were establishing new industries. The war and the revolution had almost destroyed production by 1920. Then came a rapid recovery which Soviet leaders loudly ascribed to their five-year plans. The motivating force, however, was not the energy of the planners, but a natural rebound from an abnormally low level. The planners were merely agents in the same way that the American packers were agents in a ten-fold increase in meat exports from 1914 to 1918. Nevertheless, the action of the Russians should not be disparaged. Their Herculean efforts helped in bringing coal production to a level even higher than would have been expected from the prewar record. Therefore, the solid line for Russia in Figure 1 crosses the dashed lines, which show what might have been expected on the basis of prewar progress. Consumers' goods, however, such as sugar, cloth, and

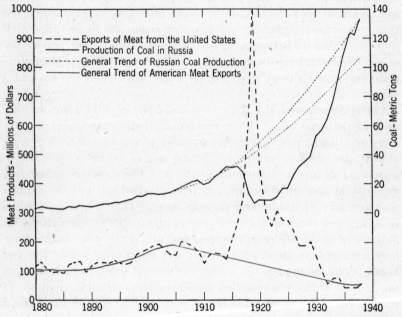

Figure 1. Coal Production in Russia and Meat Exports from the United States, 1880–1938.

shoes, did not recover so rapidly. Hence when Russia was again plunged into war in 1941 the total industrial production was apparently not much different from what it would presumably have been if there had been no previous world war and revolution.

Figure 1 also illustrates the fact that historical accidents, if such we may call them, often cancel one another. One curve goes up when another goes down. Historical accidents occur by the thousand. Some alter civilization in one way, some in another. The net result might be no changes unless some sort of evolutionary force leads to new conditions that have a trend in some definite direction. In Russia, for example, the second world war is likely to undo some of the special changes arising from the first. The net result will presumably be that in the end Russia will have moved in the general direction toward which the forces of evolution are tending.

It is hard to accept the idea that events such as the Russian Revolution are incidents rather than fundamental causes. Many economists and historians violently dispute this viewpoint. Nevertheless, such a conclusion is supported by hundreds of curves like those of Figure 1 and by the history of practically every nation. A similar sudden upheaval and gradual return to normal occurred during and after the American Civil War. It always occurs along some lines in any great crisis. There is a certain stability about the process of national development which cannot be easily overcome. The United States witnessed this stability in 1933 when the gold in the dollar was reduced by more than one third. Economists almost unanimously believed that a great rise of prices would ensue, but nothing of the kind occurred.

To take another example, for centuries the Turks persecuted the Armenians. Sometimes, as in 1895–96, terrible massacres took place. Then in 1908 a new constitution wiped out religious distinctions and gave all citizens equal rights. Turks and Armenians embraced one another in the streets and wept for joy. Henceforth, they were going to live in brotherly love. Greeks and Turks were similarly swept by a wave of good fellowship. Only a year later the Turks perpetrated a massacre in which some twenty thousand Armenians were killed in the Adana region. During World War I hundreds of thousands of Armenians were slaughtered or driven from their homes into the desert. After the war one and a half million Greeks were forced to migrate from Asia Minor to Greece. A new constitution was no match for the mighty force of differences in race, language, customs, religion, and aptitude for getting on in the world. Nevertheless, within a single generation the spread of new ideas has caused the vast majority of Turks to look upon those sad days of massacre as a temporary reversion to barbarism which they will never again permit.

The same general principle applies throughout the whole evolution of human culture and civilization. The general march of progress is directed by deep-seated forces which are only dimly understood. Less powerful forces may alter the general march temporarily. They may produce long periods of stagnation, such as the Dark Ages, or violent crises like our two modern world wars. The effect of such interruptions of the general evolutionary process may last a long time. Nevertheless, they are of secondary importance compared with the basic evolutionary urge which is the supreme fact of history. It is beyond the scope of this book to discuss the philosophical problem of whether life and especially civilization are directed toward definite goals by forces beyond the known physical laws. Our discussion is based simply on the fact that *Homo sapiens* is the most advanced product of organic evolution, and modern civilization the most advanced product of human progress. Neither man himself nor his civilization is necessarily the main objective of evolution, even if there is such an objective. Both may conceivably be vanquished by more lowly forms, such as insects and their extraordinary communal life, or by some new form of life with a better brain than ours. Nevertheless, man and his civilization may fairly be considered the supreme products yet achieved by evolution.

F. A Metaphor of Civilization and Motorcars

A metaphor will perhaps clarify our idea of the mutual relationships between the main evolutionary trend and the three great factors of biological inheritance, physical environment, and cultural endowment. Our understanding of civilization resembles the comprehension of motoring possessed by people who do not realize that the explosion of gas makes the wheels go around and who have only vague knowledge as to the location of the city toward which they are headed. The motive force of civilization is still imperfectly known, as is the type of civilization toward which we are moving. The variations in the rate of human progress from region to region and century to century, however, can be understood more readily. Just as the windings of the motorist's road are influenced by mountains and rivers, so the march of civilization is influenced by man's physical environment as a whole. On the other hand, the sharpness of the curves, the smoothness of the roadbed, and the steepness of the grades are cultural qualities. They depend on man's work and correspond to the cultural background against which historic events take place. Finally, the element of biological endowment is represented by the character of the motorist, on the one hand, and of the people in any historic epoch, on the other. Thus, the course of the car depends on (1) the general direction of the road; (2) its curves and grades; (3) the quality of the road; and (4) the quality of the driver—that is, upon all four of our factors.

Let us consider our metaphor again in relation to the evolution of civilization. Irregularities in the road, which in some places become holes, bumps, or stones, oblige the driver to keep the steering wheel in constant motion, and the car makes many little windings although it sticks to the road. Such windings correspond to the minor events of history. A major historical event, such as the Crusades or the French Revolution, corresponds to washouts which necessitate long and often difficult detours. A thoroughgoing bit of sudden sabotage, such as the wars of Napoleon or Hitler, may stop progress completely for a while and necessitate the rapid extemporization of a long and difficult detour. Nevertheless, such happenings have no effect upon the general direction of the road or upon the big curves due to the topography. Of course, not all the new developments result in delays. The banking of a curve may diminish accidents and increase speed. This corresponds to some new discovery, such as a new motor fuel. A great event, such as the introduction of machinery run by steam, corresponds to a long cut-off with a tunnel, whereby miles of winding road are replaced by a smooth, high-speed highway.

It often happens that drivers take the wrong turn at a fork. Sometimes it is easy to get back onto the main highway, but the mistake may not be discovered until the road peters out among the hills. Such events are comparable to forms of culture which follow blind alleys, in the way exemplified by nomadic camelmen. On the highway, as in the march of civilization, the course of each individual unit, whether it be car or nation, differs in detail and in speed from that of every other. No two cars, even on the smoothest road, follow precisely the same track at precisely the same rate for more than a short distance. The main course of every car, like that of every nation, is guided by the original plan of the highway unless the wrong turn is taken. When that happens, the rate of progress diminishes and the goal is not reached. The course of the road follows drawings made by engineers, and that of civilization follows the immutable constitution of the universe. No car and no nation can ever go any great distance independently of the geographic environment, but everywhere each of them can move faster and more safely in proportion to the degree to which man's cultural achievements overcome the difficulties imposed by nature. And, finally, the ultimate fate of each car and each nation depends on the quality of the people concerned.

CHAPTER 2

THE BACKGROUND OF CIVILIZATION

A. Physical Uniqueness of the Earth

In the past it was commonly held that the earth and its plants and animals were created for the express purpose of providing a suitable home for man and hence for his civilization. At the opposite extreme stands the view that the advent of man and the growth of civilization are the fortuitous result of innumerable accidents, which by mere chance have tended in a certain direction. The viewpoint suggested in Chapter 1 stands between these two extremes. According to it, the universe is so constituted that, if the physical evolution of inanimate matter reaches a certain state and remains there long enough, life can and presumably will appear. If appropriate conditions, both physical and biological, prevail over another long period, biological evolution will at length produce a being in whom reason triumphs over instinct. At that point cultural evolution begins. Its continued upward development depends on the right combination of physical environment and biological inheritance, together with cultural inventions which lead toward progress along the main line rather than blind alleys. In order to emphasize the continuity of the evolutionary process and the interdependence of the physical, biological, and cultural factors by which it is modified, a few main features of the earth's physical constitution and the biological evolution which preceded the first steps in human culture will be briefly considered in this chapter.

From a physical standpoint the earth must be almost, if not absolutely, unique. One feature of this uniqueness is that for two thousand million years, more or less, the temperature of its surface has remained almost constant. Many readers will question this. Has not the earth's temperature been repeatedly and profoundly altered by glacial periods? Yes, but although the changes of temperature during a glacial period seem to us great, they are trivial when measured on a cosmic scale. What is 20°C compared with 1,000,000°? Few geologists believe that the average temperature of the earth's surface at

16

the height of the most severe glacial epoch was as much as 20°C lower than during the warmest interglacial epoch. How great is such a difference compared with the range of temperature experienced in the universe as a whole or even in the solar system? The main part of the universe consists of hot, shining stars or else of cold, non-luminous matter in the form of dead stars, planets, meteorites, comets, and the scattered molecules of gas which presumably cause the black patches in the sky where no stars are visible even with the strongest telescope. The surface temperature of the millions of shining stars ranges from 3,000° to 30,000°C or more. Their interior is supposed to reach at least 30,000,000° in a star like the sun and perhaps 100,000,000° in others. By far the greater part of the matter that is not self-luminous has a surface temperature close to absolute zero, which is −273°C. In other words, it has become as cold as possible. Only an insignificant fraction of all the matter in the universe—only one part in many millions—has a temperature intermediate between the low level of almost absolute zero and the relatively high level of incandescence. Such an intermediate temperature can be maintained for a long time only on a body which combines many special features of size, atmosphere, and distance from its sun.

Consider for a moment the magnitude of the differences in temperature on the earth when measured on a cosmic scale. Suppose that the range from the absolute zero to 1,000,000°C is represented by the 12,000 leaves of paper which form the entire *Encylopædia Britannica*. To get paper thin enough to represent 20°, a leaf would have to be shaved into four sheets, each as thin as gossamer. Even if we take the maximum and minimum temperatures on the earth's entire surface during the whole period since life first appeared, the range is probably not more than 150°C. That is only one part in more than 4,000 or possibly 400,000 of the range of temperature in the universe as a whole. On the Fahrenheit scale it is equivalent to 270°, or from 100° below zero to 170° above. The fact that life has persisted from pre-Cambrian times onward, with no interruption so far as paleontologists can determine, makes us certain that with minor local exceptions temperatures significantly beyond these limits have not occurred on the earth for a billion years. Only a few years, or at most a few hundred, with temperatures everywhere below freezing or above the boiling point of water would presumably destroy all life.

This prolonged uniformity of temperature becomes still more remarkable when we note that it occurs at the most critical of all levels from the standpoint of chemistry. Water, at least in minute amounts, is essential for the majority of chemical reactions. For example, unless a little water is present, chlorine and sodium will not combine into common salt even if the sodium is heated to melting. Absolutely dry air and charcoal, even when red hot, will not burn with a flame and will form only carbon monoxide instead of carbon dioxide. In the absence of water the boiling point of mercury is 420°C instead of 358°. Only minute amounts of water are needed to cause almost innumerable important differences of this sort. Certain mixtures of gases, when perfectly dry, will not react chemically even when an electric spark passes through them. The entrance, however, of a single bubble of ordinary air with its moisture leads to a violent explosion when the next spark passes through. The whole field of organic chemistry is limited to temperatures at which liquid water is available.

Life in any form of which we have the slightest inkling is possible only at temperatures between the freezing and the boiling points of water—zero and 100°C. At no other temperatures can oxygen, nitrogen, carbon, hydrogen, and sometimes sulphur and phosphorus unite into the huge and highly complex molecules of protoplasm. Such molecules are the only ones that can create new molecules of their own kind. They alone have the power to cluster together and put walls around themselves, thus forming cells which have the marvelous power to divide into new cells. A single cell may give off new cells which ultimately develop into either hard white teeth or soft pink gums. It is conceivable, to be sure, that creatures with the power of reasoning may exist at temperatures which do not permit water to be liquid, but it is hard to find a physical basis for such a supposition. One can imagine some form of life at temperatures so high that the molecules are broken into their constituent atoms, but, search as we will, we find no shred of evidence that there is any foundation for such conjectures.

The amazing uniformity of the temperature which the earth has maintained for a thousand million years is emphasized by certain peculiar qualities of water. Perhaps it might be said that water has been endowed with these qualities for the express purpose of maintaining an environment fit for life. Without attempting to solve the philosophical problem thus presented, we can point out that water has a unique ability to maintain an even temperature. This is due partly to the slow rate at which water becomes either warm or cool and partly to its high demands for latent heat when it passes from ice to water or from water to vapor. Latent heat is energy that can be absorbed without causing any change of temperature. When water is evaporated, no matter what the temperature, it uses up far more heat than would be needed to raise the temperature of the same amount of water 1°F. That is why a puff of wind cools the skin. Vaporization at the boiling point (100°C) takes 540 of the heat units needed to raise the temperature of water 1°. On the other hand, when water freezes, it gives up 80 units of latent heat. Therefore, freezing checks the cooling of the surrounding air, just as evaporation checks a rise in temperature. Thus an abundance of water tends to prevent the temperature from falling below freezing or rising above the evaporation point. In this way water has a remarkably strong tendency to hold the temperature within the narrow zone where life is possible.

Another unique quality helps to maintain a large supply of water in liquid form on the earth's surface and in the air. Most liquids contract as they become cooler. They contract still more on solidifying, so that the solid part sinks. As water cools, on the contrary, it contracts only until a temperature of 39°F is reached, and then it expands. If it contracted like other substances, ice would accumulate at the bottom of bodies of water which freeze in winter. Ponds, lakes, and the ocean from middle latitudes poleward would consist of masses of solid ice topped with a layer of cold water in summer. Ice from the glacial period would still clog the ocean depths far toward the equator. Ocean currents could not carry tropical warmth poleward as they do now. Contrasts of temperature between high and low latitudes would be much greater than at present, and winds would be correspondingly violent. Other changes would occur also. The evolution of life would presumably have taken a course quite different from that actually followed, and man might never have appeared.

Free oxygen, as well as water, is necessary to life as we know it. These two substances can apparently be found together only on a planet having about the size, the speed of rotation and the temperature of the earth. Such a combination is extremely rare. It was formerly supposed that many stars must have planets similar to the earth. The theory now generally accepted is that planets are formed only when two stars come close together but do not collide. Under such circumstances an enormous tide is raised on both the near and the far sides of each star. If either of the stars is of the right size and in the right stage of development, its tides may become so huge that they break, as it were, and a great jet of matter streams out on each side. The star's own gravitation prevents part or all of this material from following the other star, but the speed of the jets sometimes prevents their falling back into their own star. If this happens, the material circles around the star and gradually coalesces into planets. This statement sounds as though planets might be numerous, but the stars are so far apart that, according to Shapley, there is only about one chance in something like a million that any given star, even though it lives billions of years, will come near enough to another to produce planets. Shapley estimates that among the millions of stars in our galaxy only one system of planets appears likely to be formed in about 6,000 million years, a period which is probably two or three times as long as that since the earth was formed.

Even if such a system came into existence, the chances that it would include a planet fitted for life are small. At least ten factors must be right if life is to be possible. These include the planet's size, density, distance from the sun, shape of orbit, speed of rotation, length of day, and degree of cooling, together with the size and stage of development of the central sun and the degree to which its radiation varies from one period to another. A planet like Jupiter, which is too large, may be so warm internally that water cannot stand on its surface. It may have an atmosphere so dense and so varied in composition that there is no free oxygen and no light can penetrate to the surface. Too small a planet may completely lose its atmosphere and thus have no water or free oxygen, as has happened on the moon and almost happened on Mars. A planet as far away as Neptune, 2,800 million miles, sees the sun as an object not much bigger than a star and never gets heat enough to raise the temperature anywhere near the melting point of ice. When the sun shines on a planet close at hand, like Mercury, only 36 million miles away, the surface must become far too hot to permit the existence of protoplasm.

A simple illustration will show how greatly a slight change from the present status would alter the conditions of life. Suppose the earth were just as it is except for the differences that would arise if the length of the day were a month instead of twenty-four hours. Everywhere the contrast between day and night would be enormously increased. Even at the equator a night of two weeks would mean a period of hard frost every month. During the long day, on the contrary, the temperature would soar tremendously and might be fatal to all life. Shifting winds of unexampled violence would blow from the cold areas of night to the hot areas of day. Perhaps plants and animals might have evolved on such an earth, but they would certainly be radically different from those known to us. If one relatively small change can make so great a difference, the present balance among the environmental factors in which life has evolved could evidently be upset very easily. Any one of thousands of possible differences in the ten factors mentioned above, as well as in various others, would make a planet impossible as the abode of life. Hence if there is only one chance of the development of a planetary system in 6,000 million years, there can scarcely be more than one chance that in 6,000,000 million years a planet fitted for life will evolve. The chances that such a planet will continue to be fit for life during 1,000 million years must be far less. The "fitness of the environment" for life, to quote the title of a significant little book by Lawrence J. Henderson, is one of the outstanding facts of science. To say, then, that an earth fit for civilization is a rarity is certainly no exaggeration.

B. Early Biological Preparation

The biological as well as the physical conditions under which civilization is possible are almost, if not quite, unique. They have reached their present stage through a long series of steps which have left their imprint upon human physiology as well as human culture. We have seen the supreme chemical and biological importance of water. A natural consequence of this is that life must have begun in water, as practically all biologists agree. Hundreds of millions of years have elapsed since plants and animals gradually emerged from the ocean. Nevertheless, the mark of the ocean is still strong on every living thing. Protoplasm cannot exist except as part of a semi fluid mass in which the fluid portion is much like sea water. The degree of concentration varies, but there must be the equivalent of about fifty parts of sodium chloride (common salt) for one part of calcium chloride. Other compounds containing sulphur, magnesium, potassium, silicon, aluminum, phosphorus, and iron are present in proportions which show much the same range of variations as in sea water. It would seem, then, that a large part of the modern science of nutrition is built up around the need of our bodies for salts nearly like those of the sea water from which our ancestors emerged untold ages ago.

Other great steps in evolution, as Huxley has well shown, are connected with other phases of physical environment. The development of a strong but flexible backbone is one of the chief of these. Such a spine is not of much use in developing civilization unless its owner emerges from the water. In water, but not on land, a spineless invertebrate may attain great size. Giant squids have been found with a stretch of 52 feet from tip to tip of their snaky, sucker-studded tentacles. On land, however, no invertebrate attains a length of more than a few inches unless it has a body like a worm which is normally supported on all sides by the ground. The wings of some butterflies, to be sure, have a spread of more than a foot, and ancient dragon flies in the Pennsylvanian era had a spread of 3 feet, but their bodies were small and light. Even the largest land invertebrates, such as worms 1 or 2 feet long, crablike crustaceans as big as a plate, or insects with bodies the size of a mouse, cannot create civilization. So far as we can see, the only creatures that can thoroughly dominate the earth are large land animals with a firm, flexible inner framework of bone.

A backbone does not appear to have originated on land. The best hypothesis seems to be that it evolved as a response to the great uplift of the continents at the beginning of Paleozoic time. The uplift gave rise to rushing streams and rockbound coasts where the waves created fierce commotion. Such waters subject feebly swimming invertebrates to severe strains. The tendency of evolution has been to develop some form of life for every environment which is not prohibitively cold, dry, or otherwise impossible. Some new device was needed if these violently moving waters were to be occupied. Squids, which are the best invertebrate swimmers, move backward by squirting out water. Crustaceans, such as lobsters, swim with many pairs of swimmerets. Such methods cannot cope with swift water. In order that an animal may swim strongly in the right direction, the best device seems to be a flexible backbone to which strong muscles are attached. At least two pairs of fins are needed. They must be on opposite sides of the body, one pair near the head and another farther back. It is hard to imagine any other line of development which would have been anything but a blind alley. Our bodily symmetry, our paired arms, legs, and eyes, our erect posture, and the ability of our hands to meet at just the place where it is easiest for the eyes to focus upon them—all these and a hundred other human characteristics depend on the backbone and the bilateral symmetry which arose apparently as a response to the challenge of swift water. This early step in evolution is one of the important factors in enabling man to create civilization. Nevertheless, it imposes a strain. Civilization demands long hours of seated work. To sit at a desk or machine day after day and bend forward as we so often do is by no means good for us.

As evolution progresses, new elements control the changes that take place. After life became adapted to the quiet ocean and then to moving waters, it was ready to advance into the great unoccupied lands. Then, as Lull puts it, the vertebrates "emerged from the limiting waters to the limitless air." The fact that we live *in* the air is even more important than that we live *on* the ground. It does not trouble us at all to get our feet off the ground, except as a figure of speech, but a few moments out of the air or with the air out of us prove fatal. Emergence into the air, like the development of a spinal column, seems to have occurred as a response to a change in physical environment. This time the change was climatic. Lungs appear to have evolved from the swim bladder which enables fish to maintain their position at a given depth without effort. In some fish a modified bladder takes oxygen directly from the air when the supply dissolved in the water becomes scarce in stagnant pools. In late Silurian and Devonian times extreme aridity appears to have provided vast areas where seasonal inundations alternated with long dry spells during which innumerable pools dried up. Creatures which could use their swim bladders as lungs and their fins as feet could live in such places when others perished. Accordingly, we live today in the air, and a large part of the work of civilized man is devoted to keeping on good terms with it. Clothing, houses, fires, and summer vacations are motivated largely by the desire to keep ourselves in comfortable relations with the air.

The fact that we are warm-blooded makes our responses to the air different from what they would be if we were cold-blooded. In fact if we were cold-blooded in the biological sense, it is doubtful whether we would have sufficient energy to create civilization, even if we could have reached our present stage of evolution in other respects. Warm-blooded animals appear to have originated in the Permian period of geology. They were apparently another response to a climatic change. Vast desert deposits are evidence of intense aridity in Permian times, and glacial deposits indicate long intermittent epochs of low temperature. Aridity, as Lull puts it, places a premium upon speed, not only because long distances must be travelled for food and water, but also because the strife between pursuer and pursued is intensified. Speed demands relatively high metabolism, and this involves a raising of temperature. Increasing cold places a premium upon the ability to maintain activity beyond the limits of summer, but such activity is possible only for warm-blooded creatures. Reptiles and amphibians, as well as insects and other invertebrates, remain dormant or otherwise quiescent in cold weather. Cold countries are almost devoid of snakes and lizards, but warm-blooded creatures, such as bears, rabbits, musk oxen, and many birds, are numerous. Because man is warm-blooded, he can live almost everywhere and carry civilization with him.

Among warm-blooded animals one type followed a blind alley; another chose the highroad toward civilization. The blind alley led into the air by way of wings, nests, and eggs. The road to civilization lay on the ground, where four limbs, relatively helpless young, and mother's milk were some of the chief characteristics of life. Existence in the air limits the total size of an animal, makes the development of a heavy, brainy head almost impossible, and spoils the fore limbs as organs for grasping and manipulating. All birds have small heads. Really large birds, such as the ostrich and the rhea, have given up the use of wings. The mere fact that birds are warm-blooded, however, and that so many flying forms nest in trees helps to develop a custom which is one of the primary essentials of civilization. It puts a premium upon care of the young by the older generation, and thus lays the foundation for ethical and moral qualities. Further development of these qualities among birds, however, is blocked by the lack of a big brain and hands.

With mammals there is no such blocking of progress. The nursing of her offspring makes the mother's relation to her young much more intimate and lasting than among egg-layers. This fosters the tendency for one generation to take care of the next in other ways, such as keeping the young clean, protecting them from enemies, and teaching them a few simple habits. Thus even among the lower mammals we see a foreshadowing of the fact that moral qualities begin with family relationships and owe their growth to mothers more than to fathers.

C. Man's Tree-Dwelling Stage

A tree-dwelling stage for mammals seems to have been an essential part of the preparation for civilization. It led to the evolution of primates, including monkeys, apes, and men. Some of the earliest mammals—little creatures no bigger than squirrels—lived in trees. Several evolutionary paths were open to them. One was to hang to the branches by means of curved claws, such as those of sloths and anteaters. This course is a dead alley, for it means slow, restricted motion. Species of this kind which have returned to the ground are still slow. They usually protect themselves by such devices as a bad odor, armor of bony plates, or spines like those of the porcupine. Another path was taken by squirrels and leopards, which cling to trees with sharp claws surrounding smooth, rubberlike pads. Such animals, unlike those with long, curved claws, can easily run on the ground. They tend to be alert and quick. Nevertheless, so far as civilization is concerned, they are in a blind alley. Their forefeet are needed for walking and therefore can be modified only slightly for purposes of holding and manipulating their food.

A third path of evolution was followed by animals which move through the trees by means of fingers or toes which grasp the branches. Such grasping is more effective if one digit—a thumb—can be opposed to the others. Hence the line of progress was the development of a hand with an opposable thumb. Such a hand is vastly more valuable on a foreleg or arm than on a hind leg. The use of hands at the ends of hind legs is greatly limited because they are not in the direct line of vision.

No matter how good the hand may be, it is of little use either for location or manipulation unless the eyes are capable of stereoscopic vision. The eyes of many mammals are placed so far apart that each eye sees a different field. This is excellent for an antelope, for example, since it enables the animal to note the approach of danger from all sides. It makes everything look flat, however, so that distances and sizes cannot easily be judged. Creatures which jump from tree to tree or branch to branch could not survive if they had such eyes. Stereoscopic vision is essential to them. Thus stereoscopic vision and hands with opposable thumbs go together. The monkeys and apes in which the hand is most perfectly developed are jumpers. Some gibbons are said to jump as much as forty feet from branch to branch. Every leap involves an unconscious but genuine estimate of distance, wind, strength of branches, and amount of energy needed to jump just the right distance. Among physical feats performed by animals few demand such keen sight, quick co-ordination of muscles, and accurate timing. Failure may mean death. Because of such requirements, strong supple hands, superb stereoscopic vision, and muscles of great delicacy and strength are essential, but they are useless without a brain capable of instantaneous and accurate estimates of distance, size of branches, and other pertinent factors.

The qualities which man acquired during the tree-dwelling stage of his evolution are among the most important of those requisite as a prelude to civilization. Without them no hunter could successfully shoot arrows; no warrior could parry the swords of his enemies. No tennis player could judge where a swift ball will light or how he must hit it to make it land on the back line out of reach of his opponent. Nor could a woman thread a needle, or a carpenter hammer his nails straight. By staying in the trees, however, the relatives of our ancestors lost the chance to bring high muscular faculties of this sort back into the highway that leads toward further development of the brain and thus toward civilization.

Of course we have no direct knowledge of the evolutionary steps outlined in this chapter. We do, however, know a vast number of facts about the past. Hundreds of able students have framed hypotheses as to how these facts fit together. When new facts have been discovered, the hypotheses which did not fit them have been discarded. Thus at last we have general agreement as to the main lines of evolution. Of course, some parts of what is said in this chapter may have to be modified when further facts are available, but the general principle of rapid evolution at times of environmental change seems unassailable. Nor can there be any question that in the long run each great environmental change has been marked by progress along the line of evolution toward civilization, as well as along many paths which come to a dead end.

D. Descent from the Trees

Reasoning in this way, geologists and anthropologists are generally agreed that our ancestors came down from the trees as the result of still another period of climatic stress. This presumably took place somewhere in Asia. Two or three million years ago Tibet and the neighboring regions constituted a well-watered and well-forested area only slightly elevated above the sea. There, presumably, our nimble ancestors with their unique combination of eye, hand, muscle, and brain jumped from tree to tree and probably chattered as busily as school girls. Little by little life became more difficult; the distances from tree to tree became longer; some of the trees that supplied food disappeared; many watering places dried up. These things happened because the climate became drier by reason of the gradual uplifting of the Himalayas and other great mountains. As the dryness increased, the forest doubtless assumed an open, orchardlike appearance, with abundant grass between the trees and many open, grassy glades, as is normal in such climates. Unless man intervenes, the presence of abundant grass means great herds of grazing animals, composed of species like the sheep, goats, horses, and cattle of Asia. Such animals, especially their young, furnish so much food that large carnivorous beasts—wolves, lions, tigers and leopards—become numerous.

In their forested grasslands, then, our primate ancestors were confronted by another of those unconscious but real choices which repeatedly arise in the progress of evolution. Should they remain in the old kind of forest as its borders were slowly pushed southward, or should they boldly attempt a new mode of life? Should they depend on new kinds of food and face dangers hitherto unknown? Of course the choice depended on the physical make-up of the animals. Those that did not differ significantly from their ancestors were obliged to remain in the old kind of forest or perish. Those that had advanced sufficiently could at least attempt to live in the new environment. Many, however, must have been destroyed. The new kind of life was possible only if the anthropoids, as we may now call these progressive primates, walked on the ground in the open grassy spaces. Except in small clumps the trees were now too far apart for jumping. As aridity increased, the anthropoids were obliged to change their food, eating a much larger proportion of meat, especially such kinds as young antelopes, small rodents, and ground birds, and also substituting hard, dry seeds of cereals for the fruits and nuts of the forest. They were also forced to be far more wary than formerly, for the big carnivores doubtless found anthropoids as good eating as sheep or colts.

It has been suggested, not unreasonably, that the ability to use sticks, stones, or other weapons for killing animals was the original step from which the use of tools developed. Anthropoids which evolved in such a way that their brains and arms permitted this ability were better fitted than their comrades to protect themselves and their children from wild beasts as well as to kill game for food.

As the mountains rose higher and shut out the influence of the ocean still more, the anthropoids had to face a long dry season. For this reason they presumably had to walk farther than before for both food and water and to be much more wary and clever in avoiding danger. Of course this whole process took a long time, and the anthropoids themselves had no idea of what was happening.

We come now to some of the most puzzling problems in the whole realm of evolution. These problems apply to stages of human culture as well as to prehuman stages. When man's ancestors went into the trees, mutations occurred not only in his feet but also in his legs, his eyes, the relative positions of his internal organs, and above all in his nervous system and brain. Again, when our particular line of human anthropoids came down out of the trees, further mutations altered the shape of the legs and teeth, the position of the viscera, the curve of the spine, and many other characteristics. Above all there occurred changes in the brain and nervous system appropriate to those taking place in the other organs. All these mutations involved hundreds of minor physiological changes—thousands, perhaps, if we consider individual groups of cells. Many of these changes are incomplete so that vestiges of the old arrangement still remain. Hence some people call man a misfit. Nevertheless, all the changes, taken as a whole, were so well co-ordinated that a new mode of life was not merely possible but successful. This same general co-ordination of a great many changes has happened time and again. It occurred when our ancestors became vertebrates, when they acquired warm blood, when they became mammals, when they went into the trees, when they came down again from the trees, and so on throughout the whole of evolution.

Can such co-ordination occur time and again as the result of mutations which depend merely on chance, or must we suppose that a definite plan of evolution is inherent in the universe? If there is such a plan, how is it working today? By his own action in creating civilization and now in developing its mechanical stage, man has changed his environment almost as radically as it was altered in earlier ages by the geological processes of continent building and climatic change. Will this fact in due time lead to any biological change in man? Or has the biological phase of human evolution been completely eliminated by man's ability to make tools? No one can answer these questions conclusively, but they are worth thinking about. We shall return to them later.

E. Man's Physical Fitness for Civilization

In the rest of this chapter let us consider the relation of man's present biological structure and functions to his fitness for civilization. We are talking about *Homo sapiens,* our own species of man, not any of the earlier, more primitive forms. Many discussions are misleading because they overlook the fact that there were several species of men before ours. These differed from one another more drastically than horses differ from zebras or donkeys. The several species of the genus *Equus* differ mainly in size, color, and minor features of bodily form. Their brains differ little in size, as compared with their bodies, and scarcely at all, presumably, in their way of functioning. The various species of man, however, differ markedly in size of brain and in relative development of the parts of the brain with different functions. The high development of the part which thinks, as contrasted with that which directly controls muscular action, is the outstanding feature in which *Homo sapiens* differs from earlier species and, of course, still more from his anthropoid ancestors.

The species of animals and the types of human culture which have the best chance to survive are generalized. Such species or types possess a wide range of qualities which are capable of development. They do not show excessive development along any one special line unless it be along the main upward road of evolution. A seven-foot ammonite with a spiral shell full of beautiful crinkles has not the slightest chance of developing a spinal cord or of becoming a land animal. A small, snail-like creature, unencumbered by a huge and intricate shell, has a far better chance.

In many respects man is an unspecialized creature. His teeth, stomach, intestines, and other alimentary organs are such that he can thrive on many kinds of food. The Eskimos, for example, have lived for uncounted generations on little except flesh; the Bedouins are nourished mainly by milk for months at a time; the inhabitants of eastern Persia get perhaps nine tenths of their sustenance from wheat; many tropical people live largely on starchy foods, such as cassava and bananas. So it goes. Man uses a great variety of foods ranging from the pure carbohydrate of sugar to the concentrated proteins of lean fish. Primitive savages eat raw grubs, roasted snakes, and bamboo shoots; civilized man eats raw oysters, living cheese mites, and even, of late, a prepared form of grass. In this respect man is extraordinarily different from jaguars which eat only flesh, cattle which eat only a limited number of plants, and a certain species of snail which can live only on a special mould which grows only on one particular species of leaf.

In regard to shelter, too, human freedom exceeds that of other species. We do not have to carry our houses with us as does a periwinkle. Even without tools we can construct rude shelters from woven grasses in the savannas, boughs in the forest, rocks in the mountains, dried mud in the plains, and snow or skins in the far north. With tools, of course, we can do far more. Our brains enable us to find or create shelter almost anywhere, whereas all other creatures find it only under a few special conditions.

Many people suppose that man's naked skin is a disadvantage in contrast to the fur and feathers of animals. This is far from true. Our lack of a hairy covering, coupled with our brain, helps us to live in practically all climates. A polar bear, because of his specialized covering of warm fur, is most uncomfortable in the summer of middle latitudes and would perish in the hot tropics. An elephant, with his thick, hairless skin, can resist insects but cannot stand low temperatures. By putting on more or less clothing, however, man can easily protect himself against all kinds of weather as well as against insects. If we had a complete hairy covering which became thick and warm in winter, we should probably want to shave it off so that we might wear clothes and thus be as comfortable as possible both indoors and out in all kinds of climates. The fact that his skin is hairless helps man to surpass all other animals in ability to live and thrive in a great variety of climates.

Lack of a hairy skin, through its effect on clothing, may have been indirectly helpful in the evolution of mental ability. The matter has never been scientifically studied, but the mere possibility is worth mentioning. Clothing tends to make the face the main factor in sexual selection. Among primitive people practically all women are mated, but those most desirable in appearance, as well as in the ability to work, are the ones whom the men are most likely to want and hence to take care of. Their children, therefore, are more likely than others to be born in good health and to survive because cared for thereafter by the fathers. As clothing becomes more complete, each sex tends more and more to judge the other by the appearance of the face rather than the body. This fact may mean that a strong body does not have so great an effect as it ought, but a good complexion and a healthy-looking face are generally signs of a good physique. They are certainly potent agents in making men seek women.

Something else, however, is more important than these signs of health, and its importance increases as civilization advances. This other factor is the expression of the face. A dumb Dora, even if her features are lovely and her complexion perfect, is far less attractive than a woman who adds to these attributes an expression of animation, alertness, and that inexplicable but most desirable quality called charm. In these days, when many people remain unmarried or marry too late to have children, the processes of sexual selection appear to be assuming a new importance. How far future generations can be helped or hindered by concentration of selection upon the face rather than upon the body no one can yet tell. There can be little doubt, however, that the hairlessness of the human body and the consequent invention of clothing have concentrated sexual selection upon the face far more in some parts of the earth than in others. This fact may have played at least a small part in making northern people more intellectual on the whole than those of low latitudes where the body is less clothed. Thus a generalized condition in respect to a hairy covering and protection from weather and insects may have been a help in raising mankind to a higher level of mentality.

Man's limbs afford another example of the value of a generalized development in contrast to the more specialized development of practically all animals. Our naked hands, to be sure, are poor weapons compared with a horse's hoofs, a wild bull's horns, or a catamount's claws. But consider how free they are to move in all directions—to pound, push, pull, tear, and hold. Our hands are capable of a hundred combinations of movement for every one that a horse's hoof can make. By holding an implement in his hand, man can duplicate the abilities of every type of foot in the whole animal kingdom and improve upon them. He can also do a thousand delicate tasks which are impossible even for the proboscis of an elephant or the fingers of a monkey. The hand is indeed highly specialized for manipulation in general, but not for any one kind of manipulation or any one type of environment.

So, too, with our feet. A yak's forefeet are wonderfully skillful in testing the sliding scree which clothes the steep slopes of the Himalayas, but they would be a great disadvantage to a camel. The camel has his own specialization in the form of big, rubbery pads, but they slip and slide and often bring death to the animal in snow or mud. Our feet can be used almost equally well on sliding stones, on sand, in mud, or in snow.

In many additional ways *Homo sapiens* is physically less specialized than almost any other animal. His relative freedom from seasonal restrictions in reproduction is an example. Mankind does indeed show a survival of a definite annual season of reproduction like that of animals, but this specialization seems to be in process of reversal to a more generalized condition. This point will be fully explained in a later chapter. What now concerns us is that among most animals the sexual attraction which leads to mating is largely confined to a definite and often brief season. One of the main reasons, of course, is that young animals have the best chance of survival if conceived at that season. Man's primitive ancestors doubtless were like animals in this respect, and modern man still furnishes abundant evidence of a seasonal waxing and waning of sexual attraction and power of reproduction. Nevertheless, the growth of civilization has made it more and more possible for children born at any season to survive. At the same time seasonal differences in sexual attraction appear to have diminished, although they still persist. They are surprisingly strong among the Eskimos, for example, and distressingly evident in sexual crimes in civilized countries. In spite of this, however, the general fact is that in the human species as a whole the mating instinct and the power of reproduction prevail more steadily throughout the year than in almost any other species of higher animal.

This tendency of the human species to mate at all seasons seems to be one of the cornerstones of civilization. Without it the men would probably be inclined to leave the women and children to take care of themselves much of the year, as happens among most animals. Yerkes has observed that during the mating season a male chimpanzee will let the female take food which at any other season he would grab with violence. He suggests that self-control of this kind may be the first faint glimmering of conscience. Certain it is that, although women have suffered a vast amount of abuse at the hands of men, almost universally they induce their mates to remain more or less permanently with them and to provide food and protection for them and their children. If *Homo sapiens* were a more specialized animal, with a definite restriction of the mating period to a particular climate and season, the chances that the two sexes would so universally stay together in this way and form permanent families would be greatly reduced.

It is generally agreed that the family is the basic group in human society. It requires adjustment, co-operation, division of labor, and mutual sacrifices among all three of its components, namely, wives, husbands, and children. Moral conduct and ethical ideas arise primarily in the family. So do the first stages of government and education. All these would disappear, or at least be greatly weakened, if mankind were so specialized that the two sexes were actively interested in each other only for a short season at a particular time of the year.

F. *Is Man's Physical Evolution Complete?*

The evidence that man is a highly generalized type of animal leads us to inquire whether biological, as opposed to cultural, evolution has come to an end. The general opinion is that it has and that biologically the people of today are not superior and may be inferior to those of two thousand or even twenty thousand years ago. The old Greeks appear to have been of a high type both physically and mentally, and so do the Cro-Magnons who left their spirited drawings on the caves of France fifteen or twenty thousand years before the Greeks. Certain it is that since *Homo sapiens* spread widely over the earth he has experienced no radical biological change. Moreover, it is clear that during this time, which may not be more than thirty thousand years, human evolution has taken the form of using hands and eyes and brain to construct all manner of devices which take the place of the slowly evolved adaptations of all the rest of the animal kingdom. The story of how we have learned to travel on the earth, on the water, in the water, and in the air has been told repeatedly. So, too, has the story of how man has made tool after tool until now his largest ones are factories that cover square miles of territory.

All this, however, neither proves nor disproves that biological evolution is at an end. We simply do not know, but there are possibilities which ought to be stated. One of them lies in the realm of eugenics. We have at last learned to separate the cohabitation of men and women, which is the basis of family life and thus of civilization, from reproduction, which is the basis of biological increase. In some lands the size of families is now being largely regulated by the wishes of parents and not by mere chance. This fact means that people with certain mental or physical characteristics may and probably will have so few children that their type will die out. Others with a different constitution may have so many children that their type will finally become dominant. In addition the most advanced countries have created conditions of living which are radically different from those under which our species originated and under which it lived until the last few generations. As a result certain mental and physical types are probably dying out because they cannot stand the new conditions of life. These changes in birthrates and in mode of life may constitute a crisis in evolution as great as that of a glacial epoch. Hence it is not impossible that a new type of man—even a new species—may originate.

Putting aside all speculation as to the future, we are faced by a definite evolutionary fact which is of great importance for the future of civilization. A new factor, cultural in nature, has entered into human evolution. The first evolutionary factor, the gradual development of seawater to a composition such that life in its simplest form was possible, appears to have been chemical. Next came two physical factors—first, the uplift of the earth's surface into continents and mountains with the development of swiftly moving waters which could be mastered only by vertebrates, and then climatic changes, one set of which apparently led some of these vertebrates out of the water and onto the land, whereas another set provided the stimulus for the evolution of warm-blooded mammals. Then the chemical and physical factors were supplemented by biological ones. Two of these were botanical, namely, forests in which four-footed creatures developed hands and stereoscopic eyes, and grasslands which resulted from movements of the earth's crust and the accompanying climatic changes. A third was zoological, namely, the grassland animals which either hunted the primates who came down from the trees or were hunted by them.

Human culture, the new factor which has now been added, does not destroy the old factors. It merely supplements them. The chemical conditions of the ocean and of protoplasm, the physical conditions of climate and the relief of the earth's surface, and the biological condition of plants and animals—all these still exert their influence on human evolution. Nevertheless, in the long run the new cultural factor may prove to be the most powerful of all. The growth of human culture, the development of civilization, and especially the recent growth of urban and industrial life may already have started a series of adaptive mutations which we cannot yet detect. They certainly seem to have altered the selective forces which determine what types of people shall survive or perish. As one factor after another comes into play in evolution—as chemical action is supplemented by physical agencies, as both of these are modified by biological factors, and as all three are supplemented by cultural factors—the problem of understanding evolution seems to become more and more complex.

In Chapter 1 of this book we examined the basic fact that in this world of ours a profoundly powerful evolutionary force is evident.

It persistently leads to development along a variety of paths, but most of these prove to be blind alleys so far as the so-called higher aspects of life are concerned. Along one main line, however, there has been persistent, although intermittent, progress toward greater complexity of cellular organization, increased powers of mind, higher stages of culture, and ultimately civilization.

In Chapter 2 we have seen that the development of life, which seemingly arose from an inherent tendency of the universe toward evolution, has been greatly influenced by differences in the physical environment from region to region and from one period of time to another. Except at the very beginning, however, new forms of life seem always to have arisen from older forms and never as purely new products. Thus throughout geological times every species of plant and animal and even every act of each individual in any given species was the result of (1) the basic evolutionary force; (2) the innate qualities of the organism as determined by its heredity; and (3) the environment, including purely physical conditions of climate, topography, and so forth, and also organic conditions, such as the numbers and kinds of plants and animals.

In due time still a fourth factor entered the scene. This factor was culture in the form of ideas, habits, and material articles which one individual is able to transfer to another by methods other than biological inheritance. From a geological standpoint the growth of culture, with its development into civilization, has been amazingly rapid. It has changed the face of the earth in ways wholly unknown before. This has been possible because only through cultural means can the experiences and achievements of many individuals be combined in such a way that a new generation starts at a higher level than its predecessor. Each generation of animals starts at essentially the same level; each generation of man, especially of civilized man, starts at a new level. If civilization is advancing, the new level is higher than the old. Nevertheless, the basic evolutionary urge, the innate qualities of the organism, and the geographic environment, including both its physical and organic phases, still continue to act.

In the study of civilization the common practice has been to emphasize cultural events and to neglect the other three phases of the subject. In the present book a different method is employed. We shall concentrate upon the influence of heredity and geographic environment, especially climate, upon the cultural events which are described in a multitude of other books. There will be no further discussion of the basic evolutionary urge because that would lead us into philosophy. Cultural events will constantly be mentioned, but there will be no attempt at an orderly recital of the historic order in which they have developed. Instead we shall consider the way in which heredity and geographic environment have influenced typical phases of the cultural development known as civilization.

PART II

HEREDITY

CHAPTER 3

THE PROBLEM OF RACE

A. Pride of Race

Heredity runs like a scarlet thread through history. One of its manifestations is racial differences, but mistaken opinions as to such differences are even more prominent. In the folklore of primitive people each minor group generally claims racial superiority, usually by reason of a supposedly unique ancestry. This superiority is generally regarded as innate, although sometimes it can be bestowed by adoption. The ancient Hebrews believed that they were God's "chosen" people. The Japanese, they themselves claim, are descendants of the gods. Their emperor is himself a god. Ancient monuments give humorous evidence that the Egyptians regarded Negroes as inferior. The Negroes in turn picture devils with fair skins. To the ancient Greeks all other people were "barbarians." Although the Romans believed that selected outsiders might deserve Roman citizenship, they took great pride in purity of race, especially in their earlier, nobler days. The medieval Crusaders fought to humble the "upstart" Arabs as well as to redeem the Holy Sepulcher. Even today, almost every nation and tribe regards its enemies or rivals as inferior in race.

This attitude is well illustrated by a Chinese emperor's snub when George III asked for a British representative and trading post at Peiping.[1]

If your reverence for Our Celestial Dynasty inspires a desire to acquire our civilization, [you should know that] our ceremonies and laws differ so completely from yours that, even if your Envoy were able to acquire the

[1] Backhouse and Bland, vol. 3, p. 352.

37

rudiments of our civilization, you could not possibly transplant our manners and customs to your alien soil. . . . Your tribute offerings, O King, are . . . accepted . . . solely because of the spirit which prompted their dispatch from afar. . . . We possess all things. . . . I have no use for your country's manufactures. Therefore . . . it behoves you . . . to display even greater devotion and loyalty in future, so that by perpetual submission to our Throne you may secure peace and prosperity for your country.

The British apparently were regarded as so inferior that even a royal envoy could scarcely acquire the rudiments of real culture. Nevertheless, the British built the world's greatest empire. Then they assumed "the white man's burden." In other words, the white man's "superiority" obliged him to manage the backward parts of Africa and Asia. The British still regard themselves as the world's born leaders. The people of the United States dispute this claim, partly from pride of race, but mainly on the assumption that citizenship in a great country gives everyone a kind of innate glory. American-born Italians, Jews, Swedes, and even Negroes boast of "our" Pilgrim Fathers. Most of them wish that all Americans could belong to one race. A strong racial cleavage permitted slavery. At first Negro inferiority was rarely ascribed to physical environment or cultural deficiency. Race was to blame. Four years of devastating civil war ensued, but the idea of racial superiority still dogs our steps incessantly.

Few people have proclaimed their own superiority more loudly than the Germans. Their shouts sound strangely like those of "one hundred per cent" Americans. Houston Chamberlain, a foremost advocate of the "Nordic myth," declared that Jesus, as well as practically every other great man, was partly Nordic. In the early days of Hitler, honest Nordic anthropologists such as Lips had to flee from Germany because they would not accept "racism" and teach that a so-called Aryan race is superior to all others. The effort of every racial group to prove itself the best is amusing when displayed by the backward Samoyedes of Siberia, for example. A similar effort becomes sheer madness when Germans reject scientific truths because Jews have discovered them or exalt such races as the Japanese simply because of a political alliance. We must remember, however, that we ourselves, whoever we may be, are almost certain to glorify our own race unduly.

The historical effect of racial prejudice is strong, regardless of whether it is based on fact or fiction. Mistaken racial views may have played as large a part as either language or nationality in moulding human destiny. The attitude of the United States toward Orientals illustrates this. If we had given the Japanese an immigration quota like that of Persia or Rumania, the Japanese would not have felt insulted, and our racial quality would not have been altered by one hundredth of one per cent in a decade. The slight racial alteration thus arising would probably have been to our advantage, for the Japanese are an able people. Moreover, the events that led to Pearl Harbor might have been greatly altered.

To safeguard the future we need exact knowledge of the innate qualities of races and especially of nations and social classes. Until we understand the actual truth as well as what people have supposed, history can never be a safe guide for future conduct. The truth seems to be that innate racial differences are much less important than innate individual differences or than those due to environment. Moreover, the external marks which are supposed to indicate racial inheritance appear to be more changeable than they were formerly believed to be. And, finally, the main importance of heredity seems to lie not in races, but in differences among individuals, family stocks, occupational groups, urban and rural types, castes, or social classes.

B. Three Attitudes toward Race

Extremes beget opposite extremes. This has been especially true of race. Examples of two extremes and of a middle view will make this matter clear. Japan ranks with Germany as a country temporarily obsessed by the "racist" point of view. Compulsory textbooks for little children contain statements which may be paraphrased thus:

Japan is the best of all countries. It is the central country of the world. Its soil, its climate, its location, and its vegetation surpass those of all other lands. Its people are descended from the gods. Their strength, wisdom, and ability are unrivalled.

Such claims are bolstered by statements like the following by Hyogoro Sakurai, a member of the Japanese Diet:

The question . . . is whether the Yamato [Japanese] race is of superior breed. Dr. Kanichi Tanaka . . . in the Tokyo University of Science and Literature says "yes." He has dealt a blow to the complacent sense of superiority among Europeans and Americans that the yellow race is inferior to the white race by publishing the results of his statistical research showing that the Yamato race is the finest race in the world. This, too, shows the importance of keeping pure by preventing any intermarriage with the Chinese.

Prof. Tanaka conducted his research since 1935 with the backing of the Japan Society for the Advancement of Science, Education Ministry, and Foreign Office, not only in Japan, but also in Manchuria, Korea, Formosa, China and North America. His statistics were based on intelligence, temperament, general psychological and physical tests. . . .

In order not to impose language handicaps on his subjects, he used only arabic numerals and diagrams. The Japanese lead all other races in intelligence, their index being 49.8. The Germans came next with 44.7. The British came third with 44.2, Portuguese 40.5 and French 40.2. Hawaiians, Italians, Spanish and Filipinos were all on the 30-point level.

The other tests are yet to be completed, but it has been made clear that although the Japanese are inferior to Europeans and Americans in stature, weight, posture, and bust, the Japanese are superior in respect of lung capacity, which is important for vitality, grasping power, running speed and accuracy of motion. In the temperament test, it has been found that adults are more introspective than children, and that the Japanese are more so than Europeans or Americans who in turn are more introspective than Negroes, showing that the more highly developed the civilization the more introspective is that race. In all these tests, the superiority of the Japanese has been amply demonstrated.

Such statements yield convincing evidence as to innate racial capacity only so far as they satisfy the following conditions: (1) the alleged tests are equally adapted to all groups who are tested; (2) the persons tested are an average sample of their race; (3) either all the racial groups have been subjected to identical conditions of climate, diet, home environment, formal education, and so forth, or the effect of these environmental differences can be eliminated.

The mere location of the Japanese tests makes it almost certain that these conditions were not complied with. The fact that the Japanese are put first, the Germans second, and the British third suggests bias because of the current political situation. The omission of Americans, whose relation to Japan was especially critical when Sakurai's statement was made, seems also to bear a political impress. We must not, however, be too hard on Japan. If America and Americans, Germany and Germans, or Britain and British were substituted for Japan and Japanese, both this quotaton and the one from school books could be almost duplicated in America, Germany, or Britain. Moreover, we must not forget that people who carry out extensive and laborious scientific investigations are almost certain to rank high in intelligence. Germans, Jews, Japanese, Americans, and British are leaders in such work. Naturally, and also correctly, they find themselves ranking high. The important question is not so much what race stands highest, but what part do heredity, physical vigor, and training play in this.

Claims to racial superiority almost invariably provoke violent opposition. In recent decades Nazi anti-Semitism has added fuel to the flame. Therefore, at the other extreme such statements as the following by Jacobs [2] are not surprising:

> No reputable scientist knows of evidence that would reveal a causal connection between the family-line heritage ("race") of a population and its language, culture, mental or emotional makeup.
>
> No matter what their regional appearance and biological characteristics are at present, all members of *Homo sapiens* constitute a group of domesticated animals of a unique kind. During the hundreds of thousands of years there occurred profound changes in the brain, nervous and glandular systems of all regional types of *Homo sapiens*. These changes were everywhere similar and resulted in a new sort of mammal. It is the one animal which in all its modern regional populations is of indeterminable mental and emotional—that is, cultural—malleability and potentiality. It is methodologically inescapable that the specific linguistic, religious, mental, temperamental, or other behavior forms or emotions of any people have to be considered products of complex historical and social forces—not biologic forces. As far as scientific method permits a phrasing of our present knowledge, the petty skeletal and external anatomy differences between populations must be treated as completely irrelevant to temperamental or cultural characteristics. Nothing seems more certain either in recent human history or in science than the lack of demonstrable molding influence of family-line heritage. The achievements and characteristics of any community seem always the products of regional historic forces and circumstances; these supply no clue to biologic quality.

The writer of this quotation apparently believes that mental traits are never inherited biologically. He appeals to heredity to explain bodily form, coloring, and appearance but draws a sharp line at "mental, temperamental, or other behavior forms or emotions." So sweeping a conclusion requires far more evidence than the author seems to realize.

A viewpoint midway between the two just presented is expressed by Hankins: [3]

> Racial differences are not those of kind . . . all races have all human qualities; but they have these qualities in different degrees of development.

[2] p. 53.   [3] pp. viii, ix.

One race may excel in physical energy, another in creative imagination. This conception does away with the notion of general or universal superiority on the part of any one race. Moreover, in view of the wide range of variation among the members of the same race, inferiority or superiority cannot be attributed to an individual on account of his race. A short member of a tall race may be distinctly taller than a tall member of a short race. So with intelligence, organizing ability, or artistic sense. Social barriers on account of race have, therefore, no basis of biological fact.

A similar conclusion is reached in the study of race crossing; there is no biological mandate against it, even in the case of widely different races. The sociological grounds for opposition to race mixture are doubtless important, but their importance springs almost entirely from the fact that race prejudice is a social force and not a theory. Offspring receive their hereditary endowments from their immediate ancestors; if the parents are of high quality, so also will be the offspring, regardless of race. . . . While we are denying the extravagant claims of the Nordicists, we also deny the equally perverse and doctrinaire contentions of the race egalitarians. There is no respect, apparently, in which races are equal; but their differences must be thought of in terms of relative frequencies, and not as absolute differences in kind. They are like the differences between classes in the same population. It thus appears that the eugenic contentions are fundamentally sound, as against the racialists on the one extreme and the thorough environmentalists on the other. From the standpoint of population quality, superior rank within a race is of more importance than race. . . . Well-endowed Italians, Hebrews, Turks, Chinese, and Negroes are better materials out of which to forge a nation than average or below average Nordics. . . . From the standpoint of the creation and maintenance of high culture, high-grade stock is more important than cultural opportunity, though the latter doubtless also is important. The progress of a people is so greatly dependent on the abilities of its few ablest men that the primary question which a theory of the racial basis of civilization must answer is, what are those conditions which produce the greatest supply of genius?

This quotation agrees in general with the viewpoint of the present volume. Instead of a theory of the racial basis of civilization, however, this book presents a wider view in which heredity, not race, is coequal with physical environment. The two together provide materials and conditions for the growth of human culture. Advances in human culture in their turn modify both physical environment and heredity. The ultimate result is civilization. The frequent failure to make a distinction between races in general and specific stocks within a race seems to be largely due to the fact that anthropology is still immature. The same is true of the failure to realize that bodily traits, including even head form, can be altered environmentally and by selection. These failures help to explain why anthropologists frequently minimize or even deny the existence of an hereditary factor in the evolution of civilization.

C. Recent Anthropological Ideas as to Race

In their passionate fight again a racism which encourages anti-Semitism, slavery, exploitation of "natives," and prejudice against Negroes, anthropologists have formulated certain definite ideas as to race. So far as external bodily characteristics are concerned race well deserves scientific study. There is little value, however, in the old classification into white Caucasians, yellow Mongoloids, and black Negroids. The three merge into one another so intimately that only a small part of mankind can be regarded as belonging purely to any one of them. Moreover, a classification according to a single minor quality has no great significance. Other types of classification, such as that of Haddon, take account of a larger number of qualities. Haddon bases his racial identifications upon the texture and color of the hair, together with skin color, stature, head form, and the shape of the face, especially the nose and eyes. He names seventeen races, including Negrito, Papuan, Pre-Dravidan, Eurafrican or Mediterranean, Nordic, and Eskimo. Coon,[4] following a revised form of the same general method, makes a classification which separates Bushman-Hottentots, Negritoes, Australoids, Veddoids, Negroes, Mongoloids, and whites. The difference between Haddon and Coon illustrates the fact that races are not definitely delimited. They are like types of mongrel dogs which grade into one another imperceptibly.

Because of this indefiniteness such expressions as the French race are meaningless. The French, like the people of practically every other nation, are a mixture of races, and it is hard to select pure physical samples of any of them. The task of picking out corresponding examples of mental qualities is far harder and perhaps impossible. Hence anthropology has made little progress in a scientific estimate of the mentality of races. The difficulty is increased by the fact that relatively pure samples of different races are rare and are found only in diverse geographical environments.

The innate mentality of a pure Negro population in Africa, let us say, cannot be fairly compared with that of pure broad-headed Alpines in Europe because of differences in environment. The two

4 1939.

groups live in different climates, eat different food, and follow different occupations. Any attempt to measure the inborn mental traits of the Dinkas, for example, must be fruitless unless allowance is made for the excessively hot climate, huge grasses, and pastoral mode of life where these tall black Negroes wander naked. Allowance must also be made for the Dinkas' stage of culture. Looking like ghosts in the pale gray film of ashes which they smear over their wholly unclad bodies to ward off insects, they stand idly on one leg beside the upper Nile. But what would they be like if trained from infancy as are the children of Danes? And could the Danes have reached their present high stage of culture in a geographical environment like that of the Dinkas? Some people believe so, but it seems improbable.

It is likewise almost hopeless to attempt to solve the problem of innate racial character by finding members of diverse races who have grown up in the same geographical environment. Groups that thus live together are not likely to be racially pure even when separated by barriers such as slavery, caste, or social classes. If thus separated, they are almost certain to differ in mode of life, diet, occupations, and training. Hence we cannot tell how far their intelligence, emotions, and social aptitudes are due to innate traits and how far to environment. Such difficulties have led many anthropologists to believe that racial character is due largely to physical or cultural environment. Being unable to find convincing correlations between temperament or intellect and the few anatomical criteria by which they commonly measure race, they maintain that there is no connection at all. More careful students, however, merely say that a convincing relationship between race and mentality has not yet been demonstrated, although it may exist.

Klineberg [5] gives an excellent example of the attitude of able and conscientious psychologists in this respect. Ranging far and wide, he discusses a remarkable variety of physical traits, including blood groups, endocrine glands, physiognomy, pigmentation, stature, head form, cranial capacity, rate of physical or mental growth, age at puberty, rates of respiration and circulation, blood pressure, basal metabolism, speed of nerve conduction, and even "racial odors." Each of these is compared with one attribute of mind or sense at a time—for example, with speed of nervous reflexes, keenness of vision, sensitivity to pain, ability to hear, sense of smell, or musical ability.

[5] 1935.

Another mode of comparison balances specific physical traits against criteria such as IQ, occupation, or advancement in school, each of which indicates many phases of an individual's mental condition. A third procedure measures each physical trait in relation to the culture, social status, economic condition, language, or schooling of large groups of people. All these comparisons are valuable, but usually they seem so contradictory that the result has been negative.

This does not mean that there is no connection between inherited physique and people's mental or social qualities. Nor does it preclude the idea that sufficiently large and well-distributed random samples of the world's main races would reveal distinct differences in mental capacities and aptitudes. It merely means that, although such differences may exist, the methods thus far employed have not disclosed them in any conclusive fashion. Part of the difficulty lies in the fact that the extremes are much the same in all races. A white or Chinese idiot is just as idiotic as a Negro or Polynesian idiot, but no one knows whether the proportion of idiots would be the same among all peoples if all conditions except race were identical.

Nor do we know whether geniuses are of higher quality and more numerous in some races than in others. It would require marvelous skill to determine whether Hammurabi and Confucius excelled Genghis Khan, or whether Shakespeare, Gandhi, or the Haitian Negro, Toussaint L'Ouverture, inherited the greatest power of mind. As to how frequently such geniuses appear in each race, history gives no answer. We can never know how many "mute inglorious Miltons" have died unknown. In encyclopedias Europeans far exceed Africans, but that fact proves nothing concerning the number of people born with high capacities. Lack of vigor because of climate, diet, or disease, or lack of opportunity by reason of isolation or backward culture, may explain the difference. It seems probable that some races excel others in the proportion of persons born with high capacities, but thus far anthropology has not demonstrated that such superiority actually exists. We shall see later, however, that small homogeneous groups of people present many indications of diversity in innate capacities, even though there are no apparent racial differences.*

* Considerable evidence suggests that some of the more primitive races are deficient in the kind of intellectual ability needed for modern civilization. For example, according to Porteus, the Australian aborigines, after a century of contact with whites, still kill game with stone-age arrows instead of making the relatively small effort which would be required to procure firearms from the white man. Almost the only innovation is that old bottles, instead of flints, are now often

D. New Anthropological Methods

New methods often solve old problems. The work of Kretschmer, Draper, Hooton, Sheldon, and others holds out hope that the relation between man's physical and mental make-up may soon become much clearer. From numerous measurements upon each of thousands of criminals, students, and others, Hooton, for example, finds that although there is no single criminal type, as Lombroso supposed, the percentage of criminals showing a disharmonic blending of physical traits is abnormally great. Anthropologists are beginning to believe that people should be classified according to the general constitution of the body as a whole, not according to a single physical trait, such as head form, or according to a few other traits which bear little relation to temperament or intellect. Thus far, to be sure, abundant data are available only for external form, but in due time information as to internal anatomy, the chemistry of the blood, hormones, and the electrical reactions of the nervous system will doubtless be available. External form bears a close relation to some of the internal conditions, but not to all and perhaps not to the more important.

The new approach to the problem of race is illustrated by the work of Sheldon. He gives figures derived from autopsies on three groups of ten or more elderly men, representing the extremes of three types,

chipped into arrow heads. Again, according to Dyk, "the rapidity with which the Polynesians accepted firearms and appreciated their worth in battle is almost unbelievable. . . . [In contrast to this] the Bushmen to this day have not been noticeably affected either by the gun or the horse or the military activities of the British and Dutch. Papuans of New Guinea are only now showing signs of unrest and possible change after one hundred and fifty years of contact with guns and powder of the whites." A similar contrast is seen between the Maoris of New Zealand, who have rapidly adopted many features of the white man's civilization, and the Indians of the high plateau of Ecuador, who have lived almost unchanged beside white civilization for close to four centuries. The anthropologist sometimes says that such contrasts merely illustrate the tenacity with which cultural traits persist. The geographer may say that the people who adopt the new methods generally have some advantage of climate, products, or contact with the rest of the world. The weight of evidence, however, seems to point to innate racial differences as at least part of the reason for such contrasts. Even if this explanation is true it must not be interpreted that backwardness in civilization necessarily means hereditary lack of mental ability. Innate inferiority is indicated only when people of a given type consistently fail to take advantage of opportunities and inventions which are freely open to them. Poverty, such as that of the Indians of Ecuador, or inertia due to climate, as among the Papuans, may explain their failures.

namely, short and fat, muscular and square, tall and thin. The average heights were approximately 66, 68, and 70 inches, but the weights varied in the opposite way, being 179, 163, and 141 pounds. The length and weight of the intestines also varied inversely with the height, the lengths being 36, 32, and 29 feet, and the weights 3.2, 2.4, and 1.7 pounds. Men with such different alimentary tracts can scarcely fail to differ significantly in tastes, activities, and habits.

The short, fat people in the first group represent the extreme of a physical type which Sheldon calls endomorphs. He uses this word because the endoderm, or inner layer of the young embryo, gives rise to the digestive system. Endomorphs have rounded faces, large bodies, small bones, and more or less "ham-shaped" arms and legs. He finds that this sort of body is associated with a definite type of temperament which he calls visceratonia. In its extreme form visceratonia is characterized by "general relaxation, love of comfort, sociability, conviviality, gluttony for food, for people, and for affection. . . . The personality seems to center around the viscera. The digestive tract is king, and its welfare appears to define the primary purpose of life." Such people tend to be affectionate and kindhearted.

People of a square, muscular type are called mesomorphs, because the mesoderm, or middle layer of the embryo, develops into bones, muscle, connective tissue, heart, and most of the blood vessels. Mesomorphs have strong, prominent bones and large bodies in which the upper part is especially developed in contrast to the lower part, which is emphasized in endomorphs. Extremes of this type appear to have a temperament in which the body as a muscular organism is dominant. Somatotonia, as Sheldon calls this kind of temperament, "is roughly a predominance of muscular activity and of vigorous bodily assertiveness." Such people have energy and push. They walk resolutely and noisily; their voices are loud and domineering. "The executive department of their internal economy is strongly vested" in their muscles. "Action and power define life's primary purpose." They assert their own rights regardless of others.

The ectoderm, or outer layer of the embryo, develops into the skin, hair, nails, sense organs, and nervous system, including the brain. Hence ectomorphs is a good name for a third human type, the slender kind among the three groups above. They are slight, fragile persons with small bones, drooping shoulders, and relatively long legs, arms, fingers, and necks. Extreme ectomorphic males, 68 inches tall and 18 years old, have an average weight of only 108 pounds, as compared with 240 pounds for extreme endomorphs of the same height and age. The habits and tastes of such persons are dominated by cerebrotonia, which is Sheldon's name for their type of temperament. In its extreme form cerebrotonia involves "roughly a predominance of the element of restraint, inhibition, and the desire for concealment. Cerebrotonic people shrink away from sociality as from too strong a light. They 'repress' somatic expressions," and avoid somatotonic conduct, such as whistling or singing, which draws attention to themselves. They also repress visceral conduct, such as spending time and thought over getting good meals. They are easily distracted and worried by noises or other outside occurrences. They shrink sedulously from attracting attention to themselves. "Their behavior seems dominated by the inhibitory and attentional functions of the cerebrum," and their motivation is the opposite of that of the other two types.

Among ordinary people the connection between bodily form and temperament is not so obvious as in the extreme types, but it appears to be just as close. Most people's bodies are mixtures of endomorphy, mesomorphy, and ectomorphy. Their temperaments are mixtures of visceratonia, somatotonia, and cerebrotonia. Mixtures in which all three types of body and temperament are well balanced are the best. Extremes are undesirable. Normally, too, the corresponding bodily and temperamental traits receive about the same relative degree of emphasis. A person with a huge intestine, for example, has a correspondingly strong desire to sit quietly after his meals and allow time for digestion.

Sometimes, however, the body tends in one direction and the temperament in another. A large intestine may be associated with a somatotonic temperament which impels a person to eat fast and then rush off to work. Such unbalanced persons are handicapped. Ideally, the digestive system, the muscles, and the nervous system are perfectly balanced, and the temperament is a good combination of hearty, affectionate good humor, alert, vigorous activity, and keen, quick, nervous responses. For the best results these attributes must be joined to a good intellect, thus supplementing bodily physique and temperament. Sheldon cites many examples of difficulties due to lack of harmony between body and temperament.

All this is highly significant as a step toward the solution of the problem of innate differences among races, although as yet it offers little more than a hope and a promise. Sheldon's facts suggest that certain types of body and temperament are relatively more abundant among Jews than among Negroes, for example. Kretschmer, Draper, and others have found that certain forms of insanity and disease tend to be associated with particular types of bodily form. The work of others indicates that bodily form and hence presumably temperament are probably inherited. Years ago Davenport found that the children of slender parents show a fairly uniform tendency to inherit the build of their parents. The children of fleshy parents, on the other hand, are only about half as likely to do so. He concluded that at least three and perhaps four hereditary factors influence bodily build.

E. A Speculative Connection between Religion and Bodily Build

The way in which bodily build and temperamental inheritance may possibly affect history is suggested by a comparison of three diverse religions. No definite conclusion is yet warranted, however, and what will now be said is highly speculative. Sheldon points out that Christianity has been historically based on the cerebrotonic virtues of self-restraint with an admixture of the visceratonic virtues which lead to affection. Christ has been almost universally portrayed as a slender ectomorph. Much of the teaching about him has centered around the corresponding cerebrotonic virtues of self-effacement, humility, non-resistance, and self-denial whereby the harmful, self-indulgent features of the affectionate visceratonic temperament are neutralized. The harsh, active, dominating, warlike qualities that go with the mesomorphic body and the somatotonic temperament are especially frowned upon in the Gospels. Nevertheless, the western Christian nations have followed an aggressive somatotonic way of life. Climate and diet with their effect upon vigor certainly have something to do with this contrast between earlier and later Christianity. Nevertheless, the question arises whether the original nature of the religion owes anything to the bodily constitution and innate temperamental type of the people among whom it originated.

This question gains more point when we look at Buddhism, a religion that is consistently visceratonic. In other words, its virtues are those of the quiet, placid type. Buddha is almost universally represented as a rather plump, well-rounded, inactive and almost stolid person. The ideal of Buddhism is quiet contemplation, which might almost be called a glorified version of the visceratonic propensity to sit still and enjoy a good smoke after dinner, even when there is work to do. Buddhism is a good expression of the better side of the visceratonic temperament which accompanies the endomorphic type of body. Hence we are again confronted by the question of how far the innate bodily and temperamental qualities of a man of great intellectual power, together, perhaps, with similar traits among the people around him, were responsible for the character of a great religion. A glance at the history of Buddhism shows that in India it has tended to die out among vast numbers of people who do not as a rule have endomorphic bodies. On the other hand, it has spread into regions such as Tibet, Burma, and China where that type of body and its accompanying temperament are dominant, and there it still survives. In this instance, however, just as with Christianity, the problem is greatly complicated by the effects of climate and diet upon bodily vigor and by the historical events which led up to the new religion.

In our own day another religion has at least made a beginning along the lines of the third major bodily and temperamental type. In Germany before World War II a new and vigorous religious movement was based squarely on the somatotonic temperament which accompanies the rectangular mesomorphic body. The Nazi cult glorifies force, vigor, activity, and little else. Christianity, because of its pacific nature, tends to repress these qualities or at least to concentrate them on peaceful and kindly purposes. The Nazi creed, so to speak, sloughs off both the visceratonic love of one's neighbor and the cerebrotonic idea of humility and non-resistance. Here again, however, we must not neglect other factors. The typical picture of a German does, indeed, show somatotonic features, although no one yet knows how common this type really is in Germany. Nevertheless, the Nazi cult, like the so-called worship of money and achievement in America, is the outgrowth of a long historical process and may also owe a great deal to its origin in a climate which stimulates vigor and activity far more than that of Palestine or India.

These facts about religion suggest an hypothesis which needs to be tested on a large scale. The hypothesis is that migrations and the natural selection to which they lead, together with the effect of climate, diet, and other environmental factors both before and after the migrations, may have caused the people of specific regions to show a preponderance of certain bodily types and of corresponding temperaments or habits of mind. Such "racial" traits in turn may predispose the inhabitants toward a certain type of religion, thus leading them to remake a religion which arose elsewhere or to adopt a new religion more in harmony with their bodily type, temperament, and physical environment. It must be clearly understood that when we talk about temperament we do not mean intellect. A strong intellect may accompany any type of temperament, regardless of whether it is indolent, self-sacrificing, alert, or of some other sort. Moreover, a strong intellect does not necessarily direct its efforts along lines that will benefit society. What happens in that respect depends largely upon cultural surroundings, especially the events of childhood. This hypothesis of religion in relation to other factors is of no value if accepted as a fact. It is of great value as a stimulant to the framing of alternative hypotheses and to the development of methods whereby the various hypotheses can be tested. It is also of value as illustrating the fact that in the great problems of civilization the effect of all three of the prime factors—heredity, physical environment, and cultural endowment—must always be considered.

Chapter 3 may be summed up by saying that views concerning race as a factor in civilization are undergoing a radical change, and no one can yet see what the final result will be. It seems clear that the truth does not lie with those who claim great superiority for Nordics, Aryans, or people of any other real or supposed race. Nor does it lie with those who maintain that racial background and biological inheritance are of no importance in determining aptitudes and capacities. The truth seems to be that biological inheritance is quite as important in man's brain and other internal organs as in his outward appearance. Nevertheless, because environment influences everyone from the time of conception onward, it has thus far been almost impossible to obtain reliable measurements of the actual conditions of heredity in one race as compared with another. Fortunately, however, new anthropological methods are coming into use. These suggest that we shall soon be able to estimate many features of innate temperament from physical build, and that in due time a new classification of people according to bodily build and temperament may be developed. When that is done we may find that great cultural movements, such as religions, or other basic historical trends take many of their qualities from the innate physical and temperamental character of the people among whom they originate. Even if this theory proves true, however, we shall still find that both physical and cultural environment also play major roles.

CHAPTER 4

THE INSTABILITY OF RACES

A. Temperamental Selection as a Racial Factor

In addition to providing other novel ideas concerning racial traits, the new anthropology suggests that these traits are not so immutable as was formerly supposed. Perhaps it would be more accurate to say that psychology and physiology are now taking an active part in the investigation of racial problems, and anthropology is therefore assuming a radically new aspect. Inheritance of bodily form and mental aptitude is assuredly persistent, but little by little, through selection and perhaps by other means, it can be changed. The work of Shapiro illustrates this truth. His associate, Hulse, measured about twenty-six hundred Japanese according to a method resembling that of Sheldon. By comparing each person's measurements with his height, Shapiro obtained twenty-one indices which give a picture of constitutional physique. The subjects thus measured belonged to three closely related groups: (1) Japanese immigrants to Hawaii; (2) their near relatives of similar age still living in Japan; and (3) their Hawaiian-born children.

Shapiro's analysis shows that the first two groups differ systematically in size and bodily proportions. The migrants are taller than their stay-at-home relatives, or "sedentes," as Shapiro calls them. In proportion to their height the men show greater width of shoulder, length of arm, length and breadth of hip, depth of chest, width of nose, and so forth. The migrant women differ from their relatives at home in much the same way as the men but to a less extent and with some differences. When the migrants are divided into three groups according to their original homes in Japan, a curious and important fact emerges. The three migrant groups are more alike than are the corresponding groups of relatives in Japan. Moreover, the bodily type most common among the migrants is more abundant among the home-stayers around Niigata on the cool northwestern coast of central Japan than among those in Fukuoka and Hiroshima in the warm Southwest close to Korea. Inasmuch as the Japanese during past centuries have migrated northward, the people of Niigata represent a greater migration than the other two groups. Thus three stages are evident: first, the normal southern type; second, northward migrants of long ago who differ from the southerners in certain respects; and third, recent migrants to Hawaii who differ from their home-staying relatives in these same respects, but more markedly, and also in others. Thus Shapiro concludes that Japanese with a certain type of physical build are temperamentally more inclined to migrate than those with a different build.

The fact that women show this tendency less than men is to be expected. In Japan women are still so subservient that the wishes of wives are less potent than those of husbands in deciding whether to migrate. The great majority of the Japanese women who migrated to Hawaii, however, were "picture brides." The decision to migrate was largely in the hands of their parents. Nevertheless, the wishes of both the wives and the prospective brides doubtless influenced the final decision. Under such circumstances we should expect the women to show the migrant type of physique to a certain extent, but not so much as the men. It should be borne in mind that most of the migrants were ordinary peasants of the less prosperous sort who went to Hawaii to serve as laborers on the sugar plantations. The steamship companies which brought them made no selection. They simply provided relatively easy opportunities for migration. The selective process operated through the temperamental and intellectual qualities of the Japanese themselves.

Shapiro's work on Japanese emigrants leads to the same general conclusion as that of Draper on diseases, Kretschmer on insanity, Hooton on criminals, and Sheldon on students and others. Definite types of bodily build appear to be accompanied by a predilection toward certain kinds of conduct. If this broad generalization is confirmed, it becomes of great historical importance. It suggests that during the centuries the mental as well as the physical qualities of different sections of a race may have been altered by migration and other selective processes. When the effect of racial mixture is also taken into account, it becomes evident that the old method of ascribing specific qualities to races which were defined only by such factors as head form and complexion is quite out of date.

B. Environmental Effect on Racial Traits

A new environment, as well as selective migration, may alter qualities which are supposedly characteristic of races. More than a generation ago Boas measured many immigrants and their children in New York City. Some were broad-headed Jews from Poland. Their children born in New York proved to be less broad-headed than the parents. Moreover, the reduction in breadth of head increased in accordance with the duration of the residence in New York. Another group of immigrants consisted of long-headed people from southern Italy. In their case, also, there was a slight but significant difference between the American-born children and their parents or brothers and sisters born in Europe. This difference, too, increased with the length of time since immigration. In this case, however, the change was toward greater instead of less breadth of head. In other words, each type of children tended somewhat away from the standard physique of the parents and toward a less extreme middle type. In spite of earlier skepticism the work of Boas appears to be a sound, epoch-making step of progress. Migration from Europe to New York seems to be accompanied by slight physiological changes whereby racial stocks at either extreme in head form become less extreme. This does not mean that broad-headed people become long-headed, or the reverse. It merely means that each group, although retaining substantially its original innate traits, becomes less extreme than formerly. This fact is highly significant because head form has been accepted as the most reliable element in most classifications of race.

Shapiro's Hawaiian study also indicates a difference of bodily form between immigrant parents and their children. On the whole the difference is not so great as between the parents and their kindred in Japan, but the children depart farther than their parents from the old type of physique which prevails in Japan. Some idea of its importance may be gathered from the percentage of Shapiro's twenty-one indices which indicate mathematically significant differences among his three groups of Japanese. The Japanese men who came to Hawaii differ significantly from their kindred at home in 76 per cent of the indices and the women in 45 per cent. The children of these migrants differ similarly from their parents to the extent of 44 per cent, the figure for both sexes being practically the same. These new differences cause the Hawaiian-born children to differ from their kin in old Japan in 91 per cent of the indices for boys and 80 for girls.

This, then, is what happens. First, the opportunity to migrate to Hawaii initiates a selection whereby Japanese with a particular bodily constitution show more tendency than others to migrate. This must mean that somehow they differ from the others mentally. Second, the children born to the migrants in Hawaii differ from their parents. When allowances are made for age, the boys average 4.1 centimeters taller than their fathers and the girls 1.7 centimeters taller than their mothers. Moreover, the new environment somehow causes the generation born in Hawaii to differ from its parents in the relation between height and other measurements, thus giving a slightly different bodily build. This does not mean that the Japanese in Hawaii are becoming like the native Hawaiians. The old Japanese inheritance is still overwhelmingly dominant, but with a difference. Whether this difference is temperamental as well as physical is not known, but the chances seem to be that it is.

C. Secular Changes in Stature

Another kind of change is also altering the bodily form of more than one race. Bowles cites statistics of stature that go back a century and a half in Switzerland and fifty years or so in many other places. They indicate a surprisingly widespread increase in stature. Among European countries data covering one or two generations are available for Norway, Sweden, Denmark, Germany, the Netherlands, Italy, and Spain. Japanese data from 1878 onward are particularly significant because they show that an Asiatic people is undergoing the same lengthening process as those of European extraction. Women share this trend with men, as is clear in Japan as well as the United States. Students at Smith, Vassar, Wellesley, Mount Holyoke, and other women's colleges are taller than their mothers or predecessors, and at Harvard, Yale, Princeton, Amherst, Pennsylvania, Wisconsin, and other places each college generation is generally taller than the last.

Among students entering Yale, according to Deegan, those more than 6 feet tall formed 23 per cent in 1941 in contrast to 5 per cent 50 years earlier. The classes entering the university in 1940 and 1941 were the tallest on record up to that time, with an average height a trifle over 5 feet, 10 inches, almost 2½ inches greater than in the 1880's. Studies of armor indicate that even among the upper social classes, which usually are relatively tall, medieval men were decidedly shorter than those of today in the same regions. Bones in Norway indicate still shorter stature in the late Stone Age. Only when we go back to the extinct Cro-Magnon people of the Old Stone Age nearly 20,000 years ago do we find men who average as tall as American college students. The increase in stature still continues, although some authorities see signs that the rate of increase is declining.

From the standpoint of civilization it is important to know whether increased stature is accompanied by changes in other respects also. Bowles' study of fathers and sons at Harvard and of mothers and daughters at Wellesley, Smith, Vassar, and Mount Holyoke shows that in both sexes the younger generation is not only taller and heavier than its parents but differently proportioned. For example, among the men of the younger generation 54 per cent of the total increase in height is concentrated in the upper leg from knee to hip. The corresponding section of the arms, on the contrary, has become actually as well as relatively shorter, but the forearm has become longer. In the trunk of the body, the abdominal lower section below the navel has increased in length more than any other part. Thus among men the increase in size is largely concentrated in the middle of the body from elbows to knees as one stands with the arms hanging down. Other changes make the younger generation more slender. The head has become narrower. So have the hips when measured from side to side, although the buttocks have become more prominent, thus increasing the girth at the hips. Among the Harvard sons the girth of the upper arms and chest, as well as of the thighs and hips, is relatively, as well as absolutely, greater than among the fathers, but curiously enough the sons can, on the average, expand their chests only 70 per cent as much as their fathers.

Among college women, differences between mothers and daughters are generally similar to those between college fathers and sons, but with some variations. Among women the lower leg instead of the upper shows the greatest relative increase in length. Narrowing of the hips and protrusion of the buttocks are more accentuated than in men. The trunk, rather than the legs, shows the greatest increase in length, and among women, as among men, the abdominal section lengthens most. In comparison with the men of their own generation, modern college women are proportionally smaller than their mothers. Both sexes have become more slender, with narrower shoulders and hips. The narrowing of the hips is especially noteworthy, as it means decreased width of the pelvic bones. Such changes raise a most interesting question which cannot yet be answered: do they indicate changes in temperament as well as in body?

D. Causes of Changes in Stature

The cause of the recent increase in stature is generally supposed to be modern improvements in diet, hygiene and exercise, or perhaps changes in occupations, but such factors can scarcely be solely responsible. In many countries the increase in stature began long before there was any appreciable change in these respects. The stature of army recruits or others is known to have increased almost steadily from decade to decade since 1792 in Switzerland, 1836 among Harvard students, 1841 in Sweden, 1852 in Denmark, 1855 in Norway, 1863 in Holland, and 1885 in Japan. Mills [1] believes that a gradual lowering of temperature has been the primary factor since medieval times and that recent warmth, especially in the decade from 1930–40, has checked the gain in height, but this needs verification. Another hypothesis is that the present increase in stature and weight, with the accompanying changes in bodily proportions, is part of an evolutionary process whose nature and causes we have not yet penetrated. This solution is unsatisfactory, but so is all ignorance as to fundamental causes. A third hypothesis, based on women's increasing freedom in the choice of husbands, will be explained later.

As a factor in civilization the change in bodily form is important mainly if it has some relation to temperament and intellect or to survival. Sargent [2] states that students with high scholastic standing are generally above the average in height and weight. The mentally proficient, as he puts it, are also physically proficient. "We may conclude, therefore," says Bowles, "that increase in stature should be considered as a good sign, for students are getting both younger physically and more fit than those of a generation ago." On a later page,[3] however, this favorable conclusion is modified: "Despite the advantage of increased stature and weight these increases are offset to a degree by the decrease in chest expansion and the decrease, especially in the female, of pelvic breadth." Bowles [4] also suggests that the recent increase in heart diseases is partly caused by taxing the heart muscles in earlier life. Tall children grow so fast, especially at puberty, that they are often weak for a while and their hearts may suffer a serious strain.

A glance at geological history suggests that excessive stature may hamper survival. Throughout organic evolution a tendency toward extreme size has systematically been a precursor of disappearance. This was true of the ammonites referred to in Chapter 1, of the huge dinosaurs in medieval geological times, and of the mastodon and mammoth. The Cro-Magnons of fifteen or twenty thousand years ago were tall, but have died out. Among modern peoples the backward Dinkas and Shelluhs of the hot plains of Sudan are among the few groups which vie with college students in height and slenderness. We do not know whether they are decadent, however, nor do we know whether the elongated heads of our tall modern people are a disadvantage or advantage.

Griffith Taylor [5] believes that such narrow heads are a sign of racial primitiveness. Analyzing the people of the world according to head form, he finds approximately the same peculiar distribution in each continent, including even Australia. In general the most primitive types with the narrowest heads occupy the margins or extreme tips of each continent, as well as isolated islands, and secluded areas protected by mountains, tropical forests, or other natural features. Toward the center of the continent and in the most easily accessible of the other portions the breadth of the heads increases. Hence until modern Europeans invaded the New World the central part of each continent was regularly occupied by broad-headed people of relatively recent origin. These people, Taylor believes, represent the latest product of evolution. At present the broad-headed type seems to be gaining in relative numbers. In world history the long-headed people of Mediterranean and Nordic race have indeed been more conspicuous in their achievements than the broad-headed Alpines and Mongoloids of Asia. This superiority, however, seems to be due largely to advantages of physical environment rather than innate competence. Some of the greatest men of all time, such as Louis Pasteur and Victor Hugo, were broad-headed Alpines.*

E. A Sample Test of an Evolutionary Trend

As a test of the relation between bodily form and human survival, the physical measurements of 3,500 men who graduated from Yale College between 1890 and 1911 may be compared with their family relationships. The men were measured soon after entering college and also at later dates. The measurements nearest the age of 19 were chosen, those at ages below 18 being excluded. The family records were taken from books issued by each class 25 years after graduation. Dividing these men into approximately equal groups according to

[5] 1919, 1921; Huntington, 1924A, p. 75.

*The short line immediately below the asterisk indicates the beginning of a somewhat technical section which the reader can omit without losing the thread of thought. The end of such a section is indicated by a longer line.

height, we find that among short men (under 67 inches) the percentage of marriage is 79, among men of medium stature (67–69 inches) it is 85, and among taller men, 89. The low figure for short men is due in considerable measure to persons who would normally be of medium height or tall, but have been stunted by malnutrition, disease, or accident. Such men, being often weak, crippled, or otherwise handicapped, are more likely than others to remain unmarried. Nevertheless, part of the 10 per cent difference in the marriage rates of tall and short men is presumably due to social selection. Other things being equal, women as a rule prefer tall men to short. This preference may help to explain the general increase in stature during the past century.

The reproductive rate of short men is lowered by sterile marriages as well as by failure to marry. The percentages of sterile marriages among short, medium, and tall Yale graduates are 24.5, 20.4, and 22.6. Both extremes are less fertile than the more normal middle type. Here, too, however, the short group includes men who would normally be in the other groups if it were not for ill health. In view of this it is rather surprising that the number of children per father is almost the same among them as among the others, the averages for the three groups being 2.44, 2.58, and 2.55. The net result is that the number of children per graduate, including the unmarried, the childless married, and the fathers, averages 1.48, 1.74, and 1.73 for the short, the medium, and the tall respectively. Thus the short men have approximately 15 per cent less children than either the medium or the tall.

If the relatively small number of children among short men were entirely due to social selection instead of to physical handicaps which are also the cause of shortness, it would help to explain the increase in stature from generation to generation. The help thus rendered, however, does not amount to much. Suppose, for example, that the average statures of the three groups are 65, 67, and 69 inches. If no other cause of progressive change in stature were in operation, the differences in the size of families among tall men and short would cause the average height of the sons to be 67.10 inches, as compared with 67.00 for the fathers. In other words, the differentials in marriage and fertility that we have just been discussing would produce an increase of only one tenth of an inch in stature from generation to generation. The actual increase among Yale students has been about 1½ inches. When allowance is made for the impairment of physique environmentally by disease and other factors, there remains little evidence that systematic increase in stature for generation after generation is due in any significant degree to a selective process which acts against short people. Thus a study of fertility in relation to stature is of no more help than improvements in diet in explaining why people are growing taller. The only alternative seems to be an unsatisfactory appeal to some unknown evolutionary force, the workings of which we can see although its origin and nature are not understood.

F. Bodily Form and Rates of Reproduction

Other evidence suggests that the shape of the body—the constitutional build—is more important than stature both as an index of temperament and as a factor in survival. In this respect the most significant aspect of bodily form thus far tested is the shape of the trunk as indicated by the ratio between the breadths of the shoulders and hips. This ratio depends on distances measured from points where the bones come close to the skin and is only slightly influenced by fat or muscle. The shoulders are normally broader than the hips. In solidly built "rectangular" people the shoulders may be no more than ten per cent wider than the hips; in extremely "triangular" people, on the other hand, this figure may rise to fifty per cent. On the basis of the shoulder-hip ratio each of our stature groups may be divided into "rectangulars" with a ratio of 124 or less, "moderates" with a ratio of 124 to 130, and "triangulars" with still higher ratios.

The family relations of the rectangular and triangular types are alike in some respects and different in others. For example, among the 3,500 Yale graduates here considered, the percentage of married men varies only from about 83 for the most rectangular types to 84 or 85 for the rest. On the other hand, Figure 2 (curve A) shows that the percentage of married men having at least one child declines rather steadily from the most rectangular types on the left to the most triangular on the right. This suggests that the rectangular men, or their wives, are potentially more fertile than the others.*

Curiously enough the significant (solid) part of curve B, showing the average number of children per father, slopes in an opposite direction from the curve above it. This means that the average size

* The dashed parts of the lines in Figure 2 are of little significance because based on very few men, only 2 per cent of the total. They suggest that extremely triangular men stand low in fertility. In the following discussion this group will be omitted.

of families increases systematically from about 2.4 children among the rectangulars to 2.7 among the triangulars, a difference of 12 or 13 per cent. The third curve (*C*) indicates that this increase occurs be-

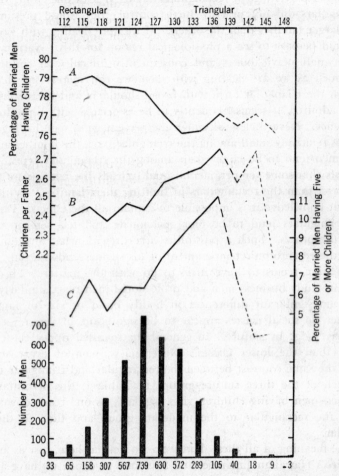

Figure 2. Bodily Build and Families of 3,500 Graduates of Yale College, 1890–1911
Numbers at top show breadth of shoulders as percentage of breadth of hips.

cause the triangulars are about twice as likely as the rectangulars to have large families of from five to nine children.

The facts represented in Figure 2 seem to indicate a connection between bodily physique on the one hand and temperament and biological survival on the other hand. Perhaps the various types choose wives who differ in fertility, but that does not alter the final result. Some quality connected with bodily shape seems to make rectangular men, or their wives, more fertile than triangulars, as is indicated by the higher percentage of rectangulars having at least one child. If the rectangulars did not practice birth control, they would presumably have larger families than the others. If we were dealing with women, it would be easy to see a physiological reason for this. Narrow hips mean small pelvic bones and consequently difficulty in childbirth. Inasmuch as we are dealing with men, we can merely say that although the triangular form with broad shoulders and narrow hips is often admired, it seems frequently to be associated with reproductive deficiency. Nevertheless, although the percentage of men having children is relatively small among the triangular type, the families among such men tend to be larger than among the rectangular type. This suggests that some temperamental quality leads the triangulars to be less strict than the rectangulars in limiting their families. With our present knowledge it is impossible to explain all these facts. Perhaps the triangulars tend to be more passionate and less self-controlled than the others. Such a possibility accords with what Sheldon says as to the cerebrotonic temperament of his slender endomorphic type. Occupation seems to have little to do with the matter. Throughout this study business men and professional men react similarly and show no significant differences in bodily build or size of families. Neither do social classes appear to be significant in this respect, if we may judge by stature. In general the so-called upper classes are taller than the lower classes. Nevertheless, men of every stature show the same contrast between the rectangular and triangular types. In each of the three stature groups in Table 1, the percentage of married men having children rises regularly as one reads downward from the rectangular to the moderate group and then to the triangular.

The meaning of all these data seems to be that here, just as among Shapiro's Hawaiian Japanese, and Sheldon's students, we have an example of a significant relation between bodily form and temperament. In the present example, however, we also find a still further relationship, namely, a connection whereby bodily constitution in one way and temperament in another influence the size of families and hence the survival of specific types. It happens that in this example the two influences seem to work in opposite directions, but under other social conditions they might operate together. As things now stand, greater powers of reproduction among rectangular men

TABLE 1

PERCENTAGES OF MARRIED MEN HAVING CHILDREN

(Based on about 1,100 men of the Yale classes of 1893, 1896, 1898, 1910, and 1911)

Ratio of Shoulders to Hips	Stature			
	Short Under 5 ft. 6 in.	*Medium* 5 ft. 6 in. to 5 ft. 8 in.	*Tall* Over 5 ft. 8 in.	*All Statures*
Rectangular (124 or less)	66%	79%	72%	73%
Moderate (124–130)	79%	83%	77%	80%
Triangular (above 130)	82%	86%	82%	84%

appear to be cancelled by greater self-control and consequent limitation of families. The net result is that the number of children per graduate, including the unmarried and childless, as well as the fathers, is only 1.57 for the most nearly rectangular third of our 3,500 men, 1.72 for the middle third, and 1.70 for the most nearly triangular third. The smallness of all these figures, of course, indicates that the type of population represented by college graduates is declining rapidly. The differences in the numbers suggest that the percentage of triangular men, like that of tall men, is on the increase. It must not be forgotten, however, that all these differences may be due to unknown factors which influence the selection of wives.

Although we do not yet know how far these tendencies extend to all parts of the population, a general principle seems clear. The physical form and presumably the temperamental inheritance of any given group of people may suffer alteration from one generation to another. Such changes may result from new environments, as among the Japanese in Hawaii and immigrants from Italy or Russia in New York. They may also occur without any noticeable variation in physical environment, but in harmony with changes in social customs, such as the freedom of girls to chose husbands, or the introduction of a new idea, such as contraception. Thus among Yale graduates the new social custom of contraception seems to have affected the rectangular men, or their wives, more than the triangular, presumably because of a difference in temperament associated with a difference in physique.

G. *The Plasticity of Races*

The main feature of this chapter and its predecessor is a series of facts which indicate a rapidly changing viewpoint as to race. Throughout history the belief that races differ markedly in innate ability has played a prominent and usually sinister part. Merely because of his color, the shape of his nose, the breadth of his head, or the slant of his eyes, every man has been supposed to inherit a tendency to be cowardly, brave, sentimental, intellectual, musical, superior, or inferior, as the case may be. Anthropology and psychology have overthrown this idea by showing that any such connection between a single physical feature, or even a small group of features, and a definite temperamental or social trait is slight. Now, however, we are beginning to suspect that when the entire body is taken into account, including all the organs and functions as well as the outward appearance, there is probably a significant relation between bodily type and temperament. The man in the street has long believed this in a perverted form which has encouraged the worst kind of racism. What we now need is full and impartial scientific analysis.

The new idea of constitutional types has been accompanied by another great change of opinion. A few generations ago, and even today in many countries, it was widely believed that race is something clearly defined and that each person can be assigned to a definite race. Now, however, it is clear that each race, even the purest, contains a great assortment of physical and mental types. In each main race it would theoretically be possible to pick out many groups with distinct temperamental and intellectual traits, differing widely from those of other groups belonging to the same race, but rather closely matching similar groups from other races. In the really vital factors of innate mental endowment the groups from different races would thus be much alike, but they would differ in head form, hair, complexion, and shape of nose and eye—the very criteria on which our present racial classification is based. Anyone who has travelled widely and observed sympathetically knows that when the barrier of language and habits is passed, he is more at home with men whose minds are like his, regardless of whether they are Chinese, Negroes, Turks, or Arabs, than with men of his own race whose intellectual and temperamental level is widely different. The most significant difference between races lies not in externals, but in the relative numbers of the various constitutional types with their diverse physical and, especially, temperamental and intellectual qualities.

Another great change is taking place in our ideas about race. There has long been and still is a strong conviction among anthropologists that head form in particular and the bony skeleton in general are good indicators of racial descent because they supposedly cannot be changed by any form of environment. They may be altered by the intermarriage of different types, but otherwise they have been supposed to continue unchanged for hundreds of generations. The work of Boas, Shapiro, and others has strongly shaken this view. Three types of change may take place in what were formerly considered permanent racial traits. First, a new environment, either through climate, food, or economic and social factors, can apparently initiate changes whereby the bodily form of children differs from that of parents. A new environment seems to have caused the children of broad-headed Russians and long-headed South Italians in New York and of Japanese migrants in Hawaii to differ from their parents. This may be partly because the new environment brings out possibilities which were previously present but could not make themselves manifest until the right external stimulus appeared. The second type of change arises through selection. Among Japanese emigrants to Hawaii we have seen that physical and mental selection are associated. In later chapters we shall see much additional evidence of mental selection.

The third type of change in hitherto supposedly permanent racial traits is represented by the prolonged increase in stature which has been widely observed among military recruits and students. It does not seem to arise through any external physical cause that we can yet lay hands on. It may, however, be the result of social selection such as that exercised by women in their choice of husbands. Another possibility is that new social customs introduce new selective forces, thus limiting reproduction among some types of people more than among others. Triangular Yale graduates, for example, are especially likely to have large families. In spite of these various possibilities the persistent increase of stature under environmental conditions as diverse as rural life a century ago and the urbanized life of the majority of college students today suggests some deep-seated cause connected with the general course of evolution. Only time can tell whether this type of change is really actuated by some great underlying evolutionary principle which is as yet beyond the reach of ordinary investigation.

The interplay of the various factors which lead to new combinations of human traits is illustrated specifically by our study of the families of Yale graduates. What seems to happen among them is that the evolutionary process which has for centuries tended toward greater stature has recently been supplemented by a new tendency arising from birth control. If the first tendency could work unchecked it would apparently produce tall people of such proportions that the women would have hips wide enough to make childbirth relatively easy. This more or less rectangular type of body, however, is apparently associated with a temperament which under our present economic and social system leads to especially severe restriction of births. Hence we are getting an undue percentage of people who combine excessive height with hips so narrow as to endanger reproduction. How much truth there is in this conclusion remains to be seen. The important point at present is that even though innate traits of both body and mind are transmitted from generation to generation with great persistence, they may at any time be modified by the impact of new environments or by new types of selection arising from new social conditions. Thus racial traits are modified in other ways as well as by intermarriage between diverse racial types. Moreover, in addition to the changes which can be definitely ascribed to known factors of environment there are others for which environmental causes are not yet evident.

One of the conditions which may be altering the quality of the people in the United States is a change in the age of mothers at the birth of their children. In 1922 and 1923, after the effect of World War I had disappeared, 65 per cent of white children were born to mothers under 30 years of age. In 1939 and 1940, although the general birthrate had fallen, this percentage had risen to 71.[6] The greatest change was that the percentage of children born to young women 20 to 25 years of age, and in a less degree to those under 20, had increased, whereas at greater ages, especially 35 to 40 years, there had been a corresponding decline.

This change should be considered in connection with the evidence that the first-born child is more likely to distinguish itself than those born later.[7] There is also some evidence that children born to mothers near the end of the reproductive period tend to be more nervous and more often defective than those born between the maternal ages of 20 and 30 years. If this is true, birth control tends to make na-

[6] *Vital Statistics*, 1941, p. 669.

[7] Huntington, 1938; Havelock Ellis, 1927.

tions stronger. Where it prevails, the proportion of children born to mothers in the period when their health is best is greater now than formerly, and the chances of producing healthy children are correspondingly greater. This may be an important element in giving vigor to America and western Europe in contrast to countries such as India, China, and Japan.

From the standpoint of the present book this whole discussion means that in studying history and civilization we must carefully distinguish between two lines of thought. The first, which now seems outmoded, insists that there are superior and inferior races regardless of environment. The innate qualities of a race, both physical and mental, are supposed to be permanently fixed. The other, which now appears correct, holds that, although races differ, each contains so many physical and mental types that some parts of it are able to rise to a high level if given the right environment, both physical and cultural. It also holds that races are to a certain degree plastic. Undoubtedly their main characteristics, both physical and mental, are passed on with high persistence by heredity. Nevertheless, if the environment, either physical or social, is sufficiently extreme, it induces changes or at least brings out possibilities and responses which were previously hidden. A race which is widely distributed over the earth's surface is almost certain to comprise a wide variety of types.

CHAPTER 5

MIGRATION AND HUMAN QUALITY

A. Migration and Illiteracy in the United States

Differences in human quality from place to place and period to period are so important and so little understood that we may well investigate them further. Much of the difference between Denmark and the Indo-Chinese state of Cambodia, for example, arises from differences in the temperament, intelligence, and vigor of the people. Cultural differences, so obvious in occupations, dress, manners, government, religion, and education, explain these mental and physiological differences only in part. Physical conditions, such as natural resources, food, climate, and location in respect to other countries, are also obviously important. In fact there is reason to believe that in due time every type of culture adapts itself to its physical environment. Behind both the culture and the physical environment, however, lies the innate quality of the people. The history of the past can never be a reliable guide to the future until we know with certainty the answers to such questions as these: What innate differences in mentality are there between Danes and Cambodians? Were the Vikings who harried the coasts of western Europe in the ninth century temperamentally more aggressive than the descendants of the modern Danes? Were the Khmers who built the wonderful ruins of Angkor Wat in the same ninth century innately more efficient than the present mild and inefficient Cambodians? And how far have the present innate qualities of both Danes and Cambodians been influenced by the physical and cultural environment of their ancestors?

As a step toward answering such questions a study of the selective action of migration will be helpful. Migrations induce changes in all three of the primary conditions which determine the level of civilization. On the physical side they bring people into contact with new climates, foods, diseases, resources, and occupations. Biologically they lead to bodily and mental changes such as we have seen among Japanese in Hawaii and Europeans in New York. Culturally migration may bring people into contact with new habits, or may stimulate them to drop old practices and adopt new ones.

The United States, with its reliable statistics, gives a clear idea of some effects of migration. Although the historical importance of migration is universally recognized, there are diverse views as to how far it is selective. The conditions among immigrants to the United States suggest that literacy is an important clue to the general intelligence and perhaps the innate ability which lead people to sort themselves into diverse groups during the process of migration. In 1920, when the great tide of immigration that preceded World War I had settled into place, the literacy of the foreign-born American population increased quite steadily from Pennsylvania westward.[1] Figure 3 shows this for farmers, for rural non-farm people, and for the urban type of population. All the way from Pennsylvania (right side of diagram) westward to Oregon, the three groups behave about alike. The curve for farm families, which is the smoothest, rises with almost perfect regularity through Ohio, Indiana, and Illinois to Iowa. There, in America's richest agricultural state, which was then a "land of promise," it rises to its maximum. Farther west in Nebraska and Wyoming, where the opportunities for farmers are not quite so good as in Iowa, the curve declines a little. Then in Idaho and Oregon, where irrigation or rainfall once more provides good opportunities for farming, the curve again rises to almost the Iowa level. Even among native whites (top of Figure 3), the ability to read and write increases from the Middle West (Indiana) to the Far West.

The significance of Figure 3 seems clear. Immigrants who can read and write generally know more than the illiterate about the location of the best opportunities. On an average they have greater resources and usually more intelligence, energy, and persistence. At any rate selection has taken place in such a way that the percentage of illiterates declines almost steadily from the ports of entry to the parts of the country with the greatest opportunities for able immigrants. Night schools and special opportunities in cities alter this arrangement but do not destroy it. This illustrates the important fact that the quality of migrants does not depend merely on the type of selection in their original homes. It depends also on new opportunities and experiences during and after the journey to the new home. The final character of migrants may depend more on such conditions than upon initial selection. This, however, does not detract from the im-

[1] Huntington, 1934.

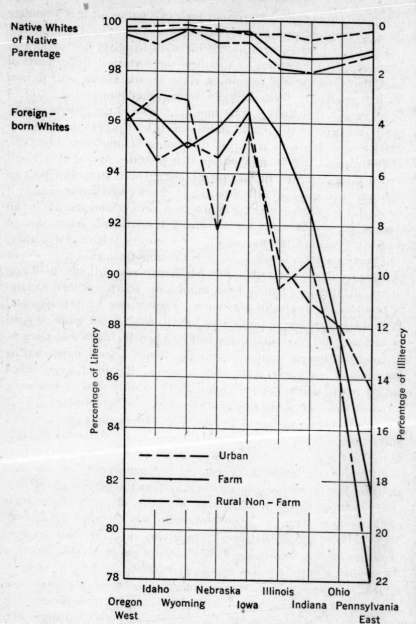

Figure 3. Literacy of Adult Immigrants in the United States, 1920.

portance of the selective process. The delicacy with which the process operates is evident in the fact that in Nebraska and Idaho a decline in opportunities is reflected in increased illiteracy. In states so far from the seacoast, however, the difficulties of a long migration have already weeded out most of the illiterates so that the increase in their percentage is slight. Still farther west great distance and good opportunities again reduce the percentage of illiterates to practically the Iowa level.

―――――――

Among the immigrants who remain in Iowa the selective process still continues. Although Iowa is comparatively uniform, the value of its farmland varies considerably because of differences in soil and topography. Table 2 shows the state of affairs in 1920, when the many immigrants of the early part of the present century had become well settled. A selective process had then distributed the foreign-born farmers of Iowa in such a way that they were especially numerous in the counties with the most valuable land. In 20 counties where the average value of farmland was below $150 per acre (column *A*) only 10 per cent (column *C*) of the farmers were foreign-born, whereas in 16 counties with land values above $250 the percentage was 24. On the poorest land only 31 per cent of the farmers were tenants (column *D*) but on the best the percentage was 53. Nevertheless, columns *E* and *F* show that on the poor land illiteracy was twice as great as on the good. Among the native whites this may have been due in part to poor schools, but among the foreign-born it must have been almost entirely due to selection, for most of the

TABLE 2

SELECTIVE MIGRATION IN IOWA [2]

A	*B*	*C*	*D*	*E*	*F*
		Percentage of	Percentage of	Illiteracy per 100,000 Persons Over 10 Years of Age	
Value of Land per Acre, 1920	Number of Counties	Foreign-born Farmers	Tenancy	Foreign-born	Native White
$150 or less	20	10	31	622	63
150 to 175	16	15	41	413	49
175 to 200	15	11	43	472	42
200 to 225	15	17	47	404	37
225 to 250	15	18	48	403	44
250 or more	16	24	53	290	29

[2] Huntington, 1924A, p. 72.

foreign-born came as adults. If opportunities for education after arrival in America had much effect on our data for literacy, the curves of Figure 3 could scarcely stand far lower in Ohio, for example, than in Nebraska. In Iowa it is clear that the more ignorant immigrants, who generally tend to be the less efficient, show a systematic tendency to go to the poorer counties in greater proportion than to the best. Then, as so often happens, the relative disadvantages of the new environment accentuate the contrast due to the original selection. The relatively illiterate poorer counties do not support such good schools as the others, and their children suffer accordingly.

B. *Migration and Farm Values*

Similar selection seems to occur among native white farmers who migrate westward in the United States.[3] Using data for 1924, when there had been time for fairly complete adjustment after the great prewar migration, we can pick out thirteen national, or racial, groups of farmers who are numerous enough to be significant. Three of these, whites, Negroes and Indians, are native-born. The rest are British, Irish, Germans, Russians, and other Europeans. The average values of the farms owned or operated by these different groups vary considerably. For example, in New England the farms of Indians had an average value of only about $2,000, and those of British-born farmers $11,000, with the others scattered between. An average of $5,500, only half the British figure, is not very creditable to the native whites, most of whom inherited their farms, whereas the immigrants had to buy or rent. Still less creditable is the fact that among the thirteen groups the native whites of New England stand eighth from the top.

Further westward, the relative position of the native white farmers improves, becoming seventh in the Middle Atlantic division, third in the East North Central, fifth in the West North Central, fourth in the Rocky Mountains, and second on the Pacific Coast. Except for a sudden upward jump in the East North Central States, which as a whole are America's most prosperous and attractive farming section, the native white farmers improve their position steadily from east to west. This suggests that in the East, on an average, they are less competent than most of the immigrant farmers. Westward, however, even though the immigrants show increasing ability, if one may judge

[3] Huntington, 1924A, p. 85.

from their literacy, the native white farmers increase in competence at a still more rapid rate. Thus they surpass first one group of immigrants and then another until they rise from eighth place to second. On the Pacific Coast only the Irish-born among our thirteen groups surpassed them in 1924, and they by only a small margin. It is interesting, however, to note that in those days, before World War II, the farms owned or run by Japanese in the Pacific States were even more valuable than those of either native whites or persons born in Ireland.

C. The Nature of the Selective Process

These two examples, based on illiteracy and farm value, seem to illustrate a definite pattern of selection by migration. The main selection of immigrants to America takes place in Europe. Many facts in addition to those here presented indicate that on the whole, but with many exceptions, the immigrants who come to a new country on their own initiative and at their own expense tend to be more enterprising than their neighbors of similar social, economic, and intellectual standing who stay at home. This does not imply that they are more intelligent than the others or that they are more enterprising than the average *of the community as a whole*. The social and ethical level from which immigration is derived varies greatly according to political, religious, and economic conditions. Therefore, when we say "more enterprising" we mean only in comparison with the particular level from which immigration is drawn under any particular circumstance. After the immigrants reach America further selection takes place in such a way that the better educated tend to go to the places where opportunities are greatest. Among farmers good opportunties may be offered by new regions not yet heavily populated, or by good soils. Abandoned, but still potentially productive, farms left by enterprising native whites in the East may offer considerable opportunities for poor farmers from Poland, for example. Thus on all sides there is selection such that the immigrants who settle where opportunities are especially great tend to be more competent on an average than those settling where opportunities are less. It is especially significant that in Figure 3 the curve of farmers not only has the same general form as those for urban and rural non-farm people but is much more regular. It shows what happens when, to a considerable degree, we eliminate differences due to such matters as voca-

tional aptitudes and previous occupations. Part at least of the drop
in the curve for rural non-farm migrants in Illinois is due to large
numbers of foreign-born miners, who, as a whole, tend to be illiterate.
The curve of the farmers, on the other hand, is based on people who
were practically all farmers before coming to America as well as afterward. Thus it is especially easy to see the relation between literacy
and migration among farmers. The same relation appears to prevail
among other groups, although occupational and national differences
make it less clearly apparent.

Among the native-born farmers a similar process of selection takes
place within the limits of their own country. It may cover several
generations, each moving farther west. In New England, the native
white farmers are the residue left after the more enterprising young
people have been removed by selective migration to cities or to the
West. This residue is adversely selected so far as enterprise is concerned, although not necessarily otherwise. In our study of farm
values it is compared with Europeans among whom a major selection
of an opposite sort has taken place. Thus, although many fine and
competent "old Americans" undoubtedly still remain on New England farms, it is not surprising that the general level of enterprise is
below that of all foreign groups except Poles, Austrians, and Finns.*
Negro and Indian farmers also stand below native whites. Because of
the adverse selection to which the native whites have been subjected,
the advantages of inheriting their land and knowing the language
and customs of the country do not enable them to own farms as valuable as those of the foreigners. Thus they have only limited success.
This may be the fault of their ancestors as well as themselves, for
those who remain may tend to be ones who inherit relatively poor
farms. The immigrants may have a real advantage because they are
in the market for farms just when many of the finest young men who
would inherit unusually good farms are ready to migrate cityward
or westward. This does not alter the fact that on the Atlantic Coast
an adversely selected native white group is being compared with favorably selected foreigners, but it helps to explain why the native
whites stand relatively low.

Such relative incompetence is by no means incompatible with the
fact that the old New England stock still supplies far more than its

* The Finns occupy farms of exceptionally low value largely because they prefer
glaciated areas with coniferous forests and lakes, like their old home. They
apparently improve these farms and get a much better living than might be
expected.

proportional share of leaders. A dreamy temperament, or an intense scientific curiosity, may make a man a poor farmer but may lead to great success as a poet, philosopher, or scientist. Emerson, Alcott, and Thoreau illustrate this truth. Far more important, however, is the well-established fact that farmers, in proportion to their numbers, supply only a few leaders such as are mentioned in *Who's Who*. City people, especially those living in the suburbs of large cities, are by far the most prolific source of leaders.[4]

West of New England the native American farmers become more and more fully the good material picked out by a prolonged process of favorable selection. Thus at the end, on the Pacific Coast, they stand practically at the top. This does not mean that they are better men than the French (including Belgians), whose farms stand just below theirs in value, or than the British, Germans, and Scandinavians, who come next, or even than the Russians, Italians, and Austrians, who have farms worth about half as much as those of the native Americans. We have as yet no means of learning with certainty which groups have the better hereditary endowment, but it is clear that qualities of some sort, either acquired or innate, make the selected native white farmers of the Pacific Coast able to compete with highly selected foreigners on better terms than those on which the adversely selected native whites of New England compete with less drastically selected Europeans.

When a single migrating group is taken by itself, it seems probable that those who migrate farthest, or to places especially difficult to reach or requiring difficult adjustments to new conditions, are likely to be the ones most highly endowed genetically as well as culturally. Migration to a neighboring city, for example, may require a more difficult adjustment for a farm boy than migration hundreds of miles west to a new farm. A trek of a few hundred miles on horseback or on foot with small children from Pennsylvania to Indiana in 1810 was far more difficult than a modern trek in a jalopy from Maine to southern California. A great truth as to difficult migrations is expressed in an old saying: "The cowards never started; the weak ones died on the way." [5]

How far the selection thus illustrated is genetic and how far merely cultural is by no means proved, nor can it be easily tested. Opinions vary widely. Nevertheless, certain general principles seem to be established. When migration to a new and untried region takes place,

---

[4] Visher, 1937. [5] Sandburg, p. 37.

people who are physically weak or of a timid temperament tend to stay at home.[6]   The physique and temperament of women are especially important in this respect.   Moreover, people with sturdy bodies, strong wills, good intelligence, and a spirit of adventure and initiative are likely to go farthest, or to the places where the opportunities appear to be greatest.   One reason for this is that such people are likely to have enough money to pay their way and get started in new homes.   Such people also tend to be thrifty and industrious.   The progressiveness of Australia,[7] illustrates the matter, as do the high qualities of both the Maoris and the whites of New Zealand.   That island is the most remote land to which the white man has gone as a settler.   The voyage thither is long and expensive.   Its dangers and difficulties in the early stages of settlement erected a barrier which was too much for the timid, the poor, the weak, and the irresolute. Today New Zealand is pre-eminent in productivity, in general prosperity, and in social progress.   The outstanding qualities of modern New Zealand are certainly due in part to an admirable climate, abundant land, and great resources in proportion to the population.   Nevertheless, it seems probable that in part they are due also to innate qualities picked out by natural selection through migration and preserved by intermarriage of like with like.   By the same token, it is probable that before it became easy to reach all parts of the United States, the early, permanent settlers in each state were of an especially competent type.   States such as California and Arizona still retain a good deal of this earlier advantage in spite of recent immigration of less drastically selected types.

D. *Recent Internal Migration in America*

Internal migration within the United States since World War I bears out the conclusion that migration is a selective process.   Lively and Taeuber,[8] for example, present Table 3, in which the entire 3,049 counties of the United States are classified according to their planes of living.   The plane is represented by an index in which rural families not on farms (chiefly villagers) are rated according to the estimated value of dwellings and the percentage of homes having radios.   For farm families the index also includes the percentages of homes

[6] Huntington, 1935A.

[7] Huntington, 1925B, Chap. XVII.

[8] p. 74.

equipped with telephones, electric lights, automobiles, and running water inside the house. From the lowest to the highest plane of living there is an almost steady change from heavy outward migration to pronounced inward migration. The poorest counties suffered a loss of 17 per cent from 1920 to 1930 in contrast to a pronounced inward migration with a gain of nearly 14 per cent in the most prosperous counties.

TABLE 3

COMPARISON BETWEEN PLANE OF LIVING AND MIGRATION

Rural Plane of Living Index, 1930	Population in Thousands	Net Migration, 1920–30, as Percentage of Rural Population
Less than 30	5,816	−17.4 *
30–59	12,446	−16.1
60–89	6,066	−13.6
90–119	6,450	−15.0
120–149	6,697	−11.0
150–179	6,850	−8.0
180–209	3,551	−0.8
210 or more	3,493	13.8

* A minus sign means loss of population.

It is especially important to discover whether there are any differences in the quality of migrants and non-migrants. In 1935, Gist and Clark looked up the records of 2,544 persons whose IQs had been recorded when they were students at rural high schools in 1922–23. From their investigation it is possible to compile Table 4, which shows average IQs according to the place of residence in 1935. Those living on farms averaged lowest in IQ—only 93—compared with 99 among their schoolmates in big cities. The average IQ increased with almost perfect steadiness from the farm group to villages and then to those living in cities of larger size. Those who left their home state averaged a little more intelligent than those who remained there. A similar result was found by Mauldin, who studied the marks of 1,221 high school students in small towns in Tennessee and South Carolina. The marks of about 600 who migrated were compared with those of the rest who stayed at home. Those who had shown superior ability in school were most likely to migrate. Superior boys were especially likely to go to the city. This agrees with other accounts of places where those who migrate are more highly educated than those who remain at home. Migration in general becomes more selective in proportion to the opportunities which young people see in places other than their homes. Gessner is another of the many who find that those going to a big city are better educated than those going to smaller places.

TABLE 4

Migration and IQ

Place of Residence	IQ
1. Living on farms	93.4
2. Rural, including both farm and non-farm (1,580 persons)	94.8
3. Still resident in Kansas	95.7
4. Rural, but not on farms	96.1
5. Cities of 2,500–10,000	97.0
6. Residing outside of Kansas	97.8
7. Cities of 10,000 to 25,000	98.2
8. All cities (964 persons)	98.3
9. Cities of 25,000 to 100,000	97.8
10. Cities of 100,000 or more	99.3

The difference between numbers 2 and 8 is highly significant, being eleven times the probable difference. There is only one chance in billions that it is accidental.

Lack of success, as well as superior ability, may promote migration. Among 2,554 rural households in Ohio, Lively and Foott found that families on relief moved 40% oftener than non-relief families and changed their occupations twice as often. Gist and his co-workers find that, inasmuch as tenant farmers have no farms to bequeath, their children are more inclined to leave the farms than are the sons and daughters of farm owners. Bernert says that during the decade from 1930 to 1940 non-white persons, chiefly Negroes, constituted 24% of the total migration from rural farm areas, although they formed only 16% of the population of those same areas in 1930. All these facts indicate that the numerous able people who go to great cities are more or less balanced by incompetents. This is one reason for the great contrasts between aristocratic sections and slums in modern cities. Thus the character of the communities at both ends of a migration may be permanently altered. Another example of this is described by Sanford in a study based on the education and occupations of men who migrate from small towns in Alabama. He found that the occupational level is becoming lower with each generation, despite the fact that the present generation has more education than its predecessors. He regards this situation as the result of selective migration, for the emigrants have higher education than their comrades who stay at home or than new people coming from outside.

An especially illuminating study of recent migration has been made by Hobbs at Plymouth in the anthracite mining region of Pennsylvania. The mining industry was on the upgrade until 1927. Then a rather rapid decline began, accompanied by a reduction of the population from over 18,000 to 15,500. Hobbs carefully distinguishes between "resultants" and other "out-migrants." The resultants are people who migrated on their own initiative. Children, dependent parents, and wives are not resultants because they are not directly responsible for their own migration. The most telling comparisons are between resultant migrants and their brothers and sisters who remained in the coal region.

The fact that families are large among unskilled laborers and smaller in the upper parts of the social scale does not explain why the "resultants" far outrank their stay-at-home brothers and sisters in intelligence and energy. Even though one father is sometimes counted twice, that is, as the father of two migrants, or of a migrant and a stay-at-home, the distribution of occupations among the fathers of the migrants and the stay-at-homes is practically identical. The percentage having unskilled laborers as fathers is 73 for migrants and 76 for their non-migrant siblings. In spite of such similarity in origin, however, more than 63 per cent of the migrants had finished high school before leaving home and 12 per cent went to college. The corresponding figures for the non-migrant brothers and sisters were 23 and 4, a large difference. Among the migrants, 56 per cent entered occupations ranging from skilled labor upward to the professions, whereas only 29 per cent of the non-migrant siblings chose similar vocations. Another way of looking at it is that among migrants who were children of laborers and servants 50 per cent attained the level of skilled workmen or higher (clerks, proprietors, or professional people), and 12 per cent entered professions. On the other hand, among the brothers and sisters of these migrants, those who stayed in the coal region show corresponding percentages of only 20 and 3.

From such facts Hobbs concludes that "there appears to be considerable justification for the belief that the superior socio-economic attainment of the resultant migrants is more a product of their individual superiority than of their superior background. . . . The resultant migrants are apparently a selected superior group." [9] This selectivity appears to have been most marked at the beginning of the decline in

9 p. 85.

economic opportunity (1927–29, at which time the demand for anthracite coal fell rapidly); it was least noticeable when economic opportunities were poor outside the coal region (1930–33). It seems
that the degree to which superior types were selected for migration
decreased after the first sharp impact of economic distress. "It also
appears that those who leave earliest, who apparently are first to per-
ceive the seriousness of the economic distress, are more favorably endowed with the elements of ambition, character, intelligence, or social background necessary to reach the upper rungs of the socio-economic ladder." [10]

Variations in the urge to migrate are illustrated in another way by
Zimmerman's study of five hundred farm families in Minnesota. He
found that the tendency to leave the farm varies according to income. In families with incomes of $1,400 or less, 32 per cent of the
children over 18 years of age migrated to cities of 10,000 population
or more, whereas among families with incomes above $1,400 the per-
centage was only 13. In other words, the urge to migrate depends
upon what Zimmerman calls the gradient between the home and the
outside world. If the home offers good opportunities, the most competent, or the most favored, groups tend to stay there, but if the home
is unfavorable, the competent and ambitious tend to be the first to
leave. This principle is illustrated in what Hobbs says of the coal
fields and in many other ways in later chapters of this book. A large
part of the diversity of opinion as to the selectivity of migration arises
from failure to note the strength and nature of the gradients which
impel migration. For this reason an investigator using the same
method in different places may obtain seemingly contradictory results, such as Klineberg [11] points out. Thomas, in her excellent review of the whole problem, brings out the fact that the relative quality of migrants and non-migrants depends largely upon the relative
attractiveness of the places where migration begins and ends. Migration, as Hobbs [12] well concludes, "is essentially a function of a
gradient."

E. Birthplace of Leaders and the Selective Process

A concrete illustration of what selective migration is doing to the
United States is found in the distribution of leaders. A study of (1)

[10] p. 78.   [12] p. 110.
[11] 1938.

American Men of Science, (2) Poor's *Register of Directors of Corporations,* and (3) *Who's Who* shows that such leaders, who represent the more competent people of the United States as a whole, are born in large numbers in certain parts of the country and are leaving some parts and congregating in others to an unexpected degree. When allowance is made for duplication, the three groups here investigated include approximately 85,000 persons. In spite of differences in detail, all three behave essentially alike in respect to the geographic distribution of both birthplaces and migrations. For each group we have calculated the number born in each state in proportion to the number of white children under one year of age.*

Table 5, showing the ten states standing highest or lowest in producing the three kinds of leaders, raises many questions. Why, for example, have Colorado and Utah, in proportion to the number of white children born there, produced six or seven times as many scientists as Arkansas or Georgia? Why does Massachusetts never fall lower than third in any part of Table 5, whereas New Mexico never

* The number of young children gives the closest available approximation to the actual number of native white births. The *Who's Who* people average about 20 years older than the scientists, and the business men (directors) fall midway. Each of the three groups, as well as the total of the three, has been given a set of index numbers based on the number of births of leaders in each decade, such as 1855–64, compared with the number of children under 1 year of age at the census in the middle of the decade. The method here employed seems not to have been used before in studies of this sort. Previous studies have been based on the number of births in proportion to the entire population. This gives an interesting set of figures but does not furnish a fair comparison of either ability or success. Unlike the method here employed it takes no account of the fact that the number of births in proportion to the population is far greater in some states than in others. For example, in 1900 no less than 15.1 per cent of the population of Utah consisted of children under 5 years of age, whereas in California the percentage was only 8.5. If the children born in all states from 1896 to 1900 should become scientists or directors or be mentioned in *Who's Who* to an exactly equal degree, the ordinary method of computation would indicate that those of Utah were almost twice as successful as those of California. The index numbers here given avoid this difficulty by assuming that the total number of births in the various states is closely proportional to the number of living children under 1 year of age at any given date. The chief inaccuracy arises from the fact that only white children have been taken into account, although the lists of leaders include a number of native-born colored people. Thus the index numbers for states with a large Negro population are a little too large in proportion to the others.

rises higher than forty-fourth? Why has the white population of great states such as Tennessee and Kentucky produced only one fourth to one third as many leaders as Connecticut in proportion to the number of children born there? In Column D the greatest contrast is between Connecticut (418) and New Mexico (41), but similar, though smaller, contrasts separate Massachusetts, for example, from

TABLE 5

BIRTHPLACES OF LEADERS IN THE UNITED STATES

Index Numbers of Births of Leaders in Proportion to the Number of Children Under One Year of Age at the Census Nearest the Date of Birth

I. HIGHEST STATES *

A. Scientists		B. Directors		C. Who's Who		D. All	
1. Colorado	68	Connecticut	304	Connecticut	226	Connecticut	418
2. Utah	61	Massachusetts	238	Massachusetts	186	Massachusetts	375
3. Massachusetts	57	Rhode Island	219	Nevada	171	Rhode Island	326
4. Connecticut	56	California	188	Wyoming	169	New Hampshire	301
5. New Hampshire	55	New York	181	Idaho	157	Colorado	300
6. Montana	54	Vermont	167	New Hampshire	153	Vermont	287
7. Wyoming	53	New Hampshire	159	Rhode Island	149	California	282
8. Vermont	51	Nevada	152	Colorado	143	New York	254
9. California	49	Delaware	138	Montana	133	Montana	248
10. Washington	48	Maine	134	Vermont	127	Maine	236

II. LOWEST STATES

A. Scientists		B. Directors		C. Who's Who		D. All	
39. West Virginia	14	Louisiana	53	Georgia	63	Florida	114
40. Texas	13	North Carolina	53	North Dakota	62	North Carolina	108
41. Louisiana	13	Alabama	51	Missouri	59	Mississippi	92
42. Florida	12	Mississippi	50	Alabama	57	West Virginia	92
43. Kentucky	12	Kentucky	49	West Virginia	53	Alabama	91
44. New Mexico	11	West Virginia	49	Kentucky	49	Louisiana	88
45. Alabama	11	Arizona	46	Texas	48	Kentucky	86
46. Tennessee	10	Tennessee	45	Louisiana	47	Tennessee	84
47. Georgia	10	Arkansas	32	Arkansas	33	Arkansas	58
48. Arkansas	9	New Mexico	19	New Mexico	16	New Mexico	41

* The District of Columbia outranks all the states, but its sociological condition is so different from theirs that it is omitted. Its presence raises the level of Maryland and Virginia, because many people who work in Washington live outside the District of Columbia.

Arkansas, Colorado from Kentucky, and New York from Louisiana. Racial origin, that is, the large proportion of Mexicans who were classified as native whites in earlier censuses, helps to account for the low position of New Mexico, but no such condition explains Arkansas with its white people of almost pure British ancestry. If the Arkansans fail to produce leaders because of poor education, it is the fault of themselves or of some such cause as malaria, climate, or the isolation due to geographical environment. Climatic differences help to explain the contrast between New York and Louisiana, but can scarcely explain why Rhode Island stands far ahead of Kentucky. A high percentage of people of Puritan descent is usually supposed to explain the high rank of Massachusetts and Connecticut, but whether it explains that of Colorado and California is not so clear.

The differing distribution of the births of scientists and directors also furnishes an interesting problem. The distance of Colorado, Utah, Montana, and Wyoming from the great eastern centers of commerce and industry and also from the West Coast doubtless helps to explain why those states, although close to the top in scientists, disappear from the upper ten in directors, whereas New York and California, as well as New England, tend strongly toward business men. But why should such relatively isolated states as Nevada and Vermont stand among the first ten in directors? Again, what is there about a group of western and northern states, Colorado, Utah, Wyoming, Nevada, Montana, Washington, and California, which brings them into the upper part of Table 5 in one column or another, along with all of New England and New York? The full answer to these questions will appear in later chapters or in a later book, as we study the three great factors which alter the progress of civilization. Cultural differences, such as the greater predominance of commerce, industry, agriculture, or education in some states than in others, certainly play a conspicuous part. So do climatic differences which alter health, energy, occupations, migration, and training. And finally, there appear to be actual biological differences between the average people in one part of the country and another.

Let us see what the geographical distribution of our three types of leaders suggests as to the relative influence of culture, physical environment, and heredity. In Figure 4 the data of Column *D* in Table 5 have been graphically mapped. The combined births of scientists, directors, and *Who's Who* people show the following outstanding features, beginning with those that are less noticeable. (1) A tendency is evident for the greatest productivity of human ability to occur along a band extending irregularly from Connecticut to California, as indicated by the dotted line. The reason for the location of the line may be climatic, but that remains to be seen. The irregularities, however, are certainly not climatic. Maryland, for example, stands high mainly because of the scientists born there. The abundance of its born leaders may be due to the attraction of scientific families to Baltimore or the suburbs of Washington by government work and famous educational institutions, such as Johns Hopkins University.

(2) An irregular decline northward from the dashed line is noticeable in almost the entire width of the country. (3) A similar but

more noticeable decline is seen toward the south. This would be even greater if we could separate colored people from whites in our lists of leaders. In general the low position of the South in Figure 4 is of climatic origin, but the indirect climatic effect is probably greater than the direct. The direct effect is mainly a lessening of the desire to work. The indirect effect includes modes of agriculture, cultural ideals, and the immigration of African slaves.

(4) Another feature of Figure 4 is the strong dominance of New England, especially the three southern states. Advantages of location, climate, migration, occupations, customs, and opportunities all help in this. Nevertheless, it is curious that New York, New Jersey, and Pennsylvania, with similar climate, occupations, and culture and with greater wealth of natural resources, rank much lower than southern New England. In fact, even New York, with an index of 254, ranks only a little above Maine (236), which stands lowest among the states of New England. The only outstanding condition which might cause southern New England to give birth to an unusual number of leaders is its Puritan people and traditions.

(5) A fifth feature of Figure 4 is the relatively high level of all the Pacific and Mountain states except New Mexico in comparison with the older and generally more populous states of the Great Plains and Mississippi Valley in the same latitude. Even Oregon, where a rank of 179 makes this condition least evident, surpasses Wisconsin (172), Michigan (174), and Pennsylvania (176). In the same way Arizona (106) stands higher than any state directly east of it until Georgia (117) on the Atlantic Coast is reached. The long migration to which the early settlers of the western states were subjected has presumably had the effect of selecting able people as the ones who finally settled there.

(6) This calls attention to the conspicuous fact that all along the Atlantic Coast the productivity in leaders has been high in comparison with interior states in the same latitude. Connecticut (418) stands two or three times as high as the entire tier of states from Pennsylvania (176) to Nebraska (159). South Carolina (180) stands equally high above the states from Alabama (91) to New Mexico (41).

(7) Thus in the interior of the country the entire area from the Great Lakes and North Dakota to the Gulf of Mexico, although highly productive of leaders in the north, is nevertheless less productive than the regions that flank it to east and west. The Appalachian Highland appears to carry low productivity of leaders unusually far north. A curious fact about this contrast between the

coast and the interior is that in all latitudes the states bordering the Atlantic Ocean have produced well nigh twice as many leaders as the least productive states in the same latitude in the interior. Here are some ratios between the index of leadership in coast states and in interior states in the same latitude:

Maine—North Dakota	1.7	Maryland—West Virginia	2.4
New Hampshire—Minnesota	1.9	Virginia—Kentucky	2.0
Massachusetts—Michigan	2.2	North Carolina—Arkansas	1.9
Rhode Island—Illinois	1.9	South Carolina—Mississippi	2.0
Connecticut—Ohio	2.2	Georgia—av. of New Mexico and	
New Jersey—Indiana	1.9	Texas	1.8
Delaware—Missouri	1.9		

If these seven features of Figure 4 * are looked at as a whole, two broad hypotheses seem warranted. First, the median band of high productivity across the country from east to west and the accompanying decline northward and, especially, southward are primarily, although probably not entirely, climatic in origin. Further study of this point will be postponed to Part III of this book. Second, the conspicuous contrasts from the East Coast to the interior and then to the West Coast are primarily due to selective migration. It seems probable that the prominence of southern New England and South

* Maps like Figure 4 based separately on *Who's Who*, scientists, and directors are all essentially alike. Minor differences, however, arise from several conditions. For example, states with few inhabitants, such as Nevada, Wyoming, Idaho, and Montana, tend to have a relatively large representation in *Who's Who* because that book automatically includes state officials, judges, etc., and a small state has almost as many of these as a large one. The same kind of overrepresentation occurs in many southern states which have given birth to few non-official persons who are mentioned in that book. Another reason why a map of the births of any one of our three groups differs from the map of all three combined (Figure 4) is that leaders born in southern New England, the Middle Atlantic States, and California naturally show a strong tendency to become directors of business concerns, as do those born in Georgia and Florida, for less obvious reasons. On the other hand, because of relative remoteness from business, the people mentioned in our three lists tend strongly to become scientists in the states lying northwest of a line between the centers of Ohio and New Mexico. The only exceptions are Nevada, California, and South Dakota. On the other hand, New Mexico, as well as Utah and Montana, tends strongly toward science in spite of the fact that in proportion to the births of white children it has produced only one fifth as many scientists as the other two states. Another minor detail worth noting is that scientists are especially migratory.

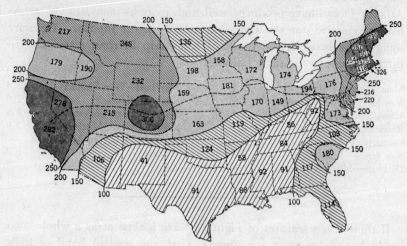

Figure 4. Approximate Number of Leaders among an Average 100,000 White Children Born in Each State. Based on *Who's Who* (1936–37), *American Men of Science* (1938), and Poor's *Register of Directors* (1938).

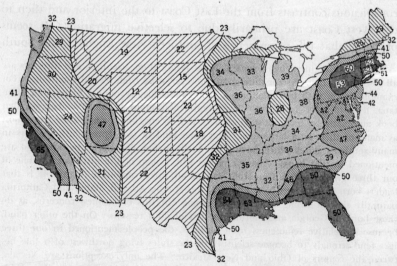

Figure 5. Percentage of Leaders Residing in the State Where They Were Born.

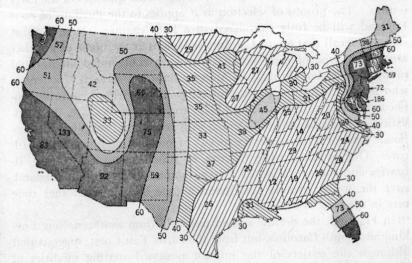

Figure 6. Leaders Received from Other States per 100,000 White Population in 1930.

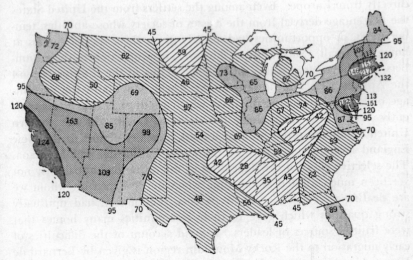

Figure 7. Leaders Living in Each State in 1937 per 100,000 White Population in 1930. Nevada appears unduly high because officials included *ex officio* are almost as numerous in a small state as in a large one.

Carolina as sources of leaders is due to the innate qualities of the early settlers. The process of selection as it applies to the Puritans of New England will be fully considered in a later chapter. Here it must suffice to recall that South Carolina is famous as the home of a rather aristocratic type of early settlers who have contributed an unusual numbers of leaders throughout American history. French Huguenots, who fled from Europe because of religious convictions, were an important element. From 1725 to 1775, according to Wallace, the cultivation of rice and indigo, together with commerce "supplied the economic basis of a coast country society of notable intelligence and culture. One of the earliest theaters in America, musical culture, libraries and the education of a large number of youths in England, gave the society around Charleston a tone and finish at that time rare in the New World."

In Figure 4, the decline inland not only from southern New England and South Carolina, but from the entire East Coast, suggests that although the settlers of the interior possessed sterling qualities of character, as well as unusual energy and initiative, the proportion drawn from intellectual and cultural levels, such as made Charleston famous, was small. This was especially true of the great migration directly from Europe. Even among the settlers from the United States the percentage derived from the classes of society whose abilities, temperament, or opportunities had already given them special success at home was small. Such families, however, in proportion to their numbers, are the greatest source of leaders. Thus in the interior beyond the Appalachians and onward to the Rocky Mountains the percentage of homes having the qualities which produce leaders has apparently been lower than along the Atlantic Coast. In the western United States the production of leaders increases almost to the New England level in states such as Colorado, California, and Montana. The selective effect of the difficulties of migration had apparently not yet been much diluted at the time when the leaders with whom we are dealing were born. Their parents, presumably, had unusually strong qualities which gave to their communities many homes that were fruitful sources of leaders. A vivid account of the difficulties of early migration to the Rocky Mountain region is given by Bernard de Voto. In addition, certain facts which will now be presented indicate that families of this type show a tendency to move away from the Middle West, thus accentuating the regional differences. Some readers may object to an hypothesis which suggests that regional differences within the United States have any connection with heredity, but, as Visher well points out,[13] no other explanation seems to harmonize with all the facts.

F. Counter-Migration and Selection

Having seen where many of our three types of leaders are born, let us inquire to what extent their birthplaces are able to retain them. Data as to this point are shown in Figure 5, which indicates the percentage of the scientists, directors, and *Who's Who* people residing in the states of their birth. The North Atlantic region (southern New England, New York, and Pennsylvania), four southeastern states close to the Gulf of Mexico, and, above all, California are the only parts of the country which have held half the leaders to whom they gave birth. Utah, however, rises almost to their level, and so do North Carolina and Alabama. Abundant opportunities in the realms of business and education and along other lines largely explain the North Atlantic prominence. The rapid growth and great possibilities of California explain the situation there. In the South the retention of home-born leaders is due to several causes, including the rapid growth of new opportunities in recent times, the scarcity of leaders born at home, as shown in Figure 4, and relatively slight competition because comparatively few leaders from elsewhere go south. In Utah the fact that many leaders are Mormons is probably a strong factor in keeping them at home. A really surprising feature of Figure 5 is that aside from Utah and California no state west of the Appalachian Mountains and north of the states touching the Gulf of Mexico has been able to hold as many as 40 per cent of its born leaders of the kinds here considered. In a vast area from North Dakota and Montana southward to New Mexico and western Texas the percentage retained at home falls below 23. Montana, Wyoming, and North Dakota, which make an excellent showing as the birthplace of leaders, lose at least four fifths of the leaders to whom they gave birth. The ancestors of the leaders migrated thither not many generations ago. The leaders born there are moving away in a significant counter-migration.

A comparison between the number of American-born leaders migrating into a state and its white population in 1930 shows what states are attracting the leaders who move away from the interior (Figure 6). The Atlantic States from New Hampshire to Maryland, together with southern Florida and the Pacific Coast, evidently have

[13] 1928.

great power of attraction. Curiously enough, the Rocky Mountain States from New Mexico to Montana also attract a good many to replace their conspicuous losses. Mining helps them to get scientists. Delaware shows the extraordinary figure of 186 leaders per hundred thousand inhabitants. Its great chemical industries largely account for this. The vast interior plains and the Southeast, especially the Appalachian region and Arkansas, show little power of attracting able men, except in Florida. Great cities, such as Chicago, St. Paul, Minneapolis, St. Louis, Cleveland, and New Orleans, raise the standing of their states somewhat, but only to a moderate level. Utah drops much lower than its neighbors. Able people are not drawn thither, partly because home-born leaders are numerous and tend to fill the relatively limited local opportunities. One of the significant facts about Figure 6 is that the manufacturing states bordering the Great Lakes have comparatively little power of attraction. At the stage of their development represented by the latter part of the decade from 1930 to 1940 they had produced a moderate number of leaders, lost at least three fifths of those born there, and attracted proportionally far less than either the new Southwest, including California, or the old Northeast.

In concluding this study of internal migration let us look at the final result. Figure 7 shows how many scientists, directors, and *Who's Who* people actually live in each state in proportion to the present white population. Inasmuch as foreign-born leaders of these types are here for the first time included, our comparisons are based on the total white population instead of merely the native whites. The outstanding fact is that from the standpoint of leadership the North Atlantic Coast is far the most important part of the United States both relatively and absolutely; California with its satellites in Nevada and Arizona shows a minor concentration, and so does southern Florida on a small scale. The rest of the Pacific and Rocky Mountain states, except Idaho, succeed moderately well in holding or gaining leaders. So does an East North Central area extending from Ohio to the upper Mississippi River. Illinois, by reason of Chicago, rises as high as Utah or Pennsylvania. The western and southern parts of the Great Plains, and especially the Ozark and Appalachian regions, find the greatest difficulty in holding or attracting leaders.

Another phase of the final result of migration is seen in the degree to which migration varies from one type of people to another (Table 6). Scientists are especially migratory. Only a handful can find work in their home towns and less than a fourth do so within their own state. Much the same is true of clergymen and educators. So far as facilities for work are concerned, authors and artists do not need to migrate so much as scientists and clergymen, but the demands of education and of earning a living take a large part of them to new states. On the other hand, business men, doctors, and especially lawyers and politicians often find it easy to establish themselves in their home states. Their careers are helped by family prestige, local acquaintance, and the inheritance of property and position. Nevertheless, the successful men of these professions sketched in *Who's Who* are far more migratory than the population of the country as a whole.

TABLE 6

MIGRATORY TENDENCIES BY OCCUPATION AND COLOR IN THE UNITED STATES

Percentage of Americans Migrating Away from State of Birth

Starred scientists	80
Other scientists	77
Clergymen in *Who's Who*	76
Educators in *Who's Who*	73
Authors and journalists in *Who's Who*	69
Artists in *Who's Who*	67
Corporation directors	66
Business men in *Who's Who*	55
Doctors in *Who's Who*	55
Lawyers and politicians in *Who's Who*	49
Negroes in the United States	25
Native whites in the United States	23

In Table 6 three pairs of associated groups are especially interesting, namely, starred scientists and other scientists, business men in *Who's Who* and corporation directors in general, native whites and Negroes. In each pair a more successful group is compared with a less successful one. Among the scientists, the ones who are starred were chosen by their fellows as the most productive of superior research. They are a little more migratory than the others. This may be partly a matter of age, for scientific success frequently causes men to be called to new positions. Among business men, the contrast is the other way. On an average the 41,600 directors mentioned in Poor's *Directory* are by no means so successful as the business men in *Who's Who*. Nevertheless only 55 per cent of the *Who's Who* men live away from their state of birth in contrast to 66 per cent of the others. This fact seems to indicate that the more successful a business man is, the more likely he is to find a good opening near home. Many of the business men in *Who's Who* are engaged in long-established family businesses, or at least got their positions through family influence. We shall find other examples where a fortunate position at home lessens the amount of migration, but this is true only for certain types of occupations. It applies, however, to native whites as compared with Negroes. About 23 per cent of the whites live outside the state of birth in comparison with 25 per cent of the Negroes. On the whole, native whites are better satisfied than Negroes. For this reason, presumably, they migrate less. All these examples emphasize the highly selective action of migration.

Millions of people in addition to the relatively conspicuous groups here discussed are constantly migrating. Among sociologists there seems to be a growing tendency to believe that migration is practically always more or less selective. If this is so, it must inevitably alter the balance of leadership, education, wealth, labor, and opportunity in the different parts of the country. We do not know how long the present tendencies have existed or how long they will continue. Nor do we know at what level of the social scale a given tendency may be reversed. It is evident that as we descend from the most successful to the least successful, the direction and frequency of migrations change. If we judge by Table 6 and use averages of large groups, we conclude that there must in any given place be some general level of home conditions above which more than half the business men, let us say, tend to remain near their birthplaces, whereas below it more than half go away. At the top, for example, among the richest families in New York, practically all sons who go into business remain in the home city or its suburbs. At the other extreme, in small, decaying villages, practically all the sons who enter business go away. In any given region, also, the kind of migration may change radically. For example, the rapid and forced migration from the Dust Bowl of the Great Plains in the decade from 1930–40 brought to California a large group of people who averaged below the previous migrants in education and wealth. Whether they averaged lower in innate ability and temperament we are not certain. It is clear, however, that if such migration, or any of the other types discussed in this chapter, were to continue, the quality of the different parts of the country would be decidedly altered.

These diverse migratory tendencies with their complex countercurrents suggest grave possibilities. The future welfare of the various parts of the country can scarcely fail to be influenced by the fact that for every hundred thousand of its white population, New York State, for example, has 127 scientists, directors, and prominent leaders and California has 115, in comparison with only 13 in Mississippi and 15 in Kentucky. If such tendencies persist long enough and affect enough people, the nature of the different sections of the country will be notably altered. Even more important is the fact that we seem to be dealing with a great principle which presumably has operated through the whole of history. People of diverse social levels and abilities migrate in different directions and to different degrees. While ordinary people are moving into certain regions, others with more than ordinary ability may be moving away. Thus the balance is altered both culturally and biologically. A constant fluctuation in these respects appears to have gone on throughout the centuries. History can never be rightly read until we discover how the quality of the people has varied from one time or place to another.

G. Migration and Social Status

Another method of investigating migration confirms the preceding conclusions and helps in framing certain definite laws. Let us examine about 1,400 people of a single family stock.[14] In this study each individual is assigned to one of five social classes in which a rank of five denotes persons who are at least locally known as leading citizens. A rank of one denotes people of little education and achievement. Each class is divided into three groups, namely (1) non-migrants residing in the county where they were born; (2) short-distance migrants who have moved to another county in their own state or into an adjacent state; (3) long-distance migrants who have moved to a foreign country or a state not adjacent to their own.

Figure 8 shows what happens to the first and last of these groups in relation to migration. Social status is indicated by the height of the lines. Size of birthplace (upper part of diagram) or of residence (lower part of diagram) is indicated by distance from left to right. Suburbs are placed to the right of cities because they represent a later and, on the whole, a higher cultural condition. Unsuccessful city people tend to go back to the farms or villages. Successful ones migrate in large numbers to the suburbs. The upper part of Figure 8 shows that non-migrants (solid line) who live all their lives in rural districts or villages have the lowest rank culturally, as might be expected. As the size of their birthplace increases, the rank of these

14 Huntington, 1934, 1935A.

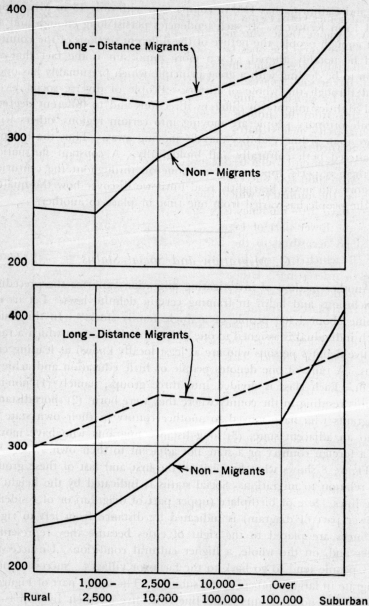

Figure 8. Cultural Rank of Migrants and Non-Migrants According to Size of Birthplace (above) and of Residence (below).

stay-at-homes keeps rising until it reaches its highest level in the sub-urbs. Among those who migrate long distances (upper dotted line), on the contrary, the ones born in rural areas or villages (1,000–2,500 population) have a much higher rank than their non-migrant kinsfolk born in the same places. As the size of the birthplace increases, the amount by which the migrants surpass the stay-at-homes diminishes. Migrants from the suburbs are so scarce that their level is not shown. Such scarcity means that so far as this particular set of 1,400 people is concerned, only a negligible percentage of those born in the sub-urbs of great cities migrate far away. This is significant. It confirms our impression that successful people, unless they follow occupations such as the ministry, which can rarely be carried on in the home town, have little tendency to migrate.

In the lower part of Figure 8 the non-migrants and migrants are classified according to the places where they ultimately live. The way in which the two lines converge from left to right and finally cross is interesting. Although non-migrants hold the lowest rank in the rural districts, their position becomes relatively higher as we go to larger places. In the suburbs they stand at the top. Here again we see that among the prosperous, well-educated people living just outside our great cities, the opportunities are so great that they feel little urge to migrate. This is directly in contrast to the effect of the relatively unfavorable rural conditions. Among the rural people of this closely related family stock the urge to migrate increases from the lower to the upper cultural level. Among the suburbanites, the opposite is the case.

Another suggestive feature of Figure 8 is that the long-distance migrants tend to be more uniform than the others, regardless of either birthplace or residence. This suggests that migration is accompanied by a kind of selection that tends to pick out a definite cultural type, just as the migration of Japanese to Hawaii seems to pick out a physi-cal type. We witnessed the same phenomenon among foreign-born immigrants. The difference in literacy between native Americans and immigrants diminishes as one goes westward from the Atlantic.

H. Laws of Migration

The facts now before us are samples of a vast body of similar evi-dence which seems to indicate that there are definite laws of selective migration. Beginning with Hawaii in the last chapter, we have seen a widespread selective process at work. The Japanese who migrate thither are a selected group in the sense that they show certain definite bodily tendencies which are presumably associated with corresponding temperamental tendencies. In the present chapter we have seen that a similar selective process sifts immigrants to the United States in such a way that the educated show consistently more tendency than the uneducated to settle in places where the opportunities are good. American-born farmers show the selective process through the increasingly high value of their farms, as compared with those of immigrants, as one goes from east to west. New Zealand and California, with their high levels of social progress, are two of many illustrations of the results produced at the end of a long migration which, in earlier days, was so difficult that it had a strong selective action. Many recent studies agree in indicating that the selective process is almost invariably an important factor in migration within the United States. They show that the nature and strength of the selection vary according to the relative advantages, real or supposed, of the places where migration begins and ends. An impressive illustration of this fact is the way in which leaders, such as scientists, directors of corporations, and persons sketched in *Who's Who,* leave some parts of the country and congregate in others. And, finally, we have seen how a small and relatively homogeneous group of people belonging to the same family stock unconsciously sort themselves out according to a definite pattern.

Such facts do not settle the question of how far the selective process is biological as well as cultural. In general, however, they seem to indicate that innate qualities, as well as training and opportunities, play a vital part in determining who shall migrate and which ones will make the more difficult migrations. The results arising from the migratory impulse sometimes seem to be contradictory, because they depend on whether the circumstances at either end of a migration are good or bad for a particular kind of person. Thus the net conclusion is that migration appears to be both socially and biologically selective, but that it acts very differently according to the individual circumstances of the persons concerned and according to the relative advantages of places at the origin and the termination of migration. Under some conditions the most competent types are the most likely to migrate; under others the opposite is true.

As a final result of this study the following laws of migration may be formulated: (1) Migration is systematically accompanied by selection. A migration forced by conquest, flood, or other disaster may seem at first to be non-selective, but after the migration the deathrate is almost certain to be altered, thus leading to at least a small selection of relatively weak types for destruction. (2) The more difficult a migration is, the greater is the selection. The factor which counts most heavily is the difficulty encountered in leaving home, journeying to the new home, and then becoming established. A short migration may be difficult and a long one easy. (3) Differences in racial, national, or social characteristics tend to lose their sharpness in accordance with the length or difficulty of the migration. If the migration is long enough or hard enough, the less competent both physically and mentally are gradually eliminated so that ultimately a rather similar temperamental type survives, regardless of origin. Chinese pioneers on the frontier of Manchukuo in the 1920's appear to have had considerable resemblance to British pioneers in Canada or German pioneers in southern Brazil.[15]

(4) The social level from which migrants are drawn varies according to the strength and nature of the impulse toward migration. The people who fled from Russia after the Bolshevik revolution belonged largely to the so-called upper classes. The criminals shipped to Australia a century or more ago included a considerable percentage of the vicious and the ignorant.

(5) The impulse toward migration, that is, the gradient down which migration flows, derives its strength partly from the conditions at home and partly from those in the place toward which migration is directed. In a Chinese flood the main impulse comes from the extremely unpleasant condition of homes and fields under water. Nevertheless, the direction in which the migrants flee depends on the height of the land and the chances of finding means of survival. When a young man in a comfortable and happy home migrates cityward, the outward push is scarcely more than a slight feeling that his home is no longer the right place. The main impulse is the pull of the city with its real or imagined opportunities for doing great things. These five laws, with numerous corollaries which spring from them, seem to apply to all human migration. Their combined action has been one of the major factors in history. Illustrations of this fact will be found in later chapters.

[15] Huntington, 1924A.

CHAPTER 6

THE PURITANS AS A TEST CASE

A. The Reality of Puritan Descent

The Puritans of New England furnish a good means of measuring the selective effect of migration. They also provide an example of the kind of results that may be expected when a genuine eugenic system is adopted. In the following discussion it may seem at first that we are glorifying a certain type of American. Further thought will show, however, that this is not the case. We do indeed demonstrate that people of Puritan stock are today unusually competent. The essential point, however, is that this competency is the result of a definite type of selection, and that such selection can produce similar results when applied to practically any kind of people. A population derived entirely from the readers of this book would probably be outstanding in general ability.

Controversy over the Puritans has been almost as heated as over the Jews. According to William Stoughton, in his election sermon of 1668, "God sifted a whole nation that he might send choice grain into the wilderness." This grain was Stoughton's own people, the 18,000 Puritans who came to southern New England as permanent settlers, mainly from 1630 to 1643. Some people disagree with Stoughton. Although the Puritans, according to C. E. Banks,[1] "came as they alleged, to find an outlet for their suppressed liberties . . . they were the 'scofflaws' of their day, often flouting contumaciously the statutes of the kingdom. [From them] we doubtless inherit our indifference to precedent, disregard of authority, and tendency to individualism." Such differences of opinion are amusing, but inconclusive. A conclusive test of the value of the Puritans to America must be strictly objective with no chance for personal opinion. Therefore, we shall follow a purely statistical method. Reliable data concerning the Puritans appear to be more abundant than for any other large and conspicuous group of migrants.

[1] p. 16.

Complete separation of people of Puritan descent from the rest of the population is impossible, but a fair approximation can be made by means of family names. Practically no one, of course, is purely of such descent, but millions are dominantly of that line. These are the people to be discussed. Many Puritan surnames have been brought to this country only once. Many others were brought in early colonial days and not again until at least five or six generations of large families had spread them to hundreds of persons on this side of the ocean. For example, at least 90 per cent of the 1,500 adult men named Huntington who lived in the United States in 1935 were descended from a Puritan who set sail for Boston with four sons and a daughter in 1635.[2] The other 10 per cent are partly, if not wholly, of similar descent from ancestors who left New England for Canada or elsewhere before or during the Revolution and then lost trace of their New England ancestry.

The name Whitney illustrates a slightly different condition. Most of the numerous Whitneys in America are descended from John Whitney who settled at Watertown near Boston in 1635. Six of his eight sons lived to manhood and had about fifty-five children. Two other Whitneys are mentioned in early records, but as nothing more is heard of them, they were probably childless or went back to England. A fourth, named Henry, of the same stock as John but not closely related, is first heard of in Long Island in 1649. He had eleven children, who were contemporaries of the fifty-five grandchildren of John. These two Whitney families increased so that 382 heads of families of that name were listed in the census of 1790. All but nine of these lived in New England or close by in New York, mostly on Long Island. Inasmuch as the name is rare in England and no other Whitneys are known to have migrated to America, five sixths of the Americans with this name are presumably descended from an ancestor who arrived in 1635, and about one sixth from a man who arrived ten or more years later. Since we cannot separate these two lines of descent, all the Whitneys are treated as if they belonged to the main group descended from a settler arriving in 1635. This illustrates the fact that the names here used do not represent a pure ancestry of a given type, but merely an ancestry in which a given type is dominant. If we could find large groups of pure ancestry, the types discussed below might differ even more than they they do now.

[2] Huntington, 1935A.

In estimating the significance of the facts which will soon be given, it must be noted that descent from a particular ancestor is far less significant than descent from the social group represented by that ancestor. Nevertheless, it is often surprising to see the facial resemblance between people of the same name, even though they are only distantly related. Inasmuch as we are here tracing descent by means of names, we are of course limited to the male line. How limited that line is may be judged from an example. Suppose that for eight generations each family consisted of two sons and two daughters who grew up and had similar families with four surviving children. The children of the first such set of four—the grandchildren of the man with whom the name starts—would comprise four boys and four girls bearing the original name and the same numbers with other names. Inasmuch as the girls would change their name on marriage, only four out of sixteen families of these grandchildren would bear the original name. In the next generation only eight out of sixty-four families would retain the name. Thus the eighth generation would consist of 64,536 descendants, but only 256—one out of every 256— would be men who still bore the old name. Too much stress, however, must not be laid on names. The really important matter is selective, or assortative, marriage. People tend to marry into families of their own kind far more than into others. They also tend to marry neighbors. Both of these tendencies were especially strong in New England throughout colonial times and well on toward the end of the last century. Cousin marriages—not first cousins, but third, fourth, and so on—were so frequent that almost all the leading families in most villages and towns were connected. Moreover, early settlers who arrived in successive years tended to establish different villages, the newcomers jumping over the older ones, so to speak, in order to pick out the best possible unoccupied land. Hence the descendants of people arriving at any particular time were especially likely to marry descendants of others who arrived at that same time. Thus the new racial stock which was being built up differed somewhat from place to place and was partially stratified into classes.

B. Finding Fair Samples

In order to pick out names representing a particular type of colonial ancestry a rigid mathematical procedure is needed. A census volume makes it easy to pick out all family names which in 1790 were borne by at least twenty-five heads of families. Among these there are many whose bearers to the extent of at least 50 per cent were concentrated in one or another of four regions, namely, northern New England, southern New England, Middle Atlantic (New York, New Jersey, Maryland *), and South Atlantic (Virginia and North and South Carolina). This purely statistical basis provides 129 colonial names belonging primarily to northern New England, 588 to southern New England, 214 to the Middle Atlantic States, and 228 to the South Atlantic. For New England the entire alphabet has been used, but for the other two regions only the first part.

For the present we will confine ourselves to southern New England. Such names as Angell, Conant, Mather, and Seymour are included there, together with the presidential names of Coolidge, Garfield, Cleveland, Lincoln,† Pierce, Taft, and Tyler. On the other hand, such widely and honorably known names as Adams, Brown, Edwards, Jones, Smith, Stone, and Williams are automatically excluded because in 1790 they were not concentrated to the extent of 50 per cent in any one of our four regions. They were borne by many Puritans, but also by many immigrants of other types. People with these names are so numerous in Great Britain that they have come to America in considerable numbers at all times down to the present. Moreover, many German immigrants have Anglicized such names as Braun, Schmidt, and Stein. Thus the seven widely used old English names mentioned above are borne by a random sample of the descendants of average migrants from Great Britain and, in minor degree, from Germany during the whole period from colonial days to our own. For this reason these seven (with the addition of Davis and Johnson, or Johnston, in our study of business) have been put in a separate category as a control on the others.

The names belonging primarily to southern or northern New England, and those of the Middle Atlantic States so far as they were also found in New England before 1692, have been divided according to the date, as given by Savage, when the first bearer of the name

---

* Pennsylvania is not available.

† The name Lincoln, with 155 out of 210 heads in southern New England in 1790 and all but one of the others in northern New England, is omitted because many "Lincoln Laundries," "Lincoln Restaurants," and so forth have been established by men with other names. Individuals of other than Puritan descent have also adopted the name quite freely. This illustrates one of the factors which cause the figures given below to be less impressive than they presumably would be if we could segregate pure Puritan ancestry.

appeared in New England. Among the southern New England names, 193 arrived in 1620–35; 233 in 1636–43; 138 in 1644–92; and 24 in 1693–1790. The number of names in each group represents roughly the amount of immigration into southern New England in each period. After 1643, when Cromwell's rebellion ended the persecution of the Puritans in England, a period of fifty years showed far less immigration than the preceding seven, while throughout the century from 1690 to 1790 immigration was greatly reduced. Poor soil, rugged hills, stern Puritanism, and blue laws made southern New England relatively unattractive in comparison with states farther south. Immigration to New England did not revive until 1830, but even after that, until the end of the nineteenth century, old New England families intermarried very little with newcomers. Thus the 588 names selected because of their dominance in southern New England after the Revolution represent a racial stock, or "kith," * as we may call it, which originated for the most part from 1630 to 1642 and then remained almost unmixed for more than two centuries except as it was joined by people who were more or less like-minded. During the last century the amount of mixing with other types of old American stock and with more recent immigrants has steadily increased. It should be noted, however, that inasmuch as the adults with whom we deal in this study were born mainly before 1900, they still carry a large percentage of old Puritan ancestry—far more than

---

* Some good term is needed for groups of people smaller than races and often derived from a mixture of races. Such groups may be nations, but may extend beyond national boundaries or comprise only a part of the people within such boundaries. In general the groups for which we need a name have a common language and culture and intermarry freely with one another. The French and Sicilians, for example, form such groups, as do the Indians who speak Quichu on the plateau of Peru. "Natio-racial," a term suggested by Hirsch, is hard to pronounce and carries too strong a racial implication. Moreover, it scarcely applies to groups like the Quichu Indians, who in no sense form a nation. "Ethnos" might be good, except that "ethnic" is too closely tied up with race in the debatable sense of the word.

Fortunately the English language contains a word which seems well fitted to our purpose. "Kith" is archaic and obsolete except in the phrase "kith and kin." There, according to Webster's *International Dictionary,* it means "familiar friends, neighbors, fellow countrymen, or acquaintance, collectively." Only "by confusion" does it mean "kindred or kin." It seems legitimate, then, to give kith a more definite anthropological meaning. We may define a kith as a group of people relatively homogeneous in language and culture, and freely intermarrying with one another.

is carried by most of the people bearing such names as Adams, Brown, and others of our random sample.

The differences between persons descended from Puritans who arrived in America early in contrast to those who arrived later are surprisingly great. The distinction between groups based on date of arrival is clearer than many people would suppose. The earliest colonists settled on the seaboard or in a few especially favorable places on rivers. In a few years small villages grew up. Later arrivals went a few miles beyond these older villages and established new ones of their own. In colonial times and down almost to our own day, as we have seen, the vast majority of people married neighbors. If they went outside their own locality, the chances were that they would marry into families of their own type. Ministers' families, for example, were especially prone to marry into those of other ministers or of deacons. Religious prejudices were strong. This fact tended to cause the earliest settlers, who were the most intensely religious, to marry their own kind. Thus, although there has unquestionably been a great amount of intermarriage between the descendants of the four groups of immigrants arriving in successive periods from 1620 to 1790, there was a real distinction so long as people stayed near the old homes.

Even when the Puritan stock migrated westward, the distinction between groups of different origin did not vanish. Hundreds or thousands of midwestern villages were settled by New Englanders and for a long time had relatively little to do with villages settled by people from other sections. Such places as Beloit, Wisconsin, with its college and great white Congregational church, still boast of their New England quality. Moreover, in many instances the people who settled in a midwestern locality came in large proportions from a particular neighborhood in New England. The assortative tendency in marriage emphasizes the distinction between different types of settlers. Thus old differences were preserved to a considerable degree well down toward the latter part of the last century. Nevertheless, none of the four groups with which we shall now deal can be counted as more than a diluted sample. Each merely represents more than the average of descent from ancestors who arrived at a particular time. Hence the clear differences which we shall find are doubly significant. If the four groups had remained completely separated, the differences would presumably be much greater.

C. A Measurement of Achievement

Having selected our Puritan names and divided them into groups according to the date when the name first appeared in America, let us see how many representatives of each line of descent now live in the United States. For this purpose, the number of entries under each name was counted in the directories of thirty-eight cities well distributed over the country.* On the assumption that among old white stock the names in the cities are representative of those in the surrounding areas as a whole, it is possible to estimate the total population belonging to each type of name in each main section of the United States.

TABLE 7

ESTIMATED POPULATIONS NOW BEARING VARIOUS TYPES OF NAMES

Date of Arrival of Names	Southern New England		Northern New England	Middle Atlantic	South Atlantic	Control (Adams, Brown, etc.)
	75–100% in 1790	50–75% in 1790	50–100% in 1790			
1620–1635	111,725	1,095,900	59,105	211,250	....	....
1636–1642	151,630	1,434,100	57,685	294,070	....	....
1643–1692	82,551	552,790	116,005	284,100	....	....
1693–1790	20,021	81,770	21,015	125,230	....	....
Total	365,927	3,164,560	253,810	1,928,515	569,200	3,130,278

The Middle Atlantic figures which are tabulated by date represent names which in 1790 were found to the extent of at least 50 per cent in the Middle Atlantic States and which are also found in Savage (up to 1692) or at least are represented in New England before 1790. These names as a whole seem mainly to represent ancestors who came to New England but soon moved on to New York, New Jersey, or occasionally Maryland. The Middle Atlantic total also includes 1,013,865 persons whose names do not occur in Savage's *Genealogical Memoir* and whose ancestors in the male line presumably come directly from the Old World to the Middle Atlantic States. They can be used as a "control" along with the widely used names of the last column. The South Atlantic total represents names occurring in 1790 to the extent of at least 50 per cent in Virginia or the Carolinas.

The next step is to find reliable statistical data whereby to measure the ability and achievements of the bearers of the various types of names. For this purpose we have chosen (1) the proportion of pro-

* This work, as well as much other statistical investigation described in this volume, was done by Charles L. Ziegler.

fessional men, inventors, directors of corporations, and persons in *Who's Who* or the *Encyclopædia Britannica,* (2) credit ratings in business, and (3) criminals and persons on relief. More than the average ability and persistence are ordinarily required to obtain an education for medicine, law, engineering, or other professions. It usually requires hard, intelligent work to make an invention and patent it or to succeed so well in business that one becomes a director of a corporation or establishes a concern that gets a high credit rating in Dun and Bradstreet's *Reference Book.* Clergymen, social reformers, and physicians tend to be altruistic and morally strong as well as intelligent. Inclusion in *Who's Who* or the encyclopedia normally indicates unusual capacities as well as achievements. A high credit rating in business denotes reliability and good management. Crime and chronic dependence on relief, on the other hand, are often signs of innate weakness as well as of misfortune.

The fact that names which rank high in the most creditable respects rank low in crime and dependence is significant. It indicates, among other things, that we are not being misled by any possible mistakes in estimating the number of people bearing each type of name. The same thing is indicated by criteria such as ratings in business. Of course, each of our groups contains a certain number of people who are not of colonial descent, but according to the laws of chance the percentage of these ought to be essentially the same in each of the large groups with which we are working.

D. Date of Arrival and Success

Figure 9 illustrates some of the main results of this study of names. The four bars in each group represent people bearing names that appeared in New England during successive periods. The periods begin with *A,* 1620–35, when the earliest Puritan immigration occurred. They go on to *B,* 1636–42, when immigration was heaviest, then to *C,* 1643–92, when the strongly Puritan type was no longer so dominant, and, finally, *D,* 1693–1790, when migration was almost at a standstill. Names characteristic of any one of three areas, namely, northern and southern New England and the Middle Atlantic States, are all included here. Bars *A, B,* and *C* largely represent New England stock. The latest bar (*D*), however, is equally strongly representative of names which may have come first to New England, but

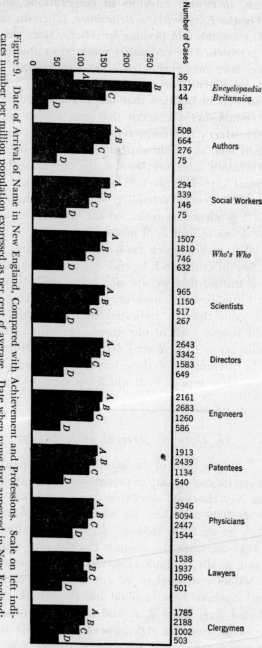

Figure 9. Date of Arrival of Name in New England, Compared with Achievement and Professions. Scale on left indicates number of cases per million population expressed as per cent of average. Date when name first appeared in New England: $A = 1620–35$; $B = 1636–43$; $C = 1644–92$; $D = 1693–1790$.

which belonged primarily to Long Island, southern New York, and northern New Jersey in 1790.*

In the scale on the left of Figure 9, a level of 100 indicates the average proportion of authors, scientists, lawyers, or others, when the entire 1,164 names employed in this study are put together. In other words, the averages as a whole are based on 84,701 † entries of professional men and other leaders in reference books and on 1,191,-380 entries in city directories which represent an estimated present population of 9,412,290 people.

The outstanding fact about Figure 9 is that 9 out of 11 groups show an uninterrupted, steplike descent from a high level for the earliest names to a lower level for the later names. Of course each each type of name includes persons with almost every degree of ability, but we are discussing averages. The departure from regularity in the left-hand group—the one for the *Encyclopædia Britannica*—is probably due to mere accident. The number of persons involved is too small to be significant except in column *B*, as appears from the numbers above the bars. The reason for the other departure, among lawyers, is unknown.

Figure 10 is like Figure 9, but is based only on people in *Who's Who*. Therefore, the number of persons is sometimes too small to be significant, as in the group for military men on the right. Nevertheless, the same steplike regularity is dominant. The only instances where bars based on more than one hundred men fail to show the expected regularity are the ones labelled *B* for educators and literary men. Their departure from the rule simply means that in those two

---

* As a matter of fact, at least 80 per cent of the two older types of names (*A* and *B*) and 75 per cent of the next type (*C*) consist of persons with names that were found mainly in southern New England in 1790. On the other hand, about 85 per cent of the persons with the latest type of names (*D*) belong similarly to parts of New York and New Jersey not more than one hundred miles from New England. This latest group, *D*, is included in order to get a sufficiently large representation of a relatively late migration which did not undergo such difficulties as beset the earlier migrants.

† This number probably becomes about 75,000 when duplications are omitted. Many of the individuals taken from *Who's Who* are included in other lists. A certain number of engineers are also directors, authors may be scientists or clergymen, and so forth. The averages are based on the following number of individuals: *Encyclopædia Britannica* and list of eminent names in Webster's *International Dictionary* 264, social workers 1,129, authors 1,958, scientists 3,946, *Who's Who*, 6,084, lawyers 7,451, engineers 9,110, clergymen 9,190, directors of corporations 11,125, patentees 15,399, and physicians 19,045. Far more than half of all these bear southern New England names.

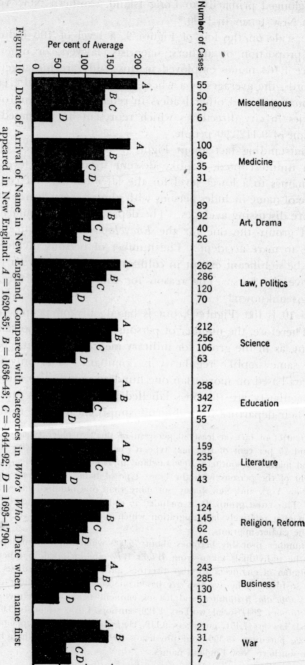

Figure 10. Date of Arrival of Name in New England, Compared with Categories in *Who's Who*. Date when name first appeared in New England: *A* = 1620–35; *B* = 1636–43; *C* = 1644–92; *D* = 1693–1790.

occupations the group with names dating from 1636 to 1642 slightly excels the one with names that first appear from 1620 to 1635.

The general meaning of Figures 9 and 10 is clear. The fact that, aside from the bars for names belonging to the latest period (1693–1790), practically all the other bars rise above 100 shows that old New England names rank high compared with the American average. This does not mean that they outrank other special kinds of names, such as those belonging mainly to people of Quaker, Huguenot, Old Dutch, or the 1848 types of German descent. On this point we have no exact information, but a general knowledge of such people suggests that they are much like the Puritan type. A group descended from a highly selected ancestry of almost any origin would presumably show similar characteristics. The important point just now, however, is that the degree of leadership among bearers of Puritan names varies in accordance with the date when the name first appeared in America. The advantage is almost invariably with the older names. Nowhere in Figure 10, and only among encyclopaedia people and lawyers in Figure 9, does either *A* or *B* fall below *C*. Column *D*, for names arriving in America from 1692 to 1790, almost invariably stands lowest.

TABLE 8

PERCENTAGE OF PERSONS WITH VARIOUS KINDS OF NAMES IN THE CENSUS SECTIONS OF THE COUNTRY IN 1935

A	*B*	*C*	*D*	*E*
	Southern New England Names Percentage in Southern New England in 1790		Northern New England Names	All Native Whites of Native Parentage in the United States
Census Division Where People Now Live	50–75% type	75–100% type		
New England	13	20	17	5
Middle Atlantic	16	14	13	16
East North Central	19	21	19	21
West North Central	12	13	11	12
South Atlantic	10	6	9	15
East South Central	7	4	6	10
West South Central	9	6	8	12
Rocky Mountain	4	5	5	3
Pacific	10	11	10	6

This close connection between descent and achievement has little to do with the place where people now live. Even those whose names were found in southern New England to the extent of 75 per cent or more in 1790 are now less numerous in New England (20 per cent) than in the East North Central States (21 per cent). Among the much larger group whose names were found in southern New England to the extent of 50–75 per cent in 1790, only 13 per cent now live there as against 19 per cent in the East North Central States, 16 per cent in the Middle Atlantic, and 10 per cent each in the South Atlantic and Pacific sections. (See Table 8.) On the whole, the present distribution of our various groups of old New England names is much like that of the entire body of native whites of native parentage except in the South. This wide geographical distribution of New England names is very important. In conjunction with the systematic contrasts in Figures 9 and 10, it indicates that the qualities connected with these names are due to an inheritance of some kind, either cultural or biological, which New Englanders carried with them as they migrated westward.

E. Success and Duration of Residence in New England

The length of time that people's ancestors remained in New England, as well as the time of first arrival, seems to have a connection with their achievements. In Figures 11 and 12, the people bearing the names that were predominantly located in southern New England in 1790 are divided into two groups according to the percentage of the bearers of the name remaining there at that time. No attention is paid to the date when the name reached America. For Group *A* the percentage is 75–100 and for *B,* 50–75. This gives a clear-cut separation according to the amount of both cultural and biological inheritance received from the Puritans. The result is astonishing. According to every one of our twenty-one criteria, the people with the greater degree of Puritan inheritance surpass those having less.

The intimate relation between success and Puritan ancestry is emphasized by the fact that names which belonged primarily to northern New England or the Middle Atlantic States in 1790 agree with the southern New England names. This is evident in Figure 13, which is based on 31,000 scientists, directors of corporations, social workers, engineers, and persons mentioned in *Who's Who.* On the left we have names that were found in southern New England to the extent of 75–100 per cent (section I), or of 50–75 per cent (section II). Then come names belonging to northern New England (III), the Middle Atlantic States (IV), and finally all of these combined (V). The four bars of each section represent names arriving in America at successive

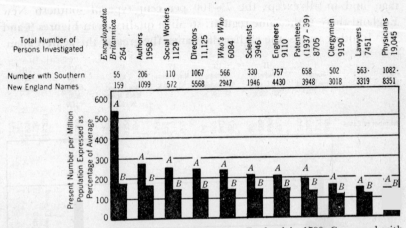

Figure 11. Degree of Residence in Southern New England in 1790, Compared with Occupations and Achievements. $A = 75$–100% in southern New England in 1790; $B = 50$–75% in southern New England in 1790. Upper figures for "Number with Southern New England Names" denote number of persons on which bar A is based; lower figures, bar B.

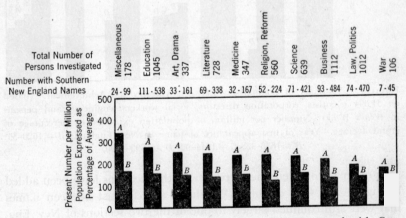

Figure 12. Residence in Southern New England in 1790, Compared with Categories in *Who's Who*. $A = 75$–100% in southern New England in 1790; $B = 50$–75%.

dates. In each case the two earlier types of names have the advantage, and in all except the 75–100 per cent type of southern New England there is the same regular, steplike quality as in Figures 9 and 10. In other words, the earlier the name, the greater the achievement.

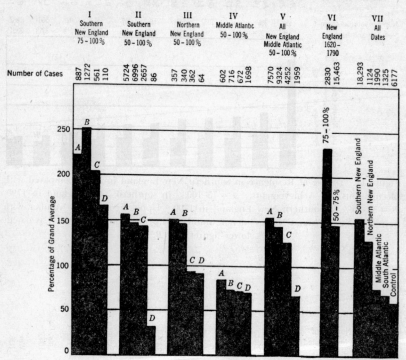

Figure 13. Summary of Comparisons between Ancestry and Achievement. (Based on 31,394 scientists, corporation directors, social workers, engineers, and persons in *Who's Who*.) Number per million of population expressed as percentage of grand average. Year of first appearance of name in New England: *A* = 1620–35; *B* = 1636–43; *C* = 1644–92; *D* = 1693–1790.

In order to complete the picture two other sections have been added to Figure 13. One of these (VI) shows the contrast between names that were still confined largely to one of the two sections of New England in 1790 (75–100 per cent), and those whose bearers had spread more widely, leaving only 50–75 per cent still near the old home. The other diagram (VII) shows a regular decline from names belonging to southern New England in 1790 (50 per cent or more) to those of northern New England, the Middle Atlantic States, the South, and finally a control group representing ordinary British migration to

America at all dates. The control is based on the following names: Adams, Brown, Edwards, Jones, Smith, Stone, Williams, and a random list of names which appeared in the Middle Atlantic States before 1790, but were not found in New England prior to 1692. The significant feature of this study is the systematic way in which early Puritan ancestry is associated with high achievement, even though the persons who bear this ancestry are now found in all parts of the United States.

F. Patentees, Religious Leaders, and Heredity

Although the strong relationship between ancestry and achievement can scarcely be doubted, its cause is by no means clear. Is it due to heredity or environment? That both play a part seems certain. The study of twins, as illustrated by the work of Newman, Freeman, and others, is probably the most convincing of the many lines of evidence which indicate that mental characteristics are the combined result of heredity and environment. Identical twins, it will be remembered, possess the same hereditary make-up because they are derived from a single ovum which divides into two separate parts instead of producing a single embryo. Careful measurements show that identical twins are much more alike than ordinary twins or than brothers and sisters who are not twins. When brought up together, they are extraordinarily alike in appearance. Even their best friends often have difficulty in telling them apart. Moreover their grades in school, their intelligence quotients, their likes and dislikes, their fluctuations in health, and many other features of their lives are amazingly similar. On the other hand, when brought up apart, identical twins show distinct differences, but still are much more alike than ordinary brothers and sisters or than fraternal (non-identical) twins would be under the same circumstances. If the environments are sufficiently different, identical twins may differ somewhat in height and a good deal in weight. If one is brought up in an unfavorable environment, he may acquire a sullen disposition or be retarded mentally so that his IQ falls distinctly below that of his more fortunate twin. Nevertheless, the resemblances, both physical and mental, still remain greater than among corresponding pairs who are less closely alike genetically.

The study of twins has led careful students to believe almost universally that people's intelligence and temperament, as well as their physical characteristics, are always a combination of the influence of heredity and environment. In individual cases, such as brothers who are trained almost identically but differ greatly in temperament, heredity may be the dominant factor in causing differences of character and achievement. In other cases, such as identical twins who live under highly diverse conditions from infancy onward, environment may account for large differences in character and achievements. Although there seems to be clear-cut and convincing evidence that heredity and environment are of approximately equal importance in determining human characteristics, many people still think that environment, especially childhood education, is far more important than heredity. This attitude has of late been rather prominent among sociologists, anthropologists, and educators.

Because of this attitude it is especially desirable to inquire how far environment alone can account for the observed facts as to patents, for example. People who take out more than one patent within a year are presumably endowed by heredity with unusually active and original minds. For example, in 1907, 1908, and 1909, Thomas A. Edison took out twenty-three, twelve, and thirty-two patents respectively. His co-workers helped, to be sure, but he was the dominating spirit. Figure 14 shows that in the field of invention the relative achievements of people with different types of ancestry vary in essentially the same way as in the various lines illustrated in the five preceding diagrams. Figure 14 is based on the percentage of patentees taking out more than one patent per year according to the records for five years. The left-hand section shows a close approximation to section V of Figure 13. It indicates that when all New England and Middle Atlantic names are divided according to their date of appearance in America, the early names are more likely than the later ones to be represented by inventors. The middle section of Figure 14, like section VI of Figure 13, shows a similar condition for names which prevailed in southern New England to the extent of 75–100 per cent in 1790 in comparison with similar names which prevailed there to the extent of only 50–75 per cent. Finally, on the right the patentees bearing colonial names belonging to each of four geographic sections show approximately the same relative numbers as the corresponding people of section VII in Figure 13. The control, which represents a population of 3,130,000, stands lowest, as usual.

Although the three sections of Figure 14 are less impressive and more irregular than the corresponding parts in Figure 13, they show the same persistent tendency for early names and strongly New England names to outrank others. Inventiveness depends to a large degree upon innate personal traits. The development of these traits is, of course, much influenced by the cultural environment in which people live. Nevertheless, it does not seem probable that the cultural environment alone could cause the differences seen in Figure 14. It is obvious that the presence of a strong strain of Puritan ancestry, especially the early type, tends to make people inventive. It seems as

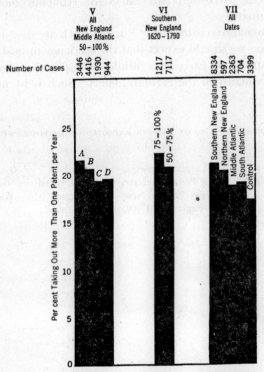

Figure 14. Colonial Names and Percentage of Persons Taking Out More Than One Patent Per Year, 1907, 1908, 1937–39. Year of first appearance of name in New England: A = 1620–35; B = 1636–43; C = 1644–92; D = 1693–1790.

though this must indicate that an innate tendency toward inventiveness plays some part in the matter.

The occupations which most strongly attract people likewise suggest that the present position of the Puritan kith depends on biological as well as social heredity. The earliest Puritan settlers were extremely religious, but their descendants, although still leaders in religion, do not put it first to any such extent as did their ancestors. In fact, relatively speaking, they neglect this field of effort far more than do people of average British stock. Rarely, if ever, has a colo-

nizing group equaled the earliest Puritans in its proportion of ministers and university graduates. These people and their companions
were the ones in whom the religious motive was most dominant.
Within a few years after 1630, however, economic as well as religious
motives began to play an increasingly prominent part in sending
Puritans across the Atlantic. After 1643 the economic motive was
apparently dominant.

If the present characteristics of the Puritan stock are due mainly to
social inheritance, we should expect that the tendency toward religion
which was so strong in early days would be especially strong now
among the descendants of the earliest comers. Such is by no means

TABLE 9

NUMBER OF LEADERS AS RATIO OF NUMBER EXPECTED ON BASIS OF POPULATION

	A Largest Proportion of Puritan Ancestry (75–100% in New England in 1790)	B Southern New England Ancestry in General	C Control Based on Seven Widely Used Names
1. *Encyclopædia Britannica*	5.7	2.2	0.4
2. Authors	2.7	1.9	0.5
3. Social workers	2.5	1.7	0.6
4. Directors	2.5	1.7	0.6
5. *Who's Who*	2.4	1.6	0.6
6. Scientists	2.1	1.7	0.6
7. Engineers	2.1	1.6	0.6
8. Multiple patentees	2.0	1.6	0.6
9. Patentees	1.9	1.5	0.7
10. Lawyers	1.9	1.5	0.8
11. Clergymen	1.6	1.3	1.0
12. Physicians	1.5	1.4	0.7

the case. Column *A* in Table 9 shows that among the 300,000 or
more people with the highest percentage of Puritan descent, 5.7 times
as many are in the *Encyclopædia Britannica* as would be expected on
the basis of population. Among the 3,000,000 who come from southern New England stock in general the ratio is 2.2 (column *B*), whereas
among another 3,000,000 bearing widely used names that represent
the average migration from England at all periods (column *C*) it falls
to only 0.4. Authors, social workers, and business directors are also
strongly represented among the two old New England types and
under-represented among the average British type. If we go down
the table to the clergy (No. 11), however, the ratios for the two Puri-

tan types drop to 1.6 and 1.3, whereas the ratio for the widely used names rises to 1.0. This means that although Puritan stock still does more than its proportional share in religious leadership, it takes still greater interest in other professions, aside from medicine.

Curiously enough, this is the opposite of what happens among people bearing widely used English names such as Jones and Smith. Their representation is lowest in the *Encyclopædia Britannica* and among authors and highest among clergymen. Although their ancestors came to America primarily for economic profit, their rank among directors of corporations is only 0.6. Such facts seem to mean that among people whose mental capacity is high, the most active minds have a special tendency to gravitate toward the types of work which at the moment are most to the fore. Alert, active minds are attracted by new or challenging occupations. Less alert minds tend to follow the ways of their ancestors. Thus the most strongly Puritan type goes in for social work about one and one-half times as strongly, relatively speaking, as for strictly religious work. This is reversed among the control group representing British migration in general. That group shows little more than half as great a tendency toward social work as toward the ministry. Hence we infer that innate mental traits have a good deal to do with the index numbers of Table 9.

G. Business Success, Heredity, and Selective Migration

A third line of evidence may throw light on the relative parts played by heredity and environment. It also supplies a forceful illustration of the laws of migration set forth in a previous chapter. Figure 15 shows the percentage of business concerns which receive a high rating in Dun and Bradstreet's *Reference Book*. Its four sections represent conditions among people residing in four geographical regions, namely, New York City, the North Atlantic area aside from that city, the North Central States from Ohio to the Rocky Mountains, and, finally, the Pacific Coast. The three bars of each section represent degrees of Puritan ancestry. The left-hand bar represents the type of name which in 1790 was found in southern New England to the extent of 75–100 per cent. Next comes the corresponding 50–75 per cent type, and on the right the northern New England names.

Figure 16 is similar to Figure 15 except that the bars indicate time of arrival of names in southern New England, namely, up to 1635, from 1636 to 1643, and from 1644 to 1790. In both figures New York City shows the usual strongly steplike arrangement with the greatest degree of Puritan ancestry standing highest. The rest of the Northeast shows a similar, but less pronounced, condition that agrees well with what we have found again and again as to Puritan achieve-

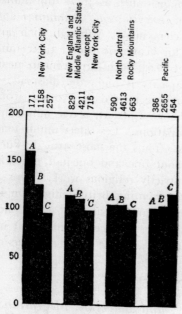

Figure 15. Dun and Bradstreet's Business Ratings, Compared with Degree of New England Ancestry and Later Westward Migration. *A* = Names in southern New England in 1790 to extent of 75–100%; *B* = Names in southern New England in 1790 to extent of 50–75%; *C* = Names in northern New England in 1790 to extent of 50–100%.

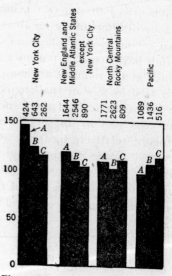

Figure 16. Dun and Bradstreet's Business Ratings, Compared with Date of Arrival of Names in Southern New England and with Later Westward Migration. Date when names first appeared: *A* = 1620–35; *B* = 1636–43; *C* = 1644–1790.

ments. In the North Central region, however, there is no significant trend either way, and all the bars are approximately equal. On the Pacific Coast a reversal occurs. This state of affairs seems curious, but it agrees with what would be expected from the laws of migration as set forth in a previous chapter.

Omitting for the moment the effects of migration, let us see what the diagrams for New York City and the Northeast suggest concerning heredity. A high rating in Dun and Bradstreet normally means both integrity and business capacity. Training and opportunity certainly play a prominent part in making men good executives. Nevertheless, success in business, especially where competition is so keen as in New York, must depend also to a large degree upon innate capacities. There is no known means of determining how far the steplike arrangement of the diagrams for New York and the Northeast in Figures 15 and 16 is due to either cultural conditions or heredity. There seems little room for doubt, however, that the two vary together and are jointly responsible for the relative standing of the different types of descent.

Turning now to the problem of migration, we have seen that there is a strong tendency for the most successful business men, as well as others, to migrate away from the country's interior, especially toward the Northeast. We know also that there are definite laws of selection through migration. On this basis the high level of the left-hand bar in the New York sections of Figures 15 and 16 means that the attraction of New York City has had an especially great effect in drawing thither an unusually large percentage of the 75–100 per cent group whose ancestry would lead us to expect most from them. Hence in the rest of the New England and Middle Atlantic group, as represented in the second section of Figures 15 and 16, the 75–100 per cent type is apparently depleted, so that those who remain rank only a little above the other two groups of old New England stock. Farther west in the North Central States the tendency for the most successful old families to stay in the East has had so much effect that the contrast between the different kinds of names has disappeared.

Finally, on the Pacific Coast, we seem to see the combined result of the tendency for the most successful types to send out only their less successful members as migrants, and of the opposing tendency for less successful groups to send out their strongest members. Hence in a distant place, such as California, the biological type that is most successful in the East is surpassed on an average by members of biological groups which in the East do not succeed so conspicuously. This is especially interesting because it agrees with what we found among suburban people, as indicated by the crossing of the lines in Figure 8. In an exaggerated way "remittance" men in western Canada illustrate the point that we are now making. Many such men are the relatively unsuccessful or erratic sons of the British gentry. Some migrate overseas because of too much drinking, unfortunate escapades, or a moody and discontented spirit. Their better balanced, or more intelligent, brothers and cousins may be successful business men, authors, or members of parliament. Some of the remittance men have good abilities and do well in Canada. Nevertheless, on the average, they do not equal the sons of competent people in less conspicu-

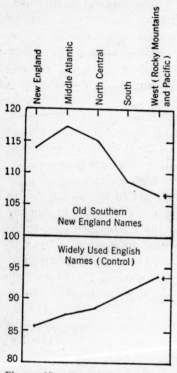

ous walks of life. The son of a clerk, farmer, or carpenter who goes to a new country is often much superior to the general class into which he is born. His intelligence, energy, and initiative cause him to succeed to an unusual degree. Thus in a new land at the end of a long or difficult migration, the normal laws of migration, as we saw in the last chapter, have a distinct tendency to equalize or even reverse the position of social classes. Between New York City and California there is the same sort of reversal as between London and western Canada. Midway between the reversed sections there must be a region where the differences disappear, as in the Midwest sections of Figures 15 and 16.

The way in which such a reversal occurs is well illustrated in Figure 17. The lines show Dun and Bradstreet's ratings for old southern New England names (above) and our seven widely used English names (below). From left to right we have sections of the United States from New England across the country westward and southward. The sections are arranged

Figure 17. Equalizing Effect of Migration, as Illustrated by Dun and Bradstreet's Ratings of Businesses Conducted under Different Types of Names. Ratings are expressed as percentages of grand average.

roughly according to the difficulty of migrating thither from New England. In the upper curve, representing Puritan names, New England itself does not stand so high as the Middle Atlantic and North Central states. In other words, it has not been able to hold its most energetic or able families of the business type in competition with New York, Chicago, and other great industrial centers. Otherwise the Puritan curve slopes steadily downward toward the right, because a large share of the most competent people of this type find satisfactory opportunities without migrating far. The other curve rises steadily toward the regions which are the most difficult to reach from the Northeast and Europe. The reason, as we saw in the last chapter, is that the most energetic and competent people who fail to find good openings near home are the ones most likely to migrate far. If we could carry these same curves further, basing them, perhaps, on the names of Americans in China, we should probably find them coming together, although they might not cross. Their tendency to converge indicates the remarkable way in which a long migration favors a selection such that at the end the migrants tend to be similar despite significant differences in the groups from which they started.

H. Crime and Dependency

Before we attempt to explain the causes of the highly systematic and illuminating differences between various kinds of names, let us examine crime and dependency. Unfortunately data on these are not available for our entire list of names. *After Three Centuries,*[3] however, contains an account of a preliminary investigation in which seven distinctively colonial names have been compared with five widely used old English names belonging to immigrants arriving at all times from the earliest colonial days down to the present. For three of the colonial names and four of the others data as to both crime and dependency were obtained from police departments and social service exchanges in seven cities (New York, Chicago, Cleveland, St. Louis, Baltimore, Louisville, and Toledo) and three states (Massachusetts, Indiana, and Michigan). Table 10 shows that in proportion to the population the representation of the colonial names in creditable categories is systematically greater than that of the widely used English names. In the less creditable categories of criminals and persons on relief the opposite is true.

On the whole, the more difficult achievements are the ones having the higher ratios in Table 10. This again suggests innate mental differences. Under ordinary circumstances it certainly requires unusual innate capacity as well as good opportunities to secure inclusion in the *Encyclopædia Britannica* or even in *Who's Who*. On the other hand, mere mention in Dun and Bradstreet requires no more than

[3] Huntington and Ragsdale.

the ability to run a filling station or a small grocery store. Table 10 is especially significant because it suggests that the right kind of descent, either biological or cultural, lessens crime and distress as well as increases positive achievements that promote civilization.

TABLE 10

RATIO OF REPRESENTATIVES OF THREE OLD COLONIAL NAMES TO THOSE OF FOUR WIDELY USED ENGLISH NAMES

Encyclopædia Britannica	16.8
Notable Americans	10.5
Cards in catalogues of libraries (Yale, Harvard, Boston, New York)	8.4
Authors	7.8
Social Register	7.7
American Association for the Advancement of Science	6.7
Who's Who in America	6.3
Scientists	4.9
Directors of corporations	3.5
Lawyers	3.0
Physicians	2.1
Inventors (patentees)	1.8
Government officials	1.6
Dentists	1.5
Business concerns in Dun and Bradstreet's Reference Book	1.3
Criminals	.6
Persons on relief rolls in 1933	.4

The facts here presented as to multiple patents, devotion to religion, business ratings, and crime and dependency all suggest that hereditary mental traits, as well as cultural conditions, enter into the differences among our various types of names.

I. The Selective Process among Early Puritans

We are now ready to amplify what has already been suggested as to the relation between modern success and the time when people's ancestors arrived in America. The secret seems to lie in something which happened at the time of migration. Taken as a whole, the earliest migrants to New England were the most completely dominated by deep religious conviction. They believed that certain things were God's commands, and they had the strength of will to act according to their beliefs. This does not mean that their beliefs were necessarily right. It simply shows that those early Puritans were intelligent enough to think for themselves, and then to stick to their convictions and act upon them in spite of opposition and persecution.

Such strength of mind is rare. Thus there was both a mental and a moral selection. Only the most intelligent people have sufficient mental depth to think out a religious problem for themselves. The extremely high proportion of ministers and of graduates of Oxford and Cambridge Universities among the earliest Puritan settlers in New England illustrates this point. Even today it is difficult to find so large a proportion of college graduates except perhaps in small college towns. The iron hand with which the Puritans suppressed their own impulses toward pleasure illustrates their moral strength, even though that strength was often wrongly directed.

Other types of selection were based on temperament and health. Boldness, courage, and physical vigor were needed, especially among the women. It was no light matter to cross the vast ocean on a slow voyage of many weeks and settle in a cold, forested land full of wild savages. Charles E. Banks [4] describes some of the difficulties.

The present generation has scant conception and practically no actual knowledge of the inconveniences which their ancestors experienced in making the voyage from England to the American continent. The most that is understood and appreciated is the diminutive size of the vessels and the long and hazardous passage required under the best conditions to reach the "stern and rockbound coast" of New England. A contemporary writer speaks of the giant seas "hurling their unfixed goods from place to place" from lack of proper stowage. . . . The only possible place for passengers was the space between the towering stern structure and the forecastle or between decks. Below this was the hold, which was used for cargo, the ordnance, and the stowing of the longboats. In this part of the ship, as we learn from Winthrop's story of the *Arbella,* cabins had been constructed, probably rough compartments of boards for women and children, while hammocks for the men were swung from every available point of vantage. . . .

It may be left to speculation how the sanitary needs of the passengers were provided for in ordinary weather with smooth seas. The imagination is beggared to know how the requirements of nature were met in prolonged storms in these small boats when men, women, and children were kept under the hatches for safety. This may be mentioned as an inevitable accompaniment of emigration in its beginning.

The selection due to temperament and health was most drastic. Many a man who wanted to join an early band of Puritan migrants was undoubtedly deterred because his wife or sweetheart dreaded the venture. Or perhaps either a man, or the woman of his choice, was

[4] pp. 6–7.

not of an adaptable temperament. Many fine people cannot easily adjust themselves to new conditions. People with constitutional weaknesses are not likely to migrate to a new and difficult country. They are not adapted to hacking farms out of the wilderness, living in makeshift shacks, and meeting the dangers of wild animals and Indians. Moreover, after the new land was reached, the physical selection was at first tremendous. Half the people who landed in Plymouth and a third of those in the first shipload to Boston died during the first year. Almost any genealogical book shows that among the earliest settlers many a man had successively two, three, or even four wives. Young mothers and their babies died in great numbers because of the harshness of the new conditions.

All these types of selection—intellectual, moral, temperamental, and physical—were more severe at first than afterward. The physical selection operated more fiercely upon the women than the men, but economic conditions and the difficulty of getting wives gave a selective advantage to the most competent men. Almost half the men who came to America in the early days never succeeded in getting wives. As late as 1635, typical shiploads of immigrants contained such proportions as these: 254 men and older boys not belonging to families, and 132 women and older unattached girls. According to Charles E. Banks, the fare of five pounds was equivalent to at least $150 or $200 in our day, and equipment had to be added. Therefore, it required a fairly substantial economic condition to bring a family, or even one-self and later a prospective wife, to America. Moreover, so many of the more successful men took second wives that the supply for less competent men was limited. For all these reasons, then, the children born in the new land were likely to inherit strong qualities from both parents and to be brought up by mothers of rare quality. It is not surprising to find unusual achievements among people descended wholly from such ancestors. The surprising thing is to find that even when such descent is much diluted, it still is important.

As soon as Boston and other early settlements blossomed into little villages with reasonably comfortable houses, the conditions of migration became easier. Newcomers did not have to camp out amid danger from weather and Indians while building log houses. They were hospitably sheltered in kind homes until they could move on a few miles into cabins already prepared. Hence, although the process of selection was still strong, it was not so strenuous as before. With each succeeding year it diminished in intensity. Moreover, the religious motive was more and more supplemented or superseded by purely economic motives.   Puritans who would not have thought it worth while to migrate in the first years of the colony concluded that it would be good for their pocketbooks as well as their souls to go to the new country.   A gradual change thus occurred in the type of migrant, and the results are manifest in their descendants.   The change continued more or less steadily through early colonial times.   Then immigration practically ceased.

When immigration revived after the War of 1812 its average quality, in spite of many exceptions, seems to have continued downward until about the end of the nineteenth century.   This deterioration occurred because the difficulty of migration steadily diminished, while the attraction exerted by tales of great fortunes grew steadily greater. Steamship agents who brought immigrants to ready-made jobs in America co-operated with makers of great fortunes in reducing the selective power of migration to a low ebb.   Energy and adaptability still counted as selective factors, but moral and intellectual selection largely ceased, and temperamental and physical selection counted for little.   Nevertheless, even when steamship agents were bringing contract laborers by the hundred thousand, migration across the sea required some courage and initiative.   Except under unusual conditions, however, it did not bring many of the more thoughtful people, or of the upper classes, or even of the most successful peasants.   Some improvement of quality doubtless occurred when it became illegal to bring contract laborers to this country.

Since World War I an enormous improvement in the mental, and presumably in the moral, quality of American immigrants has again taken place.   The quota system in itself places a certain premium upon forethought.   The migration of refugees from Bolshevism, Fascism, and the Nazi regime has brought to America large groups of unusually competent people.   The main thing that attracted the earliest Puritans to America was the opportunity for freedom of thought and action.   This same motive has again become dominant in a new wave of migrants who, in intellectual quality, may possibly be of higher caliber than the Puritans, or the Germans of 1848, for whom Carl Schurz may stand as the protagonist.   Some of these latest migrants are Jews, but far more are gentiles—Germans, Italians, Czechs, and others who could not stomach Europe's totalitarian regimes.   Today almost every American university has on its staff many men of unusual ability who left Europe because of political difficulties from the time of World War I onward.   Thus the quality of migration continually varies in harmony with the natural laws set forth in the last chapter.

This discussion of the Puritans seems to lead to an important conclusion and to leave a great problem unsolved. The conclusion is that if the selective forces are strong enough, and if the people who are selected are sufficiently isolated, the results of selection by migration may persist with amazing strength for centuries. The problem is to find ways of determining how far this result is due to the establishment of definite genetic strains which predispose people to certain lines of conduct and how far to a social organization whereby definite habits, customs, beliefs, and methods are transmitted from generation to generation as a cultural inheritance. Our study of the Puritans seems to show elements due to both causes. Whatever may be the relative parts played by environment and heredity, this study of the Puritans seems to show that a eugenic program is practical. Unconsciously, but with grim seriousness, the Puritans, like the Quakers and many other groups, made a distinct selection along what seem to be sound eugenic lines. They selected themselves in such a way that the majority of children were born in families where a sound heredity was combined with a sound training. The children thus born were for the most part obliged to marry similar children, unless they migrated or remained single. Although this eugenic policy gradually died out, the result is still clearly evident in the facts set forth in this chapter. Later chapters will develop this theme more fully. The outstanding conclusion of this chapter is that the Puritans of America illustrate what might happen to practically any other stock if it could be subjected to a stringent eugenic selection.

Note to Fourth Printing: In reviewing this book my colleague, Professor G. E. Hutchinson, suggests that the mere fact of having a name that is socially acceptable may play a part in bringing success to persons of Puritan descent. If that is true, the relation between descent and achievement ought to appear less strong when the maiden names of mothers replace the names of fathers. A test of this matter by means of Who's Who gives a quite contrary result. The use of the mother's name increases the strength of the contrasts described above. There is no reason to think that genetically the mother's effect on the child is any greater than that of the father. Therefore we seem forced to conclude that mothers who have grown up in the Puritan tradition, especially that of the earlier stocks, exert a peculiarly strong effect in giving their children the kind of training that leads to success. This does not solve the problem of how far biological inheritance enters into the matter, but it seems to verify the conclusions of psychologists as to the great importance of early childhood training. When a man says, "All that I am I owe to my mother," he apparently gives expression to considerable truth as well as much sentiment.

CHAPTER 7

CHARACTER AND INHERITANCE

A. Literary Achievements of Iceland and Newfoundland

If selection through migration is intimately connected with character and achievement, we are confronted by a principle of deep historical significance. Let us, therefore, inquire further as to how long the effect of migration may remain evident and how far it is either cultural or biological. The contrast between Iceland and Newfoundland offers excellent material for such an inquiry. These two islands in the North Atlantic Ocean lie about 1,600 miles apart. They are of similar size, about one third larger than Ireland. Both are sparsely populated, with only 120,000 persons in Iceland and 290,000 in Newfoundland, in contrast to 4,200,000 in Ireland. In both the inhabitants are primarily Nordic with an old Mediterranean and perhaps Alpine admixture.

In spite of resemblances the islands differ amazingly in culture. Among European kiths few outrank Iceland in the finer elements of civilization. Newfoundland, on the contrary, stands much lower. Reading and writing provide a good measure of cultural progress. Newfoundland has twelve daily and weekly newspapers and four monthly and two quarterly periodicals. Iceland, with less than half as many people, has twenty newspapers and an almost incredible array of other periodicals. At least twenty societies issue regular publications devoted to literature, archaeology, linguistics, history, folklore, religion, engineering, natural history, general science, agriculture, cooperatives, fishing, and other topics. There are three medical societies and one each for dentists, nurses, midwives, pharmacists, and veterinarians. The nurses, the midwives, and one medical society publish monthly journals. Newfoundland has nothing that remotely approaches this output. How a handful of doctors, nurses, or midwives among a hundred thousand poor Icelanders can edit, write, and support these magazines is a puzzle. Anyone who has tackled such a job knows how hard and thankless it is. Practically all the work is done for love, not money. Yet by all accounts it is well done.

A similar contrast appears in many other respects. Travellers report that as late as 1863 Iceland had only a single school. Nevertheless, for centuries practically everyone over ten years of age has been able to read and write. Travellers who could not speak Icelandic have been surprised by being addressed in Latin by fishermen, shepherds, or farm girls. In the early nineteenth century clergymen could and did refuse to perform the marriage ceremony for women who could not read and write, but this rule was less strict than earlier. For centuries the Icelanders have set such store by reading and writing that the children have been carefully taught in their homes. There are plenty of schools now, and every healthy child of school age attends. A few itinerant schools still move from one outlying farm to another, but today many children are brought to relatively large central schools. In Newfoundland, on the contrary, as late as 1900 a considerable percentage of the men and still more of the women in the outlying districts could neither read nor write. Even in 1935, one fifth of the children at ages seven to fourteen did not go to school.

The handful of Newfoundlanders who now receive higher education have to go elsewhere for it. Iceland, on the contrary, supports a flourishing university with schools of theology, the humanities, medicine, law, and philosophy. Iceland has also long had a normal college, a school of navigation, and two agricultural schools. It takes pride in its scientific societies, Bible Society, national picture gallery, and an archaeological society which has published dozens of volumes. Newfoundland has only a vestige of such developments. Bear in mind that Iceland's people are poor and only about as numerous as those of Fort Wayne, Indiana. One third are in Reykjavik, a little city the size of High Point, North Carolina. The rest are widely scattered over an area about the size of Ohio—eighty thousand people, whereas Ohio has six million outside of Cleveland.

One of the most amazing signs of mental activity in Iceland is the production of books and poetry. In the Danish official bibliography for 1915–34, Icelanders appear as the authors of over three thousand titles. An astonishing number of these are books of poetry. In proportion to their numbers Icelanders write about one fourth more than the Danes, whose high cultural standards are universally recognized. No official list of writings in Newfoundland is available, but three hundred books and articles in comparison with Iceland's three thousand is somewhere near the truth. The literary output is almost negligible. Until recently, more than a quarter of a million Newfoundlanders had only a single public library. In Iceland, the capital alone has long had four. There are also four main regional libraries and scores of local ones, some of which are centuries old.

In the past the contrast has been as great as at present. Newfoundland has practically no literature of its own. Iceland's superb early literature was merely a prelude to high literary achievement from that day to this. James Bryce, the famous British ambassador who wrote *The American Commonwealth,* says that Iceland has been the home of an "intellectually cultivated people which has produced a literature both in prose and poetry that stands among the primitive literatures next after that of ancient Greece if one regards both its quantity and quality. . . . Nowhere, except in Greece, was so much produced that attained so high a level of excellence." The Icelandic Eddas are the world's chief source of knowledge about ancient Scandinavia and the Vikings. The sagas, often superbly written, are a veritable mine of history. Later centuries have seen a succession of literary periods. History, religious hymns, drama, essays, and difficult types of rhyme have characterized successive fashions, but always the urge to write seems to have been strong.

The skill required for this prolonged literary output may be judged from the "rimur," or poems based on mythical and heroic tales. These begin in the fourteenth century, and are still being written. Each stanza usually has four lines with rhymes at the ends of the lines or within them. So fertile is the Icelandic mind that 2,267 different kinds of meter have been counted. An occasional rimur consists of stanzas which can be read backward or forward. Stefansson [1] quotes one as follows:

> Grundar dóma, hvergi hann
> hallar rjettu méli;
> stundar sóma, aldrei ann
> örgu pretta táli.

Read normally, this means, "His judgments are well grounded, he never leans unfairly to one side in an issue, he cultivates honor, he never shares in deception and evil." Read backward, it means, "He leans toward vile deception, he never considers honor, he twists what is right to make it wrong, his judgments are ill-grounded." Wasted work, perhaps, but thought-provoking and indicating effort. Try to make an English sentence of six words that can be read either back-

[1] 1939.

ward or forward. It is easier to do this in Icelandic than in English, but even in Icelandic it requires intense thought and extraordinary persistence to make a whole poem of this sort.*

La Peyrere, in his uncommonly penetrating description of Iceland three centuries ago, was probably right when he said:

The Icelanders were so famous for their poetry among the neighboring nations, that it was generally believed that there was a certain kind of magic hidden in their verses, whereby they could summon daemons from the infernal regions, and change the influence of the planets. Their poets are born, and not made such; for the most ingenious person among them cannot write a verse without his natural genius prompts him to it, the rules of poetry being most strict and severe; whereas such as are endowed with this qualification by nature write them with such facility that they can speak scarce anything but in meter.

Another measure of the quality of a people is its men of eminence. The *Encyclopædia Britannica* includes nine Icelanders born since 1600, in addition to several belonging to the Golden Icelandic Age when the famous sagas were written. In proportion to the average population since 1600 this representation gives Iceland three times as many eminent persons as Ireland, France, Switzerland, or Germany. Newfoundland apparently has only a single representative, Robert Bond. He was the son of a Devonshire man and was educated in England. If this comparison be considered unfair because Newfoundland had a smaller population than Iceland up to 1800, consider the fact that even during the last century Iceland has had four native sons sufficiently eminent in literature to find a place in the *Encyclopædia Britannica*. Others, such as the sculptor Thorwaldsen and the explorer Stefansson, were born of Icelandic parents in other countries.

* After this chapter had been written Beck's book on Icelandic literature appeared. It shows that within a single century a population of less than one hundred thousand people produced at least twenty-eight authors whose works are worth translating into English. Dipping into this book at random, the present author was impressed by the beauty of many of the poems. The first story he chanced upon told of an old, rather incompetent man who thought he was a poet. In the second story, selected also by mere chance, he found these words: "On days when rough seas kept the boats tied up, the sand hills were crowded with fishermen engaged in all manner of sports . . . impromptu wrestling and boxing matches, and other contests of a physical nature. . . . Sometimes all those who were best versed in lays and rhymes would gather in one of the huts to play a verse-capping game" [p. 66].

B. Political and Economic Contrasts

In politics the contrast between the islands is as great as in literature. Newfoundland has been conspicuous for fishery disputes, an enervating system of poor relief at times of poor fisheries, and a recent debacle of bad judgment and graft. Rather than go bankrupt, the island gave up its status as a British Dominion and became a crown colony in 1933. London paid its debts and set its affairs in order. Of Iceland, on the other hand, Bryce says:

During nearly four centuries Iceland was the only independent republic in the world. . . . It was absolutely unique in its constitution, for the government was nothing but a system of law courts, administering most elaborate laws, the enforcement of which was for the most part left to those who were parties to the lawsuits. In our own time [Iceland's amicable separation from Denmark] has furnished another argument to those who hold that peace and progress are best secured by the application of the principles of liberty and self-government.

Another striking difference between Iceland and Newfoundland is that Iceland appears to have suffered very little from mismanagement, selfishness, or dishonesty among its leaders. It has never had anything like the Newfoundland depression of 1860–67, when failure of the fisheries led to great distress and poverty. By supporting a large part of the population for several years, the Newfoundland government inaugurated a pitiful period of national idleness. The inhabitants fell into such a habit of expecting public aid that the country became demoralized. They profited little from this experience, for the same thing happened again in 1933. For some years previously there had been reckless borrowing in order to open mines, build railways, and encourage industries. Widespread political mismanagement had come close to grave dishonesty. When fish became scarce, poor relief again became necessary, and Great Britain assumed financial responsibility.

The Amulree Report, a careful official British study of Newfoundland's troubles, ascribes these political and economic weaknesses to faults of national character. After the period of famine and government relief in the 1860's

the people, long tired, would seem almost to have lost heart. . . . Reckless and indolent habits were engendered; and ere long nearly a third of the entire revenue went in charity. . . . A great majority of the industrial population soon learned to disregard the stigma of pauperism. . . . [In 1933]

three years of adversity have sapped physical stamina and moral courage.
. . . [The people, however] are potentially fine material.[2]

Before this time they had fallen into the habit of looking to their
political representatives for everything.

If a man lost his cow, he expected the Member [in the parliament at St.
John's] to see that the Government provided him with another. . . . If the
wharf in a settlement fell into disrepair, the Member was expected to see
that funds were provided by the government to compensate the inhabitants
for repairing it.   Notwithstanding that the material was at hand, that the
lack of suitable wharfage was a serious inconvenience . . . and that the
necessary repairs could be effected in a few hours by willing workers, men
would stand idly by and would prefer that the wharf should collapse into
the sea rather than that they should repair it for their own benefit without
public remuneration.[3]

The report also says that although there are three fishing seasons,
most fishermen limit their work to the middle one (June-July).   Only
if the catch then is poor do they fish in the fall. Severe storms and
fog are, indeed, more common then than in summer, but the fall fish
are best, because they are fat and their livers are full of oil.[4]   The
report also states that in the great paper mills at Grand Falls,[5] the
"most prosperous community in the island, . . . difficulty was at
first experienced in obtaining suitable . . . foremen or superintend-
ents, for the Newfoundlander, while a steady and intelligent worker,
is apt to shrink from responsibility and the exercise of discipline."

Co-operative movements also illustrate the contrast between Iceland
and Newfoundland.   Under the impact of natural disasters Iceland
has built up an admirable system of co-operation among both fishermen and farmers.   The government takes an active share in this.   In
Newfoundland, on the contrary, pure inefficiency permitted the collapse of a field laboratory which was established in 1888 as a co-operative enterprise for the propagation of fish and of the profitable
but diminishing lobster.   In 1900 co-operative stores were established
in Newfoundland to replace the old system by which the fishermen
were constantly in debt to merchants.   Here again political rapacity
and incompetence practically destroyed the system.   The gist of the
matter is that Newfoundland has shown less capacity than Iceland,
which has repeatedly demonstrated extraordinary ability to pull itself out of difficulty.   Iceland has rivalled the most advanced nations

[2] p. 14.   [4] p. 99.
[3] p. 82–83.   [5] p. 142.

in almost every line of endeavor not dependent on mere wealth. It has surpassed practically all others in steady education of its children and in continuous output of excellent literature for a thousand years. Newfoundland, on the contrary, has fallen far below the Icelandic standard. It has contributed little to the world in general, and has repeatedly needed special help in getting out of difficulty.

C. Printing, Health, and Eugenics

Iceland's acceptance of new ideas is another evidence of a kind of mental alertness which is rare in Newfoundland. In A.D. 1000, after a civil war, the problem of paganism versus Christianity was publicly debated at the great annual meeting of the entire island. Christianity was adopted by a deliberate vote, with provision for private worship of the old gods by people not yet ready for a new faith. One chief decided to be a Christian on land, but felt safer to follow Odin on the sea. The printing of books also indicates Iceland's hospitality to new ideas. In Mainz the date of the first printed book was 1455; in England, 1478; in Scotland, 1507. This was in Europe, in places easy of access, relatively prosperous, and with vastly more people than Iceland's fifty thousand. Moreover, the poor Icelanders, far away across a stormy sea, had just emerged from a terrible depression, and were only feebly in touch with the rest of the world. Yet in 1530 a printing-press was introduced, and between 1540 and 1600 at least forty-six books were published. In Norway it was not till 1651 (121 years later than in Iceland) that the first book was published.

In our own day a similar progressive tendency is seen in matters of health. The deathrate has been reduced from 25 per thousand in 1880 to 10 today, and is one of the world's lowest. Between 1880 and 1910 the Icelandic rate fell 42 per cent, which is the fastest decline on record except in Saxony (44 per cent), where the deathrate in 1880 was higher than in Newfoundland. The corresponding fall was only 31 per cent in Prussia, 25 in England and France, and 16 in Ireland. An even greater Icelandic triumph is the world's lowest rate of infant mortality, only 33 deaths in the first year of life per thousand births in 1937, and 28 in 1938. The rates that stood next in 1938 were 36 for New Zealand (whites only), 37 for the Netherlands, 38 for Australia, and 41 for Sweden. The whites of the United States were far behind at 47. Newfoundland, too, has diminished its deathrate, but in 1937–38 the crude deathrate in Newfoundland was one-fifth greater than in Iceland, and the infant deathrate, which is a far better index of progress, was three and a half times that of Iceland.

One reason for the relatively poor health of the people of Newfoundland is a poor diet. In 1932–33, when 70,000 Newfoundlanders were on relief, their official ration unwisely consisted of pork, flour, tea, and molasses, which is about as bad a diet as they could well have. At that time, according to the Amulree Report, "lack of nourishing food was undermining . . . health and stamina; cases of beriberi, a disease caused by inferior diet, and of malnutrition were gradually increasing." Unfortunately, the Newfoundland diet is poor at all times, being distinctly inferior to that of Iceland, where milk products largely supplement fish and imported grain. For our purposes this is significant because the natural resources of Newfoundland would apparently permit a better diet than that of the Icelanders. Moreover, the topography, the distribution of population, and the facilities for transportation make it easier to maintain a medical service in Newfoundland than in Iceland. Nevertheless, according to Lodge, the health services in Newfoundland are appallingly inadequate when judged by any European standard. Even on the readily accessible South Coast a stretch of two hundred miles with settlements only a few miles apart has no doctor at all. On the island as a whole, the hospital accommodation is only about one quarter of that which would be considered essential in England. Iceland, on the contrary, has long had government physicians who travel patiently back and forth among even the most remote settlements at all seasons.

A surprising evidence of advanced thought in Iceland is the eugenic system which was in operation at least three centuries ago, when illiterate women were forbidden to marry. La Peyrere, writing in 1644, tells us that in ancient Iceland the bailiffs had power over beggars "to kill or to emasculate them, to prevent their multiplication. They also had a law forbidding (under pain of banishment) not only a poor fellow to marry a poor woman, but also any man who had but just enough for his own sustenance to marry a woman without something to maintain herself." This efficient, though crude, eugenic policy prevailed among people whose intellectual inclinations are indicated by their devotion to chess and history, as well as poetry. According to La Peyrere, "They are great chess players, there being not a peasant in the country, but what he has a set of it, which they make themselves out of fish bones."

As a final evidence of the intellectual capacity of the Icelanders we may cite their record in America. About 1870 a migration from Iceland to the United States and Canada began under stress of political disagreement with Norway and economic difficulties due to a climatic cycle which culminated in a cool phase about that time.[6] By 1900, according to Stefansson,[7] the migration had almost ceased, after about twenty-five thousand people, one third of the Icelandic population, had migrated. They settled mainly in the Prairie Provinces of Canada and the adjacent parts of the United States. There they promptly began to print books in their own language, but rapidly became Americanized. Today the descendants of these settlers are regarded with great respect by their neighbors of other origin.

D. Physical Advantages and Disasters

The great contrast between Iceland and Newfoundland must be due to one or more of three primary factors, physical environment, heredity, and culture. Let us compare the islands physically. Both have deeply indented seacoasts with innumerable picturesque bays and islands, admirably adapted to fishing or commerce. Both are rugged, but Iceland is much more so. Much of it is occupied by volcanoes, some of which rise above 6,000 feet. Because of the altitude about 5,000 square miles are covered with snow practically all the year. Much of the rest is too rugged for human occupance, but there are low plains near the sea. In Newfoundland the highest mountains rise only 2,200 feet and the topography of large parts is fairly well adapted to human use.

One of the worst features of Iceland is frequent and disastrous volcanic eruptions. There are 107 known volcanoes with thousands of craters of various sizes. Postglacial lava flows, too rocky and rugged for occupation by man, cover nearly 5,000 square miles. Eruptions have time and again wrought disaster. In 1783 a single lava flow from Laki covered 218 square miles. The ashes that were vomited forth destroyed the grass over a vast area and led to the loss of 53 per cent of the cattle, 77 per cent of the horses, and 82 per cent of the sheep which form the main source of livelihood. The famine and distress thus arising destroyed 9,500 people, one fifth of the population. The next year another of Iceland's great disadvantages appeared in the form of an earthquake that destroyed 92 farmhouses and severely damaged 372 others. One twentieth of the people who remained after the famine were rendered homeless, or at least had to

6 Huntington. 1935B.   7 1939.

rebuild their houses. As late as 1896 earthquakes destroyed 161 farmsteads and injured 155 others. Sometimes an Icelandic volcano melts vast quantities of snow and sends down a flood that engulfs scores of farms. Throughout history, Iceland has repeatedly suffered disaster from volcanoes, earthquakes, and floods. Newfoundland has experienced little, if anything, of this sort.

Climatically the two islands are not so different as might be expected. Nevertheless, Newfoundland has an advantage because it lies 16° farther south than Iceland. Its southern part is in the latitude of Quebec, Seattle, and Budapest. In January, however, thanks to the continuation of the Gulf Stream in the Atlantic Drift, the temperature as Reykjavik, the Icelandic capital, is about 30°F, whereas that of St. John's, the capital of Newfoundland, is 20°. Reykjavik at that time is about like New York City or central Denmark; St. John's is a little cooler than Chicago. In summer the conditions are quite different. Even in the warm southwest corner of Iceland, July averages only 52°F. In other parts of the world, such summer temperatures are associated with Eskimos, Lapps, and the lowly Indians of Tierra del Fuego. It is impossible to rely on crops as a main source of livelihood. Iceland, to be sure, now raises two thirds of its small consumption of potatoes, but this is possible only because the last few decades have witnessed a partial return to warmer conditions, such as prevailed a thousand years ago. Cereals, however, will not mature, although the climate was warm enough for them until about the thirteenth century. In southern Newfoundland, on the contrary, average temperatures of 59° in July and 60° in August make the summer as warm as at Liverpool, although cold winters shorten the growing season by nearly a month. Oats, potatoes, turnips, cabbages, and other vegetables grow so well that, according to some people, inefficiency alone prevents the Newfoundlanders from having tens of thousands of farmers instead of only three or four thousand. This may be an overestimate, but certainly Newfoundland has agricultural possibilities far ahead of those of Iceland.

In Iceland, grass is the only reliable crop and the way to use it is by keeping cattle and sheep. Both islands rely on these animals considerably, but Iceland, with less than half as many people, has ten times as many sheep as Newfoundland and more cattle. It can raise livestock more easily than Newfoundland because the fifth or so of the island where vegetation grows at all is practically all grassy. In Newfoundland a thick forest has to be cleared, but when that is done there is good pasture. Iceland stores away about 200,000 tons of hay each winter and the other island half as much. The Newfoundlanders have not thought it worth while to clear the forest. They seem to prefer sheep-killing dogs to wool-bearing sheep.

Both islands often suffer from cold winters and wet summers, but these do most harm in Iceland. Joseph Banks,[8] who visited Iceland in 1772, tells of

so violent a cold in 1753 and 1754, that horses and sheep dropped down dead on account of it, as well as for want of food, horses were observed to feed upon dead cattle, and the sheep eat of each others' wool. In the year 1755, towards the end of . . . May, in one night the ice was one inch and five lines thick. In . . . 1756, on the 26th of June, snow fell to the depth of a yard, and continued falling through . . . July and August. In the year following it froze very hard towards the end of May and the beginning of June in the south part of the island, which occasioned great scarcity of grass, insomuch that the inhabitants had little or no fodder the ensuing winter for their cattle; these frosts are generally followed by a famine, many examples of which are to be found in the Icelandic chronicles.

Because of the inclement weather from 1753 to 1759 a famine carried off nearly 10,000 people, or about one fourth of the population, in addition to more than 16,000 who are said by Mackenzie[9] to have perished in the smallpox epidemic of 1707. This calamity was followed in 1762 by an epidemic which carried off about 280,000 sheep. Then came the great Laki volcanic eruption of 1783. At the end of these disasters there remained only 42,000 sheep where there had been 492,000. Horses were reduced from 36,000 to 8,000, and cattle from more than 30,000 to less than a third as many.

Similar, but even greater, disasters occurred in the Middle Ages. From 1402 to 1404, for example, a plague of unknown nature swept away nearly two thirds of the population. This tremendous affliction was succeeded by a season so inclement that scarcely one tenth of the cattle survived. Toward the end of the century, a disastrous epidemic carried off a large part of the population and produced acute and widespread distress. Such facts illustrate the terrific natural handicaps under which Iceland has labored. Newfoundland's disasters seem mild compared with these.

The forests which cover most of Newfoundland, although a disadvantage for stock-raising, are a wonderful asset as fuel, raw material, and a home for fur-bearing animals. Those of Iceland are small copses 6 to 10 feet high except in a few warm valleys where saplings

[8] 1780, pp. 49–50.   [9] pp. 52, 64.

12 or 15 feet are found. Driftwood and the bones of whales were long the chief reliance for the frames of the turf houses. Peat or imported coal serves as fuel. Lately, however, the water of hot springs—the geysers for which Iceland is famous—has been piped to Reykjavik and other places, thus giving a cheap source of heat.

In mineral resources the scales are still more unequally weighted. Newfoundland has excellent iron ore, much of it close to the water. Good coal is also well located not far away. Then, too, there are valuable deposits of copper, silver, lead, gypsum, fine slate, oil shale, and some gold. Iceland, on the contrary, has practically no mineral wealth except sulphur and Iceland spar. Both countries might develop considerable waterpower, but here, too, Newfoundland has the advantage. Because of glaciation its rivers are well interspersed with lakes to serve as reservoirs and reduce floods; the Icelandic streams are largely rushing, muddy torrents, sweeping down from high mountains and hard to control. With its coal, waterpower, metals, lumber, and fur, and its ability to raise wool, Newfoundland apparently might easily support a manufacturing industry.

The value of all these resources is enhanced by Newfoundland's location close to the ocean lanes from North America to Europe. By travelling an extra four hundred miles, great liners from New York to Liverpool could touch at Newfoundland if there were anything to take them there. They would have to go about one thousand extra miles to touch at Iceland. Then, too, Newfoundland lies only one hundred miles from railheads that connect with the whole United States and Canada, but Iceland lies one thousand miles from anything similar in Europe. Thus the facilities for commerce, as well as manufacturing, are vastly better in Newfoundland than in its northern neighbor.

Almost the only respect in which the two islands are practically equal is the fisheries. Newfoundland perhaps has an advantage because it lies adjacent to the Grand Banks, often called the world's best fishing ground. Partly for this reason the Newfoundlanders till recently have relied on fishing far more than the Icelanders. The census reports twenty times as many Newfoundlanders engaged in fishing as in farming. In Iceland only one sixteenth of the inhabitants are recorded as fishermen. Half practice agriculture, which means that they raise animals, but they often do some fishing. The Icelanders, however, are so enterprising that they now export much more fish than the Newfoundlanders. From the standpoint of natural advantages as a whole, Newfoundland seems far ahead of Iceland, but somehow the Icelanders make the better living.

E. Can Culture Explain the Island Contrast?

The present fashion of explaining historic events and circumstances almost solely in terms of culture and economics seems to be due largely to scarcity of knowledge as to physical environment and heredity. Of course the *immediate* explanation of most events is cultural. A war occurs because of a broken treaty. The treaty is broken, perhaps, because one nation prevents another from getting metals. Behind such events, however, lie demagogic leaders and an inert citizenry who have foolishly developed a type of artificial culture based on wrong principles. Denmark with its highly developed agriculture and co-operatives exemplifies an opposite procedure whereby it has prospered in spite of poor soil and practically no natural resources or advantages except climate, level land, and accessibility to markets. The good sense and energy of the Danes have played a dominant part in this.

An examination of Newfoundland in comparison with Iceland seems to indicate that the present cultural differences are largely a result of the character of the people. Character has apparently had more effect upon culture than culture has had upon character. The opposite, or traditional, point of view is well stated by Lodge in an excellent article on Newfoundland's loss of Dominion status. Newfoundland's

difficulties arise, not from obscure causes hidden in complex industrial organization, not from the complications inherent in involved international arrangements, but essentially from the dependence of a population of 300,-000 on one calling, and that calling prosecuted in a highly individualistic way. The root of her troubles is to be found in the difficulties experienced by this main industry in adjusting itself to modern circumstances. Fundamentally the fishing industry is endeavoring to produce, by methods not far different from those employed centuries ago, a foodstuff which is to be sold in a world market in competition with other foodstuffs which are the result of mass production.

There is much truth in this quotation except that the so-called "root" of Newfoundland's troubles is merely a twig which produces leaves, flowers, and fruit. If it were a real root—a basic cause—Iceland ought to suffer even more than Newfoundland. In proportion to its total available resources Iceland is far more dependent on fish than is Newfoundland. It also meets the same competition. Nevertheless, it has managed to improve its methods, compete with other people, use other resources, and thereby avoid Newfoundland's failure.

Among the purely cultural conditions of early times it is hard to find any which give Iceland a special advantage. Newfoundland has all the culture of Great Britain behind it, whereas the Icelanders left Europe while their own land was still backward, illiterate, pagan. During the succeeding thousand years Iceland has been largely isolated from Europe. The ancestors of the Newfoundlanders, on the contrary, lived in Britain close to the cultural centers of that advanced island until little more than a century ago. Moreover, during the last century they have been in relatively close contact with Europe and its civilization. For every European ship that has visited Iceland, scores have visited Newfoundland.

Moreover, if we go back to the Middle Ages the cultural handicaps of Iceland appear still greater. Under stress of several centuries of depressing climate, when crop-raising perforce came to an end and intercourse with Europe was at its lowest ebb, Icelandic culture sank rather low. In the eighteenth century also, as we have seen, physical conditions dragged Iceland down pathetically. If cultural inheritance alone were responsible for the status of a nation, such conditions would presumably have given the Icelanders a much worse start than the Newfoundlanders in 1800. The Icelanders, however, pulled themselves together. With little outside aid they again forged ahead until their culture compares favorably with that of any other throughout the whole wide world. Thus the present great advantage of Iceland over Newfoundland can be due only in part to cultural inheritance. Its main source seems to be that the Icelanders, in spite of scanty resources and great isolation, have had the innate capacity to build a much better structure than the Newfoundlanders, even though the latter had much better raw materials, and the help of the mighty British Empire. What we are here studying, then, is an example of the relative effect of environment versus heredity, for both culture and physical conditions are parts of man's environment.

F. Heredity and Original Selection in Newfoundland

Inasmuch as neither physical environment nor cultural advantages explain the contrast between Iceland and Newfoundland, we must inquire further into heredity. An interesting example of the present widespread uncertainty as to the causes of historical events is found in the following words of Lodge, whose remark that modern difficulties in the fishing industry are the "root" of Newfoundland's troubles has already been quoted.

It is relevant here to emphasize the fact that for generations a steady process of negative selection has been in operation in Newfoundland. Local opportunities for brains and energies above the average have been so limited that right up to the crisis in the United States in 1929 there has been a steady exodus to the American continent of the best individuals of all classes. In a reasonably favorable environment the Newfoundlander is a resourceful, energetic, adaptable person, and it is common knowledge that those who so went abroad achieved success. But that their departure lowered the general standard of both ability and character in the people seems to me incontrovertible. What Maine and the Maritime Provinces of Canada gained, Newfoundland lost, and that loss is manifest in the post-war political life of the island.

This sounds like a selective process whereby the hereditary composition of the population is altered. So does Tait's statement that ever since the middle of the seventeenth century there has been "a constant drain of able-bodied seamen." One reason for this, according to Prowse,[10] is that lawlessness and factional fights were common in the early days. "The violence of the mob," especially from 1833 to 1838, "helped to kill out some of the very best blood in the colony . . . the Irish middle class liberals."

In the original settlement of Newfoundland the type of selection was very different from that of the Quakers or Huguenots, for example. In the sixteenth century many fishermen from England, France, Spain, and Portugal landed in the sheltered bays of the island to cure fish, but only a handful remained in winter. For a long time the British government prohibited settlement. Nevertheless, a few fishermen and agents of the fishing firms stayed permanently and brought wives from England, so that by 1785 the population numbered 10,000. Then there was a fairly rapid migration of fishermen and others from the west of England, together with English soldiers and officers, some Irishmen, and a few loyalists from the United States. Among the 80,000 inhabitants in 1812 by far the greater number were the sturdy fishermen type. Then came the adverse outward migration to the United States and Canada.

[10] p. 451.

The present situation is about what would be expected from the migrations described above. The *Encyclopædia Britannica* [11] describes the Newfoundlanders as "open air men. They do not take kindly to mining or even to the lumber woods. On the other hand, they are born mechanics and as carpenters, builders, plumbers, painters, and other skilled workmen they are greatly in demand." Practically all descriptions emphasize these qualities, but say little of intellectual traits such as are so prominent in Iceland. Tait, for example, says that the Newfoundland fishermen "are fearless to the point of recklessness and also very law-abiding, home-loving and patriotic." MacKay points out that although the Newfoundlanders

for the most part are of West of England or Ireland stock, much the same stock by which self-government was nurtured in the American colonies and in most of Canada . . . there are profound differences . . . from the other colonies. Though Newfoundland is essentially a frontier community, its people are far from realizing economic equality, as was usually the case in other frontier communities in North America where agriculture has been the principal occupation. On the one hand, there is a comparatively well-to-do merchant and professional class; on the other, the great mass of the people, who live often in conditions of sheer poverty, in a country endowed with great natural resources.

This division into a large proletariat and a small upper class is very different from the strong approach to equality in Iceland. It is like the condition in many Latin-American countries. It seems to be typical of places inhabited mainly by people of ordinary ability who are dominated by a few able persons among whom there is no special development of the temperamental and intellectual qualities essential to idealism and constructive leadership.

G. *The Selection of the Icelanders*

From the beginning the process of selection has been more favorable in Iceland than in Newfoundland. The original Icelanders were Norse Vikings, part of whom had previously migrated to Ireland, whence they brought Irish wives and followers. The old Vikings in Norway consisted of three classes: thralls, karls, and jarls. The thralls are described in the Eddas as swarthy people, burden bearers, servants "who erected fences, manured the fields, tended swine, kept goats and

[11] Article on Newfoundland.

dug turf." Because of misfortune or lack of ability they were land-less. The karl stood higher than the thrall. The Edda says,

> He learned to tend the oxen, make a plow,
> Build barns and houses, fashion carts, and turn the furrows.

His occupations differed little from those of the thralls, but he held land, and in those days that was all-important, even though a tax or rent had to be paid. The jarls or earls, who were mainly fair-haired Nordics, were petty nobles, owners of small estates on which the karls lived as retainers and the thralls as servants. The Vikings, as we know them, were mainly the jarls with the bravest and strongest of their karls. Some of the Vikings, as is well known, invaded Scotland and Ireland. In France they became the Normans; in Sicily they founded a kingdom. A band of them, the Rus, gave a name to the world's largest country.

As incentives to the migration of the Vikings to Iceland from A.D. 870 to 930, two conditions were especially important. One was general unrest among the Norsemen. Overpopulation probably played a considerable part in this, and was rendered worse by frequent wet or cold summers which injured the crops and created discontent. The other condition was political. Harold Fairhair, a powerful jarl, made himself king and imposed taxes and other imposts upon jarls whose ancestors from time immemorial had been completely their own masters. Then, as Conybeare [12] says, there "arose a universal cry of indignation which it is not difficult to sympathize with."

As a result many jarls took their most reliable karls and left Norway, going as raiders to other places or as migrants to Iceland. Others of similar character joined them from Ireland. A dangerous, difficult migration in open boats across stormy seas to an inhospitable place such as Iceland means drastic physical selection. Even though the obviously weak have been left behind, life in the new land while homes are being established is too hard for the others unless they have unusually strong constitutions. Women and young children, as we have seen, suffer especially. During the Pilgrims' first year at Plymouth, thirteen of the eighteen married women were laid to rest in graves that were left unmarked for fear the Indians would realize the weakness of the settlers. Most of those women were young. It seems practically certain that the early Icelanders suffered similar losses.

[12] p. 21.

Under such circumstances a courageous, determined, adaptable temperament and high intelligence are quite as important as physical vigor. Such a selection, both temperamental and physical, augurs well for future generations, although terribly hard on the pioneers. Newfoundland never went through an initial selection of this kind. Numerous small villages had been occupied by the fishermen in summer long before any women arrived. Of course pioneer life in Newfoundland was hard, but it required nothing like the courage and vigor demanded of the earliest Icelanders and Puritans.

After the first migration, which was completed within sixty years, the isolation and poverty of Iceland almost prevented new settlers from coming. Hence for a thousand years the Icelanders have been the descendants of selected migrants. Much more completely than modern descendants of the New England Puritans they are derived directly from a distinct and well-known ancestry, with an unusually good inheritance both mentally and physically.[13]

The severe selection which began among the first Icelandic settlers has continued in one way or another to our own day. The agencies which have produced it include volcanoes, earthquakes, floods, cold and wet summers, stormy or foggy seasons when fish cannot readily be caught, and stormy periods when ships could only rarely bring supplies from Europe. It is significant that, in spite of all the difficulties, there has not been much migration away from Iceland until almost our own time. Again and again we find statements like that of a visitor in 1782, who says that the Icelanders "have an inexpressible attachment for their native country, and are nowhere so happy. An Icelander, therefore, rarely settles in Copenhagen, though ever so advantageous conditions should be offered him."

One evidence of the presumable continuance of selection is the deathrate. From 1876 to 1915, for example, young Icelandic men aged fifteen to twenty-four suffered about 75 per cent more deaths than is normal in comparison with young women. This was due to the dangers of fishing on stormy seas and of herding sheep amid fog, snow, and the darkness of the long winter in a rugged, volcanic country. In few, if any, other countries is there such enormous destruction of the young men in early manhood during times of peace. This is apparently a selective process. On the whole, the ones who die tend to be relatively weak physically or lacking in foresight and judgment.

[13] Huntington, 1924A, 1935A.

The final result seems to be that the Icelanders still retain a high innate intellectual capacity inherited from their ancestors in ancient Norway. The intellectual factor appears conspicuously in Icelandic literature, in the modern high level of science, politics, and general progress, and in repeated recovery from the most depressing disasters. There may, to be sure, have been some change in the Icelandic inheritance by reason of the later selective process. The modern Icelanders are often described as more cautious and serious than their ancestors, with less initiative and perhaps with greater power of self-preservation. They are also said to have become more uniform, perhaps because repeated natural disasters have carried the selective process very far, as normally happens in migrations of great difficulty. Then, too, the incipient eugenic system may have tended to eliminate the inefficient. The outstanding fact, however, is that for one thousand years the Icelanders have retained an innate capacity that has enabled them to compose some of the world's greatest literature, rise superior to physical disasters, and surpass their more fortunately placed neighbors in Newfoundland in practically every phase of culture.

H. Human and Environmental Limits

This comparison of Iceland and Newfoundland brings out an important principle which is rarely appreciated. The principle is that as the difficulties of the environment become greater, the importance of heredity increases. Another way of putting it is that as people rise in the scale of innate capacity, as well as of cultural advantages, the limits imposed by nature become less strict. In the case of cultural advantages the principle is widely recognized. In the lowest stages of culture, for example, the production of metals is limited to picking up bits of native copper, nuggets of gold, or fragments of meteoric iron. At a higher stage, production is limited to localities where high-grade ore is found close to the earth's surface. Today among the most advanced people the limits of exploitation are set by oceans, by icesheets, by great plains of deep alluvium, and by depths within the earth so great that heat, pressure, and problems of ventilation make mining unprofitable. As our technical skill increases, these limits will doubtless be pushed back.

The same principle applies to innate capacities. Both Newfoundland and Iceland furnish physical environments in which a satisfactory economic and intellectual life can be maintained only with difficulty. If the kiths of these two islands were transplanted to Pennsylvania, let us say, the differences in their culture and achievements would doubtless still be pronounced. Nevertheless, the contrast would presumably be diminished because sturdy workers like the Newfoundlanders would not be subjected to such depressing difficulties as now confront them. If they were farmers, they would be able to raise at least reasonably good crops every year, and there would be little danger of losing their cattle because of failure to make a crop of hay. If they wanted other work, they would be in the midst of a progressive region with plenty of mines, quarries, factories, and other industries which thrive under advantages such as those of Pennsylvania. As things actually are, however, Newfoundlanders live in a physical environment which is too difficult for their innate capacity.

If the Newfoundlanders had the Icelandic capacity, they would presumably have found methods of using forests, coal, metals, and agricultural possibilities more effectively than they actually have. Their more favorable location would have enabled them to adapt their fisheries to the modern economic regime more easily than was possible for the Icelanders. They would presumably have produced enough goods of one kind or another so that liners passing between America and Europe would have made regular stops at their island. The reason for believing that the Newfoundlanders might have done all these things if their heredity had been superior is that the Icelanders have done correspondingly well in their more difficult environment.

Similar instances are seen in other parts of the world. The Falkland Islanders, for example, resemble the Icelanders. Savings bank accounts there are surprisingly large and numerous. The number of bookstores in the little port of Stanley is amazing in proportion to the population. The secret seems to lie in the fact that because of a remote location in the far South Atlantic near Cape Horn, migration to the Falklands, mainly from Scotland, has been so difficult that only people with uncommon energy and initiative have gone there.

In the future the isolation of their homes, or some change which makes sheep-raising or fishing unprofitable, may start an exodus which will deprive the Falklands and Iceland of their more competent people. Such a development would be quite in accord with the general principle that the hereditary quality of any given kith may fluctuate in response to changes in the proportion of people with different kinds of abilities. The fact remains, however, that if its innate capacities are of the right sort, a kith will win a living and make progress in a physical environment so harsh or otherwise resistant that another kith, with inferior innate capacities, cannot succeed. Of course, the kind of capacities required for success varies according to the environment and the stage of cultural progress. Thus still another factor is added to those which complicate the interpretation of history. This does not alter the general principle that nature is less harsh in imposing limits upon people with high capacities of the appropriate sort than upon those with lower capacities.

I. A Social and Biological Warning

In concluding this chapter a word of warning is needed. When we say that Icelanders are superior to Newfoundlanders, we do not mean that all Icelanders are superior to all Newfoundlanders. Far from it. We merely mean that the averages are different. One kith inherits greater intellectual capacities and more favorable temperamental qualities than the other. In both kiths, however, according to one of the most basic biological principles, there are many grades, from idiots and imbeciles through morons and a great many average people to superior persons and even a few geniuses. Moreover, according to another principle of similar importance, by means of appropriate selection and isolation it would presumably be possible in due time to produce from the Newfoundlanders a kith as competent as the Icelanders, whereas from the Icelanders themselves another type of selection might isolate a kith composed primarily of sturdy, but not highly intellectual, workers like the average Newfoundlander. A basic assumption in this whole study of migration and selection is that all races and kiths display a wide range of innate capacities. The range of developed capacities is still wider, because innately competent individuals usually get better training and develop farther than others.

Human society is so constituted that competent people tend to rise to the top, thus creating social stratification. This is true in spite of the fact that unusual abilities, such as extreme originality, are sometimes a handicap. Social stratification is greatly strengthened by assortative mating whereby people who are similar in occupation, social level, ideals, and habits tend to marry one another. Such mating takes place in even the most democratic society. Moreover, in spite of assertions to the contrary, the evidence seems conclusive that this stratification is associated with differences in innate capacities, although these are far from being so great as ardent believers in heredity sometimes claim. Thus the chances that the capacity for leadership and foresight, for example, will be inherited are greater for the children of leading business executives than for those of persons chronically on relief. Human chromosomes, however, behave in such a way that either group may produce almost any grade of ability from the lowest to the highest. Hence by a continuous and prolonged process of selection it appears possible that kiths of relatively high or low capacity may arise from almost any racial stock.

The essence of the whole matter is the same for races, nations, kiths, social classes, or even small local communities. Each such group, whether large or small, contains varying degrees of innate capacity. Moreover, no two groups are exactly alike in their proportion of persons innately endowed with superior capacities for leadership, original thought, and moral strength. This fact is of the utmost importance historically. Its importance becomes still clearer when we realize that physical and social conditions constantly exert a selective action. Thus from generation to generation the innate qualities of human groups are altered by migration, war, new diets, differential birthrates, and a multitude of other circumstances. The essential fact is that people with particular types of body, intellect, or temperament are preserved under some circumstances and not under others. Two outstanding and often conflicting principles are at work: first, the human race is plastic to a degree not usually recognized; second, when certain qualities have once become hereditary, they persist with great tenacity unless some new factor causes mixture with other types or introduces some new selective process.

CHAPTER 8

THE INTERPLAY OF CULTURE AND HEREDITY

A. Commercial Leaders of India

The selective process acts as surely among Asiatics as among Americans or Europeans.[1] The Parsis of India furnish evidence that in a biologically isolated kith, the effect of selection may persist undiminished even longer than Iceland's thousand years of stormy progress. The Parsis became unique through fundamentally the same sort of selection which we have seen in connection with the physique of Japanese in Hawaii, the literacy of immigrants in Iowa, the migrations of American farmers and leaders, the achievements of persons with diverse types of Puritan ancestry, and the contrast between Iceland and Newfoundland. In each case the migrants differ from their kindred who stay at home, and the difference seems to be both cultural and genetic. Moreover, the quality of the migrants seems to vary in harmony with the difficulty of the migration or the strength of the forces which impel people to seek new homes. The immediate effect of selection by migration is seen in the comparative uniformity of New Zealanders in general and of people bearing all types of colonial names in California. A long-delayed effect is seen in differences among people descended from Puritans who reached America at different dates. In Iceland, a selection which occurred fully one thousand years ago is even now producing strong effects.

In India, a similar selection at an even earlier date raises the modern Parsis to a surprisingly high level in spite of a physical and cultural environment which is distinctly repressive. Some idea of the Parsis may be gathered from the following quotation from *The New York Times* of June 4, 1932:

Sir Dorabji Tata, head of the Tata Companies, the largest Indian industrial organization, and founder of the Indian steel industry, died today in a sanatorium in Bavaria. . . . After leaving Cambridge he became one of the leaders of the social and commercial life in Bombay, his companies being

[1] Huntington, 1926B, 1935A.

149

engaged in structural work and in operating hotels, spinning and weaving mills, oil mills, cement works, and power stations. Just before he left Bombay, Sir Dorabji signed a trust deed worth 2,250,000 pounds sterling, mainly for charitable purposes. . . . He created and endowed the Indian Institute of Science and endowed engineering laboratories at Cambridge University of which he was a graduate. He also established numerous scholarships for research work in diseases regarded as incurable. In religion he remained true to the fire worship of his sect, the Parsis. According to his modest explanation, his knighthood, awarded in 1910, was a posthumous honor to his father, Jamsetji Tata, who had wrought vast improvements in Bombay by installing hydroelectric power.

Who are these Parsis? How does it happen that this so-called fire-worshipper, this Indian Rockefeller, not only did great things at home, but endowed laboratories at Cambridge University in England? In our ignorance we often look down upon the people of India, but here is one whom even the most materialistic business man cannot fail to admire.

The word "Parsi" is essentially the same as "Persian." In the middle of the seventh century of the Christian era, the Zoroastrians, or Fire-Worshippers of Persia, were conquered by the Arabs under the powerful spur of their new Mohammedan religion. Most of the Persians forsook the old faith, and the rest were often persecuted. In A.D. 651 a remnant who were still faithful to the old religion "abandoned their houses and gardens and palaces for the sake of their religion," as the old chronicle puts it, "and lived in Kohistan for a hundred years." [2] There they suffered persecution at the hands of the Moslem Arabs. Consequently the Zoroastrians, to quote the chronicle again, "became anxious for their religion," and in A.D. 751 moved to the island of Hormuz at the southern end of the Persian Gulf. There they lived for fifteen years, but, being harassed by the Arabs, they finally set sail for India. How many thus migrated we do not know, but certainly no great number. They landed at Div, east of the mouth of the Indus, but were not welcome. After nineteen years of friction with the native inhabitants they sailed eastward in 785 to Sanjan. There they were allowed to settle and follow their own religion. They ultimately adopted the language and many of the customs of the country, but married only among themselves, like a Hindu caste.

The selection of the Parsis was like that of the New England Puritans, but even more severe. When the Mohammedans first invaded

[2] Huntington, 1924A.

Persia it took courage and determination to cling to the old religion. Yet some of the Parsis did so. Between the Arab invasion of A.D. 640 and the final Parsi settlement in India in 785, many less resolute Zoroastrians must gradually have fallen away to Mohammedanism. This is what always occurs under such circumstances. The deathrate, too, must have been high. Four different times the whole community had to move as persecuted refugees. Deaths are always numerous under such conditions, especially among women and children. Thus the Zoroastrian remnant which finally settled north of Bombay had endured a drastic selection in which intellectual conviction, moral courage, and physical endurance all played important parts. We are specifically told that this highly selected remnant came from Persia's upper classes.

Today in proportion to their numbers the Parsis are generally recognized as the most competent people in India aside from the British. The Parsis number only about one hundred thousand, half living in Bombay and half farther north. They include many of India's most eminent people. They are "proverbial" for their "sagacity, activity, and commercial enterprise." [3] They include a surprising number of successful merchants. Compared with the United States as a whole, the Parsis have two and a half times as many persons engaged in public administration and the professions and nine times as many bankers and brokers. Their business executives, as well as professional men, are often keenly interested in literature and science and in preserving and purifying their religion. In preparing this chapter, the author consulted seven books written in excellent English by Parsis of Bombay. Aside from Christianity, theirs is the only religion in India which insists upon a high moral code and upon active charity and altruism. Its basic code is, "Good thoughts, good words, good deeds." Many Parsis, like many Christians, fall far below the standards of their religion, but the lives of many others are definitely more altruistic and useful because of their faith.

Education, prosperity, and leadership go hand in hand among the Parsis. Girls as well as boys are carefully educated. The rate of literacy for both sexes comes close to European standards. The attractive, fair-skinned, dark-haired women appear frequently in public. Crime and poverty are rare. The poor are helped by the community as a whole, which supports orphanages, hospitals, and other public enterprises. The Parsis also assist others, as is indicated by

[3] *Encyclopædia Britannica*, article on Parsis.

the univerity which a Parsi merchant established in his new home in Hong Kong. Power of leadership is evident from the fact that two Parsis are the only natives of India ever elected to the British House of Commons. It is no small tribute to be chosen thus by a British constituency.

With the Parsis, as with all selected groups, one of the vital questions is how far their present position is due to cultural versus biological inheritance. The Parsis seem to afford good evidence in this respect. For several centuries, after their four painful migrations, we hear little of them except that they converted an arid waste into pleasant gardens and fields and spread slowly to new regions. For practical purposes they were almost a caste, like those of the surrounding Hindus, but with more thrift and a different religion. Although they were peaceful and almost unnoticed peasants, they are twice reported as fighting with notable courage and skill against invading Moslems.

B. The Awakening of Dormant Capacities

With the coming of the British three centuries ago, the Parsis changed significantly. A new field of enterprise was opened. Commerce was introduced and soon proved profitable. Their preceding history had given the Parsis little if any reason to be more commercial than other Indian kiths. When the new method of getting a living was introduced, however, some force led the Parsis to grasp it. Dormant capacities which had not been needed in agricultural life now found opportunity. The same thing happened again in the nineteenth century when modern manufacturing was introduced to India. The Parsis established cotton factories and then iron foundries—the earliest and most successful large modern industries in India. Their former life as farmers had not prepared them for industrial management any more than for commerce. They must have had innate qualities which fitted them for this occupation. We are often told that certain types of people cannot become good mechanics, for example, because their ancestors have had no experience in such work, and they have not seen it in childhood. The fact, however, seems to be that if people possess the right innate qualities, they can quickly learn almost any kind of work, as Seagrave well shows in his account of Burmese nurses.

In analysing Parsi success all three of the primary factors must be considered. In the realm of physical environment, a hot, moist climate, tropical parasites, and deficiencies of diet doubtless reduce the physical efficiency of the Parsis below what it would be if they lived in France, for example. Nevertheless, the Parsis are more vigorous and active than most of the people around them. One of the best measures of vigor is the deathrate. As long ago as 1881–82, according to Karaka, the rates in Bombay were 33.6 for low-caste Hindus, 30.5 for Moslems, 26.1 for other Hindus, 20.2 for Europeans, and 19.3 for Parsis. Karaka reports that the heavy weight of Parsi children, as compared with those of other local races, long ago attracted the attention of medical authorities. The Parsi population, he says, "possesses a vitality and energy inherited from their ancient ancestors, the Persians, and equal to those of Europeans living in more bracing climates than India." On the next page, however, he presents a cultural explanation of Parsi vigor: the low average mortality of the Parsi population indicates their "material prosperity . . . and the . . . comfort and cleanliness of their homes. So much is this the case that it would almost appear as if the excellent sanitary precautions of the Zoroastrian prophet were being indirectly and unwittingly followed." Non-Parsi writers support this claim for better sanitary conditions among the Parsis than among their neighbors. The Parsi diet also is better and more varied than that of most people of India.

It cannot be made too clear that when we recognize the importance of one factor, we do not thereby prove that other factors are unimportant. Climate and disease certainly reduce people's energy in India. The Parsis by no means work as hard as the Swedes or Finns, or as they themselves would doubtless work if acclimated in Sweden or Finland. This circumstance, however, does not prove that sanitation and medical care are unimportant in their effect on activity. In the same way the prosperity of the Parsis evidently helps in giving them a better diet than their neighbors, but the importance of constitutional vigor is not thereby impugned.

The condition that seems most strongly to indicate innate mental capacity among the Parsis is the persistence of alertness and adaptability through thirteen hundred years. Among some kiths, such as the Indians of the Andean plateaus, the ability to change habits seems to be very limited. The great majority live like their pre-Columbian ancestors, even after centuries of life close to people of European ancestry and habits. Among the Parsis, as among the Icelanders, the kith as a whole seems to have a rare capacity for quickly seeing the significance of new ideas and changing its mode of life accordingly. In India several groups of Christians, Jews, and others have started with cultural advantages quite as great or greater than those which the Parsis brought with them, but lack of sufficient innate capacity or some other defect has apparently prevented them from advancing. Thus the Parsis of today seem to represent a biological inheritance of all-round ability which only in modern times has found opportunity for full expression. Such dormancy of innate ability is most interesting. The selective process is apparently able to segregate capacities which may be passed on through many generations before they find full opportunity for expression. The flowering of literature in New England in the first half of the nineteenth century may illustrate this phenomenon, as may the Golden Age of Greece. The fullest flowering of all requires a combination of good conditions biologically, physically, and culturally.

C. A Long-Lived Kith *

Among the Jews the selective process can be seen at work for three thousand years or more. This kith has exceeded all others as a theme of controversy. It consists of God's chosen people, according to one view, and of a race of parasitic usurers, according to another. No other kith has so persistently produced great leaders. Although Abraham may be a symbol rather than a man, Moses, David, and Isaiah were strong, outstanding personalities of living flesh and blood. Jesus, St. Paul, and St. John represent the greatness of an intermediate epoch. Mendelssohn, Disraeli, and Einstein are outstanding Jews of later times. In our own day one of the chief grievances of anti-Semites is that in proportion to their numbers Jews are more numerous and successful than gentiles in occupations such as medicine, science, banking, and business. Even such liberal institutions as American colleges sometimes limit the percentage of Jews because they know that on a basis of scholarship alone Jewish students would be represented out of all proportion to the Jewish population as a whole. In many studies of the IQ of school children Jews rank notably high.[4] Another condition in which the Jews are almost unique is persecution. Other kiths have been persecuted as viciously

---

* Much of the material in this section is condensed from the author's book entitled *The Pulse of Progress* (Including a Sketch of Jewish History).

[4] Hirsch, 1926.

for short periods, but none has been so persistently persecuted for two thousand years.

A great anthropological controversy has raged about the problem of whether the Jews are a race. Many books have been written on this subject.[5] Much of this controversy has been a waste of energy. It has arisen from failure to realize that kiths are not races. The Jews are a kith in the same way as the Icelanders, the Puritans, the Maoris, or the Greeks. Coon's [6] convincing analysis of anthropological measurements shows that the Jews are not "simply a racial grab-bag united by a common bond of religion with no more biological cohesion than units such as radio listeners or . . . seamstresses" who may be white or black, Chinese or Eskimo. On the other hand, they display no more racial variability than such units as the Volhynians of the Ukraine or the inhabitants of a Swabian village. Like these people they include "individuals who belong predominantly to a number of distinct white subraces—as well as more numerous individuals who approach the general average for the Jews as a whole."

In other words, the Jews, to a measurable degree, differ physically from the other people among whom they live but are not a race any more than the Volhynians or Swabian villagers. To call them a race like the Nordic or Mediterranean races would be comparable to listing the English or French in the same way. Biologically they are about as uniform as is the average intermarrying social and geographical unit among other white peoples, but "they have racial peculiarities which serve to differentiate the majority of them anthropometrically from their non-Jewish compatriots and neighbors." In other words they are a kith in the same sense as the Parsis or Puritans.

If the Jews are merely a branch of the Mediterranean race more or less intermixed with other races, why do they stand out so distinctly? The answer seems to lie in the neglected fact that the process of selection depends upon mentality far more than upon the external physical traits on which races are based. This statement sounds simple enough, and most people would accept it at once. Nevertheless, if it is accepted, it demands a revolutionary revision of anthropology and history. Its truth, however, seems to have been indicated by our study of migration and selection. When we remember that there are many powerful selective factors in addition to migration, the idea of mental selection assumes still greater importance.

[5] For example, the works of Kautsky, Hertz, and Barzun.
[6] 1942, p. 34.

D. Selection and the Evolution of Religion

Let us now apply the principle of mental selection to the history of the Jews. Up to the time of Christ their history may be divided into three stages: (1) the period of the Patriarchs, the Exodus, and the Judges, until the Israelites became established in Palestine as a distinct nation; (2) the national period from David to the Captivity; (3) the period from the exile until the time of Christ. Each period presents abundant evidence of a selection in which religious inclination played a strong part.

The first period may be dismissed briefly because of doubt as to how far the reported events have been idealized for the purpose of proving that the Hebrews were God's chosen people. For the sake of convenience we shall follow the record approximately as it stands in the Bible, but the reader must remember that the facts are by no means clear. The first that we hear about the Jews is that they claim descent from a migrating Semitic family. This family, with Abraham as its founder, migrated five hundred miles or so northwest from Babylon to northern Mesopotamia and thence a similar distance to Palestine and later to Egypt. For several generations its members wandered back and forth intermarrying almost exclusively with near relatives. According to the Biblical account, Abraham was an unusually strong-minded man with deep religious convictions. His grandson, Jacob, was likewise unusually competent, although wily and selfish. Jacob's son, Joseph, appears to have been really great. Moses, who apparently belongs to the seventh generation from Abraham, is almost universally considered one of the world's greatest religious teachers. The Hebrews who migrated out of Egypt under his leadership were apparently a closely related band descended from a line in which high ability was conspicuous. Their wanderings in the desert at the time of the Exodus presumably weeded out many weaklings so that an unusually vigorous group settled in the "Promised Land." How far the selective process tended toward a religious type we cannot be sure. When we study the Arabs, however, we shall see that a desert migration almost inevitably exerts a selective effect in favor of capacity for leadership, persistence, and initiative.

After the Hebrews were established in Palestine, those who lived in Judea gradually became different from the rest.* Judea is a rocky

* The following pages are taken largely from the author's volume, *Palestine and Its Transformation*.

little plateau about half a mile high and with an area of scarcely a thousand square miles. Isolation is its keynote. It is so infertile that it does not attract either settlers or traders. The Philistine plain to the west and the gentler uplands of Samaria and Galilee to the north are far more desirable. So was the rolling plateau of Moab east of the Jordan in the centuries of antiquity when long climatic cycles gave the country more rain and a more stimulating climate than now. Moreover, the Judean plateau is not easily accessible. On the east it is protected by the Dead Sea and a steep escarpment three thousand feet high, and on the south by the desert. On the west it is separated from the fertile Philistine Plain by a row of high hills and its own steep slope. Only from the north along the center of the plateau is it fairly accessible. On the other hand, the part of Palestine east of the Jordan River is easily open to invaders from the desert, and the part west and north of Judea is open to caravans and armies from either Egypt or Syria. In the ancient days when the climate was more favorable than now, an active caravan traffic swept north and south on each side of Judea. Only those who have travelled by caravan, stopping every fifteen miles or so at some village to spend the night, can realize how closely such traffic brings a region into contact with the outside world. The ancient caravans, however, had only a slight effect upon the relatively isolated plateau, although they passed in plain sight of it. Because of such conditions, the Hebrews in Judea preserved their old culture and religious inheritance almost unchanged, whereas the rest of the Hebrews gradually became mixed with other racial stocks and lost much of their old culture and religion.

It is particularly important to note that because of its isolation Judea tended more and more to become the focus of the conservative form of the Hebrew religion. The Ark of the Covenant, around which the Temple was later built, was carried to Jerusalem, thus making that place the religious center. We have no means of knowing how far the people who were less religiously inclined drifted away from Judea while judges ruled Palestine before the days of David. It seems probable, however, that there was outward migration from the relatively harsh plateau to the more fertile land of the Philistines to the west. The story of Samson and his infatuation with the Philistine woman, Delilah, who caused his death, illustrates this. Presumably such migration was most likely to occur among persons who did not care much about their religion.

The second, or kingly, period of Jewish history witnessed a distinct separation of the Israelites into two kiths, the Ten Tribes and the Judeans or Jews. This development is vividly dramatized in the separation between the kingdoms of Israel and Judah under Solomon's two rival successors, Jeroboam and Rehoboam. According to the Biblical account, this political split intensified the selective process which was dividing the two kiths. The most religious elements among the Israelites of the northern kingdom tended to migrate southward to the old center of religion with its great Temple of Solomon and its Holy Ark. Jeroboam, king of Israel, tried to offset this migration by setting up his own religious center with two golden calves as its symbols. He apparently drove out the religious leaders who opposed this measure, and Judea became their refuge. Earnest Jews, like Quakers and other people with strong religious convictions, are ready to migrate for the sake of their beliefs. On the other hand, Judeans who did not care much about religion were especially likely to be tempted away from their poor plateau by the pleasanter and more prosperous life in other parts of Palestine. Thus, although no numerical facts are available, there was quite surely a concentration of people with strong religious ideas on the barren Judean plateau.

The great event which opened the third Jewish period might seem at first sight to nullify the previous selection, but further inquiry shows that this is not so. From 587 B.C. onward, Jerusalem was ravished by Nebuchadnezzar. The leading people were carried to Babylonia in three successive groups. We know little about those who were left in Judea except that they were poor and that Jeremiah was their prophet. Many wanted to flee to Egypt, but Jeremiah insisted that this would make Jehovah angry. Nevertheless, so many fled that Jeremiah felt obliged to go with them. Those who remained in Judea presumably included a high percentage who feared God and honored Jeremiah so much that they stuck to the old home. If this is so, the exodus from Judea left an especially religious type in the old home.

Another migration, different in form but similar in effect, occurred when some of the Jews returned from exile in Babylonia. Although there is disagreement as to details, there can be little doubt that during the preceding one hundred and forty years of residence in Babylonia many of the less religious Jews gave up their old religion. It seems equally certain that during this long period some of the Babylonian Jews returned to Jerusalem. Many who did this must have been of an especially religious type. Otherwise there would be little reason for returning. Life was difficult in Judea; the Temple was in ruins. "Why should not my countenance be sad," said Nehemiah, "when the city, the place of my fathers' sepulchres, lies waste and the gates thereof are consumed with fire?" Because "the remnant that are left of the captivity there in the province are in great affliction and reproach, I sat down and wept and mourned certain days; and I fasted and prayed before the God of heaven." Then he asked permission to return to Jerusalem..

When the Babylonian king granted his plea, Nehemiah and a company of Jews travelled six or seven hundred miles across the Syrian Desert or around its northern end to Palestine. On arriving in Judea they had great difficulty in rebuilding the walls of Jerusalem. The surrounding Gentiles put every possible obstacle in their way. Although the number of Jews who thus returned to Judea may not have been large, it sufficed to give the small Judean population a group of leaders who were able to establish a strict observance of the Mosaic law with all that this means as to marriage, migration, and the ultimate composition of the population. Jews who married women from the surrounding "heathen" were obliged to put away their wives and children or else to move to some other region. Josephus confirms the Biblical account of this by the story of a man who expected to become high priest at Jerusalem but was rejected because he had a foreign wife. Thereupon the king of Samaria, just north of Judea, advised him to keep his wife and become high priest of a new temple which the king would build on Mount Gerezim. There he was joined by many other priests and Levites who left Jerusalem because of marriages outside the Jewish fold.

This matter of Jewish law is highly important. For several centuries before Christ rigorous observance of the law was required of all Jews who lived in Judea and worshipped in the Temple at Jerusalem. Anyone who married outside the Jewish fold was cut off from the community. Moreover, all the events of daily life were regulated with extreme minuteness by religious ordinances. It was wicked to go more than a short distance on the Sabbath or to harvest even a few heads of wheat to eat as one walked along. On that day it was a religious crime even to lift a poor ass out of the pit into which it had fallen. According to the rules of the Scribes, there were thirty-nine main kinds of work that could not be done on the Sabbath. The Romans gave up using Jews as soldiers because so many things were forbidden by their religion. People who were deeply devout, deeply devoted to Jehovah, and deeply fond of their people and their home were willing to endure this annoying religious domination. The irreligious, the unpatriotic, and the rebels against restriction would not put up with it. We know that there was plenty of migration away from Judea during the centuries before Christ. We may be sure that those who were religiously minded and proud of their kith were more likely to stay in Judea than those who were irreligious, impatient over the limitations of their kith, or especially desirous of worldly gain.

Here, then, is the upshot of the whole matter. We see in the Jews an admirable example of selection which more and more tended toward a definite religious type. At first, the selection was much like that whereby desert nomads as a whole tend to become alert and self-reliant. Then, as the centuries rolled by, religious attitudes became more and more decisive. An extremely powerful cultural factor was at work. Finally, those who remained in Judea became really a "peculiar" people, a people among whom the percentage having an unusually deep sense of religious loyalty was especially great. It is not surprising, then, that when a high cultural level permitted an awakening of intellectual activity, there arose a remarkable group of religious leaders. Jesus seems to represent the culmination of a long process of religious selection. He did not, however, stand alone. His success, like that of other great leaders, depended on the presence of men of lesser stature who, nevertheless, had some of the same great qualities. His disciples and the men who wrote the New Testament are among the most powerful teachers of all time.

A long selective process, which began with the patriarchs and reached its most strenuous development during the centuries just before Christ, seems to have been the means by which the Jews became a peculiarly religious people. This process prepared the way for three great events. First, the religion of the Jews attained substantially its present form; second, Christianity arose; and third, the foundations of Islam were laid.

E. The Selective Power of War and Persecution

Since the days of Christ the Jews appear to have preserved much of their old inheritance. This is not surprising when we recall the apparent effect of heredity among Parsis, Icelanders, and Puritans. Nevertheless, the Jews, like the Icelanders, have been subjected to powerful selective forces which may have altered their general character somewhat. Moreover, unlike the Icelanders, they have added a considerable body of new and diverse recruits to their number and at the same time have lost many of their own people to the gentiles. A generation after the death of Jesus the Jews entered upon a period of terrific slaughter and selection. For several years before the destruction of Jerusalem by Titus in A.D. 70 they were in active revolt against the Romans and were also fighting furiously among themselves. The Zealots, who wanted to get rid of everything foreign, attacked the moderates, who wanted compromise. Recruits of the type most zealous in defense of religion and race kept dribbling into Jerusalem from Jewish colonies far and wide. Josephus says that 1,350,000 people were killed in the battles which he lists. Another 900,000 are said to have been taken captive and either sold as slaves or made to fight and die in the arena. Other hundreds of thousands died of massacre, famine, and disease. Some suffered thus in almost every Jewish community. Forty-six years later in A.D. 116 the Jews again rose violently against their gentile rulers in each main Jewish center. In Egypt they are said to have put to death 220,000 of their neighbors at Alexandria and elsewhere. For every gentile life thus taken, one Jewish life was usually exacted later. In Cyprus all Jews were killed or deported. In many other places the Jews were moved from place to place as captives.

Although the numbers given above are doubtless exaggerated, it is clear that in the century after the death of Jesus the Jews went through a truly terrific series of wars, massacres, and persecutions. Such events are always selective. In the first place, the more militant type tends to be killed off. Secondly, persons who are constitutionally weak, especially women and children, die in large numbers. Thirdly, the slow-witted die because they do not know how to preserve themselves. And, finally, those who are canny enough to know when to stop fighting and how to placate their too-powerful enemies stand the best chance of survival.

A parallel case is found among modern Armenians. That kith has suffered almost as much persecution as the Jews. Within the last half century hundreds of thousands of Armenians have been slaughtered by Turks and Kurds. In 1895 and 1896 about two hundred thousand were massacred, and hundreds of thousands more were robbed of everything and left almost naked in burned villages. Nevertheless, the Turks were soon saying, "What kind of people are these Armenians? Three years ago we killed half of them and took everything away from the rest. Now they eat better than we do." Then came World War I, during which vast numbers of Armenians, probably about six hundred thousand, were slaughtered or otherwise killed, and about one million others were forcibly driven from their homes in the Armenian Plateau or elsewhere to the desert farther south.[7]

Here is an illustration of what happened then and of what must also have happened time and again to the Jews.[*] Among the million Armenians who were driven south into the Syrian Desert was a high-bred girl. At the age of twelve she was driven from home by a band of rough Turkish soldiers after her father had been carried off and presumably killed. Her brother and uncle were also taken away; she heard shots and the screams of wounded men and boys whom she knew to be her own people. She and her mother, with other women and children, were forced to travel on foot over rough mountain trails with so little water and food that they fainted from exhaustion. After a week of such travel the girl was sold for sixty cents to a Kurdish chief and taken with other girls to his harem. The Kurds tried to make her become a Moslem, but she would not renounce Christianity. They tortured and killed another young woman in her presence, hoping to make her yield, but she would not. Then they beat her into unconsciousness, tattooed her face with great blue marks, and said, "We have made her a Moslem." Seizing her chance one day, she jumped from a window and fled along a mountain path. Someone saw her, and a band of horsemen gave chase. With shouts and jeers they roped her to the tail of a horse and dragged her back, bruised into unconsciousness. In spite of all this she clung to her Christianity and her kith, insisting that she would not "turn Turk." At long last a British force arrived and freed her.

If a girl between the ages of twelve and fifteen can have such tenacity and courage, it is not surprising that the Armenians as a kith are remarkable for their persistence. She was only one of many who suffered similarly. It was because of stubborn will power that she and they were finally restored to their own people and became the parents of future Armenians. This sort of thing has happened not only in our own day but time and again in the past. And it has happened to Jews even more often than to Armenians.

---

[7] *Treatment of Armenians in the Ottoman Empire, 1915–16.*

[*] These paragraphs concerning Armenians are an abridged version of pp. 139–41 of the author's *The Character of Races.*

Although selection on the basis of moral qualities is the outstanding feature of persecutions, massacres, and deportations, there is likewise a physical and mental selection. Among the Armenians who were driven into the Syrian Desert only about one quarter survived. Doctor Lambert, who for two years helped the American Red Cross take care of them, reports that the returning sufferers were half starved; they had also suffered almost intolerably from winter cold, summer heat, and the attacks of vermin. Many were ill as well as weak. Nevertheless, the physicians were continually impressed by the organic soundness of the stricken refugees. The weaklings had been destroyed.

It seems almost certain that this persecution eliminated the mentally weak even more completely than the physically weak. In the world at large there is a strong tendency toward harsh treatment of persons who are mentally weak. In times of persecution stupidity and dullness are especially likely to arouse the wrath and vindictiveness of the persecutors. This is especially probable when people are oppressed because of race, class, or some social distinction, such as religion. On the other hand, among people like the Armenians, those who are mentally most alert are best able to preserve themselves when they fall into the hands of brutal enemies. They know how to wheedle their captors into giving them a chance to procure food and shelter. The stupid merely anger their masters and bring blows and violence upon themselves. The mentally dull are likewise the ones most easily persuaded to give up their religion. Having once become Moslems, they are less likely than their more quick-witted kinsmen to return to their old faith and kith when better times arrive. Among the Armenian children, especially the girls who were carried to Moslem houses, it was the quick-witted, the resourceful, and the tenacious who ultimately escaped. Thus natural selection appears to have been a potent factor in producing in the Armenians a character closely similar to that of the Jews.

After A.D. 150, the Jews seem to show new characteristics, by reason of which they were left in comparative peace for a long time. Gibbon, who is not friendly to them, says that "awakened from their dream of prophecy and conquest, they assumed the behavior of peaceable and industrious subjects." Other historians also comment on the way in which the Jews at this time became less militant, more commercial, and more prone to accomplish their purposes by mild and indirect methods rather than by violence. Some explain the changes as due to lack of a central city or a compact country of their own after the fall of Jerusalem. Others say that after three main revolts against their gentile oppressors and several minor ones, the Jews, being canny people, concluded that submission to the constituted authorities and attention to business paid better than rebellion. A third view is that this same canny quality led the Jews to believe that the best way to meet oppression is to make the oppressor your debtor, wheedle him into giving you protection, buy him off if necessary, appear to conform to his unrighteous demands, but secretly follow your own customs and grow rich. In brief, bow before the wind and rise again.

There is doubtless truth in each of these three views, but that fact does not prove that they represent the whole truth. If the theory of selection is valid for man's mental traits, the terrible holocausts from A.D. 65–140 must have killed off a high percentage not only of Jewish weaklings, both physical and mental, but of the more aggressive, excitable, warlike, and less cautious types. Similar selection has taken place repeatedly in later times. In our own day the Nazi persecution of the Jews follows nearly the same main lines as of old. That is, it subjects the whole kith to conditions of physical stress which remorselessly kill the weaklings. It places a special premium upon quick-witted, non-violent methods of meeting persecution and upon the power to plan far in advance.

Where the Jews are left to themselves, these same qualities seem to promote success in business and finance. They also lead to remarkable success in science, literature, music, and the higher realms of culture. Moreover, where prejudice as well as other limitations are removed, the Jews seem to show a highly developed sense of social responsibility. Many of the world's greatest philanthropists have been Jews. In many local communities Jews do much more than their proportional share in projects for social welfare, such as those sponsored by community chests. In addition, the Jews seem to have acquired a special ability to resist the ill effects of life in cities. Perhaps this capacity has arisen in part through the loss of weaklings in ghettos where life is peculiarly difficult. Because of all this, the Jews have reached an advanced stage of evolution. Some of their qualities, though doubtless by no means all, resemble those which other progressive kiths will presumably acquire at some later time. Like the precociously bright child in school, they suffer because they have advanced too fast.

Another factor in Jewish character must not be overlooked. Although the Jews, as we have seen from Coon's analysis, are predominantly of Mediterranean stock, their kith contains large elements of other races. This is what would be expected from their history. There has been much intermarriage between Jews and gentiles, especially in times of peace. An early example is the Jewish women who in the first and second centuries were sold as slaves and taken to the Rhine Province as wives for soldiers. Most of them were abandoned when their husbands were transferred to other stations. Their children were accordingly brought up as Jews. Down through the centuries marriages of Jews and gentiles have risen to considerable proportions during times when the two groups were friendly, only to decline when persecution arose. If the husband is a Jew, the children are generally brought up in the Jewish fold. In other cases the strong faith of the Jewish mother sweeps the children away from the faith of the father and into her own. Another method of mixing races has been conversion. The Ashkenazim, or Polish Jews, arose mainly from the mixture of Mediterranean Jews with broad-headed, large-featured Khazars who lived in southern Russia north of the Caucasus. In the eight and ninth centuries many of the Khazars were converted to Judaism.

The Ashkenazim bring up another vital element in the problem of Jewish character. For many centuries two opposing tendencies have worked toward the same end. One tendency has been for the Jews to lose part of their number. This may occur rapidly under stress of persecution, as happened in Spain and Portugal about 1492 when hundreds of thousands were forcibly "Christianized." It may happen slowly in less troublesome times, as when Heine, Börne, Gans, Neander, and Felix Mendelssohn adopted Christianity. The other tendency is for gentiles to adopt Judaism. Although Judaism is not a missionary religion like Christianity, it has made many converts. The Roman Empire passed laws to prevent this. The Khazars, as we have seen, were converted in large numbers. Moreover, at many periods the high moral code of Judaism and its insistence on the oneness and supremacy of God have attracted individual converts. Curiously enough, such conversion has been especially prevalent in times of persecution.

From the standpoint of character, the important point is that the people who have left the Jewish faith have generally tended to be those who were unlike the standard type, whereas those who have adopted Judaism have to a still greater degree been persons who shared the Jewish mentality and aptitudes. The situation is like that of the Quakers, or Friends, as they prefer to be called. A person who is a Friend by birth is likely to have considerable of the cautious, thoughtful, industrious, and pacifist leanings of his sect, but there is no assurance of this. He may be born with a temperament which makes the Roman Catholic Church or the Salvation Army attractive to him. Such people tend to drift away from the Friends. On the other hand, suppose a person is born with such a temperament that he is strongly attracted to the views of the Friends and to their solemn, quiet worship. He is not urged to join the "meeting." In fact, he is warned that it will mean sacrifice. If he persists, however, he becomes a Friend "by election." Such Friends have even more of the Quaker character than the average Friend by birth.

Even so with the Jews. Down through the ages they have lost members who were weak in the distinctively Jewish traits of religious tenacity, loyalty to kith, and ability to endure persecution and nevertheless get ahead. On the other hand, they have gained members who were strong in these traits and who felt the appeal of a theology somewhat like that of Friends and Unitarians. Thus in spite of "racial" diversity and outward physical resemblances to the gentiles among whom they live there is reason to think that the Jews tend to preserve a preponderance of certain innate temperamental aptitudes and capacities. In this they are like the Parsis, the Armenians, and any other kith which more or less isolates itself by marrying within its own group.

F. The Selective Process in the Sahara

In estimating the historical importance of the principle of selection illustrated in previous chapters, we must remember that we are dealing with general laws which are applicable to all kinds of people and to groups of all sizes. The Mzabites of the Saharan oases some three hundred miles south of Algiers, for example, illustrate the fact that the selection arising through religious persecution has substantially the same effect upon followers of all faiths—Moslems, as well as Christians, Zoroastrians, or Jews. In the tenth century the reformed Abadite sect lived in a fairly well-watered part of Algeria about one hundred miles from the sea. Being persecuted because of their faith, they were forced to move to a less fertile area. In A.D. 1012 continued persecution drove them further south into the real Sahara Desert. There they still live to the number of about fifty thousand, shunned and cursed by other Moslems, but respected for their ability. Throughout this long period they have kept rigorously apart from all others. So strict are their rules that a man may not take his wife, or even his son under ten years of age, away from his own country, nor may he under any circumstances marry a non-Mzabite. Primarily these exclusive people are tillers of the soil, greatly skilled in irrigations. Being industrious and intelligent, however, they also carry on handicrafts which have made their ornamental woolen goods famous in North Africa. In addition to this their commercial honesty is "proverbial." They are so well educated that nearly all the men can write Arabic, although their speech is Berber.

Many people have seen a similarity between the Mzabites and the Puritans of New England. Powell,[8] for example, says that in their form of government, their extreme austerity, and their intolerance of beliefs other than their own, as well as in "energy, industry, and commercial integrity, they strongly resemble the Puritans. . . . Like the Puritans they went into exile in a remote land for the sake of their faith." Another point of resemblance is their "blue laws. [A Mzabite] found guilty of drinking wine, or coffee, or of frequenting houses of ill fame is punished by flogging. . . . Of all the Berber tribes the Mzabites have remained the freest from foreign admixture. . . . While totally lacking the cleanliness, the sociability, and the charm of manner of the Arabs, the Mzabites far surpass them in industry, in commercial enterprise, and in dependability. . . . Though they are detested by the Arabs for religious reasons, the Arabs will unhesitatingly intrust them with their last franc."

G. *Selection in Ireland*

The way in which even a small selected group may persistently display distinct qualities is well illustrated in a country as noted for moisture and verdure as the Sahara is for dryness and bareness. Here is what Morton,[9] in an interesting modern book of travel, says about a small village in southwestern Ireland a few miles from Limerick.

I came, by one of those unbelievable transitions not uncommon in Ireland, into an improbable place called Adare. I think Adare is the happiest-looking village in Ireland. It looks cozy, comfortable, prosperous, its wide road is flanked by model houses, and there are even flowers in the gardens. Everything about Adare spoke of some presiding genius. Some one loved the

[8] pp. 212 ff.
[9] p. 147.

place, spent money on it, and . . . enjoyed doing it. . . . The Earls of Dunraven, I was told, had created Adare.

As a matter of fact, the Earls of Dunraven had little to do with the matter. A century and a half ago the village had the same characteristics as now. Here is how it is described by Arthur Young,[10] a famous agricultural expert who toured western Europe in an effort to improve agriculture. How much improvement was needed in Irish agriculture may be judged from Young's exuberant delight on finding even a few people sufficiently advanced to raise turnips in addition to potatoes and wheat. The people of Adare, he says,

are different from the Irish . . . ; they put their potatoes in with the plough, in drills, horse hoe them while growing, and plough them out . . . They plough without a driver; a boy of twelve has been known to plough and drive four horses, and some of them have a hopper in the body of their ploughs, which sows the land at the same time it is ploughed. . . . They yet preserve their language [German], but that is declining. They are very industrious, and in consequence are much happier and better fed, cloathed, and lodged than the Irish peasants [although as is said elsewhere, their quantities of land are small]. We must not, however, conclude from hence that all is owing to this; their being independent farmers, and having leases, are circumstances which will create industry. Their crops are much better than those of their neighbours. There are three villages of them about seventy families in all. . . . They all have offices to their houses, that is stables and cow-houses, and a lodge for their ploughs, etc. They keep their cows in the house [barn] in winter, feeding them upon hay and oat straw. They are remarkable for the goodness and cleanliness of their houses. The women are very industrious, reap the corn [wheat], plough the ground sometimes, and do whatever work may be going on; they also spin and make their children do the same. Their wheat is much better than any in the country, insomuch that they get a better price than anybody else. Their industry goes so far that jocular reports of it are spread; in a very pinching season one of them yoked his wife against a horse, and went in that manner to work, and finished a journey [day's work] at plough. The industry of the women is a perfect contrast to the Irish ladies in the cabbins, who cannot be persuaded, on any consideration, even to make hay, it not being the custom of the country; yet they bind corn, and do other works more laborious.

The people of Adare are the remnant of a stringent process of selection. In the days of Queen Anne (1702–14), political and religious confusion led 820 families of German Protestants to migrate from the Palatinate, west of the Rhine, to Ireland. Queen Anne

[10] p. 377.

wanted Protestants there to offset the Catholics. More than half the families did not like Ireland and went back to Germany. About one quarter stayed in Dublin, and the rest (157 families) were established with government help in several little villages of western Ireland. Some of them merged with the general population, but Adare remained separate. The ancestors of the Adare people evidently underwent the usual selection incident to a religious reform, a difficult migration, the loss of those who had not the courage, strength, or skill to cultivate land in the "wild west" of Ireland, and finally a weeding out, or disappearance, of those who lacked the ability or persistence to stick to their own ways. Originally the Adare people were doubtless greatly helped by the knowledge of farming which they brought with them and by the relative excellence of their soil, as appears from Young's description of the fine trees in their neighborhood. Thus the uniqueness of their village is due to a combination of biological, cultural, and geographical advantages. If any of the three had been different, the results would have been different.

The world is full of instances similar to Adare, for example, the Mennonites, whose superb farms near Lancaster in the world's "garden spot" in southeastern Pennsylvania are described by Kollmorgen.[11] The world is also full of examples of a different sort where varying combinations of heredity, physical environment, and culture produce highly diverse results. Such diversity is manifest even among people who live near together, start at the same cultural level, and are of common ancestry but have at least one outstanding difference. One of the most important requisites of an enlightened study of geography, anthropology, psychology, sociology, and history is the universal recognition that every human situation depends upon the combined effect of heredity, physical environment, and cultural endowment. Progress in such studies has been hampered in the past by the tendency of most students to ascribe special, or even complete, potency to one of the three factors at the expense of the others.

[11] pp. 109–17.

CHAPTER 9

EVOLUTION OF DIVERGENT TYPES

A. Contrasted Character of Nomads and Sedentary People

One of the most interesting features in the evolution of civilization is the way in which the same original group of people can give rise to highly diverse types which may ultimately become well-established kiths. This phenomenon is well illustrated by nomads, but it is also clear in other groups which have undergone a somewhat different process of selection and isolation. A study of the various modes by which kiths originate is basic to an understanding of the effect which small outstanding groups of people, such as the Attic aristocracy and the Prussian Junkers, have exerted upon history and civilization. Let us begin with nomads in general. Lattimore [1] makes the following suggestive comment on the contrast between nomads and sedentary people:

There is little difference in physical racial type between the majority of Northern Chinese and the majority of Mongols. . . . It is often possible to mistake a Chinese in Mongol costume for a Mongol, or a Mongol in Chinese costume for a Chinese. On the other hand, when it is possible to tell them apart . . . it is only possible because of differences in stance, movement, expression, manner, which are intangible in the material sense, but unmistakable. They are not differences of the physique itself, but of the life within the physical structure. Yet these intangibles, which belong to outlook, culture, feeling, and the way of life, establish a cleavage.

A similar, but greater, contrast distinguishes the sedentary people of lower Egypt from the neighboring Arabs of the desert. Although closely allied in race and much intermixed, the two peoples differ in quality. Historians often speak of the uniformity of the Egyptian common people for millennium after millennium and of their slight effect upon history. The Arabs, on the contrary, are almost invariably described as alert and active, with flashing eyes and fiery tempers. Their great effect upon history is well known. In Egypt, as Toyn-

[1] pp. 70–71, 299–300.

bee [2] puts it, there is a strong contrast between the nomad who "regards the agriculturist as a stick-in-the-mud" and the agriculturist who "regards the nomad as a vagabond."

A similar difference appears repeatedly among neighboring kiths which may or may not be racially alike. For example, in the heart of Asia, the Chantos of the oases in Sinkiang (the Tarim Basin) live near the Khirghiz of the surrounding mountains and neighboring steppes. According to Younghusband, the Chantos "are the essence of imperturbable mediocrity. Shut away from the rest of the world, they live a dull, spiritless, easy, but perhaps happy life which they allow nothing to disturb." Very different from the sheltered oasis life of the Chantos among the sands of the desert is that of the nomadic Khirghiz, who wander from winter camps in the neighboring foothills and plains to summer camps in the high mountains.[3]

His mode of life makes the Khirghiz able to endure hunger, thirst and fatigue, for these are the necessary accompaniments of long rides in search of strayed cattle. He has no fear of raging fords or slippery passes and despises the Chanto or Sart of the city, who shrinks from crossing a ford where his horse may lose his footing and be washed downstream. In such rough experiences the Khirghiz learns to be self-reliant and his frequent meeting of strangers under all sorts of circumstances gives him an air of readiness and self-possession.

Coupled with this contrast between the agriculturist and the nomad is a similar contrast in their influence upon history. Ever since civilization became widely established, agricultural people have vastly outnumbered pastoral nomads. Nevertheless, the nomads have repeatedly conquered and ruled the others. Practically never has the reverse been true except when strong people, such as the old Romans or the modern British, have checked nomadic raids along the borders of agriculture.

B. A Basic Principle of Civilization

Thus we come to two crucial questions. First, how do nomads acquire their distinctive qualities? Second, how far are these qualities inherited, and how far are they the result of education and experience? The answer to both questions leads to one of the profoundest principles in the whole realm of civilization—a principle which is often ignored and often vigorously disputed. The principle is that

[2] Vol. 3, p. 17.   [3] Huntington, 1907B, pp. 125–26.

a two-fold process of selection is persistently in progress. One type of selection eliminates people who fail to reach a minimum level in certain qualities which are essential to preservation. The other eliminates customs and ideals—mores, to use Sumner's term—which tend to cause a kith to die out. This process may be intermittent, and it is often interrupted by the migration of people or ideas. By no means all persons or mores which fail to help in the process of survival are eliminated. Moreover, individuals and practices which are ill adapted to the environment repeatedly arise and may flourish greatly for a while. Nevertheless, for untold generations a relentless process of elimination has tended to adapt both people and mores to their physical environment and to the established modes of getting a living.

Thus, as time goes on, those human qualities and habits which help toward survival tend to be strengthened. This is far from meaning that every human trait, every custom, or every ideal which would help in survival is bound to arise. Nevertheless, the whole process apparently tends to produce people whose innate qualities fit them for survival under the prevailing conditions of life. At the same time there is a tendency to produce a social system in which the more basic mores also have a survival value in that particular kind of life. Thus the central core of truth in this whole matter seems to be that the process of selection tends to create a harmonious relation among our familiar trio of (1) physical environment with its limitation of resources and its effect on methods of getting a living; (2) heredity with its restriction of human capacities; and (3) the mores or culture in the three-fold aspect of material possessions, customs, and ideals.

C. Cultural Traits of Nomads

The Arabs provide a good example of the way in which a given physical environment tends in the long run to produce a definite human type both biologically and culturally. The corresponding relationships are by no means so clear under more complicated cultural conditions. Nevertheless, they are equally real and of the same fundamental sort, provided due account is taken of the entire range of geographical and cultural environments which influence human conduct. Practically everyone agrees that democracy is a notable Arab quality. The sheik and the poorest tribesman sit down together before a mounded dish of rice and a freshly boiled kid. Together they scoop up rice with their fingers or tear off bones and gnaw the meat. Is the democracy thus illustrated essential to the nomadic life? Is it a help toward survival? And does it tend to become based on hereditary qualities?

Considerable democracy seems to be essential so long as people follow the pastoral mode of life with frequent migrations from one pasture ground to another. In permanent agricultural communities the rich can put fences around large estates. They can build big houses and fill them with massive furniture, breakable pottery, heavy books, and other luxuries. They may add barns, granaries, and greenhouses. A poor family, on the contrary, can live in a one-room hovel, furnished with quilts on the floor and a few dishes. Among nomads such contrasts in equipment are impossible. The rich man's camels and horses cannot transport heavy, bulky, or breakable articles any better than the poor man's. The rich man's tent may be larger, but its general pattern must be essentially the same as the poor man's. It must also be small enough to be quickly rolled up and packed on animals every few weeks. In actual practice the food of rich and poor does not differ greatly. The difficulty of procuring, preserving, and transporting many articles aside from milk, cheese, and easily kept oasis products such as dates and cereals is too great. Then, too, in tending their animals practically all nomad men, rich or poor, do the same work, as is also true of the women. Among nomads there is far less opportunity for differences in occupation and way of life than among sedentary people.

Another condition favorable to democracy among nomads is that nomadic groups are necessarily small, rarely more than fifteen or twenty families. Everyone knows everyone else intimately, and the man or woman who holds aloof becomes unpopular. Again, nomads, far more than sedentary people, are in danger of being reduced to poverty at any moment. The rich man's three hundred camels, as well as the three of the poor man, may be all driven off by raiders. When this happens, all alike have to help one another. Thus in many ways a democratic spirit is encouraged, and democracy becomes the social ideal. Whether there is a tendency toward the development of innate qualities which make for democracy is not so clear. Perhaps non-democratic families may be handicapped in making marriages and in getting their share of scanty food supplies in time of distress. Thus a tendency for the least democratic types to die out would be created. Nevertheless, the democracy of nomads seems to be largely a cultural product.

In respect to hospitality the situation seems to be a little different. Nomads are almost invariably hospitable, at least for a short time.

Such hospitality is certainly in large measure a social trait, but it seems so important as a means of survival that it may influence biological selection. In other words, an innate temperament that encourages a churlish and stingy attitude toward strangers seems to be a real handicap to survival. The handicap is based on the fact that the nomad's life frequently depends upon the hospitality of others. When the animals stray, as they often do, the nomad must follow at once, regardless of food, water, or protection during the cold desert nights. When night comes, or at least when the second night comes, he and his horse or camel, if he has one with him, must find water and food. They make for the nearest encampment. The people there know that they themselves may soon need hospitality. If they receive strangers, they, too, in their time of need will be helped. Thus the survival of both groups is favored by hospitality.

So great are the disadvantages of the inhospitable spirit that a genuine biological selection may tend to weed out the temperamentally inhospitable type. A possible result of this hospitable spirit is seen in the fact that among the nomadic conquerors of agricultural communities one of the outstanding characteristics is friendliness to strangers and foreigners. The experience of Marco Polo when he became an official of Kublai Khan is typical of what happens under such circumstances. So is the tolerant attitude of other great leaders who sprang from nomadic stock—Cyrus and Akbar, who were friendly to all sorts of religions, Shah Jahan, who employed architects and artists from Italy, Turkey, and many other lands in building the Taj Mahal. Numerous other examples suggest that the exigencies of the nomadic life may weed out individuals whose innate traits fail to harmonize with the necessity for making hospitality a social virtue.

It must not be forgotten that this whole problem of innate versus acquired traits is still in a state of flux. The viewpoint here set forth is a middle ground between two antagonistic extremes. A final estimate of the degree to which such traits as hospitality depend on heredity in comparison with environment cannot yet be made. Certain it is, however, that social pressure makes hospitality one of the most rigid requirements of the nomadic code of honor. We can also be sure that ordinary agricultural villagers have little need of hospitality. They rarely spend the night away from home. In this whole problem, as in many others, our capacity to measure cultural influences is vastly greater than to measure genetic differences. This does not mean, however, that the genetic differences are less real or powerful than the others.

D. Biological Traits of Nomads

Because of a selective process which we shall soon describe, the part played by heredity as compared with environment in making nomads resourceful, self-reliant, and full of initiative is clearer than in such traits as democracy and hospitality. Compare the varied life of a nomad with the uneventful life of a peasant. Today the nomad's sheep, camels, horses, goats, or cattle stray during a sand-storm in the desert or during a snowstorm in the mountains. To-morrow lions in one region or wolves in another must be killed when they threaten the young animals. The next day, perhaps, raiders drive off most of the animals, and all the owners set off in pursuit. The women are left alone to manage everything. I [4] have been awak-ened at night in the Syrian Desert by gunfire, shouts, and the barking of dogs when raiders drove off the camels that had been herded a few hundred yards from a group of low black Arab tents. I have seen the men move away in two bands in the moonlight in pursuit of the raiders. In the cool morning with two other guests—native Arabs—I rode away, not speaking to the women, for to do so would have been discourteous, but leaving them to do the ordinary work of the men as well as their own. They did not know when their men might come back, nor whether another set of raiders would drive away the sheep. Nor did the men know what adventures awaited them during their midnight chase of the plunderers.

Another day the whole camp must migrate to new pastures. At dawn the women dismantle the tents and load them on camels or horses. There is so much work that five-year-old tots lead great gurgling camels by ropes fastened to wooden pins in the animals' noses. Many of the men have gone ahead with the slow-moving sheep. The women put their babies on top of camels, mount horses themselves, and travel a rough, difficult trail. At the new camping place all seems to be dire confusion, but really there is surprising order. While the men see that the animals are watered and driven to graze, the women set up the tents, organize the camp, prepare food, and then milk the sheep, goats, camels, or cows that have been kept near at hand.

Perhaps the migration leads upward from lowland pastures or win-ter villages to high plateaus where there is the best of short grass in summer. The author himself has seen the kind of migration now to

[4] 1911, p. 8.

be described.[5] Part of the women have to go on foot, carrying babies or loads on their backs and helping to drive the sheep. All have to negotiate a rough trail where in some places a slip may mean a fall of hundreds of feet down a precipitous mountainside. A pass has to be painfully surmounted in deep snow. A rushing mountain river must be crossed, although it is too deep to be forded. Frail rafts are prepared by inflating entire goat skins. The women and children crowd onto them, hugging a motley array of lambs, kids, calves, and even colts to keep them from falling overboard. The men paddle frantically, but the violent current carries the rafts far down the stream. Occasionally one overturns and its occupants perish. Meanwhile other men have equipped themselves with life buoys in the form of inflated goatskins. The unwilling animals of all kinds are pushed and beaten until they plunge into the cold flood and strike out for the opposite shore. The men plunge in, too, and swim with the animals, keeping them headed upstream and toward the opposite shore as much as possible. One grabs a sinking sheep by the head and swims with it till its feet touch bottom. Another swims violently downstream to head off a cow that has turned back. When all the animals and people are safely across, camp must be made in the open, for it is too late to set up the tents. Next day the march must be resumed. A famous old still movie called "Grass" gives actual views of such a migration in the Zagros Mountains. It shows the kind of experiences which presumably developed the bravery and stamina of the ancient Medes and Persians.

I have watched migrations among Arabs, Kurds, Turkomans, Khirghiz, and Mongols. Quick, decisive action, self-reliance, and physical exertion are almost invariably necessary. Often there is imminent danger to life and limb. Each man and woman and all but the smallest children must play some active part and do it without much help from others. Few training schools are more severe in teaching people to be brave and resourceful. At the same time, few experiences are more effective in killing off persons who are deficient in the physical or mental qualities on which the lives of both people and animals depend. The strain on women and children is especially great. Hence weaklings often perish, and their kind is gradually weeded out. Thus here we have a nomadic experience which seemingly must produce not only a strongly developed social ideal, but a decided biological effect whereby the self-reliant, the brave, and the physically tough are

[5] 1905.

preserved. Cultural development and biological selection operate simultaneously.

Another quality which seems to be favored by the selective action of the nomadic life is leadership and the power of organization. A successful migration, even though it be only ten or fifteen miles to some well-known spot, means that someone must make a plan, give orders, and see that they are obeyed. The leader must decide when and where to go. The rest must obey. Of course, long custom has led to a stereotyped method of taking down the tents, sending the sheep first, and so on. Nevertheless, differences in the weather, the likelihood of danger from raiders or wild beasts, the height to which the rivers have risen, the location where rain happens to have fallen, and many other conditions oblige the leaders to make separate plans for most migrations. For their own safety the rest must co-operate. Thus leadership and mutual co-operation are of primary value in enabling a nomadic kith to survive.

Consider how contrary all this is to the life of the peasant on his little piece of land. He and his wife rarely have to make sudden decisions. Year after year they plant and reap the same crops on essentially the same pieces of ground. Of course, they have to decide where to plant wheat and where beans, but the time of planting has been set for them by the experience of the ages. New scenes, new people, new experiences, new problems, and new responsibilities rarely confront them. They must be industrious and strong if they would feed their families, but bravery and leadership have little value in enabling them to survive. The contributions of agricultural people to civilization are indeed great, but they follow different lines from those of nomads. Moreover, in estimating their contribution to human progress it is often impossible to determine how much is due to capacities inherited from a long line of agricultural ancestors, and how much to the infusion of human stock of a more or less nomadic type.

E. Raids as an Influence on Character

Raids are in some ways the most severe of the selective processes which give character to nomads. The greatest troubles of nomads arise from scarcity of grass and water. Doughty describes the anxiety of the Arabs when the short rainy season fails in the desert. "Where is the rain?" they ask of strangers. "Have showers fallen anywhere? Why does Allah so long withhold his favor?" What can a man do when the mother animals are so starved and thirsty that they cannot supply milk? The young animals which are normally exchanged for the cereals and dates of the oases will die. The owner's own family will have scarcely enough milk. No hard sour cheese can be stored away for the season when milk is scarce. Under such conditions raids on other nomads or on the animals of the settled people in neighboring agricultural districts are practically the only way to preserve the lives of hungry wives and children. For this reason raids become not merely an exhilarating adventure but a duty. We think of raids as robberies; to the nomads they are an essential part of getting a living. To us such raids seem the antithesis of hospitality; to the nomads there is no such inconsistency. Two Arabs who slept beside me before the raid described above may have belonged to the very tribe which did the raiding. Nevertheless, as guests they were safe, and also as guests they could not help the raiders.

A good raider, and hence a good provider for his wife and children, must have the capacity both to lead and to follow. Before the Russians conquered the region east of the Caspian Sea, a Turkoman would sometimes thrust his spear upright into the ground and say, "I go on a raid. Who goes with me?" Others thrust in their spears, and finally the party started. On such a raid it is essential that one man lead and the rest obey implicitly. Failure may mean disaster. All must be able to put every ounce of strength into a great effort for at least a short time. Each man must be able to rely implicitly on his companions. In Arab raids, for example, two men often ride a milch camel and lead a horse which shares the camel's milk with them. At the time of the final dash one takes the horse while the other goes to a designated point to wait for him with the camel. Unreliability in such an affair may be a matter of life and death.

Thus capacity for leadership, soldierly obedience, fidelity to comrades, quick, decisive action, and intense temporary exertion are potent means of survival among nomads, but are of relatively little importance among sedentary tillers of the soil. The nomad may be idle when things are quiet and peaceable. The women will do the ordinary work, which consists chiefly of milking the animals and cooking. Steady industry promotes survival in the villages, but not in the desert. Among nomads, the most promising youth is one who may seem lazy but who springs promptly into alert activity and has the power of leadership. He is the one most likely to get the prettiest and healthiest girl as wife and to bring up many healthy, sturdy children.

There is direct evidence of a selective process based on the preceding qualities. For example, I asked a gray-bearded but erect old chief of pastoral nomads in the Egyptian Sudan what he thought of the British regime compared with the days of his youth when the Sudan was free. "The British," he said, "are not so bad, but their rule is disastrous to the young men. There is nothing to cultivate their character. The British prevent raids, and the young men have nothing to train them in courage and leadership. They just sit around and are lazy." The chief was then asked what happened in the old days if a young man proved cowardly when he began to go on raids. The old man shook his gray head and answered, "That was sad. We reasoned with him, but if he failed again and we saw that he was a coward, his mother said, 'You are no son of mine.' If he was married, his wife said, 'This is no longer your tent.' If he was not married, no girl wanted him, and no father would give his daughter to such a man. What became of him? We drove him out, and he went to the river."

This means that the cowardly young man was expelled from the tribe and went to the irrigated lands by the Nile to find such work as he could. The chief was asked what happened if a young man was brave enough in raids but not reliable. He answered that failure to meet a comrade at the right place at the right time was not so bad as cowardice, but in the end it, also, would send a young man to the river. A final question: "Did you ever actually see such cases?" "Yes, indeed, in my young days I saw several."

The significance of the foregoing lies in the fact that among pastoral nomads in widely scattered areas this same kind of separation between nomads and sedentary agricultural people has been going on for untold generations. The necessities of the pastoral life demand certain distinct characteristics, among which leadership, bravery, self-reliance, reliability, and adaptability are vital. If young men who are weak in these qualities remain among the nomads, they fail to get wives or are given girls whom others do not want and who are often physically deficient so that they have few children. The result is that their kind tends to die out. On the other hand, the young men in whom the requisite qualities are strongly present get the most desirable wives, and are more likely than others to have several. Thus their stock increases. If temperamental tendencies are hereditary, as most assuredly they are, it seems almost certain that prolonged biological selection must have tended to intensify innate qualities which give nomads unusual ability as soldiers, organizers, and rulers.

There is more to the problem than this, however. Young men who are failures as nomads may be successful as tillers of the soil. Some of them may be unusually strong for back-breaking work with the spade, a task which the true nomad hates like poison. Some of them may have great persistence, or a gentle hand with cattle and other domestic animals. Such men may be unusually good in taking care of their children or in the kind of foresight which plans well for food during the winter. Whatever their qualities may be, a new type of selection at once begins to act upon them and their families as soon as they give up the pastoral life and betake themselves to agriculture. Thus where crops are raised there must be a certain degree of selection in favor of those who have the qualities of physical build and temperament best adapted to promote survival in an agricultural community. There can be little doubt that the qualities of such people are different from those of nomads. There is good reason to believe that this difference is in part a matter of biological inheritance as well as of social custom.

F. Benign Selection and Chinese Hakkas

The differences between kiths are so fundamental that we may well examine an example of another kind which also illustrates the contrast between favorable and unfavorable selection. Students of China, including the Chinese themselves, recognize a deep-seated difference between the people of the North and the South. Contrary to what would normally be expected on a climatic basis, the South is progressive and the North conservative. Modern revolutionary movements and leaders such as Sun Yat Sen and Chiang Kai-shek are mainly of southern origin. The Chinese themselves say that the southerners are relatively quick to accept new ideas, easy to persuade, ready to change their habits, alert in action, radical in politics, and fond of travel. People less friendly to China say that the southerners are extravagant, pleasure-loving, and immoral, although generous and rich. On the other hand, the northern Chinese tend to be fond of home, slow in accepting new ideas, steadfast of purpose, frugal, serious, miserly, and moral. This contrast is illustrated in many ways. For example, in proportion to their population the coastal provinces from Shanghai southward supplied about four times as many of the Chinese officials holding the higher degrees of old China in 1910 as did the North and the West. In 1923, the "binding of girls' feet, the seclusion of women and the wearing of pigtails by men, had almost disappeared in South China, but were only beginning to disappear in the North." [6]

This contrast between North and South cannot be due to contact with Europe, for old Chinese sources describe it long before the arrival of Europeans. It can scarcely be due to climate, for the prolonged damp, hot, southern summer appears to reduce energy more than the cold, dusty winter of the North. It can owe little to race. The alert Hakkas of the South and certain especially backward villagers of the North both appear to be of relatively pure Chinese stock. These two groups typify the extremes of South and North. The secret of the contrast seems to lie largely in the great frequency and severity of famines in the North than in the South, together with more intense overpopulation and barbarian incursions. Such conditions have led many competent northern Chinese to migrate southeastward and cityward, while many dull ones have remained in some of the poorer villages.

The contrast between the Hakkas and these especially backward northern villages epitomizes the selective process so well that we shall examine it in detail. The Hakkas, numbering about ten million, have their main center in the mountains north of Canton and west of Foochow. Swarms of them, however, live in the cities of south China and in Formosa, Java, the Malay Peninsula, and Hawaii. There they furnish a surprisingly large portion of the more industrious coolies, better business men, and educated professional people. Good judges say that in average ability they surpass the Chinese as a whole, including even the Cantonese, who rightly make strong claims to special competence. Because they get ahead so well, the Hakkas are disliked by other Chinese, much as Jews are disliked in Europe. The Chinese of the coastal cities call them barbarous, but even in their secluded mountain home the Hakkas excel in some of the best elements of civilization. Their women, who are generally regarded as uncommonly pretty, are held in unusual respect and have never been crippled by the painful process of foot-binding. Personal cleanliness and bathing are more prevalent among Hakkas than among any other main group of Chinese. Education has likewise been especially widespread so that in the central Hakka district, even in the nineteenth century, about 80 per cent of the men and an unusual number of women could read.

[6] Huntington, 1924A, pp. 161–64; 1925B, p. 208.

G. Adverse Selection in Chinese Famines

In strong contrast to the relatively comfortable Hakkas, the miserable inhabitants of certain poor villages near Peiping rarely have enough to eat. Their fields, according to Dr. Wilder [7] of Peiping, are so small that normally the villagers do not expect their food supply to suffice for more than nine or ten months of the year. In the autumn, preparations for next year's spring work are made by placing in each house enough grain for seed and for food from planting time until the earliest crops can be harvested. Then the rest of the food is consumed during the first part of the ensuing period of idleness. The villagers are idle partly because winter temperatures like those of Chicago discourage farm work. Other reasons are absence of farm animals and home handicrafts and inability to get jobs in neighboring cities. The only other recourse is to beg. Therefore, when all except the seed and the spring portion of the food is gone, these ill-starred people seal up their doors and windows with bricks of dried mud. Faring forth into the bitter winds that sweep down from Siberia, they eke out a wretched living by begging. The strangest part of the story is that neither they nor others will break into the sealed houses, although mud bricks are easy to demolish. So common is this degree of overpopulation and so essential are the wandering and begging that it has become a point of honor not to break into a sealed house. This restraint is not due to honesty, for the wanderers will steal anything they can lay hands on elsewhere. It is merely one of those interesting social devices which are preserved because they have a survival value. If the wanderers broke into each other's houses and stole the grain, none of them would have either food or seed the following spring. Most would therefore starve to death.

Only people of low intellectual caliber would tolerate such a method of preserving life. Investigations by Dr. Wilder and such rough intelligence tests as he could make indicate that these villagers as a whole are mentally subnormal. This idea is strengthened when one inquires how people of high mental caliber would live in those same villages. If Hakkas lived there with no more land than is now available, part of them would certainly find work in nearby Peiping, Tientsin, or other cities. Many would have gone to Manchukuo. They would readily find work in these new places because tens of

[7] Huntington, 1924A, pp. 174 ff.

thousands of them have been conspicuously successful in doing so elsewhere, even in competition with the capable Cantonese. Such migration and the funds sent home by the migrants would relieve the pressure on the home villages. Moreover, if people in these northern villages behaved as the Hakkas do, they would develop simple home industries, get hold of at least a few animals, and gradually increase their livestock. The subnormal villagers, however, seem to be too dull to migrate. In Chinese cities they are not intelligent enough to compete with the people already there. It seems impossible to avoid the conclusion that their deplorable life is a result of low mentality as well as overpopulation. It is hard to imagine Icelanders behaving in any such way, no matter how unfavorable their physical environment may be.

Having said this, we at once face a question which keeps coming up. How far is this low mentality innate, and how far is it due to malnutrition and other environmental handicaps from infancy onward? Here, as in many other cases, a single set of facts does not warrant any precise conclusion. On the basis of many lines of evidence, however, two conclusions seem almost inescapable. First, a selective process, shortly to be described, has led to an innate mental contrast between the southern Hakkas and the subnormal northern villagers. Second, the low mentality thus segregated in these particular northern villages has resulted in an economic and social system in which semi-starvation is chronic. This condition still further lowers the mental powers. Thus heredity and environment apparently combine to produce the observed results.

The selective process referred to above has been more or less active since the dawn of Chinese history. It is set in motion by three main conditions: first, overpopulation arising from natural increase in numbers; second, the 'pressure of barbarous northern nomads who are especially likely to swarm into adjacent northern China at times of prolonged drought; and third, famines due to either drought or flood.

Let us concentrate on famines. Chinese history is full of them. One type arises from droughts which often last several years and are especially common and harmful in north China. At Peiping, for example, the seven months from October to April normally have a combined rainfall of only 2 inches. Even in May, which is about as warm as June in New York, the amount is only 1.4 inches. In other words, for eight months out of twelve, on an average, Peiping has a desert climate, as dry as that of southwestern Arizona from Phoenix to Yuma. The four months from June to September, however, normally get about 21 inches of rain, close to half of which falls in July. If this summer rainfall begins in May and is well spread out till September, good crops may be expected. Often, however, it holds off until late June or July. So short a rainy season does not leave time for the crops to grow and ripen. Hence famine stalks the land. The villagers in the lowlands near the rivers, to be sure, and any others who can practice irrigation get along reasonably well in spite of the drought. Their crops help the beggars who swarm into the lowlands from the drought-stricken sections. The misfortune of the lowlanders, however, comes later, for droughts are often followed by unusually severe rains. Peiping may get as much as 20 inches in a single month. As a result floods inundate hundreds or thousands of villages, killing the crops and eating away the mud walls of the houses.

Even if overpopulation, the incursions of nomads, and civil wars are not added to these climatic disasters, the result is migration on a large scale. Under the impetus of floods everyone, rich or poor, must move promptly. Under that of drought the exodus is slower, but in the end it may be almost as complete. Such movements are peculiarly selective. The more farsighted, competent, and prosperous people generally go first and farthest. Collins, in his summary of the voluminous records of the Tolan Committee of the House of Representatives Investigating the Interstate Migration of Destitute Citizens, shows what happens in America. According to an official WPA (Works Progress Administration) investigation in 1938, the heads of families which migrated from one state to another "possessed relatively far greater skill and education" than the unemployed who remained at home. Common laborers were also relatively less numerous among the migrants than in the working population as a whole. In other words, among the portion of the population which lost its economic moorings, the more intelligent and competent were the more likely to migrate to a distance.

Chinese famines, which usually produce economic stress far greater than that of the depression of the 1930's in the United States, have doubtless repeatedly caused similar or worse results in China. Moreover, the data for the United States show that after the competent have once left a blighted area, they are less likely to return than the incompetent. The competent find jobs and acquire property in other places. They have gone far and that makes it more difficult to return home. Moreover, in China the abandoned home is not a pleasant place to which to return. If migration is due to drought, the houses are still there, to be sure, but they have suffered during the owner's absence. There are no cattle or other animals at home to help make farming pay. Seed must be bought by people who have little money. A big landowner may return to look after his property, but he is not likely to take his family back for a long time. A less prosperous but competent family may send back one son to start the old life again, but the rest stay away until good times return, and by then they may not want to go back.

The incompetent, on the contrary, often have to go back as soon as possible. They have greater difficulty than the competent in finding jobs in their temporary homes, and they have not gone so far from home. If their villages have been flooded, most of the houses are in ruins. The water may not disappear from flooded lands for a year or more. In some places the fields are covered with sand, and it may take years to restore them. Many things combine to make the famine-stricken areas unattractive to anyone who is competent enough to get a good job elsewhere. Thus the worst of these areas become regions inhabited largely by poor incompetents who return because they cannot compete with more able people elsewhere. Thus in China we have a striking illustration of selective migration which separates people of the same race into an uncommonly competent group far away from the original home, on the one hand, and a group, little above the stage of morons, near the old home, on the other.

H. *Diversity of Racial Possibilities*

China is far from being the only country where adverse as well as constructive selection has occurred through migration. In one of his vivid stories published posthumously, Thomas Wolfe describes an American type which has been left stranded in some of the least favorable parts of the country. He is talking about the Mountain Whites of the Appalachians—not about all of them, but about the extreme type which is for America what the moron villagers are for China. Wolfe may exaggerate poetically, but he puts his finger on one of the most vital points in the entire study of civilization when he says that the people themselves, and not their culture or surroundings, are the cause of their own troubles.

Backward types such as the poorer Mountain Whites are not peculiar to the Appalachians. One can find them in almost every state or country which has long been settled. Here and there among the hills of Massachusetts, for example, one encounters little pockets where groups of incompetent people have been left behind by their more vigorous relatives. The incompetents marry among themselves, and incompetence is perpetuated. Such conditions are merely an example of a process which is taking place all the time. They illustrate the fact that practically any large body of people can be divided into groups which differ radically in innate characteristics and which in the long run may also differ in mode of life, habits and ideals. From any large body of people in any country, regardless of race, it probably would be possible to select a minor group which would be like the Hakkas in abilities and temperament and which might be developed into a distinct kith. It would also be possible from this same body to select a group of peace-loving people like the Quakers, or a group which would be as incompetent as the most degenerate Chinese villagers. Every racial group, every nation, every city, and even every village seems to contain possibilities whereby selection and isolation may lead to highly divergent types which might develop into kiths.

CHAPTER 10

THE SELECTIVE PROCESS IN HISTORY

A. The Power of Pastoral Nomads

The general process of biological selection set forth in previous chapters helps to explain a multitude of historical problems, but in this study of basic principles we have space for only a few. One of the most impressive historical facts is the constant repetition of a standard pattern whereby pastoral nomads from deserts or mountains invade agricultural regions, establish themselves as rulers during a period of chaos, take part in an outburst of progress when peace ensues, and then, after generations or centuries, fade into obscurity. This pattern seems to depend on the capacity of nomads for war and leadership in contrast to the capacity of agricultural people for achievements of another sort. Here, as in other cases, the capacities are the combined result of biological and cultural conditions, the effects of which cannot readily be separated. The pattern to which they lead is exemplified on every side of the vast deserts and grasslands which stretch eight thousand miles from the western Sahara to Manchuria. Circling around the desert we see the same general historical development among the Arabs in Africa and Spain, the Huns in Hungary, the Turks in Asia Minor, the Manchus in China, many groups of nomadic invaders in Mesopotamia and Egypt, and even among such little known people as the Fulah on the borders of Nigeria south of the Sahara.

No group of nomads has been more conspicuous in this respect than the Mongols. Their repeated invasions of the lands around the deserts illustrate a pattern which, with changes in details, has been repeated scores of times by other nomads throughout the course of history. Military capacity and power of leadership seem to have been common among the Mongols for reasons which we have considered in the preceding study of nomads. A conspicuous example of this came into prominence nearly one thousand years ago, near the Manchurian border of Mongolia. There for seven generations a line of nomad chiefs gained increasing power. When the seventh chief died in A.D. 1175, his son, Genghiz Khan, was a lad of thirteen. The subordinate chiefs proposed to disregard the boy's claims to authority, but his energetic mother foiled this plot by leading an army into battle. Young Genghiz apparently had uncommonly able ancestors on both sides. He showed that he was a born leader, and the warlike chiefs of the surrounding nomads soon recognized his authority and were glad to share his conquests. As the years went on, four unusually competent sons and a group of able subordinates helped him.

Genghiz first spread his conquests westward. Having disposed of other nomads, he led his wild hosts against settled agriculturists. City after city was sacked and burned. Bukhara, Samarkand, and Merv in modern Soviet territory east of the Caspian Sea, Balkh and Herat in Afghanistan, and Nishapur in northeastern Persia all felt his bloody hand. At Bukhara he said to his men, "The hay is cut; give your horses fodder," and they plundered with a will. At Nishapur everybody, old or young, male or female, was massacred with the exception of four hundred artisans who were deemed valuable as slaves to be sent to Mongolia. At Herat after a siege of six months the army was allowed a whole week of killing and burning. The claim that one million six hundred thousand persons were slaughtered shows what people then thought.

Genghiz himself never went farther west than Bukhara or farther south than the Indus River, but consider what this means. To reach India from eastern Mongolia overland by way of Bukhara involves a journey of at least four thousand miles by winding trails. Horsemen travelling with pack trains and supplies rarely make more than twenty miles a day for any great length of time. On a long trek, they must often halt for weeks to let man and beast recuperate. When the Mongols reached the Indus they were, at the very least, a good ten months' journey from headquarters. This, however, is far from being the whole story. The energetic generals and sons of Genghiz carried their campaigns much farther west to Mesopotamia, Russia, and even Hungary. On the way they started the migration which brought the Osmanli Turks into their modern home. At Budapest, where they reached the western limit of easily traversed grasslands, a full year's "fast" journey separated the hard-riding, relentless Mongols from their far eastern home.

Everywhere the victorious Mongols established themselves as a ruling aristocracy, imposing their rude desert authority on the more cultured people whom they conquered, but soon learning the ways of their subjects. In the most remote regions the Mongol rule did not last long. Nevertheless, in Persia the Ilkhan dynasty founded by Hulagu, a son of Genghiz, endured a hundred years. The most famous Mongol kingdom of this time was established in China. While his generals were bringing dire fear to Europe and western Asia, Genghiz himself began to conquer China north of the Yellow River. His sons and grandsons brought practically the whole country into the Mongol Empire. One son, Ogdai, promptly succumbed to certain weaker aspects of civilization. Leaving the final conquest of China to his generals and brothers, he gave himself up to ease and licentiousness. His nephew and successor, Mangu Khan, although retaining some features of nomad life, built a great palace at Karakorum in Mongolia. Its size, luxury, and elaborate hunting parties, as described by Marco Polo, provide an amazing contrast to the simple tent, plain food, and active exercise of Mangu's grandfather, Genghiz.

The ability which for ten generations had kept this line of nomads in the forefront was by no means exhausted when Mangu's brother and successor, Kublai Khan, came to the throne. He was one of the greatest of Asiatics. He probably ruled more people than had ever before been under the authority of one man. Before he became emperor he did something almost unprecedented. Instead of fire, rapine, and slaughter for his conquered enemies, he gave them help as soon as they submitted. As emperor, his tolerance toward religion and his active interest in science, literature, and general culture remind one of the conduct of other nomadic conquerors, such as the Arabs who built the Alhambra in Spain and the Dome of the Rock in the Temple enclosure at Jerusalem. The astronomical instruments made at Kublai Khan's behest remained in Peiping until the Germans carried them to Berlin in 1900. Marco Polo expatiates on the good government, hospitals, printed books, and other signs of progress in his day in China. The Grand Canal, for example, was much improved. Competent Turks, Persians, Armenians, Byzantines, and even remote Venetians, such as Marco Polo, were welcomed and given service as governors, generals, envoys, astronomers, advisors, and physicians. Although few Chinese were placed in high positions, the people as a whole appear to have liked Kublai Khan in spite of his hated nomad origin, his extravagance, and his oppressive methods of collecting taxes.

During the sixty years from Kublai's death in 1294 to the end of the Mongol Empire in 1355, the nine descendants of Genghiz who came to the throne are said to have been weak. This may be true, but they were faced by one of the worst physical periods in all Chinese history. The records indicate that at this time droughts and especially floods, with their accompanying famines, were more severe and numerous in North China than at any other time in Chinese history. According to Yao's record, the year 1325 is the only one in which floods are recorded during every month from January to December. Almost every province suffered. Moreover, about this time the terrible Black Death, the worst plague of history, broke out in China and spread westward. Such conditions almost inevitably bring political disruption, banditry, invasion, rebellion, or similar disasters. The remarkable fact is that under such unfavorable conditions the Mongol dynasty lasted as long as it did.

Historians have sometimes sought to explain the victories of the Mongols as the mere result of vast hordes of soldiers. A military critic finds such an idea quite contrary to the facts. According to Hart,

Fuller knowledge has dispelled the excuse of mediaeval historians that the Mongol victories were due to an overwhelming superiority of numbers. Quality rather than quantity was the secret of their amazingly rapid sequence of successes. Alone of all the armies of their time they had grasped the essentials of strategy, while the tactical mechanism was so perfect that the higher conceptions of tactics were unnecessary.

The way in which the Mongol kith established empires in widely separated parts of Asia is extraordinary. The famous Timur Lenk (Timur the Lame, or Tamerlane) established one with its center in Samarkand and its borders far away in India, Mesopotamia, Turkey, and Siberia. Though often called a Turk, he was apparently descended from the same tribal stock as Genghiz Khan. Timur compares well with Genghiz and Kublai as conqueror and organizer. His descendant, Baber (1483–1530), who conquered northern India, was of similar caliber. Baber founded the Mogul dynasty, which lasted until 1761, when the Mahrattas put an end to it. At Delhi in 1525, with only an insignificant army, he promptly routed an immense host of Indians. This was partly because he was progressive enough to adopt the new-fangled idea of using artillery, but also because of brilliant leadership. Baber's son was driven out of India, but his grandson, Akbar, one of the great names in history, returned as undisputed ruler of most of the country.

Many leaders in the kith of Genghiz Khan were great administrators as well as soldiers. Akbar is an example. On his mother's side and possibly also on his father's he was a descendant of Genghiz. He ordered careful surveys of property, and on their basis framed a mode of taxation that encouraged prosperity. He set up a semi-feudal military system and established schools impartially for Hindus, Moslems, and Parsis. Although this "greatest and wisest" of Mogul emperors was a Moslem, he tolerated other religions and actually devised one of his own, including what he deemed best in others. The Parsi religion evidently influenced him, for every morning, like the Zoroastrians, he prayed in public, looking toward the sun as the symbol of divine power.

In art, too, the Moguls showed exceptional ability. Few buildings are more famous than the Taj Mahal, the magnificent tomb of the favorite wife of Shah Jahan. A nomad kith by no means deserves all the credit for this structure any more than for the Temple of Heaven in Peiping or the Alhambra in Spain. Nevertheless, the Moguls were the guiding spirit—they gathered architects and artisans; they engineered the planning whereby these great and beautiful monuments were erected. The Taj Mahal does not stand alone. Among the many other Mogul palaces and monuments, the lovely Pearl Mosque at Agra, with its pure white marble set off by delicate tracery in gold, appeals to many even more than does the Taj Mahal.

B. The Manchus in China

The essential features of the Mongol conquests have been repeated by other nomads of both deserts and mountains so frequently that we may properly speak of the nomadic pattern of invasion, conquest, brilliant civilization, and decay. Steppe-dwelling nomads erupting from the same general region as the Mongols have imposed their rule upon the Chinese at least four times. The Khitan Tatars did so in the tenth century, the Kin Tatars in the twelfth, the Mongols in the thirteenth, and the Manchus in the early seventeenth. Similar events have occurred so often on other desert borders that they seem to be characteristic of steppes. It is widely recognized that drought and pressure of population induce nomads to invade agricultural regions. It is not so widely recognized that the nomadic life, with its stern selective process, endows the nomads with qualities which enable a few to conquer vastly larger numbers of settled people and then to dominate them for centuries. These same qualities seem to explain why nomads produce many rulers.

The Manchu dynasty, with its succession of able rulers, illustrates this last point. It was one of the longest-lived in the history of China. During the nearly three centuries of its rule (1644–1912), the Chinese Empire reached its greatest territorial extent except under the Mongols. According to Latourette,[1] the country also "attained a fresh level of material prosperity, probably higher than ever before. In the latter part of the seventeenth and most of the eighteenth century, it was the most populous and possibly the most prosperous realm on the planet. . . . From the standpoint of order and justice it was probably as far advanced as any state of the time. [The Manchu dynasty includes] two of the ablest monarchs that China ever had." One of these was K'ang-hsi (1661–1722) and the other his grandson, Ch'ien Lung (1736–97), who "appears to have been the equal of the two famous monarchs of Europe in his day, Catherine of Russia and Frederick of Prussia. . . . For nearly a century and a half, with a short interruption, China's government was in the hands of two extra-ordinarily able men."[2] Nor were these two the only great representatives of the Manchus. Tz'u Hsi, a Manchu woman of great beauty and charm, was the real ruler of China during most of the time from 1861 to 1908. (The length of all these reigns suggests that the Manchu rulers were vigorous physically.) The Empress Dowager, or "Old Buddha," as Tz'u Hsi was called in later years, is classified by Latourette[3] as "one of those remarkable women who at irregular intervals have forced themselves into the virtual rulership of the Empire." She may be compared with the Arab queen, Zenobia, and the mother who saved the chieftainship for Genghiz Khan. Women of nomad stock seem often to display unusual strength of character.

Architecture is good evidence of ability. In this respect the Manchu dynasty is pre-eminent. The Imperial Palace, or Forbidden City at Peiping, with its bewildering array of courtyards and of buildings roofed with glowing yellow tiles, is a masterpiece. So is the Temple of Heaven with its sky-blue tiles and pure white circular altar. These structures and the Temple of Agriculture are spread over considerably more than one square mile of groves and open fields. The new Summer Palace, built by the Empress Dowager among the hills outside Peiping, represents a similar magnificent use of space. Although sometimes called decadent in style, it is immensely impressive in grandeur of plan and in the way in which tiled buildings rise among trees on steep slopes or overlook lakes spanned by graceful bridges.

[1] Vol. 1, pp. 328–29.   [3] Vol. 1, p. 383.

[2] Vol. 1, p. 340.

C. *Turkish Shepherds and Janissaries*

The Osmanli Turks afford an interesting variant of the normal nomadic pattern of conquest and domination. At first they were a band of two to four thousand nomads who were driven from Central Asia by a Mongol invasion and by drought. They settled near Ankara, the present Turkish capital, in A.D. 1227. Today after seven centuries their descendants, although much mixed with other stocks, are still dominant in Turkey. At the end of the last century, Elliot described the "true" Turk as still a nomad at heart. Such a man, so Elliot says, never acts as if permanently settled. If he wants to install one of the sheet-iron stoves which are Turkish favorites although they become red-hot in a few minutes, he does not bother to build a chimney or even to carry the pipe to a window. He merely makes a hole in the mud wall of his house, sticks in the pipe and stuffs rags around it to keep out the wind. Why do more when Allah may make him move on tomorrow? Of course, this is an exaggeration, but it expresses a certain truth. In practical affairs, such as agriculture, arts, crafts, and business, the Turks have systematically lagged behind the Greeks, Armenians, and Jews whom they formerly dominated. Nevertheless, they have shown remarkable power to maintain authority over a great variety of subject people and to utilize the skills of such people.

Toynbee employs an interesting figure of speech in describing the Turks. He says that in accord with their nomadic character they have treated conquered people like sheep. Just as a shepherd trains dogs to look after sheep, so the Turks in earlier times trained Christian youths to guard flocks of subjugated people. They did this through the unique institution of the Janissaries. These were boys snatched from Christian homes in early youth. The most promising were given very careful education. Many became military leaders. The rest were farmed out for some years to Moslems and then brought together for military training. Practically all became ardent Moslems. They were taught that the one great way to get ahead was through good service as soldiers or in other allotted tasks. Family life was discouraged. Their main work was to protect the sultan and spread his power. Although mercenary soldiers appear frequently in history, no other kith appears ever to have worked out so elaborate a system whereby nomadic "shepherds" used human "dogs" to keep conquered "sheep" in order. Here, as in other cases, the conspicuous fact is that for centuries a relatively small kith, derived from desert nomads, dominated far larger sedentary kiths which were apparently more competent in many respects. The nomad kith was presumably able to do this because it inherited a talent for political and military leadership which was not so strongly present in the others.

D. Nomads of Mountains and Deserts

Mountains as well as deserts lead to nomadism and the selective process which favors boldness, hardihood, and the power both to fight and to lead. This fact is well illustrated by the history of Mesopotamia, which has again and again been invaded by nomads alternately from mountains and deserts. The strip of irrigated fertility which formed the core of the ancient empires of Babylonia and Assyria and of the medieval caliphate, as well as of modern Iraq, is bordered by deserts on the west and south and by cold, rugged mountains on the east and north. The Zagros Mountains, as we may call the whole great western highland of Iran from Lakes Van and Urmia to the Persian Gulf, still harbor nomads who are only half subdued by the modern governments of Iran and Turkey. The author of this book was once present when some of them drove away the sheep of a village under the very nose of a small military post.[4] These mountain nomads generally live in adobe villages during the winter but in summer betake themselves and their livestock to the mountains. The ruggedness and height of the mountains and the swiftness of the rivers render migrations to mountain pastures especially difficult.

Behind the Zagros Mountains to the north and east lie vast deserts and steppes which have repeatedly spewed forth Turks, Mongols, Huns, Scythians, and other nomads. Time after time these Central Asiatic nomads have burst from the dry lowland grasslands into the mountains that form a lofty barrier north and east of Mesopotamia. Sometimes they have burst clear through to the plain of the Tigris and Euphrates. More often they have lingered in the mountains for generations. Almost invariably, however, any severe disturbance among the tribesmen in Central Asia has tended to push its way through like a wave to Mesopotamia. Moreover, the Great Zagros system of western Persia is so high that many of the plateaus with the best pasturage suffer from too much snow. Hence, cold, rainy phases of great climatic cycles drive the semi-nomadic inhabitants out of the mountains, just as hot, dry phases drive them out of the desert.

[4] 1902.

Because of such conditions Mesopotamia and Babylonia have long been ground between an upper millstone of invasion by nomads of the mountains and a nether millstone of invasion by nomads of the desert. A brief catalogue of these will show how the two kinds of invasions have alternated, and how fully this part of the world has been dominated by people of nomadic stock. Three thousand years before Christ, a Sumerian civilization of unknown origin had become well established in Babylonia. Then, about 2500 B.C., Semitic nomads from the western deserts invaded the land. Their power reached its zenith under Sargon of Akkad, one of the great men of history. About 2370 B.C. Gutian nomads from the Zagros Mountains to the northeast rudely interrupted the rule of Sargon's desert kith. The Gutians were apparently much like the modern Kurds of that same region, who in winter inhabit mud villages but in summer drive their flocks upward into the mountains and live in low black tents. After ruling the rich plain between the lower Tigris and Euphrates for nearly a century, the Gutians were expelled by a new Sumerian dynasty, which apparently was not of nomadic origin. Then, about 2170 B.C., another turn of the wheel brought the Elamites to Mesopotamia. They, like the Gutians, came from the Persian mountains and were much the same nomadic sort of people. Less than a century and a half later Semitic nomads of the western desert were again on the march. They established a dynasty which is famous because its greatest leader, Hammurabi, was the first known compiler of a code of law.

By about 1900 B.C. the day of these Semitic desert folk was done. No amount of law-making could stem the incursions of the wild Kassites, who, like their predecessors, had become fighters and leaders in the hard, selective school of the desert. They came from the deserts of Central Asia and passed through the eastern mountains in much the same way as the Gutians and Elamites. The Kassite dynasty lasted remarkably long, nearly six centuries. Toward the end it was greatly disturbed by Aramaeans of desert origin, like the followers of Sargon. Then about 1200 B.C. Babylonia was overpowered by still a fourth group of semi-nomadic mountaineers, Elamites once more. A new Aramaean or Semitic group of desert origin repeated the process of invasion about 1090 B.C. The Medes from the eastern mountains and then the Persians under Cyrus from nearly the same region followed some five centuries later. Two great Median leaders, Phraortes and his famous son Cyaxares, were probably chieftains of a nomadic

Median tribe in the desert. Sykes [5] calls the Persians of Cyrus the Great "mountaineers who had hitherto been dwelling in scattered villages." They doubtles were semi-nomadic, like most of the mountain people of that region. The traditional accounts of the miraculous birth and childhood of Cyrus connect him with shepherds rather than towns. The end of another four centuries saw still a seventh eastern group invading the lowlands. These Parthians, like many other invaders, were nomads who started far to the northeast in the desert, swarmed into the Persian mountains, lived there for a while, and then swept down to overwhelm the fertile lowlands.

The Roman Empire largely checked nomadic invasions for several centuries. Nevertheless, in the second half of the third century A.D., a brief but significant Arab revolt arose close to Mesopotamia. Odaenathus of Palmyra, with a vigor and astuteness like that of the old Arab stock to which he belonged, defied the Romans. He was helped by his wife, Zenobia, "famed for her beauty, her masculine energy and unusual powers of mind." [6] When her husband's death left her with a minor son, she herself, like the mother of Genghiz Khan, led her armies. She was another of the women of nomadic stock who have been especially strong-minded.

The next desert invasion of Mesopotamia was the outpouring of Arabs in the seventh century under the impulse of the new faith of Islam. This gave rise to the famous caliphate of Baghdad and the Ommiad dynasty, some of whose members went nearly three thousand miles to Spain and founded the kingdom which built the Alhambra. Space is lacking to recount the great deeds of the Arabs in Mesopotamia and other vast areas. For centuries they led the world in astronomy, mathematics, geography, and certain other sciences. In Jerusalem, almost at the beginning of their career, the superb Dome of the Rock, or great mosque on the site of the Jewish Temple, was erected by Omar, the second caliph. For six centuries the Arabs ruled Mesopotamia. In the early ninth century there was no richer region in the world. In the end, the Arab empire of Baghdad fell under the blows of other nomads, fresh from the desert or mountains. First came the Seljuk Turks, then Saladin from the wild Kurdish tribes of the Zagros Mountains, then the Mongols, and finally the nomadic Turks who treated the conquered people like sheep.

The list of kingdoms and empires founded by nomads from deserts or mountains might be much expanded. Egypt was ruled by several

[5] Vol. 1, p. 125.

[6] *Encyclopædia Britannica*, article on Zenobia.

dynasties of nomad origin, the first known to history being the Hyksos, or Shepherd Kings, who arrived as nomadic invaders from the east about 1800 B.C. and ruled for two centuries. Even on the south side of the great deserts, where the Sahara abuts against the grasslands of central Africa, desert nomads appear frequently to have imposed their rule on the sedentary people. A recent instance of this was the Fulahs, or Fulani, who a century or two ago established a kingdom in northern Nigeria. Race seems to make little difference in the character of nomadic invaders. Semites, Mongols, and so-called Aryans, such as the Persians, all behave in much the same way. Their character seems to depend on their habitat far more than on their race.

E. Strength and Weakness of Nomad Aristocracy

We may well inquire further into the nature of this constant repetition of movements from dry regions or from cold and rugged regions to lands where crops can readily be grown. Time and again the same history is repeated. The nomads, although few in number, have a warlike ability which enables them speedily to overcome the sedentary people. They establish themselves as an aristocracy which exploits the conquered groups. At the same time they rapidly absorb the culture of their subjects, who generally surpass them in craftsmanship, industry, commerce, art, and social organization. Great leaders and a supporting group of able men are present to an unusual degree among the nomadic overlords. They often lead a conquered country into an era of high development, marked by great achievements in architecture and along various other lines of effort. We know most about the architecture because it leaves lasting memorials. Such outbursts of progress may be called the fruit produced when a sedentary culture is fertilized by the genius of nomadic leadership and initiative. Such fruit is by no means the universal result of the intermarriage of the desert and the sown, nor does it last indefinitely. Not infrequently, however, the rule of nomadic kiths has been surprisingly prolonged, as in the case of Sargon's Akkadians, the Arab caliphate, and the Turkish Empire.

A nomad dynasty normally collapses because some stronger group arises. A ruling kith often deteriorates through luxury. Having all power in their hands and being no longer called upon for strenuous exertion as in the days of nomadism, the men give themselves up to feasting, wine, and women. Weakness also ensues because the luxurious life of women as well as men often reduces the birthrate so that the nomad stock dies out. Again, intermarriage may eliminate or dilute whatever characteristics of the nomads are hereditary in origin. Then, too, the removal of the selective power of the difficulties and dangers which kill off weaklings in deserts or mountains tends to dilute the desert strength.

The brilliant period which often occurs within a few generations after the establishment of a nomadic dynasty, or indeed of any other dynasty arising in a period of great stress, appears to depend on the common people as well as on the leaders. When both are vigorous, great things may be expected. After a nomadic conquest or other period of stress, the subject peoples recover strength. The war and commotion which normally precede and accompany a conquest by nomads tend to reduce the population. Deaths occur not only in war but in the accompanying famine, disease, and dislocation of population which are almost inevitable. Such disasters are often exaggerated by crop failures resulting from climatic conditions which also act powerfully to expel nomads from their homes. This kind of diminution of population helps the farmers, and these, as is well known, have till recently composed the great bulk of all sedentary populations. Because there are fewer people than before, the amount of land available per family is larger and the less fruitful fields need not be cultivated. A good example of this in the days of Akbar will be described later.

The prosperity arising from such a reduction in the density of population is more important than most people realize. Because we now live at the end of an age when new continents have been recently occupied, we overlook the fact that throughout most of human history all countries have normally contained about as many people as they could support at the stage of culture which had then been reached. In other words, at all times and places there is a powerful tendency toward population pressure. The birthrate so far exceeds the deathrate that there are more people than can be comfortable in a given area. Immigration of the quiet sort whereby people filter into a region from less favorable sections increases the pressure. Invasions, wars, famines, and epidemics, on the other hand, lessen it, because people die off or are forced to emigrate. Moreover, such periods of stress presumably kill off many weaklings, both physical and mental, among the sedentary population. Thus the common people who are ruled by an invading dynasty tend to be less numerous than formerly and also more prosperous and vigorous.

Suppose, now, that an able nomadic kith has established itself, and that a stormy period of physical, political, economic, and social disaster has at last come to an end, leaving a much diminished population living in peace. Many types of pressure will be reduced, and prosperity will normally ensue. Thus there arises a period when people are relatively well fed, healthy and contented. Taxes are paid with ease, and reforms can be carried out. If a strong ruler with the dominating ability which is so often characteristic of nomads is in power, he has the chance to do great things. Conditions of this sort apparently had much to do with the brilliant reigns of Kublai Khan, Akbar, and others.

F. The Heartland and Geopolitik

It may seem a far cry from the nomads of deserts to German ambition for world domination. Nevertheless, the effect of grasslands, deserts, and the nomadic life upon human character has a close connection with certain political ideas which, under the name of "geopolitics," played a considerable part in bringing on World War II. In 1904 Halford Mackinder, a Scotch geographer, laid the foundations of this Germanized form of political geography by setting forth an idea which he later expressed thus: "Who rules East Europe commands the Heartland; who rules the Heartland commands the World-Island; who rules the World-Island commands the World." The World-Island is the vast continent of Eurasia, to which Africa is attached as an appendage. The Heartland is the grasslands which extend from southeastern Russia to Mongolia and are the main home of pastoral nomads.

North of the Heartland from the Ural Mountains to the coast of Siberia the population has always been sparse. South of it lie deserts and mountains with other smaller grasslands on their flanks. To the northwest and west of the Heartland, however, lie the populous parts of Europe from western Russia and Scandinavia to Spain and Greece. A good imagination sees Europe linked with China and Manchuria by way of Turkey, Iraq, Iran, India, and Indo-China to form a vast inhabited crescent draped around the Heartland. Two outliers, Britain and Japan, are located close to this "Inner Marginal Crescent." Encircling the whole, the lands of the "Outer or Insular Crescent" include the Americas, the southern part of Africa, and Australia.

The idea of zones at varying distances from an Asiatic center is by no means fanciful. Matthew has shown that during a large part of geological time the Heartland, including the neighboring deserts and plateaus, has been the region of most rapid evolution among animals. From it has spread first one great type of mammal, such as the horse family, then another, such as the cat family, and so on through an astonishing number. Taylor [7] presents reasons for believing that human evolution has followed a similar course. The earliest types of men, low-browed and narrow-headed, apparently evolved somewhere on the south side of the Heartland before the Himalayas and Tibet had been upraised to their present height. In the course of time men of a new, more intellectual type arose there, with heads that exceeded those of their predecessors in height, width, or both. These new people presumably occupied the central grasslands. The more primitive type disappeared in the main area of evolution but persisted on the borders of the grasslands or perhaps migrated away from them. This process recurred time and again with successive types of human beings, who became progressively more highly developed until finally there arose in Central Asia the present broad-headed Mongolian and Turanian types. These, with their round heads, as we have seen, are believed by Taylor to represent the highest bodily type yet evolved. Be that as it may, there seems to be good evidence that the Heartland has been an area of uncommonly active evolution among both animals and man. It has been the center of a repeated outflow of new types. Even during the historic period a human outflow has occurred time and again, as has been evident in our account of Huns, Mongols, Manchus, and Arabs.

Mackinder, like many other students of history, is much impressed by the frequent recurrence of invasions of the well-inhabited lands of the "Inner Marginal Crescent" by nomads from the Heartland. The ancient Scythians of the Russian steppes and, still earlier, the Greeks themselves were such groups. The early Aryan invaders of India were another, and probably the original Chinese a third. Such invasions have set up disturbances which propagated themselves all over both Europe and Asia. Mackinder puts it thus:

For a thousand years (from the fifth to the sixteenth century A.D.) a series of horse-raiding peoples emerged from Asia through the broad interval between the Ural Mountains and the Caspian Sea, rode through the open spaces of southern Russia, and struck home into Hungary into the very

[7] 1921.

heart of the European peninsula, shaping by the necessity of opposing them the history of each of the great peoples around—the Russians, the Germans, the French, the Italians, and the Byzantine Greeks. That they stimulated healthy and powerful reaction, instead of crushing opposition under a widespread despotism, was due to the fact that the mobility of their power was conditioned by the steppes, and necessarily ceased in the surrounding forests and mountains.

According to Mackinder, much of modern history might be written as a commentary upon the changes directly or indirectly ensuing from the Huns under Attila, who established themselves in the plain of Hungary and dealt formidable blows northward, westward, and southward against the settled peoples of Europe. The pressure of Asiatic invasions may have driven the Angles and Saxons across the seas to found England; it united the Franks, Goths, and Romans on the battlefields of Châlons against the Asiatics, thus welding together modern France. According to Weigert's summary, "even the Papacy owed prestige to the successful mediation of Pope Leo with Attila at Milan. The Avars followed the Huns, and Austria was founded as a marchland against them; Vienna was fortified. Next came the Magyars, and their incessant raids from . . . Hungary increased the importance of [Vienna], thus drawing the political focus of Germany eastward to the margin of the realm."

Mackinder claims that a large part of history can be summed up in the one comprehensive idea of the influence of nomadic pressure from Asia upon Europe and upon Western civilization. The history of India, China, and even Japan has been similarly influenced, at least indirectly. Realizing thus the great significance of the inner grasslands of Asia, Mackinder jumped to the conclusion that throughout history the control of those lands has been the most vital element in controlling the agricultural regions round about and thus in controlling the world. Hence his statement that whoever controls east Europe controls the Heartland and hence controls the world.

This brings us to geopolitics and Germany. Mackinder's work had little influence in his own home. In this respect it was like that of Houston Chamberlain's glorification of the Nordics or Gobineau's attempt to prove that there are great innate differences among races. The work of all three men, however, found wide acceptance in Germany. Just as Gobineau, a Frenchman, and Chamberlain, an Englishman, led the way to the Aryan fallacy as to race, so Mackinder, a Scotchman, led the way to the similar fallacy as to the Heartland.

Major General Professor Doctor Karl Haushofer, as he likes to be called, became enamored of this fallacy. His writings did much to make it the accepted doctrine of the Junkers, the German army, and finally of Germany as a whole. This Bavarian with the Junker type of mind followed the unusual course of taking a doctorate in philosophy at the age of forty-two, after active army service, and of becoming a university professor at forty-nine, after serving in World War I. The final fruit of his teachings was a widespread German idea that the control of the Ukraine, the rest of southern Russia, and the neighboring parts of Asia was an essential prelude to world domination. Hitler adopted this idea. He expounds it in *Mein Kampf* and put it into bloody execution during the three fateful summers of 1941, 1942, and 1943. He and his Junker advisers rationalized this faith in the importance of the Heartland into the idea that southern Russia, with its iron, manganese, coal, oil, and wheat, would become a vast industrial region under German tutelage and that with its help Germany could overthrow the British Empire and rule the world. Although the basic idea of Mackinder and Haushofer is false, it has had a most impressive influence. In this respect it is like many other false ideas, such as those concerning race, demons, and the flatness of the earth.

In the light of our study of pastoral nomads it is easy to see how the major tenet of German geopolitics arose, and how the perversion of a fundamental truth led to strange consequences. The control of the Heartland is in itself of little significance in gaining control of the world. Acre for acre, even the best of the grasslands of eastern Russia and western Asia are scarcely half or even one third as productive as the arable land of Germany, the Low Countries, and northern France and England. Industrially the minerals of the Heartland, including the oil, are probably less valuable than the iron, coal, potash, and other minerals of western Europe. As for trade and transportation, the continental location of the Heartland and the enclosed nature of its bodies of water have long been great handicaps compared with the coastal location and oceanic harbors of the west.

In spite of all this there can be no denying that the inhabitants of the Heartland have exerted a remarkable effect upon history and have dominated the world to an astonishing degree. They have not done so, however, by virtue of mere temporary control of a particular region. The main factor that has given them their power is the innate character and closely knit democratic social system which normally develop when the same kith resides for many generations in steppes or mountains where the pastoral mode of life prevails. Hence possession of the Heartland is of little import. The vital condition is that people should possess the Heartland and follow its pastoral mode of life so long that the selective process has time to weed out the cowards and the unreliable and strengthen the qualities of courage, self-reliance, fidelity to comrades, and power of leadership.

G. Mobility and Nomadism's Dead Alley

The dominance of nomads as a group has probably come to an end. Individual nomads may leave their old life and become leaders in settled communities, but there is little prospect that the feats of the Arabs, Mongols, and Turks will ever be duplicated. One reason for this conclusion is that in modern times there has been a rapid acceleration in the rate of cultural progress among settled agricultural and commercial or industrial people in comparison with nomads. Until a few centuries ago the stage of culture in the better watered lands was such that the weapons and means of fighting among the settled people were about the same as those of the neighboring nomads. Hence when overpopulation, drought, ambition, or the desire for adventure made the nomads invade the settled lands, the inhabitants there possessed no special facilities that gave them an advantage over the nomads. Under such circumstances, personal character is of special importance, and the nomads almost invariably won.

This point becomes clear when we recall what has happened when the opposite conditions have prevailed, that is, when the settled people have had better weapons and better military organization than the nomads. For example, when Rome had a strong military frontier in Syria, Palestine, and North Africa, raids from the desert almost ceased. The same thing occurred in Palestine after World War I. Under the previous Turkish rule raids along the desert border had been frequent. Within a single month in the spring of 1909 the author met desert raiders four times.[8] One night he camped among the tall rushes near the mouth of the Jordan River within sound of an Arab party which had just driven off a herd of sheep and robbed the Jordan ferryman. A few days later the camels of his Arab host were driven off as already related. Next he and his student companion foiled an attempted

8 1911.

Arab hold-up by mere talk as they looked up at the gleaming barrels of rifles. And, finally, we saw in the distance a raiding band which had stripped a big party of villagers and wounded a Danish archaeologist. Nevertheless strong British rule after World War I soon made such adventures very rare, even though the conflict for irrigated land created great friction between the Arabs and the newly settled Jews. In the same way in India, England has largely, although not wholly, prevented the nomads of the mountainous deserts and grasslands of Afghanistan and Baluchistan from making raids except on a small scale.

Mobility is a factor which has not been sufficiently stressed in the preceding chapters. Their own mobility seems to have been a major factor in enabling nomads to conquer sedentary people. The present mobility of other people is equally important in bringing the nomad's type of culture to the dead end of a blind alley. In spite of their boldness and power of leadership, a few nomads could not regularly have conquered many times as great a number of settled people unless the nomads had been able to move rapidly. Before the days of gunpowder, and still more before the days of bows and arrows, a few horsemen armed with spears and swords were a match for many times their number of footmen. They had the immense advantage of being able to surprise the enemy by a sudden charge and then retreat quickly to a point of safety. The same group of horsemen could attack at different points in rapid succession. They could outflank the enemy and even swing around to his rear. Modern methods of warfare, however, by means of motorized artillery, tanks, and airplanes now put most of the agricultural peoples so far ahead of nomads that the chances of further nomadic conquests are almost nil.

Mobility by land, water, or air has always been a great asset in war. A new or more rapid mode of transportation almost invariably helps bring victory. Hannibal found this so when the elephants which he drove across the Alps frightened the horses of the Romans, but that advantage lasted only a short time. A far more significant advance in capacity for war and also for trade was associated with the development of transportation by water. The Cretans and Phoenicians spread their culture along the seacoast. Although we know little of their history, we are sure that they, too, could surprise the enemy and get away safely if the fight went against them. The Vikings are an outstanding example of a people possessing this ability. Like the nomads of the desert, these Norsemen, whose cousins settled

Iceland, had been through a severe process of selection. Sailing and fishing on stormy seas weed out the weaklings in much the same way as do migrations. Moreover, the Norsemen were the end product of long migrations before they appear in history. When we first hear of them they were impelled outward in much the same way as the desert nomads. The impelling forces included overpopulation, bad seasons for crops and fish, the lure of wealth in less rigorous climates, their own physical energy, their bold temperament, and also political and social disturbances at home. When they fared forth to plunder or conquer, their ships gave them an advantage in mobility like that which horses and camels gave to nomads. It was easy to swoop down unexpectedly upon some coastal town in Scotland, Ireland, or France. Moreover, it was easy to sail long distances, as far as Spain or even Sicily and Constantinople. It was also feasible to sail up rivers in comparative safety. Thus the Vikings of the Russ tribe entered Russia and gave their name to that great land. Mackinder makes frequent comparisons between nomadic pirates of the desert and nomadic pirates of the sea.

For many centuries the mobile people of the steppes had little contact with those of the sea. Mobility helped to give dominance to each in its own region. We have already seen frequent examples of this among nomads. The Greeks with their numerous settlements near the Mediterranean and Black seas are notable examples of the efficacy of transportation by water. So are Venice and Genoa with their far-flung medieval trade and influence. The effect of mobility by water found broad expression in the part played by Portugal, Spain, France, and Holland in the exploration, conquest, settlement, and colonial development of the New World. Its final outstanding expression is seen in the British Empire and the great English-speaking countries of America and Australasia.

During the past hundred years the mobility of nomads and even of seafarers has lost much of its old power to give dominance in trade, war, and politics. The obvious reason is the development of faster and more efficient means of transportation by land and finally by air. Railroads and motor cars bring to the interior many of the advantages of the seacoast so far as ease of movement is concerned. From the standpoint of speed they far surpass transportation by water. They are of very limited advantage, however, in steppes and deserts, simply because the population there is not dense enough to warrant large expense for the construction of railways and roads.

Thus these newer means of transportation bring increasing advantages to the parts of the earth where plains, fertile soil, mineral resources, and a climate good for both agriculture and man provide conditions favorable for a population that is both dense and prosperous. The advantages of the steppes in transportation have largely disappeared and those of coasts have become relatively less than formerly.

The airplane diminishes the advantages of steppes and coasts still further. From the standpoint of aviation it is actually a disadvantage for a city to be located beside a large body of water. To the aviator the water is merely something that has to be crossed instead of an area which can support people and provide materials for commerce. In this respect the relation of an ocean to airplanes is much the same as that of deserts or mountains to railroads and motor cars. In other words, the ocean is an area which entails expense because it must be crossed. Of course, the seacoasts still retain other advantages. They are usually more healthful than the neighboring interior regions. They also have the great advantage of transportation by water as well as by land. There is every reason to believe that for a long time such transportation will continue to be the cheapest way of carrying the heavier and more durable articles of commerce. Nevertheless, it is clear that the supremacy which transportation by water long enjoyed has now become a thing of the past. Mobility henceforth will vary from region to region in essentially the same way as progress in industry and wealth. Those regions which are most efficient in manufacturing and which have the greatest wealth per capita will be the ones in which the transportation of goods and people will be most highly developed. Such transportation is among the powerful factors in adding still more to a country's wealth and in giving it power in politics and in war.

In the light of all this, Mackinder's study of the Heartland assumes a new significance, and the German geopolitic founded upon it becomes still more clearly an illusion. The Heartland is indeed of the highest significance as a subject of historical study, but its significance lies in what it did to its inhabitants and their culture during the course of long centuries of nomadism. With the advent of gunpowder the advantages of the steppe-men as warriors began to disappear. With the advent of transportation by mechanical power those advantages became slight. Motor transportation and aviation have done away with almost the last traces of the old advantages. So far as nomads are innately endowed with valuable qualities, their advantage will continue. From the standpoint of war and political domi-nance, however, the sun of the nomads seems to be setting. Their culture has long been following a blind alley, and now that alley appears to be nearing a dead end. The same thing seems to be true of geopolitics and the Aryan cult of race, but political geography is more alive than ever.

CHAPTER 11

JUNKERS AND NAZIS

A. Junker Origins and Character

As a final example of the power of selection and isolation and of the kiths which thus arise, let us look at what many regard as the most disturbing element in the civilization of the first half of the twentieth century. In a previous chapter we saw the fallacy of the Nordic myth and of belief in a so-called Aryan race, but we did not investigate the secret of Germany's distinctive character. Every intelligent person knows that Germany has had a profound effect upon the entire world. Does the peculiarly militaristic nature of this effect have any biological basis, or is it due merely to a system of training which has gradually given the German people an almost unique character? Our study of kiths suggests that both biological inheritance and social organization enter into the matter. The Germans are far from being a separate race, but they have been dominated by a small microkith which apparently inherits certain distinct temperamental tendencies and intellectual capacities. Under this leadership the country has developed a social system with a strongly martial slant. The microkith which is mainly responsible for this is the Junkers, or old Prussian aristocracy, who comprise only a few thousand families but have had an influence far out of proportion to their numbers.

The term Junker means "jung herr" or "young gentleman." Originally in medieval times it was applied to the sons of the nobility who had not yet been dubbed knights. Then it gradually became the designation of the proprietors of large estates east of the Elbe River. It was especially appropriate there because this region, which was formerly Slavic, came under German control largely through the efforts of the sons (junge Herren) of nobility from other parts of Germany—young men "chosen for their knightly discipline and prowess at arms." The center of Junker development lay beyond the Vistula River in East Prussia. That region, some eight hundred years ago, was inhabited by a pagan Slavic population which made much trou-

208

ble for the Christian Germans farther west. Hence, when the Crusades were drawing to an end in Palestine, a movement arose for a crusade of another kind against the Slavic infidels of the eastern Baltic region. The Order of the Teutonic Knights was formed for this purpose. This order and the "junge Herren" who joined in its pious but rough "crusade," as Griswold says, gave rise to a "proud, medieval cult of virtue and the sword [which] has largely dominated Prussian politics since the thirteenth century, and through Prussia [has] profoundly influenced the whole course of German history."

The Junkers arose in the poorest part of Germany. East Prussia belongs to the east or northeast rather than the west of Europe. Geographically it is northeastern by reason of long, cold winters, poor soil, and an agriculture based largely on rye, oats, flax, and in our day potatoes, all of which yield relatively little per acre compared with the crops of western Germany. Culturally East Prussia is east European because of its vast landed estates, tilled by a mild, subservient peasantry. The estates are much like those that prevailed in Russia until the Revolution. They have been worked cheaply for centuries by peasants who were almost serfs or by poorly paid Slavic labor brought mainly from Poland.

In regions of this sort the contrast between a small, dominating minority and the mass of the population tends to be especially great so long as agriculture is the chief method of getting a living. In East Prussia and in neighboring regions east of the Elbe River, including West Prussia, Pomerania, and Brandenburg, this has continued to be true down to our own day. The submissiveness and poverty of the peasants have co-operated with the vigor and wealth of the Junkers to intensify the social contrast between the two groups and to make the Junkers more domineering. The peasants have always been poor, inert laborers. The Junkers, on the contrary, have either devoted themselves to managing their estates and living a gay life as hunters and country gentry, or else to serving their country in the army or as high officials. Other occupations have been regarded as unworthy. The contrast between Junkers and peasants stands out as a keynote in much of German history. It is quite different from the more democratic and much pleasanter relationship of social classes in south Germany, especially Bavaria.

The good qualities and high abilities of the Junkers must not be overlooked. Fay speaks of them as "experienced in war and efficient in administration, and possessed of a strong sense of duty and loyalty. From them came many of the generals and statesmen who helped to

make Prussia great in the past, and who have ever—even today under
Hitler—formed a dominating element in the German army."

Other writers speak similarly. Griswold says:

From the Teutonic Knights the Junkers inherited an austere, almost
ascetic, sense of duty (*Pflichtgefühl*), an acute consciousness of race and
class, and the professions of arms, government and husbandry. The Grand
Masters of the Teutonic Order presided over an elaborate, quasi-monastic
administration, which formed the earliest prototype of the Prussian bu-
reaucracy that Frederick the Great founded, staffed with Junkers, and be-
queathed to Bismarck and to Goering. The piety and stern devotion to
duty with which the Knights spread the gospel of Christianity and pan-
Germanism into eastern Germany were reflected in the careers of their
descendants who colonized the region and governed it. The early Hohenzollerns had to subdue a defiant nobility before they could rule in Brandenburg-Prussia, and only made their throne secure by taking the Junkers into
camp.

Griswold goes on to speak of the Junkers as "a caste imprisoned in
its own archaic economy and social system, a caste not lacking in
stern virtues and paternalistic enlightenment, but which, for all of
that, forms a source of the spirit that holds the German people down
and back. This is the spirit of feudalism; and feudalism and economic democracy and responsible self-government cannot exist side
by side."

B. Junker History

Let us briefly review the history of this Junker kith which has
played so noticeable a part in modern affairs. The Ascanian family
illustrates the early Junkers. Like other famous German families,
such as the Hohenzollerns, Hapsburgs, and Hohenstaufens, the Ascanians came from the rugged Black Mountains in Swabia, a region
which seems to have been particularly fertile in producing able people. From A.D. 1134 to 1320 the Ascanians held Brandenburg, of
which Berlin is the capital, making it an outpost against heathen
Wends and other Slavs. Like the Teutonic Knights, farther to the
northeast in East Prussia, they spent much of their time in rough
fighting with the heathen. They regarded themselves as crusaders
in the cause of Christianity, but their deeds had little relation to the
teachings of Christ. The rule of the Ascanians ended in the early
part of a century of dire confusion. Here, just as in China in this
same fourteenth century, crops were poor because of abnormally wet
or cold summers alternating with drought. Hunger, famine, war,

and pestilence stalked the land. That was the century of the most terrible famines ever experienced in many north European lands from England eastward. It was also the century of the terrible Black Death, which swept away from one tenth to one half of the population. Prussian land-owning families that survived this period emerged stronger than ever so far as dominance over the peasants was concerned. Although there are no records by which to test the matter, it appears probable that a second selective process was at work. The first selection, that of the original Junkers, was on the basis of migration and the accompanying spirit of adventure, fondness for war, and ability to lead. The second was a selection of those who, through capacity to dominate others, were able to maintain their favored position when society as a whole crumbled into dust.

After the worst of this period the Hohenzollerns came into power in Berlin in 1460 and later became kings of Prussia and emperors of Germany. There were also other additions to the Junkers, but all seem to have been of much the same type. Their descendants had to go through other periods that tried men's souls and tested their metal. Fay tells us that in the early seventeenth century, for example, "battle, murder, starvation, and suicide . . . swept away more than half the population of Brandenburg." Berlin's population fell from 14,000 in 1618 to 6,000 in 1640, that of Frankfurt-an-der-Oder from 12,000 to 2,000, and of Prenzlau on the Pomeranian frontier from 9,000 to 600. Great as was the suffering of the townspeople, that of the peasants was worse. They suffered not only from starvation and the ravages of war, but because their weakness and need gave the Junkers an opportunity to broaden and strengthen their control of the land. Such conditions, together with the previous extravagance of Joachim II, also enabled the Junkers to steal a march on the towns by gaining the almost exclusive privilege of selling agricultural produce, which means chiefly rye, oats, and flax.

All this chaos and disorder must have tended to eliminate Junker families which lacked the physical force and temperamental hardness required for preserving and improving their position. Unless a landowner was a good fighter and manager, and unless he worked hand in glove with his fellow-Junkers, he was likely to be dispossessed by someone who was more capable. Thus it happened that as time went on the cleavage between the forceful, dominating Junkers and the patient, submissive peasants became greater than in the rest of Germany. Many other aristocracies have arisen in the same way, but in few has the selection been more drastic because in few have the difficulties due to war, famine, and similar hardships been greater. Moreover, because of the separation between the Junkers, on the one hand, and both the peasants and the townspeople, on the other, and also because of the relative isolation of Junkerland, especially East Prussia, the amount of intermarriage of Junkers and others has been very slight for many centuries. Only recently have Junkers intermarried with rich merchant families, or even to any great extent with noble families from other parts of Germany, such as Bavaria.

One reason for the scarcity of outside marriages has been the desire to keep the landed estates intact. An interesting sidelight is shed on this by the special tax fund set up by Frederick William I to support his famous six-foot grenadiers. He allotted to this fund the sums paid for permission to marry within the prohibited degrees of relationship. The main payments apparently came from rich Junkers who wanted the privilege of marrying cousins. For hundreds of years such marriages have joined with other conditions in keeping the Junkers almost as isolated biologically as the Icelanders. Hence, if the original Junker nobles attained their position because of innate qualities different from those of the rest of the Germans, there has been the best of opportunity for those qualities to be passed onward unchanged. The situation is somewhat like that of the Parsis, although the original method of selection was different.

C. Military Might of the Junkers

With such a background it is not strange that in war, politics, and certain phases of economics the Junkers have been able to dominate the social evolution of Prussia and then of Germany. From the very beginning the Junkers have been conspicuous for personal bravery, warlike skill, and the ability to organize military operations. This ability was crystallized by the Great Elector of Brandenburg, Frederick William, as long ago as 1655, when he organized the first standing army. Strong armies, composed often of mercenaries, had existed long before. This, however, was the first army which remained steadily in training during peace as well as war. It was strong in part because it was officered almost entirely by Junkers who by both biological and social inheritance were warriors and looked upon war as the noblest of human occupations. Frederick William complained of the "officiousness" of the Junkers but chose practically all his officers from among them. His successors did likewise. In 1806, according to Griswold, more than 90 per cent of the seven or eight thousand Prussian officers of all ranks were nobles, most of whom were real Junkers. In 1861, after the liberalizing reforms of Stein, five sixths of the officers with the rank of major or higher and all of the thirty-three highest generals were nobles.

Griswold [1] goes on to say that

the needs of a mass army forced the late Kaiser both to recruit officers wholesale from the bourgeoisie and, as is well known, to encourage the impecunious aristocrats in his officer corps to marry into prosperous commercial families. . . . This process substantially altered the proportions of Junkers to commoners, as did the great blood-letting and blood-mixing of the First World War. Even so, although the Nazi political machine has brought some commoners [like Rommel] to the top, the high command has remained a Junker stronghold. Von Brauchitsch, von Bock, von Rundstedt, von Reichenau, von Arnim, von Kleist, von Mannstein, first families of East Elbian Germany, [fought] Hitler's war against Russia.

A man who has in his hand a good instrument itches to use it, regardless of whether it is a golf club, a car, or an army. He is especially eager to use it if he believes that it is the best of its kind. Such an instrument in the hands of Frederick the Great, for example, enabled him to hold his own among the great empires that surrounded him. Able as he was, it would have been foolhardy for him to attack Austria in 1740 and seize Silesia in the War of the Austrian Succession, if it had not been for the standing army established by his great-grandfather, together with the capable Junker officers who helped both grandfather and grandson. A little later the fighting spirit of the Junkers, together with the army, was a decisive factor in leading Prussia to embark on the successful Seven Years' War and then to share in the partition of Poland. In the nineteenth century similar conditions precipitated wars with Austria and France. Finally, in our own day, the warlike spirit of the Junkers and their confidence in the perfect instrument of their army have played a vital part in bringing on two great world wars.

In view of this it is not strange that many people regard all Germans, or at least all Prussians, as by nature uncommonly warlike and dangerous, a biological menace to the rest of the world. Many people, however, dispute this view. They admit that many Germans, especially Prussians, have the spirit which has long made Germany Europe's greatest political and military threat. They claim, however, that this circumstance arises largely from economic and geo-

[1] pp. 7–8.

graphic misfortunes, coupled with faulty education and mistaken ideals. Here is the way they often put it. One has only to travel in Germany to see that most Germans are just ordinary people like Americans or English. Millions who have migrated to the United States are highly esteemed there. American-born children of German descent are as good citizens as those of British or Scandinavian descent. If Americans were subjected to the training which prevails in Germany, they would show the same military nature as the Germans. According to those who support this cultural view of German national character, it is unscientific to fasten the sins of the leaders upon the people as a whole. If Germany today could have a democratic type of education with emphasis upon social service and international cooperation, the German military spirit would disappear. Germany would cease to be a political menace.

The theory of kiths set forth in this book stands midway between the extreme biological view and the extreme cultural or sociological view just presented. It recognizes that biological inheritance is a real and important factor and that selection and isolation may endow a certain group of people with distinctive innate qualities which persist indefinitely. It also recognizes that diverse cultural or geographical conditions may produce radically different results, even when they act upon people with precisely the same biological inheritance. Hence when we say that the Junkers are a microkith of an especially warlike type, it does not mean that they are biologically destined to be soldiers. It merely means that if the course of history has led to emphasis on war, the Junkers will fit into the picture unusually well. Under other conditions they might fit equally well into some other picture in which their truly valuable qualities would be a blessing instead of what other nations regard as a curse.

The core of the German problem seems to be that for centuries Prussia, Brandenburg, and finally all Germany have been dominated by the small, but well-defined and competent, microkith of the Prussian Junkers. There is no direct proof that the Junkers as a group possess any distinct innate qualities or capacities different from those of other Germans, but there is considerable probability of this. Physically they are mainly of the tall, blond Nordic type, but their mental traits appear never to have been measured separately from those of other Germans. For centuries they have had success in their efforts to maintain their position, and that in itself seems to indicate innate capacity. Their activities have certainly been directed along definite channels which are appropriate to the kind of temperament which they seem to inherit. The growth of the army illustrates this. It is also certain that if other conditions, geographical, economic, and historical, had been different, the Junker kith might never have arisen, or might have disintegrated long ago. It might also have turned its energies in some other direction, as did the Parsis and Icelanders. Such qualities as efficiency and energy in administration and a strong sense of duty and of loyalty to their leaders are just as valuable in business as in war.

D. Other Fields of Junker Dominance

In politics, the second of their three main fields of activity, the Junkers have been as dominant as in war. Through skillful political maneuvering as well as warlike prowess, the little Brandenburg domain of the Hohenzollerns gradually expanded until Prussia, its modern representative, dominated the German Empire. Before the German Empire was organized in 1870 Prussia, with Berlin as its capital, controlled approximately three fourths of the states that later made up Germany, and this domination continued unchanged until World War II. At the outbreak of World War I Emperor William was more powerful as king of Prussia than as emperor of Germany. He and a Prussian Diet, composed mainly of Junkers, were in complete control not only of the real Prussia, which consists of poor Junker provinces in the northeast, but of the expanded Prussia comprising the whole of northern and western Germany. They were so powerful that they could also control the main political affairs of the rest of Germany, including Bavaria. The natural result was that at that time, even more than in earlier days, Junkers held most of the high political positions in the German Empire. At the end of World War I the Junkers greatly feared that the old political system within Germany would be broken up. If the allies had marched into Berlin and taken a hand in organizing a new government, each German state or principality might have been allotted a degree of political power proportional to its population. No such change occurred. The Weimar Republic was not a real federation of German states. It merely took a new name and perpetuated the old system of Prussian preponderance with all that this meant in the way of Junker dominance.

After World War I Hitler was able to rise to power only through co-operation with such Junkers as old General von Hindenburg. Throughout his regime they continued to control the army and most of the high political offices. Their ideas helped Hitler, but many people believe it would be more nearly correct to say that Hitler at first was permitted to gain power because his ideas helped the Junkers. The problem of race, for example, illustrates this. At the end of the last century, it suited the tall, blond Nordic Junkers to have Houston Chamberlain preach that practically all the world's great achievements were the result of Nordic blood. The later Nazi doctrine of an Aryan race satisfied them equally well. It left them their Nordic pride and at the same time gave the rest of the Germans something that served as a rallying cry to strengthen the army and the national spirit. Hitler's dreams of world conquest did not disturb the Junkers. Such dreams were not new. The pride of the Junkers in their army and their military and political might had already aroused in many, perhaps most of them, the eager desire to outdo Britain in building a world empire. That was what William II wanted in World War I.

The main point where Hitler and the Junkers parted company was in the speed with which Germany should move to attain its prospective glorious place in the sun. One group of Junkers, however, as Dorpalen well explains, agreed with Hitler in urging a prompt war. It had its way. Another party, influenced greatly by the "geopolitik" of General Haushofer, wanted to wait a decade or two or even longer. It had become convinced that the nation which controls the "Heartland" controls the world. These Junkers thought that in due time this Heartland, which to them meant mainly a part of the USSR, would develop into a great industrial region rivalling the United States. While that development was going on, they wanted Germany gradually to increase its influence there. Then, when the time was ripe, they thought that Germany could wrest from England the dominance of the world. The Russian Heartland, they believed, would serve them as a great arsenal from which to draw the sinews of war and also as a great ally, just as the United States had served Britain in World War I and was likely to do again when the second world war broke out. Hitler, however, and the Junkers who held with him moved too fast, with results that are known to all. As World War II dragged to its weary close, the great aim of the more conservative Junkers became peace without victory—a negotiated peace, which would leave Germany unchanged in its internal political structure. Only thus could they hope that the power of the Junkers would survive.

We come now to the economic phase of Junker strength. We have seen that in medieval times the Junker landowners were enabled to enrich themselves by putting restrictions on the privilege of selling agricultural products. Even if a peasant had land of his own, he was forced to sell his surplus products to his landlord. Merchants in the cities were not allowed to deal in grain, or at least not in a way that would impair the profits of the Junkers. In course of time these crude regulations were altered, but the alternations still reacted in favor of the Junkers. In later times the chief methods of favoring them have been heavy import duties on cereals, the entailment of estates, and a system of agricultural credits. Tariff duties have kept prices so high that until recently the large estates of northeastern Germany enriched their owners even though the yield per acre was small and the profits of agriculture declined. For example, in February, 1935, Australian wheat was selling in London for eight gold francs a quintal, whereas native German wheat, probably of poorer quality, was selling in Berlin for twenty-five. At that same time imported rye entered Hamburg at seven francs a quintal, but when customs duties and other expenses were added, the price became twenty-two francs in Berlin. Oats cost twice as much in Berlin as in Paris. In Antwerp Danubian barley, brought across Germany and down the Rhine, cost only half as much as native barley in Berlin. Junker landowners with large estates and many tenants in northeastern Germany were the chief beneficiaries of these high prices which the rest of the Germans had to pay for their main food supply.

The practice of entailing estates comes down from the Middle Ages. It provides that landed property cannot be sold and must go only to the legitimate heirs of the owner. It prevents large estates from being broken up and encourages the marriage of cousins. Thus it tends to preserve old conditions unchanged and to keep the Junkers in their position of dominance. In 1919, according to Griswold, there were 2,314 entailed estates in Germany, mostly east of the Elbe. Their average size was about 3,700 acres, or roughly 6 square miles. The Nazis undertook to get rid of these, but in 1938 there still remained 910 with an even larger average size than before. One of these was the estate given to von Hindenburg as a present. Still later further attempts were made to break up the estates, but their effect was largely nullified by providing a new method of insuring the ownership of land and of granting financial credits to "a new nobility of blood and soil" which includes the old Junkers. In spite of this, however, the general depression of agriculture had seriously curtailed the wealth of the Junkers by the time of World War II.

Hand in hand with their prolonged dominance in the army, in politics, and in wealth has gone supremacy of the Junkers in education. This does not mean that they have been teachers or have been highly educated. A good number, to be sure, have been university graduates and men of high intellectual ability. Far more, however, have gone to military schools, in which, according to some, the standards are lower than in universities because the students are of a less intellectual type. The influence of the Junkers on education has been exercised largely through official channels. This became well known to all the world during the Hitler regime, but the same conditions prevailed earlier, although to a less extreme degree. The Junkers have learned a great lesson: if you want people to believe something, teach them while they are children. Only with the utmost difficulty can most people overcome the deeper impressions of early childhood. Thus in the last analysis it seems that one of the great factors in giving Germany its warlike character and aggressive temperament has been the clannish persistence of the Junker kith with its control over education as well as over the army, the government, and landed wealth.

In summation, then, we find that Germany supplies an outstanding example of the importance of kiths. Starting with a process of drastic selection in a rough, warlike age, the Junker microkith has preserved both its biological and social entity for many centuries. The ability of its members has enabled them to retain and increase the rights and privileges acquired by their fathers. Initiative, persistence, and intelligence in high degree have been devoted to the preservation of a military, political, and social system which has lent itself to the glorification of war and race. There seems, however, to be no biological reason why abilities such as those of the Junkers should always be turned in those directions. A properly federated Germany might benefit from the real abilities of the Junkers without the dangers of a military, political, economic, and educational system aimed at the preservation and glorification of this one social group.

E. Kiths and the Philosophy of History

In these chapters on heredity as a factor in civilization we have seen that comparatively little importance attaches to race as the word is commonly understood. Such racial groups as "whites," Alpines, and Negroids do indeed possess a certain unity in head form, complexion, and shape of features. Mentally, however, there is no such unity. It is probably true that on the whole certain innate capacities and aptitudes are more common in one race than another. High sensitivity to musical pitch, for example, appears to be more common among Negroes than among whites, whereas whites, on the whole, probably have a greater percentage of persons with high powers of self-control. Nevertheless, the greater part of what is often called racial character is the result of physical environment and stage of cultural progress. It was formerly supposed that innate racial traits are immutable except through definite mutations or racial mixture. We know now, however, that certain of the supposedly most stable characteristics, such as head form and the proportions of the bony skeleton, may vary under the impact of new environments.

This shift of emphasis away from old ideas of race does not mean, as some suppose, that heredity is unimportant, either physically or mentally. If the environment, both physical and cultural, remains stable and there is no mutation or mixture of other groups, the same innate traits of both body and mind are apparently passed on unchanged for untold generations. This is seen in the persistence with which the Parsis, Icelanders, and Junkers, for example, have retained their fundamental ability and temperament for many centuries.

Within kiths, as well as races, the type and degree of innate mental capacity of individuals vary enormously. Unless a person is born with musical genius, good training will never produce a Beethoven; before the hard knocks of life can shape him into a glorious leader, a Lincoln must be born with exalted capacities for sound judgment, self-control, and persistence. The rarity of such geniuses makes it almost impossible for them to mate with their kind. Even if this were possible, the laws of heredity would cause most or all of the children to be far less talented than the parents. Nevertheless—and here is the crucial conclusion which many people fail to appreciate and some dispute as erroneous—if a considerable group of men and women are selected because of strongly marked innate traits, such as the power of self-control, their children as a group will show a high degree of the same traits, although not so high as the parents. If such a group is completely isolated, either physically or socially, and there is no further selection, future generations will continue indefinitely to differ from the unselected ancestral stock. If the same selective process continues for generation after generation, the type originally selected will become more firmly established and even strengthened.

A rough approximation to such fixation seems to have occurred among Icelanders, pastoral nomads, and Quakers.

As a result of these biological processes innate differences in temperament, intellect, and special talents disclose an almost infinite series of gradations. The variation in the strength of these differences is evident when we examine population units of four major grades, namely, individuals, kiths, nations, and races. Innate mental differences reach their acme when individuals such as Alexander, Aristotle, Darwin, Gandhi, Jesus, Newton, Shakespeare, and Zoroaster are compared with the common herd. The specific line of effort along which each man works is largely determined by his training and the cultural conditions of his times. The energy with which he works is greatly influenced by physical conditions such as disease, climate, and diet as well as by innate bodily constitution. The basic mental capacity for the task, however, is primarily a matter of innate endowment. All this is now so generally accepted that a whole school of historians centers its work on "the great man in history."

The importance of kiths, unlike that of individuals, is only beginning to be appreciated. A notable kith, such as the Jews, to be sure, is universally recognized as a powerful historical factor. Nevertheless, kiths as a biological, social, and historical type have largely been neglected. In this book we have discussed a few, such as the Icelanders, Newfoundlanders, Puritans, Junkers, Quakers, Mongols, Parsis, and Hakkas. Many others are equally distinct and important, for example, Hittites and Spartans; Highlanders of Scotland, Kentucky, Nepal, or Kenya; Sicilian villagers, Picts, Angles, and Normans; and such groups as the Walloons of Belgium, the French-speaking Swiss, the Irish and German colonists who hold aloof from the mixed Portuguese-Negro kith of Brazil as a whole.

Kiths vary greatly in size, permanence and degree of separation from the surrounding people. Outstanding examples of small kiths include the royal families of Europe, the patricians of old Rome, and the ancient, self-contained aristocracy of Athens, which for centuries prohibited its women from marrying outsiders. Such small kiths may well be called microkiths. Larger groups, such as the Rumanians, Prussians, or English, are macrokiths. These larger groups are often nations, although a normal kith rarely constitutes a nation. As kiths increase in size, innate qualities which distinguish them from other kiths become less evident. Almost every nation comprises many microkiths and often many kiths. Even though these have distinct innate qualities at first, the majority may intermarry so that the nation as a whole tends toward a certain average level. Then, too, a nation may contain so great a diversity of occupations and habitats that it has no uniform set of selective factors which help to preserve similar traits among all the inhabitants.

Enlarging our horizon beyond individuals, kiths, and nations, we come to races in the old sense of the word. They are so vast and comprise so many highly varied and greatly intermixed kiths and nations that hereditary mental characteristics sufficiently distinct to set them apart are scarcely discernable, except perhaps among backward types such as the Australian aborigines. Thus, although race has played a great part in history, the moving force has been the *idea* of racial superiority rather than any actual differences other than those due to environment or to dominant kiths. A true interpretation of history will recognize the reality of innate differences. It will also recognize that such differences decrease in importance from individuals to microkiths and then to kiths, nations, and finally races. As the importance of the inheritance of mental qualities decreases in this series, that of both physical and cultural environment increases.

F. The English-Speaking Macrokith

In this study of the genetic factor in history we have emphasized the selection due to migration and religion, but other conditions are likewise important. Inventions and discoveries, for example, may cause one group of people to decline and another to increase. The progress of navigation and modern machinery has drastically altered the relative numbers of Australian aborigines in comparison with the English-speaking macrokith. One Australian kith, the Tasmanians, has disappeared. The main aboriginal kith has scarcely held its own during the last century and a half.

The contrast between such aborigines and the huge macrokith of English-speaking people is impressive.

In 1600, according to Garvin's penetrating analysis, the English-speakers numbered about five and a half million; the French-speakers, sixteen million. Today the English-speakers number more than two hundred million and the French-speakers only forty-five million. Part of the ancestry of the present English-speakers, to be sure, is derived from other kiths; but, even so, the biological types represented by the British Isles have increased thirty-fold, whereas the French type has increased only three-fold. Still more extraordinary examples are furnished by Java and New England. In 1800 before new European methods of agriculture, transportation, government, industry, and medicine had reached Java, the population of that island was about three million. The new methods have led to such an increase of productivity and such a saving of life that the population has increased nearly fifteen-fold, whereas that of neighboring New Guinea has apparently remained almost stationary.

New England illustrates an even more remarkable change in about the same length of time. Up to 1650 that region had received about twenty thousand immigrants, mainly English and almost entirely from the British Isles. In 1790 with only an insignificant amount of further immigration, the population had increased to almost exactly one million, a fifty-fold expansion in a century and a half. During that same period the American Indians of New England, who were probably as numerous as the English population in 1650, actually declined. Such figures represent enormous and rapid changes in two of the fundamentals of civilization, namely, the biological composition of the world's population and the relative proportions of that population living in the various stages of culture and progress. The historical effect of such changes is almost incalculable.

G. The Kithal Theory

In this attempt at an analysis of the genetic factor in history we have emphasized migration rather than other kinds of selection merely because in migrations the selective process occurs so rapidly that its effects can readily be seen. Other types of selection, however, must not be overlooked. Some arise in the realm of health. Immunity to disease, especially to newly introduced diseases, such as measles in Borneo, may mean that people with certain mental as well as physical traits stand an especially good chance of survival. The introduction of new weapons may mean that people with alert minds and with bodies well adapted to the use of such weapons survive at the expense of others who may have more desirable qualities in other respects. A new ideal as to feminine beauty may gradually eliminate types that depart too widely from it, but may also lead to harmful conditions such as foot-binding or waspish corseted waists which diminish the fertility of those among whom they prevail. We know little of the real effect of such selection. The problem has been scarcely studied except in respect to migration. That is one reason why migration is given so prominent a place in this book.

Inasmuch as both the physical and cultural environments generally change rapidly at times of migration, the genetic factor is also more likely to change at such times than at others. Special qualities are required in order to meet the changing circumstances of a difficult migration. People must be strong physically, they must be adaptable and far-sighted, and they must have a relatively optimistic attitude. Otherwise, they generally refrain from such migration or fail if they attempt it. Even if people who lack the necessary qualities begin to migrate, they are likely to stop before going far or to go back to the place whence they came. The result is that people who have endured long and difficult migration tend to be much alike regardless of the stock from which they spring.

Nomads have much of the migrant quality because their hard life weeds out the physical weaklings and those whose temperament departs too far from the kind needed for their particular physical environment and mode of life. Thus nomad kiths tend to have qualities of leadership and warlike ability which have given them an historical influence far out of proportion to their numbers. On the contrary, in regions from which too many migrants have gone out the people often lack energy, foresight, and initiative. An extreme case of this kind is seen in the subnormal villages of north China. Mild examples may perhaps be found in such groups as the villages of southern Italy, where prolonged intermarriage, according to Gini,[2] has given all the inhabitants approximately the same genetic composition and much the same character. Ireland's peculiar political attitude in recent times may be in part the result of the emigration of great numbers of the more active and adaptable people. The vital element of this study is the idea that selective processes are constantly at work, differentiating one set of people from another and entrenching or eliminating cultural traits.

According to the interpretation set forth in these chapters, the world has seen many experiments in eugenics. Time after time an unconscious selection along seemingly eugenic lines has isolated and preserved people with decidedly more than average ability, and these have contributed greatly to the advancement of civilization. Time after time something of quite a different kind has also happened. The removal of the more energetic, intelligent, and forceful individuals has caused a region to be populated by relatively ineffective human types. Sometimes the spread of civilization has permitted an

[2] 1912.

enormous multiplication of population, as in Java and India, without regard to the innate quality of the people or the stage of their culture. Under still other circumstances, as in Iceland, the harshness of the environment has prevented the increase of what seem to be highly desirable types. Sometimes also the prompt intermarriage of a desirably selected type with unselected types has neutralized the selection and prevented results that might have been highly valuable. All such conditions have a definite eugenic bearing. They are parts, so to speak, of a vast experiment which nature has been carrying on for untold thousands of years. Now at last man has become conscious of his ability to control, or at least modify, his own biological quality. He has seen clearly that want, misery, disease, and backwardness are favored by the existence of people with low innate capacities or by the presence of too dense a population composed of people with ordinary capacities. In this book we have seen something of the selective processes by which the innate qualities of human groups are actively being altered. If good as well as bad results can be produced through the haphazard selection of migration or of occupations such as pastoral nomadism, it seems as though the favorable types of selection might be encouraged and the unfavorable ones discouraged under intelligent human direction. Hence the most important result of this whole study is that it helps to point the way toward new lines of eugenic investigation. Through these we may hope to learn more about the methods that will work best in preventing the undue multiplication of biologically inferior types of men and in increasing the number of individuals of those types which foster the upward march of civilization.

PART III

PHYSICAL ENVIRONMENT AND HUMAN ACTIVITY

CHAPTER 12

THE GEOGRAPHIC PATTERN OF CIVILIZATION

A. Measures of Civilization

Having devoted Part I of this book to the forward march of civilization and Part II to the influence of heredity upon that march, we are ready to devote Part III to the corresponding influence of physical environment. Our first objective will be to examine the geographical pattern of civilization. Then we shall inquire how that pattern is related to the earth's physical features, especially climate, and to the distribution of plants, animals, and men. As a basis for such an inquiry we need a map of civilization. As yet, to be sure, we have no reliable means of measuring civilization as a whole, but for many of its important phases exact facts are available. Demography, for instance, provides data concerning births, marriages, deaths, and the distribution of population. We have widespread statistics as to health, disease, and medical care. Vast masses of facts are available concerning agriculture, diet, housing, industry, transportation, trade, inventions, machinery, science, education, art, religion, crime, war, politics, and philanthropy.

Hundreds of items belonging to these various phases combine to constitute civilization. Diverse civilizations rarely differ because any one of the main phases is absent in some and present in others. They differ mainly because the same kind of item is present in different degrees or qualities. Thus the geographic pattern of civilization is set largely by the way in which a host of items vary from place to place. Fortunately for our purposes there is considerable agreement in the distribution of many of the main items. For example, essentially the same geographic distribution prevails in (a) the percentage of time and income given to charitable, philanthropic, or public service activitics, (b) average amount of formal education, and (c) the use of machines or electricity.

A review of the geographical distribution of certain phases of civilization in the United States by means of maps will illustrate what has just been said. The United States is excellent for this purpose. In no other country are uniform and reliable statistics available for so large a population distributed over so wide an area with such variety of geographical environment. The general type of culture is everywhere similar in spite of isolated pockets. On the whole, too, the population is fairly homogeneous, although Negroes and immigrants introduce disturbing factors. Such divergencies in both culture and race blur the broad geographic pattern less than might be supposed. Typical maps show that in general a basic pattern seems to be set by man's physical efficiency. Efficiency in turn appears to be especially influenced by climate, diet, density of population, and disease.

Few items of civilization are distributed in harmony with any one of these four factors or even with the combined effect of all of them. This is to be expected, for the distribution of almost every major human activity is affected by physical factors such as rainfall, minerals, and vegetation, by racial and cultural complications arising from migrations or differential birthrates, by occupations, customs, and practices which have grown up locally, and by outstanding individuals who happen more or less accidentally to live in some particular region. Nevertheless, although such conditions often introduce conspicuous features peculiar to some special aspect of civilization, a basic geographical pattern can generally be detected. It is like the sky, sea, land, or forest in the background of a painting. People or animals may be conspicuous in the picture, the sky may be dotted with flying birds, and the land starred with flowers. Nevertheless, the main background is plainly evident.

All this will become clear as we examine maps which illustrate variations in the intensity of diverse types of items within the United States. In the majority of cultural qualities southern New England and New York tend to be near one extreme. For example, they have many libraries and few farmers. Accordingly, on our maps, unless otherwise stated, this extreme is heavily shaded, and the opposite extreme is light. Heavy shading does not invariably indicate either good or bad conditions. It may represent a low infant deathrate or good school facilities; it may also indicate a high deathrate from cancer, a high percentage of mortgages, or a relatively large number of people without definite church affiliations.

B. Two Maps of Social Progress

Let us begin with maps of definite items which are easy to understand. Scores of others would give essentially the same result. The number of persons per room in dwelling houses is a good indication of the general social and economic level of the occupants. Something is generally wrong if there are decidedly more people than rooms in a house. Nevertheless, such overcrowding prevails locally in all parts of the United States. Figure 18 shows the percentage of dwellings with more than three people for every two rooms.* The darkest shading shows that from New England and New Jersey westward along the Great Lakes to the Mississippi River or beyond, less than five per cent of the dwellings have more than one and a half persons per room. Surrounding this area and on the West Coast there are regions which are only a little less favorable. On the other hand, in the South Atlantic and South Central states overcrowding rises to a fairly high level, with percentages above 20 in South Carolina and Alabama. Rather poor conditions extend far north in the Rocky Mountain region and there is a suggestion of the same thing in the Appalachians. Florida, on the contrary, appears better off than its neighbors farther north.

Many readers will endeavor to find a separate explanation for each main feature of the map. Overcrowding will probably be ascribed to Negroes in the South Atlantic area, for example, and to Mexicans in New Mexico and Arizona. The lower degree of overcrowding in Florida than in Alabama and Georgia will be attributed to the presence of northerners. There is truth in these statements, but let us examine the actual extent of Negro influence. Figure 18 shows that overcrowding in Kentucky (18 per cent) is almost as great as in Mississippi (19.2 per cent), but Negroes form less than 8 per cent of the population in Kentucky and close to 50 per cent in Mississippi. Again, although Massachusetts has three to twelve times as high a percentage of Negroes as Idaho, Wyoming, or Utah, its overcrowding

* In order to eliminate the effect of urban as contrasted with rural communities, the percentages of overcrowding among (a) urban, (b) rural non-farm, and (c) rural farm populations have been taken separately for each state and then averaged.

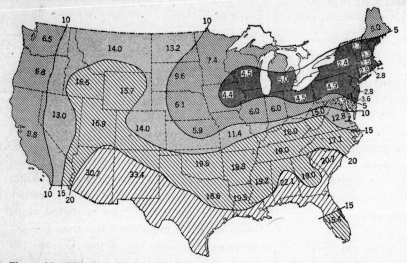

Figure 18. The Crowding of Dwellings. Percentage of dwellings with more than 1.5 persons per room, 1940. Heavy shading indicates good conditions, i.e., little crowding. Note the resemblance between this map and Figure 28.

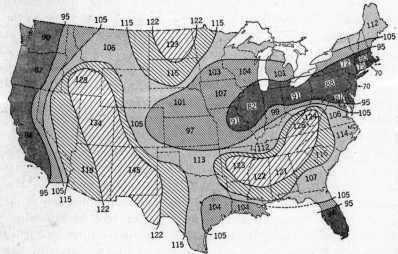

Figure 19. Net Reproductive Rate of White Population of the United States, 1940.

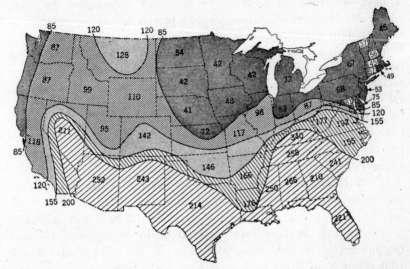

Figure 20. Homicides of Whites per 100,000 White Males Aged 21 Years or More, 1937–40.

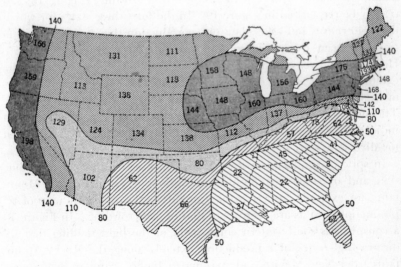

Figure 21. Economic and Social Prosperity in the United States (based on data of Thorndike and of Angoff and Mencken).

is only one sixth as great as theirs. The correlation coefficient (.45 ± .08) between overcrowding and percentage of Negroes is significant, but it indicates that only about 20 per cent of the resemblance between these two variables is due to a common cause.* This does not mean, however, that the overcrowding is due to the innate racial traits of Negroes. The overcrowded regions may possess physical or cultural qualities which lead to overcrowding regardless of the color of the population. The fact that Kentucky and Oklahoma have much overcrowding and relatively few Negroes suggests that this last supposition is true, but the possibility that some racial condition connected directly with Negroes also plays a part is not excluded.

For further light on the relative importance of race, place, and culture in setting a geographical pattern such as that of overcrowding, let us examine a different kind of map based only on white people. Figure 19 shows how far white births depart from the number needed to maintain the population at the 1940 level. Rhode Island and New Jersey have a birthrate only 70 per cent as great as is needed for this purpose; in Utah the corresponding percentage is 134 and in New Mexico 145. In spite of pronounced differences in detail, the main features of the map of overcrowding (Figure 18) can readily be recognized in Figure 19. In the forty-three states for which the 1940 census publishes data on reproduction the correlation coefficient between overcrowding and net rate of reproduction is .75. Hence these two variables agree in geographical distribution to the extent of about 56 per cent (the square of .75). There is nothing remarkable about this, for large families cause crowding everywhere. The noteworthy point is that overcrowding and reproduction both indicate that broad underlying causes set the geographical pattern for diverse aspects of civilization.

In spite of similarity in their main features the maps of reproduction and overcrowding both show distinctive peculiarities. Mountains, for example, appear to be a modifying factor in the map of reproduction, just as are Negroes in that of overcrowding. In Figure 19 a conspicuous southwestern embayment of the light shading that indicates high rates of reproduction extends along the Rocky Mountains from New Mexico and Arizona to Idaho. Similar shading extends along the Appalachian Mountains from West Virginia to Ala-

---

* This figure is based on the standard mathematical principle that the percentage of agreement between any two variables is equal to the square of their correlation coefficient, or in this case .45 × .45 = .2025.

bama and Mississippi. Its westward swing into Arkansas brings the rugged Ozark Mountains into the area of largest families. Isolation and the predominance of rural life are doubtless the intermediaries through which mountains encourage large families. The Dakotas have large families for similar reasons. Relative dryness, vast plains, and scarcity of conditions favorable for cities cause the population to be sparsely scattered on big farms, and such conditions encourage large families.

On the other hand, on seacoasts families tend to be smaller than farther inland. This is evident from New England all the way to Texas and again on the West Coast. Harbors, commerce, and the consequent growth of industries and cities are doubtless intermediaries through which seacoasts influence the size of families. Thus, although the main features of the maps of overcrowding and reproduction still remain unexplained, we have found evidence of the influence of (1) an hereditary factor (Negroes and Mexicans); (2) at least three types of physical factors—mountains, dry plains, and seacoasts; and (3) cultural conditions, such as agriculture, commerce, industry, and the contrasted habits of sparsely populated rural communities and crowded cities.

C. A Map of Self-Control

As a further step toward understanding the general geographical pattern of civilization, let us examine another type of regional difference. Homicide, including unpremeditated as well as meditated manslaughter, is a sign of two great weaknesses. One is lack of self-control among individuals. The other is the failure of public opinion, and hence of law and government, to protect human life. Figure 20 shows that the average annual number of homicides per million adult white men varies from 37 in Vermont to more than 200 in practically all southern states and 340 in Kentucky. To what is this due? Is Vermont's high standing due to religion? Can the opposite condition in Kentucky be ascribed to race? No one would deny the importance of these factors. Religious people rarely commit murder. Among Negroes in the United States homicide is about ten times as frequent as among whites. But is Vermont any more religious than the "Bible Belt," where Kansas has relatively twice as many white homicides as Vermont and Missouri three times as many? Is the murderous tendency of the Negroes due to an innate racial lack of self-control? It is true that the correlation coefficient between homicide and the percentage of Negroes stands at .87, which means a 75 per cent agreement between the two, but this may be due mainly to the poor conditions under which the whites oblige the Negroes to live. A third factor may also play a part. Human conduct may vary according to the place where it occurs, as well as according to the biological inheritance and cultural surroundings of the people.

Homicide shows a significant relation to temperature both geographically and seasonally. Vermont, which is one of the coldest states, sets the best record, and all northern states make a good showing in comparison with those far to the south. As one goes from Maine and Vermont southward near the Atlantic Coast the number of homicides per million inhabitants, when both whites and Negroes are included, runs as follows: (18), 15, 16, 19, (17), 22, 44, (37), 92, (75), 133, (118), 153, 215, and 250. The departures from a steady upward progression are indicated by parentheses. Seasonally, as well as geographically, the rates increase from cooler to warmer weather. In the months from January to June the number of homicides per million inhabitants in the country as a whole runs as follows: 45, 55, 60, 60, 63, 72. In view of what we shall see about hot weather in connection with riots in India and sexual self-control in Italy, these two sets of numbers suggest that temperature may be a factor in the distribution of homicide. Warm weather apparently is associated with lowered self-control. It also makes people feel disinclined toward steady effort. Lack of self-control is a primary factor in promoting murder. Disinclination to work is a primary factor in the failure of public sentiment to express itself in observance of law.

D. The Goodness of Life

Economic prosperity and general well-being are distributed according to much the same geographic pattern as social welfare. A map of the percentage of families having radios, for example, closely resembles that of crowded dwellings (Figure 18), except that the Mountain States show up better. The general distribution of radios is much the same in each of the three groups into which the census divides the population, namely, urban, rural non-farm, and rural farm. The most favored regions extend from southern New England to Iowa and Minnesota and along the Pacific Coast, just where overcrowding, reproduction, and homicide all fall to a low level.

Another way of testing the geographic distribution of economic prosperity is to combine many items into a single map. The most feasible way of doing this is to rank the states from 1 to 48 in each respect and add the ranks together to get an index number. Rank 1 is given to the most extreme state in one direction and rank 48 to the most extreme in the other. Angoff and Mencken have in this way prepared index numbers based on the numerous criteria listed in the accompanying footnote.* These give a map much like the maps of crowding and reproduction combined. A map of the same kind prepared by Thorndike on the basis of quite different data has essentially the same form. It is astonishing to see how closely these maps agree with those based on single items such as overcrowding, rate of reproduction, and homicide.

The higher aspects of civilization follow the same general pattern as the others. Unfortunately no widespread statistics are available for such qualities as idealism, altruism, honesty, self-reliance, originality, and artistic appreciation. In general, however, these seem to be best developed among people who excel in more readily measured qualities, such as literacy, education, the use of libraries, and gifts for philanthropic purposes. The best we can do in measuring and mapping the higher qualities is to take such statistics as are available and see what they show.

* The index is based on the following factors:

A (1) Tangible, and (2) taxable property per capita.
B (3) Per cent paying income tax, and (4) per capita income tax.
C (5) Bank clearings, (6) bank resources, and (7) saving deposits per capita.
D (8) Average value of estates of deceased persons.
E (9) Real income per capita.
F Percentage of farms with (10) tenants, (11) tractors, (12) electricity, and (13) mortgages.
G (14) Per cent of telephones among people in general.
H Per capita data as to (15) consumption of gasoline, (16) motor vehicles, (17) postal receipts, and (18) life insurance.
I (19) Average income of corporations.
J (20) Per capita value of manufactures.
K (21) Value of land and buildings per farm.
L (22) Size of farm mortgages compared with the size of farms.
M (23) Value of mineral products per capita.
N (24) Average total value of farms including machines and stock.
O (25) Average value of hogs.
P (26) Average value of cattle.

Thorndike has attempted to use statistics of this latter kind in an especially interesting way.* Instead of searching for the "worst American state," as Angoff and Mencken have done, he put together many items which "may be used as indices . . . of the general goodness of life for good people," but the result is essentially the same. Thorndike weighted his items according to their supposed importance. The weights vary from 2 for the per capita acreage of public parks up to 13 for the infant deathrate. The result is still another map closely resembling Figures 18–20. When Thorndike's index numbers and

---

* Thorndike's items are as follows:

(A) Death rates:
  (1) infants, (2) total population, (3) typhoid fever, (4) appendicitis, (5) diseases connected with childbearing.

(B) Education: Per capita cost of
  (6) schools as a whole, (7) textbooks and supplies, (8) libraries and museums;
  Percentage attendance among persons aged
  (9) 16–17 years, (10) 18–20;
  Average salaries of
  (11) teachers as a whole, (12) high school teachers, (13) elementary school teachers.

(C) Recreation:
  (14) public expenditures per capita for recreation, (15) acreage of public parks per capita.

(D) Economic and social items: the rarity of poverty in
  (16) extreme forms, (17) less extreme forms;
  Freedom from employment among children 10–14 years of age
  (18) boys, (19) girls;
  (20) per capita contributions to the support of the YMCA;
  (21) percentage by which physicians, nurses, and teachers exceed male domestic servants.

(E) Creature comforts: Per capita use of
  (22) electricity, (23) gasoline, (24) automobiles, (25) telephones, and (26) radios.

(F) Miscellaneous items which influence the pleasure and comfort of life:
  (27) Per cent of literacy in the total population;
  (28) Per capita circulation of *Better Homes and Gardens, Good Housekeeping,* and *National Geographic Magazine;*
  (29) Per capita circulation of the *Literary Digest* (when Thorndike collected his data this magazine occupied a position like that which *Time* later held);
  Deathrates from (30) syphilis, (31) homicide, (32) automobile accidents;
  (33) Relative value of schools and other public cultural centers compared with that of jails and other public facilities for criminals and incompetents;
  (35) Per capita value of all public property minus the public debt.

those of Angoff and Mencken are put together, giving equal weight to each, the result is Figure 21, which may be called a map of the plane of living. Its resemblance to Figures 18–20 is obvious in spite of differences of detail.

It may seem superfluous to present more maps, but Figure 22, representing the percentage of urban population in 1940, sums up the situation in a new way. Here in simple form we have the usual pattern, with a few departures of the kind found in almost every such map.

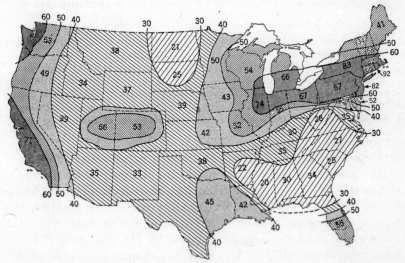

Figure 22. Percentage of Urban Population in the United States, 1940. A percentage of 68 for Connecticut is relatively much too low, because that state does not incorporate small towns and counts many thickly populated suburban districts as rural.

Louisiana and Texas, for example, outrank their neighbors mainly because recent developments, including the oil industry, have increased the size of cities, just as have pleasure seekers and tourists in Florida. Colorado, and especially Utah, rise above the level of their neighbors because mining and irrigation tend to concentrate population in cities, whereas aridity causes the density of population to be low elsewhere. In the Dakotas, on the other hand, broad plains, a rather unreliable climate, and lack of minerals and harbors provide conditions under which the most feasible way for Americans to get a living is by having the population sparse and widely scattered. In spite of such local characteristics the map of urban population clearly portrays the same basic features as the other maps.

If all the cultural features for which statistical data are available should be combined into a single map, the result would not differ much from the average of the maps already given. In fact, so far as can be judged at present, it would merely emphasize the eight main features which are mentioned in Table 11. These features would stand out with special clearness if the state showing the most extreme

TABLE 11

BASIC FEATURES OF THE DISTRIBUTION OF CIVILIZATION IN THE UNITED STATES

Major Features	*Minor Features*
1. New England–Great Lakes strip of strong intensity	5. Northeastern border area of declining intensity
2. Great Plains and Rocky Mountain area of variable intensity decreasing southward	6. Southwestern or Rocky Mountain embayment of relatively low intensity
3. Pacific area of strong intensity	7. Southeastern or Appalachian embayment of relatively weak intensity
4. Southern area of relatively weak intensity	8. Florida area of relatively strong intensity

development along the lines prevailing in or near New York were ranked as number 1 regardless of whether the trait under discussion is desirable, as in the case of prosperity, or undesirable, as in degenerative diseases. One extreme of shading would then stand for the type of culture exemplified in the general region from Boston to Philadelphia, and the opposite extreme for the type most different from this. Although New York and New England are generally regarded as fortunate, their civilization includes many unfavorable features. Mortgages and slums, for example, are especially numerous. A birthrate so low that if it continued for three generations a population of 1,000,000 would be reduced to 343,000 unless recruited from outside might be desirable in crowded China, but is scarcely ideal for America. Yet that is what a net reproductive rate of 70 in 1940 (Figure 19) indicates for New Jersey and Rhode Island. Even in Missouri and Ohio a rate of 91 means only about 750,000 people instead of 1,000,000 a century hence.

E. The Fundamental Importance of Health

In the preceding pages we have not yet found an explanation of the major features of the geographical pattern which stands out so clearly in Figures 18–22. We have seen, to be sure, that minor features are at least partially explained by such factors as mountains, racial conditions, and migrations, but these fail to explain the fundamental pattern with its heavy shading in the area from New England to the Great Lakes and on the Pacific Coast. Health and the vigor which it imparts seem to come nearer than anything else to affording such an explanation. They set a basic pattern, which is modified and sometimes erased by other conditions. Let us consider the relation of health to human progress, and then examine its distribution in the United States.

Physical vigor is basic in human progress. Other things being equal, cultural progress is favored by health and hampered by physical weakness. Vigor is needed in order that people may work hard without undue fatigue and have a reserve of strength in emergencies. It is especially important in promoting mental activity and clear thinking. Only in exceptional cases can people who lack physical vigor have the same alertness of mind and power of intensive work that they would have if in perfect health. Extra energy, over and above the mere needs of getting a living, is one of the chief factors which enable inventors, thinkers, reformers, and other leaders to exert themselves. Darwin has well said that man is not troubled so much by lack of talent as by failure to use those talents which he possesses. Physical vigor helps people to use their talents. Vigor does not mean brute strength. It means the kind of clear-eyed alertness and eagerness for work which one feels when in the pink of health. One of the main elements in acquiring fame is mental alertness and the power to persist in arduous work, even when it is discouraging. Only rarely, as in men like Robert Louis Stevenson, is this faculty strong except among persons who are physically sound and vigorous. The average lifetime of persons included in lists of famous people is close to 70 years—a good indication of a strong constitution.

Good health and high civilization obviously go together. Each, as we have seen, helps the other. Physical vigor seems to be one of four foundations without which civilization cannot make progress; civilization, in turn, is one of three chief factors in giving people health and vigor. The foundations of civilization are (1) innate capacity; (2) a physical environment with sufficient natural advantages to maintain a rising standard of living; (3) a cultural inheritance to serve as a basis on which to build; and (4) sufficient vigor so that the other three conditions are well used. Some peope insist that abundant natural resources are necessary if civilization is to reach a high level, but Iceland, Norway, Switzerland, and New England all indicate that if people are sufficiently vigorous and intelligent, handicaps along this line can be overcome. The three chief factors in giving people health and vigor are (1) innate biological endowment; (2) a physical environment which is favorable in relation to climate, food, and disease; and (3) a cultural condition in which the arts of medicine, nutrition, sanitation, and hygiene, as well as trade and transportation, have made good progress.

F. Inclination to Work

Differences in health indicate corresponding differences in inclination to work, as well as in actual capacity for work. Vigorous people prefer to work rather than sit idle. The will to work beyond the required limits is extremely important in crises, such as war, flood, or other disaster. It is one of the main factors in leading people to make inventions, explore new lands, carry out scientific experiments, initiate reforms, and produce works of art, literature, and music. In New Zealand, the most healthy of all countries, the average length of life (about 67 years) is more than twice as great as in India (27 years). This indicates surplus vigor which is used in the activities just mentioned and also in such matters as beautifying houses and grounds, reading books and papers, engaging in sports, and working for social, educational, and political betterment. The average New Zealander is so energetic that he spends not merely twice as much time and energy on such matters as the average person in India but perhaps ten times as much. Good health inclines him to devote spare time to such activities, whereas only a few unusually energetic Indians feel that way. The New Zealander may be neither more intelligent nor more virtuous than the Indian, but he has sufficient energy to make good use of his powers.

Inclination to work is even more important than ability to work. What effect, for example, does a bad cold or indigestion have upon your inclination to work? The American Institute of Public Opinion (Gallup Poll) found that in the United States between October, 1941, and February, 1943, the number of million persons suffering from colds in a given week was approximately as follows: 6½ in July, 13 in October, 18 or 20 in November and December, 21 to 23 in February, and over 15 in April. Health during these winters and the one before was better than usual, as appears from the low deathrate. Nevertheless, during the entire winter of 1940–41 about 84,000,000 persons in the United States had colds. About 50,000,000 of these persons were of working age, above 21 years. One quarter of the workers were absent at least one day because of colds. The National Association of Manufacturers estimates that the annual loss from this cause in wages alone amounts to about a billion and a half dollars a year. The real cost includes also medical care and losses due to poor work, mistakes, bad temper, forgetfulness, and poor judgment among people who have colds or who do unaccustomed work because somebody else has a cold. To this we must add a good round sum because colds weaken people so much that they contract other diseases and are ill a long time or die.

The incidence of colds is more or less typical of that of human energy as a whole. It varies with age, economic conditions, and geographical location. Children under 10 years of age suffer most—more than twice as much as young people aged 20 to 24. Many are doubtless weakened throughout life by diseases contracted as aftereffects of colds. People who are poorly nourished and badly protected suffer more than others. The Gallup Poll found that as early as November the percentage of people already kept from work by colds was 16 in the lower income brackets in contrast to only 11 in the higher brackets. During the entire winter of 1940–41 the percentages were as follows: 67 for incomes under $1,000, 63 for incomes of $1,000–$2,500, and 61 for higher incomes. Moreover, the lower income groups were especially well represented among the 13,000,000 who were kept from work by two different colds and the 7,000,000 who were kept away three times.

Big cities are less afflicted with colds than small cities; the latter, in turn, are better off than villages and rural areas. This may be merely because cities predominate in the regions that are climatically most conducive to good health. The urban belt from southern New England to Lake Michigan has fewer colds than the more rural areas. The percentage of population having colds in 1940–41 was 72 in the South, 63 or 64 from New England and New Jersey to the Dakotas and Kansas, and only 58 in the West. In a region afflicted chronically with colds, indigestion, headaches, and other minor ailments many people lack vim, although not exactly ill. They mean well but put things off, because they do not feel like working and find it hard to concentrate. Such conditions are systematically indicated by high deathrates. Thus both the inclination and the capacity for work vary in harmony with the deathrate. Even within a single country these differ greatly among social classes and from one geographical region to another. Among nations the differences are greatly accentuated.

G. The Geographic Pattern of Health

The geographical distribution of health and vigor depends largely on the combined effect of climate and of cultural conditions such as form the basis of the maps which we have just been studying. The health of the United States, as measured by the deathrate, presents a curious geographical contrast when younger and older people are compared. Figure 23 * shows that among persons under 45 years of age the basic geographic pattern of the deathrate in the United States is like that which we have seen in maps of overcrowded dwellings, homicides, density of population and so forth. Its general agreement with other maps in the present series is obvious. Low rates prevail from New England and New Jersey westward past the Great Lakes. The area of low rates expands widely in the great agricultural area from the Dakotas to Kansas. After a Rocky Mountain break in Montana and Wyoming, low rates appear again in the Pacific Northwest. In the southern part of the country the deathrates are relatively high —generally twice as high as in the North. A tongue of high rates extends into Nevada and another runs up the Atlantic Coast to Virginia. Maine falls below the standard of the rest of New England, although a deathrate of 3.6 is by no means bad. All this accords with the basic geographic pattern. Florida, however, fails to show an improvement over the states to the north of it, although such an improvement is evident in each of the four preceding maps.

In spite of its clear portrayal of the basic geographic pattern, the map of deathrates under 45 years of age has certain idiosyncrasies. For example, the best conditions of all (rates of less than 3.0) are experienced in southern New England (Connecticut and Rhode Island) and in the North Central states of Wisconsin, Minnesota, Iowa, the Dakotas, and Nebraska (best of all). This is interesting because we are often told that high deathrates afflict regions where industries, cities, and people are concentrated. Here, however, we have identically the same low deathrate in Rhode Island, the most urban state, and North Dakota, the most agricultural. Between the two, we find

* In order to eliminate irregularities due to the fact that one state has relatively many children or young people and another only a few, the rate for each state has been standardized by taking the rates at different ages, such as under 1 year, 1–5 years, and so forth, and calculating what the net rate would be if everywhere the percentage of persons in each age-group were the same as in the United States as a whole in 1940. Figure 24 has been prepared in the same way.

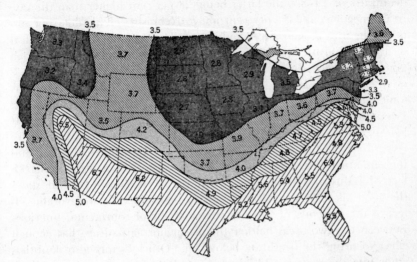

Figure 23. Standardized Deathrate at Ages under 45 Years, 1940, 1941.

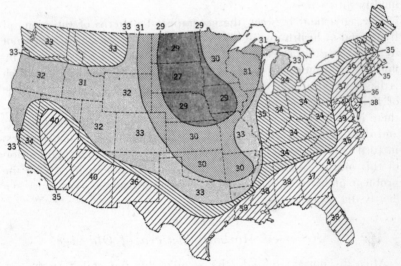

Figure 24. Standardized Deathrate at Ages above 45 Years, 1940, 1941. Note that light shading here indicates unfavorable conditions, just as in Figures 20 and 21.

deathrates of 3.4–3.7, the latter being 28 per cent higher than the rate in Connecticut and 34 per cent above Nebraska. This does not disprove the idea that urban or industrial life is less healthful than rural or agricultural life. Nevertheless, it suggests that before people reach middle age such differences in mode of life have less effect than is often supposed. It also suggests that the northern coastal states enjoy some advantage which more or less balances their urban disadvantage. Proximity to the sea is well known to have a healthful effect. It lessens the extreme of both heat and cold. Agricultural life is also recognized as being good for health. Thus in southern New England the climatic effect of the ocean may more or less neutralize the effect of industrialization, whereas in the West North Central states the good effect of agriculture tends to neutralize the unfavorable effect of the extremes of weather characteristic of continental interiors. Between the two areas neither the ocean nor agriculture has enough effect to bring the deathrate below 3.0. Other factors also doubtless enter into the matter. The important thing is to recognize the presence of the standard geographic pattern in health as well as in wealth and cultural progress and to recognize also that other conditions modify this pattern.

The agreement between the geographical patterns of the plane of living and of health during the most productive years of life does not in itself indicate a relation of cause and effect. Each certainly influences the other, and each may depend on some third factor which is basic to both. As to the relation between health and the plane of living, if the population as a whole is persistently full of vigor, there is almost certain to be progress in medicine, sanitation, hygiene, and diet, as well as in the general standard of living. Such progress in turn leads to better health and still more vigor. The recognition of this mutual relationship, however, is of little help in solving the problem of how the basic geographic pattern arises. We must evidently dig deeper.

H. Reversed Mortality Pattern of Old Age

After the normal reproductive span of life has ended at the age of forty-five or fifty years the geographical pattern of deaths changes greatly (Figure 24). The Dakotas, Nebraska, and Iowa are the only states with outstandingly low mortality after, as well as before, the age of forty-five. In those West North Central states and also in the entire South from ocean to ocean Figures 23 and 24 show essentially the same pattern. From Wisconsin and Illinois eastward, however, and to a less extent in Montana and Washington a reversal occurs. In both these regions the highly favorable conditions indicated by the darkest shading in Figure 23 give place to less favorable conditions indicated by other shadings, including even the lightest in New England and New York. Degenerative diseases, especially those of the heart, together with diabetes and nervous disorders, have much to do with this unfavorable change. Their distribution is evident in Figure 25, where light shading means many deaths. Such deaths occur mainly among older people. Their prevalence in areas where the deathrate before the age of forty-five is low must be due in part to the survival of persons who would have died young under less favorable conditions. Such people lower the general resistance at higher ages and thus lead to a pronounced increase in the deathrate. Part of the increased deathrate at older ages may also be ascribed to urban life, which helps to explain the light shading of Figure 25 from Rhode Island and Massachusetts to Illinois. Another element in the situation is the fact that outward migration of young people has left an unusually high proportion of old people in northern New England. None of these conditions, however, explains why Iowa has so high a deathrate from degenerative diseases, nor why the same basic geographic pattern is repeated so frequently.

On the basis of the maps now before us it appears that the fundamental geographic pattern of civilization in the United States must be due to conditions which are highly stimulating to health and activity during the first fifty years or so of life but which finally lead to overexertion and degeneration of the vital organs. Such activity has been a factor in causing the deathrate from infectious diseases to be reduced so that it is only one half to one fifth as great in the North as in the South. Nevertheless, it seems to wear out the vital organs so that after the end of the reproductive period the deathrate rises more rapidly than in regions which have not previously been so stimulating and which have had a higher deathrate. If infectious diseases could be sufficiently reduced in the southern United States, the average length of life in the South would apparently be as great as in the North. This, however, would not alter the fact that in the northeast from New England to the Mississippi River and on the Pacific Coast all except the older people have the advantage of conditions of some sort which especially aid their health during the most important years of life.

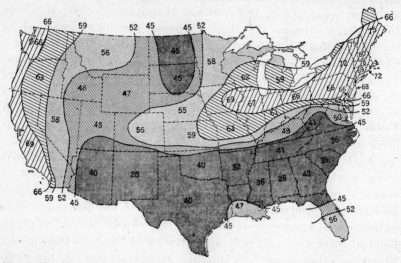

Figure 25. Deathrate from Degenerative Diseases per 10,000 Population, 1939–41. Light shading indicates unfavorable conditions. Thus this map is almost the reverse of Figures 21, 22, and 28. Not standardized, but standardization would have no appreciable effect on map.

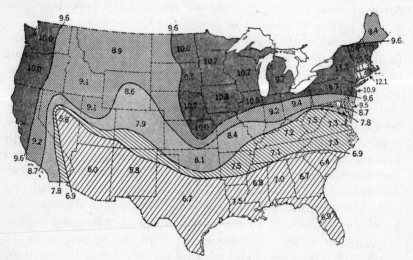

Figure 26. Ratio of Standardized Deathrate above 45 Years to Similar Rate below That Age, 1940, 1941.

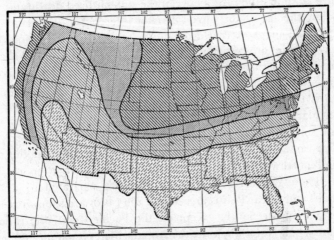

Figure 27. Climatic Efficiency in the United States on the Basis of Factory Work.
From *Principles of Economic Geography*.

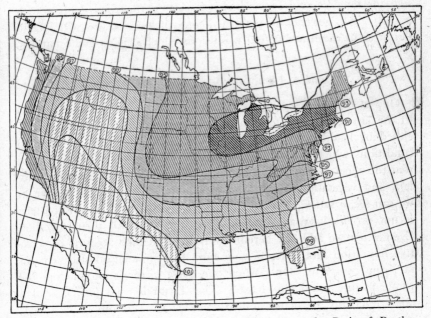

Figure 28. Climatic Efficiency in the United States on the Basis of Deaths.
Courtesy, Yale University Press.

Figure 26 shows the ratio between the standardized deathrates above and below the age of forty-five. It is of interest because of its resemblance to the maps of crowded houses, rates of reproduction, homicides, economic prosperity, and urban population. If its shadings were reversed so that the dark parts were light, the degree to which it follows their general pattern would be more clearly evident. The pattern is the feature with which we are now mainly concerned. It is particularly interesting to see the way in which this pattern stands out in a comparison of this sort, as well as when specific objects, such as radios or motor cars, are examined. Blocks of states in the northeast and northwest quarters of the country show a ratio of 9.6 or more. These two areas with high ratios are separated by a Rocky Mountain and Great Plains area where the ratios are somewhat lower. Everywhere in the South, except on the Pacific Coast, the ratios are less than 7. In Nevada and in the Appalachian region an embayment of low ratios is observed. These are the big features of the geographic pattern of health and also of the majority of human activities. The faithfulness with which such maps and many others present the same general aspect makes it clear that we are dealing with a truly basic geographic pattern. Nevertheless, we are still left in doubt as to the fundamental conditions which originate the pattern.

I. *Climatic Aspect of Basic Geographic Pattern*

One of the most logical methods of resolving the doubt expressed in the last sentence is to compare the geographical distribution disclosed by health, wealth, and plane of living with that of physical conditions which might be influential. When this is done we find that the effect of mountains, plains, seacoasts, soils, fuels, metals, rainfall, and vegetation is far from negligible. Nevertheless, so far as we can see, a satisfactory explanation of the basic geographic pattern is not provided by any one of these nor by all of them together. Even when we add the hereditary factor and take account of selective migration and differences of race, the explanation still remains far from complete. Only when one more factor is added does the whole picture stand out clearly. That factor is what may be called climatic energy, or better, climatic efficiency. Without it we see, as it were, a picture in which one clearly discerns a child, a tree, a bird, and other individual items, but in which there is no sky, no earth, no sea, no general setting or background.

Climatic efficiency means the relative efficiency which people in any given stage of civilization would have in various climates if their efficiency varied only in response to weather and climate, and if the people everywhere were exactly alike in all other respects. Figure 27 is such a map for people in the American stage of cultural progress.* It is based mainly on the productivity of pieceworkers in American factories under different conditions of weather. The primary data came from factories in Connecticut and were confirmed by similar data from Pennsylvania, North and South Carolina, and Florida and by data as to students' marks at West Point and Annapolis. Although several kinds of data have thus been combined, we have a map which shows only one thing—climatic efficiency. It is a purely physical map constructed according to exact statistical procedure from weather records all over the country. Even if there were no people, the map would remain unaltered, for it simply portrays the degree to which the climate is of the kind that encourages efficiency among modern people of European descent. For each of the more primitive stages of culture some other map is needed. People who lack clothes or fire are most efficient in climates warmer than the type that is best for us.

The map of climatic efficiency has sometimes been misinterpreted as the basis for a theory that climate is the "cause" of civilization. This is a curious mistake. The map does not even indicate the existing efficiency in different parts of the world, for that is influenced also by heredity, stage of culture, diet, and other factors. The map's true nature can perhaps best be realized by comparing it with maps show-

* This map was first published in the author's *Civilization and Climate*, 1915, but revisions appear in the third edition, 1924, and in *Principles of Human Geography*, fifth edition, 1940. The map ought to be reconstructed on the basis of a vast body of statistical material which was not available in 1915, but the labor involved in this has thus far made it impossible. There is no reason, however, to believe that a revision would alter the general appearance of the map, although details might be changed. The exact climatic status of California needs much further study. The general reliability of the map is confirmed by experiments at the laboratories of Yale, Harvard, the American Society of Heating and Ventilating Engineers, and other institutions, by studies of fatigue in England and Japan, and by experiments on animals, such as those conducted by C. A. Mills. Fortunately the original map took account of storminess, seasonal changes, and mental activity, as well as of mean temperature. The fact that it has been republished twenty or thirty times in various countries and in other books as well as college textbooks indicates that it is widely accepted as the best available indicator of the effect of climate on human efficiency. The uses made of it are illustrated in such books as A. J. Toynbee's *A Study of History* and Quincy Wright's *A Study of War*.

ing the effect of climate on the growth of trees. One such map would show how fast the American red oak would grow if the soil, slope, degree of crowding, pests, and all other non-climatic conditions were everywhere the same. It would be different from the corresponding map for white oaks. In general, the average size of red oaks would agree with what would be expected from the map, but in particular places the size would be quite out of harmony with this because of special soils or parasites, or because the forest had been cut at some time by man.

In the same way the fact that Figure 27 indicates high climatic efficiency in a certain place does not necessarily mean that efficiency is actually high just there. Other conditions, such as innate incompetence, poor diet, bad government, or wasting diseases, may prevent this. Moreover, inasmuch as climate is only one factor in promoting efficiency, there may be fairly high efficiency, but not absolutely the highest, even where the climate is poor, provided the people are innately competent and have a highly developed culture, as is true in Iceland. There can, however, be no efficiency at all if the climate is too bad. If the temperature were always 100° below freezing, everybody would perish, even if food were available. There would likewise be no efficiency if the temperature should remain for even one month at an average of 110° with a high humidity. Everyone would die. Inasmuch as there are definite climatic limits beyond which life is impossible, it is a logical necessity that somewhere between the limits there must be an optimum zone in which efficiency is highest. It is equally obvious that between the limits and the optimum there must be every possible intermediate degree of climatic efficiency. Simple as these conclusions are, they are often overlooked, and serious logical errors are therefore committed.

In relation to civilization the point of present interest about the map of climatic efficiency is its resemblance to the other maps in the series belonging to this chapter. All of the four main features of the basic geographic pattern are clearly evident in the climatic map. So, too, is one of the four minor features, that is, the southwestern embayment, and there is a hint of the southeastern embayment in Tennessee. The decline in Maine would appear if the map were more fully subdivided. Only the tendency of Florida toward the northern type is missing, and that is not to be expected because it is clearly due to a purely human cause—migration.

Another map of climatic efficiency (Figure 28), which may also be called a map of climatic health, shows the same general features as

Figure 27, but in a slightly different form and with the inclusion of the decline in the North and Northeast. The southeastern embayment is also present with its tip in eastern Kentucky. East of it lies a new feature, a southward projection of relatively good conditions along the line of the comparatively cool Appalachian Upland to Asheville, N. C. This does not appear in Figure 27 because no station at sufficient altitude was used in making that map. It is worth noting that mountains act in two opposed ways. They hamper progress by making transportation and many other activities difficult. They help, if the latitude is low enough, by improving the climate.

On the whole, Figure 28 may be a little better than Figure 27 as a map of climatic efficiency, but there is not much difference. It is just as purely climatic as Figure 27 but is based on the weather prevailing in various cities during months when various deathrates prevailed, rather than on the weather when people worked at different rates. Its resemblance to such maps as those of overcrowding (Figure 18), white homicides (Figure 20), and the deathrate under age forty-five (Figure 23) is significant. The resemblance between the two climatic maps is also significant in view of the fact that they are based on the weather of entirely different cities in different years and in relation to widely diverse human conditions.

The main significance of all these resemblances lies first in the fact that, in spite of considerable minor differences, the maps all show the same basic pattern. It also lies in the fact that the resemblances are too close and too widespread to be accidental. If the resemblances arise from some connection between climate and such factors as health, piecework, and the plane of living, it is impossible for the connection to operate in more than one direction. The other maps must get their basic pattern from climate. Nothing that man can yet do has any appreciable effect upon the weather, with its changes from day to day and season to season, or upon the climate, with its variations in temperature, humidity, and wind. On the other hand, everyone knows that human feelings, health, and activity are extremely sensitive to weather and climate. The evidence as to this is even more abundant and conclusive than is commonly realized, as will appear more fully in later chapters. Meanwhile this chapter leads to two main conclusions. First, in the United States human conditions and activities of many kinds show a geographic distribution which is evidently founded upon a persistent and powerful basic pattern. Second, the only known factor capable of producing this pattern is climate acting upon the health and vigor of the people.

CHAPTER 13

HEALTH AND NATIONAL CHARACTER

A. The Vigor of Nations

A study of health among the nations leads to the same conclusion that we have reached in respect to the United States. Health, or vigor, is a basic factor in determining the rate of human progress. Among the factors which influence health, climate plays an especially significant part in setting the geographical pattern. Deathrates afford the best available means of comparing the physical vigor of nations. In fact, no other method is available on a large scale. Physicians and experts in public health, as we have seen, believe that when large groups of people are considered, length of life is one of the best evidences of constitutional vigor and of the general energy with which the affairs of life are prosecuted. Where the average life is long, few children die in infancy. There is also relative freedom from inefficiency due to minor ailments, such as colds, headaches, and indigestion, and from greater handicaps due to more serious diseases. Moreover, the proportion of persons who continue to be productive well into old age is large.

The relative health and vigor of nine representative nations are shown in Figure 29A. The bars represent relative length of life on the basis of deaths in recent years and of the average age at which deaths will occur in the future if present conditions of health persist unchanged. The diagram is based on three measures of health, each of which has the same weight.* Local differences due to more old persons or children in one region than in another are eliminated. Only the white population of the United States is included. In Figure 29A an index number of 100 means that among the nine countries New Zealand has the greatest length of life, lowest deathrate,

---

* The criteria employed here are: (a) standardized deathrate, 1930–32; (b) expectation of life, 1932–34 or 1931–35; (c) infant mortality, 1934–39. In (a) and, to a less extent, (b) a little extrapolation, or interpolation, has been necessary, but this has no appreciable effect on the relative standing of the various countries.

and lowest infant mortality. The other countries are ranked proportionally lower. Zero would mean death of everybody at birth. All
three methods of measuring longevity give essentially the same results.

A comparison between Figure 29A and the other sections of Figure
29 shows that the relative rank of the nations in physical vigor is the

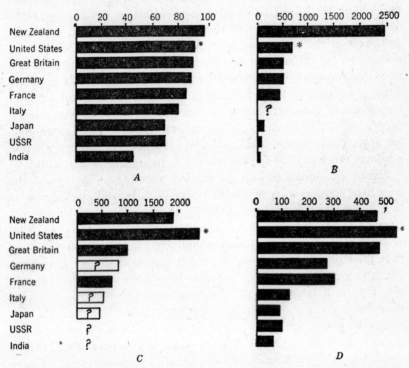

Figure 29. Relative Rank of Nine Nations: A = Health and Vigor; B = Agricultural Productivity per Man on the Farm; C = Industrial Productivity per Worker;
D = Income per Capita.

same as in agricultural production per man on the farm (29B), and
almost the same as in productivity per industrial worker and income
per capita.[1] When other countries and other aspects of civilization
are added to the data of Figure 29 essentially the same relationship is
still seen, in spite of individual discrepancies. Although New Zealand's extreme preponderance in agricultural productivity is exceptional, its leading position is normal. The amount produced by the

[1] Huntington, 1943.

* Whites only in A, entire population in others.

average man in agriculture depends partly on soil, topography, climate, and methods of cultivation, all of which are no better in New Zealand than in other well-favored regions. It depends also on markets, a condition which handicaps New Zealand because of remoteness from Europe. Then, too, agricultural productivity is, of course, influenced by the skill and intelligence of the farmers. New Zealand stands high in this. Last of all come two factors in which no other country, taken as a whole, now rivals New Zealand. One is the health and vigor of the people, as shown in Figure 29A. The other is opportunities for agricultural development. Sparsity of population permits vast ranches where one man can care for large flocks or herds. This is a major element in making the agricultural production of New Zealand extremely large. It would help little, however, unless coupled with (1) human intelligence and vigor; (2) a climate good for grass, cattle, sheep, and man; and (3) a stage of culture wherein products can be raised for sale on the opposite side of the world.

Figure 29C indicates that the relative standing of the nine countries here considered is nearly the same in industrial efficiency as in health and agricultural productivity. Industrially, however, the differences between countries are much less than agriculturally. This is largely because overpopulation and consequent scarcity of land have relatively little effect on rates of factory work. They have some effect, however, because they influence efficiency through diet, disease, the quality of labor, and the resultant impetus toward labor-saving machinery.

Income per capita (Figure 29D) is different from the average production per man because it is based on the entire population, including many who produce no goods for actual consumption. Professional men, business executives, clerks, servants, and persons engaged in repair work of all kinds belong to this group. The national income also includes receipts from investments, transportation lines, and other activities abroad as well as at home. Putting together all these varied sources of income, we still find essentially the same order, with the new English-speaking countries at the top, the big west European countries of Great Britain, Germany, and France next, Italy, Japan, and Russia lower down, and poor India at the bottom. This appears to be almost the order in which countries stand on the basis of climatic efficiency, although selective migration, diet, and density of population must also be taken into account. Thus among these nine countries the relationships of climatic efficiency, health, and plane of living appear to be the same as among the states of the United States.

B. *World Pattern of Climatic Efficiency*

This same relationship between health and modern progress holds true in countries outside the nine already considered. Figure 30 is a world map of climatic efficiency constructed in the same way as Figure 27 for the United States. In each continent this purely climatic map tends to repeat the main features which appear in North America. There are, however, considerable differences due to continental size, extension into high latitudes, and the direction and altitude of mountains. The dominant feature is that in middle latitudes each continent that extends sufficiently far from the equator has (1) a western and (2) an eastern area of relatively high climatic efficiency. In North America these high areas are clearly seen in a heavily shaded band running north and south on the West Coast and in a larger area of the same kind elongated eastward from near the Mississippi River to the Atlantic Coast in the northern United States and southern Canada. The western area of high efficiency spreads more widely north and south in vast Eurasia than in North America. From west to east it is about as wide as the eastern North American area. It includes Great Britain, France, Germany, and the neighboring small countries, together with North Italy, the well-populated parts of Scandinavia, the Baltic area practically as far as Leningrad, and a fringe of the countries east of Germany. The eastern Asiatic area of high efficiency, on the contrary, is almost limited to Japan and is not so intense as the European and American areas.

The rest of the world has only small areas of high climatic efficiency. South America has two, one in central Chile and the other in central Argentina. They are separated by lofty mountains and a relatively dry interior, just as in North America. In Africa the continent is cut off by the ocean in such low latitudes that the areas of high efficiency merge into a single small section near Capetown. It is doubtful whether any part of Africa has a climate of the "very high" type, but the height and wide extent of the African Plateau permit the climate to be of medium rank over a considerable area. In Australia, as well as Africa, the continent does not project into high enough latitudes to have an area of "very high" climatic efficiency, but a "high" level prevails in a small southwestern and a larger southeastern corner. New Zealand as a whole ranks near the top.*

Aside from these areas of high efficiency Figure 30 shows certain other major features. (3) There are mid-latitude interior areas with a climatic efficiency less than on either coast. In the two Americas these areas do not fall much below those in the same latitude nearer the sea. In North America this is due mainly to frequent storms, as will appear more clearly later, and in South America to the relatively short distance from ocean to ocean. In the Old World, however, the vast size of Eurasia leads to such extremes of temperature and such a scarcity of storms that the energizing effect of the climate falls off from the North Sea region eastward almost as fast as southward. (4) Areas of low or very low efficiency dominate low latitudes. Much of Africa, South America, Australia, and southern Asia falls into this category. (5) Areas of low efficiency prevail in high latitudes. In Asia and North America these expand widely and are sparsely inhabited.

C. World Pattern of Human Vigor

The statistics of many countries are so poor that we shall not attempt to present a map of health in the world as a whole. Instead we shall examine Table 12, which gives an index of health like that

TABLE 12

INDEX OF HEALTH AND VIGOR

1.	New Zealand	100	16.	Scotland	86
2.	Netherlands	98	17.	Latvia	86
3.	Australia	98	18.	Finland	86
4.	Norway	97	19.	Estonia	83
5.	Sweden	96	20.	Austria	83
6.	Switzerland	93	21.	Italy	81
7.	United States (white)	93	22.	Czechoslovakia	77
8.	Denmark	92	23.	Greece	75
9.	England	92	24.	Hungary	70
10.	South Africa (whites)	91	25.	USSR	70 (?)
11.	Germany	91	26.	Japan	69
12.	Canada	90	27.	Poland	69
13.	Eire (Ireland)	87	28.	Bulgaria	68
14.	Belgium	87	29.	Egypt	52
15.	France	87	30.	India	45

* New Zealand and the southeastern corner of Australia may be in the "very high" climatic type, if seasonal contrasts are less significant than was assumed in making Figure 30.

of Figure 29A. It includes all of the thirty countries for which at least moderately good data are available. Bear in mind that a high index means good health, long life, a low deathrate, widespread vigor, and a good standard of living. The difference in civilization between countries such as New Zealand and the Netherlands at the top of the table and Egypt and India at the bottom is obvious. So, too, is the general decline as one reads downward. The United States does not rank so high as it might, but any rank above 80 is decidedly high. If Negroes are included, the United States drops to the level of Canada.

Consider how strongly New Zealand and Australia are contrasted with Egypt and India. In World War I the Anzacs (Australia-New Zealand Army Corps) were famous as especially bold, adventurous, and adaptable soldiers. Their successors in World War II have done equally well. Men of the Anzac type are physically tough, learn rapidly, and adapt themselves quickly to new situations. They are obedient to orders but have none of the subservience characteristic of some armies. Almost any general would warmly welcome such men in his ranks. Both Australia and New Zealand are famous for social progress. For example, in 1941 Robert Semple, New Zealand's minister for national services, is reported as saying that no one pays hospital bills in New Zealand.

In maternity cases, instead of . . . receiving a bill as she leaves [the] hospital, [the mother] is free of obligation. . . . If she subsequently becomes ill, she is eligible for a sickness benefit. . . . We safeguard the children by making maternity safe and free from worry, and we safeguard them still further by providing free dental clinics . . . in cities, towns, and rural areas.

India and Egypt present a remarkable contrast to New Zealand in both war and peace. Only a small fraction of the Indian castes and other social groups make good soldiers, as we shall see when discussing diet. Moreover, all the soldier groups come from the better sections of the country climatically. The relation of Egyptian character to climate is well described by Olmstead, who incidentally brings out the effect of the selective process which has differentiated the agricultural people of "the River" from their conquerors among the surrounding nomads. In Egypt, says Olmstead,

we have a hot, dry climate where the main dependence for the crops is not on the rains, but on the rise of the Nile. This rise, regular as the seasons, the comparatively small change in temperature among the seasons themselves, the almost complete absence of rainfall taken in connection with

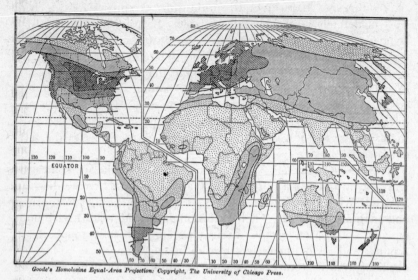

Goode's Homolosine Equal-Area Projection: Copyright, The University of Chicago Press.

Figure 30. World Distribution of Climatic Efficiency. From *Principles of Human Geography*, Fifth Edition.

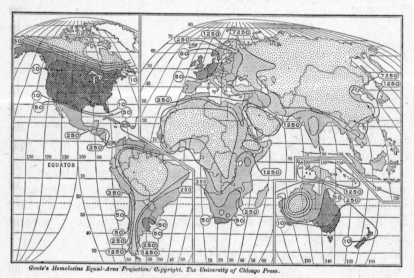

Goode's Homolosine Equal-Area Projection: Copyright, The University of Chicago Press.

Figure 31. World Distribution of Automobiles. From *Principles of Human Geography*, Fifth Edition.

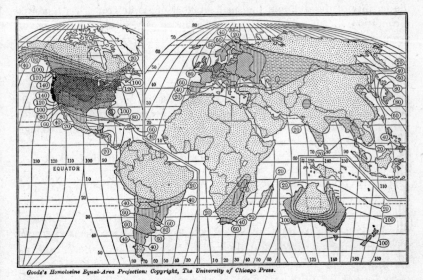

Figure 32.   World Distribution of Education.   From *Principles of Human Geography,* Fifth Edition.

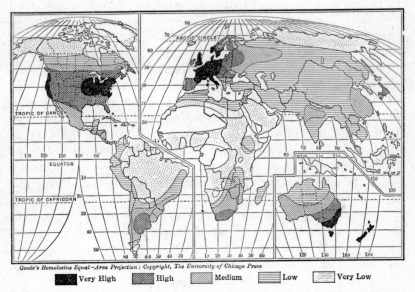

Figure 33.   World Distribution of General Progress.   From *Principles of Human Geography,* Fifth Edition.

the fertility of the soil, and the small number of staple crops, has produced a condition . . . in which all that is demanded is a steady carrying out of a routine which never changes and requires rather brawn than brain. This we find admirably reflected in the character of the peasantry, now, as in antiquity, interested only in securing enough food to live and to marry upon. But this did not seriously modify the character of the ruling class for, from predynastic times, they have always been foreigners. . . . Just because they did not adjust themselves to the climate, they became enervated and finally were killed off. . . . The unchanging peasantry, who show most strikingly the effect of climate, need be mentioned only once by the historian, after which their existence may be assumed for the further historical relation.

It must not be supposed that physical vigor alone suffices to produce civilization. If the stage of culture is low, such vigor is not accompanied by what we now consider a low deathrate. The American Indians of A.D. 1600 in New York appear to have been energetic without being civilized, and their deathrate must have been high according to our standards. Nevertheless, their energy is evident in their long, hard raids and general alertness. Its contrast to the opposite quality among millions of tropical "East" Indians is what we are interested in just now. The way in which human energy is used depends largely on people's training, stage of progress, and natural resources. The degree of energy, although influenced by heredity, depends especially on factors such as climate, diet, and disease which directly influence health.

Bearing this in mind, let us continue our comparison between health and climatic efficiency. The countries listed in Table 12 fall into four well-defined groups. (I) With an index of 90 or higher we find five new English-speaking countries, New Zealand (number 1), Australia (3), the United States (whites) (7), South Africa (whites) (10), and Canada (12). All these enjoy the combined advantages of (a) recent selective migration, (b) a relatively small population in proportion to the natural resources, (c) a high stage of culture in the original homes from which their population was mainly derived, and (d) climates which range from medium to very high in their effect on efficiency in the sections where most of the people live. An interesting feature of these countries is that because of advantages along other lines they tend to rank higher in both health and progress than would be expected on the basis of climate alone.

(II) The next group of countries comprises all others as far down as Czechoslovakia (number 22, with an index of 77). These lack the advantages of recent selection by migration and of abundant land

and large natural resources in proportion to the population. All, however, are included wholly, or in considerable part, within the European area of very high climatic efficiency in Figure 30. This advantage is apparently a great help in compensating for lack of advantages in other respects.

(III) At levels of 68 to 75 in Table 12, six countries have the advantage of only the second, or "high," level of climatic efficiency. Greece may in part owe its relatively high index of health (75) to the severe selective process which weeded out weaklings among the million or more migrants whom it received after World War I. Russia is popularly supposed to have abundant land and resources. When only the good agricultural land is considered, however, together with the relative inaccessibility of most of the mineral resources until quite recently, the Russian advantages are diminished. The other countries, Hungary, Japan, Poland, and Bulgaria, all suffer badly from overpopulation and have no special advantage from migration.

(IV) The least favored countries in Table 12 are Egypt, with an index of 52, and India, only 45. Many others belong in this group or the preceding one. They are not listed because they are not yet advanced enough to furnish reliable statistics. All the countries which appear to have index numbers as low as those of Egypt and India rank from medium to very low in climatic efficiency. Most of them also are relatively poor in natural resources and have had little advantage from recent selective migration. Many, such as Egypt, Iran, India, and China, are seriously overpopulated.

D. World Pattern of Civilization

Having found the world patterns of climatic efficiency and health much alike, let us see how they compare with that of civilization. Here, as elsewhere, we are hampered by lack of reliable statistics. Nevertheless, Figures 31 and 32 give a fairly reliable picture of two main phases of human progress. Figure 31 shows the number of persons per motor vehicle. The well-motorized regions are located where the climate promotes efficiency. Nevertheless, the United States and Canada show far greater predominance than would be expected on the basis of climate alone. This is due partly to natural resources, partly to freedom from overpopulation, and partly to the vigor arising from selective migration. In Japan an opposite condition prevails. Extreme density of population, scanty resources, and poverty, together with lack of space for roads and inefficiency among laborers and farmers by reason of poor diet, largely preclude much use of automobiles.

Another prominent feature of the automobile map is that motor vehicles are more numerous near coasts than in the interior. This agrees with the climatic conditions, for seacoasts generally promote health. Nevertheless, this phenomenon is largely due to other factors. For example, trade and hence wealth tend to be more prevalent on coasts than inland. Foreign influences reach the coast sooner than the interior. Tropical plantations are mainly located near coasts because of advantages in climate, topography, transportation, and labor. If gasoline must be imported, it is cheaper there than in the interior.

In Figure 32, showing the distribution of education, the climatic pattern is clearer than in the automobile map. Japan, for example, rises well toward the top. It is, to be sure, far exceeded by the United States, especially California, as might be expected on the basis of natural resources, wealth, and migration. It surpasses the whites of South Africa, however, rivals the best in Argentina, and falls only a little behind England, Germany, and Australia. Energetic and intelligent people can educate themselves in Japan as well as in Iceland, even though they have few resources and suffer from overpopulation. When due account is taken of factors such as these, it appears that in spite of differences in detail, the maps of motor vehicles and education, as well as of opinion, show quite clearly that the main pattern of modern civilization agrees rather closely with the efficiency and activity that would be expected climatically. This is true even though this pattern is altered by other conditions, such as density of population, distance from the sea, natural resources, diet, and stage of civilization. Innate traits also enter into the matter, as appears when Iceland is compared with Newfoundland.

E. A Map of Opinion

As a final method of studying the worldwide distribution of civilization, let us look at a map based on expert opinion. Such a map is imperfect, but a similar one of the United States shows the basic pattern quite closely in harmony with the average of the various statistical methods employed in the last chapter. Therefore this method seems to be fairly reliable. Figure 33 is based on the opinions of fifty experts in fifteen countries. These historians, geographers, anthropologists, and world travellers assigned a numerical rank to each of one hundred and eighty-five regions according to

those characteristics which are generally recognized as of the highest value . . . power of initiative, capacity for formulating new ideas and for carrying them into effect, power of self-control, high standards of honesty and morality, power to lead and to control other races, capacity for disseminating ideas, and other similar qualities. . . . These qualities find expression in high ideals, respect for law, inventiveness, ability to develop philosophical systems, education, the capacity to dominate the less civilized parts of the world, and the ability to carry out far-reaching enterprises covering long periods of time and great areas of the earth surface.[2]

The map resulting from this survey of intelligent opinion closely resembles that of climatic efficiency. Fortunately it was made before World War I, a time when international good-feeling was widespread and fair judgment was possible. Practically every area which stands high climatically stood high in the opinion of well-informed men all over the world. Areas that stand low climatically stood low in civilization.*

The map based on opinion also agrees closely with the index of health (Table 12). The correlation coefficient between that index and the rank of the same countries according to expert opinion is .94. This means practically a 90 per cent agreement, but there is reason to believe that it would be still higher if data for more countries were available, and if opinions as to the relative progress of different parts of the world were more exact. Even as things now stand, however, it seems unquestionable that in the world as a whole the level of civilization and the physical vigor of the people are closely associated, and that both agree with the pattern of climatic efficiency

[2] Huntington, 1924B, p. 150.

* The failure of Figures 31 and 32 to show the difference between Iceland and Newfoundland illustrates the difficulty of comparing one civilization with another. The map of civilization based on opinions puts Newfoundland ahead of Iceland for the simple reason that until World War II even the best informed people rarely had exact knowledge of those two islands. They thought Newfoundland was much like the advanced parts of Canada and that Iceland was cold and backward. In the map of education (Figure 32) Iceland is on the same level with Newfoundland because when the map was made, isolation still kept many Icelandic children away from school, although they were educated at home. If we could get exact data as to real education, Iceland would probably be as heavily shaded as California. Minor contradictions and errors such as these do not alter the fact that civilization in the world as a whole shows a basic pattern like that of climatic efficiency.

in their main features. Such worldwide similarities, as well as the resemblances among our varied maps of the United States, are far too great to be the result of accident. Moreover, they are duplicated in many unpublished maps. There is no possible way in which factory work, deaths, the plane of living, the opinion of experts, the use of motor vehicles, or the percentage of children in school could affect the distribution of climate. The resemblances among the maps clearly must originate with the climate.

The question, then, to which we must now address ourselves is the relative degree to which human vigor is influenced by climate and other related conditions such as diet, overpopulation, and disease. It seems logical to begin with climate because that is the factor over which man has the least control. Until we can estimate its influence we cannot rightly tell how much is due to the other factors. We see and appreciate the effect of cultural conditions on health and vigor because we can constantly experiment with them. We often fail, however, to realize how much of our experimentation has been designed to produce a climate approaching the optimum. All our vast progress in medicine, surgery, hygiene, and diet in the most advanced parts of the world would be of little advantage if everyone at all times and seasons had to endure nature's heat and cold, wetness and dryness, with no help whatever from fire, clothing, or shelters of any sort. Indeed, one may well say that without these aids little progress would have taken place. It must be remembered, however, that elsewhere, even more than in the United States, non-climatic factors play a prominent part in giving shape to the map of civilization. Density of population and diet are particularly important in this respect. In countries such as Japan they reduce the level of health much below what would be expected on the basis of climate alone. A further complication is added by wide differences in stage of civilization and by differences of heredity.

CHAPTER 14

HUMAN ACTIVITY AND TEMPERATURE

A. Biological Adjustment to Temperature

In the next few chapters we shall concentrate on climate for four main reasons: (1) aside from the distribution of land and sea, climate appears to be the most important physical factor in determining the habitability, occupations, and mode of life in different parts of the world; (2) no other known physical factor, when considered directly and indirectly, has so great an influence upon health and vigor; (3) no other feature of physical environment is so variable from one period to another, as well as from place to place; (4) we have just found that both in the United States and the world at large climate seems to set a basic pattern of civilization upon which other factors impose variations with all degrees of magnitude.

The first of these four propositions needs little discussion. It is the theme of elementary geography in childhood and of repeated attention in reading and travel. In Greenland and Antarctica vast areas are rendered uninhabitable by icesheets. Much larger areas in high latitudes and at high elevation support only a scanty population because they are cold. Huge deserts are equally effective in limiting population. Elsewhere excessive rain, damp heat, or alternations between extreme dryness and heavy rain limit man's activities. Where the population is fairly dense, the climate has a preponderant effect upon the plants, animals, and bacteria which influence man's food, clothing, shelter, diseases, occupations, transportation, and density of population.

The second and third reasons for the importance of climate are not so well understood as the first, and there is much more difference of opinion about them. The reliability of the fourth proposition depends largely upon what we decide as to the second and third. Therefore, we shall first consider the relation of climate to health, vigor, and human habits.

Among the climatic factors temperature has an especially strong effect on the distribution of civilization. Man's sensitivity to tempera-

ture appears in the fact that the average person can detect a difference of only one or two degrees on going from one room to another.
It is also apparent in the contrasted speeds at which people walk in
different temperatures and in the way they work, dress, eat, and build
their houses in arctic and tropical regions. Atmospheric humidity
and wind influence us largely through their effect on temperature.
A hot day may be fairly comfortable if dry or windy, but uncomfortable if humid and windless. Man, like all plants and animals,
has a definite optimum, or most favorable, level of temperature. This
varies from person to person and according to age and physical condition. A ten-year-old boy normally has a lower optimum than his
grandmother, who tries to make him wear a sweater when he is comfortable without it. Nevertheless, the variations between the optima
of individuals are not large. A sufficient departure below the optimum will make both the boy and his grandmother shiver; a departure
in the other direction will make them sit quietly in the shade. Under
either extreme they are inefficient.

Differences of temperature have so much effect upon civilization
that we may well study the optimum more fully. Daily and hourly
records of thousands of factory hands show that in New England,
Pennsylvania, and England piecework is done fastest and most accurately when the outdoor temperature averages about 60°–63°F for
night and day together, which means a mid-day temperature not far
from 68°–70°F.[1] Farther south, and also in the relatively warm climate of southern Japan, as Yagi has found, a similar optimum prevails at slightly higher levels up to 68°, which means about 75° in the
middle of the day. These noonday temperatures are essentially the
same as those which are most comfortable for people dressed normally
for the season and at rest or engaged in light sedentary work such as
typing. As summarized by Stone, the "comfort zone" in still air with
a relative humidity of 50 per cent has a temperature of about 70°
among Americans in winter, about 75° among Americans in summer,
and 77° among Javanese, Dutch, and Chinese in Java. In warm
weather natives of cool climates (Americans and Dutch), of warm
temperate, or semi-tropical, climates (American Negroes and South
Chinese), and of tropical climates (Javanese and Cubans) all feel most
comfortable under essentially the same conditions.

Such facts indicate a relatively uniform response to temperature
among widely diverse human stocks. In America the summer leads

[1] Huntington, 1924B.

to a temporary acclimatization like that which the Dutch or other Europeans experience in tropical climates. The winter, on the other hand, causes Negroes and tropical Chinese, as well as the rest of us, to become adjusted to somewhat lower temperatures. The significant point is that all races thus far tested seem to react to temperature in much the same way. Among Javanese lowlanders, whose ancestors for many centuries have lived where the thermometer averages close to 80° at all seasons, the most comfortable temperatures are in the lower range of those which they ever experience. Among the Dutch, on the other hand, those same temperatures are the most comfortable, although they are in the highest range of those which their ancestors have experienced for uncounted centuries.

Deaths are another good way of measuring the effect of temperature. In warm, moist New Orleans the minimum of deaths from 1931 to 1940 occurred with an average temperature of 75°F. In Houston, with about the same temperature as New Orleans but slightly lower humidity, deaths are at a minimum with a mean temperature of 73°. On the northern side of the United States at Chicago and Minneapolis deaths fall to their lowest level with an average temperature of 70°.

TABLE 13

DEATHRATES, ALTITUDES, AND TEMPERATURES IN JAVANESE CITIES, 1937 AND 1938

A	B	C	D	E	F	G	H
			Temperature				
Altitude	Death-rate	Yearly Average	Mean Daily Maxi-mum	Mean Daily Mini-mum	Differ-ence between *D* and *E*	Number of Cities	Average Popu-lation
Near sea level	23.0	79°	85°	74°	11°	11	127,000
250– 700 ft.	19.9	77°	84°	72°	12°	6	73,000
800–1,500 ft.	18.6	75°	82°	68°	14°	4	64,000
1,800–2,500 ft.	14.1	72°	78°	64°	14°	6	49,000

In Java the deathrate is greatest with high temperatures. In the cities it varies in almost direct harmony with altitude and temperature. Table 13 shows deathrates of 23 for 11 cities near sealevel and of only 14 for 6 cities at altitudes above 1,800 feet. Between sealevel and an altitude of approximately 2,000 feet the mean annual temperature drops from 79° to about 72° (column *C*). Part of the difference in deathrates doubtless arises from the decreasing size of the cities as the altitude becomes greater (column *H*). Part may be due to weather conditions other than temperature. A decline of 7°F in average yearly temperature is accompanied by a decline of nearly 40 per cent in deaths and presumably by a corresponding rise in efficiency. Although the temperature of the most elevated Javanese cities is above the optimum only a few months each year, people living still higher, at somewhat cooler altitudes, apparently have even greater efficiency. Near the equator the best temperatures for work appear to be found at a height of a mile or more above the sea. The highest indigenous tropical civilizations are also found mainly near this altitude.

TABLE 14

Percentages by Which Deaths during Worst Winter Month Exceed Those during the Best Summer Month, 1937–40 *

East		Center		West	
Florida	49	Texas	47	Arizona	54
North Carolina	38	Tennessee	46	California	41
New York	36	Illinois	36	Oregon	40
Maine	41	Montana	40	Washington	33

* In the United States the percentage of increase in mortality during cold weather is greatest in the South, although the contrast in temperature between the seasons is there at a minimum. In the East and center of the United States a minimum effect is produced in a belt from New York to Illinois and onward. Farther north the effect of cold weather increases once more (Maine and Montana). The minimum difference in number of deaths between the seasons occurs in the latitude where the climate is best for human efficiency.

At temperatures below, as well as above, the optimum the death-rate increases. Table 14 shows that in the United States the deathrate at the end of winter (February or March) is everywhere systematically greater than at the end of the warm season (August and September) by at least 33 per cent. In southern Italy [2] from 1899 to 1913 an average temperature of 42°F in winter was accompanied by a death-rate 45 per cent higher than prevailed in months with an average temperature of 65°. By contrast an average of 80° was associated with a corresponding excess of only 30 per cent. In other countries also departures of temperature below the optimum are accompanied by increased deaths and diminished energy. All over the world the best health is normally experienced when the temperature for day and night averages somewhere from 63° to 73°. Seeming exceptions, such as a maximum of deaths in northern India during December when the temperature approaches the optimum, do not alter this general rule. They simply show the effect of additional factors, includ-

[2] Huntington, 1919, p. 69.

ing the immense number of malarial mosquitoes which breed in stagnant pools after the end of the Indian rainy season. Nor is the rule altered by the fact that the optimum temperature is not the same under all conditions. In general the temperature under which people work best is a little lower than that which makes them feel most comfortable when at rest or which is associated with the lowest deathrate. This is natural, for work makes people warm. Variations in wind, sunshine, humidity, and clothing shift the optimum temperature, as everyone knows from experience. Naked savages naturally have an optimum higher than that of people who are well clothed.

The essential uniformity of the reaction of all races to temperature is altered only slightly by a few racial differences which may be interpreted as incipient biological means of protection against cold or heat. Eskimos, Tibetans, and other inhabitants of cold climates tend to have a stocky bodily build with a considerable layer of fat. People in hot climates, like that of India, tend to be slender with a relatively large surface of skin compared with their weight. Thus, the evaporation of sweat has a more effective cooling power than in fat people. Negroes have especially numerous sweat glands which cover the body with a fine film of moisture. They, as well as other tropical people, also have a deep pigment, but this is a protection against the chemical action of ultra-violet light rather than against heat. None of these developments, however, has apparently gone far enough to produce much difference in the optimum temperature of the main branches of the human family. They are of minor importance compared with the great fact that mankind as a whole appears to work best when the mid-day temperature (not the average for the whole day) is about 63° to 70°, and feels most comfortable when at rest if the corresponding temperature is about 70° to 77°. Thus, when all phases of life are considered, an average within a few degrees on either side of 65° for day and night together and a noonday average of about 68° to 75° seems best. It must be remembered, however, that factors other than temperature enter into the problem of the climate most favorable to human progress.

B. *Body Temperature and the Optimum*

This systematic and well-nigh uniform relation of temperature to human comfort and activity depends primarily on the fact that among all races the internal temperature of the body is practically identical,

98.6°F. The human body is so constituted that it functions best at temperatures of 60° to 70° for people who wear civilized clothing and at somewhat higher temperatures for unclothed people. Under such conditions most persons can carry on ordinary work without raising the body temperature much above normal. Confining ourselves to civilized people, we find that when the thermometer goes much above 70°F in humid weather or above 80° even when the air is quite dry, difficulty begins to be felt in preserving the internal temperature at the normal level. The heat places the heart, lungs, and other organs under a strain in their attempt to prevent the internal temperature from rising. At still higher temperatures, or as the work becomes more vigorous, this maintenance of normal temperature becomes increasingly difficult, a temporary fever is induced, and people quickly become tired. The rapid oxidation caused by even a slight rise of body temperature leads to an excess of toxic substances, which are not eliminated fast enough. Thus the body is poisoned, which gives a sense of fatigue. External means of counteracting this condition, such as electric fans and air-conditioning, are mainly new inventions. Inactivity is by far the most feasible way to counteract the effect of heat. Therefore, throughout human existence people have apparently found that the easiest way to adjust themselves to temperatures above the optimum is to do as little as possible.

When the thermometer falls below the optimum, as well as when it rises above that level, the body has difficulty in preserving the right internal temperature, but the net effects of the low and high temperatures upon human activity are quite different. Extremely low temperatures, to be sure, may equal hot weather in limiting purposeful activity. People who are shivering or benumbed with cold are not much more useful than those who are supine because of heat. Between extremely cold conditions and the optimum, however, there is a long interval in which there are many comparatively easy means of keeping warm—for example, clothing, shelter, fire, fat meat and other foods with abundant carbohydrates. The Canadian lumberman does not object to temperatures far below zero provided his food, clothing, and shelter are right. He also adjusts himself to low temperature by active physical work. Still another method is to use one's wits in devising new methods of protection from wind, snow, and rain, as well as from low temperature. In other words, although both high temperature and low challenge man's ingenuity, the usual response is to get the better of heat by doing as little as possible and of cold by using the body and mind as actively as possible. This contrast between protection from hot weather by passivity and from cold weather by activity is one of the most vital factors in the history of civilization. Its direct effect is obvious in such well-known facts as the tendency of tropical people to sit around and do little in contrast to that of people such as the Scotch or Swedes to be active most of the time. Such physiological differences inevitably express themselves in the culture of the people, so that it becomes good form to be idle in the tropics and to at least seem to work hard in Scotland.

C. Temperature and Early Civilization

In accord with this principle of disinclination to work at high temperatures, most of the world's main civilizations have grown up where the majority of the months have average temperatures near or below the optimum. None of the greatest types of civilization appears to have originated within 25° of the equator. Egypt, Babylonia, and the Indus region, which are often cited as places where civilization developed in hot climates, are not exceptions to this rule, nor are they regions where hot weather prevails steadily. The parts where civilization first flowered lie in latitudes 25° to 35°. In each of these places at least half of the year brings temperatures of the kind well adapted to people in the early stages of civilization, as will appear more fully later. Moreover, because the air is dry, months as warm as October and May at Cairo, for example, with averages of 75° and 77°, seem no hotter than June in Philadelphia, which has an average temperature of about 70°, coupled with high humidity.

The minor civilizations indigenous to the vast area within 25° of the equator all seem to have arisen on temperate plateaus or abnormally cool seacoasts where the temperature at all seasons remains close to the optimum. Those of the Mayas in Mexico and Guatemala, the Khmers in Indo-China, and the ancient Javanese, South Indians, and Singhalese all appear to have originated in climates cooler and more stimulating than those where the ruins of these ancient cultures now arouse our admiration. They were brought to their warm tropical foster homes by migrants who presumably had been highly selected by long and arduous journeys. This last point should be emphasized. In Part II we have seen how a difficult migration selects especially able types of people for preservation. We know that the civilization of the Mayas, Khmers, and early people of Java and Ceylon was brought from elsewhere by migrants from higher latitudes or from plateaus. During these migrations the people doubtless under-

went a selection which may have been as drastic as that of the Icelanders, Mongols, or Parsis. Such selected people, in spite of the
handicaps of tropical climate, appear to be able, for a time at least, to
maintain and even improve the arts and crafts which they bring with
them.

The descendants of missionaries in Hawaii illustrate the manner
in which unusually competent invaders of the tropics can maintain
the high civilization that they bring with them. Hawaii has been
conspicuous for the way in which a few big commercial firms have
dominated the sugar and pineapple industries, the transportation, and
the economic and social life of the islands. A large majority among
the founders and later operators of these businesses and among the
Hawaiian leaders in all fields are descended from missionaries who
completed the work of Christianizing Hawaii, and preferred to make
the islands their home rather than be transferred elsewhere. Missionaries are a highly selected group, both biologically and culturally.
Hundreds of books written by or about them show that, as a group,
they consist of people with a wide range of high abilities. In his
travels in many lands the author has systematically found that, on
the whole, missionaries are the foreigners from whom one obtains
the fullest and most unbiased facts about native people. Similar
ability is found in missionary children. In college and in later life
in the homeland they are on an average more successful than almost
any other corresponding group.[3] This is to be expected, for both
their parents are generally selected on the basis of high moral and
physical qualities, as well as of a good education and the spirit of
altruism and adventure. This gives the children a great advantage in
both heredity and training.

An advantage like that of the descendants of missionaries in tropical Hawaii has probably been one of the major elements in enabling
intruders in the tropics—the Parsis, for example—to maintain their
civilization for centuries in genuinely tropical climates. A selective
process, however, such as long and arduous migration, and a marriage system which preserves the advantages thus gained seem to be
essential if great results are to be gained. All this, however, does not
alter the fact that tropical climates of the warm humid lowland type
have never given rise to any civilization which ranks at all high.
Even so tropical a culture as that of Uganda, where the Negroes have
perhaps attained their highest level, is located high enough to be in

[3] Huntington and Whitney, 1927A.

a climate where the temperature remains steadily near the upper limit of the optimum.

D. Regions with Optimum Temperature

If average temperature were the only climatic factor, we might infer that the best of all climates are those that come nearest to having the optimum temperature at all times of the year. Such climates are found near the equator at an altitude of 5,000 to 7,000 feet in Java, Ecuador, Kenya, and elsewhere. Nairobi at 5,500 feet in Kenya comes close to the optimum at all seasons. So does Addis Ababa, the capital of Ethiopia, at an altitude of 8,000 feet. San José, the capital of Costa Rica, 3,700 feet above the sea, is a little on the warm side of the optimum, whereas Mexico City, 7,500 feet, is on the cool side. A few low, narrow strips on west coasts in subtropical and tropical latitudes also enjoy the optimum temperature at all seasons. Ocean currents from higher latitudes keep the coastal waters cool, and winds from the ocean prevent the temperature from rising too high on the adjacent shore. San Diego in California, Mogador in Morocco, and the South American coast from Lima to northern Chile are examples. Such places all have little rainfall.

The climate of places where the temperature is uniformly near the optimum is in many ways delightful. If there is moisture enough, it has an eternal springlike quality. It is at its best in a place such as the official experiment station for quinine in Java. There at an altitude of about a mile one looks across groves of cinchona trees to volcanic peaks surrounded by fertile slopes superbly terraced for rice. The pleasantly cool, yet softly warm, air gives people who have come from the heat of the enervating lowlands a thrill of joy and energy. If parasitic and infectious diseases could be eliminated and a wise diet and mode of life could prevail, well-watered tropical plateaus, with temperatures close to the optimum at all seasons, might be especially conducive to health and long life. As centers of civilization, however, such places have been intermediate between ordinary humid tropical lowlands and regions beyond the limits of the tropics. Ethiopia, the Rhodesian ruins of Zimbabwe, and the Inca and Aztec civilizations of America illustrate this point. High altitude has probably been a handicap because it affects the inhabitants physiologically and because it tends toward isolation, but lack of changes of weather from season to season and day to day has probably hampered these regions still more.

The low coastal regions where the temperature remains most nearly at the optimum at all seasons have likewise fostered a type of civilization which has risen fairly high but has been short-lived or else relatively unenterprising. This is illustrated by the coast of Peru which appears to have been the original home of an extinct, but fairly advanced, culture different from that of the highlands. The temperatures on this coast are not far from the optimum and are like those ordinarily experienced in low latitudes at an altitude of nearly 4,000 feet. For example, at Callao, the seaport of Lima in Peru, the coolest month (August) averages 62°F and the warmest (March) 71°. So powerful is the cooling effect of the northbound ocean current and the upwelling deep seawater along the Peruvian coast that one goes inland to get warm, just as in California. Farther inland, beyond the narrow coastal plain, cool air is found again among the mountains. Early civilizations of a fairly high type developed in both of the cool regions but stagnated relatively soon.

The dryness of the Peruvian coast, coupled with irrigation from the Andes, was a great advantage from the standpoint of the early development of agriculture. After the rare rainy periods hundreds of square miles which normally are absolutely devoid of vegetation become one vast garden of waving grass and lovely flowers. In such a place civilized existence naturally depends upon irrigation, and the soil is much more fertile than in the moister tropics. The dryness of cool tropical coasts, such as that of Peru, is also an advantage to health and vigor in many respects. Nevertheless, it has certain disadvantages. The dust which is raised by almost every breeze in such deserts is a serious menace to health. Nor is the constant sunshine so great a promoter of health as is often supposed. Sunshine is of value in diseases such as rickets and certain afflictions of the skin. Often, however, the very sunny parts of the world are relatively unhealthful. Excessively dry cities, such as Cairo in Egypt and Lahore in India, have some of the world's highest deathrates, whereas cloudy cities, such as Copenhagen and London, have low deathrates. Nevertheless, the favorable temperature at all seasons which is associated with the dryness of the Peruvian coast appears to outweigh the disadvantages of dryness so far as health is concerned. It seems to have been an important factor in enabling a relatively high civilization to develop on the Peruvian coast as well as in the highlands. In spite of all this, however, the parts of the earth's surface where the temperature stays near the optimum at all seasons appear to be under a distinct climatic handicap which lessens human vigor and thus retards the progress of civilization.

E. Reproduction as the Basis of Optimum Temperature

The relation of temperature to civilization is so intimate and pervasive that we may well inquire why the optimum for man is approximately an average of 65° for day and night together. Why is it not 80°, the apparent optimum of monkeys in equatorial lowlands, or 40°, which is presumably not far from that of polar bears? The usual answer is that the optimum depends upon the conditions under which man took the evolutionary steps which gave him his present adjustment to climate. Recent studies make this supposition more specific. They suggest that the optimum temperature depends upon an annual cycle of reproduction.[4] Man, in his conceited way, has supposed that he alone among animals is free to reproduce at all seasons. As a matter of fact, however, his freedom, although greater than that of other animals, is limited. Worldwide statistics indicate that the human species has an annual cycle of reproduction like that of animals, with a maximum of births in the early spring. The cycle, to be sure, is greatly modified by social conditions, such as seasonal work and migration, diet, and social status. For example, in the parts of the United States with the highest standards of living and also among the upper classes of Britain and Germany, the normal maximum of births in the early spring is replaced by a maximum in summer. This is the result of conceptions in October and November at a season when cool weather brings a widespread feeling of exhilaration, which also shows itself in the most efficient factory work of the year. This shifting of the season of maximum births seems to be the result of a high standard of living, whereby the effects of inherited adaptations to the weather are more or less overcome. It does not appear in less fortunate groups, such as those which produce the majority of American criminals, insane persons, and sufferers from tuberculosis, nor does it appear in the great masses of people in the world as a whole.[5] Among such people, when we eliminate cultural effects, such as seasonal migrations of the men in search of work, the normal animal cycle becomes evident practically everywhere.

This cycle varies according to climate. In the northern United States and western Europe the maximum of births normally occurs in

---

[4] Huntington, 1938.   [5] Huntington, 1938.

March or April as a response to conceptions in June or July. Elsewhere the maximum tends to shift to earlier dates in hot climates and later ones where the climate is cold. Where the winter temperature is below the optimum, conceptions which result in living births are normally at a maximum when the temperature approaches or reaches the optimum in the spring or summer. In warm countries, such as northern India, however, this maximum is associated with the winter months, the only ones when the temperature falls as low as the optimum.

The meaning of this seems to be that primitive man, like the animals around him, was best able to survive if the young were born in the late winter or early spring. Young animals are born in the spring because both the weather and the food are then favorable to survival. The same was doubtless true of primitive man. Our species presumably acquired its primary climatic adaptations in an intermediate type of moderately warm, but by no means equatorial, climate. From February to April in such a climate vegetation bursts forth, the birds lay eggs, and young mammals are born. Food of the kinds used by primitive man begins to be abundant and also unusually nutritious by reason of abundance of vitamins. Then for six or eight months an increasing supply of food is available so that mothers can meet the growing demands of their young for milk during a longer period than if the children were born at any other season. The inference from this is that among our earliest human ancestors those whose health and powers of reproduction were most stimulated at a definite temperature were the ones whose children were born at the time when the chances of survival were best.

Among primitive people the great majority of infants always perish. Selwyn James says that 48 per cent of the Bantu children in Africa die in their first year. So many others die later that the total mortality during the first four years of life is about 64 per cent. Under such conditions an advantage of the kind here suggested would be great. Thus there seems to have been implanted in the human race an innate tendency to reach the highest level of reproductive vigor at the temperature normally prevailing nine months before the season which gave a newborn child the best chance of survival. The primitive human stock most likely to survive was presumably the one most fully inheriting a tendency toward maximum vigor at the temperature which has now become the human optimum.

A similar condition is seen among animals, although the nature of the stimulus to reproduction varies. Among many kinds of birds, according to Rowan, Bissonnette, and others, the stimulating factor is light. The lengthening of the day in the spring induces a swelling of the reproductive glands, which have been dormant and seemingly atrophied for many months. This is associated with a restlessness which leads to migration and then to mating and nest-building. Birds inherit a sensitivity to light which causes them to lay their eggs at the season most favorable for the survival of the young. A similar effect upon mammals seems to be produced by both temperature and diet. Human reproduction, too, may be influenced by diet, for in the spring many plants contain a greater proportion of vitamin A than at any other season. The eating of such plants or of the flesh, milk, or eggs of animals that have eaten them is known to be a stimulant to reproduction. Nevertheless, the greatest factor in guiding man's annual cycle of reproduction seems to be temperature. The optimum temperature for health and activity seems to have become established as a response to a specific type of climate in which the chances of survival were greatest if a child were conceived when the mean temperature rose to about 65°F, so that it would be born early the following spring. This conclusion is not an essential part of the argument of this book, but if it is correct, it helps to explain why civilization tends so strongly to follow a climatic pattern.

The essential points of this chapter begin with the fundamental fact that physical vigor is one of the main factors in the growth of civilization. From this we go on to see that mankind as a whole has a definite level of optimum temperature at which health and vigor are best. At temperatures above the optimum, fatigue is readily induced, the inclination to work diminishes, and the easiest way to make oneself comfortable is to do as little as possible. At temperatures below the optimum the inclination to work is stimulated, partly because bodily activity promotes warmth, partly because there are many ways in which a moderate degree of inventiveness enables people to keep themselves warm artificially. Thus, if all other influences were eliminated, we should expect civilization to advance most rapidly in climates which have few or no months with temperatures above the optimum and many below, but none far below, the optimum. As a matter of fact, the actual distribution of civilization approaches this pattern but departs from it in some respects because mean temperature is only one of the climatic factors, climate is only one of the physical factors of environment, and the effects of physical environment are modified by cultural environment.

CHAPTER 15

SOCIAL CONDITIONS, RELIGION, AND CLIMATE

A. Climatic Selection of Social Attitudes

Temperature, rainfall, and other climatic conditions have as much effect upon social conditions as upon the human body. It is particularly necessary to discuss such conditions because there is much confusion concerning the direct and indirect effects of climate. To take a simple illustration, a hot climate, especially if it is humid, makes people feel disinclined to work. This encourages the more clever people to get a living with as little physical exertion as possible. Their example fosters the growth of a social system in which hard work is regarded as plebeian. Disinclination toward extra effort also leads to the neglect of medical care and sanitation, thus permitting disease to play havoc, and still further reducing human vigor. By encouraging one type of social organization and discouraging another, climate has great influence upon the development of civilization.*

The kind of contrast that we have in mind is well illustrated by two women in a hot city of northern Australia.

One was comely, dark-haired, fairly plump [and] of a merry, easy-going temperament . . . a delightful hostess. . . . Kindness of heart was one of her dominating characteristics. . . . In a sudden emergency she would work desperately to help even her enemies. Nevertheless, her idea of doing good . . . was to feed the hungry and clothe the naked . . . without . . . asking . . . why they became so. "Make them happy and let them go. It's too much work to go digging into their past lives to find out what's the matter with them." That was her attitude toward everything, including the climate. "Oh, yes, it's hot sometimes, but I love it. If it's too hot, don't work so hard. Why wear yourself out for nothing?" . . . The other woman, equally charming, was fair, slender, blue-eyed, and more nervous than her friend . . . an intense, eager sort of person. Her house would always look more spick and span than that of the other, but her guests would . . . find her

---

* This subject is especially well discussed by A. Grenville Price in *White Settlers in the Tropics.*

absorbed in other things. . . . She would have to run off to a meeting of her welfare board over in the poorer quarter. . . . A community containing many people of her sort could scarcely fail to make rapid progress. . . . This was her opinion of the climate: "Oh, I hate it. The winter is well enough, but in summer you can't do what you want to do, and it makes the people lazy and makes them careless about sanitation and food and all sorts of things. I want to get back to the South where it's cool." [1]

In these modern days of easy travel people of the first type are more likely than those of the second to settle permanently in a tropical or semi-tropical climate. Thus a process of selection through migration is tending, slowly perhaps, to concentrate the more easy-going type in the warmer climates. In the past, similar differences in adaptability have presumably given the less active type a better chance of survival in warm regions, and the more active type in cool regions. The contrasted character of the Finns and the people of Ceylon, for example, suggests biological as well as cultural differences. We cannot be sure of the degree of biological difference. First, the climate itself and the accompanying diseases and diet tend to render the people of hot regions less active than those of cooler regions. Second, under any given geographical conditions the organization of society, with its ideals, aspirations, and habits, tends gradually to assume a form adapted to the physical environment. For example, the necessity of preparing shelter, clothing, and fuel as means of combatting the cold and moisture of winter tends to promote a social system which places high value on foresight and thrift. These virtues are more needed in cool climates than in either the regular tropical types or the rare types which have the optimum temperature at all seasons. Hence we should expect that, even if human groups which have migrated into climates having a cold winter are not biologically endowed with qualities leading to foresight and thrift, they would evolve social systems which emphasize these virtues.

B. North and South in the United States

A familiar and impressive example of the effect of climate, especially temperature, is seen in the handicapped economic development of the southern United States. The alleged causes include slavery, the Negroes, the Civil War, the postwar carpetbag policy, tenancy, fluctuations in the demand for cotton and tobacco, preferential freight

[1] Huntington, 1925B, pp. 347–48.

rates, exhaustion and erosion of the soil, malaria, hookworm, and a social system which long regarded manual labor as degrading. They also include restriction of European migration, lack of capital, a poor diet based on corn, syrup, and pork, lack of educational facilities, restricted mineral resources, poor harbors, and scores of other conditions. All these factors have played significant parts. The emphatic point just now, however, is that each of them has been influenced directly or indirectly by climate.

Consider the probable development from colonial times onward if the climate had been reversed so that the South claimed the ancient glaciation, present severe winters, and relatively short summers of the North, whereas the North had never been glaciated and now had mild winters and long, hot, humid summers. Because of glaciation, and the presumable pushing downward of the earth's crust by the weight of ice, with consequent "drowning" of the seacoast, the South would have better harbors than the North. Its soil would excel that of the North because it would be largely glacial in origin, relatively new, and less leached and better supplied with plant foods than at present. Wheat, oats, corn, potatoes, and many vegetables and fruits would yield more per acre than now. Corn yields three times as much per acre in Pennsylvania as in Georgia. Idaho similarly excels Arkansas in potatoes. In each case, as in many others, the product of the cooler climate excels the other in its percentage of minerals and vitamins. Then, too, in the cooler climate, cellars are more necessary and also cooler than where the mean temperature is high. Hence the preservation of apples, cabbages, onions, and other sources of winter vitamins is much more practical than in the present southern climate. Thus for generation after generation an interchange of climates between North and South would have given the South a much better diet than it has actually enjoyed. Moreover, with such a reversal of climates the southern grass would be less bunchy, softer, and more nutritious than now. Cattle would flourish better so that milk and its products would be more abundant and better supplied with vitamins than is actually the case. In other ways, too, the health of the community as a whole would be improved, and some of the present southern handicaps would be removed.

The handicaps of the South can, to a large degree, be overcome if people will study them with open minds. Those just mentioned, for example, can probably be outbalanced by fuller utilization of the advantages of a long growing season and of modern knowledge as to agriculture and human health. They persist largely because of a few main hindrances. One of these is the fact that the necessary scientific knowledge and technical skill have only recently been developed and are still unknown to the rank and file of the population. A second is the persistence of relative inertia because of the combined effects of diet, climate, and social customs. A third is lack of capital because of the preceding conditions, together with other handicaps mentioned at the beginning of this section.

One of the first requisites in overcoming these difficulties lies in widespread recognition of the part played by man's physical environment. Most people are much like the pioneer settler whom Van Doren saw in his youth. The man had been driven out of western Kansas by drought in 1895. During the preceding three years his part of the state had received only 77, 50, and 54 per cent, respectively, of the normal rainfall. Drought was the obvious reason for his crop failures, his inability to pay the required installments on his land, and the distress of his family. Nevertheless, on the side of his old-fashioned, white-topped "prairie schooner" with its weary horses he put a big placard: "I'm going back to my relations. Damn Cleveland's administration." Like the vast majority of mankind, he overlooked nature and ascribed his troubles to some human cause against which he could vent his resentment. Often, to be sure, the human factor is a genuine link in the chain of cause and effect, but its presence does not make it wise to overlook the underlying physical conditions.

This last statement is well illustrated by the problems of slavery, the War between the States, and the present Negro question. These would scarcely have troubled the South if its climate had been like that of the North. The suppression of slavery in the North was not due chiefly to moral conviction. That arose after long experience had shown that slavery did not pay in a cool climate. In many a New England meetinghouse the slaves' gallery was still occupied after the Revolution. Slaves, however, were a luxury. In the long, cold winter there was little work for those who were field hands, but expenses for food, fuel, clothing, and housing were then at a maximum. Moreover, the climate did not foster easily exportable money crops, such as tobacco and cotton. Then, too, the combination of good food, stimulating climate, and a northern type of culture made the white northerners so energetic that it irked them to wait for slow-moving Africans. Even though the housewife had several slaves, she liked to bustle around in the kitchen herself. So, too, on the farm or in the garden the northern men were so active that they would not wait for slow, careless slaves to get in the hay when storms were threatening or to hoe weeds which were fast becoming knee-high.

In the South, on the other hand, the short, mild winter interferes only a little with farm work. It does not demand large expense for food, fuel, clothing, and housing to maintain farm people while they are idle. The climate is so favorable to tobacco and cotton that wealth was formerly amassed even with the inefficient labor of slaves. In early days, as well as now, the pervasive effect of the weather on inclination to work had to be reckoned with. In warm, unstimulating weather people may have the capacity for work, but their inclination thereto declines, and they need much rest. Thus, even without slavery, different ideals of labor were bound to prevail in the North and South.

The difference in inclination toward work had much to do with the development of diverse social ideals in these two parts of the United States. In the North the successful family was the one where everybody worked hard as well as intelligently. Hard work became the supreme virtue, as it is to this day in spite of other tendencies. In the South the successful ante-bellum family was the one that eschewed physical labor and at the same time got a good living. This system favored slavery and attached a social stigma to work with the hands. An aristocratic society was almost inevitable, because the mental ability to get a good living through slave labor is more limited than the physical ability which was so important in the North. Thus the old South distinguished sharply between aristocrats and "poor whites," as well as between whites in general and Negroes. This distinction of classes was in strong contrast to the relative democracy which prevailed in the North, where the squire might care for his own horse, cow, and garden. When slavery disappears, a system of tenancy almost inevitably grows up in regions where differences in ability to manage people and property are especially important in comparison with the ability to do manual work. In all these respects climatic contrasts paved the way for civil war.

This discussion of North and South illustrates one of the profoundest facts in the history of civilization. Social and economic systems everywhere tend to adjust themselves to geographical environment and to the occupations which provide a living in a particular environment at any particular stage of human progress. This is obvious in the contrasts between mountaineers and plainsmen, between inland farmers and coastal fishermen, or between the banana-growing people of Uganda and the llama-raising Indians of highest Peru. It is equally true, although less obvious elsewhere. A watch repairer's job is the same everywhere, but the demand for his services, the hours of work, the arrangement of his shop, the intentness with which he works, and the quality, number, and state of repair of the watches and clocks brought to him all vary greatly from place to place. Much of the difference is directly or indirectly connected with climate, which influences the comfort, vigor, and activity of the people, as well as their general prosperity. In fact, among all the factors which influence people's modes of life the two that seem to be most dominant are climate and the stage of culture already attained. Climate, of course, operates through soil, vegetation, animals, diet, clothing, housing, disease, and other factors, as well as directly. Nevertheless, its greatest social influence is probably its effect on inclination to work. This inclination depends primarily upon man's inheritance of delicate climatic adjustments, which make him extremely sensitive to differences in weather. These will be discussed in a later chapter.

C. Religion and Physical Environment

Let us widen our outlook somewhat and examine the relation of one of the dominant elements in civilization to several aspects of physical environment. Religion has been a vital factor in molding human society. It owes its character to the great ideas of supreme religious teachers, the thoughts and deeds of many minor men, and the kind of geographical setting in which it develops. It is beyond the province of this book to discuss the way in which religious ideas originate in the human mind. Nor can we do more than recognize the enormous influence of teachers such as Confucius, Gautama, and Jesus. They represent vital steps in a long evolutionary process which is still going on and whose ultimate result can only be conjectured. Their teachings, modified by the ideas of a multitude of lesser men, have led to wide differences of conduct and ideas in different parts of the world. Nevertheless, diversity of physical environment has also been effective in leading to religious differences, and among the environmental factors climate has been especially important. Without trying to separate the effects of the various environmental factors, let us look at some of the ways in which religious faith and practice have been influenced by man's physical surroundings. We shall begin with a mere external and then proceed to something more vital.

An interesting minor effect of physical environment is seen in descriptions of God's relation to man. Religious ideas cannot spread widely unless expressed in language. The language of the common man is full of imagery based on nature. Hence it was natural that in Palestine people should speak of God's protecting care as "the shadow of a great rock in a weary land." This simile means a great deal to people who live close to the hot, treeless desert, but nothing at all to those in a Siberian forest. One appreciates such a rock at noonday in Transcaspia when one tries to take a siesta in the burning sun with a temperature of 120° and no shade except that of a restless horse. The ground is hot to the touch, a breath of air feels as if a furnace door had been opened, the horse will not stand still, and the sun smites one continually. Then at evening, when the temperature falls to 80° or lower and one sits among fruit trees in a tiny oasis beside a gurgling streamlet, Mohammed's description of heaven seems very appealing:

Paradise is better than anything on earth. It is a garden in which are rivers of water, flowing springs, and branching trees with fruit of every kind. Among [the Saints] eternal youths shall pass with goblets, ewers, and cups of flowing wine. No headaches shall arise from this, nor any dimness of the senses.

To reindeer herders in Lapland, however, a God who provides a place where "the sun shall not smite . . . by day" seems positively cruel. To sit in the warm sunshine is bliss.

Japan and New Zealand illustrate another kind of contrast in religious imagery. Nearly five sixths of Japan is waste mountainland too rough for cultivation and so warm and rainy that it is heavily forested. When trees are prevented from growing, the grass which replaces them is too tough and coarse for good pasturage. Moreover, the hot, wet Japanese summers do not favor woolly beasts, such as sheep. Hence Japan has only one sheep for every two thousand inhabitants. In such a land what meaning is there in the Twenty-third Psalm: "The Lord is my shepherd. I shall not want. He maketh me to lie down in green pastures"? The Japanese psalm should read: "The Lord is my guide among sweet cherry blossoms, he showeth me still waters that reflect the glory of autumn." In modern New Zealand, however, the Twenty-third Psalm is fully appropriate. That island has nearly twenty sheep for each inhabitant, approximately forty thousand times as many as Japan in proportion to the population.

All over the world religion adjusts itself more or less to differences such as this. Even the same religion, with no change in fundamental beliefs, may alter its imagery to agree with the geographical environment. For example, Buddhism has a hot hell. This is not surprising, for in northern India late spring and early summer are terrifically hot. At Allahabad, for example, close to the birthplace of Gautama, the average temperature for day and night in May is 93°F. The *maximum* hovers around 105° or 110° day after day. Small wonder, then, that the Buddhist hell has six levels based on torture by heat. In the mildest level the people are burned and then allowed to recover before the next burning: In the next they are cut to pieces as well as burned but have a breathing space for recovery. And so on, until in the lowest hell, burning continues eternally without respite. When Buddhism migrated northward a few hundred miles to high Tibet, a hot hell did not seem at all bad to shepherds whose worst foe is cold and snow. Their mildest month is only about as warm as the coldest at Benares. So hell had to be remodelled. In Tibet, as in India, it has six levels, but torture by cold is the main punishment. In the lowest hell the excruciating ache of fingers that are being warmed after being frozen is spread eternally to all parts of the body.

D. *The Geography of Great Religions*

The moral and spiritual aspects of religion, as well as religious imagery, are intimately related to physical environment. It is not easy to measure or even define these aspects. Estimates of the importance of their various phases differ greatly according to people's training and temperament. Nevertheless, the essentials of the finest types of religion seem to include the following: (1) love, confidence, and faith, in place of hate, doubt, and fear; (2) uniform, unbreakable law, in place of arbitrary divine interference; (3) ethical personal conduct, without which ritual and faith have little value; (4) altruism and social responsibility as the basis of social conduct.

The first two essentials are a modern version of the first great commandment of Jesus, which is the same as the old Jewish commandment: "Thou shalt love the Lord, thy God." The last two are a restatement of Jesus' second commandment: "Thou shalt love thy neighbor as thyself."

When we examine the world's great religions we find a rather impressive relation between geographical environment, especially temperature, and the degree to which the religions conform to these es-

TABLE 15

Location of Great Religions

Animism, etc.	25°S–25°N, 45–70°N, 40–55°S	All continents
Hinduism	10–30°N	Practically limited to India
Islam (Mohammedanism)	10°S–45°N	North Africa, south half of Asia, East Indies
Buddhism	10–50°N	Southeastern Asia
Confucianism and Taoism	20–50°N	China
Shintoism	30–40°N	Japan
Judaism	25–50°N	Europe, North America, western Asia
Christianity	50°S–65°N	Europe, North and South America, Australia

sentials. In Table 15, eight great forms of religion are arranged in order according to the temperature of the regions where their adherents are most numerous, the religion of the warmest regions being first. This arrangement is practically identical with what would prevail if we classified the religions according to the four preceding essentials. Taking account both of the higher ideals which pertain to each religion and of the ordinary lives of the adherents, it seems safe to say that, as we pass from animism through Hinduism, Islam, Buddhism, Confucianism, Shintoism, and Judaism to Christianity, there is in general a systematic progression in five respects: (1) latitude; (2) approach to the optimum climate for civilized man; (3) religious beliefs, that is, conceptions of God, ideas as to a future life, ideals of personal and social conduct, and relation of religion to ethical conduct; (4) standards of living and general progress; and (5) physical health and vigor.

The problem now before us is to ascertain, if possible, what relationships prevail among these five conditions. Which ones lead to the others, and how far does each react to produce one or more of the others? We cannot here solve more than a small part of the problem. No one doubts that a high form of religion goes far toward overcoming the untoward effects of a poor physical environment. It is equally clear that great advances in civilization are in general accompanied by corresponding advances in religious thought and practice or at least in the feeling of social responsibility. All this is so well established that we may for the present accept it as demonstrated. The problem before us is to determine the extent to which religious and climatic differences are correlated, regardless of whether the climate is a cause or merely an accompaniment.

E. Animism and Inertia

On the basis of the four essentials of a high religion, animism seems to stand lowest. The gods, or spirits, are almost invariably looked upon with fear. Their attitude toward any particular man, or under any particular circumstances, is always in doubt. They break the laws of nature with impunity and permit their followers to act likewise. The moral conduct of animists has little relation to religion. The religious leaders—shamans, priests, medicine men—may be the best or the worst in the community. Moral quality scarcely enters into the matter. The powerful, not the good, enjoy heaven. The holy man, the religious man, is not the one who spends his life in pious contemplation or wears himself out in unselfish service of his fellows. He is the one who at a heavy price claims to control the spirits that hover all around. Rarely, if ever, does animism inspire service for the general welfare.

Consider who the animists are. A few live in cold, high latitudes both north and south of the equator—Eskimos, Samoyedes, the remoter Indians of both Americas. The vast majority are the savage tribes in the less accessible tropical parts of Africa, South America, the East Indies, and the Asiatic mainland, especially Indo-China, Malaya, and India. Practically everywhere animists belong to what are commonly called the more backward races. They include such people as the Pygmies and Hottentots of Africa, the Bhils of India, and the Negritoes of the Philippine mountains. They inhabit the parts of the earth where natural disadvantages of low or high temperature, tropical rain forest, or jungle-clad mountains make it especially hard to get a living. Even the modern white man with all his machinery and knowledge can scarcely utilize the natural resources of such regions. In World War II no part of the world presented greater difficulties than the densely forested equatorial lands of the Solomon Islands, New Guinea, and the wet east side of the Malay Peninsula. All of these are typical of the geographic regions in which animism still persists. Intense rainfall day after day makes travel exceedingly difficult. High temperature, coupled with high humidity, causes the vegetation to be so rank that horses, cattle, and sheep do not thrive. Even the tropical water buffalo, the ubiquitous hog, and the useful hen do not easily find food. These same conditions make agriculture almost impossible except in the sketchy fashion of irregular plantings of roots, such as the yam or cassava, and trees for fruit and nuts. Muddy soil most of the time and the extraordinarily rapid growth of weeds largely prevent more advanced types of agriculture. Even the white man's banana and cocoa plantations have as yet penetrated only the edges of the animist areas. In addition, tropical insects bring insidious diseases, and their bites are a constant source of irritation, even when no specific disease ensues.

Man suffers from these conditions quite as much as animals. In no other part of the world is his vitality lowered so much by the joint effects of climate and disease. Therefore nowhere else is there less inclination to work. The effect of such conditions on mental activity and on the extent to which man uses his powers of reasoning is also of the utmost importance, as will appear more fully later.

Meanwhile it is clear that in general the animist type of religion and the stages of culture which go with it tend to persist most firmly in the parts of the earth where the difficulties due to climate and other geographical features, such as mountains or swamps, are at a maximum. The question to be answered by the student of civilization does not involve the reality of this agreement, for that cannot be doubted. The real question is this: How far is the persistence, not the origin, of the animistic type of religion the result of (1) isolation; (2) innate racial character; (3) the more or less accidental absence of men of genius and of new inventions and ideas for generation after generation; (4) the mere physical difficulties of getting a living; and (5) disinclination to work and think? Then comes the question: How far are climatic conditions the direct or indirect reason for the association of these conditions with animism? Such questions cannot be answered fully as yet. Part of the answer may be found in a selective process which has caused the animist areas to be a refuge in which biologically incompetent types have been protected against abler types that have gone on to higher forms of religion. Part is found in the principles of the diffusion of human culture set forth in any standard textbook of anthropology. Still another part will be found in later chapters of this book, which show the close relation between mental activity and the degree of variability in the weather from day to day and season to season. Here we shall merely say that animism, although once doubtless prevalent everywhere, persists today only in regions where the general geographic conditions, especially those of topography and climate, have the greatest tendency to promote isolation and to discourage physical and especially mental activity.

One of the chief elements in animism is fear of the unknown. Such fear is encouraged by life in a tropical jungle. An ignorant savage, let us say, is walking in the jungle, when a stick falls on his head. He can detect no cause. No leaves stir in the branches above him; no monkey or bird moves away. It seems as if someone had deliberately thrown the stick, but no one is visible. The easiest supposition is that some creature like a man, but more ill-tempered and quite invisible, must have done it. The same line of reasoning suggests that an invisible spirit is at work when the man stumbles on a hidden root, hears a frightening sound in the dark, or is afflicted with some strange illness. A walk through the jungle in the dark becomes a painful ordeal because of the fear that evil spirits may be lurking almost anywhere. Their name is legion. If there are evil spirits, perhaps there are also good ones. The evil ones may be propitiated by the same sort of offerings, dances, and festivities which please human beings. Perhaps the good ones may be thus persuaded to grant protection against their evil comrades.

Other things being equal, animism of this kind thrives better in a forest than in open grasslands or deserts. Even the sophisticated reader of this book is more likely to be lost and frightened in a forest than in an open grassland or desert. Nor does he need to be lost in order to feel a choking tightness of the throat when some strange sound breaks the stillness as he walks in the dark in a pathless forest. Even to highly civilized people such conditions may suggest that some dangerous creature is on their trail or hiding behind the next tree. How much more likely that an ignorant savage will feel thus, especially if his physical environment, as well as his primitive culture, handicaps his powers of reasoning. It is clear, then, that a jungle inhabited by dangerous animals and full of alarming sounds and threatening hiding places provides especially fertile soil for an animistic belief in a multitude of evil spirits. This is doubtless true of forests in all latitudes. The point to be emphasized just now is that such beliefs are most likely to persist in physical environments where two conditions prevail. One is isolation due to barriers such as mountains, swamps, and forests. The other is a climate, a diet, and diseases of the sort that render people's minds inactive. In later chapters we shall see how greatly such conditions influence mental activity and the growth of science. The combined retarding effect of climate, diet, disease, and isolation appears to be at a maximum in rugged tropical jungles too wet for agriculture. Those appear to be also the regions where animistic ideas of innumerable spirits, but no one God, still persist most widely.

F. Physical Handicaps of Hinduism

Hinduism in its higher aspects stands well above animism, but as actually practiced in India it departs far from the great essentials of a high religion. This is evident in the number and low character of its gods and superstitions, its unintelligent ritual, and such practices as public prostitution in temples and the drinking of holy Ganges water full of the germs of dysentery and other diseases. It is evident in other practices which seem to us revolting, for instance, washing in cows' urine, burning widows, and condemning child widows to a life of degradation. Hinduism is mainly a religion of fear, in which the chief effort is to wheedle the gods into refraining from harm to mortals or perhaps into doing a few favors. The gods themselves are immoral and have little sense of responsibility for anyone except themselves. Deceit, drunkenness, adultery, quarrels, and revenge are everyday events in their lives. The example of the gods encourages similar practices among their followers. Nevertheless, parts of the Hindu philosophy rise to a high level. Curiously enough, these are largely connected with the old Vedas and other writings which originated north of India. They have relatively little to do with current practices or the present physical environment. Only the exceptional Hindu knows about them.

The low estate of Hinduism in recent times is associated with life in a region only second to the animist regions in the difficulties which it imposes upon man's attempt to get a living. "The wealth of Ind" is a favorite poetic expression, but only the merest handful of the two hundred million or more Hindus ever enjoy such wealth. As a whole, the Hindus are the poorest of all great religious groups aside from the animists. They cannot be much more prosperous unless their numbers are greatly reduced so that more land and greater resources are available in proportion to the population. Even if this should happen, the Hindus could not maintain standards of living like ours, unless they worked far harder and more intelligently than we do. Their soil on an average is poorer than ours, their rainfall less reliable, their yields per acre less even with equally good cultivation, their food crops less nutritious because of the leaching of minerals from the soil. Moreover, even if the Hindus discarded their religious taboo against meat, they could not readily raise cattle, sheep, and poultry of a quality like that found in the United States and western Europe. The climate, with its extremely hot dry season and its extremely muggy wet season, produces tough, harsh types of forage which do not favor the production of milk and the rapid growth of young animals. Only with much work can nutritious forage be obtained by raising grasses introduced from abroad. Moreover, the heat and the mugginess also lead to low production of milk, meat, and wool. Therefore, in order to obtain a given amount of agricultural production either through plants or animals, much more work is needed than in more favorable countries. A similar situation prevails in respect to mineral resources. They are moderately abundant in India, but on the whole their exploitation requires more work per ton than in the United States.

Unfortunately, this necessity for much work in order to produce a given result occurs in a country where both physical and mental effort are difficult. We have already mentioned an average monthly temperature of 93°F at Allahabad in May. In that month the rainfall is only three tenths of an inch. July and August are not quite so hot, averaging 85° and 83°. They each, however, have eleven inches of rain so that they are more enervating than the worst dog days in the United States. Only in late October does the weather become as comfortably cool as July in New York City. We have also spoken of the poor quality of the food. The harm done by frequent scarcity of food and by the deficiency of the cereals and other main crops in essential minerals is augmented by lack of meat, milk, eggs, fruit, and fresh vegetables—the protective foods which supply vitamins as well as minerals. Add the wide prevalence of enervating diseases, such as malaria, dysentery, and hookworm disease, and it is evident that the Hindus cannot be as energetic as the people of more favored lands. Needing far more work than we do to maintain a given standard of living, they have far less strength and inclination to work. The Hindus fall under the last part of the Bible verse which says that "to him that hath shall be given and from him that hath not shall be taken away even that which he hath."

Hindu energy has a direct relation to religion. If religion is to advance from animism to higher and higher types, people must be strong and energetic, both physically and mentally. It is much easier to grasp the idea of a local deity who lives close by and has the good and bad qualities of a man than to conceive of universal laws which always operate in exactly the same way. Again, it is much easier to yield to anger, sexual desire, or the hunger that prompts theft than to say, "Get thee behind me, Satan." And it is easier to practice non-resistance with Gandhi than to wage a long, hard fight against the alleged oppression of the English, or than to analyse and then cure the enormous difficulties which have arisen because British peace, British famine relief, and British medical service have permitted the population of India to increase enormously without enlarging the area of arable land to a corresponding degree.

Here we have branched off into a political subject, but it illustrates the kind of inertia which makes the Hinduism of India utterly different from the Protestantism of Scotland. Consider the case of an anemic, poorly fed Hindu who has been weakened by malaria in childhood and by dysentery in manhood. He lives in the enervating heat and mugginess of India. He desires to win religious merit in order to save his soul and be happier in the next life than in this. If he were a strong, healthy young Scotch Highlander, well fed on oatmeal and milk and living always in a climate which makes one want to work, he might become a self-sacrificing physician who wears himself out attending the poor. Being a Hindu, he finds it much easier to attain holiness by lying on a bed of blunted spikes, by sitting on top of a pillar for months, or by being buried up to the neck for a while. In other words, among people who lack energy religious merit tends to take the form of passive suffering rather than active work for others. In this lies one of the sharpest distinctions between the lower and higher forms of religion.

This same distinction is found in ideas as to God and heaven. In their higher levels, the tropical religions of Hinduism and Buddhism rise to the idea of a supreme God among, but above, other gods. In both religions, however, this God is passive. In Hinduism, he is Brahma, the creator, who made the world and then faded away almost into oblivion. In Buddhism the highest god is even more impersonal. He is merely the inactive, almost incomprehensible, soul of the universe. The Hindu heaven has a similar quality. The good Hindu, especially of the Brahman caste, expects to be reborn in some higher form than at present. His hope is that first he may be a higher type of man, then some kind of spiritual being, and finally may be absorbed in Brahma, the spirit of the universe. The Buddhists have a similar faith. To them the highest form of religion is simply to sit and think until their thought, as they believe, merges with that of Buddha. Heaven is merely a state of impersonal existence in which the human soul does nothing, thinks nothing, and is nothing except a part of the illimitable, quiescent soul of the universe. All this is very different from the God and the heaven of the religions which originated in the desert and have since become more northern in their aspect. In Judaism and Christianity, God has been commonly supposed to be an active, personal being who wants to play a vigorous part in man's life. Heaven, too, has been a fairly active place. We moderns may not care much for the idea of eternally playing harps and singing hymns of worship, but that is at least a more active type of heaven than absorption into Brahma or Buddha. The Moslems have retained the idea of heaven as a place of active life like that on earth, but they have made it more sensual than the Jews or Christians. This is in accord with the general principle that the religions of low latitudes tend to emphasize the gratification of the senses, whereas those of higher latitudes emphasize moral and spiritual gratification.

G. *Islam and Monotheism*

Islam comes next to Hinduism in the proportion of its followers in tropical regions. Among its adherents more than half, namely, eighty million in India and sixty in the East Indies, are tropical or semi-tropical. On the whole, however, they live in parts of the tropics, such as Java and Bengal, which are economically more favorable than those inhabited by the bulk of the Hindus. Part of this advantage is due to the good soil of volcanoes and flood plains, part to irrigation, and part to the seasonal distribution of rainfall. Few people fully realize how greatly the prosperity of tropical countries is influenced by the length and severity of the dry and wet seasons. A considerable proportion of the animists are greatly handicapped by living where rain falls too constantly at all seasons. Vast numbers of Hindus are handicapped by living where the dry season is too long, with the result that the crops often fail and still more often are scanty. The most productive parts of the tropics, such as Bengal and much of Java, have a dry season which is long enough to favor the harvesting of crops and the ploughing of land, but not long enough to create frequent crop failures and human hardship. Outside of the East Indies and northern India the Moslems live mainly in relatively dry regions west of India, as far as Turkey, Egypt, and North Africa. Poor as these countries are agriculturally and otherwise, they are on the whole more favored than the Hindu and animist areas.

Regardless of whether the economic and climatic levels are connected with the religious level, it is interesting to note that in all four of the essentials of a high religion, Islam seems to stand higher than animism or Hinduism. In its more tropical areas, to be sure, it takes on many features in common with these other religions. Nevertheless, it everywhere maintains a belief in one god and in a heaven and hell which are rewards for good or evil conduct. Its god, indeed, is painfully human. He imposes dire penalties on anyone who is not a Moslem. He interferes with his own laws in drastic fashion. Nevertheless, he is free from such human frailties as covetousness and poor sexual restraint. The Moslem heaven and hell are extremely materialistic, but the hope of a future life does serve as a motive for ethical conduct more strongly than in animism and Hinduism. Thus ethical conduct is stimulated by Islam. Nevertheless, true believers will ultimately reach heaven, even though they live sinfully. Nonbelievers, on the contrary, will never get there.

The Islamic idea of one supreme god brings up the much discussed statement that the animistic and Hindu belief in many gods and innumerable minor spirits is the natural result of life in the tropical jungle, whereas the monotheism of Judaism, Christianity, and Islam is an equally natural product of deserts. We have already seen how the tropical jungle, with its dense foliage, short field of vision, and damp darkness at night, encourages faith in a vast number of impish spirits. Consider now the effect of deserts in contrast to that of the tropical jungle. Monotheism arose in grasslands or deserts. But do deserts in themselves lead to a belief in one all-powerful, universal God? Such questions arise repeatedly in the study of civilization. They play a part in the great controversy between believers in determinism and possibilism, or free will. The extreme determinist is supposed to say that the jungle obliges people to have a polytheistic religion, whereas the desert obliges them to become monotheistic. The extreme believer in free will is supposed to say that exactly the same religious beliefs can develop in either environment. Few people actually hold either of these extreme views. The truth is that determinism and possibilism are generally combined. In the present case there is absolute determinism in one respect: the experiences of a walk through the jungle cannot be identical with those of a similar walk in the desert. On the other hand, it is quite possible, of course, for a man in either environment to fix his thoughts on any kind of god he chooses. Plain common sense, however, tells us that ordinary people will react differently in the two places. Anyone who has experienced a walk of each kind realizes this.

Consider the difference between a five-mile walk at night in the desert and in the jungle. Instead of clouds, rain, darkness, wet branches, soggy leaves, and mudholes, the desert walker encounters clear skies, dry air, bright starlight or moonlight, dry ground, and practically no vegetation. Usually the ground is hard, being composed of gravel or clay, but even if it is sandy and soft, the traveller can walk safely without watching his feet. Danger from wild beasts and annoyance from insects do not afflict him so long as he stays away from the oases. If he becomes tired, he can lie down safely almost anywhere. He can listen to the vast stillness, watch the stars and the moon, and then sleep without fear of insect, beast, man, or storm. Because of all this he also sleeps with little fear of evil spirits. Nevertheless, the sun smites him by day and the cold by night. The wind, also, is to be feared. It fills the air with blinding dust which chokes his lungs, hides landmarks, and sometimes moves the desert sand so rapidly that when the dust disappears, the traveller cannot recognize the dunes which formerly marked the way to the spring where he must drink. The desert dwellers also fear drought which may lead to the starvation of the flocks.

Note the contrast betwen the fears and hence the spirit world of the desert and the jungle. In the oases, to be sure, there is much to encourage animism. Mohammed contended with deep-seated animistic practices. Nevertheless, out in the desert, where dwell the nomads, the things that man chiefly fears are big—winds, sun, cold, heat, drought. They have little of the local, intimate quality of the jungle man's mudholes, snakes, sticks, and malevolent mosquitoes. The desert man is as free as the jungle man to believe in spirits that inhabit stones, bushes, lizards, and beasts of prey, but there is less incentive to do so. Even if he does believe in them, they are unimportant compared with big things like sun, wind, and drought. Hence it is natural for the primitive desert man to pin his faith to a few powerful gods who rule large areas. This does not compel him to believe in a single god, but it makes the transition to that belief easy and natural. It would be false to say that belief in one universal God necessarily evolves in a desert, but it is true that the evolution of such a belief is more probable there than in the jungle.

H. The Seclusion of Women

The seclusion of women in Moslem countries furnishes a good illustration of the way in which climate co-operates with other conditions in encouraging social customs which in due time become religious practices. The seclusion of women arises from the same human impulse as the private ownership of property. The possessor of something valuable wants to keep it for his own benefit. So far as women are concerned, this desire is more or less effective in most parts of the world, but rarely, if ever, is it more highly specialized than in the harem of the Arabs, the zenana of the Hindus. The seclusion of women is most fully developed in the deserts and semi-arid regions from northwestern India across Persia, Iraq, Arabia, and Syria to Egypt and Morocco. North, south, and east of this strip it declines in intensity. In recent times, for example, the veil over women's faces has been officially discarded in Turkey and Iran. High-caste women are secluded somewhat in southern India, but only in a mild form. In China, likewise, the custom is much diluted. In western China the unveiled faces of nominally Moslem women were one of the reasons which once led the Moslem chief of my caravan to say, "The people here don't have much work with God."

The seclusion of women seems to have developed most fully in the oases of Arabia where it is appropriate to the geographical environment. So long as man is a mere hunter and gatherer of wild products, he cannot seclude his women, for the women must wander around searching for edible roots and grubs. Among pastoral nomads a similar situation prevails. Even though the Bedouins of the Arabian Desert are among the most loyal Moslems, their women are not secluded like those of their fellow Arabs in the oases. Their mode of life obliges the women to expose their faces out-of-doors while milking sheep and camels, putting up or taking down tents, or caring for animals and children on a migration.

Only after agriculture was instituted did the effective seclusion of women become feasible, but not in warm, moist countries with plenty of rain. There the normal material for huts is rough, crooked branches with a thatch of leaves or grass. It is difficult to make such huts so tight that people cannot peer in, and it is uncomfortable to cook or do other work inside them in hot, damp weather. Then, too, from time immemorial, the care of the weedy crops around tropical dwellings has been woman's work. Even if such garden patches are fenced against animals, the women cannot work unseen, for the fence is almost certain to be made of rough branches which do little to keep out prying eyes. Moreover, in a climate that is humid as well as hot, clothing is uncomfortable, especially if it covers the face.

In a desert oasis the situation is different. The most available building material is dry mud (adobe). Large, sun-dried bricks can easily be piled up to form walls. In the hot, dry air, the most comfortable place during the heat of the day is inside a thick-walled adobe house with a stout roof of the same material. Hence the women prefer to stay indoors many hours of the day. In such oases, agriculture can be carried on only by irrigation. An irrigated patch affords much temptation to thieves. Inasmuch as adobe walls can be built easily and last a long time, the common practice is to surround each "garden" with a thick wall seven or eight feet high. Thus, in the cooler parts of the day, when the women work outside the house, they are still sheltered from passers-by. They get so into the habit of being sheltered behind high walls that they feel ill-treated if their men fail to build good walls for them. How free they feel behind such walls is revealed sometimes on an early morning walk in Khartoum in the hot Egyptian Sudan, for example. A glimpse through a door inadvertently left open may disclose a woman stripped to the waist in order to work comfortably. That same woman would be heavily veiled on the street.

A veil over the face is little hardship in such a climate. Both sexes crave heavy clothing in the heat of noon and again in the sudden coolness after sunset. The Arab man normally wears over his head a small shawl which is pulled far forward to shield his face and falls to his shoulders, hiding his neck. Once when I was exploring ruins in the midsummer heat of the Transcaspian Desert, my companion, a Turkoman, wore a thinly quilted red robe that fell below his knees. The second day out he said, "If I'd known it was going to be so hot, I'd have worn a thicker robe." He wanted fuller protection against the sun. The air is so dry that there is no trouble with perspiration. On the other hand, at night the desert air becomes cool so rapidly that one wants warm clothes to keep the heat in rather than out. More than once a friendly desert host has urged me to sleep with my hat on at night because it was cold. In hot deserts then, such as those of the lower Indus Valley, Arabia, and the Sahara, the oases offer physical conditions which play directly into the hands of the jealous male who wants to seclude his women from other men. Mud walls are needed and are made with ease. The women enjoy their shelter. When a woman leaves them, she is eager to shield her face and head from the hot sun by day and to wear voluminous clothing at night.

Another factor may enter the picture. The men of the hot desert may have unusual cause for jealousy. In extremely hot weather people's ability to resist emotional impulses, including those of sex, appears to be weakened. Sexual extravagance and prostitution seem to reach a maximum in the hottest parts of the world, that is, in the dry parts of a belt located ten to thirty degrees from the equator. Animists, who usually live in moist, forested regions which do not have such extreme heat as the monsoon regions and deserts, appear to be sexually less excitable than Hindus, Arabs, and other Moslems. Of course, there are plenty of other places where these weaknesses prevail strongly. Nevertheless, hot, dry cities, such as Djibouti in French Somaliland, Omdurman in the Sudan, Cairo in Egypt, Lahore in India, and Tucumán in northern Argentina provide samples of extremes. The dusty sirocco which blows northward from the deserts of Africa and Arabia brings hot, dry weather to Turkey, Greece, and Italy. Hellpach says that in southern Italy sexual irregularities increase greatly when the sirocco is blowing. The people recognize this so well that offenses committed under such circumstances are in a measure condoned.

There is other evidence that dry weather, especially when hot, is associated with a decline in self-control. We have seen how homicides in America increase in warm climates and warm seasons. In his pioneer study, *Weather Influences*, Dexter found that in Denver the school children were punished for misdemeanors five times as often when the relative humidity was below 45 per cent as when it was 80 or 90 per cent. In Turkey, I knew a missionary, a most noble character, who secluded himself as far as possible when the hot, dry sirocco blew. He feared that he would lose his temper and say something disagreeable. If lack of self-control really displays such a relationship to hot deserts, it may have co-operated with mud walls, irrigated gardens, hot sun, and cold nights in enabling the veiling and seclusion of women to become established as a religious custom in the Arabian oases.

Now let us see what happened when Islam, in its great wave of conquest, imposed its customs on conquered nations. If the conquered countries were so dry and warm that irrigation and mud-walled houses and gardens were normal, the seclusion of women could readily be introduced and would do relatively little harm to health. In the dry regions of northern India before the coming of Islam, the women of the upper classes were already mildly secluded. With the coming of the new religion the custom spread to the Hindus as well as to the people who accepted Mohammed as their prophet. As it spread eastward in the Indo-Gangetic Valley, the custom became less and less appropriate to the climate and hence more and more harmful. The Indian province of Bengal, near the mouth of the Ganges, was conquered by Islam more than seven hundred years ago. It now contains about thirty million Moslems. January there is almost rainless and about as warm as New York City in early June. At that season the religious necessity for women to veil themselves when they go abroad works relatively little hardship. From May to September, on the other hand, the temperature for day and night together averages from 82 to 86°, rarely falling as low as 75° at night. The air is constantly humid, and the rainfall ranges from five inches in May to twelve in both July and August. As a rule, the mornings are clear, but by noon clouds cover the sky. Under such conditions, even though one perspires freely most of the time, one is not thereby cooled because there is such great humidity. A stay in the stagnant air indoors is a kind of martyrdom but the outdoor air is not much better; there are no mud walls for shelter, and a cotton sheet that swathes the head and covers the face is most uncomfortable. Nevertheless, the Moslem women, especially those of the upper classes, are counted as grossly irreligious if they fail to keep themselves well covered, face and all. Thus, by being converted into a religious requirement and then being transported to a new physical environment, a relatively harmless social custom has become a great detriment to health as well as comfort. It may have helped in giving the Bengalis their poor physique.

I. Buddhism and Its Neighbors

Buddhism is located mainly in the same latitudes as Islam. In the tropical and semi-tropical regions of Burma, Siam, and south China the Buddhists appear to have a higher standard of living than the tropical Moslems in Bengal and Java, but it is not easy to judge. Japan, which is semi-Buddhist, has progressed farther than any other country in the ranks of either Islam or Buddhism. Only in the region from Algeria to Egypt and Turkey do Moslem countries seem to rival Buddhist countries in the same latitude, aside from Japan. The other chief Buddhist country in these latitudes is China. There overpopulation seems to be the greatest handicap. On the whole, the economic difference between Islam and Buddhism is slight. From the standpoint of beliefs, and still more from that of practices, it is hard to tell which religion to place higher. Both vary greatly from place to place. Among the educated people of Turkey, Islam ranks fairly high in each of the four great essentials, whereas in the wilds of Sumatra or Mindanao it retains many elements of animism. The same is true of Buddhism, which reaches a high level among educated Chinese and Japanese but is animistic among the wilder tribes of the Burmese and Siamese mountains. In fact within both of these religions we find the same kind, although not the same degree, of contrast as between animism and Protestantism. The more advanced a region is in other respects, the more its religion tends toward a high type.

The truth of this last statement is borne out by Confucianism and Taoism, which are native to China, and by Shintoism, native to Japan. These religions exist side by side with Buddhism but have advanced well beyond it. A man may adhere to any of them and at the same time be a Buddhist. In them, as in Buddhism, higher ideals are mixed with beliefs and practices which stem from ancient animism. Ordinary Chinese who are good Confucianists make offerings at the shrines of their ancestors and worship in temples dedicated to a vast number of gods. The Shintoism of Japan acknowledges some eight hundred thousand gods and counts the emperor as a god even while he is living. Certain Japanese Christians who were accused of disloyalty once sought to placate the officials by means of a memorandum saying that they worshipped four beings—the emperor first, then God, the Holy Spirit, and Jesus. The officials objected on the ground that it was disrespectful to the emperor to put him on a par with other gods.

In spite of such weaknesses Confucianism, Taoism, and Shintoism stand ahead of Buddhism in their emphasis on moral responsibility and the human side of religious duty. They emphasize ethical conduct and social responsibility as essential parts of religion. From our western point of view, they seem to lack the positive element, that is, the feeling of responsibility outside their own group. In Confucianism the golden rule is negative instead of positive. Jesus said, "As ye would that men should do to you, do you even so to them." Confucious said, "Do nothing to others that ye would not have them do to you." In Taoism the emphasis is mainly upon thinking good thoughts rather than doing good deeds. Both of these religions are passive in their code of ethics, although not to so great a degree as Buddhism. Shintoism is more active and in that respect resembles Christianity. Its main tenet is loyalty. Three kinds of loyalty bind father and son, husband and wife, friend and friend. A higher kind makes the Japanese subject ready to devote all his energy and even his life to anything that the emperor orders. Suicide by hara-kiri is a religious duty for those who fail to achieve the emperor's purposes. The essential point is that in Japan the native religion is highly dynamic and active. There seems to be a relation between this and the fact that Japan is the country in Asia where the physical environment, especially the climate, is most stimulating and most like that of western Europe and the eastern United States.

As we pass from animism up through Hinduism, Buddhism, Taoism, and Confucianism to Shintoism, we move along one of the two great lines in the evolution of religion; the other being from animism through Judaism to Christianity. We move also from regions of low energy and low standards of living to regions of higher energy, greater industry, and standards of living which are high in view of the intense overpopulation. In other words, in proportion to the possibilities of their environment and the density of the population, the animists get relatively little from nature, whereas the Shintoists get a great deal. Thus, in other phases of culture as well as religion, the Shintoists have advanced much farther than the animists. Racial inheritance and the birth of men of genius doubtless play a part in this, but behind them lies the fact that in Japan the climate gives people more energy and more inclination to work than in the animist regions. As we go from typically animist communities to those that are typically Hindu, Buddhist, Confucianist, and finally Shintoist, we move into regions that are progressively more favorable to human activity. This has been a great help in making the progress of the Chinese and Japanese in religion, as well as otherwise, more rapid than that of the people of lower latitudes. Each step of cultural progress generally makes some other step easier.

All this brings us to one of the few great principles on which the theory of civilization expounded in this book is based. Applied to religion, the principle may be stated thus: One of the great factors in the moral and spiritual level of a religion is the energy of the people. Physical vigor, as well as training, helps people to think and reason. It depends partly upon biological inheritance, but also upon health. Health in turn is greatly influenced by geographic environment, especially by climate both directly and also indirectly through diet, disease, occupations, and other indirect relationships.

J. The Varying Quality of Christianity

The connection between human energy and human progress is illustrated by Christianity as well as by other religions. We often say that during the past nineteen hundred years Christianity has spread to all parts of the earth. But has it? Certainly it has spread enormously. If we include the Russians, Christians form more than 40 per cent of the world's population. Their geographical distribution, however, can scarcely be called worldwide. Nor does this distribution suggest that Palestine was the place where Christianity started. Looking merely at the present, with no knowledge of history before the Dark Ages, one might infer that practically the only movement of Christianity had been westward and northward from Rome and Constantinople and then fanwise from western Europe to the Americas and Australia. In other directions one finds only a few insignificant old outliers, such as the Nestorians of northwestern Persia, the Armenians close by, the Christians of St. Thomas in southern India, the Copts in Egypt, and the Abyssinians in Ethiopia. There are also many small modern outliers where missionaries have made converts during the past century or two in almost all countries. Nowhere, however, except in Ethiopia, where Christians form somewhat less than a third of the population, do either the old outliers or the new form more than a small percentage of the population of any large area. In spite of immense efforts, the missionary task of Christianizing the world has made slow progress. In fact, in the long view the Christianization of both Asia and Africa has been a losing cause since the advent of Islam. Before the end of the Dark Ages, Syria, Turkey, and Egypt were largely Christianized, and the Nestorians had spread in force to Persia, China, and India. Then the tide rolled back, largely under the stress of conflict with Islam.

From the standpoint of the relation of civilization to physical environment there are three especially interesting points about all this. First, where old outliers of Christianity have persisted in geographical regions relatively unfavorable to human vigor, there has been a strong tendency toward a lowering of ethical and spiritual standards. This has often been accompanied by a tendency toward animistic ideas and practices, as in southern India and Ethiopia. Second, Christianity has rarely gained large numbers of new adherents and then in the same place risen to higher levels except when it has migrated into parts of the world where geographical conditions offer exceptionally favorable opportunities. This means primarily Europe. Religiously, the new lands settled by Europeans in temperate climates are offshoots of that continent. Third, where Christianity has become dominant in new lands with less favorable climates, there has been a notable backward tendency. In tropical Latin America and India, for example, among native converts, the far-sighted Roman Catholic Church has permitted certain animistic ideas and practices to persist along with Christianity. I have seen Indians in Latin America performing their old dances and making offerings in caves as an ostensible part of Christian worship. Aside from rare exceptions, it seems to be extremely difficult for tropical people to maintain Christianity at its highest levels. This condition is especially common among native races, but even among Europeans who live by themselves the maintenance of standards like those of the Moravians or Quakers for generation after generation, seems to be almost beyond human ability under the depressing influence of a tropical climate.

As a result of all this, the variation in Christianity from enervating tropical jungles to stimulating mid-latitudes resembles that which we have found from animism to the higher levels of Confucianism and Shintoism. The religious difference between the Swiss and the superstitious Christian Indians of Honduras or Ecuador may not be so great as between the ardent Shintoists of Japan and the animistic Veddas of Ceylon, but it is of essentially the same kind. Wherever Christianity has penetrated it seems to have raised the standards of faith and conduct at least a little. This effect tends to be strong so long as missionaries from more favored regions are present. When they leave, however, Christianity tends to lose part of the quality which distinguishes it from animism or Hinduism. This is well illustrated in Paraguay, where the traveller marvels at the ruins of fine old missions and at the semi-pagan character of the churches and the degree to which religion and ethics are divorced. On the Malabar Coast of south India, which belongs to the geographic type where animism, or at least the animistic form of some other religion, usually prevails, the Nestorian Christianity which has existed for some fourteen centuries is largely a matter of ritual and superstition. It has little relation to moral conduct. Innumerable saints take the place of local deities. Hindu rules as to caste and food prevail. The voodooism of Haiti, with its incantations and sacrifices, is a good example of animism among people who are nominally Christians. In Ethiopia, which is relatively cool because of high altitude, Christianity is less animistic than in Haiti and Malabar. Nevertheless, religion and ethics have only a bowing acquaintance, and religion does little to stimulate social responsibility.

Many Protestants suppose that such conditions are common in tropical countries because the Catholic form of Christianity prevails there. This is a mistake. Small groups of Protestants, when left by themselves in regions of the animist or tropical jungle type, face the same tendency toward a debased form of religion. This does not mean that high types of religion are impossible in unfavorable environments. It merely means that they require efforts greater than most people feel like making in such an environment. Such efforts can be made much more easily in the North Sea countries, the northern and western United States, or New Zealand than in south India or Venezuela. This helps to explain why both Protestantism and Roman Catholicism assume higher forms as one goes from Ethiopia to Holland or from Colombia to Minnesota. In the same way, ethics and religion become more closely related, until they are almost synonymous. Social welfare rather than the saving of one's own soul becomes the major religious goal. Self-sacrifice, self-control, and service become more and more the key words of religion. At the same time religious ceremonies assume less importance and rise to a more inspiring level.

On the whole, the qualities of religion seem to rise highest in the distinctively Protestant countries. This opinion may be merely the result of the author's early training and lifetime associations. Nevertheless, Protestantism appears to be the phase of Christianity best adapted to regions in which the physical as well as the cultural conditions are highly energizing, so that people do a great deal of thinking and feel inclined to make strenuous efforts, both physical and mental. One reason for this view is that in the Protestant regions other forms of religion, including not only Romanism, but Judaism, Islam, and Buddhism, rise similarly to a high level. Much of this is doubtless due to the general influence of a high culture. Such a statement merely raises one of the major problems of this book: How far does the quality of human culture in general and of religion in particular depend upon physical vigor and how far upon something else?

K. National Character and Climate

The preceding pages lead to the conclusion that climate is a primary factor in national character. Among numerous possible illustrations the contrast between Germany and India may serve as an example. One reason why the Germans are among the world's most active people and therefore so serious a problem is that an admirable climate inclines them toward activity. Their energy is evident in the hard work of the sturdy peasants, the fondness of city people for gardening and hiking, and the extreme earnestness of students and scientists. It is also manifest in military exercises which provide an outlet for activity, just as do sports in England and the United States. The life of the nation as a whole shows that the Germans are primarily a people of work and action.

This active spirit appears likewise in German philosophy. Nearly a century ago, Tolstoy penned a vivid description of the national characteristics of military officers. Then, as now, the Germans had the reputation of being extremely persistent and active in carrying out plans laid long in advance. Such qualities indicate a high degree of mental and physical vigor. It is extremely doubtful whether Germans who had lived for generations in India, let us say, would be so active. One reason for the fall of Singapore in 1942 is said to have been the laxness of British officials and officers by reason of tropical inertia. The teachings of men like Nietzsche and the new "Nordic" religion described in Chapter 4 exalt the superman whose ruthless energy overcomes all obstacles and dominates the world. This is the philosophy of the Junkers, the Nazi party, and the "Aryan" movement. A philosophy of quiet inactivity does not please the Germans.

An inactive philosophy is displeasing also to Frenchmen, Englishmen, and Americans. In general the more stimulating the climate, the more likely people are to have a philosophy of activity. Whatever the expressed beliefs of Americans may be, the thing they generally want above all else is action. The two world wars have shown clearly the relative degree of activity in different countries. Among the world's large nations, Germany, Britain, and the United States are, on the whole, the ones with the most stimulating climates. They are the three in which action, both military and industrial, has reached its highest level. Even when strong-minded citizens of those countries oppose military action, they are generally eager for active service along other lines.

India offers an impressive contrast to these western nations. Its people, as a whole, seem to be born tired. When children are conceived, the physical vigor of the parents is generally low. They are not really ill but suffer from poor nutrition and a depressing climate. The health of the mother while carrying the child is usually far from perfect, and it is possible that the reproductive cells of both parents lack vigor. Then, when the child is born, it normally begins to suffer from deficiencies of diet as well as climate.

Direct evidence of some such climatic weakening in hot climates is found in the mortality of persons born in the semi-tropical northern province of Queensland in Australia.[2] The deathrate of the inhabitants of that province was for many years unusually low. One reason is that most of those who died were born elsewhere and had been selected by migration. Another is that the children of such selected parents are naturally of great vigor, which accounts for a low deathrate among infants as well as adults. Nevertheless, in later life people pay a price for having been born in a hot climate. The deathrates prove that no matter whether the people born in Queensland remain there or migrate to some other province, their length of life averages five or ten years less than that of similar people born in the cooler provinces or in Great Britain. Something connected with their birth or early life acts as a handicap. The evidence seems to be that this is either climate directly, or the effect of climate on mode of life or diet. The conditions which lead to such a handicap in Queensland act with vastly greater force to cause the children of India to be born tired or else to become tired while they are young.

Tagore's [3] beautifully written dirge over India's subjection to Great Britain illustrates the modern Indian attitude. He is proud of the great minds of India. He wants his country to stand high among the nations and is sure that the innate qualities of the people make this possible. Nevertheless, he recognizes that the Indian people lack not only the mechanical equipment of the British but the "brute force" which makes the British accomplish so much. The Japanese say that his words are "the poetry of a defeated people." Tagore puts it differently: it "is really because we are afraid of our own weakness, which allows itself to be overcome by the sight of power, that

[2] Huntington, 1925B; A. G. Price; Cilento.
[3] pp. 53, 135, 145, 152.

we try to substitute for it another weakness which makes itself blind to the glories of the West. . . . [This] leads us to our idolatry of dead forms in social institutions which will create in our politics prison houses with immovable walls."

Many intelligent Indians share with Tagore a feeling of bitter resentment that their own people practice "the blind and lazy habit of relying upon the authority of tradition," whereas the British set up "the ideal of power over that of perfection." The Indian attitude is like that of a Korean who was talking about his country's subjection to Japan.[4] "We Koreans," he said, "have just as good minds as the Japanese, but somehow they carry out their plans and we don't. The difference between the Japanese and us is like that between you and the Japanese. You Americans, even more than the Japanese, have the power to carry out whatever you decide to do." Inasmuch as Koreans, on an average, appear to have more power of achievement than the people of India, we have here a descending scale of vigor, or of brute force as it seems to the Hindus— the United States, Japan, Korea, India. The philosophy and national character of each nation closely correspond to its place in this scale.

Gandhi and "non-co-operation" illustrate the kind of national philosophy which prevails among people deficient in physical energy. Of course, there are Indian fire-eaters who advocate resistance to Britain by violence. Nevertheless, the general inertia arising from low vitality causes the bulk of the Indian people to welcome the idea that passive non-co-operation is their best weapon. The fatalism of countries such as Persia and Egypt is another phase of this same inert philosophy. It is almost inconceivable that a well-fed nation in a stimulating climate should widely accept ideas of this kind. Norway and Holland did not succumb to Nazi domination in any such fashion. The story of Norway's resistance is one of the world's great epics. Young men climbed snowy mountains, hid for days in trees, or swam for miles in cold water in order to escape to other countries and fight against their conquerors. Old men, women, and children refused to obey Nazi orders and sabotaged Nazi plans in spite of bitter punishment. Non-resistance, however, is perfectly natural in India. Even the Moslems there accept it. They may flash briefly into fierce activity but soon the tired feeling makes them quiescent. We are sometimes told that the Hindu religion is the

4 Huntington, 1925B, p. 39.

cause of Indian passivity. It leads its devoted followers to give up the things of the world and devote themselves to quiet contemplation. This is partly true, but a religion such as Hinduism, with its passive concept of virtue and salvation, could scarcely arise and surely could not long persist among active, vigorous people. India is a conspicuous example of the way in which the philosophy, religion, and ideals of a country—its national character—as well as the social and economic systems tend to conform to bodily feelings induced primarily by climate and diet, but modified by the stage of culture.

CHAPTER 16

THE SEASONS

A. Seasonal Agriculture as a Cultural Stimulant

In view of the vital climatic relationships described in previous chapters, we evidently need further knowledge as to how climate influences mankind. Two other aspects of climate, in addition to temperature, need special study, namely, seasons and storms. Both of these influence man externally through agriculture, food, clothing, shelter, transportation, business, recreation, and habits in general and internally through their effect on physiological processes and diseases.

The stimulating external or cultural effect of seasonal contrasts in either temperature or rainfall is especially evident among grain-raising people such as have long formed the vast majority of mankind. The earliest agriculture apparently arose through the cultivation of barley and wheat. These cereals grow wild only in western Asia, especially Palestine and neighboring regions. In the more rainy climate which existed at the beginning of Neolithic times when agriculture arose, they probably were found wild as far east as Iran and also in Egypt, especially the mountainous region east of the Nile. In the countries of their origin wheat and barley ripen in the late spring. The seeds fall to the ground during the long, dry summer, sprout in the autumn, grow with the help of the winter rains, and mature their crop as the weather becomes dry in the spring. Hence the earliest agriculture probably consisted merely of gathering the seed in May or June, storing it safely through the dry months from July to September, and sowing it when the autumn rains first made the soil sufficiently moist for germination.

Casual observation must have made the Neolithic people realize that the largest yield was obtained on almost level areas where floods spread a shallow sheet of water for a while in the spring. This is most likely to occur where mountains with a cover of snow provide the lowlands with floods in the spring. A flood of this kind, which washed out the Transcaspian Railway east of Merv, once held up the author for two weeks. At the edge of the flooded area, when trains ran once more, we found a locomotive half buried in the mud and a half mile of plank walk where the track had been undermined. The walk led across a shallow sheet of water from which brown grass, beginning to be green, stood up in bunches. Such a flood plain provides four conditions which favor primitive agriculture: (1) rich, fresh soil derived from the muddy flood water; (2) many bare spaces free from vegetation that might choke whatever grain is sown; (3) bunchy vegetation that can easily be pulled up by hand without tools; and (4) the simplest kind of natural irrigation at the most critical season.

The valleys of the Nile and Euphrates are commonly considered the earliest seats of agriculture, but this is doubtful. The dense growth of reeds and papyrus in their natural flood plains is evidence against this theory, as is the size of the floods.[1] It seems more probable that the art of irrigation grew up on the flood plains of small, easily handled streams at the base of mountains. The earliest irrigation may have taken place in Egypt among the rather high mountains east of the Nile, as well as in Palestine, Syria, or Iran. All of these regions have the necessary combination of topography and climate. At the dawn of the Neolithic Age, when agriculture was invented, their climate was more rainy than now, but the contrast between rainy winters and dry summers was undoubtedly strong. When the arts of agriculture and irrigation had become sufficiently established under the relatively easy conditions of small streams, the way was open to apply them to the large and difficult problem of the reed-filled valleys of the Nile and Euphrates.

The essential point is that although the idea of agriculture may have occurred to people in all sorts of geographic environments, the geographical conditions that made it practicable for primitive people were found only in regions which had certain special conditions of climate, topography, and vegetation. Substantially the same combination, but with slight differences, is found in America. There the place of wheat is taken by the wild forerunner of Indian corn, which is believed by Mangelsdorf and Reeves to have grown in some part of South America not far from Peru. The cultivation of corn must have originated in a region with a strong alternation between a dry and a wet season. In corn regions the wet season comes in summer, and the cereal must be planted when the rains begin in the spring

[1] Toynbee.

Nevertheless, the general relationships to topography, irrigation, and the problems of saving and storing seed are essentially the same as with barley and wheat. Rice is another cereal which may have had a similar history. Its cultivation is comparatively easy for primitive man, but not so easy as that of wheat or corn. Rice is found wild in many climates, but it has been economically important among primitive people only where there are a wet and a dry season and mountains which provide both water and fresh soil for lowlands. The general opinion, however, seems to be that rice culture was not an isolated invention, but an outgrowth of the art of raising wheat and barley. Be that as it may, three conditions loom large in the evolution of agriculture based on any kind of cereals, namely, wet and dry seasons, floods, and irrigation. So far as we know, the early stages of civilization have never developed except where this combination has prevailed.

The importance of these three types of seasonal agriculture becomes more evident when we examine another type based on trees and roots. This type presumably arose in the same general environment where it still prevails, that is, in tropical regions favorable to such plants as the coconut, banana, and breadfruit, together with ground crops such as yams, taro, and manioc. Such regions differ little from season to season, although some months have more rain and others less. The trees and roots provide food at practically all seasons. Thus there is little incentive to take thought for the morrow and lay up food for a season of scarcity. Moreover, even with the most careful planning, the heat, moisture, bacteria, and insects of tropical regions make it practically impossible for primitive people to preserve fruits, roots, or even nuts for any great length of time. This has played a part in preventing the tropical tree-and-hoe type of agriculture from having any great effect in stimulating the growth of civilization. When a season of scarcity comes, as come it will sometimes, the people who depend on such agriculture promptly face starvation and many die. Such disasters impose a handicap too strong to be overcome until more highly developed methods, such as those of modern tropical plantations, are introduced from other regions.

In its effect on civilization agriculture based on cereals and seasonal floods can scarcely be overrated. When some genius conceived the idea of sowing grain on flood plains, the foundation was laid for one of the most stupendous civilizing agencies ever invented. A premium was at once placed on intelligence, foresight, thrift, industry, and self-control, as well as on the faculty for invention. People who possess these qualities must have been the ones most likely both to see the advantages of the new method and to have the will-power to carry it out. Others may have laughed at them for throwing out good food where the birds could eat it. These scoffers probably pointed out that even if the seed grew, much of the scanty crop was sure to be eaten by rodents, insects, and birds or stolen by human beings. Thus as soon as agriculture became established, there presumably arose a division into two distinct social groups. On the one side, were the scoffers, or conservatives, who still lived by hunting and by gathering wild plants. On the other side, were the relatively intelligent and determined people who were willing to go to considerable trouble and self-denial in order to gather seed at the proper season and save it for many months. It required much self-control to refrain from eating the seed when hunger pressed them severely. It required faith and courage to plant the seed, guard the crop, and wait patiently in confidence that in due time a profitable harvest would be reaped.

These two groups—early seed-sowers and hunters—must have lived more or less separately because the seed-people were tied to one spot, whereas the others were forced to wander widely. At first the seed-people doubtless still depended in part on game and wild plants. Nevertheless, they were obliged to focus their lives around their fields at planting and harvesting time. Moreover, between these two times it was worth while to be on the watch to keep grass-eating animals and birds away. After the crop was harvested it was necessary to guard the places where it was stored. Thus each agricultural family, or clan, was obliged to adopt more regular and careful habits of life than heretofore. Each also, for the time being at least, acquired a special interest in a certain definite piece of land. Thus the foundations were laid for ownership of land and for civil government in order to protect this most important property right. It also led to the building of permanent houses and villages, with all that they mean in the way of putting an end to the nomadic life and stimulating progress through co-operative effort.

The seasons were not the cause of this development, but they provided the setting in which primitive agriculture was feasible as well as profitable. Then, too, seasonal scarcity of food had much to do with giving cereals their special value as the basis of agriculture. The ripening of cereals, far more than that of bananas or breadfruit, is limited to a short and definite season, but the ripe product can be kept a long time. This is especially true of wheat and barley.

The physical separation of the early seed-people from primitive hunters and food-gatherers must have tended to cause each group to marry mainly within its own type. If innate traits become established in kiths through selection, we should expect that kiths which developed through agriculture would exceed the hunting and food-gathering kiths in their innate endowment of the kind of temperament that tends toward foresight, industry, and thrift. Moreover, the planting of crops must have greatly increased the capacity of any given area to support population. At the same time it must have reduced the mortality, especially among infants, because the supply of food was not only larger but more reliable than among the hunting people. Thus the type which practiced agriculture presumably increased faster than that which clung to hunting. Intelligence doubtless had something to do with the difference between the two types, but temperament and physique probably had quite as much effect as mere powers of reasoning. At any rate the innate qualities which bring success and ensure survival among agricultural people and among primitive hunting or food-gathering people are different. Pastoral nomads, who depend on domestic animals, form a major group with still other characteristics. A combination of the best qualities of all three types is presumably the ideal. The final truth, however, as to the relation of all this to inherited qualities of kiths cannot be known until we are better able to distinguish between the effects of environment and heredity.

Meanwhile, it is easy to see that the seasons have exercised a great effect upon the type of culture which has grown up in various parts of the world. For example, the necessity for preserving the crop when once it has been harvested has obviously been a great stimulus to inventions, both mechanical and social. A cold and humid winter is more stimulating in this respect than one which is merely dry. Even in a dry climate it is no easy matter for primitive people to preserve grain from one harvest to the next. In Yucatan, where seasonal differences of temperature are slight and those of rainfall great, the Maya Indians with characteristic lack of initiative often leave the ears of corn in the field, gathering a basketful whenever the need arises. Even during the dry season this is not a very effective means of preserving the corn, for rodents, birds, and insects take heavy toll. In the parts of Sudan and Nigeria where the dry season is long, such a method is not feasible because millet is the chief crop and the seeds readily drop from the heads or are picked out by birds. Therefore, the stimulus to invention has been greater than in Yucatan. As a result elaborate storage bins of basketlike work with a heavy thatch stand beside the native huts.

Where the winter is cold and wet still greater ingenuity is required in order not only to keep the crop safe but to provide winter clothing and shelter. All these requirements demand special care where the winter is rainy or snowy, as well as cold. Thus, although a climate with any kind of unproductive season provides a stimulus to invention, foresight, and thrift, the effect appears to be at a maximum where both winter and summer present a challenge. Nevertheless, the difficulties must not be too great. At each stage of human progress there is a certain degree or type of seasonal contrast which is especially stimulating because it demands new methods which are not beyond the power of the cultural stage already reached. In the early stages of agriculture an especially stimulating seasonal combination occurred where the winter is humid and also cool enough to prevent the ripening of crops, but not very cold, whereas the summer is warm and dry. Such conditions prevail pre-eminently near the Mediterranean Sea. Egypt, of course, had a special advantage, but its floods are not essentially different from those of Babylonia or of the Indus region where another great civilization arose. In all these places and in hundreds of flood plains of smaller streams the seasonal occurrence of floods and the annual recurrence of long periods when no crops ripen have put a premium on foresight and invention and have been especially powerful in promoting the early growth of civilization. There, even more than elsewhere, the coming and going of the seasons appear to have encouraged inventions and practices connected not only with methods of irrigation, but with laws as to the regulation of the water supply and with methods and laws for the protection of food stored up for future use. This appears to have been an important factor in stimulating the evolution of law and government and the consequent flowering of civilization.

B. The Seasons and Modern Business

Although the effect of the seasons upon modern business is not so direct as upon agriculture, it is just as real and perhaps just as great. Almost every advanced country has sharp seasonal variations in occupations, wages, trade, transportation, bank clearings, and other phases of business. Some industries, such as canning, lumbering, and the making and sale of clothing, are pre-eminently seasonal, but practically all show a considerable variation from season to season. Some, such as railroad repair work, have a strong maximum in winter; others, such as brick-making, laundry work, and the production of gas, have an equally strong maximum in summer. Retail sales soar in December because of Christmas; fertilizer factories reach the peak of activity in March.

On the whole, the seasonal industries impose a special tax on man's powers of invention and organization. For this reason many of them, such as coal-mining and lumbering, present unusual difficulties even in our modern stage of civilization. Success in highly seasonal industries generally demands that people plan with special care far in advance. To take an easily comprehended example, the owner of a small cannery which operates only a few weeks in summer has a two-fold problem which is more complicated than that of a man who runs a bakery of similar size as measured by man-hours per year. The canner must make plans far ahead so that machinery, raw materials, fuel, and labor will all be promptly ready at the beginning of his factory's short season of activity. He must also know what he will do and how his family will be supported during the many months when the cannery is not operating. Unusual foresight and self-control are needed in a family which has to rely on earnings of weeks for support during succeeding months. This illustrates the fact that in hundreds of ways the seasons act as a challenge and as an incentive to the use of man's brain. The greater the contrast of seasons, the greater in general are the demands on man's strength and skill in order to get a decent living.

If the seasons are too severe, to be sure, or if people lack the necessary innate ability or cultural progress, an unfavorable season may act as a handicap. Until recently this seems to have been true of the cold Russian winter, as we shall see more fully later. New methods of western manufacturing, heating, and transportation, however, are helping to overcome the handicap. This emphasizes our previous statement that at every stage of human progress, there seems to be a certain degree of seasonal variation which has the most effect in promoting the growth of civilization. The degree, of course, depends on people's innate ability as well as on their training and type of culture. This may be put in the form of a broad and widely applicable principle: for seasonal change, just as for temperature, there is a distinct optimum which varies with the advance of civilization and the quality of the people. A seasonal handicap which is too great for the people of Newfoundland does not appear to be too much for the Icelanders. A handicap which was formerly too much in a

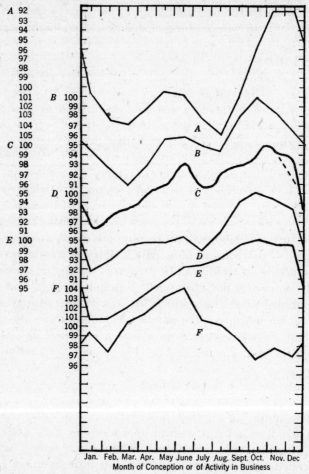

Figure 34. Seasonal Variations in Conceptions, in Business, and in Length of Life among Persons Conceived in Different Months. *A* = Deaths of infants from congenital defects, plotted according to month of probable conception, reversed; *B* = Conceptions resulting in living births in Massachusetts, New York, Ohio, and Illinois, 1936–40; *C* = Piecework in Connecticut factories, 1910–13; *D* = Relative number of wage-earners engaged in manufacturing in the United States, 1904, 1909, 1925; *E* = Persons employed in the service industries in the United States, 1939; *F* = Length of life according to month of conception. All the scales on the left indicate percentages of annual average.

purely agricultural Russia is being removed, in part at least, as the ability of the Russians to overcome the effect of low temperature increases.

The seasons appear to have an effect upon the total amount of business as well as upon the kind. Although war, pestilence, floods, and economic cycles often introduce peculiar seasonal variations, the advanced peoples of the world show a general tendency toward increased activity in industry and business with the advent of warm weather after a cool winter, and especially of cool weather after a warm summer. Figure 34, curve *D,* shows seasonal variations in the average number of wage-earners employed in all industries in the entire United States during 1904, 1909, and 1925. Among the years for which the census supplies such data these three have been chosen because they are the most nearly free from great disturbing factors, such as war and financial depression. From a minimum in January the curve rises about 3 per cent to a low maximum in June. Then it drops a little, but as soon as the weather begins to be cooler, it rises rapidly, until it is 8 per cent above the January minimum. The maximum is reached in October, but November and December stand almost equally high.

Curve *E* has much the same form as *D,* although the June maximum and July minimum practically disappear. It, too, shows a difference of 8 per cent between the most extreme months. It represents the number of people engaged in service industries in the United States during 1939. Such industries include laundries, garages, barber shops, repair shops, tailoring establishments, restaurants, and a host of other establishments which serve people's needs without producing any basically new products. The amount of employment in Great Britain also fluctuates seasonally in much the same way as in the United States. The spring maximum, however, comes a little earlier and the autumnal maximum later. This is in harmony with the mild nature of the British winter. In France there is also a systematic increase in business, industry, and other activity from summer until December, with a drop thereafter.

C. Seasonal Fluctuations in Physiological Vigor

The widespread increase of industrial and commercial activity with the advent of cool weather seems to depend on physiological as well as social conditions. The social or cultural aspect is evident in the fact that modern civilization has established a set of habits which include taking vacations in summer, observing Christmas as a time for giving presents, and slowing down the work in many factories in January in order to take inventories, repair machinery, and get ready for a new year. When we delve deeper, however, the question arises whether the persistence of the habits just referred to may not be due in part to the fact that they harmonize with the physiological conditions which happen to prevail in a particular kind of climate.

Curve *C* in Figure 34 illustrates the type of evidence which raises this question. It shows the amount of work actually accomplished by hundreds of factory operatives in Connecticut. The operatives were engaged in piecework, and their hourly earnings depended almost completely on their own inclination and capacity. They were free to earn as much in January as in October or November, but Figure 34 shows that they did not feel like working hard in January. A month earlier, in mid-December, they were spurred to extra effort by the approach of Christmas, as is evident from the way in which the solid part of curve *C* rises above the dashed part. Many other lines of evidence indicate that the curve of piecework accurately represents the way in which the changing seasons influence people's ability and desire to work in a climate such as that of the northeastern United States. Its agreement with curve *D*, showing seasonal fluctuations of industry in the United States as a whole, is noteworthy.

Curve *B* in Figure 34 also indicates a seasonal physiological variation. It shows what proportion of the two million children born in Massachusetts, New York, Ohio, and Illinois from 1936 to 1940 was conceived in each month. Seasonal differences in conceptions appear to depend mainly upon health and vigor, but mental conditions, such as a feeling of optimism concerning the future, or the reverse also enter into the matter. The curve of conceptions (*B*) agrees quite closely with the one for piecework (*C*) and wage earners (*D*), although the autumn minimum comes later in *C* than in the others. Curve *E* for service industries is also similar except that it shows only a hint of the smaller maximum in June. It has a Christmas bulge like the curve for piecework. On the whole, the four curves are so much alike that they seem to be organically connected. It is worth noting that in all four of them the difference between minimum and maximum is practically the same, 8 or 9 per cent.

At the top of Figure 34 still another curve (*A*) repeats the main features of the four below it but shows an especially strong develop-

ment of the maximum at the end of the year.[2]   This curve is based
on six million children born in the United States from 1935 to 1937.
It shows the degree to which infants conceived at different seasons
are free from congenital defects which lead to death at birth or soon
after.   It is the deathrate from such causes reversed and expressed as
a percentage of the normal.   Beginning now at the top of Figure 34,
let us see what the various curves mean when taken all together.   We
start with the fact that in the United States children who are conceived in October, November, and December are decidedly more free
from congenital defects than those conceived at any other season, but
May and June also have an advantage over the rest of the year.*

Curve *B* shows that the number of conceptions giving rise to
living births also follows this same seasonal course, except that the
difference between the two maxima is reduced.   In other words, the
children conceived in the autumn and early winter are not only born
with few defects, but they are numerous.   It is not likely that this
is due to the health of the mothers during pregnancy, for the early
months of pregnancy are the ones when the danger to the child is
greatest.   For children conceived in October or November and born
in July or August these early months are those of winter, when the
amount of illness is greatest.   The probability is that the number
and good development of the children conceived in the autumn are
due to good health and vigor in the parents—probably both parents—
at the time of conception.   The germ cells are presumably in better
condition than at any other time of the year.   The lag of curve *A*
after the other curves, especially if we allow for premature births.
suggests that the most important time in the life of the germ cells
may be when they begin to develop some weeks before they take
part in conception.

Turning next to curve *C,* we find evidence that people's general
vigor as expressed in their daily work varies in essentially the same way
as the number and vigor of the children conceived in the corresponding
months.   Then, from curve *D,* we suspect that the major seasonal
variations in the activity of manufacturing may owe their origin, or
at least their persistence, to the same variations in vigor which presumably explain the differences in the work of factory operatives
and the number and quality of children.   Going a step further to

[2] Metropolitan Life Insurance Bulletin.
* Eastman suggests that this curve should probably be shoved two weeks or more
to the right in order to allow for the fact that many congenitally malformed children are born prematurely.

curve *E,* we conclude that the service industries also follow the same
seasonal course for the same basic reason, but with a good deal of
smoothing because the demand for services is bound to lag after the
conditions which cause variations in employment and other forms
of activity. In spite of this smoothing process the curve for the service industries gives a hint of a minor maximum in June and of a
drop in July. The same reasoning which applies to the autumn applies also to the June maximum. It seems probable, then, that physiological variations in vigor lead to unusually good work as well as to
the conception of unusually good babies in June or thereabouts, and
again more conspicuously in October, November, and December.
This variation in vigor appears to be the primary reason for a widespread tendency for business to expand at the same seasons when
many babies with few congenital defects are conceived. Retail sales
follow the same seasonal trend, except that December sees a pronounced increase due to Christmas.

If the upper five curves of Figure 34 are thus organically connected, the only logical connection seems to start with the weather.
This apparently causes physiological changes whereby people's vigor
drops low in the winter, rises to a minor maximum in June, drops
somewhat in midsummer, and then rises to a major maximum in
October or November.

This is the course normally followed by health as indicated by the
deathrate, except that the maxima of work, conceptions, and freedom
from congenital defects all lag one or two months after the period of
fewest deaths. These changing conditions of physical vigor are accompanied by closely related variations in mental attitudes. People
feel growingly optimistic in the spring and still more so in the autumn. For this reason, and also because better work is done at those
seasons, there is a widespread tendency for industry and other kinds
of business to expand. Hence we conclude that the seasonal pattern
of modern life, which everyone recognizes, is set by the effect of the
seasons upon our physiological activity as well as by more obvious
external effects, such as seasons of production on farms and hindrances to movement because of snow, rain, wind, low temperature,
and floods. Christmas, for example, is a purely cultural affair, but
if it had originally been set on the first of August or March, after a
period of low energy, instead of in late December, after a period of
maximum energy, our methods of observing it would presumably be
less intense than now and different in other ways, as one readily sees
in Australia. Or, again, the fact that the year ends in the early part

of the winter, when energy is declining, is likewise purely cultural. It is one reason for the fall of industrial employment to a low ebb in January. If, however, the new year began in mid-October, when almost everyone feels like hustling, it is doubtful whether people would then be willing to pause for stock-taking and for the repair of machinery. The point of the matter is that cultural habits rarely survive and thrive if they are actively in opposition to the demands of the physical environment.

Another conclusion from this seasonal study is that part of the energy and progress of the world's leading countries is due to the constant repetition of the physiological stimulus which comes with the changing seasons. This stimulus is especially noticeable in the autumn in the United States, but it seems to be at a maximum in the spring in western Europe and Japan. This point is so important that we shall discuss it in the next section. In concluding this section we may say that three things are clear. First, the challenge of the seasons has been a great incentive to progress in civilization. Second, at any given stage of civilization there is a certain degree of seasonal variation which is most effective in promoting further advances. In other words, from the purely cultural standpoint there is a definite optimum amount of seasonal change for each stage of progress in civilization. Third, the cultural variations from season to season seem to be intimately connected with physiological conditions that manifest themselves in reproduction and in rate of work.

D. Season of Birth and Longevity *

We come now to a curious paradox which emphasizes the importance of the seasons and also shows how intimately cultural and physical conditions work together.[3] We start with the fact that in the United States infants conceived in the fall and born in the summer are especially numerous and have the lowest percentage of congenital defects. Nevertheless in the past such infants have not lived so long on an average as those conceived in June and born in March. We have already seen that man, like other animals, has a definite annual rhythm, or cycle, of reproduction. In climates like those of western Europe and the northern United States this normally leads to a maximum of conceptions in June or thereabout and of birth in the early

---

* The rest of this chapter is taken largely from the author's *Season of Birth*, where full details of evidence are given.

[3] Huntington, 1938.

spring. In large parts of Europe this June maximum of conceptions stands out strongly without any second maximum later in the year. Curve *F* of Figure 34, although representing something else, illustrates its form. This same seasonal distribution of conceptions is found in the northern United States among colored people, criminals, sufferers from tuberculosis, and those who succumb early to insanity. It is likewise found among the later children of large families but not among the earlier children. On the other hand, a strong autumn maximum of conceptions is found not only among the people of the northeastern United States as a whole, as appears in curve *B* of Figure 34, but among certain small classes of society in Europe, such as the English gentry and the princely families of the continent.

In all the preceding examples the autumnal maximum of conceptions is found among an especially prosperous or vigorous class of society, whereas the less prosperous or vigorous people in the same regions show the normal rhythm, with a maximum of conceptions in June approximately. In the eastern United States the average first child is born into an economic status which is almost the highest in the world. The average sixth child there, however, as things now are, is likely to be born in a relatively low economic level. In comparison with other countries, the comfort of the northeastern United States has long been extremely high. The high economic status of the English gentry and of the princely families of Germany needs no proof. Thus there is a curious contrast between the seasonal trend of births among the fortunate and the less fortunate social classes within the United States, England, and Germany; and there is a similar contrast between the prosperous, well-fed northeastern United States and other countries. Such facts suggest that unusually good conditions of diet, shelter, and general mode of life tend to shift the maximum of conceptions from early summer (about June) to the autumn (October or November) with subsequent change in the date of maximum births from March to July or August.

This brings us back to our paradox: Although the autumn maximum of conceptions in the eastern United States according to the "prosperity" rhythm was even more intense in the past than now, length of life has varied in harmony with the more basic animal rhythm. Length of life is one of the best means of estimating general vigor. A long life normally indicates a good innate constitution. People who possess such vigor often live to a ripe old age, even though they appear frail. Taking mankind as a whole, the healthy and vigorous tend to live long and accomplish a great deal in comparison with the ill and feeble. Strangely enough, however, curve *F* in Figure 34 shows that children who are conceived when their parents reach the peak of vigor indicated by the October or November maximum of the other curves do not live so long as those conceived at the minor maximum in June. This happens in spite of the advantage of such children from the standpoint of congenital defects. Curve *F* is based on a random sample composed of 39,000 ordinary Americans born in the eastern United States, mainly from 1800 to 1880, and living beyond the age of 2 years. The 3,500 conceived in June and born in March lived on an average 3.8 years longer than the 3,000 conceived in October and born in July.[4] Those conceived in May and July were also long-lived, whereas the ones conceived in November and December were almost as short-lived as those conceived in October. Between the extremes the change in longevity is gradual. When the 39,000 people of curve *F* are divided into four groups according to place of birth, the same general relation between longevity and season of birth is found to prevail along the whole Atlantic seaboard. Among the 11,000 persons in the *Dictionary of American Biography,* a similar, but less pronounced, variation in length of life is evident. Gini[5] has found a similar condition in Rome. In Great Britain, to be sure, no such variation is evident among the people in the *Dictionary of National Biography,* but this probably means that the British climate comes so close to the optimum that all seasons of birth are favorable, at least for the upper classes.

The explanation of this strange seasonal contradiction between longevity and number of births is not yet clear. The normal maximum of births in the spring may mean that the parental germ cells are especially stimulated by rising temperature until the optimum is reached. Perhaps the unusually high percentage of vitamin A contained in spring herbage plays the same part in reproduction that it does in health, according to W. A. Price. Thus in May and June diet as well as temperature become favorable for the conception of healthy children, especially among people who consume plenty of milk, eggs, and greens. Whatever the cause may be, the outstanding fact is that at least as late as the last century some kind of physiological endowment still caused Americans and Italians to have the greatest vigor if they were conceived and born at the season which is best according to the basic animal rhythm. This rhythm presumably dates back to the days when man was primarily an animal. On the other hand,

4 *Ibid.*   5 Gini, 1934.

the maximum of conceptions among prosperous people in the autumn may mean that at that season modern improvements in diet, in the warming of houses, and in other respects are creating conditions which increase the rate of reproduction in a manner such as formerly occurred only in the spring.

E. Season of Birth and Eminence

The birthdays of eminent people agree with length of life in suggesting that children born according to the animal rhythm possess unusual vigor. Data for many countries indicate that such people are especially likely to be born according to that rhythm, except in one respect. Their birthdays reach a maximum in February or even January, a month or more earlier than those of ordinary people. The greater the degree of eminence and intellectuality, the greater is the tendency to conform to the animal rhythm, but with a slight displacement toward an earlier date.[6] For example, among 298 supremely eminent persons whose biographies in the *Encyclopædia Britannica* exceed five columns, the births per day in February exceed the yearly average by 32 per cent, whereas those in June and July fall 27 per cent below the average. On the other hand, among 1,830 persons with biographies of two to three columns, the births per day are equally numerous in February and March and are then only 9 per cent above the average, whereas those in June and July number scarcely 15 per cent below the average.

This peculiar seasonal distribution of the births of leaders suggests that physical vigor as well as innate mentality is needed if people are to acquire fame. There is no known reason why the parental genes that bear inheritance should combine more favorably at one season than another, although this may be possible. On the other hand, the evidence as to length of life leaves little doubt that, other things being equal, children born near the height of the normal seasonal cycle of reproduction have in the past been endowed with greater vitality than those born at other seasons. The fact that variations in vigor, longevity, and achievement are so closely tied up with the season of reproduction seems to indicate that man inherits as definite a reproductive response to the seasons as do birds or other animals. The same principle governs all life from plants, through animals, to man. The only difference is that with man the power to think and reason adds a great series of further complications.

[6] Huntington, 1938.

F. Resistance of Infants to Disease

Seasonal variations in deaths at different ages afford another indication that man inherits a remarkably sensitive adjustment to climate, as is fully set forth in *Season of Birth*. Unfortunately the necessary statistics are available only for a few countries and for early periods. Interest in specific diseases has largely crowded climate and weather out of the data for illness and death. The statistics of Belgium in the first half of the nineteenth century, however, are remarkably good for our purpose, being highly detailed and accurate. Less detailed data from other places, such as New York City, agree with them.

Before the days of modern hygiene, hot weather brought terrible danger to infants. In New York City the deathrate among children under five years of age used to be two or three times as high in July and August as in May, June, or October, and 50 to 75 per cent higher than in February and March. Many cities were far worse. The chief factor in this terrific increase of deaths in hot weather is digestive diseases. For this reason among our primitive ancestors only the most sturdy children were presumably able to live through hot summers.

The Belgian statistics suggest that mankind still inherits an unknown mechanism which originally helped infants to endure summer heat, provided they were born in early spring. Curves A to F in Figure 35 show deaths by months among Belgian infants at different stages of the first two years of life. Each horizontal line represents the average daily deaths at the age in question during the year as a whole. The curves show the percentage by which the deaths at each season depart from the yearly average, regardless of whether the general rate at each age is high or low. Thus we are able to make fair comparisons between the seasonal fluctuations of the deathrate at various ages.

The upper lefthand curve (A) of Figure 35 shows that in Belgium, the February deathrate of infants under a month old was formerly 26 per cent greater than the average for the year as a whole, whereas the July rate was 19 per cent less than the average. This low summer deathrate by no means contradicts our statement as to the bad effect of hot weather. It simply indicates that the Belgian climate approaches the optimum so closely that the summer is not hot enough to bring serious harm to newborn infants. The diseases of winter,

however, raise the deathrate considerably. The next curve (*B*), illustrating deaths during the third month of life, is almost flat. The
range from the lowest to the highest points is only 12 per cent instead

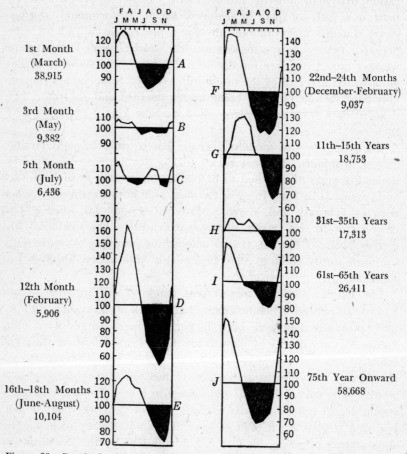

Figure 35. Deaths by Month and Age in Belgium, 1844–50. Heavy shading indicates a deathrate lower than the yearly average for the age in question. The
number of deaths on which each curve is based is indicated. All curves are
smoothed by the formula $\dfrac{a + 2b + c}{4} = b'$. From *Season of Birth*.

of 45, as in the first month. Something now causes the children to be
almost immune to the seasonal ailments of both summer and winter.
Deaths, of course, are still numerous compared with what they will
be later in life, but their causes are only in small measure those with

marked seasonal variations. This curious immunity to seasonal diseases continues for 3 or 4 months and then disappears. Meanwhile, however, the children become old enough to get bacteria into their systems, so that the curve for the fifth month (*C*) shows a mild increase of deaths during warm weather. By the time children are 12 months old (*D*), they have changed greatly. They are now so sensitive to seasonal diseases that their deathrate is about three times as great in March as in October.

During the second year of life the curious changes of sensitivity seen in the first year are repeated, but on a diminished scale. In curve *E* for ages 16 to 18 months, the range from lowest to highest deathrates is only 47 instead of 110, as it was at the age of 12 months. The next curve (*F*) shows that when the children are 22 to 24 months of age this contrast has increased so that the range is about 90. Curves for intermediate ages, as given in *Season of Birth,* indicate that the change from one to another of the conditions shown in Figure 35 is regular. We seem to be dealing with a systematic change whereby young children become more or less sensitive to seasonal disease according to their age.

A possible explanation is suggested by the names of months attached to the diagrams in Figure 35. Let us suppose that a child is born in mid-March, according to the primitive rhythm, in a climate with a moderately strong contrast of seasons. At first it needs no special protection against hot weather (curve *A*). By mid-May, however, danger from heat and from parasites of the alimentary tract has become imminent. Something then gives the child a relative immunity, which continues for 3 or 4 months (*C*). In mid-September, however, when the danger from hot weather is past, the immunity begins to lessen. By the twelfth month of age, which is February for children born in March, the apparent immunity has vanished completely (*D*). Protection against summer diseases and heat is not needed. The next summer, however, when the child born in March is 16 to 18 months old (*E*), the danger from summer heat again increases, but not so much as the first year, because the child's digestive system is more firmly established. So again the power to resist seasonal diseases also increases. In other words, human beings appear to inherit an intricate and highly delicate sensitivity to seasonal changes of weather. This sensitivity adapts them to a particular kind of climate, which is presumably the one in which certain important phases of evolution occurred.

G. A Peculiar Reproductive Adaptation

Older people, as well as infants, inherit delicate adaptations to special conditions of weather. The normal animal cycle of reproduction exposes the maximum number of mothers to the dangers of childbirth from February to April, a period when the health of the community as a whole is almost at its worst. The Belgian statistics suggest that this danger is at least partially obviated by a protective device similar to that of infants. At his particular season people in the reproductive ages of life show a tendency unlike that of people who are either younger or older. In Figure 35 the seasonal curve of deaths among children 11 to 15 years of age (G) is almost perfectly regular, with a maximum in April and a minimum in November. A few years later, when people enter the reproductive stage of life, the effect of the seasons is reduced to small proportion (H in Figure 35), just as among infants 3 to 6 months of age. Thus the deathrate of potential parents shows much less than the normal tendency to rise at the season when births reach a maximum according to the animal cycle. Later in life (curves I and J) the deathrate varies more and more closely in harmony with temperature, being highest in January.

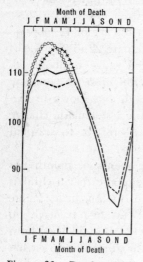

Figure 36. Deathrates of Adults at Reproductive Ages in Belgium. From *Season of Birth.*

A still more extraordinary climatic adjustment is shown when separate mortality curves are drawn for men and women at the reproductive ages of 25 to 40 years. The lines of circles and crosses at the top of Figure 36 indicate the deathrates which might normally be expected.* Instead of following these lines the actual deathrates flatten off from February to May. The women's curve flattens more than that of men, so that the sex which needs the most help gets it. Thus two especially critical periods of life, namely, the onset of hot weather in infancy and the time of childbirth, are marked by what seem to be hereditary protective mechanisms. At another critical period, the time of concep-

---

* In this figure the vertical scale has been made relatively greater than in Figure 35 in order to give a clearer picture of the difference between the sexes.

tion, a third mechanism gives special vigor through the effect of the optimum temperature and, probably, of diet. All these mechanisms, however, lose most of their value unless the birth of children follows the normal seasonal cycle.

The Queensland statistics quoted above (page 304) sum up the effect of all these inherited mechanisms when people of sturdy European stock migrate to a climate which is too warm and has little seasonal stimulus. The loss of five or ten years of life because of birth in such a climate may be compared with an average loss of nearly four years in the United States through birth in summer rather than in March. Thus we have before us certain facts as to (1) the longevity of Australians born in different regions; (2) the longevity of Americans born at different seasons; (3) the proportion of eminent persons born at different seasons; (4) the curious fluctuations in the power of infants to resist seasonal diseases; and (5) the equally curious way in which, during the reproductive period of life, both sexes, but especially women, show a reduced sensitivity to disease during the unhealthy season of late winter. All these conditions seem to point toward a selective process whereby the physical type most closely adapted to a certain definite kind of climate was preserved and other types were eliminated. As a consequence of some such process the climatic conditions under which people are now conceived or born, as well as those under which they live, have much to do with vigor and achievement throughout life. Such facts as these illustrate the reasons why the maps of climatic efficiency discussed in an earlier chapter are of basic importance in the study of civilization. When all these lines of physiological evidence are combined with the facts as to the seasonal relationships of agriculture and business, the influence of the seasons upon human vigor and upon the progress of civilization becomes still more evident.

CHAPTER 17

WEATHER AND STORMS

A. Ebullient Americans

The peculiar and almost effervescent activity of Americans living in the northern United States is widely recognized. Europeans often say that Americans act first and think afterwards. Modest Americans are often ashamed because their tourist compatriots hurry back and forth across Europe with loud voices, bustling manners, and incessant concentration on "doing" the whole continent as fast as possible. Miss Kuo, a brilliant young Chinese woman, describes this quality when speaking of her journey from China via Europe to America.

The Americans were enjoying themselves as only Americans can. In Marseilles [they] had certainly been more vigorous than any other people I had seen. Now [on a ship crossing the Atlantic] they were playing with a gusto almost furious in its zeal. . . . Every day I appreciated that the average American is keener about life and more active in his work and play than his English cousin. Compared with him the Frenchman . . . has long ago lost his zest for living. . . . Between Europe and America there is as great a difference as . . . between America and China. Throughout that voyage I was deliberately imbibing the ozone of American vigor.

This characteristic activity of Americans is doubtless due partly to selective migration, but it seems also to be closely associated with the changeable weather of the United States. In the preceding chapters on temperature and seasons we have said relatively little about weather. Everyone recognizes its importance as a help or hindrance in farming and transportation and as a factor in daily work and play. Few people, however, realize the close connection between the weather and national character.

The behavior of little children is especially interesting in this respect. In the northern United States many a small child runs most of the time instead of walking. Nowhere else, so far as I have been able to ascertain through wide travel and conversation, does this habit prevail to such an extent. After living a few years in this country, even the best-bred little European children tend to become as boisterous as equally well-bred little Americans, provided they come to America early enough. On the other hand, little Americans who live in Europe or other foreign regions tend to be quiet and "well-mannered" in comparison with their cousins in the northern United States. In many families which have migrated to America, the children who spent their early years elsewhere are less ebullient, or whatever the right word may be, than their brothers and sisters born after the parents had been in America a few years. Nowhere else is there such insistent emphasis upon action and still more action. And nowhere else, as we can probably say without boasting, is there greater capacity for rapid action. The temperament which this implies appears to become established early in life and shows considerable resistance to change thereafter. All grades of lesser activity are found in other countries. They range from active British, Germans, French, and Japanese to relatively inactive Persians, Hindus, and the inhabitants of equatorial lowlands. Such differences are among the basic factors in producing differences in civilization.

The intensity of American activity is almost universally explained as the normal result of putting active people into a geographical environment blessed with plenty of room to expand and plenty of resources awaiting development. This is true so far as it goes, but we ought to go farther. When the preceding statement is broken down into its component elements, we find ourselves faced by the same three major factors—inheritance, physical environment, and culture—which we find in practically every great problem. In Part II of this book we saw reason to believe that selective migration has tended to give the United States an unusual proportion of persons with a biological inheritance favorable to an active, alert, pioneering disposition. As for physical environment, the opportunities and resources of a great new country have undoubtedly been tremendously stimulating to American development. It is by no means clear, however, that selective migration and abundant resources are alone sufficient to explain the American temperament. They have not produced such a temperament in South America or even in Australia and New Zealand. An additional factor, apparently climatic, is needed. In the preceding chapter we have seen that the coming and going of the seasons, especially the onset of autumn, produce a physiological effect which seems to harmonize with the American national temperament, but ordinary storms seem to be still more important in this respect. Like the seasons, they influence man indirectly through agriculture and in other ways, and directly through a physiological stimulus. The net effect of selective migration, vast resources, abundant opportunities, a stimulating climate, and the culture derived from Europe has been a new brand of culture in which activity plays an especially dominant role.

B. The Nature of Storms

To most people the word "storm" means primarily rain or snow. In the following chapters it means much more. A storm includes changes in atmospheric pressure, winds, temperature, ozone, atmospheric electricity, ionization, dust, and sunshine, as well as in humidity, clouds, and precipitation. All these apparently have at least an indirect effect upon human activity and temperament, and most of them have a distinct direct effect. Differences in rainfall, for example, are universally recognized as highly significant. They lead to deserts in some places, high productivity in others, and climates too wet for agriculture elsewhere. As yet, however, there is little recognition of the outstanding differences associated with two distinct types of rainfall. One type includes (a) *convective rain,* which is due primarily to the rising of bodies of warm, moisture-laden air under the influence of the sun's heat; and (b) *orographic rain,* due to the rising of air when it flows against the side of a mountain. When rain of these two types comes to an end, the air at any given point on the earth's surface is not much different from what it was at the beginning. After a certain type of summer shower, for example, or after almost any tropical rain, including even a hurricane, the air has almost the same temperature, humidity, movement, and other qualities as before and hence is not particularly refreshing.

The other type of rain is technically known as "cyclonic." This term does not imply cyclones of the violent kind that sometimes overturn houses. It means merely an ordinary storm such as comes every week or so in the United States and western Europe. As such a storm passes over us, a cloudy day is followed by rain and then by clear skies. The center of a cyclonic storm is an area of low barometric pressure hundreds of miles in diameter with winds blowing in a different direction on each side so as to make a great whirl around the center. Such a storm, especially in the United States, is accompanied by a change in the wind and the arrival of relatively cool, dry air. The rainfall of tropical regions is almost entirely of the first, that is, convective or orographic type, whereas that of middle latitudes is dominantly cyclonic. Both kinds of rain are equally valuable in supplying water for agriculture and other purposes, but showers of the convective or orographic type fall far behind cyclonic storms in their effect upon human health and activity.

Cyclonic storms occur regularly at all seasons in western Europe and much of the United States and less frequently or regularly in adjacent regions, together with Japan, central Argentina, New Zealand, and a small section of southeastern Australia. Regions such as the Mediterranean lands, California, central Chile, southwestern Australia, and the extreme tip of South Africa get cyclonic storms in winter, but not in summer. In the USSR they occur quite frequently in summer, but in winter are relatively rare, although sometimes severe, especially in Siberia. In a narrow strip along a few west coasts, such as those of Chile and especially California, the inflow of air from a cold ocean, alternating with heating of the land by the sun, provides a substitute for storms in some respects.

The concept of storms as great whirls of air with winds circling around them—the concept which gave rise to the term "cyclonic"—has been modified by a new concept stressing the opposing movements of great masses of air. Each storm represents the meeting of a vast mass of warm, moist, "tropical" oceanic air, moving obliquely away from the equator, and a similar mass of cold, dry, "polar" or continental air moving obliquely toward the equator. The early stage of a normal storm in the northern hemisphere, especially on the east side of a continent or in the interior, is usually marked by rising temperature and winds from a southerly quarter. These result from the approach of tropical air masses. The polar air, because it is cool, is slightly heavier than the tropical air. Therefore, when the two meet, it tends to press under the tropical air and lift it up. The upward movement causes the tropical or oceanic air to expand and therefore grow cooler. Hence much of its relatively abundant water vapor is condensed into clouds and rain. Near the center of the storm the rain often ceases temporarily, the clouds perhaps break away, and the wind dies down before changing its direction. This represents a neutral space near the meeting point of the two air masses. The cold wave which follows the change in the wind represents the equatorward sweep of the polar air.

C. Storminess and Agriculture

Cyclonic storms of this sort influence civilization in many ways. One of the most obvious is the encouragement of agriculture. Storms provide frequent periods of rainfall interspersed with sunshine, a kind of alternation which is especially favorable to the majority of crops. Cyclonic storms also help the farmer by supplying rain at all seasons. How important these two benefits are may be judged from a study of crops. If rainfall were distributed evenly throughout the year, each month would have 8.33 per cent of the yearly total. In the entire world there are only five main regions where a rainfall sufficient for agriculture is distributed so evenly that no month, on an average, has less than 5 per cent of the annual total. The two largest of these areas face one another across the North Atlantic. They are (1) western Europe from Ireland and Great Britain across central and northern France, Belgium, Holland, Denmark, and Germany to western Poland; and (2) the eastern United States and southern Canada from Halifax and Milwaukee to eastern Texas, but not including Florida. A similar but smaller Japanese area (3) lies in nearly the same latitude as the North American area, but a little nearer the equator. Two other small areas are located in similar latitudes in the southern hemisphere. One of these (4) is located between latitude 30° and 40° on the East Coast of South America from the southern border of Brazil through Uruguay to Buenos Aires and beyond; and the other (5) includes a little of Australia from Sydney to Melbourne and most of New Zealand. These, it will be noted, are the most advanced parts of the world. Within the North American area a triangle with its corners near Halifax, Philadelphia, and Cleveland comes nearer than any other considerable area to having uniform rainfall at all seasons. Among the world's large cities, Boston and New Haven, with 75 per cent as much rain per day in June as in February, come nearer than any others to having uniform precipitation at all seasons.

The five areas with cyclonic rain at all seasons include by far the greater part of the agricultural land where two great advantages prevail. One advantage is a large yield per acre. The other, which in the long run is probably more important, is reliability of the crops from year to year. Only in strictly limited areas of two other types does the general productivity of the land rise so high. One type includes regions such as California and Egypt, where irrigation gives a steady supply of water at all seasons. The other consists of scattered and relatively small tropical areas, the so-called plantation regions, where rather abundant rain during most of the year is interrupted by a short drier season which helps the crops to ripen but is not severe enough to cause those that are still growing to dry up.

Figure 37 illustrates the importance of abundant reliable rain at all seasons when combined with favorable temperature.[1] It shows the value of all the main crops on an average acre of cultivated land in Europe and neighboring regions. The value of each crop per pound is reckoned as the average price in many countries during many years and is counted as the same everywhere. A considerable part of the difference between the high index numbers of western

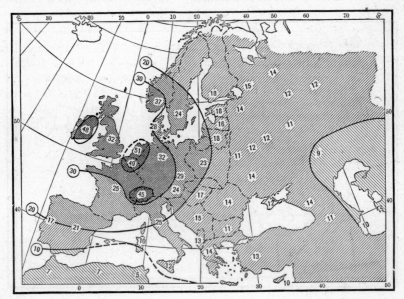

Figure 37. Value of Main Crops per Acre in Europe. From *Principles of Economic Geography*.

Europe (30 to 50) and the low ones of North Africa and the Caspian region (below 10) is due largely to cyclonic storms which bring frequent rain at all seasons to western Europe, whereas the regions farther south and east often suffer from prolonged dry spells. Methods of cultivation and types of crops, soils, and seasonal extremes of temperature also play a considerable part in influencing the yield of crops, but storms are especially valuable because they tend to insure at least a moderate production every year.

The benefit derived from the occurrence of storms at all seasons is clearly illustrated in Figures 38 and 39, which show the reliability

[1] Huntington, 1940A.

of the crops in the United States and Europe.[2] In the lightly shaded
areas the difference in yield from one year to another is slight. The
relative uniformity of the rainfall permits the farmers to know what
they can count on. It lessens the danger of debt, want, and misery
by reason of unforeseen crop failures, such as are common in the
heavily shaded areas. Here, too, other factors, including low temperature and unseasonable frosts in the north, are significant, but
the good effect of storms is dominant. In other continents a similar

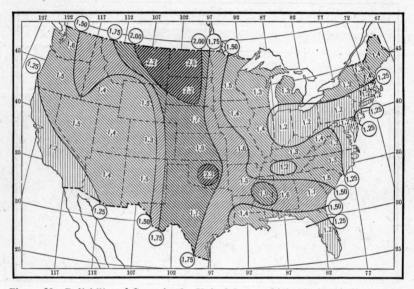

Figure 38.   Reliability of Crops in the United States.   Light shading indicates high
reliability.   From *Principles of Economic Geography*.

condition prevails.   Japan, for example, which is the only part of
Asia with rather abundant cyclonic storms at all seasons, enjoys far
the largest yield of crops per acre on that continent and suffers least
from crop failures.

Such conditions stimulate the progress of civilization by encouraging people to try new methods. In places where drought and frost
often ruin the crops, a feeling of despair or fatalism tends to prevail. Bad weather foils the farmer so often that when new methods
are suggested he says, "What's the use? If God sends rain, the crop
will be good. If he doesn't, we starve." People need the challenge
of difficulty, but they become apathetic and fatalistic when the diffi-

[2] *Ibid.*, pp. 86, 229B.

culties are too great. In thoroughly cyclonic regions, on the contrary, the farmer is almost certain to get at least a reasonably good crop each year. If he tries improved methods, the chances are large that his extra effort will not be wasted. This encourages a progressive attitude in contrast to the fatalistic, inert attitude so common in regions where unreliable rainfall causes sharp alternations between good crops and poor. Such psychological contrasts help to explain

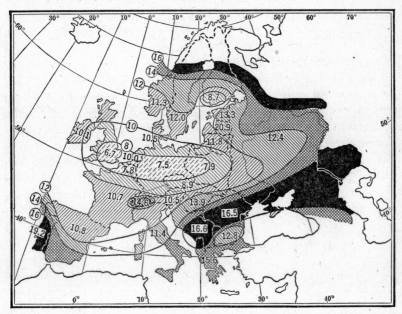

Figure 39. Reliability of Crops in Europe. Light shading indicates high reliability. From *Principles of Economic Geography*.

many historical events in which "national character," especially optimism and initiative versus fatalism and apathy, plays a part.

Cyclonic storms encourage progress by presenting a challenge which is great enough to be highly stimulating, but not great enough to be permanently discouraging. The challenge can be met without undue difficulty if people are energetic and use their heads. For example, on fair days in regions of frequent storms the farmer must hurry with his plowing and planting because rain will soon interfere. He must cut his hay with an eye to drying it before the next storm. When it is drying he must be constantly alert to rake it up or store it away before it gets wet. In the spring and fall he must guard against sudden frosts. By hurrying on days when storms are threatening he can often save grain, fruit, vegetables, or other products. Because of storms he must shelter his animals, tools, and harvested crops with far more care than in regions where a long dry season prevails. Storms occasion much trouble by piling up snowdrifts in winter and by causing sudden floods like those that have afflicted Johnstown, Dayton, and Cincinnati. The cold waves that follow storms may ruin the peach blossoms in New Jersey or Georgia or spoil the orange crop in California or Florida. Blizzards may kill sheep and cattle by the thousand unless prompt measures are taken to insure safety. In such ways and many others the frequent and sudden changes of weather accompanying the meeting of opposing air masses and the shifting winds of cyclonic storms act as a stimulant. They challenge the farmer and others to greater alertness and activity than in the far more extensive regions where changes of weather are usually more gradual and droughts and related disasters more frequent. They also encourage the growth of a social system in which great stress is laid on the dynamic qualities which are needed to meet such diffi- culties. The suddenness and severity of storms in the United States are highly stimulating in this respect. The passive Egyptian peasants know nothing of any such stimulus.

D. Storms as a Physiological Stimulant

The physiological, as well as the agricultural, effect of storms ap- pears to be an influential factor in national character. The reason is that storms act as a stimulant to health and activity. When a storm is approaching, the atmospheric conditions tend to be relatively un- pleasant. People say that the air feels heavy. Really it is light. It seems heavy because it makes people feel dull or slightly inert. A moderately warm day before a storm may be most delightful, but not at all stimulating. On such a day in the spring or autumn one longs to stroll in the woods, sit on the sunny lawn, or somehow enjoy oneself without making much exertion. Careful observation shows that after the rain begins to fall this disinclination to activity disappears. While the rain is falling one settles earnestly to work. Toward the end of the storm, even though rain is still falling, the air often changes its quality and has a stimulating effect. This usu- ally increases rapidly when the wind changes and cool air flows in. On evenings when a storm is coming to an end, old people are less likely to fall asleep over their reading or sewing than on an evening when a storm is brewing. The exhilarating quality of the weather the day after a storm is well known. Children and animals show it in their play. Adults walk unusually fast. Physicians have devoted much attention to the way in which sufferers from rheumatism, epilepsy, arthritis, and many other diseases feel badly on the approach

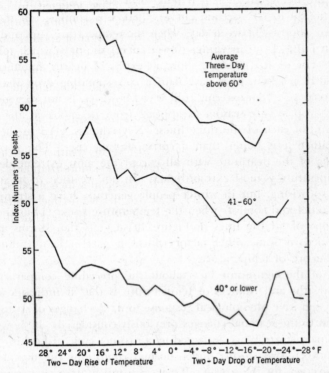

Figure 40. Deaths from All Causes at Ages above Five, Compared with Two-Day Change of Mean Daily Temperature, New York City, 1883–88. The seasonal fluctuation in deaths has been eliminated, so that the curves show only variations above or below the seasonal average.

of a storm but recover and feel unusually well when the storm is over.[3]

The effect of storms on health is extraordinary. It is summed up in a study of daily deaths during 6 years in New York City.[4] Inasmuch as changes of temperature are the best available indicator of the alternating arrival of warm and cool air masses, such changes are compared with daily deaths in Figure 40. The figures at the bottom

[3] Hinsdale, Dec., 1938; Petersen.   [4] Huntington, 1919, 1930.

show the number of degrees Fahrenheit by which the average daily temperature changed in the two days preceding death. The upper curve shows what happens in warm weather when the general temperature averages above 60°. If the temperature rises as much as 15°F from one day to the next, deaths are approximately 30 per cent more numerous than if it falls 15 or 20°. In medium weather, averaging 40 to 60° (second curve), there is a similar, but less pronounced, contrast between days when the temperature rises and those when it falls. Even in winter (lower curve) the days which follow a two-day rise of 16° or more show an excess of deaths amounting to at least 10 per cent over days with a corresponding drop that does not exceed 18°. An extreme cold wave, however, is not so good as a milder drop at any season, as appears from the hook at the right-hand end of each of the three lines. Nevertheless, even in the coldest weather it is better than a corresponding rise. The persistent lowering of the deathrate with all except the most extreme declines in temperature is most extraordinary. In hot weather, to be sure, it is not surprising, but in winter people generally have a strong feeling of relief and comfort when the temperature rises. Thus the general slope of all the lines in Figure 40 suggests that storms are accompanied by some other factor which in part at least counteracts the influence of temperature.

One of the significant facts about the preceding comparison between deaths and changes of temperature is that it indicates an extremely sensitive physiological response to daily changes of weather in addition to the seasonal changes previously considered. It shows that an ordinary storm is accompanied by a distinct cycle of health. Halfway between two storms under normal conditions the deathrate is about average for the season. Then, as a warm air mass sweeps over New York, for example, either from the ocean, as is common in winter, or from the southwest, as often happens in summer, the air becomes warmer, and deaths increase just about in proportion to the increase in temperature. When the storm breaks, a change soon takes place. The lowering of temperature during the storm and the influx of cool air as the storm passes its climax are accompanied by an improvement in health which again is closely proportional to the change of temperature. In other words, a normal storm is introduced by weather which increases the discomfort of many ill persons and brings death to others. As it passes away this effect is reversed, and many people who would otherwise have died survive the crisis of their disease and perhaps ultimately recover.

A similar response to the weather is apparent in persons who are in good health. Most people are conscious of a feeling of exhilaration at the end of a storm, even if they pay little attention to an opposite feeling of relative inertia which is widespread in the "heavy" air before a storm. Such feelings are far from being imaginary. They are based on definite and measurable physiological "tides," as Petersen has well shown. He finds that the rates of pulse and of breathing, the blood pressure, the composition of the blood, and various other bodily functions all vary systematically with the coming and going of tropical and polar air masses.

The discovery that the human body is so sensitive to the weather leads us to inquire whether the harmful and the beneficial effects of storms neutralize one another. Is the net effect of storms good or bad? An answer is found in the daily deaths in New York City.[5] Deaths of persons over five years of age have been tabulated according to overlapping periods of ten days, the first period being the first to the tenth days, the next, the second to the eleventh, and so on. Thus about 2,900 periods, each including ten consecutive days, are taken into account. These are divided according to average temperature, one group having a mean ten-day temperature of 80° or more, another 75° to 80°, and so forth. For each period the average difference between the mean temperatures of successive days is computed regardless of whether the temperature goes up or down. A high average means variable weather with rapid alternations of rising and falling temperature. Using this method, we find that moderately variable weather is the best for health at all seasons and at all temperatures. In Figure 41 the solid lower line shows the deathrate at the end of periods with moderate interdiurnal variability of temperature, that is, during periods of frequent but not severe storms. At all seasons, from the coldest on the left to the hottest on the right, this line is lower than either the dashed line for periods of great variability or the barred line for those with little variability.

The best condition for health apparently occurs when the change from the average twenty-four hour temperature of one day to that of the next averages about 3°F in summer and 7° in winter. The reason for this difference is that in winter, when great changes are the rule, we become hardened to them and at the same time protect ourselves so that we do not feel their entire impact so fully as in summer. Nevertheless, extreme changes, such as accompany cold bliz-

5 Huntington, 1930.

zards and hot foehn winds in continental interiors are too severe for almost everyone. The surprising fact, however, is that in a climate like that of New York, uniform weather day after day is as undesirable as highly variable weather. The barred line in Figure 41, indeed, shows that in winter it is worse. This agrees with the fact that the highest deathrates normally occur in cold, clear spells of unchanging weather, especially when the ground is frozen but not

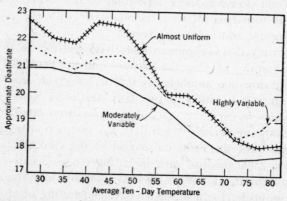

Figure 41. Daily Deaths in New York City at End of Ten-Day Periods, Compared with Average Temperature and Interdiurnal Variability of Temperature. "Moderately variable" (1,157 ten-day periods) differs in meaning according to the average ten-day temperature as follows:

Mean Temperature	Moderate Variation	Mean Temperature	Moderate Variation
76°F or higher	3°	31–40°	4–6°
56–75°	3–4°	26–30°	5–7°
41–55°	4–5°	25° or less	6–8°

The "highly variable" curve is based on 538 periods more variable than the above, and the "almost uniform" curve on 473 less variable.

covered with snow, and the wind fills the air with dust. On the other hand, in summer high variability is worse than uniformity because usually it includes extreme hot waves.

Another indication of the effect of storminess on human activity is directly connected with business. A study of the amount of work done by pieceworkers shows that in both Connecticut and Florida, more work, on an average, is done when the weather is variable than when it is uniform.[6] An extreme change of temperature, to be sure, especially a great drop in winter or a great rise in summer, is un-

[6] Huntington, 1924B, pp. 139 ff.

favorable. On the whole, however, an interdiurnal change of about 5°F in Florida and 6 to 10° in Connecticut is accompanied by enough extra work so that a climate with such qualities has a distinct advantage over one with either uniform temperatures or excessive changes. The agreement between factory work and deaths in this respect seems clearly to indicate that frequent, but not excessively severe, storms are a distinct advantage from the standpoint of human health and efficiency as well as in agriculture.

Such conditions have the good effect of helping Americans to accomplish a great deal. The combined result of selective migration, great resources, and a very stormy climate is that the American social system emphasizes action and activity and seems to pay too little attention to a more leisurely and thoughtful way of life. Americans of the northern United States accomplish more than Europeans but also lose a good deal in the way of quiet enjoyment. In addition, they wear themselves out physically. This is probably one of the main reasons for an unduly large deathrate from degenerative diseases, such as those of the heart and kidneys. Mills [7] has shown that the distribution of such diseases corresponds closely to the degree to which the climate is stimulating. Herrington and Moriyama have shown that it also agrees with the extent to which the urban and industrial mode of life prevails. There is no conflict between these two ideas. The fact is that, in a broad way, when allowance is made for factors such as transportation and the location of sources of power and raw materials, the industrial mode of life is distributed over the world in close agreement with the degree to which the climate is stimulating.

The important point just now is one to which we keep returning: the organization of society, together with its ideals and modes of thought and action, tends to evolve toward a condition in harmony with the physical surroundings. Thus in the United States we see a social system closely in accord with the stimulating seasonal changes and storms which characterize the climate. We also see that the combined effect of the climate and the social system is so strong that children are especially active here, manufacturing and other forms of business forge ahead with a zest rarely seen elsewhere, and people die from degenerative diseases to an unprecedented extent.

This brings us back to the Chinese opinion of Americans with which this chapter began. By reason of its storminess the climate of

[7] Mills, 1939.

the northern United States is extremely stimulating. The maximum stimulus is found in the interior, in the North Central States and northern New York, where the combined effect of frequent storms and strong changes of weather is close to a maximum. Such a climate drives people ahead at a great rate. No one storm may do much, but neither does one explosion in a gasoline engine. Many storms, however, coming one after another, drive people ahead at a rapid pace, just as many explosions drive a motor car. But just as an automobile may be driven so fast that it wears out from undue speed, so may the body be overstimulated by the rapid impact of storm after storm. This apparently is an important factor in the restlessness and activity which characterize the northern United States. It shows itself in the active and boisterous children and the widespread tendency for people to be always doing something.

The influence of storms may be summed up in a metaphor which was originally published in 1915.[8]

The influence of climate upon men may be likened to that of a driver upon his horse. Some drivers let their horses go as they please. Now and then a horse may run away, but the average pace is slow. Such drivers are like an unstimulating climate. Others whip their horses and urge them to the limit all the time. They make rapid progress for a while, but in the end they exhaust their animals. They resemble climates which are always stimulating. In such climates nervous exhaustion is likely to prevail and insanity becomes common. A third type of drivers first whip their horse to a great speed for a mile or two, and then let them walk slowly for another mile or two. They often think that they are accomplishing great things, and they are better off than the two types already mentioned, but they still have much to learn. They are like a climate which has a strong contrast of seasons, one being favorable and the other unfavorable. Still a fourth kind of driver may whip his horse sometimes and sometimes let him walk, but what he does chiefly is to urge the animal gently with the voice, then check him a little with the rein. By alternate urging and checking he conserves the animal's strength, and in the long run can cover more distance and do it more rapidly than any of the others. Such a driver resembles a climate which has enough contrast of seasons to be stimulating but not to create nervous tension, and which also possesses frequent storms whose function is to furnish the slight urging and checking which are so valuable in the total effect, although each individual impulse is almost unnoticeable.

[8] Huntington, 1924B, p. 152.

CHAPTER 18

REGIONS AND SEASONS OF MENTAL ACTIVITY

A. Geographic Variations in Mental Activity

"Thinking is as biological as digestion," says W. A. Price.[1] Therefore, it is readily influenced by climate, diet, and disease, as well as by education, mode of life, and other cultural conditions. This idea should be considered in connection with two important features in the history of civilization: first, the persistently increasing dominance of the north, and second, the variations from century to century in the general psychological status of individual countries and of the world as a whole. The first feature is obvious in the movement of the center of human progress from Babylonia and Egypt to western Europe. The second appears in the fact that sometimes confidence and assurance predominate widely among the nations, whereas at other times uncertainty and instability prevail.

These psychological reactions are generally supposed to arise from economic, religious, political, and other cultural conditions. This is true. Nevertheless, an hypothesis which inserts another factor may supply an additional element of truth. A peculiar psychological condition may arise because of (1) cycles of weather and hence of disease, diet, health, and temperament. This may lead to (2) economic, political, religious, and other changes. These latter produce (3) their own psychological effects, which in turn lead to further cultural changes. Thus for decades or centuries the weather may assist other conditions in giving a particular psychological aspect to certain periods of history. The Dark Ages and the Revival of Learning occurred at opposite phases of a long climatic cycle. Storminess apparently reached a low ebb in the Dark Ages but was abundant and violent in the fourteenth century. These two periods were likewise times of psychological contrast. The Dark Ages were characterized by widespread depression of mental activity, whereas the Revival of Learning ushered in a period of alertness and hope.

[1] p. 14.

343

In order rightly to evaluate this hypothesis, and still more in order to appraise the validity of our map of climatic efficiency, we must examine the distribution of mental activity geographically and also in relation to seasons and weather. The good sense and scientific temperament of northern peoples, such as Scandinavians and Finns, are widely recognized. Some people call Denmark the most civilized of countries. Icelanders in the far north and Falkland Islanders in the far south are notable for their intellectual activity. In Alaska white Americans tend to become great readers. The Eskimos are reputed to have especially keen minds. Such facts suggest that mental activity is unusually great in high latitudes. On the other hand, the Arabs in their hot desert are often said to be mentally alert. Astronomy, geography, and our numerals bear witness to this. In China we have seen a reversal of the usual rule that the parts of a country in the higher latitudes make the most progress, provided they are not too cold for agriculture. In the high latitudes of South America, as far south as the Falkland Islands, the Alacaluf savages, with their bare bodies protected from furious winds only by fur capes, seem to be among the world's most backward and inert people.

Such contradictions indicate that mental alertness depends on a variety of factors. We have seen that selection through migration is one such factor. It apparently accounts, in part at least, for the alertness of Icelanders and South Chinese. Education is assuredly a powerful stimulant of mental activity. So are natural resources that can be used if people exert their wits. Climate and weather are simply other factors in this same series. They receive special treatment here because they are little understood as yet and because their cyclic variation seems to have influenced some of the greatest historical changes. The highest mental achievement is possible only when favorable conditions of many kinds exert a combined stimulus. Our task just now is to try to separate climatic effects from those of heredity, culture, and the non-climatic physical environment.

A good measure of intellectual activity on a large scale is the circulation of books by libraries, especially ordinary city libraries. People read serious books more frequently when their minds are active than when they are inert. Library statistics, most fortunately, are generally well kept. Librarians tend to be co-operative. Hence such statistics afford a vast reservoir of material for a study of intellectual activity. Data from thirty city libraries well distributed over continental United States, together with six in Canada, two in Australia, and one each in Hawaii, Cuba, Panama, New Zealand, and Argentina, provide a wide basis for study.[2] Among those forty-three libraries, twenty-eight in the United States and Canada furnish data for the central library without the branches. Table 16 shows that when these cities are divided according to latitude, there is a steady

TABLE 16

Percentage of Non-Fiction in Library Circulation

(Weighted Averages, Generally for Twenty Years, 1920–1939)

Cities	Percentage
Eight most southerly cities (Tampa, Houston, New Orleans, Jacksonville, El Paso, Savannah, Shreveport, San Diego)	28.9
Eight next cities (Atlanta, Los Angeles, Oklahoma City, Nashville, Richmond, Oakland, Kansas City, Cincinnati) (41.3 if Los Angeles is omitted)	51.3
Six more northern cities (Baltimore, Denver, New Haven, Chicago, Boston, Hamilton, Ont.)	53.5
Six most northerly cities (St. John, N. B., Minneapolis, Portland, Ore., Seattle, Spokane, Vancouver)	55.2

rise from 29 per cent of non-fiction in the most southern cities to 55 in the most northern. The circulation of magazines shows a similar distribution. For example, in proportion to population, northern states subscribe to the *Saturday Evening Post,* the *Ladies' Home Journal,* and *Country Gentleman* far more than southern states. The Dakotas surpass Texas and Oklahoma by 50 per cent or more, and Montana similarly surpasses Arizona.[3]

An unusual but highly sensitive kind of evidence is found in the degree of accuracy with which people report their ages in the census.[4] Figure 42 is typical of a condition found more or less in all censuses. The curves indicate the number of people reported at various ages in 1910 or 1920. At that time the total number of births was steadily increasing in practically all parts of the United States. Under such circumstances data obtained from mentally alert people give curves which slope regularly downward from earlier to later ages, like those for the native whites of native parentage in Minnesota in 1920 (upper left). Even among such people there is some inaccuracy. Boys of nineteen or twenty, for example, sometimes report themselves as twenty-one, thus making a hump in the curve. Among mentally inactive people gross inaccuracies prevail, as appears in the Negro curves (lower right). Even numbers are preferred to odd;

[2] Huntington, 1941.
[3] Huntington, 1940A, p. 611.
[4] Huntington, 1927C, p. 300.

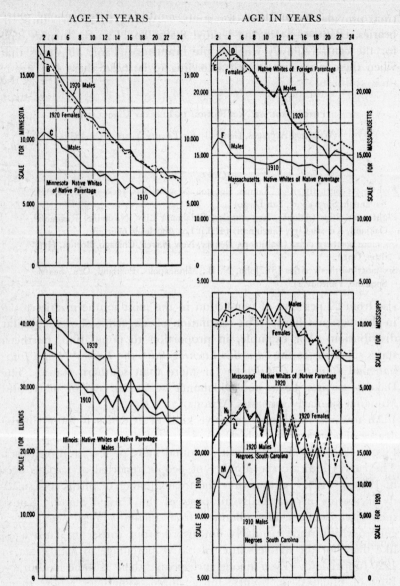

Figure 42. Accuracy in Reporting Ages. Scales indicate number of persons.
Courtesy, *Scientific Monthly*.

twelve is an extreme favorite, as are multiples of ten among older people. Russian data suggest that such inaccuracy is due more to mental inertia than to lack of education. Although the settlers in Siberia are a vigorous and competent group selected by migration, their children are less literate than those of older regions such as the Ukraine. Nevertheless, these same children, when adult, state their ages more accurately than the Ukrainians.

In statistics of age it is easy to estimate the degree of inaccuracy by adding up the departures from a normal curve. When the accuracy

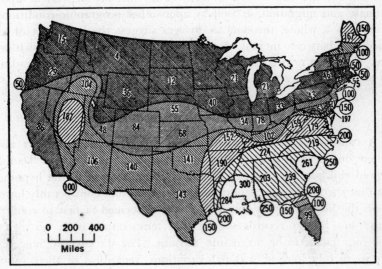

Figure 43. Map of Accuracy in Reporting Ages. Courtesy, *Scientific Monthly*.

of native whites of native parentage in the United States is thus tested, we get the map shown in Figure 43.[5] Accuracy is there indicated by dark shading and low figures which mean small departures from a perfectly smooth curve in diagrams such as Figure 42. A systematic increase in accuracy from south to north is one of the map's outstanding features. This breaks down in Florida because of the recent influx of people from farther north. It also breaks down in northern New England, partly perhaps because of the prolonged outward movement of the more alert types to cities and the West. Another noteworthy feature is that in all the more recently settled states from Texas and the Dakotas westward, except Nevada and Idaho, the

5 *Ibid.*, p. 302.

errors in reporting ages are less than in states in similar latitudes farther east. Thus Figure 43 apparently shows the combined effect of climate and selective migration upon the mental alertness and accuracy of a rather uniform racial and cultural group, native whites of native parentage. The relatively small contrast between East and West may be due partly to an actual difference in innate capacity, but differences of this sort between the old white populations of the North and South can scarcely account for the large difference in accuracy. Both types of regional contrast may be due in part to education, but the educational differences in turn are dependent upon climate and migration, as well as upon other geographic conditions. Taken as a whole, the data as to ages suggest the same sort of association between mental alertness and low temperature which we have found in respect to German and Indian philosophy, the reading of serious books, and the circulation of magazines.

B. Seasonal Variations in Mental Activity

A connection between weather and mental activity appears also when one season is compared with another. A study of Danish school children long ago led Lehmann and Pedersen to the hypothesis that there is a mental optimum of temperature considerably lower than the physical optimum. Later studies seemed at first to confirm this,[6] but library records suggest that temperature is by no means the only factor to be taken into account. For the present, however, let us merely look at seasonal variations, regardless of their cause. Townsend Lodge, for example, has found that intelligence tests of the same person vary according to the seasons. When four groups of children from superior social and economic backgrounds (171 children in all) were given four successive tests at six-month intervals, the average group ratings between November and April "were invariably higher than when the same children were tested between May and October." Figure 44 illustrates other types of evidence which give a more detailed picture of seasonal variations in mental activity. Students' marks at West Point and Annapolis, the percentage of persons passing civil service examinations, and the number of applications for amendments to patents received at Washington all have maxima in spring and fall, with minima in summer and winter. The spring maximum is systematically higher or more pro-

[6] Huntington, 1924B.

longed than the autumn maximum, whereas the summer minimum tends to be lower than that of winter.

Rossman [7] has shown that patents afford an unusually good indication of seasonal variation in a high type of mental activity. During the year or more which generally elapses between the filing of

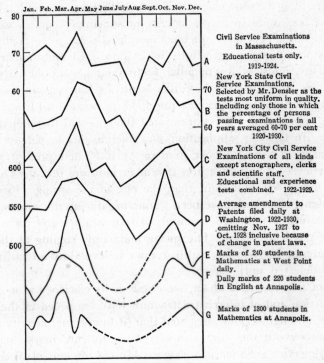

Figure 44. Seasonal Fluctuations in Mental Activity. From *Principles of Economic Geography*.

an application and the granting of a patent an inventor often gets a new idea. Unless his original application is promptly amended, he must apply for a second patent to cover the new idea or leave the field to someone else. Naturally the inventor is eager to apply for an amendment as soon as the necessary drawings and specifications can be prepared. Therefore Rossman's curve of average daily applications for amendments to patents gives an especially reliable picture of seasonal variations in mental activity. This applies primarily to

[7] *See also* Huntington, 1938, pp. 379–82.

the northeastern quarter of the United States where the great majority of American inventions originate.

The curve for patents shows several significant features. From a medium level in January it rises to a broad maximum including March, April, and, to a less degree, May. The date when drawings and specifications arrive at the Patent Office, however, is considerably later than the time when the new idea flashes into mind. Therefore, the maximum inventive activity presumably occurs as early as March or even February. In later months the inventive faculty apparently works at a progressively lower rate until midsummer. Inasmuch as August and September both stand low in the curve for patents, we infer that the inventive faculty is least vigorous in July and August. One might expect the opposite because vacations often provide opportunities for concentrated thought and the preparation of data. In October, applications for amendments to patents jump temporarily to a level higher than in April. Their prompt return to a low level in November and December indicates that the October peak is much less important than the one in the spring. Probably it represents ideas that have been simmering during the summer and are made use of under the stimulus of cool weather and the accompanying physical energy. The spring maximum, coming at the season of almost the poorest health, cannot be explained so easily and will be deferred until later.

One of the best tests of an hypothesis is its efficiency as a means of prediction and of inferring what must have happened in the past. Krynine, an engineer, has suggested that, if intellectual activity really varies throughout the year as indicated by students' marks, patents, and civil service examinations (Figure 44), the amount of discussion in scientific meetings ought to show a similar seasonal trend. This supposition has been tested by means of data for three large engineering societies (civil and chemical in New York and general in Chicago) which hold regular monthly or bi-monthly meetings from September to May or June. In each society the average number of persons who discuss papers presented at all the meetings for twenty years or more is counted as 100 per cent and the number for each month is expressed as a corresponding percentage. Combining the percentages for the three societies, we get the result shown graphically in Figure 45. Of course, the number of persons who discuss a paper varies greatly according to the subject and the speaker. When many years and three different societies are considered, how-

ever, the chances of having a good speaker and. an interesting subject
are essentially the same in all months.   Therefore, Figure 45 gives
a good idea of the degree to which highly intellectual men feel inclined to comment on scientific papers.   Its strong maximum in
March and minor maximum in November agree almost perfectly
with what would be expected on the basis of the hypothesis suggested

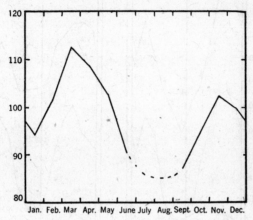

Figure 45.   Average Participation in Regular Meetings of Engineering Societies.
The curve is based on percentages of the weighted average of (1) The American
Institute of Chemical Engineers, New York, 1893–1912, with 11.1 participants per
meeting; (2) American Society of Civil Engineers, New York, 1893–1921, 4.0 participants; and (3) Western Society of Engineers, Chicago, 1900–18, 7.5 participants.

by Figure 44.   This agreement confirms the idea that mental activity
of many kinds has a definite seasonal trend which is different from
that of physical health.

C. Seasonal Variations in Library Circulation

Variations in library circulation confirm the conclusion that mental activity varies seasonally with little regard to health.   They furnish an especially good measure of seasonal fluctuations in mental
activity because exact data are very widely available.   Figure 46
shows the average daily circulation of non-fiction (solid lines) and
fiction (dashed lines) during twenty years in eight urban centers of
North America which form a series from Calgary in the north to
Panama in the south.   Data for other cities in similar latitudes both
north and south of the equator show essentially the same seasonal

swing, provided allowance is made for six months' difference in the seasons.

The curves for non-fiction (solid lines) all swing from high in the late winter or early spring to low in midsummer, just as do the

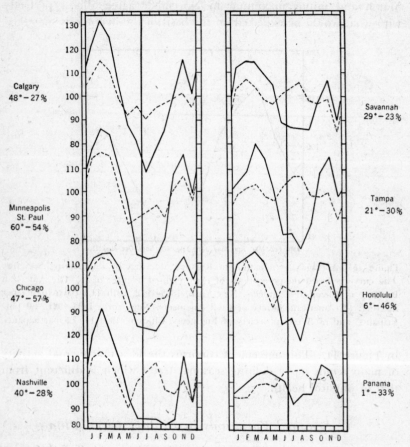

Figure 46. Seasonal Circulation of Fiction (dashed lines) and Non-fiction (solid lines) by Libraries in Eight Urban Centers. Numbers under city names indicate (1) the difference in average temperature between the warmest and coldest months, and (2) the percentage of non-fiction.

curves for mental activity in Figures 44 and 45. The amplitude of the swing from maximum to minimum tends to diminish from north to south. At Calgary in western Canada and at St. Paul and Minneapolis the contrast between summer and winter is great. At Panama, it is slight. Other features include a second and lower maximum in November (October in Panama) and a sharp drop in December due to Christmas, followed immediately by recovery in January. In the southern hemisphere, allowing for the reversal of seasons, there is no drop in winter. Christmas, with its days of shopping and gaiety, causes a marked decline in the use of libraries in both hemispheres, but south of the equator this merely intensifies the summer minimum.

A less noticeable, but no less significant, feature of the seasonal curve of non-fiction is that the maximum shifts its date as one goes from north to south. At Calgary there is a sharp peak in February. At Minneapolis, St. Paul, Chicago, and Nashville, the peak is still in that month, but March is almost as high. At Savannah the two months are equal, as they are at New Orleans, which is not shown in Figure 46. At Houston, the maximum returns to February, but Tampa and several other southern cities swing to March. Finally, at Panama the maximum of intellectual activity comes in April. A wave of mental alertness apparently starts in the north with a strong maximum in February and sweeps southward with diminishing vigor.

Now compare the curves for fiction and non-fiction. They are alike in having a maximum of more or less prominence in the late winter or early spring and in having it occur later in the season as one goes southward, although this breaks down in the curve for fiction at Honolulu. They are also alike in having a minor maximum in November and a minimum in December because of Christmas. There is, however, a noteworthy difference: the effect of the seasons is greater upon non-fiction than upon fiction; the non-fiction curve rises higher and falls lower than the other. A still greater difference is that the curves for fiction generally have at least a hint of a summer maximum which increases toward the south. In the north at Calgary, this is barely visible. At Minneapolis and St. Paul it becomes larger; at Savannah it equals the winter maximum; at Houston and Tampa it exceeds this maximum and at Panama completely dwarfs it. At Chicago, however, and at other places, such as Boston, in the regions which are climatically most favorable for efficiency, the summer maximum disappears and the curves for fiction and non-fiction run almost parallel.

It is easy to explain some of the features of Figure 46 and hard to explain others. The late autumn maximum must be partly a cultural accident resulting from the December minimum due to Christmas. This cannot be the whole explanation, however, for this autumnal maximum is evident in all the curves of Figures 44 and 45, but not in the library curves for the southern hemisphere. This suggests that the advent of cool weather is everywhere a mental stimulant but that when the weather becomes too cold or severe, there is a decline in such activity. The winters of the parts of the southern hemisphere for which we have library data are so mild that low temperature seems to have no effect in reducing library circulation there. If very low temperature really lessens mental activity, the maximum in late winter or early spring becomes more difficult to explain but we will defer this for the moment.

The summer maximum in the reading of fiction appears to be predominantly climatic, although cultural conditions play a part. It represents an effort to pass the time in the easiest possible fashion. It is a sort of escape mechanism set in motion by heat and encouraged by vacations, the dates of which are set mainly by the weather. Vacations, however, appear to be only a minor factor. Many people in Winnepeg and Boston take summer vacations, but these lead to only a little visible increase in the reading of fiction. Moreover, as a rule, especially in the South, the circulation of fiction begins to increase by the end of May, before vacations are common. The increase is closely proportional to the degree to which heat and humidity make the weather enervating. Relatively speaking, it reaches its greatest strength at Panama, where the main feature of the curve for fiction is an irregular rise from a minimum in January and February to a maximum from June to August. The minimum occurs when the temperature averages 78°, but fresh trade winds and relatively dry air, with a rainfall of less than 1 inch per month, make the weather fairly pleasant. When the maximum occurs, the temperature still averages close to 78°, but there is little wind, the monthly rainfall amounts to 8 inches, and the air is exceedingly sticky and humid. The smaller maximum of fiction-reading in November accompanies a second maximum of rain with 12 inches per month and an average temperature of 77°F. This is the lowest temperature of the year, but rain and mugginess combine to produce such sticky, uncomfortable weather that the Americans who are the patrons of the Panama library feel a strong inclination to while away the time with stories.

D. A New Seasonal Factor

The library data, with their worldwide scope, high degree of accuracy, and broad representation of people as a whole, suggest new ideas about weather and mental activity. For one thing they oblige us to modify the hypothesis of a mental optimum of temperature. At Calgary in latitude 51°N the maximum reading of serious books occurs in mid-February, when the temperature averages only 13°. At Tampa, New Orleans, and Houston it occurs in March, when an average of 62° to 66° for day and night together provides the optimum temperature for physical health. At Panama the corresponding maximum occurs in April, when the thermometer averages 78°, with about 85° at noon. Thus the kind of mental activity indicated by the reading of serious books reaches its highest level at a wide range of temperature, and the hypothesis of a mental optimum at temperatures between 40° and 50° finds no support.

This does not mean that mental activity has no relation to temperature. Quite the opposite. When the big seasonal fluctuations

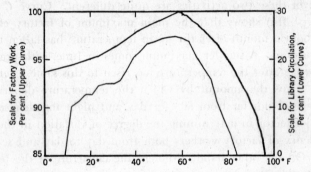

Figure 47. Library Circulation in Boston and Piecework in Connecticut, Compared with Mean Temperature. Upper curve: Efficiency of 310 men and 196 women in New Haven, New Britain, and Bridgeport, 1910–13; lower curve: Percentage of days having library circulation at least 10 per cent above seasonal normal, 1928–39.

in library circulation are eliminated, the minor ones agree with those of factory work. In Figure 47 the upper curve shows the average amount of piecework accomplished per hour in three Connecticut cities by five hundred factory hands, each working at the same job and at the same rate of pay for at least a year. These workers achieved most when the average temperature for day and night together was approximately 60°, that is, on days when the noonday temperatures approached 70°. Above that temperature their work fell off much faster than below. The lower curve is based on carefully corrected daily library records.* It shows what percentage of days had a circulation at least 10 per cent above the normal for any particular date. Aside from minor irregularities, the resemblance between the curves is obvious. The only important difference is that the library curve drops suddenly to zero at temperatures of about 10° and 80°F. During the entire 12 years from 1928 to 1939 the library circulation in Boston did not rise 10 per cent above normal on a single one of the 14 days with average temperatures below 13° or the 49 with temperatures above 80°. This merely means that in very cold or very hot weather people tend to stay away from the library. Factory workers, on the contrary, generally go to work on such days. They work slowly, but, of course, their rate of production never has a chance to fall anywhere near zero.

The fact that daily fluctuations in library circulation and in factory work show essentially the same relation to temperature must be considered in connection with the fact that the main seasonal fluctuations in these two activities are quite different. Curve *C* in Figure 34 (p. 314) shows that the main maximum of factory efficiency comes about a month after the mean temperature has fallen to 58°F in the autumn. A smaller maximum comes in June, with practically the same lag after the temperature has risen to this same level in the spring. Thus the amount by which the temperature departs from an average of not far from 60° for day and night together seems to be a major factor in determining the degree of variation in the physical efficiency of factory workers both from day to day and season to season. On the other hand, although the departure of the temperature from the 60° level appears to have an intimate relation to daily

---

* The circulation of practically all libraries varies according to (1) the day of the week; (2) season of the year; (3) specific events, such as the opening and closing of schools; and (4) changes from year to year because of conditions such as the depression which threw people out of work in the early 30's, thus leading to increased visits to libraries. In order to eliminate such divergencies, the following procedure has been followed: (1) Each day of the week has been treated separately, and a corrective factor has been applied so that each day gets the same weight regardless of whether it has the heavy circulation of Saturday and Monday or the light circulation of Wednesday and Thursday. (2) Each year has been weighted according to its average daily circulation. (3) The circulation for each week in the year, from the first to the fifty-second, has been expressed as a percentage of the average for that week during the entire twelve years, thus eliminating the effect of the seasons and of special seasonal events, such as vacations or press of school work. The following dicussion and illustrations are based on the first four weekdays, Monday to Thursday.

fluctuations in library circulation, it obviously has little to do with the big seasonal fluctuations. It looks as though the library maximum in February or March were the result of what may be called a seasonal tide of unknown origin upon which variations of temperature merely raise waves. Thus once more the hypothesis of a mental optimum at temperatures between 40° and 50° finds little support. The data for patents, students' marks, and civil service examinations seem to support it merely because they happen to come from a climatic region where the mental maximum is in March. The actual fact seems to be that the temperature which is best physically is also best mentally, which is what would normally be expected.

This leaves us with no explanation of why scientific discussions, library circulation, students' marks, and other evidence of mental activity reach a maximum in the late winter or early spring regardless of temperature. Any hypothesis which explains this must also take account of another curious feature. In many of the regions for which we have library data, that is, in Canada, the northern United States, Australia, New Zealand, and Argentina, the seasonal peak of intellectual (library) activity is superposed upon the low level of health which normally prevails at the end of a cool or cold winter. Thus a state of strain is presumably produced because an impulse toward vigorous mental effort is opposed by a contradictory impulse toward physical relaxation. It is this contradiction, apparently, which so often causes February and March to be a period of tenseness and nervous exhaustion, especially in the northern United States.

These curious relations between temperature and mental activity oblige us to inquire whether either cultural conditions or climatic conditions other than temperature are competent to produce the observed effects. What factors can cause mental activity to vary so that a maximum appears strongly during extremely cold weather in February in latitudes above 50° and then moves equatorward like a vast wave of declining size? The work of schools, clubs, lectures, and educational movements does indeed reach its highest intensity at this season, but this is merely the result to be expected from the mental condition which promotes serious reading, inventions, scientific discussion, and good preparation for classes and examinations. The real problem is to ascertain whether there is any physical condition, such as diet or weather, which varies from season to season and place to place in the same way as the various types of mental activity. Among climatic conditions other than temperature the familiar ones, such as barometric pressure, humidity, rain, wind, sunshine, and storminess afford little help in solving the problem. Nor have we yet been able to find help in any combination of familiar climatic conditions or in any of their effects, such as diet, clothing, and degree of outdoor life. The southward sweep of the seasonal maximum of mental activity is the opposite of what would normally be expected on a climatic basis. It acts, to be sure, like a climatic condition such as the monsoon winds and rains of India, which begin in the south and gradually work northward during the course of two months. It proceeds in the wrong direction, however, according to what would ordinarily be expected on the basis of the weather. Search as one will, it seems impossible to find any familiar factors, either cultural or physical, which offer a satisfactory explanation.

The conditions described above suggest that the maximum of intellectual activity in March, let us say, is due to causes different from the ordinary weather conditions which bring (1) the well-known and almost universal maximum of disease and death in January and February; (2) the maximum of reproductive vigor in May or June; and (3) the maximum of physical activity in October or November. The only conditions yet suggested, climatic or otherwise, which seem able to account for the peculiar seasonal distribution of mental activity and the equatorward movement of the wave of maximum activity are atmospheric electricity and atmospheric ozone. We shall discuss the latter at this point, but later we shall see that variations in atmospheric electricity seem to be closely connected with some of the most important variations in human psychology. Moreover, ozone and atmospheric electricity are closely related to one another. Therefore it is easy to confuse the effect of the two.

Ozone, it will be remembered, is oxygen with three atoms instead of two in each molecule. This makes it a very powerful oxidizing agent. It is also a strong catalyzer. Hence minute quantities start chemical processes that continue long after the ozone is exhausted. In very small quantities, such as one part in twenty million or even one hundred million parts of air, ozone gives air the delightful quality known as freshness. Thus it appears to be a genuine stimulant to health and especially to mental alertness. In amounts greater than one part in ten million of air ozone may be dangerous. Such amounts are rare in nature. Air without ozone seems "dead." Such air is common, especially in warm, humid weather and in the tropics. On the other hand mountain air, country air, outdoor air, and the air of cold waves—in fact practically all kinds of air which have the repu-

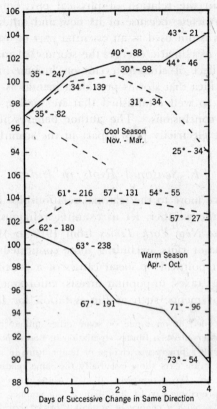

Figure 48. Library Circulation in Boston, 1928–39, on Successive Days with Rise (solid line), or Fall (dashed line) of Temperature. The days included under day 0 have the same temperature as the preceding day or differ from it by only 1° to 3°F. Days 1, 2, 3, 4 are successive days with a change in the same direction. In the body of the diagram the figures for degrees indicate average mean temperature, and the others the number of days. The short broken line indicates what would be expected normally on the basis of falling temperature in winter. All days, both fair and rainy, are included.

tation of being stimulating—contain a minute trace of ozone. We shall return to this subject later.[8]

The ozone hypothesis has thus far been little tested, and its relation to atmospheric electricity is not yet clear. If the hypothesis is

[8] Huntington, 1941.

correct, it helps in explaining some significant trends in history. Nevertheless, it is not essential to the main line of thought in this book. The author believes that ultimately ozone will take its place as an integral factor in the relation of physical environment to human progress. Nevertheless, because of its new and untested nature, the ozone hypothesis is not used as an essential part of our later study of the distribution of climatic energy, the stormward march of civilization, and the effect of climatic cycles on human history. On the other hand, the idea that storms provide a mental as well as physical stimulant seems so well established that we shall use it freely as a basis for other conclusions. The author believes that both ozone and atmospheric electricity play a part in the stimulus arising from storms.*

E. Seasonal Riots in India

Returning once more to the seasonal relationships between mental conditions and the weather, let us examine religious riots in India. The files of *The New York Times* from 1919 to 1941 contain accounts of 148 major riots, excluding those connected with actual rebellions, or with political or social causes of a general nature, such as protests against taxes, unpopular arrests, enforcement of new laws, and popular movements, such as the agitation for Indian freedom.

* An interesting sidelight on ozone or some other unknown factor connected with air masses is observed when library circulation in Boston is studied in relation to successive days with a progressive change of temperature in the same direction. Both fair days and rainy days show essentially the same relationship. They are combined in Figure 48. Day 0 represents all days whose mean temperature differs from that of the preceding day by less than 2° in summer and 3° in winter. Day 1 is the first day with a change of at least 2 or 3° according to the season. Later days represent further change in the same direction, regardless of the amount of change. Rising temperature (solid lines) has the relationship that one would expect. In summer (lower diagram) the average library circulation drops steadily day after day as the temperature rises. In winter the reverse occurs. One would expect that with falling temperature (dashed lines) the opposite would take place. Not at all. In summer the circulation rises to a high level on the first day of cooler weather and remains there as the weather grows still cooler. In winter (upper diagram) instead of going downward according to the short line of dashes, as one would expect, the circulation rises on two successive days, and only on the third day does it begin to decline. This suggests that the infall of polar air is accompanied by something which at first overcomes the normal effect of lowered temperature. The days when lowered temperature accompanies rising library attendance are the ones when ozone is most abundant, but whether ozone produces the observed effect remains to be seen.

Most of the 148 riots were of a religious nature. They originated in clashes at times of festivals or in minor events such as the following culled from the *Times:* Moslems throw beef on the steps of a Hindu temple; others cut branches from a sacred Hindu tree to make room for the banners of a procession; Hindus beat a Moslem vendor who drove away a sacred bull that feasted on his vegetables; a Hindu laundryman washes clothes in a pond attached to a Moslem mosque. Such riots usually involve Moslems and Hindus, but clashes between sects within each main religion or with other sects, such as the Sikhs, are also common. The greater number occur in the cities of the United Provinces and the Punjab, where Moslems and Hindus are intimately mixed, but they extend to Calcutta on the east and Bombay on the west. Minor riots by the hundred are a distinct and ominous feature of northern India.

TABLE 17

SEASONAL DISTRIBUTION OF LOCAL INDIAN RIOTS

January	6	June	9	November	2
February	11	July	16	December	6
March	10	August	22		—
April	29	September	13	Total	148
May	19	October	5		

The nature of the conditions which immediately incite these riots has been often discussed but never settled. They obviously arise from tension between different faiths. They are a powerful factor in keeping religious antagonisms alive and tense. Hence a knowledge of their causes is highly important for the political and economic welfare of India. Religious festivals are often said to be the cause. Table 17 shows that this is not true. The chief Moslem festivals occur at the New Year and the feast of Ramadan after the month of fasting when no food may be eaten between sunrise and sunset. The Moslem year, however, is so short that $33\frac{1}{2}$ of them are equal to only $32\frac{1}{2}$ true solar years. Hence during the period covered by our data these festivals occur almost equally at every season. This fact does not help much in accounting for 29 riots in April against 9 in June, or 22 in August against 2 in November. Hindu festivals, on the other hand, are so dated that they would lead us to expect few riots in midsummer and many in January, March, and October, but in Table 17 these three months with a total of 21 riots do not equal April or August alone.

Idleness and the congregating of villagers in the cities when there is little work in the fields are also said to set the date for riots. The course of events supports this idea at some seasons but opposes it at others. In northern India the agricultural year begins when the ground is softened by the first monsoon showers in June (May in Bengal). Thus the decline in riots from April to June accompanies an increase in agricultural work, and the rise in riots in August comes during a lull in farm work before the harvest. In August, however, the extreme muddiness of the roads, the heavy and almost daily showers, and the extremely damp, hot mugginess of the weather keep people at home, thus tending to reduce the likelihood of riots at the very time when they are most numerous. From September until November the harvesting of the summer crops and the planting of winter crops keep the peasants busy and coincide with a decline of riots to their lowest level. By the middle of December, however, the main work is at an end and the time is at hand when leisure, money, energy, and visits to the city, as well as the most important Hindu festivals, all combine to favor riots. Nevertheless, the riots remain at a low level from mid-December to mid-February. March and April, on the other hand, are again a busy season, for the winter crops must be harvested. Riots then rise to a maximum.

Another possibility is that scarcity of food, entailing high prices and hunger, leads to riots. The food supply is lowest in August and early September before the summer harvest begins. Riots then reach a maximum. Food is most abundant in the autumn when the main crop has been harvested. On this basis we should expect few riots, and that is what we find. On further investigation, however, we again find scanty food in February, before winter crops are harvested, and abundance in April after the harvest. At these times the number of riots is the opposite of what would be expected on the basis of food. Thus here, just as with idleness, close agreement at one season is neutralized by strong disagreement at another.

Weather as a promoter of riots has hitherto been neglected. Nevertheless, its effect seems to agree with the distribution of riots. The comfortable season in northern India begins in mid-October. By that time the average temperature for day and night from Lahore to Lucknow, where riots are especially common, has dropped to about 70°. The heavy summer rains are over and the mud is drying up, but the earth is still moist. Pleasant temperatures, about like New York in May, continue until February, but other things become less pleasant because drought parches the earth. After February the temperature rises rapidly until monthly averages of 80° or even 90° are reached in April and 85° to 95° in May. The air is blisteringly hot, and the wind raises clouds of dust. The April maximum of riots occurs when extreme heat and drought are most widespread. We have seen that homicide in the United States and lack of sexual control in Italy also increase with hot weather.

May in Bengal and June farther up the Ganges see the "bursting" of the southwest monsoon and an extraordinary transformation. A comforting breeze blows quite steadily, clouds shield the sun, showers fall, the dust is laid, the temperature drops a few degrees, the death-rate lessens, and farm work begins. Naturally enough, all this is accompanied by a decided decline in riots.

Unfortunately these pleasant conditions soon disappear. During July the wind dies down, the air is saturated, and the monthly rainfall rises to 7 inches at Lahore, 13 at Calcutta, and 25 at Bombay. For week after week average temperatures of 80° to 90° make the weather as bad as the four or five most muggy days ever experienced in New York City. Tempers become short, and riots reach a second maximum in August. Then step by step with better weather serious riots decline from 22 in August to only 2 in November. Thus, though festivals, idleness, city crowds, and the food supply are doubtless important, the agreement between riots and the effect of the weather on personal comfort is so close that it appears to be the main cause of the seasonal fluctuations in riots. It should be noted, however, that in very hot cities—especially when rainfall is heavy—the number of riots declines at the most extreme high temperatures. As the weather gets hot, people apparently feel more and more uncomfortable and irritable, their power of self-control declines, and they riot under relatively small provocation, especially in dry weather. At still higher temperatures, however, the heat seems to sap people's energy so that greater irritation is needed to make them active. When the weather is rainy and humid, as well as hot, the tendency toward inertia is stronger than in dry weather, and the rain itself doubtless reduces riots by keeping people at home.

The conclusions derived from Indian riots are supported by the findings of Dexter years ago as to arrests for assault and battery. Basing his study on about 40,000 arrests during eight years in New York City, he finds that the seasonal curve of arrests

is most beautifully regular, showing a gradual increase from January . . . to July . . . and a decrease for the remainder of the year. . . . One must conclude that temperature, more than any other condition, affects the emotional states which are conducive to fighting . . . [Figure 49] shows unmistakably that except for the very highest temperatures, the number of assaults increases with heat.   That is what Shakespeare had noticed, and the data corroborate in a striking manner the wonderful observational powers of the great master. . . . The general showing is one of marked deficiency for low temperatures with a gradual increase to . . . maximum excess in the 80°–85° group, at which point a sudden drop takes place.   This final decrease . . . seems without doubt to be due to the devitalizing effect of the intense heat of 85° and above. . . . For fighting purposes one must have not only . . . inclination, but also . . . energy. . . . Heat of any considerable in-

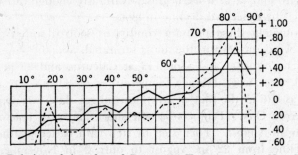

Figure 49.   Relation of Assault and Battery to Temperature in New York City, 1891–97 (after Dexter).   Solid line: 36,627 males; dotted line: 3,134 females.   Note the decline at the highest temperature, just as in Indian riots.

tensity seems productive of emotional states, furnishing the former (i.e. inclination), but at a certain point the latter is depleted by extra demands made upon it by the processes of life.

The important point is that people's temperament fluctuates in harmony with the weather.   It is easy enough to accept this as an explanation of the seasonal cycle in religious antipathies and riots in India, but the general principle extends much farther.   It applies to the actions of the Congress of the United States, for example, when tempers are frayed by hot weather, especially in the days before air conditioning was introduced.   There is a widespread impression that hasty legislation and personal violence in the form of fist fights formerly rose to a maximum under such conditions.   It is worth noting that in the United States Negro riots occur most often in unusually hot weather, as happened in 1943 during June in Detroit and early August in New York.   Their primary cause was irritableness at a time when there was already tension between two groups, just as in India.   The condition which brought them to a head was apparently the discomfort and lack of self-control associated with hot weather. In the world as a whole the tendency toward lack of self-control in politics, in sex relations, and in many other respects rises markedly in hot weather and in hot countries. This is not the only reason for the frequency of political revolutions in low latitudes, but it must play a part.

F. The Seasons, Insanity, and Crime

As final evidence of the influence of the seasons on mental reactions, let us examine the seasonal distribution of outbreaks of insanity and crime. Abundant evidence is summed up in Figure 50,[9] which illustrates (1) the outbreak of insanity in Italy, England, the United States, and Germany; (2) suicide in Italy, France, and England; and (3) sexual offenses in France and Germany. Each of the sixteen curves (eighteen if we count the dashed lines for women) is at or near its maximum in June. All likewise, if smoothed to eliminate minor irregularities, show a minimum in winter. On an average the maximum in June is more than 80 per cent above the minimum in December. Homicides also are most numerous in June but remain abundant till autumn. Insanity, suicide, sexual crimes, and homicide all indicate mental weakness which causes people to do the wrong thing under conditions where stronger minds would behave differently. Curiously enough, these signs of weakness occur at just the time when other lines of evidence indicate physical well-being. June, as we have seen, is a time of good health and maximum conceptions, especially in western Europe. Children conceived then or a little earlier live longer and are more likely to be eminent than those conceived at any other time.

It is not difficult to understand why sexual crimes reach a maximum when the reproductive faculties are most active, but why do insanity and suicide also increase? The answer seems to be suggested in what was said in Chapter 16 (Section *D*) as to the excessive percentages of criminals, insane persons, and sufferers from tuberculosis conceived in June. At that time the physical stimulus which merely leads to health and increased powers of reproduction among normal people apparently overstimulates those who are poorly poised, weak of will, oversexed, or otherwise abnormal. Moreover, in the late spring many people who are physically below par and unable to pro-

[9] Huntington, 1938, p. 409.

duce children at other seasons appear to experience a reproductive stimulus which enables them to become parents. The results of the stimulus of the reproductive season upon both kinds of parents—the temperamentally weak and the physically weak—seem to appear not only in insanity, suicide, and crime among people of the parental

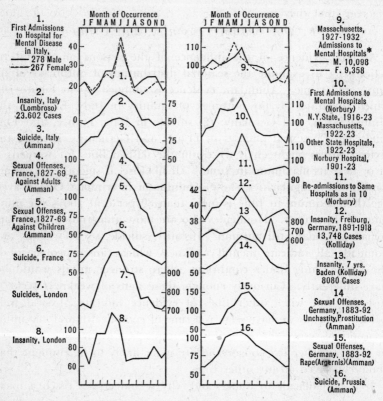

Figure 50. Seasonal Incidence of Insanity, Suicide, and Crime. From *Season of Birth.*

generation, but in a crop of relatively handicapped children. These children suffer unduly from congenital defects. Like their parents, they are also the type which provides many individuals who experience nervous breakdowns leading to insanity or show the kind of lack of self-control which leads to crime. This, then, is what happens when people who are below par temperamentally or below the threshold of reproduction at most seasons are stimulated by the advent of the annual season of reproduction according to the animal cycle.

On the other hand, among temperamentally normal people who are also normal in being well above the reproductive threshold, the stimulation arising through the advent of the season of maximum reproductive capacity leads to the conception of children who are so vigorous that they raise the average span of life and provide much more than the normal proportion of leaders. Such relationships are significant as an indication that man's psychological as well as physical conditions are powerfully influenced by the changing weather of the seasons. If this statement is correct, it seems logical to suppose that a corresponding psychological effect is produced by different types of climate and by different phases of climatic cycles. Thus again we see that human history and the progress of civilization must be closely tied up with climate.

G. *Types of Seasonal Psychological Reactions*

The essence of this chapter is that psychological as well as physiological conditions vary in harmony with climate and weather. We began with the widely recognized but little studied fact that the people of high latitudes are, on the whole, more intellectual than those of low latitudes. We found that in the United States the relative library circulation of fiction, as compared with non-fiction, and the degree of accuracy with which people state their ages both confirm this idea.

Passing next to the problem of seasonal variations of a psychological nature, we find that there are four different types. (1) School children in Denmark seem to have been the first group in which seasonal differences in mental activity were carefully measured. Similar differences have now been found in intelligence quotients, students' marks, ability to pass civil service examinations, library circulation, inventions, and the kind of alertness which leads people to take part in scientific discussions. Wherever any of these lines of activity has been followed through the year a strong maximum is found in the early spring or late winter and a smaller maximum in the autumn. The summer minimum is normally lower than that of winter. The importance of this lies partly in its demonstration of the ultimate relation between mental alertness and weather. It also lies in the fact that, although this seasonal swing is strong and unmistakable, it does not agree with seasonal fluctuations of health, temperature, or any other familiar condition to which it might owe its origin.

(2) The seasonal fluctuations of certain other psychological conditions agree with temperature. Irritability of the kind that leads to riots and the crime of assault and battery is particularly significant in this respect. It increases greatly as the temperature rises to a high level but declines when the weather becomes hot enough so that the weakening effect of heat overcomes the feeling of irritation which it engenders. (3) In a previous chapter we saw that the inclination to work declines markedly at high temperatures and also at low, so that it has its own strong seasonal swing. (4) Finally we have found that psychological manifestations of still another type follow a third seasonal trend, different from that of either mental activity or irritability. This fourth type is evident in the outbreak of insanity and the occurrence of suicide and sexual crimes. It seems to owe its origin to the coming and going of the season of reproduction as inherited from a distant past before our ancestors had learned to protect themselves from the weather and to lay up supplies of food for seasons of scarcity. Thus four different types of psychological reactions to the seasons all go on at once. In the climate of the northern United States and western Europe a main maximum is approximately reached by mental alertness in March, by insanity, suicide, and sexual crimes in May or June, by irritability and a tendency toward violence and rioting in July, and by inclination for physical work in October or November. The fact that so many different types of seasonal fluctuations are taking place simultaneously is probably one of the main reasons for the long postponement of exact knowledge as to the effect of weather and climate on mental activity and psychological status.

CHAPTER 19

PSYCHOLOGICAL REACTIONS TO WEATHER

A. Mental Activity and Storms

The psychological reactions which sway the course of history are influenced by variations in the weather from day to day, as well as from season to season and region to region. The main factor in producing daily variations is cyclonic storms with their constant alternation between masses of warm, moist, tropical air and cool, dry, polar air. We have already seen that such storms are an important factor in physical health. It will be recalled that the advent of tropical air when a storm is brewing is accompanied by pain among sufferers from many diseases and also by a rise in the deathrate even in winter. The succeeding inflow of cool polar air toward the end of such a storm is accompanied by a corresponding diminution of pain and decline in deaths. Except in extreme instances the good thus done by this later phase of a storm more than balances the preceding harm, as is evident from deaths in New York (Figure 41).

A study of library circulation leads to a similar conclusion as to mental alertness. A storm is normally preceded by a tendency toward diminished use of books and followed by increased use. The net effect is an increase in intellectual activity in comparison with what would presumably occur in perfectly uniform weather. If this is true, the geographical distribution of progress must be influenced by cyclonic storms with their alternation of tropical and polar air masses. Inasmuch as variations in storminess are a main factor in climatic cycles, we also infer that the differing phases of such cycles must tend toward diverse psychological trends.

Let us see what happens to library circulation during an ordinary transition from tropical to polar air. This transition is usually accompanied by rain, but even without rain essentially the same meteorological changes occur in other respects. Hence for our present purposes all transitions from a day or two of warm southerly winds (a tropical air mass) to a day or two of cool northerly winds (a polar air mass) may be counted together as storms. In Figure 51 nine American cities are arranged according to their geographical location. Seattle, Oakland, and Los Angeles represent the West Coast from north to south; Minneapolis, Nashville, and Houston represent the middle of the country; Boston, Richmond, and Jacksonville, the East.

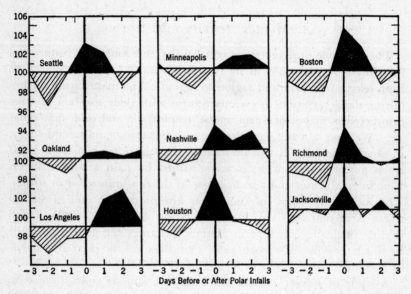

Figure 51. Daily Library Circulation in Nine Cities in Relation to Polar Infalls of Air on Fair Days from April to October. Heavy shading indicates above average.

The height of the curves represents the average library circulation on different types of days during the warm season from April to October inclusive.* The center of each curve (day 0) is based on the average circulation of all days which fulfill the following conditions: (1) average 24-hour temperature lower than that of the preceding day by at least 2°F; (2) preceding day not of the kind defined under (1); (3) no precipitation or less than one tenth of an inch, thus avoiding the effect of rain and snow in keeping people at home. This means that day 0 is normally the first day of an infall of polar air. Day 1, which

---

* In tabulating the library data, Fridays, Saturdays, and Sundays, which are not used in this particular study, and holidays and days with rain or snow are left as blanks. These blanks occur hit or miss, so that they are about equally distributed in all parts of each curve.

follows, generally represents a continuance of this infall. Similar conditions may prevail on day 2, but by day 3 the effect of the polar infall is likely to have disappeared. In similar fashion day −1 normally represents an infall of tropical air, and days −2 and −3 represent the same thing in diminishing degrees.

The uniform way in which each of the nine diagrams of Figure 51 shows a low level on day −1 or −2 and a high level on day 0 or 1 indicates that in the warmer part of the year tropical air is normally accompanied by low library circulation and polar air by high circulation. In winter similar conditions prevail in the southern and central tiers of cities, but farther north the more severe cold waves keep people at home, so that visits to the library are reduced. This contrast between mild and severe weather is illustrated in Figure 52, showing Boston's library circulation by seasons for 12 years. Bars here take the place of the curves of Figure 51, but the sequence of days is the same. Day −1, with its relatively warm, tropical air, shows a systematic change from a library circulation well above the average in January and February to practically average in March and April, nearly 8 per cent below average in July, and back toward the average during the rest of the year.* Warm, tropical air is evidently accompanied by library circulation below normal not only in summer but continuously from April to December. One would expect that warm days in April, October, and November would encourage people to go to the library, but the contrary actually happens. Day −2, which often has tropical air, behaves in somewhat the same way as −1, but not so regularly or conspicuously.

Now look at day 0 when polar air begins to be dominant. In January and February such days have a trifle more than the average circulation, but this may be accidental. In March and April they stand at the average. Thereafter, they show an excess which rises to 7 per cent in July and continues at a diminishing rate through November. The next day (day 1) being also characterized by polar air, but not so regularly as day 0, behaves just as one would expect. It varies in about the same way as day 0, but not so notably.

The strength and persistence of the contrast between tropical and polar air is well shown in Figure 53. On the left the fair days of all

* December is omitted because the Christmas season of shopping and holidays causes a great decline in the use of libraries. The first half of January is also omitted because there is then a reaction whch sends the circulation uncommonly high.

seasons during 12 years in Boston are added together.* Day −3 on the left and days 2 and 3 on the right represent approximately average conditions on days with all kinds of weather. As might be ex-

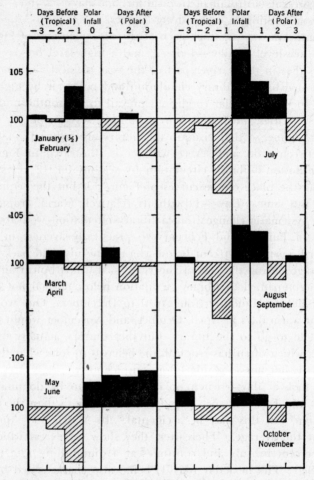

Figure 52. Seasonal Variations in Daily Library Circulation in Boston, 1928–39, in Relation to Polar and Tropical Air Masses, Fair Days Only.

pected, their library circulation is also average. Days −2 and especially −1, however, stand out clearly as times when library circulation drops decidedly below the average. This happens in spite of the fact that in winter the warmth of tropical air is very pleasant, as one

* Note that the scale here is much greater than in Figure 52.

realizes almost any day when cold weather gives place to warm. On the other hand, days 0 and 1, with polar air, stand out equally clearly because of high library circulation, even though they include most of the coldest days of winter, as well as the cooler days of summer.

The right-hand section of Figure 53 is especially impressive. It is based on all rainy or snowy days of 12 years. Because we are now dealing with rainy days, the contrast between tropical and polar air

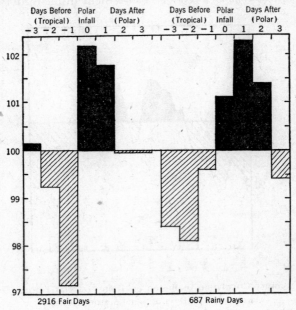

Figure 53. Daily Library Circulation in Boston, 1928–39, on Fair versus Rainy Days in Relation to Polar and Tropical Air Masses. All seasons combined. The large black areas exceed the corresponding lightly shaded areas by 9% on fair days and 48% on rainy days, the weighted average being 13%.

is stronger and more prolonged than in the diagram for fair days. Therefore days −3 and −2 represent tropical air; day −1 is transitional; and days 0 to 2 represent polar air. The tropical air masses are evidently accompanied by low library circulation and the polar masses by high circulation. The rainy days of all seasons behave essentially alike in this respect.

Rainy and snowy days, of course, have a lower circulation than fair days, but the average difference for the year as a whole is only 2.5 per cent. The slightness of this difference arises from the curious situation illustrated in Figure 54, showing average library circulation on rainy days at all seasons expressed as a percentage of the corresponding circulation on fair days. From mid-September to mid-April the rainy days rank 2 to 10 per cent below the fair days, but during the rest of the year they generally exceed the others. This excess is due to the fact that when a wave of cool polar air puts an end to rain during the daytime, people flock to the library in great numbers. They feel a renewed sense of vigor, and the weather is generally neither so cold nor so hot as to make them disinclined toward ac-

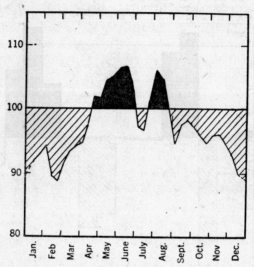

Figure 54. Library Circulation in Boston on Rainy Days as Percentage of Circulation on Fair Days at Same Season, 1928–39.

tivity or toward going out of doors. The really cold days are usually fair. The drop in Figure 54 during July probably means that in the warmest weather, even after the rain has come to an end, the heat is great enough to handicap the impulse toward activity.

B. Cumulative Effect of Small Impulses

Differences in library circulation from day to day may seem like a minor point for discussion in a book on civilization, but they have an immediate bearing on one of the major historical problems. Why were people's minds so alert and why did civilization make such active progress in ancient Egypt, Greece, and neighboring lands? In the climatic pulsations of historic times a major feature appears to have been variations in the movements of polar and tropical air masses. At their stages of highest development ancient Greece and Egypt appear to have been distinctly more stormy than now. Much of the extra storminess occurred at seasons when the average temperature (50° to 70°F) is like that of Boston at the season when Figures 52 and 53 show that the coming of polar air, even on rainy days, has the greatest effect in stimulating library circulation. Athens has such temperatures from mid-February through May and again from early October to mid-December. In Cairo they last from early November to mid-April. Thus in ancient Greece and Egypt, for half the year or more, the climate apparently provided a pronounced mental stimulus of the kind that now at certain seasons inclines Bostonians to go to the library in especially large numbers when rain comes to an end in the morning and cool polar air brings a feeling of alertness.

The facts just presented leave little doubt that, regardless of rain or shine, people's impulse to draw books from the library is subject to constant fluctuations in harmony with the coming and going of the tropical and polar air masses which bring storms. It is likewise clear that, except in the coldest weather, moist, tropical air, even if it has cooled off considerably since leaving the ocean, has a depressing effect. On the other hand, dry polar air has a stimulating effect which is very obvious in summer and which persists into the winter long after the temperature has fallen low enough to be disagreeable. This may indicate that some atmospheric condition other than temperature—perhaps ozone or atmospheric electricity—gives the cool air a stimulating effect which is lacking in the tropical air, even when that air has become as cool as it normally does in Boston in November. If the matter is looked at more broadly, the daily library data both at Boston and throughout the United States indicate that mental activity is dampened by the kind of weather which normally prevails in tropical countries and stimulated by the kind that prevails in fairly high latitudes except when they become excessively cold.

This brings us to the question of the net effect of the coming and going of the different kinds of air. The answer lies in the fact that the heavily and lightly shaded areas in Figure 53 do not quite balance one another. Putting fair and rainy days together, we find that in an average storm period of 7 days, the increased circulation on the 2 days when polar air most fully predominates exceeds the decrease on the 2 days when tropical air predominates by 0.23 per cent. In other cities, a similar difference is found.

At first sight a stimulating effect of scarcely a quarter of 1 per cent on each of 2 days seems scarcely worthy of further consideration, but that is by no means true. Consider again an illustration which we have already used in respect to storms and health. After an automobile engine is geared to the wheels of a standing car the first explosion of gasoline gives the car a speed which is certainly slow but is infinitely greater than when the car stood still. The next explosion may double that speed, the third may add 50 per cent to the speed already attained, the fourth may add 25 per cent, and so on until the car is moving so fast that the extra speed due to each explosion is negligible, only a minute fraction of 1 per cent. Nevertheless, if no more explosions occur the car will stop. Even if a single cylinder refuses to function, the car runs irregularly with a slight check in speed each time the cylinder fails to do its part.

The action of storms upon people's health and mental activity is closely similar to that of the explosions in an engine. If there are no storms, life moves onward at a pace set by various other stimuli, such as the necessity to work for food, clothing, and shelter, the standards set up by society, the kind of diet, medical service, education, and so forth. If we add another constantly repeated stimulus, such as cyclonic storms, the pace is increased. The effect at first is very evident. It is illustrated by what an old Maya Indian in Yucatan once said about the occasional "northers" which occur when polar air sweeps unusually far south to that tropical peninsula: "People work hardest the morning after a norther, after the wind has ceased, and while it is cool. On such days the women bake the tortillas much more quickly than usual, and we get away to work early." [1] If Yucatan had a good norther every few days, instead of at rare intervals, the general speed of life would presumably be appreciably increased. Perhaps the women would set to work with their grinding stones the night before, so that flour for the tortillas would be ready in the morning and the men could get to work early.

Daily work, as well as library circulation, shows the stimulating effect of polar air masses.[2] Figure 55 shows hourly amounts of piecework and students' marks on days with different degrees of interdiurnal change of temperature. Among cigar makers in Florida during

[1] Huntington. 1912.   [2] Huntington, 1924B, p. 140.

the summer (three lower curves) the best work is done with a drop of 2°. The warm uniform weather which prevails at that season ap-

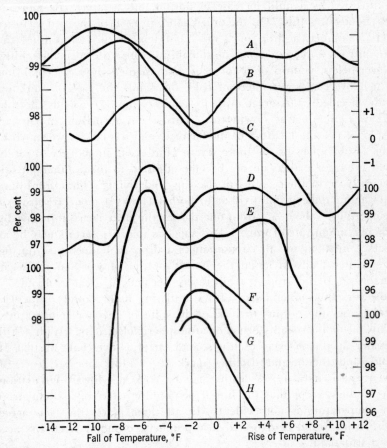

Figure 55. Factory Work and Students' Marks in Relation to Changes of Temperature from Day to Day. Courtesy, Yale University Press. A = 300 men in two Connecticut factories, 1910–13; B = 256 girls in two Connecticut factories, 1911–13; C = 400 students in mathematics and English at West Point and Annapolis, 1909–13; D = 760 cigar-makers at Tampa, Florida, factory A, October-March, 1912, 1913; E = 400 cigar-makers at Tampa, factory B, in winter, 1913; F = 400 cigar-makers at Tampa, factory B, in summer (April-September), 1913; G = 380 cigar-makers at Tampa, factory A, in summer, 1912; H = 380 cigar-makers at Tampa, factory A, in summer, 1913. From *Civilization and Climate*.

parently reduces people's ability to withstand more than a very slight amount of cooling. Nevertheless, even the mildest rise in temperature reduces the output of work. In winter these same cigar makers show a different and rather curious response to changes in the weather (curves *D* and *E*). A moderate rise of temperature is accompanied by a mild increase in output, but a larger rise more or less neutralizes this. On the other hand, in each of the two factories here examined a drop of 2 or 3° in temperature diminishes the amount of work somewhat, presumably because the men feel chilly. Nevertheless, a drop of 3 to 6° is accompanied by some condition which overcomes the effect of cold and sends the rate of work up quite decidedly. A great drop, 7° or more, however, sends the rate of work plummeting downward. This is not surprising in view of the poor heating facilities of the factories and the lack of warm clothing. Cold waves of the more severe kind occur in Florida so rarely that the cigar makers do not become adjusted to them either physiologically or in their habits of dressing and living. The astonishing fact about these people is that in both factories a moderate drop of temperature (about 5°) from one day to the next is accompanied by the maximum rate of work. This suggests that two factors may be at work. First, under all circumstances a drop in temperature during the winter tends to lessen the hourly output of work in the cigar factories. If the drop in temperature becomes as great as about 5°, however, some other factor of a stimulating nature comes into play and causes the output to increase in spite of the low temperature. This factor is probably ozone or atmospheric electricity. With a still greater drop, the effect of this second factor is overcome by that of cold, and the output declines markedly. This same sequence of events also characterizes deaths in New York and library circulation in Boston, except that the initial benumbing effect of a slight drop in temperature is not evident. In all three places the facts agree with what would be expected if atmospheric ozone or electricity acts as a stimulant.

The two curves at the top of Figure 55 illustrate what happens to piecework in Connecticut on days with various types of interdiurnal change of temperature. These curves are like those for winter in Florida, but with significant minor differences. Factory hands in Connecticut, both men and women, work most slowly when there is no interdiurnal change of temperature, or a drop of only 1°. They work fastest with a drop of 6 to 10°, but fall off a little with still stronger cold waves. Their speed is also stepped up when warm waves arrive, but not so much as with cold waves. This is due mainly to the good effect of warm weather in winter, for these curves cover the entire year. Taken as a whole, the two Connecticut curves show that when all seasons are considered the amount of work done when the variable, stormy type of weather prevails is greater than with the more uniform type.

Curve *C* in Figure 55 brings us back once more to mental activity. It shows the marks of students at West Point from late September to late May and at Annapolis from mid-October to the end of April. Practically no hot weather is included. Nevertheless, the main feature of the curve is the falling off of the marks with a rise of temperature in contrast to an improvement when the weather becomes cooler. The most severe cold waves, to be sure, are detrimental, just as they are to library circulation, to health as indicated by deaths, and to piecework in both Florida and Connecticut. Nevertheless, even in strong cold waves the marks are as high as in uniform weather and higher than when the temperature shows any considerable rise. Thus the relationship of the coming and going of polar and tropical air masses to the intellectual performance of students, as well as to the practical work of factory hands, is substantially the same as to library circulation and deaths. All these various expressions of human vigor appear to be depressed by tropical air, stimulated by polar air, and in general to show a net improvement as the result of the alternation of air masses in ordinary storms. Intellectual activity seems to be especially sensitive in this respect.

C. Hurricanes and Intelligence Quotients

An extreme example will impress on our memories the outstanding effect of alternating air masses and storms upon mental activity. On September 21, 1938, southern New England was overwhelmed by a hurricane such as had not been previously experienced for more than a century. It so happened that at the hour of the storm the freshman class at Massachusetts State College in Amherst was scheduled for one of three psychological tests. The previous day on the Army Alpha test the class ranked 4 per cent above the average of sixteen preceding classes, but this was no more than the normal accidental variation. The next day, while the hurricane was actually in progress, the class met for a test prepared by the American Council of Education and taken that year by 355 freshmen classes. The wind rose to 80 miles an hour, the room became so dark that the lights had to be switched on, trees crashed to the ground, and one of them broke the electric light wires, leaving the room so dusky that it was hard to read. It was expected that the examination would show poor results. The third test was postponed for a day in order that the students might help clear up the wreckage. Then the students were so tired or otherwise disturbed that they averaged 10 per cent lower than the two preceding classes which had taken identically the same test.

Not till months later were the hurricane papers read and graded. Ordinarily Massachusetts State College stands in the 75th percentile among the colleges taking the test. That year it rose to the 95th, far above any rank ever held before or since. The students had evidently worked with extraordinary intensity and concentration. The author knows just how they felt. During that same hurricane he was writing in New Haven in an office with thick stone walls and windows so high that only sky and a high tower are visible to one who is seated. He knew that the wind was blowing furiously and the rain was being whirled upward, but he was writing so fast that he did not want to look out of the window. When he stopped writing, the rain was over and the sky was clearing. He was amazed that he had written so much. He was also amazed to see great elms lying prone across the street. Such trees were so numerous that it took him an hour to drive home instead of ten minutes.

Something connected with that hurricane evidently acted as a powerful mental stimulant. Just what it was we cannot say with certainty. It was not temperature, for that suffered only a very slight change, much less than in an ordinary storm. It was not the atmospheric humidity, for that was essentially the same as in other storms. Perhaps the wind had something to do with it, but in the examination room at Amherst and in the author's office the windows were closed, and there was less movement of the air than on many other occasions. There was no lightning, so that an electric effect of that sort is eliminated. Two things, however, were quite unusual. One was the rapid fall in barometric pressure followed by a rapid rise during the period when the mental stimulation was highest. The other was an almost unparalleled rapidity of increase in the ozone content of the air. While the examination was in progress the atmospheric ozone was increasing so fast that Professors Peters [3] and Ritchie of the chemistry department at Massachusetts State College both report that half an hour more or less after the end of the examination they perceived a decided smell of ozone. It was so strong that

[3] p. 491.

Professor Peters thought of going indoors for fear that it might be dangerous.

The outstanding fact about all this is that the severest storm in a century was accompanied by a remarkable mental stimulus, which was clearly not due to unusual conditions of temperature, humidity, or wind. In its essential nature, although by no means in its degree of intensity, the effect was like that which makes people sing or whistle at the end of a storm or hurry to the library to get a book that they have long purposed to read. It was also like the easing of aches and pains experienced by sufferers from various diseases and the almost miraculous recovery of persons who are at death's door, which occur at such times. Other related occurrences are a temporary drop in the general deathrate, high marks among students, and fast. accurate work among factory hands as diverse as cigar makers in Florida and brass workers in Connecticut. To return once more to the metaphor of an automobile, the hurricane produced an extreme acceleration like that of a racing car that can attain a speed of three hundred miles an hour within half a minute.

The convergence of these many lines of testimony makes it highly probable that the importance of ordinary storms lies quite as much in their direct physiological effect as in their indirect effects. Two of the greatest indirect effects are that they favor agriculture by bringing rain at all seasons and encourage alertness and forethought by obliging people to be constantly on the alert to guard against sudden changes of weather. Nevertheless, an even greater effect seems ultimately to be exerted by the direct action of the weather in altering bodily functions, such as the rate of breathing, the flow of blood, the chemical composition and abundance of the secretions of the glands, and the general operation of the nerves and other organs. As yet, the nature of these physiological changes is only dimly understood. Their reality, however, cannot be doubted. It is demonstrated by the extraordinarily delicate responses to weather and climate which we have seen in relation to reproduction and by the vigor, longevity, and achievements of people born at different seasons or in different climates. It is illustrated by the marvelous way in which infants seem to be endowed with some kind of hereditary mechanism which gives them resistance to seasonal ailments at just the time when such resistance is most needed according to the primitive seasonal rhythm of reproduction. Equally marvelous is the innate resistance to seasonal danger of which we have found some evidence during the reproductive stage of life, especially among women. Lastly we find that the physical and mental alertness which determines how well the daily work of life is done displays this same close relationship to weather and climate.

When these various lines of evidence are put together, it seems hard to avoid the conclusion that human vigor, both mental and physical, varies constantly in response to atmospheric differences, which thus have a direct effect upon civilization and progress. This is equally true whether we look at contrasts of climate from one geographical region to another, at differences from season to season, or at variations from one day to another. This being so, we see why it is that a map of climatic energy, such as Figures 27 and 30 (pages 245 and 256), must be based not only on the average temperature, but upon changes from season to season and day to day. We also see that even when we disregard the influence of disease and diet, which are closely associated with climate, the geographical distribution of human vigor and of the capacity to make progress must be closely related to that of climatic efficiency.

CHAPTER 20

THE DISTRIBUTION OF CIVILIZATION

A. Regions of High Efficiency

Having gained a somewhat comprehensive idea of the nature and significance of the map of climatic efficiency, let us turn back to page 256 and examine Figure 30 in greater detail. North America and Europe share the climatic supremacy of the world so far as our particular stage of civilization is concerned. The northeastern quarter of the United States, together with a strip of southern Canada, excels from the standpoint of storms and polar infalls. Western Europe excels from that of temperature. Both continents owe a great deal to their location in the main storm belt which circles around the earth's northern magnetic (not geographic) pole. The corresponding southern belt lies too far south to have much effect on man. Although extremes of temperature cause climatic efficiency to decline toward the interior in both continents, cyclonic storms keep all parts of the northern United States and southern Canada well within the limits of the high or highest level of climatic efficiency. In the eastern United States cyclonic storms sweep into relatively low latitudes more often than in any other part of the world. This is one reason why the American South has a more stimulating climate than the corresponding Asiatic region in China. Some of the North American storms, with their meeting of polar and tropical air masses, sweep inward from the North Pacific Ocean but more originate in North America. The extremes of temperature accompanying some of these storms lower human efficiency, but the net effect is to give the United States what appears to be the world's most stimulating climate.

This cyclonic climate may be too stimulating. We have seen that it apparently has much to do with American traits, such as excessive eagerness for action without due planning, boisterousness among children, and the prevalence of degenerative diseases among older people. These handicaps are accentuated by the urban type of life, which in turn is in part a response to the activity stimulated by the highly cyclonic type of climate, as well as to abundant resources and the temperament arising from selective migration. Herrington and Moriyama have shown statistically that the correlation between degenerative diseases and the degree of urbanization (Figures 22 and 25) is close, but the correlation between such diseases and climatic efficiency (Figure 27) is closer. The overstimulation indicated by the degenerative diseases represents, so to speak, the wearing out of imperfect human machinery which is run too fast. It is apparently a price paid for the kind of energy which enabled the United States to do a colossal job of manufacturing in a very short time during World War II. It is quite possible that innate ability, natural resources, and the cultural endowment derived from earlier generations are more important than climatic efficiency as primary conditions of civilization, but in the United States, as in the entire world, the broad *geographic pattern* of civilization conforms more closely to climatic efficiency and the weather than to any other factor.

The effect of storms in setting this geographic pattern is so great that we may well follow the American storms eastward and see what happens. The low barometric pressure arising from the tropical water that sweeps northward from the West Indies toward Iceland and Scandinavia provides a pathway, so to speak, whereby many American storms cross the Atlantic to Europe. There they join with prevailing westerly winds in giving western Europe a stimulating climate with frequent changes of weather and yet with relatively few extremes of heat and cold such as are the worst climatic feature of the area of highest climatic efficiency in North America. This European cyclonic climate, as experienced within six or seven hundred miles of the Strait of Dover, does not stimulate activity so much as the American cyclonic type. In this respect it is the better of the two. In fact, for all-round permanent efficiency among modern civilized people, the world's best climate is apparently found in a rough rectangle with corners near Liverpool, Copenhagen, Berlin, and Paris.

Other candidates for first place climatically include the American region from New Hampshire to New Jersey, and the Puget Sound region. A very narrow strip along the California coast, although relatively deficient in cyclonic storms, is also a candidate for high honors, as are New Zealand and the southeastern coast of Australia. None of these climates is so stimulating as that of the Great Lakes region of North America, but there the stimulus seems to be too great. When size as well as quality is considered, the stormy part of western Europe seems to be the most favored of all regions for climatic efficiency in our stage of civilization. The northeastern United States from southern New England to the Great Lakes and beyond probably stands second.

B. *The Asiatic Handicap*

In Europe and especially Asia the value of the climate as an aid to civilization declines quite steadily eastward. The general level of progress falls off similarly. The North Sea portion of Germany is more advanced than East Prussia. The Baltic States stand ahead of western Siberia. Poland and the Ukraine surpass Central Asia, Mongolia, and the region east of Lake Baikal. Sheer distance from advanced countries helps to keep the more remote regions backward, but the handicap of remoteness and isolation would largely vanish if the climate were good, as is well seen in New Zealand. Omitting other factors, which undoubtedly play a large part, let us concentrate on the relation of climate to the backwardness of Asia. The main factor is Eurasia's sheer size, which injures both climatic efficiency and agriculture in three chief ways: (1) by extremes of temperature; (2) by scarcity of storms and rain; (3) by contrasts in rainfall from season to season and year to year with consequent droughts, floods, and famines.

In summer, masses of polar air can settle southward over northern Asia, thus helping to give southern Siberia an admirable climate for a few months. Even in summer, however, when heat and consequent low atmospheric pressure open a path for cyclonic storms, oceanic air masses can rarely bring much moisture to the interior from the west because of distance, from the south because of mountains, and from the east because air masses in middle latitudes normally move eastward rather than westward. Hence both rain and the stimulus of changing air masses are scanty over most of the interior of Asia even in summer. Only a narrow strip of Siberia extending from the southern Urals to Lake Baikal has summer temperatures and rainfall well adapted to both agriculture and human efficiency. Farther north and in the highlands farther east the temperature is too low. Farther south extreme dryness, great heat, and the absence of storms combine to give the lowlands a disadvantage, and the highlands, such as Tien Shan and Tibet, are generally too lofty.

In winter the disadvantages of the entire Asiatic interior north of the main mountains are aggravated. All continents tend to become warm or cold much faster than oceans. This is especially important in large continents and in latitudes high enough so that the days are long in summer and short in winter. Accordingly, eastern Russia, and still more the vast Asiatic regions farther east, become relatively hot for their latitude in summer and extremely cold in winter. These extremes in themselves, especially the prolonged low temperature, are unfavorable to health and efficiency. The extreme cold of winter also does harm by causing the air to contract and become heavy, so that a vast area of very high pressure is formed. This acts as a buffer, barring out storms that might enter from the west. Some such storms follow the belt of open water and low atmospheric pressure that extends into polar latitudes along the coast of Norway. Some swing along the Baltic Sea, where the presence of open water well into the winter creates a slight trough of low atmospheric pressure. In this connection it is interesting to note the high cultural level of the Finns and the Baltic States, as well as of Norway. Russians say that their countrymen in the Leningrad region are the "Yankees of Russia."

Some of the winter storms from the Atlantic cross Germany north of the Alps, but in winter they usually fade away in Russia and never reach Central Asia. Others cross southern France, or even Spain, and bring winter rains and the stimulus of storms to the Mediterranean, especially north Italy. They give the Gulf of the Lion south of Marseille a reputation for storminess in winter. They make the Po Valley, more markedly than the Leningrad area, a relatively "cyclonic" and active region that contrasts favorably with a less cyclonic and less active region in the south of the same country. Northern Italy gets some storms and rain in summer as well as winter, but in Sicily the long summer is practically stormless. Waterpower from the Alps now encourages industrial activity in the Po Valley, but north Italy was outstandingly active industrially in the great mercantile days of Venice and Genoa.

In winter the Mediterranean storms sometimes cross Turkey, or even Palestine, and reach Iran. Some, indeed, in an attenuated form, persist into northern India, but here their influence falls to a minimum. Farther east some cross the Burmese mountains into China. There they revive somewhat and are re-enforced by new storms, thus bringing a mild degree of storminess to central and southern China.

It is obvious from all this that Asia as a whole gets little of the benefit to agriculture and health that comes from cyclonic storms. Some storms, to be sure, penetrate Siberia in summer and a few traverse the southern countries in winter. The few that penetrate the interior in winter are generally accompanied by such violent winds and intense cold waves that they do more harm than good. Such conditions join with extremes of temperature and rainfall in placing most of Asia under the handicap of low efficiency, both agricultural and human. Out of Asia's seventeen million square miles about three fourths (four times the size of the United States) are agriculturally almost useless because of aridity or low temperature. A level of climatic efficiency above the medium grade is rarely exceeded even in latitudes where North America and Europe reach the highest level. The quarter of Asia where agriculture is feasible is also subject to great handicaps. In the best parts of Siberia, along the western section of the transcontinental railway, the summers are so short and cool that relatively few crops can mature. Elsewhere, from the Amur River in Siberia around through China, Indo-China, India, and Persia, to Turkey the rainfall is everywhere highly seasonal. Consequently the average yield of crops per acre is limited, and danger from drought, flood, crop failure, and famine is frequent. From China to India this marginal part of Asia also suffers from extremes of humid heat. Nowhere does climatic efficiency rise much above medium, and in many regions it falls lower.

Turning back to inner and western Asia, we find that the Heartland belongs to the Asiatic area of medium climatic efficiency. Therefore we inquire whether Part II of this book is inconsistent in ascribing high energy and ability to the nomads of that region. There is no inconsistency, only a demonstration that the geographical distribution of human ability depends on many factors, among which biological selection and climatic efficiency both play a part. The reader does not need to be reminded that the basic thesis of this book is that differences in civilization arise from the combined effect of biological inheritance, physical environment, and cultural endowment. Any one of these, if strong enough, may largely overcome the others. For example, New England stands high in climate and culture, but certain villages fall far below the normal level of progress. The reason seems to be lack of innate ability. Many inhabitants are mentally subnormal. In the Heartland, on the contrary, natural selection appears to have given the nomads a biological inheritance which more or less compensates for climatic handicaps so far as alertness and military capacity are concerned.

C. The Good Fortune of Japan

The transition from inner Asia to the eastern coast is of the utmost significance for civilization. Its most obvious phase is from deserts to lands, such as China, where the rainfall suffices for agriculture on a large scale. Then, too, as the coast is approached, cyclonic storms appear. Their full effect becomes apparent in Japan. That is the only part of Asia where cyclonic storms are numerous and effective. There the weak storms which circumvent southern Asia revive in strength. They are also re-enforced by new storms which arise locally or start as tropical hurricanes in low latitudes far out in the Pacific Ocean. Moving westward toward Asia these tropical typhoons, as they are there called, swing northward and then northeastward along the coast, just as our hurricanes do when they approach Florida or Texas and swing north as ordinary storms. Hence Japan lies in a stormy strip where masses of polar and tropical air often meet. Agriculture is greatly benefited, because rain falls at all seasons. Tokio, for example, averages 4 inches per month from October to March, as against 6 during the warmer half year, whereas the ratio at Peiping is only 1 to 3. The relatively even rainfall gives Japan much larger crop yields per acre than China and greatly reduces the risk of crop failure and famine which is so deadly on the mainland.

A no less significant result, not fully appreciated as yet, is that storminess makes Japan decidedly stimulating climatically. The climate of the Pacific Coast of Honshu, the main island, from Sendai northward closely approaches the optimum for the stage of technical progress found in the United States and western Europe. It is, however, too cool for the stage thus far reached in Japan. To get the full stimulus of a climate with an average temperature close to freezing in winter people need woolen clothing, houses with walls of something sturdier than bamboo and paper, and methods of heating at least as effective as stoves. Lacking these by reason of scanty resources, overpopulation, poverty, earthquakes, and long-established habit, the Japanese find that their best climate lies farther south, from Tokio to Osaka and Hiroshima. There the winters are admirable, like those of southeastern England but with more sun. The three summer months, however, are so hot, rainy, and muggy that they seriously reduce both physical and mental activity.* This illustrates the extremely important fact that the optimum climate varies according to the stage of technical development. Nevertheless, Japan has decidedly the best climate in all Asia from the standpoint of both

* Mean temperature: in January, Tokio 37°, London 39°; but in August, Tokio 78°, London, 62°.
   Precipitation: in January, Tokio 2.1 inches, London 1.9; in August, Tokio 4.6 (September, 7.5), London 2.2.

agriculture and human activity. This is true even though the death-rate in Japan is higher than in almost any other civilized country. The high deathrate merely indicates that other factors, for example, extreme overpopulation and poor diet, also exert great influence. On the other hand, the stimulating cyclonic climate, unique in Asia, is one of the basic reasons why the Japanese proved so stalwart in World War II.

In the parts of the world not yet mentioned in this chapter, progress and climatic energy agree in their geographical distribution, just as in North America, Europe, and Asia. Nevertheless, although the major features of the two kinds of geographical distribution agree, local divergencies are common because of other factors. The smaller the units of observation, the greater are the differences due to non-climatic factors. The Parsi quarter in Bombay, for example, belongs to a much higher stage of civilization than the poorer Hindu quarters. There can be little doubt, however, that in both quarters the level of health, activity, and enterprise is lower than it would be among these same people in a climate such as that of Buenos Aires or Melbourne. Looking at the matter more broadly, we see that the general cultural level of the Bombay Presidency differs from that of central Argentina and southeastern Australia in essentially the same way as the climate.

D. Limitations of the Climatic Theory

Several objections have been raised to the theory that climatic efficiency is basic in setting the geographical pattern of civilization. It is said, for example, that the climatic pattern is frequently overshadowed by isolation, as in Tibet and the southern Appalachians; by innate biological traits, as in Iceland and among the Parsis; by overpopulation, as in Japan; by recent migration within the limits of a single culture, as in Florida; and by the introduction of an advanced culture, as in tropical Hawaii and northern Australia.

This objection disappears when two essential points are remembered. First, climatic efficiency, as we have seen again and again, is only one of the many agencies which influence the geographic pattern of civilization. Indeed it is only a single phase of climate, and its effect is modified by the other phases as well as by soil, minerals, and other physical conditions. The geographic factor, in turn, ranks with heredity and cultural endowment as only one among three major factors that influence the level of civilization. Such being the case, the outstanding fact is not local departures from the cultural level that would be expected on the basis of climatic efficiency, but the broad geographical agreement between the patterns of civilization and climate.

The other essential point is that the theory of climatic efficiency must not be stretched to cover non-climatic matters. High climatic efficiency does not provide inventive brains; it merely stimulates such brains. It does not supply natural resources, even though the climates that are best for human energy are also admirable for agriculture and animal husbandry, and happen in some cases to be located in regions well supplied with minerals. Climates which promote efficiency merely help in developing the possibilities provided by the geographical environment. In short, not even the most stimulating climate insures the presence of a high civilization. It merely aids in the attainment of such a civilization.

This last point deserves amplification. The Indians of New York State, for example, the famous Five Nations, had merely the rude culture of the Stone Age, although they lived in one of the world's most stimulating climates. In spite of their low culture, however, they were notable for their activity and alertness. The climate, although not the optimum for their stage of culture, apparently stimulated them much as it stimulates the present inhabitants of the same region. The absence of civilization was due to a variety of reasons, some of which can only be guessed. We do not know, for example, whether the absence of iron tools among the American Indians was due to innate lack of inventive ability or to mere accident. We do know, however, that in their rainy, forested environment the absence of such tools and the consequent difficulty in felling trees and digging up grass or the weedy sod of old fields made agriculture very difficult except in especially favorable spots such as the flood plains of rivers. We also know that the Indians of New York could not possibly use domestic animals for wool, milk, plowing, and transport, because no wild animals fit for these purposes existed anywhere near them. Even if the bison had not lived far away, it was too big and stupid.

On the other hand, in spite of the limitations of agriculture, the Indians of the Five Nations showed remarkable advancement in social, military, and political organization, and in those handicrafts for which they had both the need and the raw materials. In these respects, as well as in energy, they surpassed the Indians of less stimulating climates. Many of these others, however, such as the Aztec and Pueblo tribes, had a higher civilization because they lived in a milder climate more closely approaching the optimum for their stage of culture. Agriculture by means of irrigation was there possible, and the climate was dry enough so that good protection from the weather could be secured by means of easily constructed houses of adobe. Thus the American Indians seem to be in harmony with the theory of climatic efficiency.

The fact that in Hawaii and tropical Queensland the white people preserve the highest type of civilization in climates which are relatively unstimulating illustrates another type of evidence which is sometimes presented that climatic efficiency has little to do with the level of civilization. The first thing to understand about this is that such climates are not typically tropical. They represent the best type found anywhere in tropical lowlands aside from the cool coastal variety of Peru. In their effect on human efficiency they probably stand not far from midway between the North Sea type, which our stage of civilization seems to find most favorable, and the worst type as found in steadily hot, humid, equatorial rain forests. A careful examination of the culture of Queensland and Hawaii makes the effect of this intermediate climate clear, provided the biological and social endowments of the people are also considered. Biologically the "British" population of Queensland, and still more the "American" population of Hawaii, has been highly selected through migration. Culturally both groups have been constantly in touch with Europe and America. Hence, if such conditions as climate and contact with more backward cultures did not intervene, we should expect the highest level of activity and progress in both places.

What we actually find in Hawaii and northern Queensland differs from this expectation. Among the really permanent residents of these regions, that is, those who do not go "South" or to "the mainland" for education, vacations, general recuperation, and the benefit of a stimulating climate, the pace of life is leisurely compared with that of San Francisco or Melbourne, let us say. This is not due to differences in stage of civilization or innate capacity, but mainly to diminished energy because of the less stimulating climate. This climatic difference is reflected in the social system. Leisurely rest and social amenities get more time than in more bracing climates, whereas such matters as serious reading, inventions, new projects, and the promotion of education, health, and good government get less. Activities of this latter type are by no means absent, but they proceed more slowly than among people of similar ability, character, and training in more stimulating climates. Moreover, they are largely led by people who frequently go to the more bracing climates for education, recuperation, and stimulus.

Then, too, the basic needs of life—food, clothing, shelter—can be satisfied with less work in the tropical climates than in the cooler ones. Thus lowered energy is accompanied by a lower demand for that same energy wherewith to maintain a reasonable standard of living. This difference in degree of activity has not yet had time to produce any great cleavage between the tropical and the cooler types of European culture. The growth of such cleavage is retarded by constant interchange of populations. Nevertheless, the difference in tempo is clear. In spite of the high qualities sorted out by selective migration, the social system in both Queensland and Hawaii is assuming a character appropriate to a climate that is not particularly stimulating. If these regions were left entirely to themselves for generations, the distinctive quality of their culture would doubtless become more conspicuous. Thus the life and character of these modern migrants of European stock are in harmony with the theory of climatic efficiency, just as are those of the American Indians in their stimulating climate, the British in their "efficient" climate, and the Pygmies in a climate at the opposite extreme.

E. Tropical Civilizations

Another objection sometimes urged against the climatic part of the efficiency theory of civilization is that notable civilizations have existed for centuries in tropical climates that are comparatively unstimulating. Evidences of such civilizations are found in regions of three main types: (1) tropical highlands, such as Mexico with its Aztecs, Peru with its Incas, Yemen in southern Arabia, and Zimbabwe in Rhodesia; (2) cool west-coast deserts, of which the only conspicuous example is the Pacific Coast of Peru; (3) warm, rainy forested lowlands, such as northern Ceylon, Cambodia in Indo-China, Java, Guatemala, and Yucatan.

All of these civilizations were located in places that are geographically more favored than the average within the tropics. The highland civilizations of Yemen, Rhodesia, and Mexico occur in climates where the temperature never departs far from the optimum. The Andean civilization had its center in a somewhat cooler and more stimulating climate. At Quito, on the equator, 9,400 feet above the sea, the average temperature is practically 55° at all seasons. At Cuzco, the ancient Inca capital, 13° farther south and 11,000 feet above the sea, the warmest month (November) also averages 55°, but the coolest is 47°. Still farther south, but lower down (8,000 feet), the monthly averages of Arequipa range only from 56 to 58°. Such temperatures impel people to be active. That is presumably one reason why the Indians of the Andean plateau run so constantly when they carry loads on their backs with straps over the forehead.

The relatively low temperature of the Andean highland stimulates invention, as well as activity. People have to make inventions or suffer from the cold. The agriculture of South America apparently arose in the lowlands or foothills east of the Andes in the general region where Argentina, Paraguay, and Brazil come fairly close together about 20° or 25° south of the equator. From there it was presumably carried equatorward and upward by migrants who moved slowly forward from generation to generation. As they went north the altitude at which their corn would grow best naturally became higher. Finally, however, the migration took these pre-Inca people into such high country that the temperature was too low for comfort and health. Then there occurred one of those significant combinations of climate, natural resources, human ability, and cultural inventions which seem to be at the basis of all great progress in civilization. The climate apparently stimulated both bodily and mental activity. That, however, would not have made such a cold place as Cuzco highly favorable for a relatively advanced stage of civilization unless there had been some means of keeping warm. Such a means was present on the high, cold grassy uplands of the Andean plateau. It took the form of two wool-bearing animals of the camel family, the llama and alpaca. Nowhere else in America was there any easily tamed animal which could be kept in herds and used as a source of wool. Moreover, the llama could also be used as a pack animal.

Before wool could be made into clothing someone had to make some extremely important inventions. The incentive to do so was there in the chilly evenings. The challenge to do so was present in the woolly animals, but these two conditions were not enough. People with alert, inventive minds were also needed. At some stage of their progress the old Peruvians must have been of high quality, for otherwise they could scarcely have made so many of the most fundamental inventions—first, the domestication of animals, then spinning, weaving, and the fashioning of warm clothes, also the art of loading and driving animals, and afterward that of making trails for them and carrying on trade by their means.

Other conditions also combined with the climate and the llamas to hasten the progress of Andean civilization. When the migrants came to the higher levels of the plateau, they found conditions under which irrigation was much more necessary than lower down because the climate was drier. It was also more difficult than in the gentler topography that they had previously been accustomed to. Irrigation canals that required high engineering ability were constructed, winding along steep mountain sides. Terraces, too, were needed on the hillsides. Still another condition joined with the presence of wool in enabling the migrants to protect themselves against low temperature. In the regions of relatively mild rainfall to which they had come, dried mud can be used not only to plaster dwellings made of branches or stones but to build entire houses. This is a great advantage because clay of reasonably good consistency is widely distributed and can easily be used. Moreover, adobe walls of dried clay are especially good as a means of keeping out both the cold at night and the heat of a vertical sun. A new and valuable crop, the potato, played a semi-climatic part in encouraging civilization in Peru, for it is found wild only on the high, cool Andean plateau. It must have added considerably to the security of the population against crop failures and famine.

From the standpoint of direct as well as indirect effects on human efficiency, the climate of tropical highlands has advantages in other respects as well as temperature. First, the updraft of air under the warm tropical sun and the corresponding downdraft at night make mountain climates more variable and to that extent more stimulating than those of neighboring lowlands. Second, if either atmospheric ozone or atmospheric electricity is a stimulant, highlands have an advantage which is largely independent of temperature. The amount of ozone in the air and the potential gradient of electric currents increase steadily upward. In places as high as Cuzco or Mexico City they are relatively large compared with sealevel. Even if ozone and electricity are not factors, tropical highlands have a kind of climate close to the best for a certain stage of cultural progress, although it is not the best when a higher stage is reached.

The second, or cool, dry lowland, type of tropical civilization also has special advantages. Its temperature is close to the optimum all the time. At the port of Callao in Peru, near Lima, oceanic currents cause the coolest month to average only 62° and the warmest 71°. These are almost ideal temperatures. The development of the lowland Peruvian civilization in this extremely dry desert was also helped by the fact that numerous small and easily handled streams from the high Andes favor irrigation. The temperature is never too hot or too cold for corn. Cotton grows wild, thus helping to provide material for clothing. Means [1] describes the coastal valleys as having one of the best diets in the world by reason of potatoes, maize, squash, beans, sweet potatoes, peppers, and many fruits, nuts, and spices, together with an abundance of varied seafood as well as game birds, deer, and other wild animals in higher valleys.

The location of the third, or wet lowland, type of tropical civilization, depends largely on soil, as well as on seasons of rainfall. The majority of tropical soils are so badly leached that they have lost most of their soluble minerals. Hence they are not good for cereals. Crops grown in them tend to be deficient in minerals, vitamins, and fats, so that they provide a poor diet. The Cambodian region, where the magnificent ruins of Angkor Wat are located, and the lowlands of northern Ceylon, which also once supported a relatively high civilization, are favored with alluvial soils or with muddy streams for irrigation whereby the soil is renewed. New alluvial soils and a limestone type not badly weathered are found in the Maya region of Guatemala and Yucatan. Java is especially favored with rich volcanic soils, as is Guatemala. In both Java and Guatemala ancient civilizations existed in the highlands, as well as the lowlands. Another important factor in the location of lowland tropical civilizations is a rainfall of the "plantation" type, abundant but not excessive. Its chief advantage, as we have already seen, is a good amount of rain most of the year, combined with a dry season not severe enough to injure moisture-loving crops but long enough to favor their ripening and to make cultivation and weeding practicable. Climates with this kind of favorable combination of moderately wet and dry seasons are rare in the tropics. They are especially important because they favor the growing of rice or corn, which forms the basis of the kinds of agriculture most favorable to tropical civilizations.

F. The Human Factor in Tropical Civilizations

From the human, as well as the physical, standpoint all three types of tropical civilization have common characteristics which differentiate them from non-tropical civilizations, such as those of Egypt, Mesopotamia, and northwestern India. First, they all appear to be

[1] p. 11.

intrusive, that is, we have not yet found evidence of a gradual development from more primitive stages, such as are found beneath the Asiatic and Egyptian types. This suggests that their early stages of development took place elsewhere. When they arrived at the locations where we now find their ruins their bearers had already attained at least the rudiments of civilization. For example, according to Means, both the highland and lowland civilizations of early South America were founded by people who already understood the rudiments of agriculture, pottery making, and weaving. This seems to have been true of the founders of all tropical civilizations.

If the cultures that blossomed into tropical civilizations were intrusive, it is practically certain that they must have been brought by migrants from some other region. This is the second great human fact that seems to be common to all tropical civilizations. The story of the coming of such migrants to Ceylon is well known, and practically the same general set of events occurred also in Cambodia and Java. For example, in the fifth century A.D. Java began to be the goal of voyagers, traders, and bold adventurers from India. According to Kennedy,[2] the typical "procedure was for a prince of some Indian ruling house to come to the Indies [Java] and there insinuate himself into the graces of a native chieftain. Acting as advisor, oftentimes marrying the chief's daughter, the Hindu would then establish . . . a state government copied after the Indian model." This quotation oversimplifies the matter, but it suggests what must have happened, namely, a vigorous selective migration. The famous pyramidal temple of Boro Budur, the most impressive memorial of this period, was built about the time of Charlemagne (A.D. 742–814). Episodes from the life of Buddha are carved in stone along nearly three miles of terraced walls rising tier after tier to a small lofty dome. The greatest political period came later, in the fourteenth and fifteenth centuries, when the empire of Modjopahit, with its capital in eastern Java, ruled most of the Dutch East Indies, Philippines, and Malay Peninsula. The overthrow of this empire is usually ascribed to the introduction of Mohammedanism.

A third characteristic common to all three types of tropical civilization is that they perish through senescence, giving birth to no surviving successors that surpass them, and leaving scarcely a trace in any later civilization. They perished thus in spite of a rather long life in certain cases. The Mayan civilization probably lasted at least

[2] p. 33.

fifteen hundred years, if we include both its earlier stage in Guatemala and its later stages in Yucatan with its medieval revival. Nevertheless, when the white man arrived in America, the distinctive arts and social habits of the Mayas had practically vanished. The Indians of Yucatan scarcely had any traditions of their people's ancient grandeur. The Inca civilization was already decadent when the white man arrived. All tropical civilizations have disappeared in a way that suggests premature senescence. None has passed on the torch of culture to other civilizations. Even in Java, where Europeans found a kind of gentle, decayed culture, analogous in this respect to that of modern Iran, the present natives show little of the originality and industry which gave rise to magnificent temples such as that of Boro Budur. Contrast all this with the way in which Babylonia transmitted civilization to Assyria and Syria, Egypt to Palestine and Crete, the Indus region (non-tropical) to modern India, Greece to Rome and western Europe, and China to Korea and Japan. Today none of the leading types of civilization owes more than a few minor items of its culture to any of the three types of tropical civilization.

We are now ready for a tentative final conclusion as to tropical civilizations. We have seen that in every instance the geographical location of such civilizations has special advantages of climate, soil, native plants, or native animals. Climatically, however, there is a wide range from warm, moist, unstimulating lowlands, such as those of Ceylon, Java, Cambodia, and the lower parts of Guatemala, to the cool and relatively stimulating, although monotonous, highlands. We have also seen that all the tropical civilizations are alike in being intrusive, in being due to immigrants from some other region, and in disappearing without leaving progressive successors or exerting any appreciable influence on the rest of the world. The lowland cultures show these last three qualities with special strength. Every one of them had progressed far toward its highest stage when it first appeared within the tropics. The earliest traces of the Mayas indicate that they had already developed their marvelous calendar through generations of accurate observation. They also had made one of the world's small handful of supreme inventions, namely, the art of writing. The people of Ceylon, Cambodia, and Java merely took the culture that had originally evolved in northern India outside the tropics and added a few relatively minor items of their own. On the other hand, the civilization of Peru went through many stages of growth after it reached the highlands. Thus, in general, the amount of development of these civilizations after they reached their tropical homes was least in the unstimulating lowlands and greatest in the relatively stimulating highlands.

The course of events becomes clearer when we take account not only of the climate and resources, but of the quality of the people. In fact the principles of biological selection set forth in Part II of this book go far toward solving the mystery of tropical civilization. Means [3] puts his finger on the crux of the problem when he says that in order to attain civilization people need not only a stimulating climate and raw materials well fitted to their work, but also "an indefinable factor" which is "apparently psychological." The Incas, who were the latest native rulers to dominate Peru, apparently possessed this unknown quality. It seems quite likely that, according to the terms employed in this book, the Incas were a kith that had acquired especially strong qualities during an unknown period of migration, mountaineering, and wandering with their herds of llamas. As described by Means, they had a character and played a part like that of the Mongols in China, the Moguls in India, and the Turks in Asia Minor.

Going back to tropical civilizations as a whole, we may inquire as to the place of origin of the migrant groups which brought their primitive culture to low latitudes. The culture of the peninsulas and islands of southeastern Asia appears to have had its origin in the Indus region, where the record of human progress is almost complete from primitive times. For Yemen the corresponding location was presumably north of the Arabian Desert. Little is known as to the exact place of origin of the Mayan and Peruvian civilizations. A final conclusion can be reached only after there is agreement as to where corn (maize) was first cultivated. It was formerly supposed that this occurred in Mexico, but Mangelsdorf and Reeves, as we have seen, favor a location east of the Andes and 20–25° from the equator. From there the art of agriculture may have been carried across the Andes to the dry coast and even through Ecuador and Colombia to Central America and finally to the Maya region of Guatemala. This suggests great possibilities for selective migration and for the evolution of a kith such as the Mayas. [4]

It is probable that migration was at the basis of all tropical civilizations. Migrations are practically always selective. The more difficult they are, the greater is the probability that people of unusually

[3] p. 25.   [4] Huntington, 1914A, p. 184.

high quality, physically, temperamentally, and intellectually will be segregated. If migration brings such people to the more favored parts of the tropics, as it presumably did in the cases now under consideration, the stage is set for a sudden outburst of civilization. This might last hundreds of years if the competent invaders retained their biological inheritance unmixed, if new migrants of the same type arrived, or if some other selective process was in operation. On the other hand, degeneration and the decline of civilization would normally result from intermarriage with less competent people, from the gradual weakening effect of the climate, or from the growth of luxury and licentiousness.

The Parsis illustrate the extraordinary way in which high ability and achievement may persist in a tropical environment if a high biological inheritance is strictly maintained. The British in India and the Dutch in Java illustrate the way in which a high culture from a more bracing climate may enter a country and create buildings and engineering works utterly beyond the power of the indigenous peoples. If the Dutch should die out in Java and that country should cease to have contact with the rest of the world for centuries, the ruins of Dutch structures might be as outstanding as are those of the Mayas in Yucatan or the Khmers in Cambodia. Thus tropical cultures, as a whole, whether ancient or modern, harmonize with the conclusion that there is a strong relation between climatic efficiency and civilization, but allowance must always be made for natural resources, heredity, biological selection, and the stage of culture which migrants bring with them. All this is merely another way of stating the basic fact that civilization depends on the combined effect of heredity, physical environment, and cultural history.

CHAPTER 21

COLDWARD AND STORMWARD

A. Primitive Comfort and Fire

One of the most frequent criticisms of the theory of climatic efficiency is that the center of civilization has moved from warm regions, such as Egypt and Babylonia, toward cool, stormy regions, such as those around the North Sea. In reality this fact is one of the best evidences of the truth of the theory. It is supposed to be an objection merely because of failure to realize that the optimum climate varies according to the stage of progress. Consider the situation of our most primitive ancestors before fire, clothing, and artificial shelter came into use. Such naked people, sleeping in caves at night and taking shelter beneath leafy trees at time of rain, would be uncomfortable at temperatures as low as 60°. Porteus vividly describes the torpor of the naked savages of tropical Australia when the desert nights drop to a temperature of 50°. Curled up against one another beside the gray ashes of a dead fire, they seem almost unable to move until the warm sun has shone on them an hour or two.

Elsewhere in tropical lowlands the slightly clad and poorly housed natives dread temperatures below 70°. Long habit and low vitality generally cause them to react by sitting inertly huddled up instead of by exercise. High temperatures also make them inert, but the kind of inertia thus caused is more comfortable than that due to cold. In winter we ourselves, as a rule, can usually sit more comfortably with the temperature at 76°, let us say, than at 62°, although both are about equally far from the ideal. A naked tropical savage similarly suffers less from 85° than from 65°. Consequently among the most primitive people, without fire, clothing, and artificial shelter, the best climate from the standpoint of health and activity, as well as comfort, appears to be one where the temperature rarely falls below about 60°. In other words, for such people the optimum climate is one where days with a noonday temperature of 75° or so, such as is voted most comfortable by inactive people of many races in summer and in the tropics, are the coolest that are normally experienced with any great frequency. Such a climate is found today near the Tropic of Cancer in Calcutta (65° in January) and near the Tropic of Capricorn in Rio de Janeiro (68° in July). In summer an average of 80° or more (86° in May in Calcutta, 78° in February in Rio) can be endured much more easily by naked savages than by clothed modern white men. The way to meet its debilitating effect is simply to wear little clothing and avoid exertion. That is far easier than to work out methods of protection from low temperature, as must be done in higher latitudes, especially where coolness is often accompanied by rain and wind.

The progress of human culture gradually changes the optimum climate until it becomes one in which the warmest instead of the coolest season has noonday temperatures of 74° or so. The reason for this is that as mankind becomes more civilized the discomforts of the cooler seasons tend more and more to be removed. This transition deserves careful study.* It is obvious that as soon as man learned to build fires, wrap furs or skins about himself, and construct artificial shelters, he could be comfortable under conditions of temperature, wind, and rain that previously had been bad for health and efficiency as well as comfort. Thus he was enabled to live in climates where the weather's physical, mental, and economic effects are more favorable to progress than in steadily hot climates. When once the ideas of fire, clothing, and shelter had become established, they must have acted as a great stimulus to further inventions. Vital questions at once arose. How can a fire best be kindled? How can it be kept going during rain? How can the skin of an animal be preserved so that it will keep a sleeper warm at night and not smell to high heaven? How can branches and leaves be fastened together to keep the rain from trickling onto his neck while he is

---

* Gilfillan was the first to develop the idea of a systematic change in the optimum climate in harmony with advances in man's technological skill. Stefansson and Markham, however, appear to have reached this conclusion independently. The latter's book contains an especially good study of certain aspects of the problem. Many other authorities agree that man's growing control over nature has led to a coldward march of the center of civilization. The present author (1924B, pp. 295 ff.; 1927B, pp. 155 ff.) has pointed out that movement toward more stormy areas has been as important as toward those that are cooler. In general the center of active progress in civilization has migrated from relatively unstimulating warm regions with few storms, where the winter is the most comfortable season, to stimulating regions with many storms, where the summer is the most comfortable period. The controlling factor in this migration has been man's ability to create a comfortable, healthful artificial or indoor climate in cold and stormy weather.

asleep? Through such questions all sorts of environmental conditions act as a challenge to human ingenuity, and every major new invention broadens the scope of the challenge.

Under normal conditions only a few people of the more intelligent or persistent type employ a new invention at first. A separation into diverse social groups composed of users contrasted with non-users frequently arises in this way. This in turn may be associated with a selective process which gives rise to biological differences akin to those which we seem to have found between Parsis and their neighbors. Thus, although we start with the physical fact of discomfort due to meteorological conditions, human culture soon comes into play, and we have inventions to reduce the discomfort. The inventions in turn lead to biological differentiation.

An imaginary sketch of the history of fire will illustrate this point and help to explain the coldward march of civilization. By using a simple example we can illustrate certain processes which in later times become so complicated that it is hard to recognize the underlying principles. The art of making and preserving fire presumably originated in a climate which was warm in general but had a season cool enough to be uncomfortable to primitive, fireless men who were also practically naked and shelterless. It is not likely to have originated in a steadily hot climate, for no sufficient incentive is there available. The comfort to be derived from a fire is scarcely worth the labor of making and preserving it. Where certain months are cool enough to be uncomfortable, on the contrary, early man must have enjoyed the heat of accidental fires, such as those set by lightning, long before he found out how to make them himself. The incentive to invention recurred afresh every year. On the other hand, the original taming of fire is not likely to have occurred in a climate with a really cold winter for the simple reason that it is highly doubtful whether primitive man could survive in such a climate until he had fire to help him.

One of the early effects of fire must presumably have been to induce selective migration and a greater increment of population in some groups than in others. This assumption is based on repeated known instances of what happens under similar conditions. The making of fire by primitive means, such as the rubbing of two sticks together, requires considerable skill and persistence. The preservation of a fire out of doors hour after hour and day after day also requires considerable persistence, especially among wandering hunters. Thus the users of fire were confronted by two rather perplexing alter natives, either to keep the fire going all the time or achieve the difficult task of starting a new one when they needed it. New inventions, as a rule, are used at first by only a few people. If the invention is practical, its users tend to be intelligent, persistent people who feel the need of the new device. Iron tools, waterwheels, railroads, and radio all illustrate this. If the same thing was true of primitive man, as there is every reason to believe, the use of fire must at first have spread most rapidly among the more far-sighted, energetic, and determined members of some group or groups which lived near the coldward border of the region then inhabited by man. We may reasonably picture a stage when the sparse population of certain regions of that sort consisted of two types. One comprised relatively competent people who had learned to use fire and were thereby stimulated to make new inventions, including in due time those connected with cooking. The other was a less competent group who did not think the profit to be gained from fire was sufficient to pay for the labor involved.

Other things being equal two such groups are bound to increase at different rates. The new invention helps to preserve the lives of its users. It saves them from contracting diseases which are fostered by exposure to cold and wet. It helps to ward off wild animals which might kill little children. It encourages inventions, such as the spear with a point shaped in the fire, and especially the art of cooking. Such inventions give their users the great advantage of a food supply more abundant and perhaps better than that of their neighbors. The result must be a higher rate of survival among their children than among those of the non-users.

Another factor also enables the fire-users to increase more rapidly than the others. With the help of fire they are able little by little to spread into cooler climates where the non-users do not follow because they cannot there be comfortable. Thus selective migration occurs. In the newly occupied regions, people of the more intelligent and competent type can intermarry only with one another, whereas their former comrades in the old home intermarry not only with one another but with the non-users of fire. Thus the intelligent fire-using type becomes established in the newly occupied regions and the culture of those regions becomes higher than that of warmer regions. The center of cultural progress and the optimum climate both shift from warmer to cooler regions. Cool weather no longer has its former ill effect on comfort and efficiency. On the other hand, in the new region the ill effects of undue heat are lessened because the hot period is not so long as in the warmer climate. In due time, to be sure, the biological advantage of the new region may diminish through influx of the less competent type. This will happen if overpopulation, war, pestilence, climatic change, or other difficulties drive the less progressive type out of its warm home or if the means of making and using fire become so well established that it is easy for incompetent people to use them.

We may sum the matter up by saying that the presumable effect of the invention of fire was (1) to create a division of the population into fire-users and non-fire-users; (2) to stimulate other inventions among the fire-users; (3) to cause their numbers to increase faster than those of the non-users; (4) to enable part of the fire-users to migrate into regions previously unoccupied because too cool and there to increase rapidly; (5) to shift both the optimum climate and the center of progress into regions cooler than the previous optimum; and finally, (6) to cause the newly occupied regions with their newly acquired arts to become so well established that the less competent types of people pour into them.

B. The March of Civilization

As time went on and new species of Homo arose, man's ability to protect himself against both cold and rain by means of clothing and shelter, as well as fire, gradually increased. Nevertheless, for tens of thousands of years, these methods were of little effect. Even in ancient Babylon and Egypt clothing was predominantly ornamental rather than protective. Fires indoors were unpleasant because they were kindled directly on the floor with no means of getting rid of the smoke except through the open door or a tiny unshuttered window. The dry climate, to be sure, was a help in keeping warm because it made it possible to construct little huts of sun-dried clay which were fairly effective as a protection against cold nights and against the comparatively small rainfall of the short rainy season in winter. Thus the Babylonians and Egyptians were able to be reasonably comfortable during a winter which was considerably cooler than the optimum for more primitive people. During about half the year they were stimulated to activity by temperatures below the optimum for comfort. They also had to exercise forethought and do much work in order to provide food and shelter for a long season when no crops ripened and cool nights were uncomfortable. This presumably tended to make them more active and progressive than the people who lived in warmer regions where food was available most of the time and little protection from the weather was needed.

From that day to this there has been a gradual improvement in man's ability to protect himself from cold and rain and snow and a corresponding movement of the center of progress to climates where storms, as well as low temperature, provide a progressively increasing stimulus. In Ur of the Chaldees and central Egypt the average temperature during the three winter months is approximately 50 to 55° and the rainfall only 1 to 5 inches. In the three summer months the temperature averages 85 to 90° and there is no rain. Today in the main centers of European civilization within a few hundred miles of the North Sea the temperature of the three summer months comes nearer to that of the winter in the earlier centers than to that of the summer. It averages about 63° with a total of 7 inches of rain. The winters, on the other hand, average about 36° with 5 inches of rain. Nowhere else is the winter so warm in a region where summer temperature and storminess *at all seasons* are also so favorable. Places such as California and New Zealand have few storms at some seasons.

The coldward, stormward march of civilization is so far-reaching a phase of history that we may well examine some examples. Let us look at a stage of technical development somewhat beyond that of early Egypt. For the ancient Greeks the optimum climate was cooler than for the Egyptians, but warmer than the present optimum for people with the most highly developed technology. The Greeks had learned to build fireplaces of a sort, but they knew little of chimneys. If smoke annoyed them and they wanted to be warm and comfortable on a cold day, they sat out of doors, well clothed, and in a sunny spot well sheltered from the wind. Another method was to bring into the house a pan of live coals, as is common in Turkey to this day. The author and his hosts have often sat on the floor around a pan of live coals with their legs under a quilt which also covered the pan. If one kept his hands outside the quilt, they became so cold that writing was scarcely possible. Farther in the interior of Asia the author's eyes have run with tears because he tried to write up his notes while supper was being cooked over an open fire in the corner of the room. Part of the smoke escaped through a tiny window a foot square. The rest filled the room except near the floor for a foot or two. It was not so bad if you lay down. That was what the men did while the women cooked. Such conditions are a great handicap to any kind of productive indoor work in cold weather. They are also a hazard to health. In ancient Greece the discomfort and in-

efficiency arising from cold weather and primitive heating arrangements were by no means so great as they are now in colder regions
such as Central Asia, but they were great enough to hamper many
kinds of activity during the cooler months.   •

The effect of primitive heating arrangements is paralleled by that
of difficulties in getting rid of rain. Thatched roofs in rainy countries and flat roofs of sun-dried mud in the drier ones have a strong
tendency to leak or collapse in wet weather. In Turkey I have seen
houses where heavy, rain-soaked mud roofs fell in and killed sleeping households during a winter storm. Such conditions illustrate
the fact that one of man's greatest struggles has been to protect himself against rain as well as low temperature and to protect his household goods and his place of work as well as himself against both rain
and snow. Part of this struggle has dealt with architecture and part
with devices for heating houses and providing warm clothing. With
successive steps of progress along these lines the center of climatic
efficiency has shifted away from places where optimum temperatures
prevail only during the coolest weather and toward those where they
prevail in the warmest weather. The tendency has also been away
from dry climates where protection against rain is easy and toward
more humid climates where cyclonic storms aid agriculture and provide the kind of stimulus which we have been examining.

C. Windows and Light

Inventions pertaining to light as well as heat have helped to change
the nature of the optimum climate. One of the best aids in the
progress of civilization is work which keeps people busy indoors in
the evening, on dark days in cold weather, or at other times when
outdoor work is difficult. This is especially important in winter
when the sun sets early, the air is cold, and storms with rain, snow,
and wind are frequent. In order to realize this fully one needs to
have the experience of trying to write, mend clothes, or repair an
implement by the light of the primitive stone lamps which until recently furnished the chief source of light in large sections of Turkey,
Persia, India, and China. Even if one can see to work, the strain
on the eyes is severe. Poor light enforces idleness on vast numbers
of people not only during hours of darkness, but by day when rain,
wind, or low temperature makes it unpleasant to open the shutters.
The word shutters is used advisedly instead of windows. Even in
the United States thousands of homes of white as well as colored

people in the South have no glass windows, no electric lights, and only rather poor smoky kerosene lamps. When the weather outside is unpleasant, the openings which ought to have glass are closed by wooden shutters, and there is only a dim light inside.

Imagine the blow to the work in thousands of office buildings, factories, schools, libraries, and homes if the only source of indoor light were blazing pine knots, or antique "Roman" lamps in which a thick wick floating in olive oil hangs over the side and burns with a dull flame that is half smoke. Try to imagine what would happen to transportation by train, trolley car, automobile, steamship, or airplane if such lamps were the best available source of light. A large part of the activities of civilized life would be impossible except by daylight and in weather warm enough, dry enough, and sufficiently free from wind so that people could work comfortably with the shutters open. Three things would happen under such conditions. First, a great number of the activities of modern civilization would be seriously curtailed everywhere, and the world would slip back to an earlier stage of civilization. Second, the curtailment would be at a maximum in high latitudes. It would vary in proportion to the handicaps arising from short winter days, low temperature, and cloudy, rainy weather. Third, the areas of optimum climate, best health, and highest activity and progress would shift to lower latitudes.

This picture of life without window glass emphasizes the importance of technical inventions in shifting the climate of greatest efficiency coldward and stormward. Although glass windows existed in Roman times and were used in large churches and public buildings in Italy and western Europe from the twelfth century onward, they have been available to ordinary people only since the seventeenth century. In what is now the United States, according to Knittle, that century "was almost glassless. . . . Men lived and died in the more isolated sections [of New England, for example] without ever having seen the substance called glass." Not till about 1650 was the making of glass window panes well established, and thereafter for a long time they were a luxury, not a necessity. Some idea of the effect of glass upon civilization can be gained by comparing the light, airy model houses of the poor in modern Sweden with the large, lofty, but inexpressibly dark and dingy one-room, cave-like structures which are preserved in Skansen Park in Stockholm as examples of the homes of princes six or seven centuries ago.

The coldward march of the optimum climate still continues. Thanks to the invention of power-driven machinery and to the other technical changes which have accompanied it, it is now vastly easier to live in a cool or even a cold climate than it ever was before. Two centuries ago most of the world depended on wood for fuel. There was no such thing as steam heat or even "central heating," to use the British term for the American method of depending on furnaces. Nor was it anything like so easy as now to manufacture warm woolen clothes for everybody, even the poor. In a climate as cold as that of Winnipeg, averaging $-3°F$ in January, it would have been almost impossible to heat a large building like a modern factory, school, or auditorium in winter. It was difficult to travel in winter because the only way to go was coldly on foot or still more coldly in an open horse-drawn sleigh. Under present circumstances. the protection against cold which Winnipeg enjoys through the direct and indirect use of fire makes the winters there less to be dreaded by many—perhaps most—people than the heat of the summer in Memphis, Tenn., where the average in July is 80°. Winnipeg has the advantage of an almost ideal summer temperature averaging 67° in July, whereas Memphis has the advantage of a mild winter averaging only 41° in January. Under modern conditions of comfort in cold weather, the climate of Winnipeg comes nearer to the optimum than than of Memphis, whereas a century or two ago Memphis approached the optimum more closely.

D. *The Modern Influence of Fire*

The growth in technical knowledge which changed the optimum climate toward a cooler, more stormy type must have had a deep influence upon the survival and increase of one type of people in comparison with another. The reality of such an influence is evident when we examine the well-known facts as to what has happened under the impetus of modern machinery driven by steam and electricity. The invention of such machinery became possible only when five essential factors were combined: (1) people with relatively high innate capacity; (2) strong motives for action in the form of desire for higher standards of living, eagerness for social approval, or sheer curiosity as to how new physical or chemical combinations would work out; (3) conditions of climate, diet, and so forth that gave these people the kind of energy that makes them work overtime on scientific problems; (4) supplies of fuel readily available. The final result would have been altered if any one of these conditions had been different.

What actually happened was that people in certain small areas where the combination of these four conditions is especially good began to use fire for power and thereby increased marvelously. This helped to shift the centers of human progress into colder regions, thus making the climate of Winnipeg, for example, more favorable than that of Memphis. We have already quoted Garvin's comments on the English-speaking people. In A.D. 1600 they numbered about 5,000,-000 in England and Wales; 500,000 in Scotland, and 100,000 in Ireland. The French were already 16,000,000 strong and were increasing faster than the English. Then the geographical location and national character of the British led them to colonize America. Nevertheless, by 1790 the English-speaking world had increased to only about 16,000,000, whereas the French-speakers, including those in Canada, Switzerland, and other countries, numbered over 26,000,000. Then new methods of using fire as a source of power began to show their effect. England was the first country to seize the new method. It began to manufacture goods to be sold all over the world. It built steamships wherewith to distribute these goods and carry its own people abroad. The story of this vast expansion is too well known to need repetition. By 1940 the English-speakers in the world, 210,-000,000 in number, were about fourteen times as numerous as a century and a half earlier, whereas the French-speaking population had scarcely doubled.

The growth of the English-speaking population might have been considerable even if sailing ships and horsedrawn vehicles had continued to be the chief means of transportation. It is doubtful, however, whether the increase would have been anything like so great as it actually was. Nor is it likely that without the help of fire-driven machines the English-speakers would have so largely absorbed the speakers of French, Spanish, Dutch, and other languages in North America. Moreover, it appears that in general the earlier migration under the stimulus of steamships and steam engines tended to be more competent than the later migration. In later times, when migration was relatively easy, many of the migrants to new territory were less adventurous, resolute, and active than their predecessors.

In such ways, as well as in many others, there is a close parallel between the effect of the introduction of fire thousands of years ago and the invention of new ways of using fire scarcely two centuries ago. Of course, there are also great differences, which cannot here be discussed. A vast array of conditions co-operated with the use of fire to produce the modern growth of industry and the related increase in people who speak English, especially in those who are biologically of English stock. The outstanding fact is that in its broad effects the introduction of machinery driven by the power of fire was like that of many other great inventions throughout human history. The use of fire, the art of agriculture, the smelting of metals, the use of animals for beasts of burden, the sailing of the sea in ships, and the great art of writing, each in its own way has given an advantage to a certain type of people. That type has then tended to expand faster than other types and in many places has more or less replaced some of the others. In this way both the biological composition and the geographical distribution of the earth's population are continually subject to great changes which are reflected in the major movements of history. The next revolution of this sort may arise through the biological effect of eugenics. That nation which best and soonest learns to improve the innate quality of its people seems to have the best chance to inherit the earth.

E. The Transformation of Russia

Russia provides an especially good example of the relation of technological progress to the optimum climate for efficiency and thus to the geographical distribution of civilization. Almost everyone was surprised that Russia fought so well in World War II. At first most people thought that she would collapse in three months. Few thought that she could resist Germany more than a year. She did so well, however, that the pendulum swung to the opposite extreme. The Russians were acclaimed as more competent than the Germans, regardless of the fact that for years seventy million Germans fought Russia, held off Britain and the United States, and kept many subjugated countries under control. Nevertheless, in recent times the Russians have shown a degree of energy, initiative, skill, and good judgment which few people had formerly expected.

This outburst of previously throttled capacities is generally ascribed to release from the old czarist despotism and to the Russians' new feeling of ownership not only of their land, but of their government. Another factor, however, may also be equally important, namely, a partial release from the deadening effect of intensely cold winters with their prolonged darkness because of high latitude and persistent cloudiness.

At the beginning of the present century nearly 80 per cent of the Russians were peasants, or villagers whose life was almost completely dominated by that of the peasants. Even in the cities the majority of the people lived in almost the same way as the peasants. An outstanding fact about the peasant was the contrast between the idleness of the men in winter and their long exhausting hours of heavy work in summer. This contrast was due to the climate. In Moscow, for example, the temperature in October is the same as in November in Chicago, and April is as cold as Chicago's March. Hence the ground is frozen for close to six months. Most kinds of farm work are also impossible for a long period because of mud. There is, to be sure, no such thing as the "autumn rains," about which uninformed newspaper men continually talked during World War II. October in Moscow has only half as much rain as August. Nevertheless, even though the rainfall decreases from summer to winter, lessened evaporation and frequent light frosts cause the fields and the dirt roads to become muddy in the autumn. In the spring the melting of the deeply frozen ground produces mud so deep that plowing is generally impossible until well along in May.

Because of all this, for about seven long months each year there was formerly little for the men of central Russia to do. The care of the farm animals took a little time, but their number was pitifully small, an average of less than two cattle and one horse for each farm even in the best of times. It was difficult to keep more because the long winters demand much hay, and the short summers give little time for preparing it. Poultry was scarce for similar reasons. Moreover, the long winter nights and prolonged cold greatly reduce the production of both milk and eggs. Hence the incentive to keep animals was reduced by the same conditions which lowered their value. Since the animals were so few in number, it is not surprising that they were often housed under the same roof as the people, and it was the women's work to care for the cows and hens. As southern Russia is a prairie country lumbering is possible only in the North. Home occupations, such as making plows or harness, were difficult because the small, tightly sealed windows afforded little light even by day, and the long nights (seventeen hours without the sun in Moscow in December) were lighted only by candles or tapers so ineffective that all kinds of work were greatly discouraged. Then, too, the houses were so tightly sealed to keep out the bitter cold and were so full of people, with animals close by, that the air became foul and depressing. As a result, the men among the Russian peasants, as they themselves put it, had little to do except lie on the warm adobe bench through which the smoke passes to the chimney and "spit at the ceiling." Moreover, the villagers who were not peasants and also the proletariat of the cities were under almost this same handicap. They, as well as the peasants, grew soft in body and soft in mind, because of idleness due to cold, darkness, and mud.

In the spring when the mud at last disappeared and plowing became possible, a complete change was necessary. If land enough for a family was to be plowed and sown in time for the crop to ripen before the early frosts, the peasant had to work to the point of exhaustion throughout the long day of high latitudes. This was no easy task for men who were soft from months of idleness. Such alternation between enforced idleness and exhausting work appears to have been a major factor in creating the kind of mental inertia which makes it easy for a small minority to dominate a huge majority.

Another curious effect of the cold, dark Russian winter seems to have been that as a rule Russian women have in the past been much more alert and energetic than the men. The American engineer in charge of building the great dam on the Dnieper River says that when he wanted to send a railroad crane off to work by itself, he preferred to have a woman in charge. The men, although technically better trained than the women, were likely to hook the derrick onto too big a load and tip it over. Then another derrick was needed to pull the first out of a ditch. To the western mind it was a surprise to find women in charge of travelling cranes. It was still more of a surprise to find that even as laborers and in many other ways Russian women in the early years of the revolutionary era were widely reported to be more competent than men.

The reason for the women's relative efficiency seems to be that they had reached a cultural stage such that they were not continually depressed both physically and mentally by alternations between idleness and overwork. Throughout the year they have always had to work quite steadily. Cooking, the care of children, and other household tasks prevent them from being idle in winter, but in summer even in the harvest field their labor has not been so exhausting and so deadening to mental effort as that of the men. Because of all this there grew up in Russia a social system in which the men were proud of their competent women but were not ashamed of their own idleness and inefficiency. The ideals thus arising pervaded the cities as well as the villages. Thus winter temperatures far below the optimum seem to have had much to do with relative inefficiency and lack of alertness among Russian men and superior efficiency and alertness among the women. The weakness of the men in turn made it easy for a few more active and determined people to impose their will upon the vast majority, both under the old czarist regime and under the new Bolshevist regime which has been almost equally dictatorial, although more popular.

Since the Russian Revolution this old ideal has been changed, and the men are becoming as good workers as the women. Thus the innate abilities of the Russians express themselves more fully than formerly. It is customary to attribute all this to the new ideology introduced by the revolution. Without the machine age, however, with its factories, electric lights, and universal education, the new ideology would probably deteriorate or fall by the wayside. In order to be effective it needs the conquest of cold winters and of the back-breaking work of the summers, a conquest which has come through modern machinery. Tractors, for example, are a marvelous help in getting the fields plowed in time for sowing.

The machine age was on its way in Russia before World War I. Near the beginning of this book (page 12) we saw that, contrary to the usual belief, it probably would have arrived at almost the same rate without the revolution as with it. Without any revolution Japan experienced a vast change in this respect, and even in England the difference in public education between 1900 and the present is impressive. Regardless, however, of debatable probabilities, the introduction of machinery and education has enabled the Russians to make a good beginning in overcoming the handicap of long, cold winters and exhausting work in summer. Well-lighted and well-heated factories permit millions of persons to work almost as well in winter as in summer. Electric lights in many houses, even among the peasants, make winter work easy instead of difficult. They permit people to read and thus strengthen the new desire for education. Communal recreation halls, properly lighted and heated, stimulate not only reading but intelligent discussion of public affairs and the spread of new ideals. The introduction of tractors speeds up and eases the work of harvesting and especially plowing, which has always been the main bottleneck in Russian agriculture. In many other ways, machinery, sanitation, medicine, printing, and other elements of western civilization have reduced the two-fold handicaps of idleness in winter and overwork in summer.

The gist of the matter is that since 1900 Russia has been penetrated by new cultural conditions which enable people to overcome the depressing influence of long, cold winters. This is essentially the same process as that whereby the discovery of how to kindle and preserve fire enabled our primitive ancestors to live comfortably where the winter was cooler than had hitherto been desirable. From that early discovery down to the introduction of good stoves, glass windows, electric lights, and proper ventilation the process of providing optimum climatic conditions artificially has gone steadily forward. Russia is merely a conspicuous example of the process in our own time. Great as has been the improvement of man's relation to climate in that country, however, it is doubtful whether the Russian climate will ever become the optimum, no matter how great the future technological advances. Nevertheless, if atmospheric ozone is an important stimulant, Russia will presumably reap special benefit, because its cold winter air is well charged with that form of oxygen.

One other climatic condition may have played a significant part in Russia's recent metamorphosis. Table 18, prepared by Schell, shows the departure of the mean annual temperature from the normal at Leningrad, Moscow, Archangel, and Sverdlovsk by decades for 110 years. In all places there is clear evidence of an appreciable rise in temperature since 1870. The decade from 1931 to 1940 was even warmer than its predecessor, its temperature in Russia as a whole being 1.69°C (3.0°F) higher than that of 1831–1840.

TABLE 18

DEPARTURE OF TEMPERATURE (IN DEGREES CENTIGRADE) FROM NORMAL BY DECADES IN RUSSIA

(*after Schell*)

	Archangel	Leningrad	Moscow	Sverdlovsk	Average
1831–40	−0.49	−0.83	−0.33	....	−0.55
1841–50	+0.36	−0.23	−0.18	−0.35	−0.10
1851–60	+0.19	−0.01	−0.13	−0.17	−0.03
1861–70	−0.35	−0.46	−0.64	−0.03	−0.37
1871–80	−0.70	−0.52	−0.39	−0.14	−0.44
1881–90	−0.29	+0.08	−0.03	−0.15	−0.08
1891–1900	−0.67	−0.10	−0.11	−0.17	−0.24
1901–10	+0.02	+0.25	+0.23	+0.24	+0.19
1911–20	−0.10	+0.30	−0.21	+0.17	+0.09
1921–30	+0.58	+0.34	+0.39	+0.73	+0.51
1931–40	+1.42	+1.15	+1.19	+0.80	+1.14

At Sverdlovsk, which represents the great Ural region, the temperature has risen almost steadily for a century. At the other three places the increase has been less regular, but recent years have been the warmest since records were kept. An average difference of 1.7°C between the first and last decades of the table may seem small, but it equals the difference between New York and Baltimore. It is at least one tenth—some say one fifth—as great as the difference between the temperature at the height of the glacial period and now.

TABLE 19

SEASONAL EXCESS OF TEMPERATURE (IN DEGREES CENTIGRADE) IN RUSSIA IN
1931–40 COMPARED WITH 1871–80

(Average of Archangel, Leningrad, Moscow, and Sverdlovsk [Ekaterinburg], *after Köppen
and Geiger with additional data from Schell*)

January	0.3	May	2.0	September	1.8
February	1.3	June	1.8	October	1.1
March	0.7	July	2.2	November	2.1
April	2.2	August	2.3	December	2.1

Table 19 shows how seasonal temperatures changed from the 1870's to the 1930's. Every month shows some increase in temperature. The increase is greatest in summer when the crops most need warmth. It averages 2.1°C for the whole six months from April to September and also in the early winter. It helps to explain the success of the Russians in opening ocean transportation to the mouths of the Siberian rivers. The main reason for such success is doubtless the improvement in icebreakers, meteorological observations, and other aids to navigation, but the reduced thickness of the ice must not be overlooked. When Nansen's ship, the *Fram*, drifted across the Arctic Ocean in 1893–95 the voyage took 19 months, and the average thickness of the ice was 140 inches. When the Russian icebreaker, *Sedov*, drifted over practically the same course in 1939, the voyage took only 6 months, largely because the ice averaged only 86 inches in thickness.* Thus although the recent Russian outburst of energy is doubtless largely due to new ideas, it would be a mistake to overlook the actual change in temperature as well as the improved means of coping with cold weather.

* Dzerdzejevsky says that the yearly temperature at the time of the *Sedov's* journey averaged 3.9°C warmer than at the time of the *Fram*.

The weather records of Tables 18 and 19 bring up the problem of climatic cycles and their effect on history, but this will be deferred to a later chapter. The point to be emphasized now is that the optimum climate varies according to the stage of cultural development. Inventions of many sorts, from the earliest fire-drill to electric stoves, have persistently altered the climatic optimum. Hence the centers of progress have moved from regions with the most desirable temperature in winter to those where the summers have the most favorable temperature and the winters are not too cold to be made artificially comfortable.

CHAPTER 22

DIET AND NATIONAL CHARACTER

A. A Neglected Factor in History

Diet is as important as climate in determining health and vigor. Its influence, to be sure, is more local, so that it has less effect on the major features of the geographical distribution of civilization. Nevertheless, if we focus attention on diet alone, it almost seems to be the main factor in determining the level of efficiency in different parts of the world. In this respect it resembles heredity, climate, natural resources, cultural inventions, education, and psychological motivation. Each, when viewed close at hand without due perspective, seems to fill most of the horizon.

Everyone recognizes the importance of diet. Temporary hunger makes us irritable. Poorly fed people rarely accomplish much and are especially sensitive to disease. Increased use of milk, eggs, fresh vegetables, and fruit has improved the health and efficiency of millions of people. Nevertheless, even in the prosperous United States, tens of millions still suffer seriously from malnutrition. In China and India the great majority of people are undernourished. Van Paassen, writing of Holland, says that even in that advanced country many recruits shortly before World War II "were overjoyed to be in the army . . . [where] they could at least eat their fill and have meat more often than once a week. . . . I knew children who never saw a glass of milk. At home we never saw butter, only margarine, in that land of famous dairy farms."

From the standpoint of civilization and history the most important aspects of diet are as follows. (1) The quest for food has probably been the most potent of all forces in making people work and in encouraging early inventions. (2) Agriculture, which is the main method of obtaining food, has been of paramount importance in the early development and growth of the civilized mode of life. (3) Diet, through its effect on health and vigor, is one of the main factors in determining efficiency and thus has a great effect upon national character and progress. The first and second of these propositions deal with the indirect effects of food. Much more might be said about them, but they are familiar, and enough for our present purposes has been said in previous chapters. The third proposition also finds general acceptance, but the part played by diet in determining national character has not been sufficiently emphasized.

A few examples will illustrate the way in which diet influences both health and mental reactions under experimental conditions. Rose and Gray describe an institute for children where the diet was adequate in carbohydrates, fats, proteins, and bulk, but there was not much milk. An additional pint of fresh pasteurized milk per day for each child raised the average annual rate of growth during a period of 4 years from 3.9 to 6.9 pounds in weight and from 1.8 to 2.6 inches in height. A similar experiment by McCollum brings out the effect on mental alertness as well as health. In a well-run institution an additional daily quart of milk apiece made 42 children not only grow faster but become much more active, bright, and hard to manage than the remaining 200 who were not thus fed. After another such experiment the management actually reduced the milk on the excuse that this measure would make discipline easier.

Some idea of the effect of an insufficient, though otherwise excellent, diet on character may be obtained from a much quoted experiment carried on by Benedict and others at Springfield College, Massachusetts. Each of eleven students was restricted in food until his weight was reduced 10 per cent. Then for 3 months he ate just enough to keep his weight unchanged, but never as much as he wanted. A diminution of ability was found in the following tests: tracing of drawings, discrimination of musical pitch, cancelling numbers, addition, sensitivity to electrical stimulation, speed of movement of hand and eye, strength of grip, ability to maintain a low pulse rate under exertion, and capacity for improvement with practice at clerical tasks. Some capacities, such as memory, power of eye sight, and ability to find the right path in a maze were not affected, nor were reactions to words, numbers, and things seen, but no one knows what might result from more prolonged or more intense undernutrition. If the Chinese and Hindus, for example, respond in this same way to the deficient nutrition which frequently is their lot, the relative stagnation of their culture is partly explained.

Benedict found also that among his experimental subjects interest in sex diminished decidedly while they were underfed and revived with great strength when food was again eaten abundantly. This suggests a possible factor in the sexual excesses of India. The great majority of the people there suffer from lack of food at certain seasons, but at harvest time they suddenly have enough. Many other facts indicate that an inadequate diet, even if of high quality, not only weakens the majority of mental powers but may lead to unfavorable reactions when food is once more abundant. Our own ancestors in Europe frequently suffered from diets that were deficient either in quality or quantity, and the effect of this on history must have been great.

B. Diet and Physical Efficiency

Let us look at human groups larger than those of the experiments mentioned above. The Masai and Kikuyu, two African tribes, illustrate the difficulties which confront the investigator who tries to separate the effects of diet from those of other factors. These two kiths live side by side on the high and fairly cool plateau of Kenya astride the equator in central Africa. The Masai are pastoral nomads who travel about in the higher grasslands with their cattle, goats, donkeys, and sheep. They have the reputation of being great fighters, and their social organization is based on war. The dominant group is the young men, who are not allowed to marry until they have spent years as warriors. The Kikuyu are agriculturists, living in permanent villages. They have a much less favorable reputation than the Masai, being commonly considered less courageous, more treacherous, and in general less "noble."

The Masai are physically, as well as temperamentally, much superior to the Kikuyu. At age 25, according to Orr and Gilks, the Masai men are about 5 inches taller and 23 pounds heavier than the Kikuyus. The corresponding differences among women are 3 inches and 27 pounds. The Masai women, as measured by a dynamometer, are as strong as the Kikuyu men. The two kiths also have different diseases. The Kikuyu children, but not those of the Masai, suffer from rickets and anemia, both of which are due primarily to malnutrition. Deformed bones, which are often the normal result of rickets, are found among about 53 per cent of Kikuyu children in contrast to only 13 per cent of the Masai. The contrasting figures for certain other diseases are for anemia 43 and 10 percent, bronchitis 28 and 4, ulcers 33 and 3. The Masai, however, suffer greatly from constipation and arthritis, which are rare among the Kikuyu. Nevertheless, the Kikuyu are physically much worse off than the

Masai. Among 17,000 Kikuyu men called out officially as carriers, 65 per cent were at once rejected on medical grounds. After a hundred-mile march 17 per cent of those first accepted were rejected as physically unfit. No similar data are available for the Masai, but the general opinion is that the rejections would not be half as great.

The explanation of this combined mental and physical difference illustrates one of the most complicated and fundamental problems in the evolution of civilization. Orr and Gilks think that diet is far the most important factor, but heredity, climate, and culture must also be considered. The Masai are racially Hamitic, and the Kikuyu are Negroes of Bantu stock. This may account for the difference in physical build, but nobody knows how far it is responsible for the differences in health and mentality. Selection through the nomadic in contrast to the agricultural life may also have a good deal to do with the relative competence of these two African kiths. As for climate, the Masai—at least those now under discussion—live at a somewhat higher elevation and hence in a cooler and more stimulating climate than the Kikuyu, and this may influence their health and alertness. Culturally the contrasted occupations of animal husbandry and crop-raising lead to different ideals and habits, and each kith may also have its peculiar habits for still other reasons.

Even if these other factors play a large part in the contrast between the Masai and Kikuyu, the effect of diet must not be overlooked. The Masai live mainly on milk, but meat, including all the internal organs together with blood, is eaten as much as possible. The young warriors live wholly on milk, meat, and blood. The women, children, and older men also eat bananas, beans, millet, and maize. The Kikuyu eat these latter products, but have little meat or milk. Orr and Gilks estimate that in the men's diet 60 per cent consists of maize and millet and 25 per cent of sweet potatoes. Thus they have far too starchy a diet and lack vitamins. The women eat these same articles in large amounts but have a better diet than the men because they add legumes and plantains (bananas) quite liberally. They likewise have a virtual monopoly on green leaves, seeming to know that these with their vitamins are essential for the birth of healthy children. Taken as a whole, the Masai seem to have an advantage from the standpoint of vitamins and minerals, but no one knows how much of their superiority is attributable to these in comparison with heredity and climate. A similar difficulty in distinguishing among the effects of diverse factors is found all over the world.

C. *Diet and Health in India*

Let us consider an example in which the effect of diet can be quite definitely isolated. In order to do this we turn to experiments wherein the diets of different kiths in India were fed to animals. From the standpoint of diet India ranges from absolute vegetarians, who eat mainly rice, to nomadic tribes whose main food is milk and meat. One of the outstanding dietary experiments is that of Mc-Carrison.[1] Having separated healthy young white rats of the same closely inbred stock into seven groups of twenty each, as nearly similar as possible in age, weight, sex, and other characteristics, he fed each group on food selected and prepared according to the standard diet of the Indian kiths named in Table 20. All other conditions were the same for all groups, both before and during the experiment. Nevertheless, at the end of two and one-half months the average weight and percentage of increase varied as in Table 20.

TABLE 20

Growths of Rats on Indian Diets

(*after McCarrison*)

Diet	Average Final Weight in Grams	Average Percentage of Gain
Sikh	235	60
Pathan	230	58
Mahratta	225	54
Gurkha	200	40
Kanarese	185	35
Bengali	180	33
Madrasi	155	23

The Sikh diet proved so good that McCarrison [2] adopted it for his experimental rats. During five years, among rats averaging about one thousand in number,

there was no case of illness, no death from natural causes, no maternal mortality, no infantile mortality. It is true that the hygienic conditions . . . were ideal . . . but the same care was bestowed . . . on several thousand deficiently fed rats (of the same stock) which developed a wide variety of ailments. . . . It is clear, therefore, that it was to their food that this freedom was due. If man himself did not provide in his own person the proofs

[1] 1921, 1936. [2] 1936, p. 1060.

that a diet composed of whole cereals or a mixture of cereal grains, milk, milk products, pulses, and vegetables, with meat or eggs occasionally, sufficed for optimum efficiency, this experience with rats would do so. It is not, therefore, unreasonable to conclude that if by minute attention to three things—cleanliness, comfort, and food—it is possible to exclude disease from a colony of cloistered rats, it is possible greatly to reduce its incidence by the same means in human beings, and to produce a race whose physique is as nearly perfect as nature intended it to be.

The results of the Sikh diet contrast strongly with those of the diets of the Bengali and Madrasi. The Bengali diet consists mainly of rice, which is deficient in protein, fats, vitamins, and minerals, and is made still worse by being milled, polished, and then washed, so that even the vitamins and minerals contained in the dust of the husks are removed. Little milk is used. Gangulee [3] gives the annual consumption of all milk products in Bengal as equivalent to only eight gallons of fresh milk per capita in contrast to six times as much in the Punjab, the home of the Sikhs, and twelve times as much in the United States. Religious scruples, as well as overpopulation and great seasonal extremes of heat, rain, and drought, reduce meat consumption to a low level. Fresh vegetables and fruit enter into the diet only sparingly, largely because of inertia on the part of the people. The Madrasi diet differs only a little from this and has a similar effect.

In another experiment McCarrison fed one group of rats on the Sikh diet and

the other on a diet such as is commonly used by the poorer classes in England . . . white bread, margarine, over-sweetened tea with a little milk (of which the rats consumed large quantities), boiled cabbage and boiled potato, tinned meat and tinned jam of the cheaper sorts. This has many faults, of which vitamin and mineral deficiencies are the chief. . . . Members of the well-fed group lived happily together. They increased in weight and flourished. . . . The other group did not increase in weight . . . they were badly proportioned; their coats were . . . lacking in gloss; they were nervous and apt to bite the attendants; they lived unhappily together and by the sixtieth day . . . began to kill and eat the weaker ones amongst them.

It was therefore necessary to segregate them. At the end of 190 days, corresponding to about 16 years of human life, the survivors of both groups were killed. Postmortem examination showed that among the rats fed on the poor British diet two were afflicted with polyneuritis,

[3] p. 312.

a nervous disease due to deficiency in vitamin B_1, and many with diseases of the lungs, stomach, and intestines. The rats on the Sikh diet suffered only from pneumonia, but even from that only half as often as the others.

Contrasts associated with these different diets are seen in people's susceptibility to disease as well as in the growth of rats. Deathrates from pulmonary tuberculosis, leprosy, beri-beri, gastric ulcer, and diarrhea and dysentery are high with poor diets and low with good. Heart diseases, as well as rickets, are four times as common in southerly Madras as in the Punjab, 20° farther north. Diabetes and mental diseases are three times as common, and other ailments show a corresponding increase in frequency. A large number of diseases which depend more or less directly on nutrition are excessively common where the diet is bad. The contrasted effects of these different kinds of diets caused McCarrison to believe that "the level of physical efficiency of Indian races is, above all else, a matter of food. No other single factor—race, climate, endemic disease, etc.—has so profound an influence on their physique, and on their capacity to sustain arduous labor and prolonged muscular exertion."

This statement may seem extreme when we consider the depressing effect of damp heat and the tremendous ravages of malaria. Moreover, it must not be overlooked that infant mortality is higher in the north of India than in the south, probably because of the intense summer heat and the dust and bacteria which are blown far and wide in the dry season. Malaria, too, is especially bad in the north because of stagnant pools. Then, too, climate must be considered. In Britain, for example, although people are much better fed than in Madras, there is about three times as much tuberculosis. These other factors, however, can scarcely explain the great contrast between northern and southern India, especially in leprosy, beri-beri, and ulcers of the digestive tract. Even when the fullest allowance is made for all these circumstances, there can be little doubt that McCarrison's conclusions contain a truth which is of the utmost importance in the evolution of civilization and the course of history.

D. Diet and Mental Alertness

From the standpoint of civilization our interest extends beyond physical health to mental efficiency. Are we justified in thinking that diet has any such effect upon mental alertness as it appears to have upon the health of both men and rats? Experiments such as have just been described should be considered in connection with a statement made long ago by McCay: [4]

As we pass from the Northwest region of the Punjab [where live the Sikhs] down the Gangetic Plain to the Coast of Bengal [where live the people whose diet proved almost the worst for the rats], there is a gradual fall in the stature, body-weight, stamina and efficiency of the people. In accordance with this decline in manly characteristics it is of the utmost significance that there is an accompanying gradual fall in the nutritive value of the dietaries.

In order more clearly to evaluate the effect upon character properly ascribable to diet in comparison with other factors, let us examine the qualities which make good soldiers. We will take the seven kiths whose diets were used for McCarrison's rats, and will see what is said about them in four authoritative sources: the *Imperial Gazetteer of India,* the *Cambridge History of India,* the *Encyclopædia Britannica,* and Balfour's *Encyclopaedia of India.* In doing this let us concentrate on two points: first, evidence as to the relative rank of the kiths as soldiers, and second, the causes to which the observed characteristics are consciously or unconsciously assigned by the reference books. Bear in mind that for two centuries, as the *Encyclopædia Britannica* [5] puts it, the various Indian kiths have been "exhaustively studied" in order that the native army may be

filled more definitely than heretofore by the martial classes and races . . . while the less warlike races were largely eliminated. . . . In the immense population of India the number of men of martial proclivities and even of personal courage is a very small proportion of the whole. For instance, the entire Sikh community [which provides a large percentage of soldiers] . . . barely numbers three million. . . . The great mass of the people, educated and otherwise, are quite devoid of any martial potentiality.

As a result of this prolonged study "the Native Army consists of the pick of the manhood of the various indigenous races."

Among these picked men the most pre-eminent are the Sikhs, who live mainly in northern India, especially the Punjab. Before World War II they were found not only in the Indian Army, but serving as haughty policemen in distant cities such as Singapore and Hong Kong. They defeated the Gurkhas in 1809 and are often considered the only Indian troops able to stand against the Pathans on the Afghan frontier. How good all three of these kiths are as soldiers may be judged from a statement in the *Cambridge History of India:* "One

4 1910, 1911.   5 1929 edition, "India: Defense."

of the most interesting and satisfactory conclusions reached by critics who studied the conduct of various classes in [World War I] . . . related to classes regarded as respectable soldiers, but not in the first rank [the first rank being British, Germans, Australians, Americans, etc.]. Of Pathans, Gurkhas, Punjabi Musilmans, and Sikhs much was expected, nor did they disappoint their advocates." The Sikh, says Balfour, "owes his excellence as a soldier to his own hardihood of character [inheritance?], to that spirit of adaptation which distinguishes every new people [selection like that of the Puritans], and to that feeling of common interest and destiny implanted in him by his great teachers [the inspiration of a cultural system?]."

The *Imperial Gazetteer,* likewise, hints at a biological quality in the bravery of the Sikhs, but lays more stress on education through difficulties:

Founded as a religious community, towards the end of the fifteenth century, by Nanak . . . based on monotheistic worship, absence of forms, ceremonies, and castes, and the equal acceptance of good Hindus and Mohammedans by God, Sikhism was at first a blending and union of the best in opposing creeds [religious selection]. But in the course of a century the persecution of the Mohammedans converted this peaceful sect into a military and religious commonwealth of magnificent fighting men . . . [which] became a most formidable instrument of war, and only terminated its splendid career after fighting six pitched battles with the British. The admirable qualities of the soldiers of this army were innate . . . [British generals] did something towards the training of the troops, but the material and the martial ability were already there [biological inheritance]. . . . [The Sikhs] and their descendants have proved to be the finest and most loyal soldiers of the native army, second to none in the whole empire for constancy, fidelity, and military prowess.

The Moslem "hillmen" known as Pathans, whose diet appears to be almost as good as that of the Sikhs, live in northwestern India on the Afghan border. They are not praised by our four authorities quite as much as the Sikhs. This is largely because writers on India tell mainly of wars waged against the Pathans rather than with their co-operation. It is universally recognized that these admirable fighters are so bold that one of Britain's great problems has been to check their fierce raids on the lowlands near the Afghan frontier. They are more or less nomadic keepers of sheep among the mountains. The *Cambridge History* emphasizes the strictness and vigor with which they carry out the three main provisions of their code of honor: (1)

the right of fugitives to asylum and protection; (2) open-hearted hospitality, even toward enemies; (3) revenge for insults and injuries,
with consequent blood feuds that last a long time. In general the
Pathans have the qualities which are normally associated with nomadic or semi-nomadic keepers of flocks and herds. Their raids are
like those of other nomads whom we have already studied. Our previous conclusions as to the effect of selection and mode of life upon
the character of nomads apply closely to the Pathans.

The Gurkhas, "the warlike race of Nepal" in the lower Himalayas
north of eastern India, are reported by Balfour as seeing "in foreign
service nothing but the prospect of glory and spoil. Their individual
courage is represented as not more remarkable than their innate sense
of discipline. They possess all that individual confidence each in all,
which grows out of national victory and success. Wherever there has
been fighting on the Indian frontiers ever since . . . 1838, these hardy
troops have rendered the most valuable service." The *Cambridge
History* says that this "warlike race of hardy hillmen . . . provided
the finest native troops of India" in the days before the Mutiny of
1857. We have already seen that they are ranked with the Sikhs
and Pathans by experts who studied World War I. How highly they
are esteemed in India is evident from the fact that while the usual
minimum height for native Indian troops has been five feet, four
inches, this figure is reduced to five feet for Gurkhas so that a goodly
number of these small mountaineers may enlist.

In McCarrison's experiment the Mahratta diet almost equalled the
Pathan diet and was well above the Gurkha diet. Nevertheless, in
this discussion of character the Mahrattas are placed after the Gurkhas, because that is where they seem to belong as soldiers. Their
home is on the Deccan Plateau east or southeast of Bombay. The
same experts who praise the Sikhs, Pathans and Gurkhas for their
work as soldiers in World War I say that the Mahrattas "displayed a
fine fighting spirit," but the implication is that they did not quite
equal the others. Balfour says that these people of the Indian plateau southeast of Bombay are "good, hardy, active soldiers, capable
of endurance." In war a Mahratta soldier thinks "of nothing but
the result. . . . For this he would strain his wits, renounce his pleasures, and hazard his person." The *Imperial Gazetteer* says that when
the Mahrattas overran India at the end of the eighteenth century,
"constant war had turned a race of husbandmen inhabiting a hilly
region into predatory soldiers. Hardy and active, small in stature

but wiry . . . they ravaged nearly every part of India. . . . But the Mahrattas were not soldiers by reason of inherited qualities . . . and it is now not easy to draw from this race even the limited number of soldiers that we require."

The three kiths whose diets proved least favorable when fed to McCarrison's rats belong to the vast section of the Indian population which is considered unwarlike. Balfour speaks of the "non-resistance" of the Kanarese. He says that in all the great armies which the British have formed during the past century, not more than a few thousand of this kith have become soldiers. For two or three centuries armies seem to have crossed their country in the southwestern part of the Indian peninsula without opposition.

Bengal, where the Ganges and Brahmaputra rivers form their great delta, is dismissed with even less praise than Kanara. It is "inhabited by a population traditionally unwarlike and apathetic."[6] For this reason, apparently, it has in the past been far more subject to brigandage than most sections of India. "Its people are for the most part, as Lord Canning said,[7] "less warlike and turbulent than those of Upper India" [where live the Sikhs and Pathans] . . . . Large sections of them are timid, apathetic, and peculiarly susceptible to the domination of unscrupulous terrorism." Balfour goes still farther:

> Though good looking, the mass of the Bengali are small and effeminate in appearance, remarkable for timidity and superstition, as well as for subtlety and art. . . . During many ages the Bengali has been trampled upon by men of bolder and more hardy breeds. Courage, independence and veracity are qualities to which his constitution and his situation are equally unfavorable. His mind is weak, even to helplessness, for purposes of resistance, but its suppleness and its tact move the children of sterner climates to admiration, not unmixed with contempt. . . . All [Bengal's] millions do not furnish one sepoy to the native army.

Finally we come to the Madrasis of the southeast coast of India. Speaking of early times when the British did not yet understand the great differences in the warlike qualities of the various Indian kiths, the *Cambridge History*[8] says that the Madrasi troops from the northern circars "were inferior both in discipline and courage to the Carnatic battalions (Kanarese). . . . Nevertheless the poor quality of the recruits obtainable even in the Carnatic was noticed as early as 1788,

---

[6] *Cambridge History*, vol. 6, p. 21. [8] Vol. 6, p. 157.
[7] *Ibid.*, p. 36.

and in 1795 the Madras government proposed to draw recruits . . . from Bengal and Bombay . . . but the scheme was an utter failure. . . . It was found impossible to keep the Bengal recruits with the colors."

Although it is easy to criticise such offhand appraisals of entire kiths, it is clear that there is a vast difference in character between Sikhs, Pathans, and Gurkhas, on the one hand, and Kanarese, Bengalis, and Madrasis, on the other. Within each kith, of course, there are wide variations among individuals. Moreover, in non-military characteristics the relative rank is by no means the same as in the qualities needed by soldiers. The Bengalis, or at least their higher castes, are generally regarded as among the most mentally alert people of India. Nevertheless, after two centuries of trial the British military authorities are practically unanimous in believing that the northern people of India, especially certain kiths, make good soldiers, whereas the southerners and the eastern Bengalis make poor ones. It is also clear that this contrast is much like the contrast in the diets of these various kiths. If diet influences people in essentially the same way that it does rats, as physiologists generally agree, the diets of the northern and southern kiths would cause a marked contrast in physical vigor, even if all other circumstances were uniform. Such a contrast is bound to show itself in temperament. Almost everyone is braver, more aggressive, and more venturesome when he feels fully fit than when he feels ill or merely below par.

In spite of this general agreement between diet and soldierly qualities, the rate of growth on various diets (Table 20) does not rank the seven kiths in the order which seems correct on the basis of soldierly quality. The Gurkhas apparently belong with the Sikhs and Pathans, and it is impossible to determine which kith stands highest. This is the more remarkable in view of the small size of the Gurkhas. Thus other factors seem to be at work. One of these is probably climate. As nearly as can now be determined, the Gurkhas live in the best of the climates inhabited by the seven Indian kiths. Let us assume for the moment that all the people of India are sufficiently inured to heat so that any monthly temperature averaging 73°F or less seems comfortable or is stimulating if it is too cool for comfort. We will also give the hot places an advantage by supposing that an average of 74° is comfortable with less than 3 inches of rain, 75° with less than 2 inches, and 76° with less than 1 inch. On this basis the yearly number of comfortable or stimulating months is approximately as in column *C* of Table 21. Columns *A* and *B* show the rank and percentage of gain in the diet table.

TABLE 21

Dietary and Climatic Rank of Indian Kiths

	A	*B*	*C*
	Per Diet Table		
	Rank	Per Cent Gain	Number of Comfortable Months
Gurkhas	4	40	8–10 months or even more at higher levels
Pathans	2	58	7–9 months according to height of mountain homes
Mahrattas	3	54	6–7 months according to altitude of Deccan Plateau
Sikhs	1	60	6 months, with remainder of year excessively hot
Bengalis	6	33	4 months, but these 4 quite good
Kanarese	5	35	3 or 4 months
Madrasis	7	23	1 month

We see at once that, whereas the diet of the Gurkhas would lead us to expect them to rank more like the Kanarese and Bengalis than like the Sikhs and Pathans, the climate introduces a factor which helps to explain why as soldiers they actually stand on about the same level as the Sikhs and Pathans, in spite of their small stature.

Still another factor, namely, selection or kithal heredity, must be considered, but no numerical values can be given to this. We can only point out two facts. First, the Pathans, as already stated, appear to have been subjected for many generations to the selective action which makes nomads and mountaineers especially vigorous. Second, the Sikhs are the only one of these kiths that has experienced any appreciable selection similar to that of the Puritans and Icelanders. That an important religious selection took place among them in early days seems clear. People do not accept a new faith unless there is something in their temperament which responds to that faith. The temperament which chooses to join the Salvation Army is by no means the same as that which prompts people to become Unitarians or Roman Catholics. Most of the original Sikhs were Jats, that is, members of the Rajput warrior caste who settled on the land as cultivators. Moreover, after the Sikhs became known as a fighting race, it seems probable that later converts were people who had more or less of the fighting spirit. From such facts we conclude that in India, and presumably elsewhere, the degree to which kiths produce good soldiers depends on innate quality plus physical vigor. Physical vigor in turn depends to a high degree upon the direct effect of diet and upon its indirect effect through disease, but it is also much modified by climate and heredity. Diet, in turn, depends to a large degree upon climate, but also upon stage of culture, and so does disease, either directly or indirectly.

Finally another factor enters into the picture, namely, the social system with its habits regarding food, clothing, and shelter, and its ideals as to what is good form. The Bengalis, Madrasis, and Kanarese would doubtless have better health if their religion did not forbid them to eat meat. A removal of this prohibition, however, and a complete change of heart in the matter would not do much to make their diet as good as that of the people of the Punjab. The reason is simply that their climate, with its prolonged hot, humid weather and consequent huge grasses as big and tough as reeds, is not favorable for cattle. Even if there are plenty of cattle, neither their milk nor their flesh is as nutritious in Bengal as in northern India for the simple reason that the moist heat permits rapid weathering of the soil, and the heavy rains leach out the minerals almost as fast as they decay and become soluble. Actual analysis shows that in Bengal average cow's milk contains only 30 or 40 per cent as much ascorbic acid (vitamin C) as in England. Thus we see that the Hindu reverence for cattle reaches its greatest force and is most strictly applied in regions where cattle are of relatively low value for food. It seems safe to say that if Hinduism could become established in a region such as England, which is pre-eminently favorable for cattle, the religious prohibition of the use of beef would almost certainly soon be modified. Almost any belief or custom can be introduced into almost any part of the world, but the degree to which it is accepted and the length of time that it persists are greatly influenced by its adaptation to the physical environment.

Examples of the effect of diet on physical and mental vigor might be multiplied indefinitely. Everywhere the well-fed people tend to be more vigorous than those who are poorly fed, as everyone recognizes. What we do not yet recognize so clearly is that in the long run and when large numbers of people are averaged together, diet has a profound effect upon mental activity. The better-fed people are alert, aggressive, adaptable, and even original to a much greater degree than their poorly fed comrades. This is evident enough in armies. The old saying that an army marches on its belly is true. But it is also true that if an army is well fed for years before it has to fight—yes, if its parents, too, have been well fed—it has a great advantage over one that is well fed only in time of war. Military leaders all over the world now recognize the necessity for good food in the army. Nevertheless, most people still fail to realize that the diet that has prevailed for generations is one of the major factors in determining the character of nations and kiths and in settling the fate of wars and the rate of human progress.

CHAPTER 23

AGRICULTURE, DISEASE, AND DIET

A. *The Nature of Primitive Diets*

Agriculture has been a powerful factor in lowering human efficiency as well as in advancing civilization. Is this surprising? It should not be, for practically every great step of progress is accompanied by drawbacks which are not rectified for a long time. The greatest and most revolutionary advances entail the greatest dangers. Motor transportation has brought an appalling deathrate from accidents and frightful ravages in war. Power-driven machinery accentuated the overcrowding of cities and the horrors of slums and has had much to do with the practical extermination of some of the best human stocks because of the low urban birthrate. In the same way agriculture, especially through its relation to overpopulation, diet, and health, has brought vast evils whereby large parts of the world are devastated.

From the standpoint of physical fitness the most pitiful parts of the world are relatively warm countries with dense populations engaged almost exclusively in agriculture. India, China, Egypt, and even Japan illustrate this, as do many tropical regions in Africa and South America. In such countries misshapen jaws, defective eyes, clubfeet, open sores, and a host of diseases have an especially strong effect in reducing human efficiency. The conditions there are much worse than among either the most advanced people or the more primitive types that live by hunting, fishing, and the gathering of wild products. The well-proportioned bodies and comparative health of the South Sea Islanders before the coming of the white man, for example, are largely responsible for the cult of the "noble savage"—the idea that a return to the simple life of his primitive ancestors would remove most of man's troubles. The way to get rid of these, however, is not to turn back the march of civilization, but to learn why troubles exist and then correct them. The first requisite is knowledge. The second is education so that the knowledge may be converted into practical application.

The most important effect of agriculture on efficiency probably arises from malnutrition. We have seen how much of the backwardness and misery of India, for example, is due to this cause. One of the main reasons for poor nutrition is that agriculture has lowered the quality of man's diet and at the same time made it possible for far more people to subsist. Mechanical methods of preparing food have gone still further along this same sad path until the typical "modernized" diet has become appallingly poor. By "modernized" we do not mean the diet now eaten by the more intelligent and prosperous people of Europe and America, but the kind that is still eaten there by people at the lower economic levels and in many other countries by the great majority of the population. In such a diet, bread, cereals, potatoes, and other forms of starchy food play a dominant part; the rest is largely composed of protein foods, such as beans, together with carbohydrates in the form of sugar and vegetable oils. Such a diet is far from ideal.

The ideal diet, it would seem, must be essentially that to which man became adjusted during his long, slow evolution. Among most of the ancestors of modern Europeans and Americans an agricultural diet has prevailed less than two thousand years. There is no reliable evidence that in that brief span any appreciable change has occurred in the inherited dietary requirements which had become established during a preceding period perhaps a thousand times longer. One reason for believing this is that other omniverous animals, such as rats, show similar requirements. Yerkes has shown that, although chimpanzees are normally vegetarians, they thrive on the same kind of all-round diet that is best for man. As we learn more about diet, the ideal keeps swinging nearer to the essential features of the primitive type, except perhaps in respect to cooking. The prolonged use of fire may have given us a biological adjustment to food that is cooked.

What, then, was the primitive diet which man has replaced by a new type based on agriculture and has recently modified by modern machinery. The keynotes of such a diet are: (1) the entire consumption of each article of food in a fresh condition, (2) a great variety of kinds of food, and (3) food grown in natural soils where there has been little deterioration due to prolonged cropping and to the wastage of plant foods arising from the erosion of upturned soil by rain and wind. Any animal that was killed was eaten at once either raw or only slightly cooked. Every part was consumed, including the internal organs, the walls of the stomach and intestines, the brain, and the marrow of the bones. This custom still prevails quite widely, although not among great numbers of people. For example, as a guest of nomadic Khirghiz in Central Asia I have shared in a feast consisting entirely of sour milk, mutton broth, a few little cubes of bread fried like doughnuts, and a huge wooden-bowl of boiled mutton. On top of the meat lay the most prized part of the feast, a boiled sheep's head. As a kind of dessert for our meal, the host gouged out an eye and gave it to me as the greatest delicacy. The next in honor ate the other eye, and the rest ate tongue, brains, and ears—everything except the skull. The eye tastes rather gluey, but it contains an unusually high proportion of vitamin A and is actually about as good food as can be found.

Let us return to the subject of primitive diets. If nuts are ripe, the savages eat them until they can eat no more. In parts of Africa, if locusts or grasshoppers plague the land, they are eaten fresh, just as are juicy white grubs by Australian aborigines, and slimy raw oysters by fashionable clubmen. Sometimes the locusts are dried, ground to flour, and later made into a kind of bread which is affirmed to be tasty by missionaries who have had the courage to eat it. If a patch of some wild cereal is turning yellow, its milky seeds, still rich in vitamins, are eaten in large quantities, hulls and all, before they are ripe as well as afterward. The more primitive Arabs in Palestine sometimes offer a guest green heads of wheat, toasted over a fire. I can testify that they are good. At other times our primitive ancestors ate a field mouse here, a little bulb there, then perhaps a small fish, some berries, or the stem of a succulent plant.

The general character of a primitive diet may be summed up as follows: (1) both plants and animals are eaten according to the exigencies of the moment; (2) the larger meals generally consist of only one article; (3) unless they are prohibitively rough or hard, all parts of that article, whatever it may be, are almost invariably eaten; (4) when large quantities of a single article are not available, small amounts of many varied kinds are eaten at frequent intervals, and such food, even more than the larger supplies, is consumed in its entirety; (5) all kinds of food are eaten fresh and with little or no cooking; (6) vegetable foods are likely to be eaten as soon as they are mature enough to be edible, although seeds and nuts are also eaten long after they have become dry and hard; (7) the intervals between meals are variable in length, often only an hour or two, but sometimes a day or more. It is interesting to see that modern research is in many ways taking us back to these primitive conditions as the ideal. Haggard and Greenberg, for example, say that the maximum capacity for work is attained with small meals every few hours. Another school of thought advocates eating only one main type of food at a time; for example, protein food at one meal and starchy foods at another. There seems, however, to be almost full agreement that in the long run a combination of all kinds of food is the ideal, including plenty of carbohydrates to produce calories of energy, plenty of proteins to aid in growth and the replacement of tissues, and plenty of vitamins and minerals to cause the glandular system and the blood to function properly. All this leads to the modern idea of basic foods, such as the cereals, to provide energy and heat, and protective foods, such as milk, meat, eggs, fresh vegetables, and fresh fruits, to provide bulk as well as vitamins and minerals.

B. Modern Requirements in Diet [1]

Let us see what all this means in terms of modern science. Stiebling and Ware say that a diet is not really well balanced unless about 53 per cent of its calories are derived from the protective types of food. Contrast this with the diet of China where Buck's [2] careful studies indicate that only 4 per cent is thus derived. For China as a whole cereals supply approximately 83 per cent of the energy derived from food. Dry legumes, such as beans and peas, together with vegetable oils derived from soybeans, cottonseed, sesame, and other sources, supply another 9 per cent. Sweet potatoes and similar starchy roots account for 4 per cent. All these together total 96 per cent. Of the remaining 4 per cent all animal products—milk, meat, and eggs—contribute 2.3 per cent, green vegetables about 1 per cent, and fruits only a fraction of 1 per cent.

The main reason for the extreme inadequacy of the Chinese diet is lack of land, or rather, overpopulation. China has three or four times as many people as it can feed on a good diet. Such a diet requires several times as much land and labor as a diet composed mainly of rice, wheat, or corn, with beans, for example. In overpopulated countries there is not space enough to raise such a diet. What little land a farmer has must be devoted almost exclusively to the crops which will supply at least a fair amount of protein in addition to a large amount of carbohydrates. In India, China, and Japan, and even among the poorer people in many European coun-

[1] Huntington, 1943.   [2] pp. 410–11.

tries the farmer who devotes an acre or two of land to fresh vegetables and fruit to be used by his family, or who raises cows so as to have a steady supply of milk for his children, is likely to find that he has not enough wheat, rye, rice, potatoes, or dry beans to keep his family supplied with calory-producing foods throughout the winter. Or if he raises fruit, vegetables, milk, and eggs, he feels obliged to sell most of them to the more prosperous city people. If his family eats them, there will be no money with which to pay for clothes, tools, and taxes.

Hundreds of millions of farm families are forced to base their plans upon the assumption that the order of importance in diet is, first, carbohydrates to supply heat and energy, second, proteins, and only third, and far behind, the protective foods that furnish vitamins, acids, and minerals. Sometimes, as in Japan, this order of importance and the consequent failure in the third respect are due to lack of land; sometimes, as in much of the USSR, to limitation in the kinds of crops that can be raised, or to the shortness of the growing season and the consequent inability to cultivate more than a few acres or raise more than a small crop per acre. Sometimes they are due to the fact that poor soil or a dry climate leads to such poor yields per acre that a large area has to be cultivated in order merely to raise enough of the main starchy foods and proteins. Deterioration of the soil through the removal of the upper nitrate-bearing layer by rain and wind also lowers the amount of both minerals and vitamins in the crops. Undue repetition of the same crop without fertilization has a similar effect. This is especially common in the tropics, where the soil is badly leached because of heat and heavy rain and loses much of its good quality after a few crops have been taken off. The evils thus arising are aggravated because the most slipshod agricultural practices generally prevail just where the soil and climate have the worst effect on the crops. In many regions the diet is defective in protective foods largely because of inertia and disinclination to work, which are due not only to a debilitating climate, but to a poor diet which could be remedied if the farmers felt more energetic.

Most unfortunately a good diet is expensive. It demands more land and more labor than a poor diet and more expense for transportation and storage. Some idea of its expensiveness may be gained from Table 22, in which M. K. Bennett shows the relative cost of the amount of food of other kinds which will supply the same number of calories of energy as one dollar's worth of wheat in the United States or of rye in Germany. In the United States it costs fifteen

TABLE 22

INDEX NUMBERS OF RELATIVE COSTS OF TYPES OF FOOD

	United States	Germany
Wheat or rye	$ 1.00	$ 1.00
Lard	1.24	1.65
Sugar	1.43	1.35
Milk	8.00	3.00
Inferior cuts of meat	11.00	10.00
Eggs	15.00	9.00
Cabbage	17.00	10.00

times as much, for example, to get a day's calories from eggs as from wheat. On a calorie basis, potatoes, rye, corn, and millet cost less than wheat, whereas most kinds of fruit and vegetables cost more than cabbage.

C. The Diet of the Nations

The great importance of diet renders it worth while to make a statistical comparison of the diets of various countries. The best method yet available seems to be based on the percentage of the protective foods. Statistics for these foods are by no means so accurate as those for the cereals and potatoes, but they give at least a correct general picture. We shall use three methods. First, the League of Nations has published tables giving the per capita consumption of five main types of protective foods. These show, for example, that the annual consumption of milk in all forms, including butter and cheese, ranges from about 1 gallon for the average person in Japan to 20 in Rumania, 50 in Poland, 80 in the United States, Belgium, and Germany, and 144 in Finland. The consumption of meat runs all the way from only one or two pounds per person each year in much of India to 35 in Italy, 80 in Sweden, 135 to 140 in Great Britain and the United States, and 236 in New Zealand. Eggs show a similar variation from 40 or so per year in Egypt and Russia up to 100 in Holland, more than 200 in the United States, 300 in Canada, and actually 400 in Ireland. The figures for fruits and vegetables are not so accurate as for animal products. Nevertheless, we have such facts as these: practically no bananas are imported into Russia in normal times in contrast to about 10 pounds per capita in France, 15 in England, and 30 or so in the United States. The average person in the United States, including all ages, uses about 150 pounds of fresh vegetables each year and about 200 pounds of fruit, whereas in Italy the corresponding figures are about 40 and 90, and in India much less.

Another method of measuring diet is to calculate the value of the average diet per person if prices were everywhere the same. On the basis of prices in England from 1925 to 1934, Colin Clark finds that the values range all the way from $22 in Japan and $23 in the USSR to $88 in Argentina. India, and especially China, fall considerably below Japan. The United States stands at $64, on a par with Australia and slightly above France and Switzerland. Anything above $60 is considered ample. Inasmuch as the average value of a year's food in the Scandinavian countries, Great Britain, and Germany ranges not far from $50, those countries are apparently not sufficiently well fed. Argentina ($88), New Zealand ($81), Uruguay ($77), and Canada ($76) rank high because they consume much meat, but it is doubtful whether their diet as a whole warrants such high ratings.

TABLE 23

DIET OF ECONOMIC CLASSES IN ENGLAND

Approximate farm cost of food for one person for one year in dollars (*after Colin Clark*)

| | Classes of Society | | | | | | Ratio |
	I	II	III	IV	V	VI	I/VI
Wheat products, cereals	3.4	3.5	3.5	3.5	3.4	3.1	0.91
Potatoes	2.6	2.7	2.8	2.8	2.8	2.6	1.00
Sugar	1.9	2.2	2.5	2.7	2.8	2.9	1.52
Tea, etc.	2.1	2.6	2.8	2.9	2.8	2.6	1.24
Total non-protective foods	10.0	11.0	11.6	11.9	11.8	11.2	1.12
Milk and milk products	6.9	12.7	14.8	16.8	19.2	21.9	3.18
Meat	12.4	16.8	19.8	22.3	24.2	26.4	2.12
Eggs	1.4	2.0	2.5	3.0	3.4	4.3	3.07
Fruits and vegetables	2.1	3.8	5.6	7.8	10.3	15.1	7.20
Total protective foods	22.8	35.3	42.7	49.9	57.1	67.7	2.96
Grand total	32.8	46.3	53.3	61.8	68.0	78.9	2.40

Some idea of the nature of the diets which cost different amounts can be gained from Table 23, which Clark has taken from official data. It shows the relative costs of the various types of food entering into the diet of six classes of people in England. Class I comprises the poorest 10 per cent of the population and Class VI the wealthiest 10 per cent. Each of the intermediate classes contains 20 per cent. The ratios in the last column show how the consumption of different types of food by Class VI compares with that of Class I. The prosperous, well-fed people of Class VI eat only 91 per cent as much wheat and other cereals as the poor people of Class I, but they eat fruit and vegetables which cost more than seven times as much (7.20).

Number IV in this table represents approximately the average for the United States; Great Britain and Germany fall between II and III; Poland and Czechoslovakia are intermediate between I and II. In Japan and Russia the average level of diet falls below the level of the most poorly fed 10 per cent in England (I). In India and China the conditions are still worse. There the non-protective foods probably have about the same value per person as in England, but the protective foods probably fall below $5 on an average, not half as much as among the most poorly fed 10 per cent in England. It will be noticed that in England the value of the non-protective starchy foods is about the same for all economic classes but reaches a slight maximum in Class IV. That class represents people who are comfortable but not well-to-do. Among people with more money, the consumption of non-protective foods actually declines, their place being taken by milk, meat, eggs, fruits, and vegetables. The average well-fed American can scarcely realize how much his work would deteriorate and his liability to disease increase if his sixty dollars' worth of protective foods per year were reduced to five or ten dollars' worth as in China or India.

Still another method of determining the value of the diet in different parts of the world has been based by M. K. Bennett on the calories of energy in the food consumed by the average man at ordinary work. This differs considerably from country to country, according to the stature and weight of the people, the climate, and the degree of wealth—for example, Java, 2,607 calories; India, 3,122; Italy, 3,709; Great Britain, 3,965; the United States, 4,022. On the basis of the calories in its customary diet and the percentage of adults and children in the population, Bennett estimates the approximate number of calories in the total food supply of each country. Inasmuch as good statistics are available for the non-protective foods (chiefly cereals and potatoes), the number of calories which they provide can easily be determined. The difference between this figure and the estimated total requirement must consist almost entirely of protective foods, together with sugar and vegetable oils. The percentage of the diet formed by these non-starchy foods, which are neither cereals nor potatoes, provides a rough measure of the quality of a diet. This method has the advantage of being free from reliance on imperfect statistics for fruit and vegetables, but has the disadvantage of relying on equally imperfect estimates as to the calories supplied by the average diet in most countries.

In order to get the best possible estimates of diet in the world as a whole the three methods described above have been combined in Table 24. From the data supplied by the League of Nations, two sets of index numbers have been calculated. Both, of course, include cereals, sugar, potatoes, etc., but one is based also on milk, meat, and eggs, for which the statistics are fairly good; the other on these three types of food plus fresh vegetables and fruits, for which the statistics are poor. The methods of Clark and Bennett have each been used for a similar set of index numbers. Fortunately all four sets show essentially the same general conditions, although there are discrepancies in detail. Table 24 gives the results when the four are combined in such a way that each has approximately the same weight.

This significant table shows that four new English-speaking countries are the best-fed parts of the world. If diet alone determined vigor, New Zealand, Canada, the United States, and Australia would show the greatest energy. One other new country, Argentina, also stands high, and Uruguay may come in the same class, but both countries consume too much meat in comparison with vegetables and fruit. The fact that Great Britain, as well as Switzerland, follows close after Australia makes it clear that under normal conditions the English-speaking parts of the world hold an almost unrivalled position in diet. The next seven countries (Nos. 8 to 14) form a compact group along the west coast of Europe from France through Belgium and Holland to Scandinavia. These, as well as Britain, are countries where the climate is especially favorable to cattle, so that milk is abundant and there is a good supply of meat. Vegetables grow well in the more southern parts. The close resemblance between the distribution of a good diet and an invigorating climate is worth noting, but differences due to density of population, as in Argentina and Japan, for example, are in evidence.

Below France in Table 24 we find five countries which hang on the outskirts of the preceding group and have climates with greater extremes of one sort or another. Hence they are not so favorable to a wide range of protective foods. Austria and Czechoslovakia are excellent for fruits and vegetables but are not quite such good cattle

TABLE 24

Index Numbers of Diet

(Numbers in parentheses indicate how many of the four types of index numbers are available when one or more is missing.)

America and Oceania		*Europe*		*Asia and Africa*	
1. New Zealand	100				
2. Canada	97				
3. United States	92				
4. Australia	92				
————		5. Switzerland	86		
		6. Great Britain	83		
7. Argentina (2)	80	————			
————		8. Sweden	78		
————		9. Belgium	76		
————		10. Denmark (3)	75		
————		11. Norway (3)	74		
————		12. Germany	71		
————		13. Netherlands	70		
————		14. France	70		
————		15. Austria (3)	68		
————		16. Finland	68		
————		17. Czechoslovakia	66		
————		18. Ireland (1)	61		
20. Mexico (1)	57	19. Estonia (2)	59		
21. Chile (1)	56	————			
		22. Italy	47		
		————		23. Algeria (1)	44
		24. Bulgaria (3)	42		
		————		25. Egypt (1)	36
				26. Japan (2)	29
				27. India (1)	29
		28. Rumania (2)	26	————	
				29. Java (1)	26
		30. USSR (2)	26	————	
				31. Philippines (1)	21
				32. China (2)	17

countries as the Netherlands, for example. Finland and Estonia are too cold for great production of fruit and vegetables; Ireland is too wet and cool for most fruits and vegetables. Farther down in Table 24 Mexico stands close to Estonia and Ireland. It is somewhat surprising to find these countries above both Chile and Italy, but the estimates for all these countries except Italy are not reliable.

The position of Rumania and Russia is far below that of Italy according to all the available statistics, but may not be quite so bad as an index number of 26 would indicate. The nutritive value of the Italian diet corresponds roughly to that of the next to the lowest economic class in England. Rumania and Russia actually fall below Japan in spite of the intense overcrowding of the last-named country. To find a parallel in the United States we must probably go to our most poorly fed five per cent. The trouble, of course, is not so much deficiency of food, but the monotonously poor quality. Russia, for example, eats chiefly bread, potatoes, and tea with cabbage for a season, a little milk and meat, a fifth as many eggs as the United States, and not much else many months of each year. In all these poorer countries there are, of course, people whose economic level permits them to have a fairly good diet. In warm sections of Russia, such as the Crimea and the irrigated fruit-growing areas east of the Caspian Sea, the diet improves, as it does in the Caucasus and the Asiatic sections where flocks and herds abound.

In the Soviet Union as a whole, however, one of the chief reasons for poor diet is that cold winters and short and often droughty summers make it difficult to raise both fruits and vegetables. Another is that, in spite of the common opinion to the contrary, both Russia and Rumania are overpopulated agriculturally. On an area of cultivated land not much larger than that of the United States, the USSR has four times as many farmers. The land there, on an average, does not yield as much per acre as that of American farms, nor can it be made to do so without expensive and revolutionary changes in agricultural methods. If the Russians attempt to cultivate a larger area than at present, they will have to use land where the yield per acre is even smaller than now. Such facts help to explain the low agricultural productivity per man in Russia as shown in Figure 29B (page 251). This low productivity leads to a poor diet, and the poor diet lowers the level of health and initiative. The activity of the Red Army in World War II doubtless owes much to the fact that the soldiers were much better fed than the rest of the people.

In estimating the quality of the diets of the nations two additional factors must be kept in mind. First, the proportion of vitamins, and especially of minerals, varies greatly according to the soil. Hence the same product may vary considerably in food value from place to place. McCarrison [3] found that rice grown under constant irrigation had a third less protein and less vitamin B than similar rice watered only by rain. This fact illustrates one of the great disadvantages of the tropics. Constant warmth and abundant moisture lead to rapid disintegration of the soil. Heavy rains soon wash out the soluble plant foods which would otherwise be available for growth. The result is that in vast sections of the tropics the soils are of a lateritic quality, badly leached, and reddish in color because their iron still remains after many other ingredients have been washed away. Such soils produce only scanty crops, and even those are of poor quality. This is one reason why vast tropical areas, such as the Amazon Basin, are scantily populated by relatively weak people. India, China, and Japan may have been seriously weakened because for many centuries irrigation may have carried away the plant foods faster than new ones were supplied by fresh material brought in by muddy canal water.

The second factor to remember is that even when advanced countries improve their diet by making it more varied, they often injure it in other ways. Although wheat, eggs, milk, fruit, and butter still retain their familiar appearance, as Carrel puts it, mass production has modified their composition. Chemical fertilizers increase the abundance of crops, but do not replace all the exhausted elements of the soil. The nutritive value of cereal grains and vegetables declines. As if this were not enough, "super-refinement of natural foodstuffs," as Furnas and Cook well say, "has probably been as successful in promoting American ill-health in the past two generations as the most virulent disease germ. . . . Stripping cereals of their outer coats and refining sugar . . . removes 75 per cent of the minerals." Polished rice in the East and white flour in the West are two of the wholly needless means of undermining modern health.

D. Diet and Indian Nationalism

The extent to which diet enters into political and economic history has never been adequately investigated. A single example must suffice. The Nationalists claim that in India two centuries of British domination have lowered the standard of living. Huge British sal-

[3] 1928.

aries, they say, and the cost of an army have been paid by taxes wrung from half-starved peasants. British exploiters of natural resources have become rich at the expense of laborers whose wages buy less and less from decade to decade. If the British would abandon India, all would be well. The British reply that they have prevented famine, built railroads to carry food to the starving, and constructed superb irrigation works providing a living for millions of people. They have ended such abuses as the drowning of girl babies and the custom of suttee, whereby a widow is burned on her husband's funeral pyre. They also justly claim that they have preserved peace, thus preventing the constant wars which formerly brought rapine, famine, and pestilence to millions.

As is customary in political disputes, neither side has paid much attention to the most basic facts. The Nationalists are right in saying that the standard of living has fallen since the British came to India. The British are right too; the advantages which they have brought to India would far outweigh the disadvantages if it were not for the ominous fact that the peace, reforms, famine relief, and other benefits brought by the British have co-operated with Indian lack of self-restraint and with a religion which demands sons carry on funeral rites. This combination has permitted the population to increase enormously. Drowned babies, burned widows, and children who die of hunger leave no offspring, but if such people live, they help to increase the 350 million people who now live where approximately 100 million lived three centuries ago.

Let us go back to the days of the Mogul emperors, whose nomadic strength made them masters of the Indo-Gangetic Valley about A.D. 1600. The probable population of India and the supply and price of food at this time have been carefully investigated by V. A. Smith and Moreland.[4] From the long statistical tables of Abul Fazil, biographer of Akbar, as well as from other sources, it appears that in northern India there were then probably 30 or 40 million people in an area which now contains about 180 million. This relatively small population utilized only the most fertile land and therefore presumably got a greater return per acre than now. Inasmuch as abundant good land was obviously available, it seems highly probable that the average size of family holdings was also greater than at present. For both of these reasons we should expect a correspondingly large income among the peasants. The available facts indicate that this was true.

4 1920.

Smith shows that in A.D. 1600 a laborer's daily wage bought twice as much food as in 1900 and a still larger amount compared with today. This does not mean that the peasants lived in luxury. They went about almost unclothed, and their houses were no better and perhaps worse than at present. Even such simple luxuries as sugar were rare. The peasants were oppressed by heavy taxes and rich landlords. Nevertheless, they must have been much better fed than now. Otherwise, they would not have had such a surplus that rice, wheat, millet, and gram cost half as much as now in proportion to a day's wages. It is especially significant that mutton and especially ghee, or butter, were relatively even cheaper than cereals. This means that, in spite of taxes, exorbitant rents, and peonage, the peasants had not only more but better food than now.

The relative prosperity and comfort of the days of Akbar are closely associated with famines, wars, and pestilences which killed people by the million. A famine which began in 1595 continued four years and was so terrible that children were sold for a song and cannibalism became frequent. It was accompanied by a pestilence so violent that the roads were actually blocked with corpses. Again in 1630, three years of poor rainfall were followed by a complete failure of the rains. Famine, cannibalism, and pestilence again ensued. Such conditions usually lead to extreme poverty and misery for a while, but after a few years the people are actually better off than before. Their numbers are temporarily less than formerly, but the same amount of land is available for cultivation. Thus the food supply is enlarged in comparison with the population. That this happened in the Mogul Empire is evident from what happened after the famine of 1630. Wages went up because workers were scarce, but the price of food, after rising to great heights during the famine, went back to the old level. In other words, people lived more comfortably than before. The same thing happened in the fourteenth century in Europe after the Black Death, the greatest of all known pestilences. In India the famine of 1630 was followed by the reign of Shah Jahan, the period when the Mogul empire attained the greatest magnificence. This was a time "of increasing order and tranquillity." It was then that the lovely Pearl Mosque at Agra and the delicate but stately Taj Mahal were erected. There can be little doubt that one of the conditions which made it possible to construct such buildings was due in part to an increasing food supply which made the people more healthy than usual, and also more vigorous, more contented, and better able to pay taxes and work on public projects.

E. Diet and Japanese Prowess

Although adequate statistics are not available, it seems probable that in China and Japan the general course of events has been much the same as in India. Periods when the population was reduced to low levels by famine, war, pestilence, or other calamities appear to have been followed by relatively prosperous periods when the resources were not overtaxed. Then the diet must have been more abundant, with more than now of such protective foods as meat, milk, fruit, and vegetables. The people were doubtless correspondingly vigorous. Such conditions are favorable to a rapid increase of population. Hence in due time one or more of the following alternatives must occur: cessation of growth of population, introduction of new methods of getting a living, lowering of the standard of living, or some means such as war, pestilence, famine, suttee of widows, drowning of infants, or migration whereby part of the population is removed.

Japan illustrates the difficulties arising from an undue increase in population. The average size of farms in that country is even smaller than in India and China, only about two acres. Nevertheless, the standard of living is higher because the yield per acre is greater. On an average, taking all cereals together, Japan gets about 4,700 pounds per acre, whereas Germany gets 3,000, France and Italy 2,300, the United States 2,000, and India 1,800. A high degree of native skill, the application of modern methods, and a climate peculiarly well adapted to rice account for such high production. This in turn enables Japan to enjoy a standard of living far higher than that of India and well above that of China. Nevertheless, the rapid growth of population has threatened this standard alarmingly. Imperfect records indicate that in A.D. 610, the population was 5,000,000, and in A.D. 736, 8,600,000. By 1723, when more trustworthy records begin, it had increased to 26,000,000. Then it remained almost stationary for a century and a half while Japan was closed to the outside world, being 26,900,000 in 1846 and 33,100,000 in 1872. Ancestor worship was presumably as strong during this stationary period as at any other time, but high infant mortality and other causes kept the population down. After 1870 a rapid increase brought the population close to 75,000,000 in 1940. One of the fundamental reasons for this rise seems to have been new methods of getting a living. Foreign commerce, western manufacturing, and notable improvements in the yield of crops all had an effect. Some new land was also brought under cultivation, although this meant using poorer soil or steeper slopes than formerly. Medical methods, on the other hand, helped to increase the population by lowering the infant deathrate from 200 or more per thousand infants to not much over 100. The deathrate among older people was also reduced slightly. Meanwhile births remained at the high rate of almost 35 per thousand inhabitants. Only in 1938, when the absence of husbands in China began to take effect, was there a definite drop below 30.

At first new methods of supporting the population were employed largely because they were in line with the progress of the rest of the world. Then they were adopted in a definite but ineffectual campaign to make the food supply sufficient for the growing population. Nevertheless, as late as 1917, for example, 1,652,000 babies were born, and only 609,000 persons died, thus leaving a million more people to be fed. We cannot tell whether this increase was appreciably influenced by ancestor worship and national ambition, but these two features of Japanese mores militate strongly against a lowering of the birthrate.

Faced with this ominous increase in population, the Japanese, since World War I, have made renewed efforts to find food for all their people. Migration into Manchuria, Formosa, and other areas has provided practically no help. The Japanese do not like to colonize in climates unlike their own. They hate cold weather and probably cannot endure it well because of lack of vitality, due partly at least to poor nutrition. For the same reason they do not stand the tropics as well as people of European stock. Finally, the pressure of population on the food supply led to the definite policy of Japanese expansion into Manchuria, China, and then Indo-China and the East Indies. Behind all this lies the stark fact that, although Japan, even more than India and China, craves a high standard of living, it has great difficulty maintaining even its present low standard. Moreover, like those countries, its system of ancestor worship and subjection of women leads the people to try almost every other possible method of reducing the pressure of population before trying birth control. The war that began in 1937 was actually a blessing so far as it lowered the birthrate and killed off weaklings. Some day the Japanese may learn that this same blessing might be obtained without the attendant suffering if ancestor worship could be abandoned and birth control could become the handmaid of a sound system of eugenics.

This does not quite end the matter. Weston Price, in his remarkable book on diet, shows that a diet deficient in vitamins exerts a particularly bad effect on the jaws, teeth, and eyes. He made hundreds of comparisons between people who had always lived on one of the primitive diets described above and those same people when they adopted a so-called "modernized" diet, composed primarily of white flour, polished rice, sugar, beans, jams, and so forth. He gives a convincing array of examples of the way in which cavities in the teeth appear in large numbers after only a few years of the new diet. The trouble is due to lack of vitamins and minerals. A much more significant finding is that women who adopt the new diet find hitherto unknown difficulties in childbirth. Worse still, the children of parents who have taken up the new diet also suffer. They tend to have malformed jaws and teeth. Like so many of us who claim to be highly civilized, these children have upper jaws that project over the lower ones, teeth that are out of line, and impacted wisdom teeth that have to be extracted for lack of room. The outlines of the face become contracted as if the middle part had been pushed in. An unusual number of children with clubfeet and other more or less obvious malformations are born. Such obvious external imperfections must presumably be accompanied by internal defects.

One evidence of this is the fact that the children of parents who have long eaten a diet deficient in vitamin A tend to have imperfect eyes. This is extremely interesting in view of experiments on pigs which Price describes. Several experimenters have raised pigs on diets from which vitamin A had been removed. When both parents have been thus fed for a considerable time their young show various deficiencies, especially in their eyes. Sometimes the eyes are merely imperfect, sometimes rudimentary. Now comes the extraordinary and hopeful part of the experiment. After it had been well proved that deficiency of vitamin A produces such results, another experiment was tried. Pigs which had been born with defective eyes because of their parents' malnutrition were fed on the best of diets with plenty of vitamin A. When such pigs were bred the eyes of the piglets were normal, although those of both parents had been defective.

All this has a direct bearing on the success of the Japanese in both war and peace. Scientific Japanese, as well as foreigners, recognize that the ordinary Japanese diet is one of the worst. It leaves Europeans and Americans with a hungry feeling most of the time, no matter how much they eat. The trouble, of course, is that it consists mostly of rice, flour, pickled roots, and fish, with practically no milk, very little meat or eggs, only an insignificant amount of fruit, and not much in the way of green vegetables if the year is considered as a whole. The Japanese suffer from just the effects that would be expected from such a diet. Their teeth are extremely bad. The typical caricature of the Japanese is a man with buck teeth and an overhanging upper jaw. A gold tooth is rather "the thing" in Japan. Another noteworthy trait of the Japanese is the great number who wear glasses, nearly one third of the population, according to some estimates. So great has been the demand for glasses that before World War II a large industry had grown up, and rather poor glasses made of quartz were being sold to the United States and other countries. Both the teeth and the eyes seem to indicate that the great majority of ordinary Japanese are born with defects because their parents were badly nourished.

These defects bring up the problem of the quality of the Japanese as soldiers. No intelligent person can fail to realize the existence of certain strong qualities which we cannot but admire. Nevertheless, the experiences of World War II seem to show that the Japanese cannot stand the tropics so well as Americans and British. The soldiers are indeed much better fed than the people at home, but their diet while soldiers does not seem sufficient to overcome the effects of the lifelong poor diet of their parents and of their own poor diet during childhood. Thus the soldiers lack the stamina which comes from a good diet long before birth and all the time thereafter. Such conditions may explain the relatively poor showing of the Japanese in the air. Again and again we read accounts of poor Japanese marksmanship. Such marksmanship is what would be expected from people whose eyes are imperfect because their parents did not eat enough vitamin A. We might go on to show how physical deficiencies, due primarily to overpopulation and consequent poor diet, run through the whole range of Japanese achievements, as well as through those of India, China, and many other countries in varying degrees.

Some idea of the quality of Japan's diet and medical service may be gained from Figure 56. The bars on the left show the value of the Japanese diet from the standpoint of protective foods as given in Table 24 (page 441). Their relative length is essentially the same as in Figure 29 (page 251) where physical vigor, productivity, and income are compared. In spite of its highly developed agriculture Japan is evidently one of the most poorly fed countries. The right-hand side of Figure 56 shows the degree to which medical care has been developed. It is based on the number of physicians, dentists, and hospital beds

in proportion to the population.[5] In this respect Japan excels both
France and Italy, but comes nowhere near the level of New Zealand,
the United States, and Germany. It is interesting that Japan and
Germany both stand relatively higher in medical care than in many
other respects. This is perhaps what might be expected among alert
people who suffer seriously from overpopulation. They feel the need
of improvements in their medical services in order to overcome other
handicaps. Taking into account the diagrams of Figures 56 and 29,
together with the known effects of climate, we conclude that, although
Japan is greatly helped by the cyclonic factor in its climate, it is

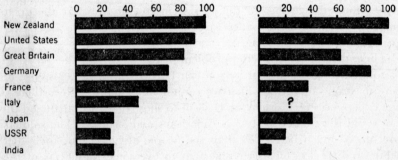

Figure 56.   Nutritive Value of Diet (left) and Medical Care (right) in Nine
Countries.

badly handicapped by a poor diet due to overpopulation and consequent low agricultural productivity per man (not per acre), and to
hot, wet summers which are not favorable for milk, meat, and fruit.
The poor diet, in turn, seems to have an adverse effect upon health,
vigor, and mortality and thus upon industrial productivity as well as
upon competence in war. Nevertheless, the energy and skill of the
Japanese and the stimulating quality of their climate during much of
the year have already led to a rather surprising degree of medical
progress. If these conditions lead to sound measures for a gradual
reduction in the rate of growth of population, technical progress will
have a chance to raise the standard of living.

F. Diet and Physiological Fitness

The crux of the problem of diet and agriculture is that the introduction of agriculture, perhaps ten thousand years ago, started a

[5] Huntington, 1943.

gradual swing away from the varied and nutritious primitive diets to one that would maintain life among the largest possible number of people regardless of its effect on health and vigor. As the population of any given area became more dense, it was discovered that the easiest way to supply a family with food was to concentrate upon the most productive cereal, with beans and other leguminous crops to supply protein, and with vegetable oils, such as those of olives, sesame, and sunflower seeds, to supply fats. This, of course, tended toward a kind of malnutrition which people often fail to realize but which makes them inefficient and easily subject to disease. In China, according to Adolph, the diet is so starchy that a large part of the people do not expect to have a movement of the bowels oftener than once in two or three days or even longer. This tends to make them sluggish. One of the queer things about all this is that when people become accustomed to a diet, even though it is of poor quality, they like it and believe that it is good for them. Even among people as advanced as the English many refuse to eat fruit after the American fashion. They do not want it and do not realize what a help it is in keeping fit. In the same way the Chinese assert that rice is the best of foods. As a matter of fact, they do not eat rice because they like it. They like it because they eat it from childhood onward.

One of the greatest pieces of good fortune is to be born in a region where fruit and vegetables grow well, and still more in one where cattle and hens thrive lustily, and milk and eggs are widely used. Buck [6] says that in China the most common number of hens on farms is 3, and the average of all kinds of poultry for every hundred farms is 459—less than 5 per farm. Here are some other Chinese averages per hundred farms: all kinds of work animals, 105; hogs, 101; sheep and goats, 76; cows for milk, 5. In Iowa, on the other hand, the number of work animals per farm is over three times as great as in China without allowing for trucks and tractors. Cattle for milk and meat are about 400 times as common as in China, poultry 30 times, hogs 25, and sheep 7. Such data illustrate the way in which the development of agriculture has made it possible for the number of human beings in a given area to increase enormously but has at the same time exposed people to the terrible handicaps that arise from overpopulation and poor diet. The way in which the Chinese, for example, have developed an agriculture which carefully apportions the land to starchy cereals, protein-bearing beans, and similar products,

[6] p. 246.

with just enough of the protective foods to sustain life, is marvelous. At the same time, it is pitiful, for it has condemned untold hundreds of millions of people to a lifetime of relatively low vitality with little of the exuberant energy felt by a well-nourished healthy man in an invigorating climate.

One of the most urgent phases of the problem of agriculture and the food supply arises from the fact that the less favored nations are beginning to think that they, too, should enjoy high standards of living like those of western Europe and America. This is impossible under present conditions. A standard of diet such as the readers of this book enjoy requires three or four times as much farm land as is available for the average person among the thousand million or more who inhabit Asia. Milk, meat, eggs, fresh fruits, and vegetables require far more space for a given number of calories than do cereals. There is not land enough to allow any such amount of space to every person in the world. In fact, practically all the good land is already in use. Of course, there are vast unused tropical areas which may some day become productive, but until greatly improved methods are available such land cannot be cultivated profitably. If it is used, or if people try to cultivate the unused land in a country such as the Soviet Republic, crops have to be planted under conditions of climate and soil where the return per acre is low. On such land, no matter how much the methods of agriculture are improved, a given amount of labor and expense will not bring so large a return as upon the better land already in use. The upshot of the whole matter seems to be that one of two things must happen: Either the standards of living of many countries—yes, of the majority of the world's people—must decline because of increasing density of population, or the birthrate must be lowered until the growth of population ceases to outstrip the growth in man's ability to produce food and the raw materials which are needed to maintain a high civilization.

CHAPTER 24

CYCLES, RHYTHMS, AND PERIODICITIES *

A. The Nature of Cycles

The whole history of life is a record of cycles. In the vast geological periods plants and animals of one great order after another rose to importance, flourished, and declined. In prehistoric times successive species of manlike creatures passed across the stage. In the historic period nations have risen and fallen; types of civilization have grown great and decayed; science, art, and literature have been full of vigor and originality only to fall into deadly weakness and conventionalism. In modern business few things are more disturbing than the cycles which seem to become more extreme as time goes on. In each of these examples some form of existence or type of activity starts in a certain condition, goes through a series of changes, and comes back to essentially the same condition as at the beginning. An explosion, for example, sets still air in violent motion. There is a loud sound and buildings fall. Then the whole thing dies down. The air may be full of smoke and dust, but so far as motion is concerned, it has returned to its old condition of stillness. The life cycle of plants and animals also illustrates the matter. It starts with nonexistence, passes through many stages, and ends once more with nonexistence.

Although this coming-around-to-the-place-of-beginning is the basic idea of the word "cycle," there is much more to it. In order to understand the full significance of the word, three other ideas must be added. One of these is repetition. Reproduction illustrates this. A species of plant or a nation may fulfill its life cycle and disappear without leaving a successor. If an individual plant produces seeds, however, a new cycle arises from the old, and this may be repeated indefinitely. Thus the reproductive cycle has a quality unknown to the cycle of an individual life. In any given species it is normally shorter, but it contains within itself the necessity for repetition. With

* The author most cordially thanks Edward R. Dewey, Director of the Foundation for the Study of Cycles, for active and most helpful co-operation in preparing this chapter and the next two.

453

some cycles there is doubt as to whether they belong to the first type or are repetitive. Cycles of civilization and of business are of this doubtful sort. Some people hold that each civilization and each business cycle contains within itself the seeds of a successor. We are told that action and reaction are equal and opposite in business as well as in physics. Others hold that each such cycle is complete in itself. New civilizations and new fluctuations of business, they say, arise only in response to a repetition of some external impetus like that which produced the first cycle.

Cycles in civilization and in business not only repeat themselves almost as surely as do the cycles of reproduction, but come and go with a certain degree of regularity. Thus, a third element, the idea of rhythm, is added to those of coming-back-to-the-beginning and of repetition. If an explosion occurs today and not again for six months, and then not for twelve years, there is no rhythm. The rhythmic quality is introduced only if the explosions occur at fairly regular intervals.

The most highly developed type of cycle involves still a fourth element, namely, periodicity. By this we mean a regular recurrence at specified and hence predictable intervals. The day with its phases of light and darkness is of this kind. So are the seasons and tides. Many people are beginning to suspect that definite periodicity goes much farther than this. They think that it is found in cycles of business and even in the rise and fall of types of civilization and the long eras of geology. This definite periodicity is supposed to have its origin in purely physical conditions which repeat themselves as regularly as the motions of the planets or the waves of different lengths which constitute heat, light, and electricity. Such physical cycles are superimposed upon one another in bewildering profusion. The length of some is only a fraction of a second and that of others, millions of years. When the effects of all these periodic cycles are added to those of rhythmic but not periodic cycles, the result is bound to be highly complex. For that reason many events which are really due to the combined effect of many periodic causes are commonly supposed to be hopelessly irregular and unpredictable.

In the following chapters we shall examine various cycles which have a bearing on the evolution and present condition of civilization. All of them are clearly rhythmic and some appear to be definitely periodic. We shall begin with short cycles that can be observed within a single lifetime. Then we shall examine others which can be detected only by examining the records of history. Only a minute fraction of the entire field can be covered. That is enough, however, to suggest that life as we know it is influenced by at least three kinds of physical conditions, each of which has its own cycles. One of these is the weather, in the ordinary sense of the word. Another is the electro-magnetic field of the solar system in general and of the earth in particular. The third is the composition of the atmosphere, with its variations in ozone and perhaps in other respects. In their effect upon the earth and its living beings the three types of cycles are mingled like threads of different colors in a tangled mass of string. Moreover, they are apparently tied together again and again. Hence it is often impossible to disentangle them. Nevertheless, we shall attempt to draw a few threads out of the tangled mass.

B. The 35-Year Brückner Cycle

Three centuries and a half ago Sir Francis Bacon talked about a physical cycle which has now become well known:

There is a toy that I have heard, and I would not have it given over, but waited upon a little. They say it is observed in the Low Countries (I know not in what part), that in every five and thirty years the same kind and suit of years and weathers come about again; as great frosts, great wet, great drought, warm winters, summers with little heat, and the like, and they call it the prime; it is a thing I do the rather mention, because, computing backwards, I have found some concurrence.

Although this "toy" has not been wholly "given over," it has certainly been "waited upon a little." At last, however, it is coming into its own, and is raising a host of fascinating problems. As long ago as 1891, Brückner [1] published an interesting set of facts as to dates of wheat harvest and wine making, the freezing of rivers and their opening to navigation in the spring, the rise and fall of enclosed lakes like the Caspian Sea, and other natural occurrences, mainly in Europe. Thus he showed clearly that the weather of Europe varies definitely in cycles with an average length of about 35 years. At one phase the European climate is oceanic, with relatively wet, cool, stormy summers and mild, moist winters. At the opposite extreme it is continental with relatively dry, sunny, warm summers and cold, clear winters. The length of the cycle ranges from 17 to 50 years, but departures from the normal balance one another and the maxima of "continental" or "oceanic" conditions average about 35 years apart.

[1] 1891.

Many other investigators have found evidence of a cycle of this same length. Carpenter [2] and Junger, for example, concluded independently that insect pests in Europe since 1700 have reached a general maximum at an average interval of approximately 36 years. The dates of maximum ravages are as follows: about 1700, 1740–43, 1780–83, 1815, 1850–53, 1880–83, and 1920–24.

Agriculture and human prosperity in general are greatly influenced by the Brückner cycle. Sir Richard Gregory puts it thus:

Although the . . . rainfall may vary widely from one year to the next, the . . . water . . . stored up on the land . . . in soil, lakes, and glaciers varies far more slowly. . . . If . . . ten years fall in the wet half of a Brückner cycle, the quantity of stored water will be great. . . . In the dull rainy countries of northwest Europe, warm dry years are favorable for crops and vegetation, and on the whole the dry half of a Brückner cycle will yield better crops than the cool, wet half, although there may be wide variations from one year to the next. An agricultural community must take the bad years with the good, and trust to the surplus from a rich harvest to tide over a year of dearth, but at the end of the warm half of the cycle the community will be prosperous, while at the end of the cold half it will be poor. Hence waves of emigration and the movements of peoples are closely related to cycles such as Brückner's, which in this way may leave their mark on history.

Ireland affords an excellent example of the effect of climatic cycles.[3] In 1739 a Brückner cycle appears to have reached the maximum of its cool wet phase in a summer frost which ruined the potato crops. Then for a century the cycle came and went without again reaching so great an extreme.* This was perhaps due to the milder phase of a greater cycle composed probably of three Brückner cycles. Thus Ireland had many relatively warm, dry summers which favored big potato crops and permitted the population to increase rapidly. A century after the great summer frost, however, the oceanic phase of a third Brückner cycle gave warning of its approach by six seasons of relatively poor crops between 1831 and 1842. Nevertheless, the popu-

---

[2] p. 139.

[3] Huntington, 1915.

* In the eastern United States the year "eighteen-hundred-and-freeze-to-death" (1816)—the "year without a summer"—occurred a little more than two Brückner cycles after Ireland's very cold year. At New Haven the coldest summers (June, July, and August) ever experienced since records began in 1778 were 1812, 1816, and 1817 (3.2°, 5.2°, and 3.2°F cooler than average, with July, 1816, 7° below average).

lation kept on growing until the census of 1841 showed 8,300,000. Then came the climax from 1846 to 1848—three years so damp that a fungus disease caused the potato crop to be largely a failure. Two or three hundred thousand people died of starvation and fever. The British government provided work for over 700,000 persons. That did not suffice, and over 3,000,000 were at one time being fed. Because of the famine, the system of absentee landlordism, which had prospered in years of good crops, seemed unbearable. A rebellion broke out in 1848. A tremendous migration also took place, mainly to America. In five years the population had diminished to 6,000,000, a drop of about 20 per cent.

During the succeeding dry continental phase of the Brückner cycle, Irish emigration fell off so much that from 1871 to 1875 the population scarcely declined at all. Then the cycle swung around to the oceanic phase once more and in the later seventies and earlier eighties the crops were very poor. Again the Irish flocked to America, and from 1881 to 1891 the Irish population declined 9 per cent. Thus the Brückner cycle was a main factor in one of the most wholesale migrations known in history. Brückner [4] has shown that the cycle produced a similar, although less drastic, effect in Germany. Dewey finds its influence clearly in the number of immigrants to the United States. Its effect has also been noted in many other countries.

C. The Great Diversity of Cycles

The 35-year Brückner cycle is only one of many. Throughout nature the same general sequence of events repeats itself at more or less uniform intervals. Ordinary storms, although less regular than the seasons, are an especially familiar cyclic occurrence. Apples, pecans, and many other crops have a 2-year cycle, with abundance one year and scarcity the next. Health and the deathrate fluctuate from season to season and also irregularly in longer cycles. In October, 1942, the deathrate in the United States, for example, suddenly stepped up some 8 or 10 per cent above the seasonal average for the three preceding years. In the late summer of 1943 it declined almost to the old level, but in December a rapid upward trend carried it fully 50 per cent above normal. Pneumonia was chiefly responsible for this, but deaths from other causes increased also. Business cycles of inflation and depression are one of the most ominous signs of our times.

[4] 1910; see also Huntington, 1915, p. 172.

A growing recognition of the importance of cycles in crops, health, prices, business, politics, and almost everything else has recently led to the development of a science of cycles and even to the establishment of the Foundation for the Study of Cycles mentioned above.*

It will be a vast boon to mankind when we learn to prophesy the precise dates when cycles of various kinds will reach definite stages. This would be easy if (1) there were only a few cycles; (2) each were absolutely uniform in length and intensity; (3) no cycle produced delayed effects or interfered with any other; and (4) a given cycle were equally developed in all parts of the earth. Not one of these conditions exists. Investigators have described cycles of hundreds of kinds and with scores of different lengths. Aside from such things as the wave-length of light, practically no cycle is absolutely uniform in length. Even the day and year fluctuate a little, although always returning to a length that can be predicted far in advance. The way in which one cycle interferes with another is illustrated by the Gulf Stream. Its waters may be unusually hot and abundant because of extra heat from the sun. That same water, not yet wholly cooled, may make the coast of northern Europe unusually warm a year later, although at that very time the sun itself is emitting less heat than normal. The inter-relations of one cycle and another become vastly more complex when we take account of the effect of weather on crops, crops on animals, animals on man, and then of both crops and animals on prices, and weather on health. The matter becomes still more complicated when we examine the delayed as well as the im-

* The diversity of the interests which led to the formation of the Foundation for the Study of Cycles is shown in connection with the Foundation's annual medal. Although the judges in 1943 included an astrophysicist, a biologist, a climatologist, an economist, and a zoologist, they felt inadequate to judge the great variety of publications which appeared in a single year, even in wartime. Therefore they called upon numerous scientific societies, which appointed over twenty advisors in fields as varied as astronomy, paleontology, mycology, and mathematics. The foundation's international character appears from the following board: Canada—Charles Camsell, Commissioner of Northwest Territories; F. Cyril James, Principal of McGill University; Great Britain—Patrick A. Cooper, Governor of the Hudson's Bay Company; Charles S. Elton, Oxford University; Julian S. Huxley, London Zoological Society; United States—Charles G. Abbot, Smithsonian Institution; Copley Amory, Chairman of the Board; George Baekeland, Bakelite Corporation; William Cameron Forbes, Chairman of the Carnegie Institution of Washington; Ellsworth Huntington, Yale University; Wesley C. Mitchell, Director, National Bureau of Economic Research; Harlow Shapley, Harvard Observatory. The Director is Edward R. Dewey, 274 Madison Avenue, New York, N. Y.

mediate effect of all these conditions, together with those of many other social, political, economic, and psychological conditions which vary in cycles and influence the general flow of business and the conditions of civilization.

———————

It used to be thought that the best way to study cycles is to examine long tables of statistics by the mathematical process known as harmonic analysis. At least twenty other methods, however, are now available and it is realized that the chief value of harmonic analysis lies in its suggestion of intervals of time that ought to be studied by the newer methods.[5]

A good example of harmonic analysis is Beveridge's [6] study of wheat prices in Europe from 1500 to 1869. He gathered a large number of tables of prices from nearly fifty places in six regions, namely, Scotland and England, the Low Countries, France, North Germany, South Germany, and Austria. Each region received equal weight. Inasmuch as the data are drawn from a wide field and represent a period and area where agriculture was the dominant economic factor, there can be little doubt that the peaks and elevations of their plotted curve "reflect substantially the harvest conditions" of the year in question.

A siege of a single town, as of Paris in 1590, may cause a rapid rise and fall of prices there, but the fate of a single town does not seriously affect the general index number. A general war, like the Thirty Years' War, or that of the Napoleonic period . . . may raise . . . the general level of prices, but after such a widespread destruction of goods and depreciation of money, prices cannot show a rapid and comparable fall. The only cause which can reasonably account for the characteristic peaks of the curve . . . is a fluctuation in the yield of harvests. That this was, in fact, the cause can be shown . . . practically in all cases by historical records.

Beveridge recognizes that since 1800 the so-called credit cycle enters into the matter, but "subject to one or two reserves the [prices] must be accepted as essentially a reflection of harvest success and harvest failure." [7]

In Figure 57 the left-hand side sums up the length and intensity of all Beveridge's cycles. The number of cycles is astonishing, but some of the longer ones may be combinations of short ones. Two cycles,

[5] Dewey, 1943.   [7] 1921.
[6] 1922.

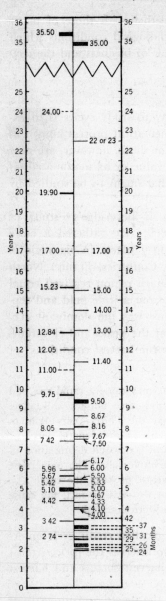

with lengths of about 5 and 35 years, stand out strongly both in the price of wheat and in various weather records. Seven, with lengths of 5.7, 9.8, 12.8, 15.2, 19.9, 54.0, and 68.0 are about as strong as the first two in prices, but appear only faintly or not at all in the weather. Six more are mildly evident in both prices and weather, and hints of others are indicated by fine dotted lines.

The right-hand side of Figure 57 compares Beveridge's cycles with those found by Brunt in an elaborate harmonic analysis of rainfall, temperature, and atmospheric pressure in twelve European cities where records for at least a century are available.* The thickness of the lines on the right indicates the relative number of records in which Brunt and others whom he cites find the various periods. In addition to the 28 cycles shown here, Brunt describes 16 more with a length of less than 2 years. This illustrates the extreme complexity of the problem.

The most obvious approaches to agreement between Beveridge and Brunt fall near 3½, 5, 8, 9½, and 35 years. One of the minor agreements is 7.50 years, according to Brunt, and 7.42 years, according to Beveridge. This is interesting because this cycle seems to be important in other respects. A prolonged study of annual tree growth, annual layers of clay deposited on lake bottoms (varves) and the laminae which

Figure 57. Cycles in Wheat Prices for Three Centuries (*after Beveridge*) (left), and in Weather for a Century in Europe (*after Brunt and Others*) (right).

* The basic data are as follows: (a) rainfall at Milan, Padua, London, and Edinburgh; (b) pressure at Edinburgh and Paris; (c) temperature at Edinburgh, Stockholm, London, Paris, Berlin, and Vienna.

represent similar layers in rocks has convinced Gillette [8] that one of the most basic climatic cycles is 7.47 years in length. Clayton [9] finds essentially this same period (7.54 years) in barometric pressure all the way from latitudes above 60° in Siberia and Iceland to the tropics in Calcutta. He also finds it very clearly in sunspots and calls attention to the fact that it is practically one third of the period (22.3 years) covered by changes in the electrical polarity of sunspots.

Gillette [10] concludes that other cycles occur in both an upward and a downward series where three is either the multiplier or divisor of 7.47. Multiplying by three gives a cycle of 22.4 years, which agrees with one found by Brunt in European weather (Figure 57). This is really the dominant sunspot cycle, although the 11-year cycle is more familiar. A normal sunspot is double, with two vortices, one of which follows the other. During any given 11-year sunspot cycle the more easterly vortex is electrically positive and the other negative. During the next 11 years these relations are often, perhaps always, reversed and the easterly vortex is negative. Thus at the end of a little more than 22 years a full electrical cycle has been completed.* Abbot [11] has found a strong rhythm of about this length (23 years) in the weather of widely separated places. He has used it as the basis of what have been called "startlingly accurate forecasts." There is a hint of a 22- or 23-year period in stock prices, according to Dewey. Schumpeter finds it in wholesale prices.

Going on with the multiples of 7½ years, we come to 45 and 68 years. According to Abbot, the weather repeats itself more closely at an interval of 46 years than of 23. Moseley [12] has made fairly successful predictions of rain and floods on the basis of a 90.4-year cycle, which is almost exactly 4 times 22.5 years and 12 times 7½ years. Dewey finds hints of a 68-year cycle in cotton prices, for which the record goes back to 1731. This agrees quite well with Beveridge's 68-year cycle mentioned above and with a cycle of 66 years which C. E. P. Brooks [13] has found in floods of the Nile. Gillette [14] says that by means of varves in Lake Saki in the Crimea he has "determined the length of the 67-year cycle with great precision. It is ex-

---

[8] 1942A, 1942B. [10] 1942A.
[9] 1943.

* It is important to note that even within the limits of a single 11-year cycle some of the sunspots may be electrically reversed in comparison with the majority, as George E. Hale long ago discovered.

[11] 1935. [13] 1926.
[12] 1939. [14] 1942B, p. 1.

actly 67 years long between its peaks of rainfall." Numerous other cycles in this same series might be described if space allowed.

D. Crop Cycles and Economic Depressions

Although we cannot discuss most of the cycles shown in Figure 57, the 8-year cycle may be mentioned before we turn to the highly significant 3½ and 9- or 10-year cycles. Although inconspicuous in the wheat prices of Europe and only moderately prominent in the weather there, the 8-year cycle is quite well developed in the United States. In the central states from 1881 to 1921 Moore[15] found it in both the weather and the average yield of the chief crops. According to Dewey, what may be the 8-year cycle (7.8 years) ranks second among the cycles in the price of cotton from 1731 to 1940. The importance of the 8-year cycle in America as compared with Europe illustrates a frequent characteristic of cycles, namely, their greater development in one region or period than in another. We shall soon see that the persistent 11-year sunspot cycle is clearly evident in some parts of the United States and in certain conditions such as storm tracks, but can scarcely be detected in other parts and in other phenomena, such as temperature.

Moore believed that variations in rainfall and hence in crops are a major factor in cyclic changes of American prices, but this view is not widely accepted. Crops undoubtedly dominate prices in countries that are mainly agricultural, but not in those that are industrial. Where agriculture is dominant, good crops mean low prices for food, and the general price level is determined largely in that way. The importance of crops in the history of civilization is tremendous, as we have already seen in the history of China and the development of Chinese character (page 183).

Even in the United States up to 1873, as Clayton points out,[16] each major financial disturbance took place in close association with low rainfall and poor crops. This was true, for example, in 1825 and 1837–39. The next two years of financial crisis, 1847 and 1857, fell between years of deficient rainfall, although they themselves did not thus suffer. Since then, however, during the period of increasing industrialization, financial crises show a tendency to come at the end of periods of good crops and to be intensified later by bad crops. This,

---

[15] 1914, 1923.   [16] 1943, pp. 424–25; 1902.

at least, is what happened in the big depressions that began in 1893 and 1929. This change in the relation between crops and prices suggests that as man's control over nature increases, his response to any given natural condition may change and even be reversed. This is obvious when a tunnel causes travel between two cities on opposite sides of a high mountain chain to be much easier than between two places that are equally far apart on a plain without a railroad. Nevertheless, it is also possible that the early financial panics, which were formerly ascribed to poor crops, may have been influenced by some other variable. This presumably had a psychological influence which re-enforced the effect of the crops at certain times.

E. The 41-Month (3.4-Year) Cycle in Business

The preceding suggestion as to the psychological effect of certain physical cycles is based partly on a 41-month cycle (about 3.4 years) which appears in a surprising number of data as to prices, production, and sales, according to Beveridge, Hoskins, Dewey, and others. King gives a chart which indicates that whooping cough also varies in a cycle which he called 3.2 years, but which other methods of analysis would put at 3.4 years. This cycle must be clearly distinguished from another, slightly longer, cycle of about 4 years which Elton [17] and others have found in the number, migrations, and epidemics of lemmings, mice, squirrels, and the foxes that prey on them in regions as far separated as Norway, Newfoundland, and Canada. Shelford [18] apparently finds it in the collared lemming of the Churchill region south of Hudson Bay. Thus there appear to be two cycles which differ about half a year in length and are evident in quite different ways. The shorter, which is our main subject, appears primarily in business. The other is primarily a cycle of abundance in animals. A similar pair of cycles, with lengths of about 9 and $9\frac{2}{3}$ years, respectively, will be discussed in the next chapter.

In modern business the 41-month cycle was noted at least as long ago as 1909 by Jevons in his much-quoted work on the relation of sunspots to cycles. It was carefully studied by Kitchin in 1923 and has been repeating itself ever since. Mitchell, for example, in his famous book on cycles, presents a series of evidences of the duration of economic cycles in the United States from 1878 to 1925, as indicated by the activity of business, bank clearings, and so forth. Each

[17] 1942.   [18] 1943.

of eight ways of measuring these conditions gives 41 to 43 months, generally 42, as the average length of a very persistent cycle. "These," says Mitchell, "are the most precise measurements of the duration of business cycles we can get for the present."

One way in which modern methods bring out more or less hidden cycles is seen in Chapin Hoskins' analysis of the 41-month rhythm in the production of pig iron, as published by Edward R. Dewey,[19] Director of the Foundation for the Study of Cycles. Iron and steel are so important in the economy of the United States that their production is often considered an index of business in general, especially the heavy industries. The solid line in Figure 58 shows the monthly variations in pig iron production in the United States from 1900 to 1940. At first glance it appears to be highly irregular, with little evidence of rhythm or cycles. Distinct cycles, however, become evident when we employ the method used in Figure 59 by Chapin Hoskins, who in 1938 drew Figures 58–59 in their original form. In Figure 59, instead of the actual tonnage, he expressed the tonnage of any given month as a percentage of the tonnage of the same calendar month a year earlier. This eliminates many of the short irregularities and minimizes long rhythms and any general trend that may exist. Percentages of this kind are constantly published as evidence of the course of business.

When such percentages for pig iron are plotted, we get the solid line of Figure 59. This marches across the page more regularly than the corresponding line in Figure 58. The interval of time between successive main peaks, or successive main valleys, tends to average approximately 41 months. If we take this period and the median height of the peaks and valleys, we have the basis for a standard wave wherein the same rigid cycle is exactly repeated time after time, as appears in the fine dashed lines. Dots at the top and bottom of the diagram indicate the exact months of maxima or minima according to the standard cycle. Brackets indicate a surrounding period of about nine months within which a majority of the tops (or bottoms) have occurred. Maxima or minima which occur within these limits may be said to return "on time."

Let us compare the standard cycle of Figure 59 with what actually happened. The first two minima and maxima (numbers 1 and 2) are

[19] 1940.

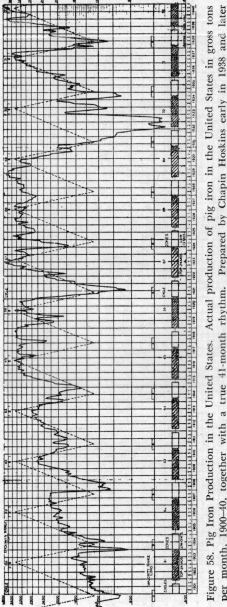

Figure 58. Pig Iron Production in the United States. Actual production of pig iron in the United States in gross tons per month, 1900–40, together with a true 41-month rhythm. Prepared by Chapin Hoskins early in 1938 and later brought up to date by him. From *Putting Cycles to Work in Science and Industry*, by E. R. Dewey.

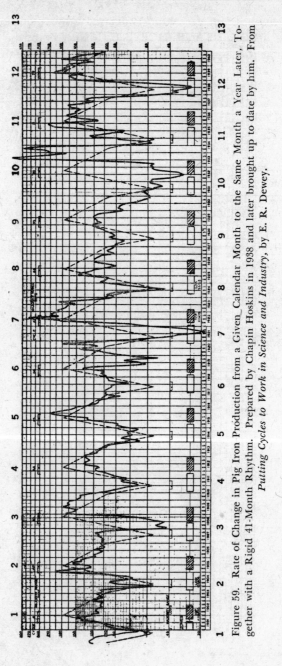

Figure 59. Rate of Change in Pig Iron Production from a Given Calendar Month to the Same Month a Year Later, Together with a Rigid 41-Month Rhythm. Prepared by Chapin Hoskins in 1938 and later brought up to date by him. From *Putting Cycles to Work in Science and Industry*, by E. R. Dewey.

on time. Number 3 of each kind is delayed a few months, due possibly to the financial depression of 1907. Note, however, that after this distortion the bottom reverts to the standard position, and the maximum and minimum labelled 4 are both on time. Then we should expect World War I to disrupt the rhythm, and so it does, but only slightly. Minimum 5, which should have come just when war was breaking out, is double, while maximum 5, at the end of 1915, falls one month outside the bracket. A most remarkable fact now emerges. In 1916, and still more in 1917, the United States was making strenuous efforts to increase production as much as possible. Figure 58 shows that these efforts produced a sort of plateau of production, but this was interrupted by valleys. Figure 59 indicates that in spite of all efforts, both 1916 and 1917, in comparison with previous years, behaved about as would have been expected on the basis of the 41-month cycle. Minimum 6 is delayed only a little after its standard date in November, 1917, and maximum 6 arrived just on time at the beginning of 1919.

After World War I three events interfered with the 41-month cycle: (1) the production of pig iron was suddenly reduced because war orders were cancelled; (2) it increased again because of postwar demands for new goods; and then (3) it fell off in 1921 in harmony with the 41-month cycle, but reached its minimum practically on time in spite of financial depression. Moreover, maxima 7, 8, and 9 and minima 8 and 9 all occurred on time. The great depression which began with the crash of 1929 again threw pig iron production out of its steady rhythm, but only for a short time. Numbers 11 and 12 of both maxima and minima in Figure 59 are on time. Even in World War II the basic rhythm of 41 months still persisted. This is the more extraordinary when we recall that the part of Figures 58 and 59 up to 1938, with its standard cycle, was first drawn in that year. The standard cycle was in effect a prediction which has actually come true.

Going back now to Figure 58, we find new meaning in the irregularities of pig iron production. The 41-month rhythm is evident, even though it is much pushed about by the general increase in business, the two great wars, and several financial depressions. Thus it seems clear that if we are to understand the course of business, we must take account not only of the factors usually considered, but of a persistent cycle of 41 months which somehow affects people's ability or desire to work or buy. This does not mean that old ideas as to the causes of cycles are thrown overboard. Overproduction, poor financial methods, new inventions, political interference, and many other factors all play vital parts in determining the general course of business. The new factors presented in this book merely add complexities with which the student of business must cope. Nevertheless, if the conclusions here set forth are correct, the newly discovered physical periodicities are of special importance in producing rhythmic variations. They hold forth a hope that we may ultimately predict and finally reduce the fluctuations to which they give rise.

F. Psychological Periodicities

Another impressive example of the 41-month cycle is seen in the stock market. Stock prices are notoriously subject to erratic changes because of conditions which often seem trivial—reports of projected legislation, rumors of war, the possibility of large business mergers, and so forth. Nevertheless, Chapin Hoskins has shown that stock prices as measured by changes in the Dow-Jones Index of Industrial Common Stock Prices fluctuate persistently in a cycle of 41 months. At almost every date when the dashed lines in Figure 60 * indicate the maximum of a standard 41-month cycle, the Dow-Jones Index is close to its time of most rapid increase. Although the depression of 1929–32 threw stock prices out of the normal rhythm, by 1936 the old relationship to the standard cycle had been restored. In 1902 and 1939 the curve of stock prices looks as if its peaks had been bitten out by some other factor, but the general rhythm remains clear. More remarkable still is the fact that in March and April, 1943, more than five years after Hoskins first drew the original of Figure 60, a sharp peak occurred within a month of the time that would be expected on the basis of the 41-month cycle.

We might go on at great length with this study of the 41-month cycle. Dewey [20] says that "out of more than 500 different kinds of economic series that have been analysed by the Foundation for the Study of Cycles and by others who have worked in this field, I would judge that more than half show a tendency toward rhythmic fluctua-

---

* For this curve the author is indebted to Edward R. Dewey as well as to Chapin Hoskins. Figure 60 is constructed in the same way as Figures 58 and 59.

[20] Personal communication.

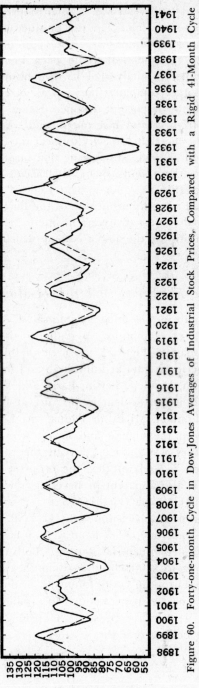

Figure 60. Forty-one-month Cycle in Dow-Jones Averages of Industrial Stock Prices. Compared with a Rigid 41-Month Cycle (*after Dewey*). Long variations and secular trend are eliminated by using 7-month moving averages and expressing them as percentages of their own 40-month moving average.

tions of something like this interval. . . . It is present . . . in the prices of many commodities and . . . the production and sales . . . of many individual corporations."

Dewey also shows the practical value of a knowledge of such rhythms. For example, an analysis of its own business and that of others convinced a great company that a peak of business in 1937 would be followed by an important decline. Hence during 1936 the company refrained from capital investment, and when the expected peak arrived had just the right capacity to meet the demand. Then, during the low period of 1938, anticipating that business in 1939 and 1940 would increase, they boldly spent $10,000,000 for new capital equipment. By spending this money at a time of depression they helped a little toward smoothing out one of the fluctuations in business. They also saved at least two years in interest charges and obsolescence, to say nothing of the lower cost at which they probably made their purchases.

G. *Atmospheric Electricity and the 41-Month Rhythm*

We are now ready to inquire into possible causes of this persistent and widespread cycle of 41 months. Is it due to the weather? According to Brunt's analysis (Figure 57), a cycle of this length can be detected in atmospheric pressure at Edinburgh and in temperature at Edinburgh, Stockholm, London, Berlin, Paris, and Vienna, but it is everywhere weak. It is not evident in pressure at Paris or in rainfall at Edinburgh, London, Milan, or Padua. At London the average difference between the highest and lowest temperatures of the cycle during a century was only 0.4°F. In the plotted curves of temperature the cycle is so faint that the ordinary eye cannot detect it. This cycle is also apparent in Beveridge's wheat prices, but there, too, it is relatively weak (Figure 57).

A cycle of 44 months has been found by C. E. P. Brooks in Nile floods.[21] Clayton[22] finds one of 45 months in atmospheric pressure at nine widely distributed equatorial stations. Both of these periods, however, are too long to represent the 41-month cycle. Moreover, neither they nor the European cycles found by Brunt and Beveridge seem to be anywhere nearly strong enough to produce the persistent development of the 41-month cycle seen in business. Therefore it seems impossible to believe that the weather in its ordinary forms

[21] 1926.   [22] 1943, Vol. 2, p. 272.

can explain the 41-month cycle as a whole. A generally accepted conclusion as to this whole matter is well summed up by Clayton [23]: "When one looks at the regularity of certain natural cycles such . . . as [are] shown by certain insects and fish [as will appear in a later chapter], it seems impossible that such regularity could be brought about by the irregular changes which are found in the weather." He also says that "if such cycles are associated with solar cycles, it seems more probable that the living objects are influenced directly by changes in solar intensity." We would add that the effect is probably produced through changes in the earth's atmosphere which are induced by the sun, but are not of the kinds most readily evident in the weather.

When we turn to the sun, a most interesting fact appears. Sterne [24] of the Harvard College Observatory has determined that the solar constant, as measured by the Smithsonian Institution, fluctuates in a compound rhythm, one part of which is 40.8 months in length, as appears in the upper part of Figure 61. According to Sterne, there is only 1 chance in 250,000 that the rhythm is accidental. Dewey, by fitting a 41-month rigid cycle to Sterne's data, shows how far the ideal and the actual cycles agree. The agreement is far from perfect, but considerable similarity is evident. This suggests a possible solar cause of the 41-month cycle. Solar heat is not necessarily the basis of this, for the solar constant, very imperfectly to be sure, indicates many kinds of solar activity, including ultra-violet light, infra-red rays, and electrical waves. Thus the 41-month cycle may be derived from the sun, but may be due to other factors much more than to temperature, rainfall, atmospheric pressure, and ordinary weather.

Before the present author knew of Sterne's work, he had prepared the lower curve of Figure 61. This shows a significant resemblance to those of the solar constant, on the one hand, and the stock market, on the other. It was prepared in order to test the hypothesis that atmospheric electricity, influenced presumably by the sun, may affect the human reactions that govern fluctuations in the stock market, in iron production, and in other business activities. Tests of the electrical data showed that the condition most likely to be effective was apparently the variability of the electrical current (potential gradient) between the air and the earth. The lower curve of Figure 61 shows the average of this at Eskdalemuir in southern Scotland

[23] 1943, Vol. 1, p. 83.   [24] 1939, 1940.

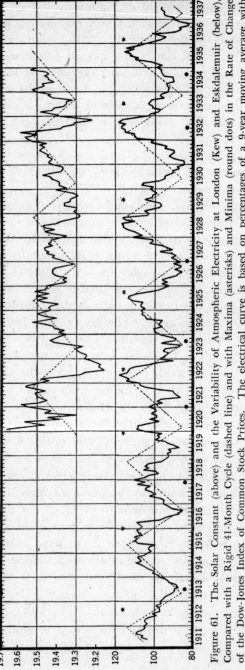

Figure 61.   The Solar Constant (above) and the Variability of Atmospheric Electricity at London (Kew) and Eskdalemuir (below), Compared with a Rigid 41-Month Cycle (dashed line) and with Maxima (asterisks) and Minima (round dots) in the Rate of Change of the Dow-Jones Index of Common Stock Prices.   The electrical curve is based on percentages of a 9-year moving average with seasonal trends eliminated.   The solar curve was prepared by E. R. Dewey.

and Kew near London.*   In spite of minor discrepancies the electrical curve clearly fluctuates in a cycle of 41 months, and its maxima keep coming back to the expected dates.

Perhaps the most remarkable thing about Figure 61 is the time relations which it indicates.   Although the two curves were prepared entirely independently, their dating coincides quite closely.   The regular sequence is for a maximum of the solar constant to be accompanied, or more often immediately followed, by a maximum in the variability of atmospheric electricity.   At almost this same time the solar constant itself drops off quite suddenly.   Thus it looks as if a sharp decline in the solar constant were associated with great variability in the electrical condition of the earth's atmosphere.

The maxima of electrical variability in turn are generally soon followed by a change from a bull market to a bear market on the stock exchange.   This is indicated by the asterisks which in Figure 61 indicate turning points in the rate of change in the Dow-Jones averages.   Except at the end of 1919, when World War I had disrupted matters and the solar constant itself had gone off the 41-month cycle, each maximum in the rate of change in the stock market falls within 3 to 12 months after a maximum in electrical variability.   This is about the lag that would be expected between a physical cause of this sort and its effect on business.

* The observatories at Eskdalemuir and Kew publish monthly data for observations at 6-hour intervals beginning at 3 A.M.   Thus the average change during four 6-hour periods is available.   The average of these four changes gives a good idea of the variability of the electrical current in any given month.   The data have been adjusted so that each observatory has the same weight.   The average of the two gives a better 41-month cycle than either alone.   The degree of betterment may be judged from the fact that the correlation coefficient between the rigid cycle and the actual observations at Eskdalemuir alone is .47 ± .03, and at Kew somewhat less, but for the two observatories together it is .60 ± .024.   For the sake of easy visibility the potential gradient curve has been partially freed from cycles other than that of 41-months by (1) expressing the electrical variability for each individual month as a percentage of the average value for that month, thus eliminating a strong seasonal cycle with maxima in February and minima in June; (2) by expressing the resultant values as percentages of a 41-month moving average in order to eliminate or minimize long cycles and secular trends; and (3) by using 7-month moving averages in order to get rid of some of the shorter cycles.   Nevertheless, it is obvious that the final curve still retains strong evidence of cycles which have not been eliminated.   All this illustrates the great difficulty in segregating any particular cycle from data which represent the effect of a number of cycles and of what seem to be mere accidents.   It also illustrates the fact that we have as yet made only a beginning in this respect.

The jump from electrical conditions in Great Britain to business affairs in New York seems big, but scarcity of both records and funds for further research prevents a closer tie-up. Hence our conclusions are valid only on the assumption that the electrical condition of the atmosphere varies in essentially the same way on both sides of the Atlantic Ocean. There is considerable ground for this assumption. The earth's electrical field is known to act as a unit. Auroras, for example, are evidence of peculiar electrical conditions in the far outer atmosphere. They become manifest all over the northern hemisphere at the same time. Stetson [25] and others have shown that radio transmission is another phase of atmospheric electricity which is closely dependent upon variations in solar radiation. Moreover, the probability that the same solar cycle dominates the atmosphere over wide areas is increased by the fact that when we average the observations at two observatories 300 miles apart, we find that the 41-month cycle is much clearer than when one observatory is taken alone. Then, too, the relationship between the 41-month cycle in the solar constant and in the potential gradient gives reason to think that we are dealing with a solar cause which acts in essentially the same way over vast areas. Hence, in spite of scanty knowledge, there seems to be a sound basis for the working hypothesis that electrical variations in the atmosphere of the sun induce corresponding variations in the atmosphere of the earth, and that these in turn are associated with psychological rhythms in human beings. Such close and reasonable relationships as we have seen between the solar constant, atmospheric electricity, and human psychology are not likely to occur by chance.

The nature of the physiological effect of atmospheric electricity, if such there be, has not yet been investigated experimentally, but it seems to pertain primarily to the nerves. When electrical variability increases, people apparently feel relatively buoyant and optimistic. They are therefore ready to risk their money on stocks and in other ways, with relatively little attention to unfavorable signs in business and politics. At the same time consumers, merchants, manufacturers, and others feel a similar stimulus. Therefore they increase the size of their orders, open new lines of activity, and make plans for enlarging their business. Thus the ascending phase of a cycle is generated.

The impetus thus received produces its full result quickly in some instances and more slowly in others. If it is simply a question of in-

25 1937.

vesting a few spare dollars, the response to the environmental stimulus may take place with little delay. The effect of this on stock prices, however, is far from instantaneous and may not be fully felt for months. How quickly it will be evident depends partly on the strength of the stimulus, partly on the previous trend of business, partly on the well-recognized conditions of the credit cycle, and partly on many other factors. Hence the amount of lag and the closeness with which events follow the solar cycle will inevitably vary greatly. Still greater variations will occur in business in general and in prices as a whole. For example, increased optimism among retail dealers in stockings, neckties, and similar articles will show its main effect on manufacturing some time after the maximum effect has been produced in the stock market. The lag in such goods as building materials will be much longer. The reverse of all this seems to occur when atmospheric electricity becomes less variable with an apparent decrease in its stimulating effect.

The final test of this electrical hypothesis of mental activity must await prolonged experiments. Meanwhile its probability is increased by recent studies of electric currents within living organisms. The measurement of such currents between one part of the body and another has already led to significant results. As Burr puts it, "wherever there is life there is electricity." Stated more specifically, this means that every "animal possesses a true [electrical] field. . . . Changes in biologic activity [of the kind associated with] growth and development produce just as significant variations in the electrical pattern as do heart and brain waves, . . . ovulation, [and] cancer. It is inconceivable that such a widespread phenomenon should be a by-product of life, for it is so intimately bound up with fundamental biological processes that it disappears at death." If each organism is thus the center or source of an electromagnetic field, it seems inevitable that alterations in the general field of the surrounding atmosphere must influence the field of the individual organism. Thus there seems to be a definite mechanism whereby atmospheric electricity may influence mental activity.

Here, for the present, we must leave the matter. We have seen that cycles of many lengths and kinds are widely prevalent. Some, such as the 35-year cycle of Brückner, are primarily evident in the weather and in its effect on crops. Their influence ramifies outward, however, into public relief work, politics, rebellion, migration, and many other matters which are thus influenced. Other cycles, such as those of $7\frac{1}{2}$ and 8 years, present fruitful fields of study but are beyond our present line of investigation. The 41-month cycle is so widespread and clear in literally hundreds of types of business that we can scarcely pass it by. In searching for causes we find this cycle only vaguely in ordinary weather. On the other hand, it is evident in the variability of atmospheric electricity and in the solar constant. Thus we are led to the working hypothesis that variations in the sun influence the electrical conditions of the earth's atmosphere. These in turn apparently exert a psychological effect upon man. Or perhaps some more pervasive cause influences the whole solar system and shows its presence by means of changes in the sun, in the earth's atmosphere, and in human reactions.

CHAPTER 25

TWO INTRIGUING CYCLES *

A. The Nine-Year Cycle in Prices

This chapter is devoted to two cycles which have nearly the same length but are of quite different kinds. In connection with the 41-month cycle of business we found that among mice and other small animals there is a somewhat longer and quite distinct cycle of about 4 years. The 41-month cycle appears to be closely connected with the variability of atmospheric electricity. The possible causes of the 4-year cycle were not investigated.

Coming now to cycles of 9 or 10 years, we again find a shorter and a longer cycle. The shorter, averaging approximately 9.2 years in length, appears primarily in business affairs, especially prices. Like the 41-month cycle, it may be connected with atmospheric electricity, although the records are too short to give any certainty. The longer cycle, like that of 4 years, is primarily evident in the numbers of animals and in the physiological rather than the psychological aspect of human affairs. It has an average length of 9.6 or 9.7 years and seems to be associated with atmospheric ozone much more than with either weather or atmospheric electricity. For convenience we shall call these two the 9-year and $9\frac{2}{3}$-year cycles. These terms are merely convenient approximations. We shall begin with the 9-year cycle but shall devote most of our space to the other.

A good example of the 9-year cycle has been worked out by Dewey [1] in Figure 62. In the lower diagram the dashed curve (based on 9-year moving averages) shows the general trend of wholesale prices in the United States; the solid line shows the course of prices when the 41-month cycle is eliminated by a 3-year moving average. In the upper diagram the differences between the two lines of the lower diagram are shown as they would be if the trend were horizontal, that is, if there were no trend at all. From 1832 onward the departures

---

* This is another of the chapters in which the author has been fortunate in having the active co-operation of Mr. Edward R. Dewey.

[1] 1940.

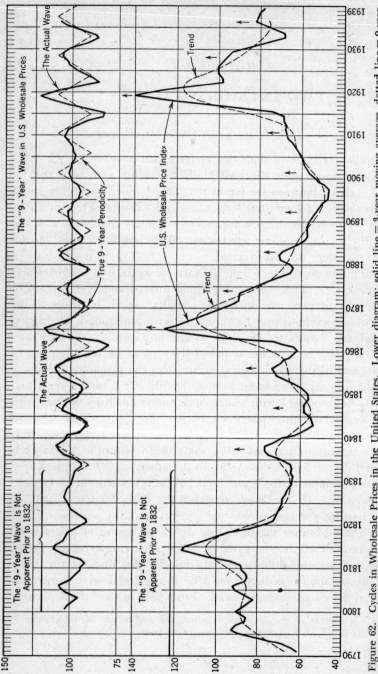

Figure 62. Cycles in Wholesale Prices in the United States. Lower diagram: solid line = 3-year moving average, dotted line = 9-year moving average; upper diagram: solid line = 3-year moving average of lower curve expressed as percentage of 9-year moving average.

From *Putting Cycles to Work in Science and Industry*, by E. R. Dewey.

show a regular agreement with the rigid 9-year cycle represented by the straight dashed lines. Before 1832 the agreement breaks down, perhaps because the components of the price index were changed in that year, but possibly because of some change in the economic or physical environment.

Incidentally, the lower part of Figure 62 shows a price cycle of about 50 years. Its three main maxima are associated respectively with the War of 1812, the Civil War, and World War I. The commonly accepted idea is that the wars have dominated prices. This is true to a large extent. Careful examination, however, indicates that if we omit the 15 or 20 years after the outbreak of each war, the remaining years suggest a cycle, which Dewey estimates at 54 years. Even if peace had prevailed, this would apparently have produced moderate maxima at this interval. Beveridge found a rhythm of this length in European wheat prices from 1600 onward and hence presumably in the weather. Dewey finds it in wheat prices in England back to about A.D. 1200. He also finds it in cotton prices in the United States since 1731. The Punic Wars of Rome are among those which are sometimes cited as possible indicators of a rough periodicity of half a century.

To return to the 9-year cycle, another good example is shown in Dewey's [2] curves of stock prices. The upper diagram of Figure 63 represents a price index as it appears when smoothed by 3-year moving averages (solid line) and 9-year averages (dashed line), just as in Figure 62. The lower diagram shows departures of the 3-year averages from the others. The persistence of the 9-year cycle is remarkable. It seems to be associated with a similar cycle found in the sun. At any rate Clayton,[3] Anderson, and many others have found one or more cycles of about this length in sunspots.

If the sun influences the course of prices, it may do so electrically, as has been suggested in respect to the 41-month cycle. The shortness of electrical records, however, and the inconstancy of a given cycle from place to place make it difficult to come to any firm conclusion. In Figure 64 the upper curve shows quite clearly that at Kew, after the 41-month cycle has been eliminated, the electrical curve has a single well-developed cycle of 18½ years. A dashed line

[2] 1940. [3] 1943.

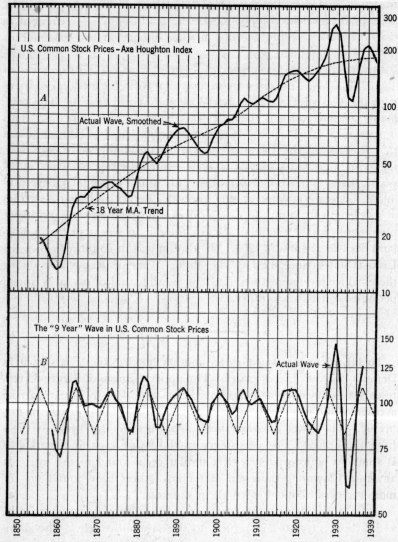

Figure 63. Nine-Year Cycles in Common Stock Prices (*after Dewey*). Solid line above = 3-year moving average, dotted line = 18-year moving average; solid line below = the solid line above expressed as a percentage of the 9-year moving average.

brings out the fact that in the low phase of this cycle there is a hint of another peak, thus suggesting a cycle of about 9.2 years. On the other hand, the Eskdalemuir curve (lower line in Figure 64) gives no hint of either a 9- or an 18-year electrical cycle. Moreover, its general trend is convex instead of concave, as at Kew. In view of the good agreement between the 41-month cycle at Kew and Eskdalemuir this disagreement in the longer cycle would be disconcerting were it not that the weather frequently displays just this sort of inconsistency. Many observers from Helland-Hansen and Arctowski[4] to

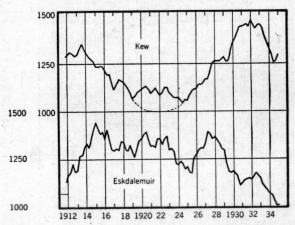

Figure 64. Electrical Potential Gradient of Earth-Air Current at London (Kew) and Eskdalemuir. Three-month totals of 41-month moving averages.

Abbot[5] and Clayton[6] have found examples of conformity between two places in one cycle, and opposition, or apparent lack of relation, in another cycle. We shall see a good example of this later in studying sunspots and storms.

Figure 65 is interesting in connection with the possible $18\frac{1}{3}$-year electrical cycle of Figure 64. It shows that in the eastern United States for one hundred years a surprisingly regular cycle in real estate activity has had a length of $18\frac{1}{3}$ years. The building industry in the United States has a rhythm of the same length. It is hard, however, to see how there can be a connection between the two cycles unless the electrical cycle in New York is in opposite phase from the one in London. In that case the maximum of building would come 6 years after the maximum electrical stimulation. That is about the

[4] 1912, 1919.   [6] 1943.
[5] 1935.

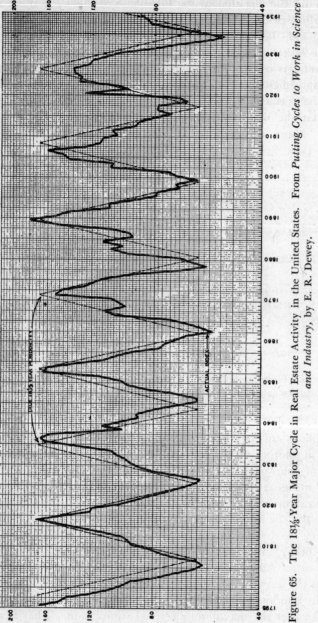

Figure 65. The 18½-Year Major Cycle in Real Estate Activity in the United States. From *Putting Cycles to Work in Science and Industry*, by E. R. Dewey.

lag that one would expect in work like building, where capital must be accumulated, plans drawn, and contractors engaged. The reality of any such relation, however, is so doubtful that the agreement in length between the oft-repeated building cycle and the once-repeated electrical cycle may be pure accident. The chief reason for mentioning the 18-year building cycle is to call attention to its amazing regularity, and to the fact that it is approximately twice the length of the

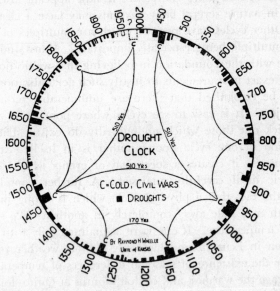

Figure 66. Clock Diagram of Droughts and Civil Wars (*after Wheeler*). Numbers around the circle indicate dates A.D.

9-year price cycle and about one third the length of the supposed 54-year cycle of prices. This again is just under one third of a cycle of 170 years which Wheeler [7] finds in droughts and in civil wars (Figure 66). His diagram, where time is arranged like a clock, also shows a still stronger cycle, three times as great (510 years), which is marked by the recurrence of prolonged and widespread droughts over wide areas.

————————

Figure 66 is in harmony with an idea which is strong among many students of cycles. They suspect the existence of certain basic short

[7] 1943.

cycles, such as those of 41 months, and 7.5, 9.2, and 11.2 years. They find reason to suppose that longer cycles are often multiples of these basic ones. In many cases the multiples seem to be stronger than the original short cycles. This matter, like many others connected with cycles, is still in the stage where our greatest need is more exact information. That is why the Foundation for the Study of Cycles is so important. Nevertheless, the evidence is piling up rapidly and is becoming more and more coherent. It now appears distinctly possible that in nature several basic rhythms may have a clear-cut periodicity. Other cycles have periods which are multiples of these, the three-fold multiple being especially important. Many students, however, agree with the Foundation in believing that we do not yet have sufficiently exact measurements to justify such generalizations.

It must be recognized that there are innumerable pitfalls in this whole subject. It is easy to see cycles where none exist. It is also hard to pick out those which undoubtedly do exist. The intricate superposition of one cycle upon another is in itself a tremendous obstacle because it creates a succession of events which seem quite unsystematic until carefully analysed. A further complication is added by the fact that a physical cycle which is strong in one part of the earth may fade away completely in another. We see this in the case of temperature. If one were acquainted only with the equatorial region in Ecuador and had only a short weather record, one might deny the existence of seasonal differences of temperature. On a long average the warmest and coldest months at Quito, for example, differ only 0.7°F. At Verkhoyansk in Siberia, on the contrary, the difference is 119°F, but in the same high latitude as Verkhoyansk the corresponding difference falls to 18° on some of the Norwegian islands. When we understand such contrasts and differences, as we do in the case of temperature, they cease to puzzle us. Similar differences in other conditions, such as atmospheric electricity, may be puzzling simply because we know so little about them.

B. *The Interplay of Psychology and Botany*

Even if the preceding conclusion as to the psychological effect of the electrical activity of the sun is correct, it by no means indicates that such an effect is the dominant cause of fluctuations in prices. The effect of at least two other factors is illustrated in Figure 67, one being human events, such as wars, and the other the weather through its effect on vegetation. The upper three curves show the general price level in the United States, Great Britain, and Germany, according to Schumpeter's data. They represent percentages of a 9-year moving average. In the early 1860's prices fell tremendously in the United States because of the Civil War, with its interruption of trade in cotton and other commodities. Then in the later sixties there

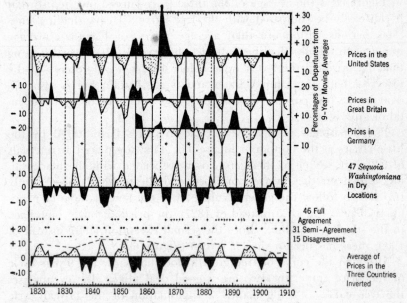

Figure 67. The 9⅗-Year Cycle in World Prices Compared with Tree Growth in California. The price curves are based on departures from a 9-year moving average. In the upper part of diagram: * = financial crisis in England; • = maximum of foreign trade in Europe and North America.

was a correspondingly sharp rise. The effect of panics and financial depressions can also be seen. Schumpeter did not carry his curves beyond 1910 because World War I created such a disturbance in prices everywhere. Such events are evidently among the main factors in determining prices in all countries.

In spite of distinctively human events the price curves in Figure 67 all show a strong development of the standard 9-year cycle. Note how closely the curves for the three countries fluctuate together and reach maxima at average intervals of 9 years. Thus a psychological effect, due presumably to some environmental, perhaps solar, condition, seems to be a second factor in determining the level of prices.

This does not end the matter. The next curve (fourth from the top) suggests that the weather, acting presumably through the growth of crops, also influences prices. This curve, however, does not represent crops. It shows the rate of growth of 47 sequoia trees in California, as indicated by the thickness of their rings of growth.[8] The trees grew in relatively dry places, so that they were quite sensitive to variations in rainfall as well as temperature. The lowest curve in Figure 67 is the average of the three price curves, inverted so that it can easily be compared with the tree curve. Heavy shading indicates periods with more than average prices, or less than average tree growth. Light shading indicates the reverse. It is worth noting that the break in the 9-year cycle before 1832 not only occurs in the prices of both the United States and Great Britain but is also evident in the tree curve. This suggests that it may be of environmental origin.

The persistence of the 9-year cycle in prices is indicated by the little circles at the bottom of Figure 67. They are placed at intervals of 9.2 years. Nine of them are closely associated with the black valleys which on the reversed price curve indicate high prices. Only two fail to follow the general rule. After the first of these (a maximum of prices in 1825 instead of 1827), the prices at once come back to the standard rhythm. Since the second exception (1907 instead of 1909) there has been a similar return (Figure 62).

Although the curve of tree growth does not show the 9-year cycle of the price curve, the two are a good deal alike. Dewey analyses the tree curve as being mainly a combination of the 11-year cycle and two or more shorter cycles. The result is a curve which resembles the price curve in many ways and may indicate that certain factors influence both trees and prices. This is evident from the extent to which the two curves resemble one another, as indicated by the signs between them. Plus signs, 46 in number, indicate years when the curves of trees and inverted prices move upward or downward in harmony, and are on the same side of normal. Zeros (31) indicate neutral years in which the two curves agree in one of these respects but not in the other. Minus signs (15) indicate disagreement in both respects. If we divide the neutral years equally between agreement and disagreement, we get 61½ agreements and 31½ disagreements.

The degree of relation between trees and prices in Figure 67 may be judged from correlation coefficients. Omitting the Civil War

[8] Huntington, 1914A.

period of disturbed prices (1861 to 1866) in the American and British figures, but not in the German, we find the following correlation coefficients between sequoia growth and prices: United States, $-.28 \pm .07$; Great Britain, $-.39 \pm .07$; and Germany, $-.75 \pm .04$.* All of these are statistically significant. They indicate that up to 1910, prices tended to go down when the sequoias grew well and up when the trees grew slowly. They also indicate that at least half of the variation in general prices in Germany was due to factors that coincided with influences affecting the growth of the Big Trees in California.

The connection between tree growth and prices is presumably due to the weather. Its greater strength in relation to Germany than to Britain apparently arises from the fact that sequoia growth and German prices depend on local weather much more than do prices in the United States or Great Britain. The weather affects American prices mainly through wheat, corn, cotton, oats, potatoes, and tobacco. These grow in climates of varied types, no one of which is much like that of the sequoias. In fact, the rainfall in the western and southeastern parts of the country shows considerable tendency to vary in opposite directions.[9] Hence the effect of the weather on prices is the result of conditions which often work in opposite ways at different places. Therefore it is not surprising that sequoia growth and American prices show only a slight correlation.

In Germany, on the contrary, the best weather for crops is like that which is best for sequoias. The California trees are especially influenced by (1) the temperature of the year as a whole, especially from October to December; and (2) the water stored up in the ground from previous seasons.[10] High temperatures favor rapid growth with little regard to the immediate rainfall, although the rain of the two preceding years is of much importance. Thus sequoias grow best when one or two rainy years end in a warm autumn and early winter, followed by a warm summer. Essentially the same conditions are best for crops in Germany. Hence rapid sequoia growth in California and good crops with consequent low prices in Germany prevail when oceanic air from the west brings warm autumns which are followed by warm summers. Of course, the short fluctuations of the weather in Germany and among the Sierras are by no means the

---

* If we include 1860–66, the coefficients become: United States, $-.22 \pm .07$; Great Britain, $-.34 \pm .06$.

9 Huntington, 1925A.

10 Huntington, 1925A, p. 167.

same. Nevertheless, the two regions occupy similar locations in respect to the continents and oceans, and when periods of several years are considered, they appear to behave much alike in respect to cycles of weather.

The kind of weather that is best for sequoias is good for crops in Britain, but not in the interior of the United States, where heat and drought are the worst enemies of crops. British agricultural prices, however, have long been greatly influenced by those of America. Hence the relation of sequoia growth to British prices ought to be intermediate between the strong German and the weak American relationships. That is what our correlation coefficients indicate. Thus the price curves of Figure 67 seem to show the effect of the weather, as well as of wars, financial depressions, and solar activity.

Other conditions of business are doubtless similarly affected. The asterisks in the middle of Figure 67 indicate British financial crises, as interpreted by Burton. These tend to occur when prices are high and the sequoias are growing slowly. The round dots indicate that since 1870 foreign trade among advanced countries (the United States, Great Britain, Germany, France, Italy, Belgium, and the Netherlands) has also tended to reach a maximum under similar conditions. The average interval from one British crisis to another, or from one peak of trade to another, is 9.6 years. This interval suggests the animal cycle that we shall soon consider, but perhaps it is due to a number of factors which work together. In spite of such difficulties the preceding discussion helps in our study of civilization. It indicates that prices depend on many conditions, among which the effect of weather on crops joins with the 9-year price cycle and a great variety of economic and human events. It also confirms the idea that a full explanation of fluctuations in business is impossible unless we understand how much is due to environmental cycles in contrast to purely economic or human reactions.

C. The 9⅔-Year Cycle Among Animals

We turn now to one of the clearest and most pervasive of cycles. In Figure 68 the upper curve shows the number of letters received by the New Jersey Agricultural Experiment Station in respect to tent caterpillars.[11] The obnoxious webs of these insects, found mainly on

11 Headlee.

wild cherry and apple trees, stimulated letter-writing considerably in 1915, more in 1924, and most in 1935. This suggests a cycle of about 10 years, but three maxima are not enough to establish the true length. The data of Shelford and Flint, however, appear to indicate that chinch bugs come and go in a cycle which averaged 9.6 years during the 120 years from 1820 to 1940. This destructive, dark-colored,

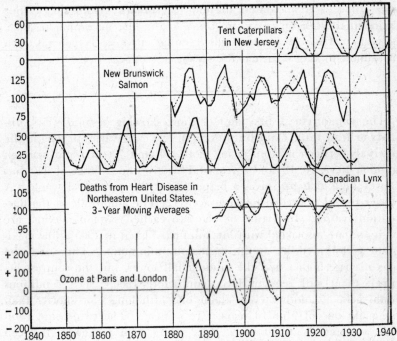

Figure 68. The 9⅔-Year Cycle in Animals, Man, and Ozone. The ozone curve shows the amount by which the ozone of any given year differs from that of the fifth preceding year, after secular trends have been eliminated.

white-winged little insect is a major pest of cereals in the United States and Canada. In Illinois its numbers vary from a few hundred to 70,000,000 per acre. The last three main maxima there occurred in 1914, 1923, and 1934, each being a year before the corresponding maximum of the tent caterpillar.

Above the insects in the scale of life, the salmon of the Restigouche River [12] in New Brunswick (second curve from the top in Figure 68) exhibit a cycle which seems almost identical with that of the tent

[12] Phelps and Belding.

caterpillars and chinch bugs 700 to 1,400 miles away. For two generations an exclusive fishing club, which controls many miles of the Restigouche, has insisted on full records of how long people fish and what they catch. When we eliminate a secular trend, or general upward tendency due perhaps to improved methods of fishing, the average hourly catch of fish per fisherman shows five clear maxima between 1880 and 1930. The last of these occurred in 1924, at the same time as a maximum in tent caterpillars. Going back four cycles in the salmon curve, we come to the first maximum in 1886, 38 years earlier. Huntsman finds a similar curve in the general catch of salmon in the Maritime Provinces.

The salmon curve, like most of those showing organic cycles, displays at least three main features. (1) The cycle varies in length, the intervals between maxima being 9, 10, 12, and 7 years; and between minima 10, 7, 10, 12, and 8 years. This gives an average of $9\frac{3}{4}$, but Dewey finds that $9\frac{2}{3}$ gives a better fit for the curve as a whole. A longer record is needed for accuracy. (2) The amplitude of the fluctuations varies. In Figure 68 the two earliest salmon maxima are high and are associated with low minima. Then in 1905 a low maximum is followed by an inconspicuous minimum. Thereafter the maxima rise higher and the minima fall lower, but the contrast between them still remains less than before 1900. Such conditions could arise if another cycle about one fifth longer or shorter than the main one of 9 or 10 years were present. The two would coincide at intervals of 50 years, thus giving high maxima. Between these maxima they would more or less reduce one another, thus seeming to produce long cycles. Data for many more years are needed before we can be sure of any such additional cycle. (3) Another typical feature of the salmon curve is that more or less complete reversals sometimes occur. In 1914, when the 9- or 10-year cycle would lead us to expect a maximum in the salmon curve, we find a depression, as if a piece of the curve had been bitten out. On the other hand, the minimum that might be expected in 1889 is replaced by a slight maximum, that of 1909 is flattened, and there is a seemingly superfluous minimum in 1903. Such conditions suggest the presence of still another cycle, considerably shorter than 9 years, but this remains to be tested. Thus the salmon curve, as a whole, is clearly dominated by a cycle of about $9\frac{2}{3}$ years. It may, however, represent at least two others, and no one knows how many more, and it is almost certainly influenced also by accidental occurrences.

In interpreting curves such as those of Figure 68, two points must be remembered. First, so far as we yet know there is no evidence that the cycles here mentioned are uniform in length and intensity in any such way as the year and the day. Such uniformity may indeed exist and be hidden by a large number of other cycles, perhaps equally uniform, as Beveridge [13] and Dewey seem to think, but these investigators, like the rest of us, are awaiting further evidence.

Second, practically all curves that illustrate the phenomena of life and many that illustrate purely physical conditions act as if they were due to the combined effect of several cycles. We cannot say that this has yet been fully demonstrated in respect to living organisms. Nevertheless, it is quite generally believed that the virulence of influenza epidemics, for example, depends on at least three cyclic factors: (1) human powers of resistance, (2) the weather with its seasons and storms; and (3) the potency of the virus, which seems to wax and wane for unknown reasons. In purely physical occurrences the combined action of several cycles is obvious. Everyone knows, for example, that there are regular daily and seasonal cycles of temperature and that the daily cycle varies according to the season. In Alabama, for instance, the daily range amounts to 20°F in winter and 30° in summer. A third type of cycle, quite irregular and due to storms, repeatedly upsets the daily rhythm and greatly disturbs that of the seasons. A rarely warm winter night may even have the same temperature as a cold summer day. The annual and daily cycles are still operating, but another cycle has temporarily overcome their effect.

Tides, as Logan suggests, illustrate this same point. They are absolutely regular in origin, but lunar and solar cycles together produce an irregular curve of high spring tides when sun and moon pull in the same direction, and low neap tides when they pull at right angles. The shape of coastlines introduces further complications. Thus in the China Sea and elsewhere gravitational and other forces which normally produce two tides a day produce only one.[14] The life of a fisherman is influenced by complex tidal cycles and still more complex weather cycles. The effect on fish is added to the direct effect on the fishermen. Other complications are added by the effect of the weather on bacteria and viruses and thus upon the health and vigor of the fishermen. In view of all this it is not strange that curves of organic activities show all sorts of irregularities, with traces

[13] 1922.   [14] Paul C. Whitney.

of many cycles. The principle of multiple cycles, which is thus illustrated, offers a key which may ultimately disclose order and regularity in many aspects of weather and life where chaos now seems
to reign.

———————

Many investigators have found a cycle of 9 or 10 years in the abundance of grouse.[15] At a still higher level, Elton and Nicholson's curve
of furs brought to the Hudson's Bay Company (middle diagram in
Figure 68) shows that the lynx population of Canada varies in essential agreement with that of salmon and caterpillars one or two
thousand miles away in New Brunswick and New Jersey. Data for
the lynx show the same cycle of about $9\frac{2}{3}$ years from 1725 to the
present. When data for only 1840 to 1904 were available, the
length of the cycle appeared to be $9\frac{3}{4}$ years. Later data show that
the maximum has returned on time in four successive cycles. When
older data also are considered, Dewey places the length of the cycle
at about 9.65 years. The lynx curve suggests that other cycles, longer
or shorter than 9 or 10 years, are at work, but thus far these have
not been analysed. Note the low maxima in 1858 and 1877 and the
flattened minima, 1852 to 1855 and 1861 to 1864. Other animals,
such as the Canadian marten, fisher, mink, muskrat, and snowshoe
rabbit, also show essentially this same cycle of a little less than 10
years, together with hints of other cycles both longer and shorter.

The second curve from the bottom in Figure 68 is especially significant because it shows that man has a $9\frac{2}{3}$-year physical cycle of
essentially the same length as that of insects, fish, and fur-bearing
mammals. It indicates that the deathrate from heart diseases [16] in
the northeastern United States follows a 9- or 10-year rhythm. The
relative irregularity of this curve may indicate that human health
is influenced by a greater number of circumstances than is the reproduction, health, and survival of animals.

D. Ozone and the $9\frac{2}{3}$-Year Cycle

The lowest curve in Figure 68 suggests an answer to some of the
questions which arise in respect to the widespread and strongly developed $9\frac{2}{3}$-year cycle. Its resemblance to the other curves is obvious. It shows that atmospheric ozone, as measured in Paris and

15 Bump, N. Criddle, Leopold.
16 *Vital Statistics Rates in the United States, 1900 to 1940.*

London, varies in what appears to be the same cycle as that of tent caterpillars, salmon, lynx, and deaths from heart disease in the United States and Canada. Does this mean that atmospheric ozone is the basis of the cycle? An affirmative answer involves far-reaching consequences as to the history of civilization and man's future adaptation to all sorts of climates from the equator to the poles. Before we can be sure of the final answer, many questions need to be cleared up, and other possible causes of the cycle must be investigated.

First, let us see why the ozone curve of Figure 68 is based on European instead of American data and what effect this has on our conclusions. The only good records of ozone covering any considerable length of time are those of Greenwich Observatory in London from 1877 to 1910 and of Montsouris Observatory in Paris for about the same period. The ozone at these places was measured by means of the change observed in the color of litmus paper when exposed to the air. The paper was compared with a standard set of colors. This method is now considered quite crude. It measures other minor atmospheric ingredients, such as nitrous oxides, as well as ozone. The records thus obtained have been used by very few investigators and were discontinued everywhere before World War I. Nevertheless, the ozone records have a real value in showing variations from hour to hour, season to season, and year to year. In their crude form, before analysis, the records do not show the 9⅔-year cycle nearly so clearly as it appears in Figure 68. The data for each city indicate a cycle which may be the 35-year Brückner period, or some longer cycle with both ends cut off.* Our first step is to eliminate this by using

* Curiously enough, this cycle forms an upward arc in London and a downward arc in Paris. This is the kind of seeming contradiction which repeatedly crops up in the study of weather and cycles. It may be due to changes in the direction of the wind and in the amount of smoke from the cities. Montsouris lies south of Paris. When north winds blow, the atmospheric ozone falls to a minimum because it is taken out by the dust and smoke of the city. South winds, on the contrary, bring pure country air with much ozone. Greenwich, too, is much affected by winds from its city, but not in the same way as Montsouris. If there were no cities, the largest concentration of ozone would probably come with northeast winds. It is known that during a Brückner cycle there is an oceanic phase with different winds from those of the opposite continental phase. Such changes in the winds may cause the two cities to behave differently in a long cycle without destroying a similarity in a shorter cycle due to some other cause. Such discrepancies illustrate the great difficulties that beset the study of cycles. For our present purpose the best course is to eliminate the long cycle by taking the departures of the actual ozone data from what would be expected if the long cycle progressed with full regularity.

departures from the general smoothed course of the curve. When
this is done we get the curve shown in Figure 69. Here there are
many irregularities due to minor cycles. Nevertheless, the 9-year
cycle is clearly visible. Its agreement with the lynx cycle is evident
from the asterisks which indicate the maxima of that cycle. The
lynx maxima of 1876, 1886 or 1887, and 1896 all come close to ozone
maxima. In 1905 and 1906, however, the ozone maximum has been
bitten out in the way that we often see in such curves.

In the ozone curve at the bottom of Figure 68 the irregularities of
Figure 69 are eliminated by expressing each year's ozone as a per-

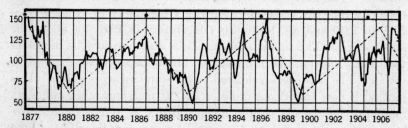

Figure 69. Ozone at London (Kew) and Paris. In averaging the two records each
of the 12 calendar months is treated as a separate unit and receives the same weight
at both places. Seasonal trends are eliminated by using percentages of monthly
averages. Secular trends are eliminated by using percentages of a 115-month moving average. Minor variations are eliminated by means of 7-month moving averages.
The 4 asterisks indicate maxima of lynx in Canada.

centage of the ozone 5 years earlier. Thus we compare opposite
phases of the $9\frac{2}{3}$-year cycle. London and Paris have been put together in such a way that each has the same weight.

The result of all this is the surprisingly regular curve at the bottom
of Figure 68. The average interval between the maxima of this
curve is about 9.5 years. One sees at once that the ozone maxima
fall at almost the same dates as those of the animals, and two or three
years before those of deaths from heart diseases. Thus we have found
a physical cycle which agrees with the $9\frac{2}{3}$-year cycle in length and
has its maxima at the time one would expect if atmospheric ozone
really is a stimulant to reproduction and to a kind of activity which
tends gradually to exhaust people whose hearts are weak.

The coincidence between ozone and organic life in the $9\frac{2}{3}$-year
cycle must be considered in connection with two other similar circumstances. One is the annual cycle wherein both ozone and the
use of libraries show a wavelike progression of the maximum from

February in high latitudes to April near the equator (page 352). The other is the brief and irregular cycle of storms with its dearth of ozone when a tropical air mass brings a feeling of inertia before a storm and its exhilarating effect when a storm comes to an end (page 379). The experience of students during the New England hurricane of 1938 will be remembered as an example of this. Thus three wholly different cycles, with periods of $9\frac{2}{3}$-years, 1 year, and a few days, agree in suggesting that fluctuations in the amount of atmospheric ozone may be a direct factor in producing rather widespread physiological results which are especially evident in the numbers of animals and in deaths from heart diseases, as well as in human feelings of energy. The numbers of animals must depend on variations in the rate of reproduction or death, or more probably on both. The variations in heart diseases presumably arise from some kind of stimulation which induces a type of activity that may be desirable for people in sound health but is dangerous for those with weak hearts.

E. The Insufficiency of Ordinary Weather

The problem of the relation between physical and organic cycles is so important that we may well pause briefly to inquire more fully into the question of how much evidence there is as to a $9\frac{2}{3}$-year cycle of weather. There is some such evidence, but it is vague compared with the sharply defined curves of Figure 68, and it does not come from Canada. For example, Beveridge [17] says that European wheat prices (Figure 57) show a cycle of 9.75 years. Nevertheless, when his data are plotted they give only a faint impression of any cycle of 9 or 10 years. In the same way Brunt's harmonic analysis discloses a 9.5-year cycle in rainfall at London and Edinburgh and in atmospheric pressure at Paris. There is no trace of this cycle, however, in rainfall at Milan and Padua, in atmospheric pressure at Edinburgh, or in temperature at six cities of Sweden, Great Britain, France, Germany, and Austria. Nevertheless, Brunt cites other investigators who have found a similar periodicity in the mean position of the high-pressure belt of the southern hemisphere east and west of South Africa, in the atmospheric pressure of Australia, and in Nile floods during a long period. Thus the evidence seems to

[17] 1921.

show that over a wide range of the earth's surface the weather is distinctly affected by a cycle of between 9 and 10 years.

In spite of the wide distribution of the 9⅔-year weather cycle, it is doubtful whether the differences between the extreme phases of temperature, rainfall, and pressure in this cycle are by any means strong enough to produce effects such as those seen in salmon and lynx, for example. In London, when the effect of the seasons is eliminated, the difference between the highest and lowest monthly temperatures in Brunt's 9.5-year cycle is less than 0.3°F. The corresponding difference in rainfall is only 0.12 inches. Such differences are trivial compared with the contrasts in the curves for lynx, salmon, and heart diseases. If this cycle exists in American weather, it is apparently no stronger than in Europe. It seems improbable that such slight differences in the weather should lead to such great differences in reproduction and health. Nevertheless, the existence of an atmospheric cycle of the right length is important. Such a cycle may be manifest in ionization, ozone, or electrical potential more clearly than in rain, temperature, or sunshine.

Failure to find an explanation of the 9⅔-year cycle in ordinary weather suggests that the sun may give rise to such a cycle through some form of energy other than heat. In other words, can this cycle be solar in origin, but not climatic in the ordinary sense? Many investigators have found a cycle of about 9 years and another of about 10 in sunspots. The solar constant, which pursues a course different from that of sunspots, may have a 9⅔-year cycle, but as yet the record is too short to give any certainty.

F. Other Possible Causes of Cycles

In addition to weather, several other causes of fluctuations in the numbers of animals have been suggested. Hamilton,[18] speaking of the 4-year cycle, thinks that in years when mice are scanty the males often fail to find the females at the oestrous period, which recurs every 4 days but lasts only a few hours. Even if such failures occur, however, this does not explain why the reproductive season is short. One would expect the opposite, for in years when mice are so scarce that they cannot readily find one another, the food supply is normally more abundant than usual in proportion to the number of

[18] 1944.

animals. Shelford and Flint have sought an explanation of the increased productive vigor along quite different lines. They suggest that fungi may influence the reproductive rate of chinch bugs but do not explain why the fungi have a $9\frac{2}{3}$-year cycle. Bacterial diseases are believed by many to be the reason for the catastrophic decline in populations of rabbits, mice, and other creatures after periods of excessive multiplication, but there seems to be little evidence that other bacteria or fungi lead to increased fertility.

Another possibility is sometimes advanced in explanation of cycles in the abundance of furs. This is discussed by Elton and Nicholson as follows:

> It is frequently suggested that cycles shown in fur returns might be caused by changes in prices. . . . This is not an important factor. . . . In the early days, and still to a great extent, trappers brought in any valuable skins they could catch, and for long periods at a time received the same tariff prices at the posts, although in London the prices did vary inversely to the supplies sold at auction. There is also a great deal of evidence, both for rabbits and lynx . . . about fluctuations observed by trappers in the field . . . from tracks in the snow and other signs.

The inadequacy of other explanations, the approximately uniform length of the $9\frac{2}{3}$-year cycle throughout vast areas, and the synchronism or reasonable lag of its phases in different kinds of animals all suggest that Elton is right in postulating an environmental cause of a more or less world-wide or cosmic nature. Beveridge [19] suspected something like this in respect to the 35-year cycle and several other cycles which he found in the price of European wheat. Like most investigators, he has no doubt that the main factor in the production of good or bad crops is the weather. Nevertheless, he is impressed by the fact that many cycles in wheat prices are either not matched at all by known weather cycles or only by cycles too insignificant to produce the observed results. Therefore he suggests that "though the most obvious way in which physical factors would affect the harvest is through the weather (e.g., by causing at certain periods excessive rain, cold, or storms), another possibility cannot be excluded. Some physical factors, electrical or other, in the sun or in the earth may affect the growth of corn [wheat] without causing an appreciable change in what is ordinarily known as the weather." Shelford and Flint in their study of chinch bugs searched for such an environmental factor, but were not satisfied with their results.

[19] 1921, p. 446.

After discarding seasonal temperature and rainfall as ultimate causes, they turned to sunspots and ultra-violet light. They find that the last comes closest to having a significant correlation with the number of chinch bugs. The bugs tend to be numerous when such light is weak and scarce when it is strong. The correlation, however, is not clear, and the available data (1924–38) are not sufficient to permit any definite conclusion. We shall return to ultra-violet light later.

G. Objections to an Ozone Hypothesis

The failure of ordinary weather, as well as of other conditions, to explain the $9\frac{2}{3}$-year cycle encourages the investigation of variations in ozone, but the evidence yet available is scanty. The close agreement between the ozone cycle and the animal cycle, however, is a strong argument. Another is that atmospheric ozone in extremely small amounts, one part in twenty or thirty million of air, is known to be a most effective physiological stimulant. According to Yaglou,[20] it gives to air the delightful quality known as freshness. Practically every kind of air that is considered especially desirable has more than the average amount of ozone.[21] This is true of outdoor air compared with indoor air, of country air compared with that of cities, of mountains versus lowlands, high latitudes in contrast to low, the day after a storm in contrast to the day before, clear desert air in contrast to dusty air or to that of regions with lush vegetation, windy air as compared with still air, and the air near waterfalls, breakers, and windswept whitecaps in comparison with that over water that is quiet.

Two of the chief objections to an ozone hypothesis are lack of experimental evidence and the fact that the ozone curve of Figure 68 comes from western Europe, whereas our data as to the $9\frac{2}{3}$-year cycle are American. The only thing to be said about the first objection is that the sooner an adequate series of experiments is undertaken, the better. As to the other objection, such data as are yet available seem to indicate that fluctuations in the general supply of atmospheric ozone are world-wide, although minor circumstances of wind, rain, temperature, vegetation, and dust lead to great contrasts locally. The contrasts arise partly from the fact that ozone is quickly removed from the air by moisture, dust, vegetation, and any other condition

[20] 1931, 1933, 1934. [21] Huntington, 1941.

which encourages oxidation. They are also due to the fact that ozone is readily carried by the wind.

On the other hand, a tendency toward world-wide uniformity in cycles of ozone seems to be inevitable because of the way in which the main supply originates. At a height of ten or fifteen miles the earth is surrounded by an atmospheric layer in which there is a relatively high concentration of ozone. The amount, to be sure, is only one part in hundreds of thousands of air, but if people had to breathe air with any such content, they would soon die because of the ozone's irritating effect on the mucous membranes. The ozone in this layer is formed mainly by ultra-violet light, which acts upon oxygen in such a way that molecules with three atoms instead of two are formed. In pure, dry, cold air the ozone can last indefinitely. Thus when ultra-violet radiation is abundant, the ozone layer all around the world tends to become more concentrated.

Because of its three molecules instead of two, ozone is comparatively heavy and sinks slowly earthward. Thus in due time it reaches the lower part of the air, where it meets water vapor, dust, and eventually vegetation, animals, and the soil. All of these tend to take ozone out of the air. The speed with which this occurs varies greatly according to climate. In warm, moist regions the ozone largely disappears even before it reaches the earth's surface, and whatever remains is used up almost at once as soon as it gets to the plants, dust, and moisture close to the ground. This appears to be one of the reasons why tropical air is enervating. In higher latitudes, and in deserts so long as they are not dusty, the length of time that ozone can retain its identity becomes shorter in proportion to the increase of the air's vapor content and dustiness. The world's coldest and least dusty air, and also that in which the absolute amount of water vapor is least, is found over the vast masses of ice which cover Greenland, the Arctic Ocean, and the snow-covered northern parts of Asia, North America and Antarctica. Even if no sunlight reaches those places for months in winter, ozone continues to settle slowly downward through many miles of air and to accumulate in the lower atmosphere.

The result of all this is that by midwinter the concentration of ozone in the far north and south has reached a high level. This may be one of the reasons why Arctic travellers have much to say about the stimulating quality of the winter air and the general good temper of the Eskimos at that time in spite of intense cold. In summer, too, although there is less ozone than in winter, the amount at high latitudes is still relatively large. This may be one reason why crops which escape frost grow luxuriantly in high latitudes, giving yields per acre that are almost unparalleled elsewhere.[22]

At all times of the year, but most of all in winter, the movement of polar air masses downward from high altitudes and equatorward from high latitudes brings some of the ozonized air to the regions where people chiefly live, especially to the stormy middle latitudes of North America and Europe. Each cyclonic storm in the northern hemisphere is likely to end with the inrush of a mass of cool, dry, dust-free air charged with ozone, much of which was originally formed by ultra-violet light at high levels far above the earth's surface. One of the handicaps of the southern hemisphere is that the paths of storms pass mainly over water. Hence atmospheric vapor largely takes the ozone out of the polar air masses before they reach the land. Ozone is also added to the air by electrical action, by the rush of the wind through spray in rain, and by the radioactivity of minerals. Nevertheless, the main supply comes from the upper air.

During the autumn and winter, as the ozone increases in high latitudes, the movements of air masses spread the increase to lower latitudes. The beginning of this process perhaps helps to make autumn a stimulating season. The maximum effect, however, is not felt till later, as we saw in respect to libraries. Since the ozone arrives in this way, its maximum naturally occurs later and later as lower latitudes are reached. In other words, looked at in a broad way, a wave of ozone presses out from high latitudes with a maximum in the late winter in the far north and at later and later dates farther south. This agrees with what we have seen in respect to libraries, on the one hand, and the mental activity of people of high latitudes, on the other hand.

For our present purposes the important point is that the accumulation of ozone and its equatorward sweep are not local occurrences. They pertain to each hemisphere as a whole. Hence there is reason to believe that if some solar or cosmic condition causes the strength of the high ozone layer to vary in a $9\frac{2}{3}$-year cycle, an ozone cycle of that same length in the lower air will be almost world-wide. Like seasonal changes of temperature, however, it may be almost imperceptible at low levels near the equator. Moreover, it is quite possible that a cycle of ordinary weather, by changing the winds and rainfall, may locally blot out the ozone cycle, or even reverse it, as we suspected from the contrast between London and Paris in the

[22] Albright.

long ozone cycle. On the other hand, if this kind of interference is eliminated, ozone cycles which do not have the same length as ordinary weather cycles may show up clearly as synchronous over wide areas. Hence in spite of manifest difficulties of interpretation, it seems possible that in a broad way the ozone cycle is a world-wide occurrence. It presumably has the same phases everywhere except as these are locally altered by cycles in winds, rain, or storms which arise through some other type of solar or cosmic activity. This seems to be as far as we can go until further exact measurements are available.

H. Environment versus Heredity in the 9⅔-Year Cycle

The effects of the ozone cycle, as well as its causes, suggest problems which can be stated far more easily than they can be solved. In the study of cycles, just as in education and most of the affairs of life, we are confronted by the inevitable question of environment versus heredity. In respect to cycles the environmental viewpoint is well represented by Elton,[23] who founded the Bureau of Animal Population at Oxford University. For many years he has sought far and wide for natural rhythms to match those of the abundance of animals. At first, sunspots seemed to provide a hopeful lead, but as the body of facts increased, it became clear that the main animal cycle in Canada is decidedly shorter than the sunspot cycle, which has an average length of about 11.15 years. The search for a weather cycle of approximately 9.6 years proved equally unfruitful. Nevertheless, Elton still feels that the cycle must be environmental.

The lynx cycle illustrates Elton's ideas. He discusses the common idea that the number of lynx depends on that of the snowshoe rabbit, or Canadian hare, and that the hares increase in numbers because of unusually favorable weather during the breeding season, or because some unknown conditions of weather provide an uncommonly good supply of food for the young. He also shows very clearly, as do many others, that the sudden decline in the number of rabbits arises from epidemics, as happens with other animals, especially mice. He then goes on to show that as yet we do not know of any factor in the weather which varies in a cycle like that of the lynx, rabbit, and other animals. He finally reaches this conclusion: [24]

[23] 1929.
[24] Elton and Nicholson.

It is also possible that the factor, at present unknown, which keeps the cycle in step over such large regions, may affect the lynx directly, i.e., through its rate of reproduction or physiological condition in other ways. . . . We have at present no clue at all to the nature of the factor controlling this enormous wildlife rhythm in the northern forests, except that it seems almost certain that climatic fluctuations must play a controlling part. The cycle operates exactly parallel on both sides of the Rockies. . . . The introduced snowshoe rabbits on Anticosti [Island in the lower St. Lawrence River] have developed a cycle corresponding to the mainland one; the whole of Canada keeps in step without ever getting out of phase.

In a later publication [25] he goes still farther. Speaking of the migrations of lemmings which occur every three or four years in Scandinavia and are sometimes quite dramatic, he says, "So we are left, as with the British cycle [of mice and voles], with a good many hints of some great cosmic oscillation, expressing itself in periodic upheavals in the biotic community, but we still lack the full key to the problem."

Quite a different viewpoint is taken by Allee,[26] who represents the primarily biological viewpoint. It seems to him probable that

swings in population density [among animals] are an expression primarily of interlocking factors inherent in the loosely integrated population. This view does not imply an absence of effect by the physical environment . . . but it does suggest that the physical environment plays a remote subsidiary role. If this suggestion is accepted as a working hypothesis, the implication is that the lack of a close balance in population numbers, year after year, results primarily from the biotic relations within the population in question and between it and other populations of plants and animals with which it is associated, rather than the oscillations being the result of some imposed cosmic periodicity. If we can accept the irregularities as an inherent part of the phenomena at hand, rather than struggling to fit the data into a periodicity of given average length, I believe we will be better prepared to make needed advances in the solution of these complex, but highly important population problems.

Some light on the relative value of these two viewpoints is shed by Table 25, which compares the dates of maxima among animals with the dates of maximum ozone. The most significant fact here is that among the twelve items in the table nine have their maxima within a period of practically three years centering on the maximum of ozone. It seems impossible that insects, fish, rodents, and carnivores

---

[25] Elton, 1942.   [26] p. 562; S. Criddle.

living far apart and having life spans which range from a few weeks to several years should all independently have an inherent biological rhythm of the same length, and that this rhythm should in one case persist unchanged for 200 years. It seems still more unlikely that the rhythm should be so adjusted that the animals all independently attain their maximum numbers within periods of 3 years which happen to center on years when ozone is at a maximum.

TABLE 25

DATES OF MAXIMUM NUMBERS AMONG ANIMALS IN RELATION TO OZONE *

Fisher or pekan	5.7 years before ozone maximum
Muskrat	2.7 " " " "
Snowshoe rabbit	1.7 " " " "
Marten	0.7 " " " "
Mink	0.3 years after ozone maximum
Chinch bug	0.5 " " " "
Red fox	0.7 " " " "
Skunk	0.9 " " " "
Lynx	1.2 " " " "
Salmon	1.5 " " " "
Tent caterpillar	1.5 " " " "
Deaths from heart diseases	3.0 " " " "

* Based in part on data for 1840 to 1940 supplied by the Hudson's Bay Company to E. R. Dewey.

The fact that deaths from heart diseases fall outside these 3 years does not lessen the concentration of effects near the time of ozone maximum. The progress of heart diseases is generally slow. Hence one expects deaths to lag considerably behind any form of general stimulus which leads to them. Moreover, after the maximum of ozone, as well as before it, there is a period when that form of oxygen is still relatively abundant and hence quite strongly able to exert whatever harmful effect it may have on people with weak hearts.

The departure of the muskrat's maximum from the period close to the ozone maximum has not yet been explained. It may be connected with the fact that the muskrat, alone among the animals here considered, lives both on land and in the water. It is peculiarly subject to the influence of rain and flood. Huntsman thinks that rainfall also affects salmon, whose young fry are especially likely to be eaten by birds when the streams are low and free from mud. In this connection it should be noted that the salmon which form the basis of our records are generally 5 years old. They are caught when they come back to the rivers to spawn. On the other hand, the rabbits whose skins are sold to the Hudson's Bay Company are mostly less than 1 year old, having been born the summer preceding the winter when they are trapped. Most of the other fur-bearers are caught at this same age or during the next year or two. Hence it appears that the salmon of our records are older than the other animals. They are the result of eggs laid 3 or 4 years before the ozone maxima. Thus their period of most rapid reproduction falls at a date somewhat earlier than the maximum of muskrats and only a year or two after the minimum of ozone. This suggests that among aquatic animals, such as salmon and muskrats, the incidence of the ozone cycle, or at least of the $9\frac{2}{3}$-year cycle regardless of its cause, may be different from its incidence among animals which live wholly out of water.

Among all the animals in Table 25 the pekan, a large marten, is the only one in which the $9\frac{2}{3}$-year cycle appears to be reversed. Data as to this animal are scarce and the number of skins is small. No explanation of its idiosyncrasies is yet apparent.

Let us return now to the many animals, including man, which seem to be strongly affected by some kind of physiological stimulant which produces its maximum effect not far from the time when there is most ozone in the air. The approach to uniformity among these many types of animals, as it appears in Table 25, becomes still more impressive when we take account of the fact that some breed rapidly and some more slowly. Insects, which lay hundreds or thousands of eggs and have several broods per season, can theoretically increase a thousand-fold in a year. Rabbits with litters of four several times a year could increase ten-fold in a year if all the young lived and reproduced. Lynxes, on the other hand, with only one to an occasional maximum of six young at a birth and one set of offspring each year, cannot do much more than double their numbers each season. Even at that rate they could theoretically increase sixty-four-fold in six years.

After any or all of these animals have become unduly numerous it is easy to see how they can be killed off with great rapidity by epidemics. There is abundant evidence as to the extraordinary rate at which this occurs.[27] It is also evident that the increase in creatures such as rabbits tends to be checked by the ravages of the lynx and other flesh-eaters. This checking will, of course, become more and more severe as the flesh-eaters increase in number. Thus the prob-

[27] Elton and Nicholson; Elton, 1929, 1931; Green, 1938; Green and Evans; Green, Evans, and Larson.

lem to be solved is not the occurrence of the drop in numbers after the maximum is reached, but of the rise to a maximum. This will be considered in the next section. The conclusions to which we have been led thus far are as follows: (1) the $9\frac{2}{3}$-year cycle must be environmental, as Elton and others have believed; (2) in ozone we find an environmental condition with a sharply defined periodicity which agrees both in length and timing with that of many animals to a remarkable degree.

I. Cycles in Reproduction

We have seen that there are two critical factors in the production of cycles of abundance among animals, namely, rate of reproduction and rate of death. The evidence as to epidemics is so clear that it scarcely needs further mention. Many writers have described, for example, the way in which rabbits die by the thousand. Their dead bodies sometimes litter the ground. When an epidemic comes to an end the survivors are often so scarce that there seem to be none at all.

The relation of reproduction to cycles is not yet clear, but important clues are available. In their study of chinch bugs Shelford and Flint concluded that ordinary weather does not fully explain variations in the numbers of that insect. They note, to be sure, that a large population of chinch bugs is correlated with (1) light rainfall in May and June; (2) a warm growing season from March to October; and (3) light rainfall from August to October. Nevertheless, before the weather of any given season has a chance to influence the rate of reproduction, "there is an unexplained difference in the vigor of chinch bugs on emerging from hibernation in different years."

In order to test this curious reproductive relationship, Shelford and Flint took chinch bugs when they first emerged from hibernation in the spring of each year from 1917 to 1925. Dividing the bugs into groups, they kept them "in the laboratory under several different conditions of light and temperature, including constant and variable temperatures and humidities." The bugs of each year, regardless of the environmental combinations under which they were kept, "showed a comparable degree of reproductive vigor or general weakness, indicating that the physiological condition in each case had been established before the bugs were placed in the experiments."

The variation in vigor showed itself in the number of offspring and also in the number of generations produced in a single season. There were three or four generations in vigorous years, compared with only one in the poorest years. The best year from the stand-point of the bugs—not the farmers—was 1925, when the total rate of reproduction was almost two hundred times as great as in 1917 and 1921. A heavy rainfall in October and November appears to have had some association with vigor on the part of the bugs, but the investigators do not regard this as sufficient to account for the great differences. The vigor "was obviously determined previous to bringing the insects in from the field. . . . It is apparently not pos-sible to ascribe this vigor to hormones. It may be the result of autumn or winter conditions. Possibly it may also be due to the presence or absence of certain fungus organisms on or in the bodies of the bugs. However, the sum total of this experience indicates that the physiological condition of the organism is an important factor."

A similar condition prevails among mammals. MacLulich [28] has found that in the first year after the population of snowshoe rabbits has fallen to a minimum in the $9\frac{2}{3}$-year cycle the females produce only two young per litter. The number rises to three the next year and then to four during the year of greatest increase. Thereafter it is three for one year, and then only two during the succeeding period of decrease. Thus we seem to have here the same sort of reproduc-tive variation as in chinch bugs. Other students, however, dispute this. Green and Evans think that the essential factor is epidemics which they have studied with special care. The normal rate of re-production, they say, is all that is needed to increase the population of rabbits or mice enormously. The coming of epidemics sweeps away most of the animals, and a new growth in number begins.

If variations in the rate of reproduction were reported only among rabbits, we might accept Green's view, but they are by no means con-fined to those animals or to the $9\frac{2}{3}$-year cycle. Carpenter quotes three authors (Voelkel, Grossgeim, and Nechleba) as saying that be-fore outbreaks of grasshoppers, the size and weight of the pupae in-crease. Hamilton [29] states that in central New York State mice in-crease regularly in a cycle of 4 years, with special abundance every 16 years. As the cycle approaches its crest the breeding season begins early and lasts long until it is almost continuous. The size of litters also increases. A pestilence of unknown origin finally reduces the population, but something else appears to be responsible for a re-lapse back to a lower stage of reproduction. Hamilton also reports a

[28] 1935; Preble.   [29] 1937, p. 265–67; 1941.

similar condition in the deer mouse, short-tailed shrew, chipmunk, and red squirrel. Howell finds it among the jumping mice of the Cascade Range in Washington, but there the reduction in the size of litters begins in the actual year when the mice are most abundant. Clearly, then, we are dealing with factors which exert a powerful effect upon the rate of reproduction among a wide variety of animals.

In concluding this chapter two main points may be stressed. One is the clear distinction between the 9.2- and the $9\frac{2}{3}$-year cycles. The first is especially evident in prices and seems to be more or less psychological in nature. Its cause is not clear, but there are hints that it too, as well as the 41-month cycle, is associated with the sun's electrical effect upon the earth's atmosphere. The $9\frac{2}{3}$-year cycle, on the other hand, is evident primarily among animals, although also important among men. The evidence is still slight, but there are indications that the cycle is associated primarily with ozone, which in turn depends largely on ultra-violet light.

The second point is that, as we go from mammals, insects, and fish to trees and crops, the $9\frac{2}{3}$-year cycle becomes less distinct. If we go in the other direction from animals to human health (heart diseases) it also grows less distinct. This suggests that the conditions which give rise to the cycle have a particularly direct effect upon animal vigor. They may have an equally strong effect upon plant growth, but other factors, such as rainfall, sunshine, and temperature, interfere with this more than with the effect on animals. In the same way, the effect on human health, and even upon the activity of man's mind, may be just as direct as upon the reproduction of animals, but here, too, the direct effect is masked in several ways: first, by ordinary weather, both directly and also indirectly through the yield of crops; second, through cultural conditions, such as legislation and the disturbances of war and politics; and third, by other environmental cycles which may be electrical in nature and may produce psychological reactions.

CHAPTER 26

BROADER ASPECTS OF ENVIRONMENTAL CYCLES *

A. Cycles in Mass Psychology

In this chapter we propose to bring together the various threads of our study of cycles and present a broad electrothermal hypothesis which has a bearing on many phases of life. We shall begin by describing the work of four investigators who differ widely in their interpretation of the way in which the atmosphere influences man but agree that many different types of influences, including those on which they lay most stress, are largely summed up in the short cycles of ordinary storms. This prepares the way for the next chapter, where we shall find that the course of history seems to have been much influenced by long climatic cycles in which changes in the location and intensity of cyclonic storms have probably been the chief variable. Before we consider the long cycles, however, we shall endeavor to gain a better idea of the causes of cyclonic storms and their relation to the solar system as a whole. That will introduce us to the electrothermal hypothesis as a framework within which all the activities of life find a place.

Tchijewski,[1] a Russian, has published some challenging conclusions as to the effect of short cycles of weather and their relation to sunspots. Regardless of whether his conclusions are right or wrong, the facts on which they are based are significant. He reports, for example, that epidemics of cholera in the world as a whole, of influenza in Russia and India, and of typhus fever in Moscow and many other places come and go in harmony with sunspots. He also concludes that "mass movements," by which he means revolutions, wars, strikes, popular agitations, and so forth, decrease or increase more or less simultaneously all over the world. He describes them as "forming what may be called one universal cycle of historical events." During most

* Here, again, the author owes much to the co-operation of Mr. Edward R. Dewey.

[1] See also Huntington, 1941.

centuries this cycle repeats itself nine times; that is, it follows the 11-year sunspot cycle. According to Tchijewski's extensive tabulations, only 8 per cent of all mass movements in the fifteenth to the twentieth centuries took place during the 3 years of minimum solar activity in each sunspot cycle; 10 per cent occurred during the succeeding 2 years of increasing solar activity; 53 per cent during the 3 years of maximum activity; and 20 per cent during the 3 years of diminishing activity.

Tchijewski also finds an agreement between solar activity, on the one hand, and labor movements, strikes, terrorist activities, and Jewish pogroms in Russia, on the other hand. He finds that lynchings in the United States, parliamentary movements in England, and the amount of migration show a similar relation to the sun. Hence he concludes that "paroxysms in the activity of large human mass movements tend to coincide with periodical intensity of sunspots." He also presents evidence of related changes in human feelings from day to day. His conclusions were gaining considerable acceptance in continental Europe before World War II.

The apparent connection between sunspots and human activity is ascribed by Tchijewski to increased electrical activity of the sun at sunspot maxima. He holds that at such times electrically charged particles are shot out by the sun in unusual numbers. This leads to increased ionization of the air, thus supposedly stimulating mankind both physiologically and psychologically. "Therefore," says Tchijewski, "solar disturbances tend to aggravate social crises, if such crises happen to exist at the time of greater solar activity." If we disregard the debatable question of whether the sun's effect is produced by "charged particles" and "ionization," or by some other means, such as electricity or ozone, this conclusion is essentially the same as that derived from our study of the 41-month cycle in prices, the stock market, and business. The chief difference is that Tchijewski recognizes only the sunspot and storm cycles, whereas our data seem to indicate that plants, animals, and men are influenced by many diverse cycles, which may or may not be of solar origin.

An hypothesis allied to that of Tchijewski has been advocated by Wheeler [2] on the basis of a psychological analysis of an extraordinarily wide collection of data from the entire historic period throughout the world. One of the most important pieces of evidence is Sorokin's [3] comprehensive list of aggressive international wars, such as

[2] Unpublished manuscript.   [3] 1937, vol. 3.

those of Alexander, Caesar, Napoleon, and Hitler, and civil wars including rebellions, revolutions, and other uprisings against established governments. Such data lead Wheeler to believe that the course of history oscillates between two main psychological types, the extremes of which may be broadly defined as follows:

Nationalistic Type	Individualistic Type
Political centralization, wars of aggression and, ultimately, dictatorship and tyranny.	Political decentralization, civil wars, and anarchy, leading ultimately to reforms springing from the people.
Totalitarian economic systems, including socialism, communism, and fascism.	Individualistic economic systems, encouragement of competition, free trade, etc.
Aristocratic forms of social organization, luxury, small families, and at their best stage "golden ages."	Democratic organization of society, relatively simple life, large families, and at the worst stage "dark ages."
"Classical" literature, etc.	"Romantic" literature, etc.

In analysing wars, personalities, discoveries, and other conditions, Wheeler noted that oscillations between his two psychological types agree quite well with the annual growth of the giant sequoia trees of California. He accordingly constructed a curve of "world climate," based on the growth of many kinds of trees and on a great collection of historical records of climatic events such as floods, droughts, cold spells, good or bad harvests, famines, and so forth. He also assumed that sunspots can be used as an indication of temperature. In many instances a close relation between this climatic curve and historical changes seems clear, but in others it is doubtful.

Wheeler holds that climatic variations are the main cause of psychological cycles in history. He identifies his two psychological types with the characteristics which are commonly associated with warm and cool climates, respectively. A tendency toward the nationalistic type is supposed to prevail in warm regions and in all regions when short climatic cycles assume a warm phase. The individualistic type is similarly associated with a lowering of temperature. The foundation for this belief is that

since the time of Greece . . . observers . . . have been in almost complete agreement regarding important correlations between man and climate. In cooler climates man is more vigorous, more aggressive, more persistent, stronger physically, larger, braver in battle, healthier, and less prone to sexual indulgence. In warm climates man is more timid, smaller, physically weaker, and less courageous but more inclined to physical pleasures, more effeminate, lazier, and less aggressive. Peoples of cooler climates [have] treasured liberty, [been] averse to slavery, built democratic communities. Warmer climates, it was noticed, were conducive to the more reflective pursuits. The birth rate was much higher in colder regions even though there were more women, proportionally to men, in the warm countries. . . . The warmer races were considered to be emotionally less stable and dependable.[4]

In support of these rather widely held ideas Wheeler lays much stress on experiments in which both he and Ogle and Mills [5] have found that mice raised in moderately cool air differ physically and psychologically from those raised in warm air. Physically they are larger, stronger, and mature earlier. Although less sexually inclined, they breed earlier and produce larger, more frequent, and more vigorous litters than the mice raised in warm air. Psychologically, they are more alert, learn their way to food in a maze more quickly than the others, and remember it better. Abundant evidence, some of which has been set forth in earlier chapters, indicates that similar conditions prevail among men. Hence Wheeler concludes that the psychological fluctuations which he finds in history are due primarily to variations in temperature, although changes in rainfall and storminess are also stressed as important.

In assessing the reliability of this conclusion at least three climatic facts must be considered. First, variations in temperature within such short periods as a decade are generally slight. Differences in annual averages are rarely more than one tenth as great as the 15° to 30° which separated the types of experimental conditions under which the mice were raised. Second, although slight changes of temperature do occur in the same direction over large parts of the earth, there are other areas where the change is reversed. Third, unless the whole idea of an optimum temperature is wrong, a rise of temperature in a cold region can scarcely have the same effect as a similar rise in a warm region. In the cold region increased warmth is likely to be stimulating because the temperature approaches the optimum. In the warm region a similar rise of temperature will be harmful because it increases the departure from the optimum. In spite of these objections Wheeler's work is impressive because his vast assemblage of historical data seems to indicate that psychological cycles of many lengths and amplitudes are somehow connected with climate in some such way as is suggested by Tchijewski's sunspot cycles and by the 41-month and 9-year business cycles.

[4] Wheeler, 1943, p. 33.
[5] See also Ogle, 1934, 1936; Mills, 1939, 1942.

Petersen, as we saw in a previous chapter, has done an immense amount of work which establishes the fact that individuals are constantly subject to short physiological cycles which are obviously connected with the weather. This is evident not only in such outward signs as the rates of the pulse and of breathing but in variations in important chemical constituents of the blood and other bodily secretions. Both Petersen and Mills lay much stress on changes in atmospheric pressure as a cause of such physiological changes, but there is little experimental evidence to support such a view. Petersen generally presents his results in such complicated diagrams that it is difficult to assess their true value. Nevertheless, here, just as in Wheeler's psychological analysis, we have the raw materials of cycles which fall into a definite pattern. Cycles of the same sort both physiologically and psychologically appear to vary all the way from the contrast between a patient's feelings last night and this morning and the difference between the Dark Ages and the Renaissance.

B. *The Dülls' Electrical Hypothesis*

A pair of German workers, the Dülls, seem to have come nearer than anyone else to discovering the primary causes of psychological cycles. Up to the present, they say,[6] the findings of research in respect to such problems "have been confined to establishing the fact that the appearance of impressive changes in the atmosphere has approximately coincided with similar changes in the organism." Such research

has not yet been able to explain by means of what physical and physicochemical mechanism the life functions have been influenced. Variations in air pressure, temperature and moisture, air pollutions and alterations in the ionic content of the air . . . do not enter into the question as decisive factors. What is certain is the frequent occurrence of definite effects from distant influences. Numerous experiments have proved the biological effect of short electric waves. Parasitic electric waves of varying length and of considerable amplitude and range occur not only during thunderstorms, but also . . . [when electricity flows back or forth] at the discontinuities of the atmosphere [which are] recognized as especially disturbing to the organism.

These discontinuities are places where air masses of different types meet at "cold fronts, warm fronts, occlusions, inversions, etc." They are characteristic features of cyclonic storms such as regularly domi-

6 1938B.

nate the weather in Europe and the United States. Sudden electric disturbances which affect mankind are "found in the earth's atmosphere after the sudden inbreak of electro-magnetic waves and electric particles caused by solar eruptions."

The work of the Dülls is so suggestive that we may well look at some of their evidence in detail. In Figure 70 the arrows indicate

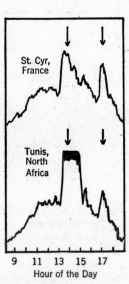

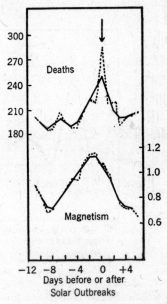

Figure 70. Solar Eruptions (arrows) and Variations in Atmospheric Electricity at St. Cyr (Paris) and Tunis *(after Düll).*

Figure 71. Deaths, Compared with Magnetic Disturbances *(after Düll).*

the outbreak of two solar eruptions of incandescent gas at an interval of about 3 hours. In such eruptions the gas shoots from the solar atmosphere at enormous speed and may rise 100,000 miles. The jagged curves of Figure 70 are instrumental records of atmospheric electricity at St. Cyr in France and at Tunis, 800 miles away in North Africa. They illustrate the fact that electrical instability in the earth's atmosphere is intimately associated wih similar instability in the sun's atmosphere. Radio observations and magnetic disturbances confirm this. There has been much confusion, however, because people fail to distinguish between the *average* of the electrical gradients of the air and their *variability*. For example, Kahler and Chree [7] concluded that there is little or no relation between sunspots and the average potential gradient of atmospheric electricity at Potsdam and Kew. They used the size of sunspots and the average potential gradient on electrically *"quiet"* days. Bauer,[8] however, had already shown that "it is the *variability* in sunspottedness, rather than sunspottedness itself, which may approximate to a true measure of the

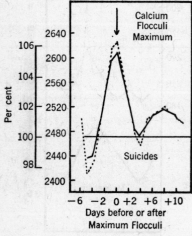

Figure 72. Suicides Compared with Heavy Concentrations of Calcium Flocculi on Sun's Surface (*after Düll*). Suicides in Berlin, 1917–19, 1930–32; Copenhagen, Frankfurt-am-Main, Hamburg, and Zurich, 1928–32.

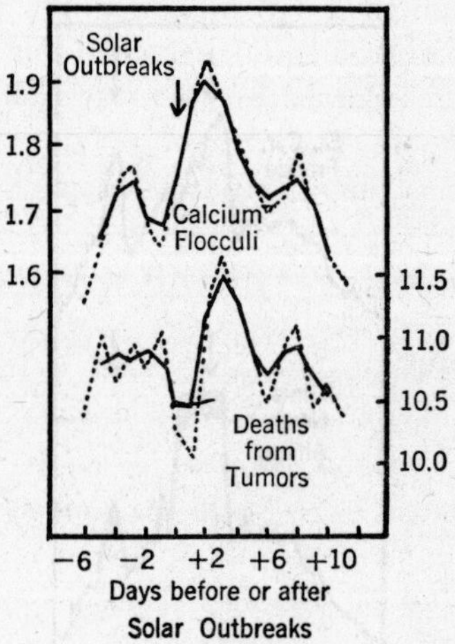

Figure 73. Solar Outbursts (arrow), Calcium Flocculi, and Deaths from Tumors (*after Düll*).

kind of solar activity which may be related to geophysical phenomena." This seems to be equally true in respect to solar activity in relation to psychological conditions of the kind now under discussion.

Some of the Dülls' findings are summed up in Figures 71–74.[9] In all of these the dotted line represents the original data; whereas the solid line has been smoothed by the formula, $\dfrac{a + 2b + c}{4}$. In Figure 71 the arrow indicates the 15 days during February, March, and April, 1930, when Copenhagen, Frankfurt-am-Main, and Zurich had the most deaths from suicide, mental disorders, and diseases of the

[7] p. 7.

[8] *See also* Huntington, 1923.

[9] 1938B, p. 108.

nerves, sense organs, and circulatory system. The upper curve indicates the deaths from these causes on the 12 days before and the 6 days after the days of maximum mortality. The lower curve indicates the amount of magnetic disturbance on these same days. The two curves run almost parallel, but the magnetic curve reaches a maximum a little before the other. It is not at all likely that a curve based on 3,700 deaths would agree in this way with an electromagnetic curve by accident. The possibility of an accidental agreement is rendered still more remote by the fact that similar comparisons for the other three seasons give almost identically the same result.

In Figure 72 [10] the arrow indicates 735 days when especially numerous calcium flocculi on the sun's surface betokened special activity in the solar atmosphere. The curve shows how suddenly suicides in Denmark, Germany, and Switzerland increase when the sun becomes excited. This close connection between a nervous reaction and solar activity suggests the same sort of relationship that the 41-month cycle seems to show between the solar constant, atmospheric electricity, and business. The practical importance of this relationship may be gauged by the scale of percentages on the left of Figure 72. The highest point of the suicide curve is about 7 or 8 per cent above the lowest point. This by no means indicates that nervous disturbances due to atmospheric electricity are the main cause of fluctuations in the number of suicides. In Figure 50 (page 366) we saw that the seasonal variation of suicides in connection with the annual rhythm of reproduction averages about 80 per cent. Suicide also varies in harmony with economic conditions. In the northwestern United States, for example, the rate rose about 35 per cent from 1927 to 1932 under the influence of economic adversity. Other cycles can also be detected in suicide, and the finding of cycles due to many different causes is to be expected.

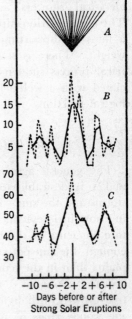

Figure 74. Strong Solar Eruptions in 1936 (*A*), High-Frequency Electrical "Showers" (*B*), and Deaths from Tuberculosis (*C*) (*after Düll*).

[10] *Ibid.*, p. 111.

Suicide is not the only form of death which is related to short changes in solar activity.   Figure 73 [11] shows how calcium flocculi on the sun's surface and deaths from tumors in Europe vary before and after days of new outbreaks of activity in the central zone of the sun. Figure 74 [12] portrays the relation between days with strong eruptions in the sun's atmosphere, on the one hand, and both high-frequency electrical "showers" and deaths from tuberculosis, on the other hand. The close relationships suggested by all these diagrams, together with a mass of supporting material cited by the Dülls, have cumulative weight.   There is scarcely room for doubt that through some electrical process sudden disturbances of the sun's atmosphere are associated with a well-defined influence upon man's health and psychological reactions.

C. Sunspots and Storms

The general agreement as to the importance of cyclonic storms makes it desirable to gain a clearer idea of the relation between storms and the sun.   First, however, let us clear the ground by showing how little evidence of the sunspot cycle can be seen in the separate elements of the weather aside from cyclonic storms.   Curiously enough, the sunspot cycle seems to be more evident in the growth of plants than in the temperature and precipitation which promote that growth.   Douglass [13] finds the sunspot cycle in his long records of tree growth, although at certain periods it becomes very faint.   In the woody rings of pine trees at Eberswalde he found the sunspot cycle reproduced almost perfectly for 100 years.   In Figure 57 (page 460) a cycle of 11.0 years in European wheat prices, one of 11.4 years in European weather, are indicated, but both are faint and neither is of quite the same length as the average sunspot cycle (11.15 years).

It has long been known that the earth's surface tends to be relatively cool when sunspots are numerous and warm when the opposite conditions prevail.   This happens in spite of the fact that the sun gives out more heat at sunspot maxima than at minima.* [14]   The difference in the earth's temperature between sunspot maxima and minima, however, is probably too slight to be of appreciable signifi-

[11] *Ibid.*, p. 112.   [13] 1919, 1941.
[12] *Ibid.*, p. 113.   [14] Huntington, 1923.

* The present author believes that this is due to some electrical or other effect of the sun whereby the contrast in atmospheric pressure from one place to another is increased when the sun is active.   Such an increase would intensify the circula-

cance in its effect on living beings. Recent studies confirm this and throw some doubt on the earlier idea that the difference is greatest at the equator and diminishes poleward.[15] Köppen, for example, on the basis of data for the nineteenth century said that the difference amounts to 1.0°F in the torrid zone and 0.8°F in the temperate zones. More recently, Adams and Nicholson [16] have found that at a string of equatorial stations girdling the earth the temperature of the 3 years nearest sunspot minimum in each of several sunspot cycles averages only 0.4°F higher than in the 4 years nearest maximum. Thomson,[17] on the basis of four sunspot cycles at nine stations spanning Canada, finds the corresponding difference to be 0.6°. There is great irregularity, however. In Calgary, for example, 1893, a year of maximum spots, was the coldest on record, but 1928, also a year of sunspot maximum, was within 0.4° of being the warmest on record. Thus sunspots can scarcely be used as a means of predicting future temperatures or of estimating those of the past.

In many parts of the world there is no apparent correlation between sunspots and rainfall, but in others the correlation is high. For example, for long periods at a time the lakes of central Africa, especially Lake Victoria, have risen and fallen in close harmony with sunspots.[18] The same is true of Nile floods and summer rain in Toronto. Atmospheric pressure comes closer than either temperature or rainfall to agreeing with the 11-year sunspot cycle, but it behaves differently in different places. Clayton [19] shows that in a broad band around the equator and also in Australia the pressure goes up when sunspots decline and vice versa. Somewhat farther from the equator

tion of the air horizontally and, especially, vertically. This would cool the lower air somewhat and warm the upper air proportionally.

After the preceding note was in print, there came to hand an article by Schell, which shows conclusively that the contrast between the atmospheric pressure at high and low latitudes varies in harmony with the degree to which sunspots remain high or low for long periods. Continued high spottedness is associated with a strong tendency for atmospheric pressure to be above normal in high latitudes and below normal in low latitudes. In other words, when the sun's atmosphere is much disturbed, masses of air appear to be moved from lower to higher latitudes. Such conditions seem to indicate some form of electro-magnetic effect of the sun in addition to the well-known thermal effect. The same is true of the present author's discovery (1942B) that the interdiurnal variability of atmospheric pressure at New Haven is correlated with the position of sunspots on the disk of the sun as seen from the earth.

[15] 1914; Huntington, 1914B, pp. 488–89.

[16] p. 10.

[17] pp. 223–24.

[18] C. E. P. Brooks, 1923.

[19] 1940, pp. 39–40.

there is no apparent relation, and then in higher latitudes a reversal occurs, so that many sunspots and high pressure go together. This is another of the many examples where solar relationships, or the phases of cycles, are reversed from one place or period to another.

In spite of such agreements Clayton's conclusion is that

there is no sharply defined 11-year period in the weather elements in any part of the world. . . . The weather elements are much more variable than the sunspots. . . . [There is, indeed,] a real relation between weather conditions and monthly means of solar radiation and monthly sunspot numbers, but in the average the amounts of the changes in pressure, temperature, and precipitation are not large. Either there are large disturbing causes, or as seems probable, the phase of the effect is not constant at any one place, being sometimes positive and sometimes negative according to some law not yet fully disclosed.[20]

This undisclosed law, with the seeming contradictions which result from it, is well illustrated by the fullest data yet available as to cyclonic storms. At the top of Figure 75 the sunspot curve shows six maxima between 1880 and 1940. Alternate ones are high, thus suggesting a period of 22 years as well as one of 11 years. The next curve, *B*, employs the storm track data worked out by Kullmer. It shows the relative number of storm tracks (storm centers) which each year crossed the part of Canada lying south of Hudson Bay and roughly between Quebec and Port Arthur on Lake Superior. For the most part the two curves are remarkably alike. The first five maxima practically coincide, although there is a slight tendency toward a lag on the part of the storms. Both curves have a hump in 1898; both display a double crest in 1905 and 1907; and in both the maxima are alternately low and then high until 1930. From 1884 to 1930 the two are so much alike that it seems almost certain that storms on the earth are connected with storms on the sun. Then a curious thing occurs. The curve of storms turns completely away from that of the spots. The dashed part of the storm curve shows that for 8 years the number of storms changes in the opposite direction from that of sunspots. Then the two agree once more.

This puzzling state of affairs becomes still more puzzling when we move west to the part of Canada between Lake Winnipeg and the Rocky Mountains. There most of the curve of storms (*C*) still follows the sunspot curve quite closely, but there is the same sort of reversal as farther east. This time, however, the reversal occurs twice, lasts

[20] 1926, pp. 38-39.

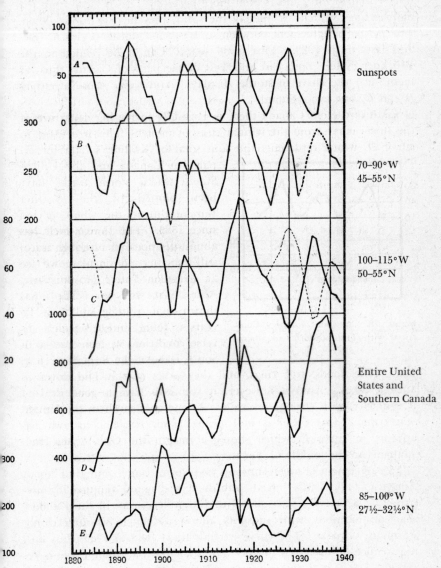

Figure 75. Sunspots (upper curve) and Kullmer's Storm Track Numbers in the United States and Canada. Location of curves is indicated by figures for latitude and longitude. Storm track curves are smoothed by the formula $\dfrac{a + 2b + c}{4} = b'$.

longer than before, and is even more perfect. This is clear from the dashed lines, which are merely the solid lines turned upside down. The period of agreement between sunspots and storms begins in 1887 and lasts until 1923. This is 36 years. Can it be related to the Brückner cycle? Both east and west of the parts of Canada thus far mentioned the curve of storms displays features like those of curves *B* and *C,* but less regular.

Southward from Canada there is a rapidly increasing departure of the storm curve from the regular sunspot model. This is evident in curve *D,* which represents the sum total of Kullmer's data for all

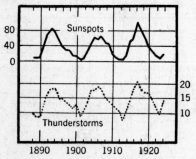

Figure 76. Sunspot Numbers Compared with Thunderstorms in Siberia *(after Septer).*

parts of Canada and the United States where storm tracks have been plotted by the Weather Bureau during the whole period since 1883. The 11-year cycle has almost disappeared, although traces still remain. In its place we see an irregular double sunspot cycle. Abbot,[21] it will be recalled, has shown that a cycle of 22 or 23 years is found in such widely diverse conditions as temperature in South Dakota, the level of African lakes, Nile floods, tree rings, and the varves of clay laid down in ancient lakes. Always, however, it seems to have a good deal of irregularity, with curious reversals. As one goes south in the United States the 22-year cycle, as well as the 11-year cycle, fades away, as appears in curve *E,* which shows storms in the Gulf States from Alabama to the middle of Texas.

The agreement between sunspots and storms is not limited to North America. The Dülls[22] have published a diagram (Figure 76) prepared by Septer[23] which shows that thunderstorms in Siberia fluctuate in harmony with sunspots almost as closely as do cyclonic storms in Canada. The curve extends from 1888 to 1924, thus failing to include either of the periods when the Canadian curve is reversed. Data for testing the reversals are not available. The important point, however, is that for 36 years in Siberia, just as in Canada, storms and sunspots vary in close harmony.

The first conclusion to be drawn from all this seems to be that sunspots are intimately connected with the storminess of the northern parts of both North America and Asia. Sometimes, in Canada at least, storms and spots vary together, and sometimes in opposite fashion, but in both relationships the agreement is equally good. Another conclusion is that as we go east or west from the central part of the broad American band where storms are most numerous, the agreement between storms and sunspots persists, but becomes less clear and the dates of reversal change. Thirdly, as one goes equatorward from the main storm belt the secondary 11-year cycles, that is, the alternate ones with low maxima, tend to disappear, leaving a 22-year cycle. Still farther south this, too, disappears, or at least becomes greatly distorted.

Two possibilities may be suggested. First, the terrestrial storm cycle as a whole may be due to the sun's electricity rather than its heat. Solar heat, of course, is overwhelmingly the main agent in causing differences of weather from season to season and latitude to latitude. This does not prevent other conditions from also playing a part. If solar electricity is a factor in storms, its effect would naturally be concentrated in certain zones of the earth and fade off farther away, just as is true of solar heat. The sun's heat produces its greatest effect where the rays strike vertically, with almost negligible effects where they are horizontal. Electrical effects, on the other hand, tend to be concentrated in zones surrounding the magnetic poles, and probably over great land masses more than over oceans. This may explain why cyclonic storms, on an average, follow arcs that center in the magnetic, not the geographic, poles. This is true in both hemispheres. Moreover, the arc of the minor Japanese storm belt swings around concentrically with the minor magnetic pole located in northern Asia.

An electrical hypothesis also offers a possible explanation of the occasional reversals between solar conditions and their apparent effects upon the earth. Reversals such as appear in the dashed lines of Figure 75 may arise from the changeable magnetic polarity of the leaders, compared with the followers, in the pairs of vortices which constitute normal sunspots. In addition to a change in the polarity of sunspots when each new cycle begins, there are other irregular changes of a similar sort at undefined times. These may account for the fact that within the main storm belt the reversals between sunspots and storms occur at different times, as is evident when the dashed lines of sections *B* and *C* in Figure 75 are compared.

Another possibility is that both sunspots and storms arise under the stimulus of the electro-magnetic field of the solar system as a whole. If such is the case, the sun would naturally be the dominant factor in establishing the general field. When its electrical activities are stimulated, there would presumably be a strong response on the earth. At the same time the great elctro-magnetic field of the solar system must constantly be altered by the movements of the planets and the moon. Thus minor complications and local reversals may be superposed upon the larger ones due to the sun. Many facts which cannot here be set forth seem to demand a supplementary electrical hypothesis of storms in one or the other of these forms, in addition to the universally accepted thermal theory of the general distribution of climate. The great stumbling block in accepting an electrical hypothesis is doubt as to whether electrical forces are powerful enough to produce the observed results.

Regardless of whether an electrical explanation of storms depends solely on the sun, or on the sun together with the planets, the facts thus far available seem inexplicable on a purely thermal hypothesis. Moreover, an electrical supplement to the accepted thermal theory of weather seems to be indicated by such facts as the agreement between the 41-month cycle in the solar constant and in atmospheric electricity. The safest working hypothesis seems, therefore, to be that cyclonic storms represent the effect of the electro-magnetic field of the sun and the solar system superposed upon the still greater effect of the sun's heat.

D. The Electro-Thermal Hypothesis

The facts which we have been considering lead to an electro-thermal hypothesis still broader than has yet been indicated. The gist of this is that the earth, in its flight through space, receives energy of practically all wave lengths, and that many or possibly all such waves have some relation to life. The marvelous discoveries of physics have shown that electro-magnetic waves cover a range of at least 80 octaves. An octave as here used is the interval from a given wave length to another that is twice as great. Some waves have a length of 5,000 miles or more and sweep forward at the rate of about 25 cycles per second. They are used on high-tension power lines. Some have a length of only one trillionth part of a millimeter and pass at the rate of 1×10^{21} (1 with 21 zeros after it) per second. They help ionize the air at high levels so that it reflects radio waves and thus makes radio communication possible.

Some of the characteristics of these various types of waves are shown in Figure 77. Shorter than the waves of electric power lines in length, and correspondingly more frequent in their cycles, are the long waves of radio, which occupy more than 5 octaves. Then comes the broadcast band, only 1½ octaves in extent. Short radio waves (about 4 octaves) and ultra-short radio waves (5 octaves) come next. Then a band of 8 octaves of so-called micro-electric waves brings the electric waves to a junction with the infra-red heat waves. These, in turn, at their lower limit of length and their upper limit of frequency pass into waves of light. Strange as it may seem, visible light, which seems to us almost the central fact of our physical world, occupies only a single octave. Then come the invisible ultraviolet rays or waves, followed by X-rays of various kinds, gamma rays, and finally the marvelously short and frequent cosmic rays. Waves of most of these highly diverse types come to us from the sun, but primarily cosmic rays, as Perrine [24] puts it,

[24] p. 38.

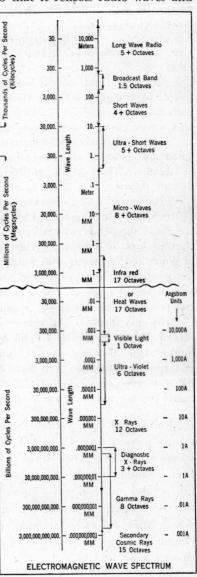

Figure 77. Electromagnetic Wave Spectrum (*after Perrine*). Courtesy, *Scientific Monthly*, LVIII, No. 1, January, 1944, p. 36.

are apparently high-speed particles which come to our earth from inter-stellar regions . . . perhaps from beyond . . . our Milky Way. . . . When they strike our atmosphere, secondary cosmic rays are produced. These latter rays possess great energy and are capable of passing through several feet of lead. . . . They have been detected in the deepest mines and deepest lakes after having passed through hundreds of feet of rock and earth and water.

It was a great sally of the imagination when man first regarded a wide variety of seemingly different kinds of waves as examples of a great category, the electro-magnetic. Visible light, ultraviolet waves, infra-red waves, heat waves, electric waves, x-rays, radium rays, and secondary cosmic rays are, after much study and reflection, regarded as waves of the same kind. Their distinguishing physical characteristics are wave length and frequency of vibration. Their origins are different, their capabilities are different, their uses are different, but all are members of the same family.

All the waves in the electro-magnetic spectrum [as the 80 octaves of Figure 77 are called] carry power. They are all forms of radiant energy. They are not of themselves color, they are not light, chemical action, heat, photo-electric effect, or sunburn. When waves bearing widely varying amounts of power and oscillating with widely varying frequency are received, the effect produced by them in the receiving material or receiving device may be heat, light, color, speech, music, chemical or physiological change. The effect produced depends almost as much on the receiving device as . . . on the frequency involved. Of course one would hardly expect the ultraviolet rays of the sun to actuate a radio receiving set, or radio waves to tan the human skin. However, with the provision of the appropriate transmitter and receiver, ultraviolet rays have been used to carry speech and music for a distance of a hundred feet. Infra-red light, quite invisible to the naked eye, has been used for secret signaling in daylight and darkness.

Although all these various kinds of electro-magnetic waves are constantly passing through the air, the world has just begun to be conscious of any except the single octave of light and several octaves of heat. Sunburn, to be sure, made us conscious of ultra-violet waves, but we did not distinguish them from visible light. Now at last all this is changed. The wave lengths longer than heat are used for power lines and radio, those shorter than ultra-violet for X-ray machines, and the new science of electronics is finding uses for still shorter wave lengths.

The time seems ripe for still another change, which may in the long run be more important than the mechanical harnessing of this vast extent of wave lengths. This new change involves the recognition and then the practical application of a two-fold revolutionary idea. The first part of this is that organic activity of all types, from the lowest functions of plants to the highest functions of man, is constantly being influenced by many hitherto unrecognized wave lengths. The second part is that many, and perhaps all, of these forms of energy vary rhythmically and often with a definite periodic ity. Everyone recognizes that living beings are constantly affected by cycles of light and heat with a definite length—day and night, summer and winter. And even light and heat are rhythmic wave motion. Now at last we are beginning to realize that we are also influenced all the time by cycles in electro-magnetic energy with wave lengths both shorter and longer than those of light and heat. Thus far we have definite evidence of the biological effect of only two main types among these other wave lengths, namely, ultra-violet on the short side of light and electric waves on the long side of heat. Each of these, like light and heat, seems to influence life directly and also indirectly through its effect on the air.

Let us see how this works in the case of ultra-violet waves. The direct effect of ultra-violet, as distinguished from visible, light has become well known during recent decades. It burns the skin and also tans it. It produces the same healing effect as vitamin D upon certain diseases, especially rickets. Our study of animal cycles suggests that indirectly ultra-violet light may be far more important than directly. We have seen that it is the main source of ozone in the earth's atmosphere. When it strikes the upper air it converts part of the oxygen into ozone. Thus a layer of relatively abundant ozone is formed at an altitude of ten or fifteen miles. If the ultra-violet were not thus intercepted and utilized, it would reach the earth's surface in such amounts that life as we know it would be impossible. A brief exposure to sunshine would burn us as badly as hours in the hottest sun that we now experience.

The ozone layer appears to influence life in two ways. First, it apparently plays some part in determining what kind of weather we shall have. Second, we have seen that the ozone molecules settle slowly downward because they are fifty per cent heavier than ordinary oxygen. Then, too, the remnant of ultra-violet that shoots through the ozone layer keeps on making more ozone. When this has settled down into the troposphere, or the part of the atmosphere where active upward and downward movements occur, it is often carried swiftly down the rest of the way by a method far more active than mere floating downward through the other molecules of the air. In stormy weather when cool, heavy polar air masses push their way under warm, light tropical masses the polar air brings with it a relatively high concentration of ozone. In addition to this some ozone arises from electrical activity, radio activity, and sources such as the wind whisking fine spray through the air.

The net result of all these conditions is that the amount of ozone in the air increases in general from the earth's surface upward, but also varies constantly in amount at the surface. It may fall to zero by night, in still air, or in the tropical air masses that sweep in before storms. It may rise quite high by day, in windy air, or during and after storms. It also varies in a pronounced yearly cycle, as we have seen, with little in summer, much in winter. Again, it varies in longer cycles, especially that of 9⅔ years. Details of all this still remain to be worked out. Nevertheless, the evidence indicates that if ozone has such importance as we seem to have found in animal cycles, use of libraries, and people's feelings during storms, the indirect effect of ultra-violet waves upon the chemical composition of the air is decidedly greater than the direct effect. Just as the sun's heat produces indirect effects through atmospheric pressure, winds, and moisture, so the ultra-violet wave lengths seem to exert a vitally important effect through ozone and the chemical composition of the air.

Beyond the infra-red waves on the long side of the electro-magnetic spectrum, and well beyond the part of which we are conscious through the senses, electrical energy seems to produce still other effects upon life, both directly and indirectly, perhaps leading to variations in prices, business, mass psychology, suicides, and certain deathrates. Thus the hypothesis that the solar variations, either directly or through their effect on the air, may induce psychological variations seems worthy of further study.

E. Summary of the Electro-Thermal Cycle Theory

Let us summarize the last three chapters. Our most important finding is that human life and the progress of civilization are influenced by three distinct but closely interlocking types of cycles in addition to the more obvious cycles of the day and the year. The most familiar of these is cycles of ordinary weather. No one doubts the existence of these, for everyone sees the effect of unusual heat or cold, rain or drought, sunshine or fog. Variations in the growth of plants, including all kinds of crops, are directly dependent on such cycles, and are influenced by them far more than by any other factor. Weather also influences the reproduction and growth of animals, both directly and through plants and the food supply. Although the direct effect of the weather on man is great, as we saw in earlier chapters, it is far less than upon plants and less than upon animals, because man is so skillful in protecting himself. The indirect effect of the weather on man, however, is for this very reason greater than upon animals and far greater than upon plants. Cycles of weather have been and still are among the chief stimulants to invention, thrift, and foresight. Thus we may say that as we go from plants to animals and man the direct effect of cycles of temperature and moisture diminishes, whereas the indirect effect increases.

The next great type of cycles is especially evident in animals. It shows itself primarily in physiological processes, especially reproduction. The only known factor which shows the required periodicity and seems competent to produce the observed result is variations in atmospheric ozone. Thus the most tenable working hypothesis seems to be that in addition to cycles of temperature and moisture, there are cycles of ozone, which are especially associated with the reproduction of animals. Man also appears to be influenced, but not so much as animals. Nevertheless, cycles of ozone may have a great effect upon the growth of civilization if they influence mental activity in the way suggested by variations in the use of libraries.

The third cyclic type is primarily human and psychological. At any rate it is only in human beings that we have as yet found clear signs of it. It displays itself in business and prices in a most interesting way. Similar rhythms are found in atmospheric electricity. The evidence is sufficient to warrant the working hypothesis that atmospheric electricity, due presumably to the sun, but perhaps also to the whole solar system, is a cyclic factor closely related to psychological reactions. The three types of cycles, due supposedly to heat, ultra-violet radiation, and electrical radiation, appear to be so intimately connected that it is often difficult to separate them. Nevertheless, further investigation will be facilitated if we differentiate between cycles of temperature and moisture, the clearest effects of which are seen in plants, cycles of ozone most closely associated with animals, and electrical cycles most clearly related to man.

A combination of the thermal, ultra-violet, and electrical conditions which underlie these three types of cycles is clearly evident in cyclonic storms. This seems to be a crucial fact. We know beyond question that during an ordinary storm the air experiences systematic changes in (1) pressure, (2) movement both horizontally and vertically, (3) water content, (4) temperature, (5) amount of ultra-violet light reaching the earth's surface, (6) ionization, (7) ozone, and (8) atmospheric electricity. We know, too, that plants, animals, and man all respond immediately and in diverse ways to the changes that accompany such storms. The ease of procuring food, the appetite for food, susceptibility to disease, reproductive activity, mental alertness, and psychological attitudes are only part of the many conditions that vary with the coming and going of storms. This combination of influences appears to explain why the present distribution of progress and of civilization in the world as a whole varies so closely in harmony with that of cyclonic storms, as explained in Chapters 12 and 17. It also helps to explain how man's gradual conquest of cold, damp, and unpleasant weather by means of fire, clothing, shelter, window glass, and other means has gradually made it feasible to live comfortably in parts of the earth where the climate is highly stimulating. The center of civilization during the past few thousand years has gradually shifted not only from warmer to cooler climates, but from those with few cyclonic storms and presumably with little of the stimulating effect of atmospheric ozone and electricity to those with a maximum of these stimulating conditions. This appears to be one of the vital elements in the history of civilization.

The gradual shift from less to more stormy climates does not explain the full effect of climate on the location of centers of civilization. Another factor is found in cycles of storminess longer than those with which we have dealt in previous chapters. If we are correct as to the three types of cycles which are summed up in storms, variations in storminess lasting scores or hundreds of years must have been a vital element in the progress of civilization. We shall direct our attention to these in the next chapter.

CHAPTER 27

HISTORIC PHASES OF CLIMATIC CYCLES

A. Records of Historic Cycles

If short cycles of storminess and related atmospheric conditions produce noteworthy effects both economically and psychologically, it seems inevitable that longer and more severe cycles must produce still more noteworthy effects. The problem of historic climatic cycles is well discussed by C. E. P. Brooks in *Climate through the Ages*. He emphasizes two points. First, there can no longer be any doubt that during historic times the climate of the earth has fluctuated in cycles having a length of centuries. Second, our knowledge of details is in many places still scanty; changes in rainfall may have taken place in opposite directions in diverse parts of the earth. The outstanding conclusion, however, is that the historic cycles have been characterized by changes in the intensity of the atmospheric circulation, in the direction of the wind, and in the amount and severity of the storms. The storm belt as a whole may have shifted.

Let us look at some of the lines of evidence which indicate the occurrence of such cycles and of related conditions in human history. For this purpose the best evidence lies in actual climatic records, but these do not go back very far. For example, in Figure 78 Gillette [1] shows that records for New England rainfall and Nile floods vary closely together and suggest a cycle at least 150 years in length. A much longer record (lower solid line of Figure 79) is based on the thickness of the rings of growth of about 450 giant sequoia trees in the high Sierras of California, as explained in *The Climatic Factor*. [2] The trees show clear evidence of short cycles of a few decades and of others centuries in length. One cycle, for example, extends from approximately the time of Christ to about A.D. 200; another from 200 to 600; then to 1000, 1330, and 1680. The intervals vary from 200 to 400 years and average about 340.

[1] 1940A.
[2] Huntington, 1914A.

The two upper curves of Figure 79 show that other kinds of changes far away in Asia vary in fairly close harmony with tree growth in California. Both were constructed without knowledge of the trees. The middle solid line represents climatic pulsations in western and Central Asia on the basis of historic records, ruins, and lake levels, especially those of the Caspian Sea, as interpreted in *Palestine and Its Transformation*. Gaps without data are numerous in the records of lakes and ruins and are of necessity bridged merely by smooth

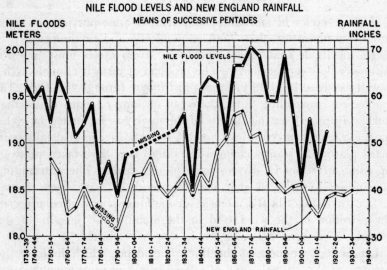

Figure 78. New England Rainfall and Height of Nile Floods (*after Gillette*). Based on 5-year totals.

curves. The upper curve represents caravan travel across the Syrian Desert, as estimated by Grant [3] from a careful study of historical records. It, too, is based on data that are full of gaps, for it is no easy matter to estimate how often caravans cross the desert. Grant believes that the Syrian caravan travel has always varied primarily in response to the degree of peace, prosperity, and strong government among the surrounding nations. This belief is correct, except that the word "primarily" should perhaps be omitted. What we are now trying to discover is whether economic and political conditions have fluctuated in the same cycles as weather. The right kind of climate, which in this part of the world means many storms and relatively

[3] p. 46.

abundant rain, would promote prosperity and at the same time make it easy to cross the desert. In modern times, until motor cars were introduced, scarcity of water was far more important than any man-made condition in making it difficult to cross the Syrian Desert from Damascus to Baghdad, for example. A direct route was rarely followed except in exceptionally wet seasons or by the hardiest of ex-

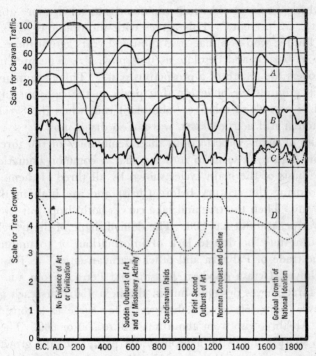

Figure 79. Interpretation of Historic Climatic Cycles: A = Caravan Travel in Syria *(after Grant)*; B = Lakes and Ruins in Asia; C = Sequoia Growth in California; D = Climate and Culture in Ireland *(after MacAlister)*.

plorers. Caravans swung north as far as the magnificent ruins of Palmyra, and then struck the Euphrates River as soon as possible.

In ancient times, however, the direct crossing was frequent and seems to have presented no great difficulties, at least during certain centuries. For example, Dougherty [4] says that Nabonidus, who became king of Babylonia about 550 B.C., set up headquarters in Teima in northwestern Arabia, and his son sent him couriers and food sup-

[4] p. 161.

plies by camel from Babylonia across what is now the worst kind of desert. Today Teima is a wretched little village, but must have been large and well watered then. Even in the days of Bakri, the Arab historian (1040–94), Teima "was located on the shore of . . . a lake whose length was a parasang. This lake must have filled the depression where Tema [Teima] now exists, north of the elevated ruins of the ancient city." Hence Dougherty concludes that "the supply of water which Tema of old could command was much more abundant than [at] . . . present." This agrees with the opinions of explorers such as Philby, who says that "two thousand years ago or more Arabia was not as barren and desolate as it is now. . . . The present desolation covers the record of a prosperous past." There are many other historical grounds for believing that peaks in the caravan curve correspond to periods of relatively abundant rain when the Syrian Desert, although still a true desert, was not so dry as now.

In spite of many imperfections the resemblances of the three solid curves in Figure 79 seem to indicate that a common climatic cause is at the basis of the main cycles shown by all three of them. They all rise during the century before Christ and are high in the first century A.D. Then the tree and lake curves both drop, but rise again to a lower peak about A.D. 200. The domed shape of the travel curve at this time may be due to lack of information, or to undue stress upon the trade of Palmyra and other "caravan cities," as Rostovtzeff calls Palmyra, Gerasa (modern Jerasa), and Petra. From A.D. 200 to 300 all three curves descend, but in the next 150 years each goes its own way. From 450 onward, however, they agree to a considerable extent. All three rise from about A.D. 450 to 550 or 600. Then they all drop sharply, implying a pronounced period of slow growth, low lakes, many ruins, and little travel across the desert. A gradual rise brings all to a high level about A.D. 900. A century later a return to favorable conditions, or at least their continuance, appears in all three respects. Then comes an outstanding feature in the form of a big drop leading to low tree growth between 1150 and 1300. In the lake curve, to be sure, this does not begin so soon as in the others, and in the caravan curve there is a sudden drop soon after A.D. 1200, but such discrepancies are quite likely to represent lack of information. The next event is a strong maximum of all three curves in the fourteenth century, followed by a minimum about 1500. Then come a high point not far from 1600 and a low near 1700. The last feature is a disagreement about 1800.

Estimates of the significance of the agreements and disagreements just described are bound to vary. Consider what we have before us: (1) a caravan curve based wholly on Syria and avowedly sketchy because of scanty information and lack of numerical data; (2) a curve of lakes and ruins based mainly on Central and western Asia, sketchy, but with a good many exact points fixed by the levels of the Caspian Sea; and (3) a tree curve, every point on which has been exactly measured, but in which the general slope, especially before A.D. 600, is uncertain because of difficulty in making allowance for the changing rate of growth as trees become older. In spite of these imperfections, the three curves agree fairly well in their main features except for a century and a half in their early part, where information is scanty, and a century toward the end, where the abundance of records has probably led to a mistaken idea as to the relative importance of caravan traffic.

In view of all this it seems probable that the main fluctuations of all three curves are due primarily to a common cause which must be climatic. This involves the assumption that the major climatic cycles of western and Central Asia agree with those of California. There is ground for this assumption in at least two facts: (1) modern records of rainfall in the Sierra region and Jerusalem show a significant positive correlation; [5] (2) Syria and California have similar climates because of similarity in latitude and continental position. The reasonable conclusion seems to be that in a broad way the long cycles of climate which are plainly evident in the growth of the sequoias are the same as the climatic cycles of western Asia.

B. A Dry Phase of Historic Cycles

Let us amplify our study of historic cycles of climate by examining evidence of phases drier than the present. Enclosed lakes, especially the Caspian Sea,[6] furnish good evidence along this line. Exact knowledge in contrast to mere hearsay as to this great lake begins when the tree curve of Figure 79 indicates the climax of a long period of declining growth. Huns from the desert were then making fierce raids on Persia. Therefore the Persians built the so-called "Red Wall," which now remains as a line of mounds extending 150 miles eastward from the southeast corner of the Caspian Sea.[7] At that

---

[5] Huntington, 1925A.
[6] Huntington, 1907B; Brooks, 1926.
[7] Huntington, 1907, p. 340.

time, to quote Rawlinson,[8] the Caspian Sea "must have been at a very low level . . . if it be true, as the Russian surveys report, that remains of masonry along the line of the wall can be traced below water for eighteen miles from shore." The most reliable tradition, according to Rawlinson, relates that the wall was built by the Sassanian king, Firuz, between A.D. 459 and 484.

Further evidence as to ruins beneath the waters of the Caspian Sea is described in *The Pulse of Asia*. At Derbent on the western shore a great wall of the same sort as at Aboskun was probably built in the fifth or sixth century A.D. Its base is said to be slightly under water. In the bay of Resht, according to Brückner,[9] houses of unknown date stand in the sea, although certainly built on dry land. Sokolof[10] relates a Persian account of the ruins of a submerged city near the mouth of the Kura, or Cyrus, River. Finally, at Baku the present author has seen the towers of a well-preserved caravanserai projecting above the water some distance from the shore. Their base lies fifteen feet below the water level, which Brückner has taken as zero. Lenz[10] believes that the caravanserai dates from before the founding of Baku in its present site in the fifth or sixth century; but Brückner, on the basis of architectural resemblances, considers it of Arab origin, dating from the twelfth century. However this may be, the walls of Aboskun and Derbent seem to establish the fact that in the fifth century the level of the Caspian Sea was lower than today. The climate in Russia, where the great Volga River collects most of the water of the Caspian Sea, must then have been drier than now, or else the temperature of the Caspian area was higher than now with consequent greater evaporation.

During the Middle Ages the Caspian Sea rose considerably above its present level and then fell again. The reliable Arab geographer, Istakhri, records that when he visited Derbent about A.D. 920 the old wall projected into the lake so far that six of its towers stood in the water, which means 29 feet above Brückner's zero. This cannot have been due to a shifting of the course of the Oxus River away from the Sea of Aral and into the Caspian Sea, as some have supposed, for Istakhri says that the river then entered the Sea of Aral. How far the Caspian Sea fell in the next two or three centuries we do not know, but, according to Sheikh Sefi-Eddin, at the beginning of the fourteenth century the water began to rise at the rate of about 32

[8] 1866–67.   [10] Cited in Huntington, 1907.
[9] 1891.

inches a year. In the winter of 1306–07 it reached a certain holy grave 37 feet above the present datum level. Then it began to fall, but, according to Hamdulla, the Persian, in A.D. 1325 Aboskun was still under water. Somewhat later, according to Brückner, "Bakui informs us that early in the 15th century the sea swallowed up a part of the former city of Baku, and that in his time the water stood at the level of a still existing mosque," 16 feet above the datum level. Thus there can be little question that the Caspian Sea stood low in the Dark Ages and high in the Middle Ages, with many minor fluctuations imposed on these large ones. Nor can there be much question that these fluctuations were of climatic origin.

Other lakes agree with the Caspian Sea in indicating long periods of aridity as well as of moisture. For example, in modern times the little Armenian lake of Göljük, 12 miles long, sometimes overflows to the upper Tigris River, but in dry periods has no outlet and becomes impregnated with borax.[11] Long ago there must have been a prolonged period when it stood low, for ruins of a submerged village can be seen where now the water is normally 20 to 30 feet deep. In the midst of the village on a hill which is now a small island stand the ruins of a monastery supposedly belonging to the sixth century. The location of an old road shows that the lake must once have been several miles shorter than now. The low and high levels of both the Caspian Sea and Lake Göljük agree in general with the fluctuations of the California sequoias and the degree to which the Syrian Desert was traversed.

Another kind of evidence of dry periods has come to our attention in Wheeler's [12] clock diagram of droughts (Figure 66, page 483). This is based on the world as a whole, and is much influenced by Chinese records, which are full of famines due to drought. Nevertheless, the eras with most droughts agree with low levels in the three curves of Figure 79. For example, droughts were abundant from A.D. 440 to 470. At that time the tree curve is low. So is the curve based on Asiatic ruins and lakes, and that was the time of the Red Wall. The next period of droughts centers in A.D. 630 to 660, and is reflected in a low level in all three curves. A similar agreement is seen near 1290, 1460, and even 1825. The drought periods centering near 970, 1150, and 1650 are clearly evident in some of the curves, although not in all. The mild drought spell of A.D. 800 is the only one that fails to appear clearly in the other lines of evidence. Thus it seems quite certain that historic cycles of climate include phases

[11] Huntington, 1907B, p. 353.   [12] 1943.

when for decades or even centuries droughts spread widely in far separated parts of the earth.

C. Humid, Stormy Climatic Phases

The rainy, stormy phases of climatic cycles are generally easier to recognize than the dry warm phases. In eastern England, for example, according to Godwin and Clifford, the relics of vegetation in the fenlands indicate that about 500 B.C. after a preceding warm period "the climate became both colder and wetter; the lime tree practically vanished." At this same time Greece was well-forested and densely populated, and the California sequoia trees grew rapidly. As late as early Roman times the climate in Ireland apparently continued to be so cool and wet in summer that there were no bees there. This does not sound important to us, but to people like the Romans, who relied on honey for sweetening, it was of great importance. Other facts also indicate stormy, wet, cool summers. By the seventh century A.D., however, the climate had changed so much that the laws governing the remarkably high Tara civilization of Ireland are full of minute regulations concerning bees. These laws, as well as abundant other evidence of a highly developed and widely distributed agriculture, indicate relatively dry, warm summers.

The effect of increased storminess is especially evident in border regions where the desert and the "sown" lie close together. Butler, for example, paints a vivid picture of the effect of such storminess in Syria soon after the time of Christ.

Among the regions which were once populous and highly civilized, but . . . are now desert and deserted . . . few . . . were more closely connected with the beginnings of our own civilization than the desert parts of Syria and northern Arabia. . . . The results of the explorations of the last twenty years have been most astonishing. . . . Practically all of the wide area lying between the coast range of the eastern Mediterranean and the Euphrates, appearing upon the maps as the Syrian Desert, an area embracing somewhat more than 20,000 square miles, was more thickly populated than any area of similar dimensions in England or the United States is today if one excludes the immediate vicinity of the large modern cities. . . . An enormous desert tract lying to the east of Palestine, stretching eastward and southward into the country which we know as Arabia, was also densely populated. . . . How far these settled regions extended in antiquity is still unknown, but the most distant explorations in these directions have failed to reach the end of ruins and other signs of former occupation. . . . [p. 77]

The traveler who has crossed the . . . more or less populous coast range of northern Syria and descended into the narrow fertile valley of the Orontes, encounters in any farther journey toward the east an irregular range of limestone hills lying north and south and stretching to the north-east almost halfway to the Euphrates. These hills, . . . 2,500 . . . to 3,500 feet above sea level . . . are gray and unrelieved by any visible vegetation. On ascending into [them] the traveler is astonished to find at every turn remnants of the work of men's hands, paved roads, walls which divided fields, terrace walls of massive structure. Presently he comes upon a small deserted and partly ruined town composed of buildings large and small constructed of beautifully wrought blocks of limestone, all rising out of the barren rock which forms the ribs of the hills. If he mounts an eminence . . . he will be still further astonished to behold similar ruins lying in all directions. He may count ten or fifteen or twenty. . . . From a distance it is often difficult to believe that these are not inhabited places; but closer inspection reveals that the gentle hand of time or the rude touch of earthquake has been laid upon every building. Some . . . buildings are quite perfect but for their wooden roofs which time has removed, others stand in picturesque ruins, while others still are level with the ground. On a far-off hilltop stands the ruin of a pagan temple, and crowning some lofty ridge lie the ruins of a great Christian monastery. Mile after mile of this barren gray country may be traversed without encountering a single human being. Day after day may be spent in traveling from one ruined town to another without seeing any green thing save a terebinth tree or two standing among the ruins. . . . No soil is visible . . . except in a few pockets in the rock from which it could not be washed by the torrential rains of the wet season; yet every ruin is surrounded with the remains of presses for the making of oil and wine. Only one oasis has been discovered in these high plateaus. . . . [pp. 81–82]

Passing eastward from this range of hills, one descends into a gently rolling country that stretches miles away toward the Euphrates. At the eastern foot of the hills one finds oneself in a totally different country, at first quite fertile and dotted with frequent villages of flat-roofed houses [because irrigation from mountain streams is possible]. Here practically all the remains of ancient times have been destroyed through ages of building and rebuilding. Beyond this narrow fertile strip the soil grows drier and more barren, until presently another kind of desert is reached, an undulating waste of dead soil. Few walls or towers or arches . . . break the monotony of the . . . landscape; but . . . this region was more thickly populated in antiquity even than the hill country to the west. Every unevenness of the surface marks the site of a town, some of them cities of considerable extent. . . . [pp. 85–86]

We may draw certain very definite conclusions as to the former conditions of the country itself. There was soil upon the northern hills where none now exists, for the buildings now show unfinished foundation courses which were not intended to be seen; the soil in depressions without outlets is deeper than it formerly was; there are hundreds of olive and wine presses in localities where no tree or vine could now find footing; and there are hill-sides with ruined terrace walls rising one above the other with no sign of earth near them. There was also a large natural water supply. In the north as well as in the south we find the dry beds of rivers, streams, and brooks with sand and pebbles and well-worn rocks but no water in them from one year's end to the other. We find bridges over these dry streams and crudely made washing boards along their banks directly below deserted towns. Many of the bridges span the beds of streams that seldom or never have water in them and give clear evidence of the great climatic changes that have taken place. There are well heads and well houses, and inscriptions referring to springs; but neither wells nor springs exist today except in the rarest instances. Many of the houses had their rock-hewn cisterns, never large enough to have supplied water for more than a brief period, and corresponding to the cisterns which most of our recent forefathers had which were for convenience rather than for dependence. Some of the towns in southern Syria were provided with large public reservoirs, but these are not large enough to have supplied water to their original populations. The high plateaus were of course without irrigation; but there are no signs, even in the lower flatter country, that irrigation was ever practiced; and canals for this purpose could not have completely disappeared. There were forests in the immediately vicinity, forests producing timbers of great length and thickness; for in the north and northeast practically all the buildings had wooden roofs, wooden intermediate floors, and other features of wood. Costly buildings, such as temples and churches, employed large wooden beams; but wood was used in much larger quantities in private dwellings, shops, stables, and barns. If wood had not been plentiful and cheap— which means grown near by—the builders would have adopted the building methods of their neighbors in the south, who used very little wood and developed the most perfect type of lithic architecture the world has ever seen. It is perfectly apparent that large parts of Syria once had soil and forests and springs and rivers, while it has none of these now, and that it had a much larger and better distributed rainfall in ancient times than it has now. [pp. 101–03]

D. Man and Nature at Palmyra

Famous and beautiful Palmyra illustrates Butler's conclusions and shows how human inventions co-operate with climatic cycles in influencing history.[13] Mountains on both sides oblige the drainage of

[13] Huntington, 1911, pp. 337, 372; 1935B, pp. 586-590.

several thousand square miles to converge near the ruins of this greatest and most superb of Rostovtzeff's caravan cities. Hence there has always been water there, and this, as well as the mountains, has made Palmyra the focus of routes that converge from as far south as Damascus and as far north as Aleppo. Nevertheless, before the Christian era Palmyra, then known as Tadmor, was not conspicuous, although large enough to be mentioned in the Bible and elsewhere. During the early centuries of the Christian era, however, it rose rapidly to fame. In the third century under Odenathus and his famous Arab queen, Zenobia, it reached such size, wealth, and power that it challenged Rome. It was conquered, however, and was laid waste in A.D. 272. Since then it has never recovered a tithe of its former glory, although some sort of town has generally been located there.

The secret of Palmyra's rise to power lies mainly in three things: first, the ability of its desert leaders; second, the rainy phase of a long climatic cycle which permitted neighboring regions to have the population and prosperity described by Butler; and third, the introduction of a new invention. Of course the prevailing conditions of history, the ambitions and wars of Rome, and the general geographic location also enter into the picture, but we are concerned with the special conditions which permitted Palmyra to be both populous and wealthy.

The invention which stimulated Palmyra was the Persian *kariz*. This is a tunnel dug in the broad, gently sloping, beachlike expanses of gravel and sand which normally lie at the base of mountains in dry regions. Sometimes such expanses are many miles wide and extend for hundreds of miles along the base of a mountain range. In dry regions all the small streams and many of the large ones sink into this beachlike gravel and never reappear except, perhaps, in small springs which are often salty. Part of the water, however, can be led to the surface by digging tunnels which begin deep down in the gravel near the mountains. These slope so little that their depth below the surface gradually declines, and finally they open into ditches. They appear to have been a Persian invention but are now found all the way from western North Africa to the center of Asia.

This type of tunnel was apparently introduced into Palmyra about the time of Christ. Before that a small oasis was supported either by a perennial stream flowing on the surface or by springs. During the early centuries of the Christian era, however, an elaborate system of tunnels was pushed far toward the mountains in several directions. Each new tunnel increased the water supply and presumably enabled Palmyra to become larger and more prosperous. Step by step with this went an increase in commercial activity, political power, and the civic pride which caused rich merchants to adorn the city with temples, huge colonnades, marvelous tombs, and many statues of themselves. So the city reached its zenith about the middle of the third century A.D.

The increase in water due to the tunnels could not last indefinitely. Even if the abundant rainfall indicated by Butler had remained constant, the tunnels were bound to lower the level of ground water, just as wells have lowered the level around London, for example. This would diminish the flow of water even if there were no change in rainfall. What probably happened, however, was that when the Romans sacked Palmyra in A.D. 272 the rainfall was already declining in harmony with the decline of tree growth in California (Figure 79, page 531). This was about the time when many ruins in Central Asia, such as those which will soon be described at Niya and Endereh, were also abandoned, according to Stein. The tunnels fell into disrepair, and the quality as well as the amount of their water probably deteriorated. Today the old tunnels are functioning and have even been enlarged. Nevertheless, the water suffices for only a few thousand people, perhaps one tenth as many as formerly. Because it flows so far underground it has a nauseating sulphurous smell and salty taste,[14] whereas of old it was famed for its good quality. When several rainy years come together, however, both quantity and quality improve, but it is doubtful whether the best years now exceed the average of the most humid centuries.

E. Prosperity of Ancient Palestine

Some idea of the change in the habitability of western Asia since the early Christian era may be gained from Figure 80. Along the border of the Syrian and Arabian deserts the area that was once densely populated, but is now almost uninhabited, extends for some 600 miles between Aleppo and the Gulf of Akaba at the head of the Red Sea. Figure 80 illustrates part of this strip.[15] Solid dots indicate places in Palestine that are now inhabited; crosses indicate ruins. The little map in the corner shows the topography, and the

[14] Huntington, 1911, p. 363.
[15] Huntington, 1935B, p. 500; 1940B, p. 502.

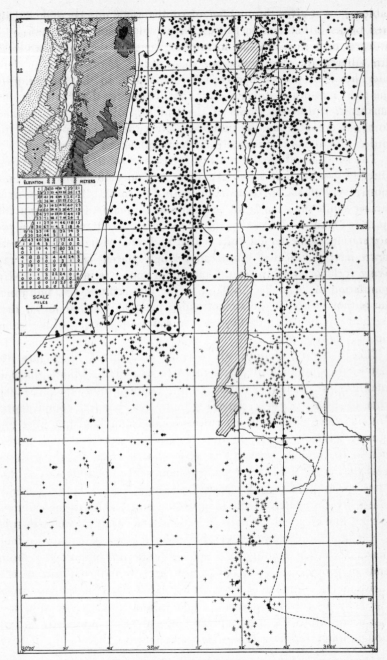

Figure 80. Ancient Ruins and Modern Villages in Palestine. From *Principles of Human Geography*, Fifth Edition.

table below it gives the number of ruins (upper number) and inhabited places (lower number) in each rectangle measuring a quarter of a degree on a side. In the northwest quarter of the main map modern villages are more numerous than ruins. Many of the modern sites, however, were also occupied in the past, so that in antiquity the total number of villages was probably greater than now. In the northeast, within the limits of the winding solid line, villages and ruins are about equal in number. Everywhere else, including the entire Jordan Valley, ruins are far more numerous than villages.

The ruins are especially noticeable east and south of the Dead Sea. Directly east of that salty lake there are only 13 modern villages, mostly very small, in comparison with 345 ruins. The entire area farther south than the Dead Sea contains 9 inhabited places and 282 ruins. There the largest inhabited place is scarcely more than a police station. The largest ruin is that of Petra, with its superb rock-hewn temples, theater, tombs, and "high places" carved from the living rock for worship on the mountain tops. It must have had a population of 20 or 25 thousand in the first century A.D., but when the author visited it the stream which formerly watered it was dry. We had to go half a mile upstream to water our horses and get water for the night's camp.[16]

The remaining sections where ruins predominate in Figure 80, that is, the Jordan Valley and the area east of the middle Jordan, contain approximately 600 more ruins, making a total of about 1,200. Some of these were never anything more than hamlets. Some represent successive villages which cultivated the same land but were differently located. Some, on the other hand, represent large towns, such as the famous caravan city of Gerasa (modern Jerash) with its great theaters of solid limestone, its "naumachia," or 500-foot pool for water sports with seats for several thousand people, and its colonnaded street over half a mile long with almost 600 limestone columns bearing finely carved capitals. Jerash still has water enough to support a population about large enough to fill one of its two ancient theaters. It has nothing like enough water to support the thousands of people who must have lived there in the early part of the Christian era. Among the remaining 1,200 ruins in the dry areas few could now be reoccupied. The trouble is that the rains are insufficient for crops except in exceptional years, and there is not enough water for irrigation. Hence it appears that in the heyday

[16] Huntington, 1911, p. 222.

of the ruins, soon after the time of Christ, Palestine alone must have supported half a million, or perhaps a million, more people than now.

F. Ancient Meteorological Records in Egypt

The distribution of ruins in Palestine, as shown in Figure 80, agrees with the oldest known meteorological record.   This was kept by Claudius Ptolemaeus of Egypt in Alexandria in the first century A.D.   He could not, of course, measure temperature, and he had no rain gauge, but he gives data for winds, rainy days, thunderstorms,

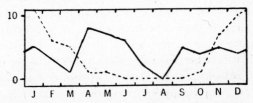

Figure 81. Number of Rainy Days per Month at Alexandria in the Time of Ptolemy (solid line) and Today (dashed line).

and special occurrences.   Hellman,[17] who made the main study of the record, was impressed by its scientific quality.   He was puzzled, however, by the fact that it indicates a high percentage of south and west winds in summer instead of the monotonous north wind which now prevails practically throughout that season.   Another surprising feature is that in Claudius' day thundershowers were experienced in summer, although today they are unknown.   Another less accurate record, the Calendar of Antiochus (about A.D. 200), confirms that of Claudius.   Between these two comes a record kept by Ptolemy, the geographer, probably between A.D. 127 and 151 . (Figure 81.)   As described by Murray [18] it apparently covers only a year, but it confirms the other records in showing many rainy days during the present dry months of April, May, June, September, and October.   Thus it appears that in the early Christian era the climate of northern Egypt, even in summer, was subject to cyclonic disturbances with frequent west winds and occasional thundershowers.   Hellman wondered whether the record might belong to some place such as Salonika, nine degrees of latitude farther north on the other side of the Mediterranean Sea.   He expressly states that there is no evidence of this,

[17] p. 332; also Huntington, 1935B, pp. 576–78.
[18] p. 83.

but one of two things must have happened; either the record must be moved north, or the storms of the north must have moved south.

The ruins found in Palestine make it clear that in the early years of our era cyclonic disturbances followed more southerly paths than now, thus giving greater rainfall and greater variability of weather to North Africa and western Asia. Alexandria lies in a zone of rapid climatic transition. Although only 100 miles north of Cairo, it has 8 inches of rain per year against only 1 inch at Cairo. Inasmuch as Alexandria lies in the same latitude as the Dead Sea, southern Palestine likewise is a marginal area with a rapid southward decline in rainfall. A marginal belt of this sort is just the place where the effect of climatic cycles is most evident. Moreover, the regions where the map of Palestine shows the most ruins are mainly at the western base of mountains, or at the top of plateaus, where an increase in westerly winds would be especially effective in bringing more rain.

There is no reason to think that a climatic change such as is here postulated is beyond the limits of reason, or that it is the most extreme phase of historic cycles. Surprisingly large changes have occurred since exact records were kept. For example, the record of temperature at New Haven, Conn., began in 1780. The coolest twenty consecutive years during that time ended in 1875 and the warmest twenty in 1938. The average temperature for the earlier twenty years was 48.6°F and for the second, 51.1°, a difference of 2.5°.* This is equivalent to moving New Haven south to Atlantic City. Other places show similar cyclic changes in recent times. A 20-year period with 25 per cent more rain than some other 20 years is common. In New York, where the rainfall is especially steady, the years 1884 to 1903, which were the most rainy twenty since the record begins in 1825, had 27 per cent more rain than the driest twenty, from 1833 to 1852. At Rome the precipitation for 33 years (1884 to 1916) averaged 29 per cent more than for another 33 years (1827 to 1859). The dry and wet periods in New York and Rome appear to be substantially, although not perfectly, the same.

G. *The Former Good Fortune of North Africa*

The conditions which we have seen in Palestine and Egypt continue westward in North Africa. Cyrenaica, with its thousands of an-

---

* The five months from November to March averaged 3°F warmer in the later period than in the earlier; June, July, and August show a similar change of only 0.6°. Thus the climate has become distinctly less rigorous.

cient dolmens and its later magnificent cities such as Cyrene, is an example. So, too, is the way in which the inland Cyrenian cities, as de Cosson describes them, decayed earlier than those nearer the coast, where the rainfall is more propitious. Farther west in Tunisia the same sort of change is evident. In the following quotation Powell [19] paints the colors rather brightly, but in the main he comes close to the truth:

For hour after hour [on the road from Tunis south to Kairouan] we traverse waterless and treeless wastes, their yellow-brown expanses broken here and there by patches of bright green where peasant farmers are striving to wring a meager living from the arid soil. The hills which fringe the horizon have been stripped of their forest clothing by fire and wanton destruction, and now they rise, naked and grim, against the hot blue sky. It is hard to conjure up a picture of those golden days when to Horace an African farm was a synonym for boundless fertility, luxury, and wealth; or to accept the assertions of the early chroniclers that, before the Arabs laid the country bare, one could ride from Tripoli to the Atlantic with trees to shade him all the way.

Yet if the ancient writers are to be believed, what is now an exception must at one period have been the rule. Vast areas of plain and mountain, now destitute of tree or shrub, must have been green with forest or jungle. Great numbers of savage beasts once roamed a region which today can show no wild animals save prowling jackals and occasional gazelles. From the Tunisian forests came the wild beasts which were used not only in the arenas of Roman Africa but in the Colosseum of Rome, itself. Elephants roamed the land in herds and were used as the first wave of attack by the Carthaginian armies; it is recorded that Juba lost the battle of Thapsus because his elephants, recently captured in the forests, were untrained. The Roman mosaics preserved in the museums at Sousse and the Palace of the Bardo depict hunting scenes in which the game were lions, tigers, leopards, deer, and wild boar. . . .

The traveller in Tunisia cannot but be impressed by the evidences which he sees on every hand of the enormous population and amazing prosperity of this region under the Romans. The whole countryside is strewn with reminders of this vanished civilization, for Byzacium, as the Romans called [Tunisia], supported a numerous agricultural population and was dotted with flourishing cities and towns. Everywhere rise the ruins of cities, buildings, aqueducts, and arches, monuments, monoliths, and heaps of sculptured stones. Yet, despite these indisputable proofs of a one-time wealth and greatness, it is difficult, nay, almost impossible, to realize that dense forests once spread themselves over yonder naked hills, that great cities stood on

[19] pp. 102, 115.

their flanks, and that from these arid steppes came the grain which fed the mouths of Rome.

Of all the monuments of this departed glory, the most impressive, the most astounding, is the amphitheater at Thysdrus, or, to give it its Arab name, El Djem. Set in a solitude of orange sand, where the Sahel runs out in the Sahara, it is one of the most remarkable structures that I have ever seen. . . . It is so large that it completely conceals the native town which lies behind it. Though used by the Arabs for centuries as a quarry, it was so colossal, so strongly built, as to defy their attempts at destruction. The achievement of building it is the more astounding when one remembers that the stones used in this mountain of masonry were hauled by gangs of slaves and teams of elephants and yokes of oxen, over roads specially constructed for the purpose, from quarries twenty miles away. . . . Of Thysdrus, the splendid city which once stood upon the site of El Djem and which gave to Rome three emperors named Gordian, nothing remains save the amphitheater and some stones and marbles built into the wretched native dwellings. The construction of the amphitheater is attributed to Gordian the Elder, who sat on the imperial throne in the first half of the third century A.D. [when Palmyra was in its prime].

H. The Psychological Factor Again

In assessing the historical importance of the various phases of climatic cycles, especially of the stormy phase, we must bear in mind that the effects are psychological and political as well as economic. Long ago Fraas put his finger on the psychological factor: [20]

An intellectual activity like that of the times of the Greeks, when Alexandria was the center of all the arts and sciences, a true world's university, with the richest library on earth; or as that which existed from the times of the Platonists up to the first centuries of the Christian era, when the greatest thinkers of the church, such as Origen, the Gnostic, developed their philosophical-religious systems—such a movement of thought demands, as an absolute necessity, a different climate, and a moister air, than that now prevailing in Egypt.

Among all the differences between the past and the present in Mediterranean lands and western Asia none is more important than the great change which has come over the human spirit. The Greeks especially, but also the Egyptians, Hebrews, Syrians, Persians, Carthaginians, and others, all displayed a greater degree of energy, initiative, and progressiveness than is seen today among the vast majority

[20] Huntington, 1907B.

of their successors. Some historians attribute this to the fatalistic quality of the Moslem religion. It seems probable, however, that this religious quality is merely the natural reflection of the change which has come upon mankind psychologically. That change is essentially the same as that which appears in Americans on a small scale in the contrasted phases of the 41-month cycle. At one stage they are optimistic and eager to do something new. At the opposite phase they are pessimistic and inclined to put on the brakes. Greece, for example, was great during the inspiring optimistic phase of a major climatic cycle.

The cycles that we have been studying seem to consist primarily of changes in the number, intensity, and paths of cyclonic storms. We saw in previous chapters that storms, with their changes in temperature, humidity, atmospheric electricity, and ozone, are among the most powerful of natural agents in their stimulation of mental alertness. It has long appeared probable that increased storminess had much to do with giving the people of Palestine at the time of Christ, for example, a degree of energy, as well as of economic prosperity, which they do not now enjoy. If our conclusions as to the relation of cycles in reproduction, health, and mental activity to atmospheric electricity and ozone are correct, there is more reason than before for thinking that the alertness of ancient people arose in considerable measure from a degree of storminess greater than at present. Evidence of the truth of this conclusion seems to be accumulating.

CHAPTER 28

WORLDWIDE CLIMATIC CYCLES

A. An Example from Central Asia

If climatic cycles have exerted any such economic, and especially psychological, influence as is set forth in the last chapter, it is worth while to inquire to what extent the evidence indicates similar cycles in widely separated regions. Of course, we cannot expect that a given type of climatic variation will produce the same effect everywhere regardless of whether a given place is dry or moist, hot or cold. An increase of storminess in one climate may be highly beneficial, whereas in another it may ruin the crops and be depressing psychologically. Therefore we shall select a series of widely scattered places which have considerable resemblance in climate and shall analyse them to see how far they are alike.

Let us begin with Central Asia. By reason of the vast size of the continent, climatic fluctuations are there especially extreme. In the Tarim Basin, near the very center of Asia, the Niya River east of Khotan flows northward from the lofty Kunlun Mountains and gradually disappears in the sandy desert of Takla-makan.[1] Most of the year it irrigates the oasis of Niya, with about 4,000 people, but during the greatest floods, in late spring or early summer, it bursts the temporary irrigation dams and flows to the desert unhindered. Formerly the river flowed at least 80 miles north of the oasis to a point fully 30 miles beyond the extreme limits of normal modern floods. There, to quote the famous archaeologist, Sir Aurel Stein,[2]

amidst the drift sand of the desert, [we find] the remains of an ancient settlement, [named Chadota in] the early documents written on wood and leather, which I excavated. . . . From these documents . . . and from [other] abundant relics of ancient life . . . it is certain that this now sand-buried settlement was abandoned to the desert at the close of the third century A.D. The extreme dryness of the climate has allowed all these relics to survive in wonderful preservation, e.g., the trunks of dead trees still rising

[1] Huntington, 1907B.   [2] pp. 4–5.

above the sand in arbours and orchards near the deserted habitations. . . .
Certain it is that no amount of engineering skill could now make the waters
of the Niya River reach the point near the southern end of the dead settlement where a fallen footbridge, lying across a dry bed, still proves them to
have flowed once. There is thus afforded an indisputable proof of a great
shrinkage in the volume of the river since the third century A.D.

In spite of this clear statement Stein does not fully believe in climatic cycles as a factor in history. His writings illustrate the objections which have prevented many scholars from accepting this idea.
His first point is that the climate must always have been dry. Otherwise writings on wood, leather, and even paper could not have survived so long. It is doubtful whether any climatologist who has investigated Central Asia, Arabia, or the Sahara has the slightest idea
that those regions have been anything but deserts at any time during
the historic period. There are, however, many degrees of desertness.
Oases may come and go while the desert remains. For example, if
the rainfall in the Tarim Basin were twice as great as now, the annual precipitation on the plains would nowhere exceed about 4
inches, and in many places would be less. So far as the preservation
of old wood and leather is concerned, there is little appreciable difference between 2 inches and 4, especially when these articles are
well covered with sand. Nevertheless, if the rainfall were doubled on
the surrounding mountains, where in some places it probably amounts
to at least 20 inches even now, the volume of the rivers would be far
greater than at present, and all the ancient settlements could be reoccupied. According to Hoyt and Langbein, a three-fold increase of
a monthly precipitation of 2 inches at an average temperature of
about 40°F results in approximately a six-fold increase in the volume
of rivers. Of course, the exact ratio depends on the topography, but
the principle is clear.

Stein's second objection to the theory of climatic pulsations is
based on conditions such as prevail at Endereh, some 70 miles southeast of Chadota. He says:

There the remains of an old settlement, smaller than Chadota but of similar type, are proved by documents I excavated to have been abandoned also
towards the close of the third century A.D. Hsüan-tsang, the great Buddhist
pilgrim, passing there in the first half of the seventh century A.D., saw it in
ruins. But significantly enough the river still passes within easy reach of
the site, and I found its water still ample to irrigate the fairly extensive cultivated area of a modern colony established some six miles further down the
river. Both [this site and Chadota] derived their water from rivers fed by

the snows and glaciers of the same high K'un-lun range to the south, and yet there is [a] marked difference in their respective positions at present as regards irrigation resources. It is clear that the assumed desiccation could not have affected the oases uniformly. Hence the question naturally arises whether the reason for the simultaneous abandonment of both oases ought not to be looked for elsewhere. . . .

Now it is certainly noteworthy that the time of abandonment here and at several other ancient sites of the Tarim coincides with the period when . . . the domination of the Han dynasty ceased. This had assured peace and order, [but at its end these] gave way for several centuries to internal strife and invasions. History proves that effective Chinese political control over the Tarim basin has always meant . . . security and prosperity for the petty states that share its oases. The collapse of that control, as the experience of the last few years sadly illustrates, has invariably been followed by wars and rapid economic retrogression.

These passages from Stein are quoted at length because they illustrate the difficulties experienced by careful and conscientious students. They also illustrate the need for additional knowledge and for following the principle of searching for multiple causes. Although Stein describes Endereh correctly, his description is not complete. After his visit the present author [3] explored the surrounding country more fully than Stein had been able to do. I found that in ancient Buddhist times a dense population dwelt along the eastern side of the river for a distance of at least fifteen miles north and south, and an indefinite distance east and west. I also found that the entire population supported by the modern river numbers about eighty. These people get their living partly as shepherds, feeding their sheep on reeds and salty vegetation supported by the spring floods. They cultivate a little land but say that the crops are worth while only if the land rests two years after being cultivated for one. The reason for this is salt in the irrigation water. The river flows underground much of the sixty miles after leaving the mountains and thus becomes saline. This, rather than any limitation of the water supply, is the main reason why a region that was formerly well populated is now practically deserted. A diminution in rainfall not only lessens the size of a desert stream, but increases the percentage of its volume that flows underground and picks up salt.

Dead trees, standing like gaunt skeletons after hundreds of years, prove that a long period of uninterrupted cultivation must have elapsed in order to allow poplars to attain a diameter of four feet.

[3] Huntington, 1907B, pp. 213–20.

They also indicate that the river in their day must have been less salty than now, for water as saline as that of Endereh soon stops the growth of trees. Recent attempts to use the large volume of water in the lower Tarim River for irrigation have proved abortive because of salt. Trees and crops grow well at first, but the evaporation of the irrigation water soon proves ruinous. The importance of this factor is often overlooked. A change in salinity thus helps to explain the fact that at Endereh thousands of people once prospered in an area where the present occupants, although numbering scarcely a hundred, find difficulty in getting a living.

In the part of the Endereh ruins farthest downstream, great age is indicated by the absence of any trace of houses, by the finely broken and primitive character of the pottery, and by the occurrence of archaic stone hammers and flint knives. Farther upstream, relics of later times in the forms of forts, temples, houses, and gardens are scattered over many square miles. The lesser age of these compared with the relics farther downstream is evident in clay walls and in the undecayed stumpy trucks of mulberry, white poplar, and other trees still standing in orchards. It is also evident in the size and ornamentation of the fragments of pottery and the occurrence of grooved millstones. Features of still later date are evident farther upstream in the most southerly ruins. There, about three miles south of the main "stupa," or shrine, discovered by Stein, I found a large mud fort of Mohammedan age, which was not seen by him. Thus we have evidence that in successive cycles the maximum degree of storminess has declined, as is suggested by the general slope downward to the right in Figure 79.

B. Forests and Desiccation

Here in the great heart of Asia the most widespread evidence of climatic changes during the last two or three thousand years is the death of vegetation over large areas.[4] Out in the desert, beyond the place where the rivers divide into fingerlike branches and then disappear in the sand, plants of many kinds have been killed by drought on a vast scale. For a distance of at least seven hundred miles from east to west their remains still stand after long centuries. Literally thousands of square miles are covered with mounds of every height up to fifty or sixty feet where tamarisk bushes have fought a losing

4 Huntington, 1907B, pp. 179–81, 262–78.

fight against the lowering level of ground water and consequent erosion by the wind. Other thousands are covered with wild poplars that have long been dead, or with beds of ancient dead reeds that sometimes extend twenty miles beyond the present limit of floods. Few travellers have seen these because they lie far off the caravan routes, but the author crossed them at intervals for several hundred miles. It has been asserted that the destruction of forests causes a diminution of rainfall, but nowhere does there seem to be any conclusive evidence of this. In the Tarim basin the opposite has evidently occurred; a diminution in the water supply has caused the destruction of forests without the intervention of man.

Another line of evidence shows that ancient roads, including great trade routes, have been abandoned because the water supply has declined. One such road formerly ran south of the salt lake and swamp of Lop Nor.[5] At rare intervals it is traversed today. The present route is a day's journey shorter than the old one. It takes a short cut across the salt flats of what was once a bay of the lake, around which the old road had to make a big circuit. An older road was still longer because it had to swing around the lake when it stood at an even higher level. Two old strands at heights of twelve and thirty feet above the old lake bed show these lake levels very clearly. Above them some higher, older strands indicate that since the glacial period the lake has stood for long periods at several different levels.

C. Widespread Uniformity of Cycles

The impression of relatively widespread uniformity in the timing of climatic cycles which we have derived from the trees, lakes, and caravans of Figures 78 and 79 is matched by a similar uniformity in other widely scattered evidences of greater rainfall. Three examples, each from a different continent, will show how closely the conditions in the heart of Asia, at places such as Chadota and Endereh, are repeated far away. The first may be dismissed briefly by means of a map. Figure 82 shows the extent of the modern and ancient oases at Merv about four hundred miles east of the Caspian Sea.[6] Scattered far and wide over both the old (unshaded) and modern (shaded) parts of the oasis there are numerous flat-topped kurgans, or tepes, as the Turkomans call them, at least forty of which are located well beyond the limits of modern cultivation. There are also several

[5] Huntington, 1907B, pp. 180–81.   [6] Huntington, 1908.

large rectangular forts, the thick and lofty mud walls of which have
been reduced to mere rows of hillocks or rounded ridges. Houses
of the ordinary sort must have existed, but their sites are marked
only by low mounds or an accumulation of pottery. The apparent
density and wide distribution of the population in the past, as com-

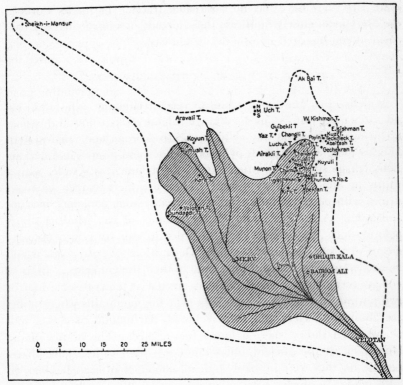

Figure 82. Old and New Oases at Merv. $T =$ Tepeh or Kurgan (clay tumulus
for village).

pared with the present, are impressive. Wherever villages exist today
there are traces of ancient occupation; but there are also large areas
which must once have been densely peopled, although now deserted.
Among low sand dunes and on deserted clay plains great tracts are
covered with potsherds far more thickly than in any of the modern
villages. In Figure 82 the limits of the present irrigated area are
drawn through the ends of the canals without regard to the extensive
unoccupied lacunae that lie between. The lacunae are so large that

much of the region now presents the aspect of a desert in which there are mere patches of cultivation. The limits of the formerly irrigated areas are drawn just beyond the outmost ruins, but it is hardly probable that the ancient inhabitants built large and important villages at the extreme limit of cultivation. Outside of these places there must have been a strip of cultivated land where the villages were so small that they have left no noticeable traces. Taken as a whole, the Merv oases closely duplicate those already described in the Tarim basin fifteen hundred miles away to the east.

D. North America's Waterless Ruins

Evidence that the moist phase of certain climatic cycles was considerably more rainy than the average climate today is found in America in much the same way as in Asia. In Arizona and northwestern Mexico there are hundreds of inconspicuous and almost unnoted ancient village sites which often extend for as much as a mile, with a width of almost half as much.[7] They are mere barren expanses strewn with pottery, flint knives, arrowheads, stone hammers, hearths, and ashes. A notable feature is the number of flat grinding stones before which the women knelt in order to rub corn into flour by means of a smaller, longish stone. Generations of hard work would be needed to wear many of the stones to their present shape. In some villages rectangular lines of boulders erected at intervals of a foot or two outline ancient walls, especially near the mountains where stones are abundant. Here and there a broad, flat mound of clay a foot or two high shows where a house was located. The houses of the Hohokam, as the ancient inhabitants are often called, have disappeared, for they were probably built of adobe, or of branches wattled with mud. In almost every village an oval hollow surrounded by a low wall covers an area one or two hundred feet long by half as wide—not a reservoir, as one at first supposes, but probably a ceremonial precinct. Little else remains. Yet these were no transient encampments, but permanent agricultural villages. Pottery to a depth of two feet or more suggests that the villages were filled with busy people for centuries.

The location of these Hohokam ruins in respect to water and arable land is essentially the same as that of the Asiatic ruins already described. By assuming that this was the case, and acting accord-

7 Huntington, 1914A.

ingly, the author was able to discover many ruins that were unknown to his guides. He simply studied the map, decided where the topography would favor villages if there were more water, and then hunted for the ruins. The normal location is on the edge of the lowest available gravel terrace, just above broad expanses of rich alluvial land. The exceptions are in alluvial plains so broad that there are no gravel terraces within a reasonable distance. Among twenty-five ruined villages examined by the author in the part of southern Arizona and Sonora surrounding Tucson, not one was located primarily in a position favorable to easy defense. Even when defendable sites were close at hand, they were not utilized for the main village, but only in a secondary fashion as refuges, apparently in times of trouble.

One of the most significant facts about the ruins in Arizona and Sonora is their relation to water. Fully half of the twenty-five just mentioned lie from half a mile to eight miles from the nearest permanent spring or perennial stream. It is hard to see where inhabitants of such places could now get drinking water. It is equally hard to see how so many villages could have found water for irrigation. Indian corn was the great staple crop. Except in unusual years it cannot be grown in this region without irrigation. The total rainfall of southern Arizona from April to September normally amounts to only seven inches. The available water supply is now fully used for irrigation, but hundreds of ancient sites have no supply.

A good example of ruins with no adequate water supply and of a river that once flowed farther than now is seen along the lower Altar or Magdalena River in Mexico, 120 miles southwest of Tucson. Caborca, with about 1,500 people, is the last town irrigated by the river. "Beyond Caborca," as Sauer and Brand [8] say, "the . . . Altar loses itself in the desert. . . . Caborca is and has been through most of historic time about at the western limit of the permanently settled country." Nevertheless, at Buzani, 14 miles farther downstream, the present author found seven modern families of cattle raisers. Most of the year their water comes from a well 200 feet deep. When I saw it the water was being drawn up in big leather buckets attached to ropes tied to the saddles of horses. This was a new-fangled method, however, for neither cattle, horses, nor deep wells were within the range of the facilities of the prehistoric Indians. They must have relied on surface water or shallow wells for drinking water,

[8] p. 100.

and on irrigated corn fields for food. Today the Buzani cattle raisers plant corn in favorable years, but in 1910, for example, they planted nothing because the preceding winter had been so dry that there was no water in the river.

This Buzani site closely reproduces the conditions at the Central Asiatic site of Endereh, described above. There I found modern shepherds, a medieval mosque, and still older ruins. At Buzani the modern cattle herders were preceded by a Spanish mission in the eighteenth century. Recent ruins around the mission church indicate a population of 40 to 60 families. These people must have lived by agriculture, for so large a number of cattle herders could not have been supported in one place. Close by there are the remains of a larger and older prehistoric village. Pottery, seashells, and grinding stones cover 30 or 40 acres of a site that was evidently long inhabited.

Some 10 miles below Buzani the dry bed of the ancient Altar River is bordered by another ancient village site about a mile long and one third as wide. Its area was greater than that of modern Caborca with its 1,500 people. In the heart of a genuine desert, 4 or 5 miles farther down, still another ruin was found. Within a mile of where the river would empty into the Gulf of California if it had water enough, a bed of pottery thickly scattered for a mile or more indicates an agricultural village that was occupied for a long time and must have been irrigated by the river which now comes to an end 60 miles away. All these sites on the lower 55 miles of the Altar River would be excellent places for villages if the river were large enough. In our day, however, villages simply cannot exist.

In spite of such evidence some students still cling to the old idea of climatic uniformity throughout historic times. Therefore they attempt to find local explanations of the obvious difference between the past and the present. These are usually mere suggestions with little real evidence behind them. It is easy, for example, to assert with Sauer and Brand [9] that the abandonment of settlements such as are here described took place because the people were "exposed to injury by nomadic raiders [who] . . . destroyed the valley farmers, but did not have the wit to take over the economic system they broke up." Such an assumption simply begs the question. It assumes that the later Indians were innately inferior to their predecessors, a point as to which we have absolutely not a shred of knowledge. It fails to take account of the known fact that fluctuation, not uniformity, is the cli-

9 p. 74.

matic rule. It also takes no account of the fact that the conditions
just described in northern Mexico are an astonishingly close duplicate of those in Sinkiang, Transcaspia, Iran, the Indus Valley, Syria,
Yemen, North Africa, and Peru. In all these regions and many others
some of the most puzzling aspects of the historic picture become clear
if we accept the hypothesis that there have been centuries when the
water supply was distinctly greater than now.

E. Depopulated Peru

Large areas in the southern, as well as the northern, hemisphere
are dotted with ruins in locations too dry to be now inhabited. In
Peru, for example, aerial surveys in the dry belt along the seacoast
west of the Andes disclose an extraordinary number of old ruins and
an almost incredible number of mountain sides terraced for cultivation, but now unused. The drier portions of the high Andean plateau show similar conditions. It is noteworthy that these conditions
do not prevail near the equator in Ecuador, but increase gradually
as one goes south. They reach a maximum in the regions of transition between the equatorial type of climate and that of the trade
wind deserts.

The region around Arequipa, 16° south of the equator, illustrates
the matter especially well.[10] This pleasant little city of about 50,000
inhabitants lies at a height of 7,500 feet in the valley of Rio Chili.
The average annual rainfall is only 4 inches. In half the years it is
less than 3. Five sixths of the rain comes during January, February,
and March. Obviously agriculture is impossible without irrigation.
Arequipa is surrounded by the imposing volcanoes of Pichu,
Chachani, and El Misti, where Harvard University maintained an
astronomical observatory from 1891 to 1937. Thanks to the mountains, the Rio Chili provides water enough to irrigate abundant gardens and support one of the most pleasant Andean cities. Nevertheless, even in the immediate vicinity of the city there is much idle
land which might be cultivated if there were more water. The surrounding slopes at first sight appear utterly barren and so uninterest-
ing that it is doubtful whether one traveller in a thousand pays much
attention to them. Yet for mile after mile practically every slope is
covered with terraces, canals, and the remnants of ancient villages
extending one or two thousand feet above the city. These neglected

10 Huntington, 1935B, pp. 578–79.

and almost undescribed evidences of a former dense population must cover many thousand acres. It would be an interesting and scientifically profitable job to map them.

An old canal, which the author followed for half a mile, illustrates a condition which is repeated hundreds, perhaps thousands, of times in South America, and probably tens of thousands of times in the world as a whole. From the site of an ancient ruined village, at an altitude of about 9,500 feet near the present village of Chikauta, the canal can be followed past scores of abandoned terraces to its head in a small valley on the slopes of Pichu Pichu. There I found two Indian families living in hovels of mud and stone which are probably much like those of the ancient villagers. Lack of water prevents them from practicing agriculture, but they raise sheep and llamas. They say that a spring near the head of the old canal supplies enough water for their animals during the four moister months, but that the rest of the year they have to drive their animals to another spring farther down the valley. If there were water enough in this little valley, it would be easy and profitable to rebuild the old canal and use the terraces for corn and other crops.

The wide distribution of such dry canals, waterless terraces, and uninhabited ruins seems to be explicable only on the hypothesis of more abundant rainfall than now during many centuries in the past. Other possible causes of the abandonment of the ruins around Arequipa have been suggested, but do not seem valid. These include recent and amazingly swift uplift of the Andes. This explanation is inadequate because ruins of similar age lie close to sea level. Another favorite suggestion is that the introduction of sheep, horses, wheat, and other Old World products and the modern growth of cities have introduced new methods of getting a living so that the Peruvians no longer find it necessary to cultivate the poorest of their land. This can scarcely be true, for even now the Peruvians cultivate an amazing number of tiny scraps of land lying high on the mountain sides and so steep and inaccessible that they seem almost worthless. The only advantage of such land is that it has rain enough for crops or can be irrigated. Except in these respects it is greatly inferior to the much broader pieces of almost level land which lie on the abandoned terraces near Arequipa. If water could be secured for the old terraces, the Peruvians would be incredibly stupid to leave them unused while going to arduous labor in cultivating tiny scraps of land high up on the steep slopes.

F. Wide Prevalence of Land Hunger

This brings up the problem of overpopulation, an aspect of civilization which is often misunderstood. Persons who do not realize the worldwide scope of climatic changes often assume that abandoned dry areas could again be cultivated if human conditions were right. We are told that all the anciently cultivated land could be made fruitful if nomad raids were prevented, if the modern people had better "wits" and were more skillful in irrigation, if they would work hard enough, or if they really needed more land. The author's experience in the border zone of Palestine between the inhabited area and the ruins (Figure 80) sheds light on these suppositions.[11] In 1909, as often before, there were renewed efforts by the settled people to extend agriculture once more into the abandoned areas. Unfortunately the rain was scanty in the winter and spring. The crops in the border zone failed completely. At Beersheba, for example, I saw hundreds of acres of wheat where the crop consisted merely of scattered little stalks six or eight inches high and not furnishing wheat enough to replace the seed. The attempt to expand the cultivated area had resulted in an actual loss of food. This occurs whenever the rains are deficient. Nevertheless, the settled people keep pushing their operations out into the desert as far as possible. In spite of repeated failures, they occupy every bit of available land where there is any hope of getting a living, even temporarily.

This eagerness to get more land is found not only in Palestine, but in practically every long-settled region. It arises from the fact that the population almost everywhere is in what may at least be called a condition of "saturation," if not of overpopulation. In the vast majority of regions the people are desperately land-hungry because their fields are too small to support them in comfort. On the borders of Palestine this induces them to cultivate marginal land where two crops out of five are failures. In Peru it induces them to climb one or even two thousand feet up steep slopes in order to cultivate tiny patches of soil where a fall might literally send a man rolling helplessly down hill to his death. In Sinkiang (the Tarim basin) it induces people to use salty water for irrigation, although they know by sad experience that it will ruin their fields in a few years and oblige them to move on. Similar conditions are almost universal. All the good land is used normally except in rich countries where wealthy

[11] 1911, pp. 113 ff.

people may keep some good land idle. That which remains unused is relatively poor. The people who try to cultivate it are bound to adopt an almost incredibly low standard of living and are likely to find themselves faced with famine every few years. They cannot establish comfortable permanent villages such as the ruins indicate in the past. It stands to reason, then, that good, level, easily accessible land would never be left idle for centuries if crops could be raised on it. Yet in the world as a whole, millions of acres of such land, which once was cultivated, are today unused for lack of water.

Misgovernment and nomad raids have only a temporary effect in preventing the cultivation of land that will yield reliable crops. The year when the crops failed at Beersheba, as described above, was so dry that the nomads were short of both water and grass. So they pressed into the settled lands of Syria and Palestine on every side, often pasturing their flocks and herds on the ruined grain fields of the border villages. They robbed the villagers right and left, stripping them naked sometimes, and carrying off their clothes as well as their animals. This same thing has happened time and again in the past when rain was especially scanty. Nevertheless, the villagers show little tendency to give up their fields on the open plateau east of the Jordan, although there they are fully exposed to Arab raids. They might go to many protected valleys where raiders on horses and camels could not easily attack them, and where ruins show that people have lived in the past. They do not go because there is no water. They stick to the places where they can raise crops, or else come back to them when driven away temporarily, just as the people around Vesuvius remain on the fertile volcanic slopes in spite of sulphurous smoke, ashes, and lava.

One of the most important questions that faces the historian is how far the abandoned villages in the dry regions from Central Asia to Peru could be watered and reoccupied if people were more skillful in the arts of agriculture and irrigation. There is no doubt that improvement is possible, just as in almost every human activity. Mere skill, however, could accomplish little in regions where the ruins are so located that no permanent supply of water is available and where the rainfall is insufficient for agriculture without irrigation. It is extremely hard to get water out of dry valleys, and impossible to get it from skies without clouds. In places where a considerable, although apparently diminished, supply of water is still available, the opportunity to improve matters is probably greater than with the small water supplies, but the hope of improvement is curtailed by the fact that ancient irrigation works of the larger sort, such as are found in Syria, North Africa, and Peru, were so well engineered that modern man cannot do much better without great dams that require the most expert engineering. The mere presence of well made old engineering works suggests a supply of water greater than at present and large enough to be worth working for.

In the smaller irrigation projects, the ancient methods were apparently the same as those of today. The skill with which modern Peruvians, Syrians, and Persians utilize every tiny spring and lead water out of gravel beds at the base of mountains is extraordinary. It is difficult to see how anyone could do much better except at an intolerable expense. It seems quite certain that if the water supply today were equal to that of the time when the ruins flourished, the modern people could cultivate as much land as their ancient predecessors.

This survey of evidence as to greater water supplies during certain centuries in the past than at present might be farther expanded, but the general conclusion would remain unchanged. The abundance and location of ruins which are now insufficiently supplied with water seem to afford conclusive evidence that some widespread cause has been at work producing similar results in all climates of the types here considered. When identical phenomena are found in widely scattered regions, the normal scientific method is to inquire whether there is any one set of causes to which they all can be ascribed. The failure to do this, or more exactly the failure to appreciate that the phenomena actually are worldwide, has led people to invent all sorts of possible local causes for the presence of ruins without a corresponding water supply. The possibilities include melting of glaciers, exhaustion of artesian waters, uplift of mountains, breaking of underground water courses by earthquakes, shifting of stream channels, deposition of alluvium to such a depth that a river gets lost in its own deposits, deforestation, erosion of the soil, ravages of nomadic raiders, loss of the art of irrigation, increasing salinity of the soil because of irrigation, growing stupidity or barbarism among the people, misgovernment, introduction of Mohammedanism, intentional burial of springs by man, ravages of unrestricted grazing, and diversion of trade.

These are not all of the asserted causes of the wide prevalence of ruins without sufficient water, but they illustrate the diversity, the local character, and often the purely hypothetical and untested nature of the supposed causes. Many of these alleged causes, to be sure, bear some relation to climatic cycles, but generally they are expectable results rather than causes. Of course cultural conditions have co-operated with climatic cycles, as we saw in reference to the gravel tunnels at Palmyra, but that is a different matter. The logical method is first to inquire whether any single set of conditions is sufficiently widespread and powerful to produce the amazingly uniform results seen all the way from Central Asia to Peru. Climatic cycles are the only known condition of this sort. They also explain the much less obvious evidences of periods drier than the present. Therefore in any study of the decline of ancient empires, we ought first to ascertain the effect of such cycles and then interpret the human events in the light of the basic physical conditions.

G. Climatic Cycles and Migration

The relation of climatic cycles to the outburst of nomads from their homes in the steppes has been much discussed. In *A Study of History*, for example, Toynbee [12] has published a full list of historic migrations of nomads from the deserts and steppes of Asia and Africa into the surrounding agricultural lands. He has also indicated movements in the opposite direction. These latter normally take the form of slow cultural infiltrations in contrast to the rather sudden eruptions of considerable numbers of people which characterize the outward movements from the desert. Toynbee's conclusion is that there is a genuine and deep-seated connection between climatic pulsations and both kinds of migration. Outward migrations from steppes and deserts tend to be associated with periods of aridity, or at least of diminishing rainfall; movements in the other direction occur most frequently when the rainfall increases.

Toynbee provides so full a body of data that we may well test his results by comparing them with indices of climate such as the droughts of Figure 66 and the caravan travel, lake levels, and tree growth of Figure 79. Instead of the tree curve of that diagram, however, let us use another (Figure 83), which represents the growth of 330 sequoia trees in California, according to Antevs' interpretation. The basic data are the same as in the tree curve of Figure 79, but Antevs uses a method which eliminates the general change of climate that seems to be indicated by the distribution of ruins and the an-

[12] Vol. III, pp. 395–444.

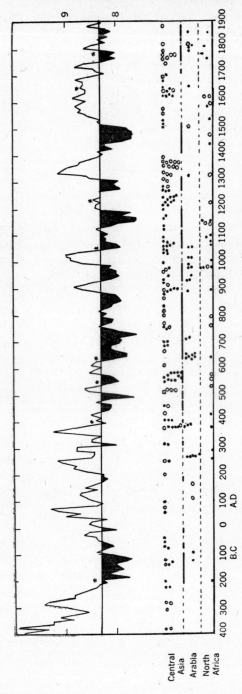

Figure 83. Nomadic Migrations and Cycles of Tree Growth in California. •Outward movements from steppes and deserts; °inward movements to steppes and deserts; *especially widespread or strong outward movements; — duration of dry periods. (The curve is based on Antevs, Table 2, columns *d* and *h* as far back as 250 B.C., and before that on Huntington, 1914A, Table G, column *F*.)

cient high level of lakes such as the Caspian Sea and Owens [13] and Pyramid Lakes [14] in the United States. Thus the tree curve of Figure 83 shows approximately the way in which variations in the California climate have caused the growth of the sequoias to depart from the average of each particular period, regardless of whether the second century B.C., for example, was more or less dry than the seventh and fifteenth centuries A.D.

All of the nomadic outbursts recorded by Toynbee have been indicated at their proper dates by solid dots at the bottom of Figure 83. The corresponding movements back to the desert have been similarly indicated by open circles. Both types of movement have been divided according to whether they are associated with Central Asia, Arabia, or the Sahara. It is unfortunate that we have to compare these Asiatic and African movements of population with a climatic record so far away as California, but no other continuous, homogeneous climatic data go back far enough. Moreover, we have seen that fluctuations of rainfall in California and western Asia appear to be genuinely correlated.

Viewing our problem as a whole, the first question is whether nomadic migrations outward from deserts show any clear tendency toward association with periods of slow tree growth, as shown in Figure 83, or of many droughts, as shown in Figure 66 (page 483). In Figure 83 the heavily shaded areas and the heavy black lines toward the bottom of the diagram indicate that the 2,300 years there represented were divided into 1,200 years of relatively fast growth and 1,100 of slow. On an average there were 5.2 nomadic outbursts per century during times of fast growth and 7.8 during times of slow growth, a difference of 50 per cent. On the contrary, movements in the other direction, back into the desert, have occurred at the rate of 3.7 per century in the years of fast growth and only 2.6 (30 per cent less) in the times of slow growth. This looks like a real relationship.

Another way of looking at the matter is to take periods when the nomadic outbursts were especially widespread or severe. As a test of these qualities, Toynbee lays special stress on the simultaneous occurrence of outbursts in more than one general region. On this basis he selects the periods centering near the asterisks in Figure 83, and to these we have added the period of the great Arab outpourings when Islam first arose. With these we may properly include two

[13] Gale.   [14] Jones.

earlier periods which are emphasized by Toynbee, but which occurred before the beginning of Figure 83. Both of the early periods belong to times of notably slow growth among the relatively few sequoias which date back so far. The first was the two centuries from about 1350 to 1150 B.C. which "saw the Libyans pressing upon the west bank of the Nile out of the Libyan Desert and the Aramaeans breaking out of the North Arabian Steppe into Syria." Two minor incidents of migration or unrest during this period were the conquest of Palestine by the Hebrews and the Trojan War of Homer. Toynbee's second period of active nomadic outburst occurred about 700 B.C., when the Cimmerians and the Scythians arrived at Iraq and Anatolia in the course of their eruption through the territory between The Pamirs and the Caspian Sea. At the same time the Arabs, erupting out of their desert, were pressing upon the upper Euphrates from the opposite direction.

We come now to the periods of nomadic outpouring designated by the asterisks in Figure 83. At the turn of the second and third centuries B.C., as Toynbee puts it, the Hiongnu at the eastern border of the Central Asiatic desert were pressing upon China, while at the other end of the Eurasian grasslands the Sarmatians were crossing the Don and occupying the western border of the steppes up to the Carpathian Mountains. This was a time when tree growth had been rapidly declining for 80 years and had at last fallen below the average. In other words, it was a time when one would expect the nomads to be in such distress that they would be ready to follow any leader who promised relief. The thing that counts most, of course, is the degree of change in the rainfall and pasturage within a short time. A great change of this sort must have occurred at this epoch, if the California trees truly represent the main fluctuations of the Asiatic climate. Skipping six centuries we come to "the turn of the fourth and fifth centuries," and again find almost the same situation. In the far east the Juan Juan were breaking in upon northwestern China. In the center the Huns were overwhelming Iran and its neighbors, and on the west they were spreading into Europe across the broad plains between the Caspian Sea and the Urals. At the same time in the south the Arabs were again pressing upon the Euphrates region and Syria. Still farther away from China the Berbers were invading the Roman dominions in Cyrenaica and even in the far northwest of Africa. Turning to Figure 83, we find that at this time tree growth once more declined very rapidly. It fell below the average, to be sure, for only a decade, but the degree of change was large. Next we come to "about the middle of the sixth century of the Christian Era when the (pseudo) Avars—with the Khazars at their heels—were sweeping out of the heart of the Steppe across the Emba and the Volga and the Don and the Carpathians into the Hungarian Alföld, and the Khitan were pressing upon China between the Khighan Range and Korea." Here Figure 83 puts us squarely in the first part of a severe period of slow tree growth. The clock diagram of Figure 66 (page 483) indicates that terrible droughts were approaching but had not yet become serious.

Among the principal eruptions that are on record Toynbee includes next the outpouring of the primitive Moslem Arabs which began about A.D. 632. At this time the California trees dropped into one of their worst periods of growth, and droughts became numerous. Toynbee next skips forward a long way to the middle of the eleventh century. The Seljuqs were then erupting into Iran and onward to Turkey. The Cumans were advancing into Russia north of the Caspian Sea, while the Banu Hilal (Beni Hilel) were breaking out of Arabia across Syria and Egypt and were surging onward toward Tunis. The Murabits were doing likewise out of the western Sahara into the Sudan on one side and Morocco and Spain on the other. The desert people were pressing outward all along a vast stretch of country extending five thousand miles from Central Asia to northwestern Africa. At this time, again, just as in so many other instances, the growth of the California trees fell off greatly, and once more Figure 66 shows that a bad series of droughts was beginning.

The next conspicuous desert eruption seems at first sight to differ from the others in its climatic relationships. It took place in "the first half of the thirteenth century [when] the Tatars or Mongols erupted out of the Eurasian Steppe on almost every front simultaneously." We have already seen what these bold conquerors did and how tremendously they influenced the world. In neither Figure 83 nor Figure 66, however, is there any serious suggestion of a climatic cause for their spread over Asia and into Europe. This is a radical departure from the rather remarkable uniformity which we have found in the apparent climatic relationship of all seven of the previous great epochs of migration. Two points, however, should be noted. First, although Figure 83 shows a good many dots indicating desert outbursts at this time, every one of these from 1200 to 1280 indicates a movement of one or another group of Mongols. This was not a time of widespread migrations, but merely of fiercely intensive migration from one particular center—Mongolia. Furthermore, as we have seen in a previous chapter, the Mongol outburst was peculiar because of the degree to which it represents wars of conquest entered into under the leadership of Ghengis Khan and his highly competent kinsmen. He was a leader so great that he inspired his warlike people to conquer the world, although their economic condition at home, if the tree curve and the chart of droughts are any guide, may have been improving for some time.

The great spurt of tree growth during the fourteenth century after the Mongol outburst is conspicuous in Figure 83 because of the large number of open circles, which denote the spread of the influence of agricultural people and their culture into the steppes. Similar, but less impressive, conditions are seen during the periods of rapid tree growth before 250 B.C. and about A.D. 75, 250, 510, and 911. Curiously enough, however, the period of rapidly declining tree growth and terrible drought which culminated about A.D. 1490 is practically free from desert migrations. Equally unexpected, so far as the trees are concerned, but fully to be expected in view of the droughts in Figure 66, is Toynbee's selection of the middle of the seventeenth century as a time of notable migrations. "The Calmucks were flooding over their Mongol kinsmen's ranges toward the east and over the alien Kazaks' ranges towards the west, the Shammar and the Anazah were breaking out of Arabia and were crossing the Upper Euphrates into Mesopotamia." Finally Toynbee considers the beginning of the nineteenth century an important time from the standpoint of nomadic outbreaks. In Figure 83, however, we have placed the asterisk at 1780, because that seems to fit the beginning of the outward movements of both the Wahabi from northern Arabia toward Syria and Iraq and of the Fulas out of the western Sahara into Nigeria. If our procedure is correct, this last period of desert outbreaks is like most of the others in falling at a time when the California trees indicate the unfavorable part of a climatic cycle. Droughts became abundant just after the dates (1800–10) given by Toynbee. The outbreaks of the Wahabi and Fulas are perhaps scarcely great enough to be of much importance.

Let us sum up what we have found as to nomadic outbursts and climate. Among the ten periods which Toynbee selects for special emphasis the first seven and probably the last all occur at times when two things are happening: A rapid decline in tree growth is just taking the curve of Figure 83 below the average, and a period of severe cold droughts is about to begin. This suggests a genuine relationship. So, too, does the fact that during periods of less than average tree growth the occurrence of nomadic outpourings is much more frequent than during periods of the opposite character, whereas when the trees grow well the movements into the desert are almost as numerous as out of it. The other two periods of restlessness in the steppes are different. The one centering in 1230 seems to be explained by the genius of Genghiz Khan and his kinsmen. The other (1650) is flatly opposed to what we should expect from the trees in California, but comes just at the expectable place before the outbreak of severe droughts. Perhaps one of the many curious inversions of cycles, which we have repeatedly seen in climate, accounts for unusually rapid tree growth at this time. In spite of this doubtful instance the evidence as a whole seems to indicate a real and close connection between climatic cycles and outbreaks of nomads from the steppes. The close agreement between the tree curve and droughts, except in the seventeenth century, is an added reason for believing that both Figures 83 and 66 represent climatic fluctuations that were widespread in middle latitudes, and that have had much effect on human actions.

This brings us back to the problem of why nomads so frequently surge out of their homes, conquer settled communities, and establish themselves as a ruling class. In Part II of this book we saw that the selective action of desert life seems to segregate nomadic kiths that have the active, alert, resourceful, and self-reliant character which is a vital factor in this whole problem. Now we see that climatic pulsations appear often to set the date when people of this sort surge out as both destroyers and conquerors. Such surges, however, do not occur every time there is a dry period, as is apparent at the end of the fifteenth century. Moreover, they may occur in what appear to be relatively moist and climatically favorable periods, as in the early thirteenth century. The fact seems to be that at least four main factors must be duly weighted in order to understand the outbursts of nomads, namely, the climate; the inherent quality of the people, especially as manifested in their leaders; the pull exerted by the wealth and opportunities of the agricultural lands; and the push exerted by overpopulation.

Let us begin with overpopulation. During periods of increasing rainfall the nomads in the steppes probably increase in number faster than the settled people around them. This is because their food supply and their wealth in general increase more rapidly than those of agriculturists. The reason is clear. Flocks and herds can double their size in a few years if there is pasturage enough. That means twice as much food, twice as much wealth. A change of rainfall from 10 to 20 inches, for example, on a given area in the United States increases the number of cattle that can be grazed there three-fold, according to Chapline and Cooperrider. Bowman [15] says that in Australia three acres are needed to support a sheep if the rainfall is 12½ inches per year, but only one acre with twice that amount. With lower rainfall, such as occurs in steppes and deserts, similar conditions prevail, and there is an additional effect because large areas lack water for both man and beast. If the rainfall increases, new springs appear, and new areas are open for the flocks. The land of agricultural people does not increase in any such fashion, even though the yield of crops per acre may rise considerably with additional rain.

Nomads are no exception to the practically universal rule that population tends to increase rapidly when abundant and expanding resources are available. It continues to do so until the land supports the maximum number that is possible under the prevailing standard of living. Hence, unless people die because of epidemics, war, and starvation, a century or two of good rainfall almost invariably means a considerable increase in the number of nomads. The density of population approaches a level where it exerts a definite and often strong outward push impelling the nomads to seek new means of livelihood. Their natural response is raids upon one another and then attempts to take possession of other people's land.

The outward push of overpopulation is enhanced by the pull of the wealth and the good grazing grounds of the agricultural people on the borders of the desert. This alone may lead a group of nomads to raid their settled neighbors. Troubles thus started may spread and grow until they lead to far-reaching movements of plunder and conquest. Frequently, probably usually, the push of overpopulation and the pull of the neighbors' wealth act together.

Sooner or later, when the nomadic population has become quite dense, a period of diminishing rainfall is likely to occur. The absolute amount of rain is relatively unimportant. It is the diminution which counts. A drop from 10 to 5 inches may have a more violent

[15] p. 184.

effect than a drop from 20 to 10. In Chapter 9 we saw why raids are an honorable part of nomadic life. Now we see that when the rainfall declines, the natural nomadic response is enlarged raids and attempts to occupy new lands with good water and grass. The degree to which this happens varies greatly according to the density of the population. If people are so scarce that there is plenty of water and pasturage in spite of a diminished rainfall, there is no special tendency toward raids. The annual migrations within a tribe's own domain simply become wider. Thus, although a diminution of rainfall may be a powerful incentive to outbursts from the desert if there are people enough, it may also have no visible effect so far as outbursts are concerned.

Finally, we must not overlook the role played by individuals. This is especially evident in Genghiz Khan and Mohammed, but on a smaller scale it must be equally true of many others. It is especially interesting that the two outpourings from the desert which have had the greatest effect upon history have both occurred under the inspiration of men who rank among the world's supreme leaders. Enough has already been said about Genghiz. As for Mohammed, soon after his flight from Mecca (A.D. 622) severe droughts arose in many regions, as appears in Figure 66. The Arabs were apparently placed under the same kind of strain which the author saw east of Palestine in the dry spring of 1909 when he had personal experience of at least four raids.[16]

Milk was scarce, the young animals were dying because their mothers could not feed them. The women and children were suffering, and the men were worried. Thus it was in 1909, and it was doubtless far worse about A.D. 630.

Then came the word of Mohammed. To people in dire distress any new idea appeals powerfully. Perhaps they had been sinning, and the one God preached by the prophet was angry and had sent the curse of drought. Already they had begun to move out into the greener lands about them when the seer . . . began to preach war. The new religion served as a rallying point. Hitherto tribe had fought against tribe for the water and pasture of their own land and its fringes. Now [beginning in A.D. 632] Mohammedanism gave unity. Arab ceased to devour Arab. Under the banner of the Prophet the tribes united to overwhelm the world. Religion was an essential part of the great Mohammedan dispersion. Hunger and drought were equally essential.[17]

---

[16] Huntington, 1911, p. 335.   [17] *Ibid.*, p. 371.

The survey of the dry, the warm, and the moist phases of historic climatic cycles which we have made in the last two chapters might be expanded almost indefinitely. We might also discuss the problem of cold phases. These have doubtless existed, but it is difficult to separate them from the dry and the wet phases. The first result of our survey is the conclusion that diverse and independent lines of investigation in regions as far apart as California, Syria, and Central Asia all show essentially the same sequence of climatic cycles. This conclusion is based on conditions as diverse as Nile floods, tree growth, caravan travel, lake levels, ruins, and droughts. Going on from this, we found widespread evidence that one of the most prominent phases of historic climatic cycles is periods that were drier than now. This is especially evident in the low level of lakes and the occurrence of droughts, but it also appears in the way in which travel across deserts declines. A less easily detected phase of climatic cycles is characterized by higher temperature than is at present normal. Naturally the evidence of this is found mainly in countries such as Ireland and England, where the temperature is close to the lower limit for agriculture, and crops such as grapes cannot now grow. A most puzzling problem is posed by the apparent difference between a wet-warm climatic climax about A.D. 1000 and a wet-cold climax three centuries later.

In our survey of historic climatic cycles the main space has been given to the phase when there are more storms and rain than now. This is the easiest to detect, although there is no reason to believe that it is any more important than the others. Future study will doubtless differentiate between the warm-wet and the cold-wet phases, but here we have made little attempt to do so. Our emphasis has rather been placed on five points. The first is the way in which almost identically the same conditions of shortened rivers, lessened agriculture, and villages and towns abandoned for lack of water are found all the way from Central Asia through Palestine and North Africa to Arizona and Mexico and then onward to Peru. Second, on the whole, the moister phase of climatic cycles has tended to become less extreme as the centuries have rolled on. Third, in the moist phase of the cycles vast areas appear to have been far more densely populated and prosperous than now. Fourth, climatic cycles appear to have intensified the effect of overpopulation, personal ambition, religious fanaticism, and other conditions in inducing hordes of nomads to burst out from the steppes of Asia and Africa, thus setting the world in commotion. Fifth, and perhaps most important of all, is the conclusion that the climatic cycles which we have been examining seem to have exerted a definite effect upon the alertness and activity of the human mind. In this, even more than in their economic and political effects, lies an impelling reason for seeking further light on the problem of cycles, which are still very dimly understood.

CHAPTER 29

GEOGRAPHICAL OPTIMA OF CIVILIZATION

A. Factors in an Optimum

Let us now apply the conclusions of preceding chapters to a few outstanding features of history. The title of this chapter contains the term "optima" instead of "optimum." The reason is evident if one recalls earlier chapters. The optimum or most favorable physical conditions for human progress vary according to both the innate quality of the people and their stage of culture. People of high inborn ability, such as the Icelanders and Parsis, may be stimulated to purposeful and progressive activity by physical circumstances which are repressive to people of lesser innate ability. Then, too, as we have seen abundantly, the kind of physical environment which is best for the early stages of human culture is far from being best for more advanced phases. Hence each particular combination of innate ability and stage of progress has its own optimum physical environment.

In order to illustrate the differences in these optima we shall begin with the people among whom agriculture first became established. We shall then pass on to higher levels in Babylonia, Greece, Ireland, and Europe. We must consider to what extent each stage represents the conquest of some new phase of nature. For example, man is continually seeking new and better materials from which to fashion tools. The primitive quest for flint was essentially the same as the modern search for aluminum ore. Fire is another important physical manifestation which man has continually sought to utilize in new ways. By means of agriculture many plants have become servants of humanity. Agriculture, however, could scarcely have attained its present value had not man discovered how to convert clay into pottery, thus providing means for preserving food as well as for cooking it. Another step was the subjugation of animals by domesticating them. That was important in the realms of transportation, war, and government, as well as of food and clothing. Other materials for both clothing and shelter have likewise been brought into the service

573

of man. Somewhere along the march of progress man learned the art of writing. This involved a wide search for materials on which writings, and hence ideas, could be preserved from generation to generation. At another stage the waters of the earth began to be subjugated and man sailed the sea in ships. Metals were one of the most difficult materials with which man wrestled. After they were well subdued he began to employ fuels as a source of power as well as heat. Today electricity, radioactivity, and a vast variety of chemical reactions vie with discoveries in medicine and heredity as claimants to a high place among man's conquests of nature.

Thus stone, wood, bone, fire, plants, clay, and animals; materials for clothing, building, and writing; the waters, metals, and fuels of the earth; electricity, radioactivity, and chemicals; and finally the viruses and bacteria of disease, and the genes of heredity—all these form a roughly progressive series of environmental factors which man has successively attempted to conquer. As each of them has been brought into the picture through new discoveries, and as the supplies and uses of each have been diminished or increased through human agencies, the location of the areas best fitted for the progress of civilization has been changed. The change has been greatly complicated by man's progressive adaptation to cooler and stormier climates, and by climatic cycles which have influenced plants and animals as well as human beings.

B. The Earliest Civilized Optimum

Inasmuch as civilization began when agriculture and a definite form of organized village life became established, the qualities of the place or places where agriculture probably evolved have much significance. Only a few limited areas provide a good environment for primitive agriculture. One of these far excels the others. We have seen that, as a stimulant to invention, thrift, and the development of society, the type of agriculture based on cereals far surpasses the tropical type dependent on trees and roots. This stimulating type must have originated in a region where wheat, barley, rye, oats, maize, rice, or millet was growing wild some ten thousand years ago. Each of these cereals is now the basis of a certain phase of agricultural civilization. The world's wheat countries include the Mediterranean lands, western Asia, Iran, northern India, northern China, western Europe, Australia, the western plains of Canada, neighboring parts of the United States, and parts of the Argentine plains. North Africa represents the barley type. For an agriculture dominated by oats we turn to Scotland, Norway, and Quebec. The rye type is found in Europe from Germany eastward and northward. The maize type is located primarily in the western hemisphere from the Corn Belt of the United States to that of Argentina. The rice regions extend from central Japan and central China to Indo-China, the East Indies, and the wetter parts of India. Millet is the main crop in north central China, central India, and the part of Africa south of the Sahara.

It seems probable that the wheat type of agriculture surpassed all the others and became the parent of modern civilization for three main reasons. First, wheat is, on the whole, the best of cereals. Second, when agriculture first arose, the climate apparently approached the human optimum more closely in the region where wild wheat was found than in the native habitat of any other important cereal. Third, the animals of that same region afforded another environmental advantage unrivalled elsewhere. The good qualities of wheat need no description. No cereal can be prepared for food more easily. None keeps better in damp weather. None except oats is more nutritious and better balanced as to carbohydrates, protein, minerals, and vitamins. Oats are the best in these respects; millets, the worst.

The relation of the native climate of wheat to man may be judged from the fact that wild wheat has been found by Aaronsohn in the highlands of Palestine. Under the relatively moist and stormy climate which must have prevailed for long periods in the past it probably grew at many spots in the uplands of the region from Cyrenaica eastward across Sinai, Palestine, and northern Arabia to southern Iran. This was at least climatically possible. We have already seen that for primitive people, such as were then experimenting with agriculture, the best climate has a winter just stormy enough to be stimulating but not so cool and wet as to create much discomfort and bad health. The corresponding summer is so dry that high temperature does a minimum of damage to health and efficiency. Wild wheat, more fully than any other cereal, thrives in this same climate. The native climate of barley is similar to that of wheat, but drier and humanly less desirable. Rye and oats belong to climates considerably cooler and more humid than this early optimum and not best for men until a rather high stage of culture is reached. Rice and corn apparently belonged originally to climates which in winter are almost ideal for primitive man, but in summer are so wet and muggy that they sap people's energy. The millets also are largely natives of climates with hot, wet, oppressive summers and dry winters. Their climates go beyond those of corn and rice in extremes of alternating drought and rainfall, as well as heat. Thus the wild wheat region had a great advantage through the fact that its climate was especially good for primitive man as well as for the best of cereals. This fact was presumably of vital help in developing agriculture and in making it the precursor of new inventions, ideas, and institutions.

C. Domestic Animals and Civilization

In addition to the best of cereals and an admirable climate for man the habitat of wild wheat had another great environmental advantage in its native animals. Omitting carnivorous beasts, fowls, and insects, which have played relatively minor parts in this respect, the qualities which most enhance an animal's value as an aid in advancing civilization may be summed up as follows, although of course no one animal can have all of them: (1) The animals must be gregarious and sufficiently timid so that many can be herded by one person; (2) they must be polygamous and must grow fast enough so that within a reasonable time superfluous males will furnish abundant meat; (3) the females must have large udders and be gentle enough so that they can be milked; (4) the animals must bear wool or fine hair fit for cloth; (5) they must be small enough and gentle enough so that an average man or woman can handle them; (6) they must be large enough so that they can carry a load, the best size being such that the animal can carry a full-grown man and a little more; (7) they must have hard hoofs of a kind that can dig into the ground and get a grip which enables the animals to draw plows or carts; (8) they must be intelligent enough so that they can readily be taught to obey commands; and (9) they must be accustomed to travelling long distances at a fairly good speed so that they will be available for use over long distances as pack animals or to carry travellers.

In Table 26 the larger domestic animals are rated according to their standing in each of the nine qualities mentioned above. All can be herded. One has only to picture himself herding twenty cats or dogs to realize how important the gregarious habit is in making animals useful. Grasslands are the main place where mammals are found in large herds. All the animals of Table 26 live in grasslands. Pigs and cattle, however, prefer border tracts where tall grasses are interspersed with trees. They seek safety by hiding amid the vegetation rather than by flight. Hence their gregarious habits and their power to travel fast are weak compared with those of animals which live on plains where the grass is short.

TABLE 26

QUALITIES OF ANIMALS

(The number of x's indicates the relative value for specified purposes.)

	1 Gregarious habits	2 Meat producers	3 Milkers	4 Wool producers	5 Size for managing	6 Size for travel and transport	7 Hoofs for pulling	8 Intelligence	9 Endurance in travel
Pig *	x	xxx	—	—	x	—	—	—	—
Goat *	x	xx	xx	—	x	—	—	—	—
Sheep *	xxx	xx	x	xxx	x	—	—	—	—
Llama	xxx	x	—	xx	x	x	—	—	x
Reindeer	x	x	x	x	x	x	—	x	x
Cattle *	x	x	xxx	—	x	xx	x	x	x
Water buffalo, yak, etc.	x	x	x	—	—	x	x	x	—
Ass *	x	x	x	—	x	x	xx	xxx	xx
Horse *	x	x	x	—	x	xx	xx	xxx	xx
Camel *	x	x	x	x	—	x	—	x	xx

* Readily available to inhabitants of native habitat of wheat.

All the animals in Table 26 are good sources of meat. Prejudice or lack of acquaintance with young tender animals is the main reason for thinking otherwise. The pig's pre-eminence as a meat producer is increased by its large and frequent litters. Goats and sheep rank high, partly because they often have two young at a birth and reach almost full size in half a year. It is doubtful, however, whether mere productivity of meat has done much to promote human civilization.

Milk and wool far excel meat as aiders of civilization. We have already seen that the health and vigor arising from a diet with plenty of milk are basic factors in human progress. That country is fortunate which has plenty of cattle or goats to furnish milk. Wool has been especially helpful to civilization because it enables people to be comfortable in cool climates. Woolen clothing has been a significant factor in facilitating migration into cool, stormy, stimulating climates where cotton or silk clothing would be inadequate. Furs are good in severe weather, but not in that which is merely a bit cool. Wool can be converted into clothing adapted to either a summer evening or an arctic night. Few factors have done more than wool to facilitate the coolward, stormward migration of the main centers of human progress.

Going on now to column 5 in Table 26, we come to the characteristics of the animals themselves rather than the materials which they supply. In order that man may easily manage a herd the individual animals must not be too large. The water buffalo is so big that it is hard to manage, and so is the camel. Sheep are so small that the shepherd would often be glad if they were larger and he had only half as many. The ass is a convenient size for managing and might perhaps be given two crosses in column 5 of Table 26. A more important point as to size is that an animal should be just large enough to carry a man and his equipment (column 6). The ass is a trifle too small for this, though in Turkey or Egypt one sometimes sees two full-grown men riding a single poor little beast and dragging their feet on the ground. The camel is too large. The wild horse and ox are about right. That is one reason why they have become so useful.

It is not enough, however, to have an animal of the right size. Certain other qualities are needed, and in several of these the horse is superior. Hard hoofs (column 7) enable an animal to dig its feet into the ground when pulling a plow, drawing a cart, or scrambling up a hill. In this respect cattle are far better than soft-footed animals like the llama and camel, but their cloven hoofs are inferior to the single hoofs of the ass and horse. The relatively small weight of the ass makes that animal much less useful in this connection than either cattle or horses. Nevertheless, the western world is wrong when it laughs at the humble donkey and overlooks his extreme usefulness. Anyone who has shared the author's experience of travelling with a caravan of donkeys and riding selected animals can scarcely fail to class them with the horse for intelligence (column 8).

Finally, column 9 of Table 26 shows that three animals, the ass, horse, and camel, are especially superior in endurance. They can travel all day in a way that is impossible for any of the others. This is because their original home was dry, open steppes with short grass and a long dry season. Therefore they were compelled to travel long distances at frequent intervals. In dry seasons they naturally eat up the forage close to the few springs which still flow, and then may have to travel many miles between supplies of dry grass and a drink of water. Ability in this respect has been especially important as a factor in civilization. It has made these animals, especially the horse, the best in the world as a means of travelling long distances, carrying loads, and serving the purposes of trade and war. They have been a potent influence in bringing diverse regions into contact, and such contacts are among the greatest stimulants to progress.

The values of the wild animals originally available in the native homes of the various cereals vary greatly. The hot millet region south of the Sahara supports more animals than almost any other part of the world, but they are not of much value. Heavy rains when the weather is hot may cause the grass to reach a height of ten or fifteen feet. The normal response to such growth is almost incredibly large herds composed of many kinds of antelopes, mixed with giraffes, zebras, and ostriches, with elephants not far away. None of these animals has ever been of much use to man except as a source of meat, skins, and ivory. The zebra, which might otherwise be admirable, appears to be too nervous for practical purposes. None of these African animals can be milked, none produces wool, and none is well fitted for riding or hauling. In the partially wooded recesses of the grasslands, to be sure, African cattle are found, but they are reputedly untamable. Even if they could be tamed, the African animals south of the Sahara would not be very promising material for domestication. Moreover, they live in a climate which predisposes mankind to take life easily.

In America, before man occupied the country, the grassland animals were less varied than in Africa. The little South American llama and its cousin, the alpaca, were the only reasonably large ones fit for domestication. They were easily tamable and supplied good wool for clothing. The llama could carry loads but was too small to be ridden, and had neither the weight nor the hoofs for drawing carts or plows. Nor could it be milked. Although it was a useful adjunct to corn and potatoes in the development of Inca civilization, its value was far inferior to that of cattle, asses, and horses. In North America the chief grazing animal was the bison. It was too big, too stupid, too untamable, and too migratory to be domesticated. Wild sheep of the mountains might possibly have been tamed, but without beasts of burden they would presumably have been only a minor factor in advancing civilization. Thus neither of the Americas was well supplied with animals fit for domestication. Australia, with its jumping kangaroos, was even less fortunate, having neither an edible cereal nor a usable grazing animal.

The rice region of Asia was the native home of two species that made really good domestic animals. The banteng of Java is thought by C. Keller to be the wild stock from which the most widely used types of modern cattle are derived. The water buffalo also comes from southeastern Asia. These two have been of great help in developing the civilization of the Far East and India, but they by no means supply all the desirable qualities mentioned in Table 26.

Oats and rye both belong to cool wet climates, where the wild ox of Europe, the mouflon type of mountain sheep, and the sharp-backed pig are native. C. Keller believes that the "heavy calm" Russian strain of horses was tamed in some European region where these cereals might grow. None of the European animals, however, has proved to be as good as the related Asiatic species, which have now largely displaced them.

Turning now to the wheat region of North Africa and western Asia, we find a grouping of animals much more favorable than in the native habitat of any of the other cereals. Wild species of horses, sheep, cattle, pigs, camels, and goats are all found in the part of Asia extending from Turkey and Arabia to northern India and Sinkiang. In other words the habitat of these animals surrounds and includes the area where wild wheat is indigenous. Conclusive evidence of this is seen in the bones dug up among ruins. At Anau, east of the Caspian Sea and just north of Iran, the Pumpelly Expedition found the bones of cattle, sheep, and horses to which Pumpelly [1] and Duerst assign a date before 8000 b.c. Whatever the exact date may be, the lowest layers at Anau are certainly among the oldest known relics of town-dwelling agricultural man. In somewhat higher, but nevertheless very old, layers the bones of pigs appear, and then of goats and camels. Farther south, at Susa among the mountains of Iran two hundred miles east of Babylon, a similar assortment of bones has been found in some of the oldest layers of ruins. There can be no doubt, then, that at least five thousand years ago all the more important animals listed in Table 26 except the ass were familiar to the people of Iran and had probably been domesticated for a considerable time. The ass is generally agreed to be a North African animal and to have been domesticated in Egypt at an early date. Thus it, too, belongs

[1] 1908.

near the wheat center. In addition, a heavy type of hen, derived from India, presumably reached the Mediterranean region by gradual dissemination across Iran. Other lighter breeds appear to be of eastern Mediterranean origin. Certain good breeds of dogs also originated somewhere in southwestern Asia. Thus the wild forms of all the domestic animals which we now consider most important must have been present within reasonably easy reach of the general habitat of wild wheat when agriculture first arose.

In an earlier chapter we saw that agriculture of the kind based on cereals presumably originated in a region of mountains and plateaus interspersed with alluvial basins where streams debouching from the mountains could easily be used for irrigation. Iran is this sort of place, and so are parts of western Arabia and North Africa. Evidence set forth by the author in *Season of Birth* suggests that in order to find a climate like that to which man seems innately to be adapted, we have to go back to the glacial period, and to the part of the wheat region at an altitude of a few thousand feet. This does not prove that agriculture and civilization originated in Iran, Mesopotamia, Syria, or Libya. It does prove, however, that in this general region, especially on gently sloping basin floors at the foot of mountains in southern Iran, we find a set of environmental conditions unusually well fitted to encourage the development of agriculture and to stimulate the domestication of animals and the growth of transportation, travel, and intercourse with other people. The essential point is that one particular region combines the cereal, the animals, the topography, and the climate best fitted for the stage of culture which prevailed when agriculture was evolved. That region is the one where civilization developed most rapidly.

D. Civilization in Babylonia and Egypt

Let us move onward to Sumeria, later known as Babylonia, and to Egypt before their days of glory some four to six thousand years ago. What region was then most favorable to the growth of civilization? By that time agriculture, government, social organization, war, art, commerce, and certain forms of science had become quite highly developed. Nevertheless, metal tools were still unknown, navigation was little more than the art of floating down the river on logs or inflated skins, and protection against cold winds and chilly rain was still in its infancy. Because of this last fact the climatic optimum was still about the same as when agriculture was inaugurated. Certain other things, however, had changed. Man's power to control rivers and use them for irrigation had greatly increased. His need for building materials had likewise grown because agriculture had permitted the accumulation of wealth, thus fostering a desire to construct large and imposing structures. Then, too, the population had grown so great that abundant labor was available for building palaces and temples. New occupations, such as those of the carpenter, mason, and jeweler, had arisen. Diversity of products had led to a great increase in trade and in the number of travelling merchants. And, finally, the great art of writing had been invented. People were seeking for means of preserving their thoughts, their financial accounts, their sorrow for the dead, their loyalty to the gods, and, above all, their victories.

For people in this stage of development the best part of the world was still the same general region as before, but now the great river valleys took on a new importance. The flood plains of the Nile, Tigris and Euphrates, and Indus became the most favorable of all regions. The great amount of water and of level fertile soil made it possible for innumerable villages to be located close together and for small cities to grow up as centers of trade and of government. That in itself was a highly stimulating condition. The rivers supplied not only water, but quiet waterways whereon people who did not yet know how to make ships could safely convey themselves and their goods on rafts. Another natural asset was the clayey soil which was widely available. It supplied a remarkably abundant and cheap material for houses that were fairly cool in summer and warm in winter. In the form of sun-dried bricks, which in due time were burned, clay could be used for surprisingly high, large buildings. Mud structures eight or ten stories high have existed for centuries in southern Arabia. In Egypt and Iran the greatest monuments of the past are built of stone, but they are modelled on structures of clay.

Alluvial clay aided the advance of civilization in other ways not generally noted. It put the keystone into the arch of agriculture, so to speak, by supplying a means whereby grain and other products, such as dates and oil, could be preserved. If clay had never been fashioned into bowls and jars, people would not so readily have become fully dependent upon agriculture. They could scarcely have preserved their grain a whole year against the ravages of insects, rodents, and wet weather. The arts of agriculture and pottery-making went hand in hand, each stimulating the other. In the alluvial plains of great rivers clay for pottery, as well as for houses, is almost everywhere present. It is generally of better quality, less sandy and more cohesive, than in the alluvial deposits of smaller streams, such as appear to have favored the first beginners in the art of agriculture.

Another advantage of abundant good clay was that it provided an excellent material for written records. Writing was one of the world's greatest inventions. It preserves the wisdom of one generation for the next. It stimulates thought, for when an idea is permanently inscribed one wants it to be worth more than what is said today and forgotten tomorrow. Nowhere else are the records of early times so numerous as in the clayey plains of Babylonia. The Egyptians depended less than the Babylonians upon clay because their river supplied another kind of writing material in the form of papyrus growing in the swamps. If that plant had not existed, they might have used clay tablets, which are more durable than papyrus. Both Egypt and Babylonia have climates so dry that clay tablets can survive thousands of years. In both countries the rivers supplied an effective medium for writing and thereby added still another to the geographic advantages of those particular regions at that particular stage of development.

Finally, if our analysis of the effect of selection on character has been correct, the Babylonian and Mesopotamian regions, and Egypt to a less extent, profited by proximity to deserts and mountains inhabited by nomads. Nomadic raids did, indeed, bring chaos, but they also brought strong types of masterful people. Then, too, a distinct stimulus must arise from the close contact of such diverse types as dwellers in the vast riverine oases, mountaineers who repeatedly brave the perils of flood and storm, and desert men with their self-reliance and power of leadership. No one who examines the checkered history of invasions from deserts and mountains can doubt the influence of nomadic kiths on history. The real problem is to determine the exact nature of the influence, its magnitude, and the extent to which its favorable and unfavorable aspects have counteracted one another. We are confronted by possibilities which may be of the first importance, but so slight is our knowledge that most historians have never even thought of them, and many dismiss them as not worth considering.

E. Greek Navigation and Trade

Our next stopping point along the path of history is Greece from the seventh to the fourth centuries B.C. A new relation between history and geography now confronts us. Since the days of early Babylonia and Egypt two great inventions had been made. One was the art of fashioning iron into tools with a cutting edge. The other was the building of seagoing ships, which was presumably first accomplished by the Phoenicians. This art was not fully practicable until iron axes were available for hewing timber. In addition, man's ability to protect himself from the weather had increased somewhat through improvements in the arts of weaving, architecture, and, to a slight degree, heating. Hence man could now live quite comfortably in climates somewhat colder and more humid than those of Babylonia and Egypt. Other arts, especially pottery-making, had also made progress, and the number and quality of the materials that enter into trade had increased.

Early in the seventh century B.C. coined money, another great invention, also began to act as a stimulant to trade. Hence the need for travel and transportation increased still more, and good means of transportation became more important than ever before.

Under these changed circumstances what conditions were most conducive to progress? The first part of the answer is that competent people, good crops, good diet, the right density of population, good health, and ready intercourse with the most progressive parts of the world stood in the forefront just as they had in the past and will in the future. The second part is that proximity to the sea, good harbors, and forests near sealevel now assume a sharply increased importance. Let us look at this second part. One of the extraordinary facts about history is the way in which at each successive stage man finds some geographical environment which is especially fitted for that particular stage. In the first of the stages discussed in this chapter wheat, domestic animals, and regions geographically adapted to the simplest type of irrigation are the dominant environmental factors. In the next stage, after man had become skilled in irrigation, he desired wider fields in which to exercise this skill. Within easy reach of his old home he found them in the form of the flood plains of great rivers. These are especially favorable to the growth of a dense, permanent population where the arts of peace can flourish and a complex social, political, and religious system can develop.

After metal axes and wooden ships had added the sea to the natural conditions which man was able to control, there was a new and great need for safe harbors, many islands, and calm seas. The Aegean Sea supplied this need. The drowning of large areas beneath this sea gave rise to a vast number of safe harbors and hundreds of islands, many of which lie within sight of one another, so that even in a small open boat the early mariner could safely go almost everywhere. This tremendous advantage was increased by the fact that the Aegean Sea is open toward the south, so that the mariner could follow the coast to older centers of civilization in Syria and Egypt, or go across the open sea to those old leaders by way of Crete and Cyprus when he became more skilled. In the other direction the Bosphorus opens a way to the plains of the lower Danube and Russia, to the sub-tropical region of Colchis at the eastern end of the Black Sea, where tea is now extensively raised, and to the whole north coast of Asia Minor. Thus as a place in which to use the power to build ships, control the sea, and employ coined money as a means to facilitate trade, it would be hard to find a better location.

A full picture of the geographical advantages of ancient Greece includes various other facts. One is that the climate, then as now, in spite of climatic cycles, had a long, dry summer with few storms and little danger even when small boats sailed out of sight of land. Another is that during the greatest days of Greece the contrast between wet winters and dry summers was apparently less marked than now, Hence forests fit for ship building and for fuel with which to smelt ores grew close to the sea instead of only on the higher mountains. Semple, in her great book on the Mediterranean,[2] says that

Strabo, on the authority of Eratosthenes, states that the forests of the . . . plain [of Cyprus] were once so dense that they formed an obstacle to tillage. . . . Though they were invaded for fuel to smelt the copper and silver from the local mines, and for timber to build whole fleets of ships, nevertheless consumption did not keep pace with the growth of the forests until, by legal enactment, the act of clearing the land was made to convey title to it. So dense a mantle of trees would indicate a heavier rainfall in Cyprus than the meager 15 to 23 inches recorded in recent decades. . . . Even in Strabo's time [born about 63 B.C.] a forest covered the western peninsula of Acamas, which was exposed to rain-bearing winds.

Loss of the soil on slopes has been one of the worst effects of the dry phases of climatic cycles during the Christian era. On the mountains of Laconia, according to Semple,[3] "poor oak brush, preyed upon by goats . . . represents the degenerate successor of the pristine oak forests. . . . [In those old days] oak and beech groves were widely distributed over the mountains of Greece, and furnished mast for

[2] p. 272.   [3] p. 278–79.

large herds of wild and domestic swine." From all this it is clear that in the best days of Greece the Aegean region was pre-eminently adapted to building ships as well as to sailing them. This alone would not account for the greatness of Greece, but it was a great help, for trade and travel are marvelous stimulants to progress.

Another factor in the ancient greatness of Greece is that the little Attican area was then peculiarly fortunate in its central and easily accessible location in respect to the Aegean. The Athenians claimed that their city was "the metropolis of the Ionians." It attained this high position partly because a location in the rain-shadow east of high mountains makes Attica the driest part of Greece. Athens gets only 15 or 16 inches of rain per year, less than a third as much as Corfu west of Greece. Even in the more rainy phases of ancient cycles agriculture in Attica was comparatively unprofitable, except on the best lands which belonged almost wholly to a relatively few powerful old families. Barley grew better than wheat. Exports of grain were prohibited much of the time. Hence the Athenians, like the early New Englanders, turned from agriculture to industry and commerce. This transition brought many foreign merchants and skilled artisans with new and sometimes valuable ideas. Industry was aided by the fact that Attica has an abundance of an unusually fine kind of clay, as well as excellent marble. The exceptional artistic skill of the people enabled them to make beautiful and widely sought urns for water, huge jars for grain, oil, and wine, and other ornamental wares. Sheep throve in all Greece, especially Attica. Their wool was another resource which the exceptional artistic ability of the Athenians converted into fine cloth that sold for a good price in coined money. In exchange for such products of human skill the Athenians imported grain, lumber, and other supplies.

F. Kith and Climate in Athens

The fact that the Aegean region was such a center of industry, trade, and intercourse with other countries only partly explains the greatness of Greece. Another factor must lie in the innate abilities of the people. No one can doubt that Solon, Thucydides, Plato, Aristotle, and many other Greeks were born with minds of far more than average ability. Nor can anyone doubt that life in Athens and other Greek cities was highly stimulating. Such conditions, however, do not explain why geniuses were so numerous, nor why the geniuses themselves were so alert, active, and persistent. Here, just as in many other cases, genetic as well as cultural and geographical factors must apparently play a part.

In considering the genetic factor, let us confine ourselves to Athens, but remember that conditions elsewhere were in many ways similar, although less extreme. There seems to be good evidence that Athens was inhabited by a kith somewhat like the Parsis, who are described in Part II of this book. Thucydides speaks thus of the time before written records are available:

In ancient times the people [of Hellas] were migratory and readily left their homes whenever overpowered by numbers. . . . The richest districts were most constantly changing their inhabitants . . . for the productiveness of the land increased the power of individuals; this in turn was a source of quarrels by which communities were ruined. . . . Attica, of which the soil was poor and thin, enjoyed long freedom from civil strife, and therefore retained its original inhabitants. . . . Through immigration it increased in population more than any other region. For leading men of Hellas, when driven out of their own country by war or revolution, sought asylum at Athens; and from the very earliest times [were] admitted to citizenship.

From the context it appears that this process continued for an unstated time after the Trojan War. The "leading men" who thus came to Attica were presumably Achaean and Ionian Greeks for the most part, although some may have belonged to the more primitive Pelasgian stock.

The result of this slow trickling of leaders and others into Attica is seen in the organization of society about 700 B.C., when written history begins. All power was then concentrated in a highly exclusive hereditary aristocracy. This had apparently arisen through the ability of the leaders to gather into their own hands the ownership of the best lands and to hold such land in large blocks which could not be alienated from the family. This aristocracy, far more than any other class of society, produced the great majority of leaders. Within the aristocracy the rules of marriage were as strict as among the Parsis. A man, to be sure, might have as many children as he chose by women of the lower classes, but these were not accepted as members of the aristocracy. In Athens, according to Herbert J. Rose,[4] the full phrase for marriage meant to take a woman for the begetting of legitimate offspring. No woman of the aristocracy was allowed to marry outside her own limited group or kith. If a man had a daughter, but no sons, to inherit his lands, he could compel the nearest male kinsman

[4] pp. 173, 178.

to marry the daughter, even if the kinsman had to divorce a wife in order to do so. The object was to have male children in the direct male line as nearly as possible. This idea of continuing the inheritance in the male line without admixture of foreigners or of persons of the lower class was strong almost everywhere in Greece. In Athens, as Grote says, "the extinction of a family, carrying with it the suspension of religious rites, was held . . . to be a misfortune not merely from the loss of the citizens composing it, but also because the family gods and the names of deceased citizens were thus deprived of their honor and might visit the country with displeasure." Grote says elsewhere that as late as 300 B.C. "the observant visitor Dikaerchus professes to detect a difference between the native Athenians [by which he apparently means the upper classes] and the Atticans [or ordinary inhabitants] as well in physiognomy as in character and race."

How important all this is in explanation of Greek greatness will be known only after long exploration of the possibilities here suggested. For the present we can merely say that the Athenian aristocracy presents a most interesting analogy to the Parsis, Icelanders, Jews, Puritans, Junkers, Hakkas, and other outstanding kiths. In each instance some sort of selective process appears to have segregated people of unusual ability. Then isolation, either geographical or social, converted the selected group into a kith which kept itself biologically distinct.

In Greece and Athens, just as everywhere else, the flowering of genius is helped or hindered by many conditions, including density of population, climate, diet, health, and vigor. In Greece from 800, or more clearly from 600 to 400 B.C., there appears to have been a more or less regular increase in storminess, followed by a slight decline till about 300 B.C. and then a rapid decline. Local evidence in Greece and neighboring countries points to this conclusion, and so do the facts as to Alpine glaciers and the sequoias of California. If we accept this interpretation, the capacity of Greece to support population increased in a general way for several centuries before the climax of the Golden Age in the days of Pericles (490–429 B.C.). This means that there was no severe pressure of population upon the food supply except as cities grew large under the impetus of industry and commerce. Therefore, relatively speaking, the people as a whole were well fed and to that extent healthy and prosperous. Such conditions are vastly more conducive to the flowering of genius than are those which apparently prevailed from 250 to 150 B.C., when rainfall and crops were declining, and prosperity and population were waning.

Health, as W. H. S. Jones well points out, appears to have been deteriorating at that time not only because of poorer food and less stimulating weather than formerly, but because of the inroads of malaria, which previously had not been severe.[5]

The stormy phase of the long climatic cycle which culminated four or five centuries before Christ must have had a good deal of effect upon the alertness of the Greek geniuses. As nearly as we can tell, the climate at that time had approximately the following characteristics.[6] (1) The greater stirring up of the air then than now by storms presumably lowered the summer temperature a few degrees and possibly raised the winter temperature. There is no reason, however, to think that the difference in temperature between then and now was of much significance. (2) The rainfall was apparently considerably greater than now. It doubtless came chiefly in winter, but storms presumably began earlier in the fall than now, lasted later in the spring, and occurred occasionally in a mild way in the dry summer. (3) This increased rainfall was the result of an increase in the number and perhaps the severity of storms. Its economic effect was doubtless felt chiefly in better crops, better pasturage, more food, more milk, more meat, and in general a better and more healthful standard of living than now or than in the dry phases of past climatic cycles. It must also have been felt in the mentally stimulating effect of frequent changes in temperature and humidity, and of cold waves with their invigorating temperature and increased atmospheric ozone and electricity. Athens would profit especially in this way because its relative dryness would permit it to get the stimulating effect of polar air masses more fully than would places where greater moisture would lessen the effect of both ozone and electricity. Thus storminess appears to have been an important factor in the prosperity and greatness of Greece.

This discussion does not include all the conditions which made Greece great. Nevertheless, it rounds out a series of circumstances which favored a great outburst of genius. The series starts with the selective migrations of the Achaeans, Ionians, and Dorians, which presumably eliminated weaklings and purged the immigrant population of many persons who lacked intelligence, initiative, and determination. Then came the development of an aristocracy in almost every Greek state, thus giving rise to uncommonly competent local microkiths. Such an aristocratic group was especially strong and exclusive

[5] Huntington, 1919, p. 136.　　　　[6] Huntington, 1924B, pp. 400–02.

in Athens, where genius flowered most fully. Next we have climatic conditions such that for two centuries or more there was a general improvement economically and presumably in diet and health. Finally, Greece, especially Athens, was greatly stimulated by cultural conditions which led to the mastery of the sea and the growth of trade. The form of the land, with its drowned bays and islands, adds to our series of factors a geographical feature which had much to do with the greatness of Greece. Thus that country, like the upland home of wild wheat and then the great river plains in a warm, dry but not tropical climate, was pre-eminently fitted to be the center of human progress at a definite stage in the evolution of civilization.

CHAPTER 30

AGES OF DARKNESS AND REVIVAL

A. The Anomaly of Ireland

Ireland and Greece, at opposite extremes of Europe, offer an instructive contrast. One is too wet, the other too dry. One has been a notable center of trade and progress; the other has persistently been rather isolated. Perhaps the greatest contrast is this: When Greece was producing an amazing assemblage of geniuses, Ireland was the home of wild cattle-raisers just emerging from the Stone Age; six or seven hundred years after Christ, on the contrary, when Greece was poor, miserable, and almost forgotten, Ireland stood close to the top in learning and civilization. Let us concentrate upon this latter fact, this strange cultural contrast at the height of the Dark Ages. Climatic cycles and migration both played a part. From the time of Christ to about A.D. 650 a progressive, although irregular, deterioration took place both climatically and culturally in Greece, whereas the opposite was occurring in Ireland. Both places became drier and probably warmer, with a disastrous effect in Greece and an astonishingly good effect in Ireland.

Our first accurate historical knowledge of Ireland comes from the Romans. Strabo, whose latest writings date from about A.D. 20, describes the Irish as mere savages. Even in England, in relatively warm, sunny Kent, Julius Caesar, who went there in 55 B.C., says that "the greater part of the people never sow their lands, but live on flesh and milk and go clad in skins." Such conditions doubtless prevailed much more fully in Ireland, where many people migrated with their cattle from summer to winter pastures. Pomponius Mela, about A.D. 43, when Rome conquered Britain, speaks of the Irish climate as unfit for grain, but comments on the luxuriance of the grass. Solinus, about A.D. 218, also speaks of the luxuriant pastures and the warlike and inhospitable inhabitants. He it was who said that there were no bees in Ireland. Such scanty notices give only an inkling of the physical conditions in those early days, but like many other phenomena in Great Britain, Europe, Asia, and even California, they

591

suggest a relatively cool, stormy period which up to about A.D. 200 rendered Ireland almost unfit for the cultivation of grain, thus obliging people to rely largely on cattle.

The third century sees a great change. In California the growth of the Big Trees slackened; in Central Asia town after town was abandoned, apparently because of a failing water supply. Between these two limits Palmyra was being toppled over, never to recover; Greece was falling into a state of torpor, poverty, and depopulation which lasted for centuries. In England, however, things looked quite bright. There, at this time, the vine was probably introduced.

Although the facts are meager they are consistent in suggesting that in the third century A.D. the climate in the British Isles and elsewhere was changing from a stormy phase with a cool wet summer to a milder phase with a fairly warm, dry summer. In the new phase the summers, on an average, were presumably warmer and the winters colder than now. In other words the climate of England and Ireland apparently became more continental than at present. The percentage of winds blowing from an easterly, landward quarter must have been large compared with those from a westerly, oceanic quarter. In the British Isles easterly winds tend to be warmer than westerly winds in summer and colder in winter. At both seasons they are relatively dry.

B. Grape Vines and Prosperity

A brief examination of the history of the grape vine in the British Isles will illustrate certain major climatic swings which seem to have influenced the history of both Ireland and England. In our day the English summers are too cool to ripen grapes except in unusual years or in protected locations. This was also true in the days of Tacitus. He must have known England rather well, because his wife was the daughter of Julius Agricola, who from A.D. 78 to 85 was one of the best rulers Roman Britain ever had. He says that "with the exception of the olive and vine and plants which usually grow in warmer climates the soil [of England] will yield . . . all ordinary products." Two centuries later, however, an edict of the Emperor Probus (A.D. 276–82) suggests that vineyards had begun to be raised there.[1] What we know about the climate elsewhere makes this seem probable. At any rate the edict of Probus gave permission to Britons, as well as to all Gauls and the people of Spain, to cultivate vineyards and make

[1] Simon, vol. 1, p. 2.

wine. Four centuries later the habit was well established, for in the seventh century religious houses in Britain paid special attention to growing vines and making their own wine. Simon [2] says that vines "were actually grown in . . . the North, in the Midlands, in East Anglia, and in the South . . . by religious houses with a fair amount of success." He also points out that "in the extreme part of Normandy bordering on Brittany wine was made in the Middle Ages all along the coast, but vines have ceased to be cultivated in this district for many centuries. All the ancient vineyards of Normandy, Brittany, and Northern France, which enjoyed a period of repute, have also long ceased to exist." Then Simon lays the blame on man. "The soil," he says, "was more favorable to vinaculture than now . . . after being impoverished by so many centuries of culture." This explanation fails completely when we recall that in Italy, Greece, and Palestine vines have grown in great abundance continually for two or three thousand years.

A few further citations as to the history of the vine in England may be worth while. The Venerable Bede (673–735) says that in his day the vine was raised "in some places." The laws of Alfred (871–99) say, "If anyone does damage to the vines of his neighbor . . . let him make good whatever is claimed." Edgar (957–75) made a gift of a vineyard at Wycet, together with the vinedressers on the estate.

At the time of the Norman Conquest vineyards were quite numerous. In the Domesday Book (1085–86) thirty-eight vineyards appear in addition to those of the crown. One is said to yield twenty casks of wine in good years. Another had an area of twelve arpents (probably 15 acres). The Isle of Ely, which is no island, but an inland district north of Cambridge, was called by the Normans the Isle of Vines. Shortly after the Norman Conquest the Bishop of Ely received a tithe from the vines grown in his district. In abbey chronicles vinedressers are mentioned as part of the staff of laborers in the reign of Henry I (1100–35). Toward the middle of the twelfth century William of Malmesbury [3] tells us that the vale of Gloucester "exhibits a greater number of vineyards than any other county in England, yielding abundant crops and of superior quality; nor are the wines made here by any means harsh or ungrateful to the palate, for in point of sweetness, they may almost bear comparison with the growths of France."

[2] Vol. 1, pp. 7–8.   [3] Simon, vol. 1, p. 12.

Referring to a period of special prosperity and warmth in the early years of Henry III, so conservative a writer as Thorold Rogers says that "wine has sometimes grown in England, though not perhaps so frequently as has been imagined. . . . The vine was cultivated and wine was manufactured from home-grown grapes as far north as Ditchingham in Norfolk. Nor was the price at which the product was sold an indication of its quality being much inferior to ordinary Bordeau or Gascony."

During the reign of Henry III (1216–72) there appear to have been great extremes in the climate of Britain. Britton,[4] for example, quotes an entry which says that in 1239 in Scotland "no rain fell and the wines were so strong that no one could drink them without water." This suggests an uncommonly good grape crop far to the north in Scotland—a crop due to a hot summer in which the climate approached that of a dry country like Italy. On the other hand, in 1257 the winter is said to have been so cold in England that fig trees were killed. The idea of grapes in southern Scotland and fig trees in southern England seems rather strange in view of the present climate. Many other references to vineyards might be cited, including statements as to royal vineyards in nine different years between A.D. 1143 and 1231. After 1250, however, such references become scarce and ultimately disappear. Nevertheless, the Bishop of Rochester sent a present of wine, raised near that place, to King Edward III, who began to reign in 1327. Simon [5] gives the latest reference to royal vineyards as 1392. On the whole, however, he is clearly right when he quotes Twyne as saying that the decay of the culture of the vine in England dates from the reign of Henry III. He appears to be wrong, however, in implying that this occurred not only when but because "the possession of Guyenne had been permanently assured, and . . . the great influx of French wines, which characterized the reign of King John [1199–1216], had shown the husbandman that land could be turned to better account in England." This last statement illustrates the almost universal tendency to saddle man himself with the responsibility for events which are really due to nature.

Now for a look at the present conditions of nature and their effect on the growth of grapes in England. In his book on British gardening George Nicholson's whole article on grape vines assumes that they are to be raised under protection. There is no hint that they are expected to produce fruit unless raised under cover or trained against warm walls. Rogers says that "at the present time . . . it would hardly be possible, I imagine, to ripen English grapes sufficiently for the production of the thinnest of beverages. [Vineyards] were attempted in many of the southern counties and the record of such cultivation lingers in local names."

There are still grape vines in England. A very famous one at Hampton Court was planted in 1769. At Cumberland Lodge (Windsor) a huge vine has been known to bear two thousand pounds of grapes in a year. It must be remembered, however, that these vines are carefully raised on the sunny side of houses or walls. Moreover, they are often unable to ripen any fruit at all. There is no indication that vineyards like those of the past could now be raised anywhere in England.

Since 1300 there appear to have been cycles in grape culture, as in many other things. Cooper,[6] for example, concludes that English wines can never have been drunk in English society because Chaucer (1340–1400) refers invariably to foreign vintages. The more probable interpretation is that the cold and wet spells for which the late thirteenth and the fourteenth centuries are famous made people give up raising vines so that no English wines were available in Chaucer's day.

The conditions which prevailed about 1500, during a relatively warm climatic phase, can be judged from a statement in the conscientious descriptions of Polydore Vergil,[7] who came to England in 1501 and spent the next ten or twenty years in writing a history of that country. He says, "They plant vines in their gardens rather for a covert and commodity of shadow than for the fruit, for the grapes seldom commit to ripen, except a hot summer ensue. . . . The earth, as we have rehearsed, is not good for wines, but instead they use ale or beer made of barley."

These facts about wine give us a means of estimating the difference between an ancient warm, dry phase of British climate and the present cool phase. At Greenwich, which is almost the warmest place in England, the temperature of June, July, and August from 1841 to 1920 averaged 61.3°F. From 1851 to 1900 the similar average for four French towns, Paris, Châteaudun, Angers, and Nantes, which lie on the very northern edge of the grape-raising portion of France, was 64.3°. Only seven years out of the eighty at Greenwich were as warm as this. It must also be remembered that wine was raised in

6 p. 100.   7 See Henry Ellis.

York and perhaps even in Scotland, where the summer temperature now averages no more than 58 or 59°. Hence it seems probable that when English grape raising was at its best the summer temperature must have averaged as much as 5°F higher than in the last century. This would be equivalent to moving England southward from 3 to 5° of latitude. The winters in the grape-raising period, as we have seen, were apparently colder than now because the climate was more continental.

The climatic facts here presented have an intimate bearing on history. Macalister,[8] in fact, believes that climate affords the best clue to the main ups and downs of Irish history. His view is illustrated in the lowest curve of Figure 79 (page 531), where high points indicate oceanic weather with wet, rainy, unproductive summers. In such periods Irish agriculture languishes and in many places disappears. Famines arise, and the people turn more and more to cattle as a means of subsistence. Low places in the curve indicate continental conditions with east winds, dry and relatively warm, sunny summers, and cool but also sunny winters. Cormac mac Airt, the "first real personality" in Irish history, began to rule in A.D. 227, when indications of the approach of a dry climatic phase are widespread from California to Central Asia. At Tara, his capital, where extensive ruins can still be seen, he is said to have founded schools of military science, law, and literature. The progress thus started reached its climax about A.D. 650 to 700. One stage is illustrated by St. Patrick, who came as a missionary about A.D. 440, when Tara was the chief seat of Druidism. After the conversion of Ireland to Christianity the pace of progress increased. Art flourished, as is evident in beautiful gold work found in ruins. Other examples of progress include laws, schools, and missionaries. The Brehon laws are one of the most elaborate codes ever written. In addition to twenty pages concerning bees and honey, hundreds of others deal with practically every phase of life.

Monastery schools were one of the most remarkable features of this period. In the second half of the fifth century Prince Enda established a school which attracted students from all over Ireland, even though it was located on the wet west coast in Galway, which is now quite unproductive and sparsely populated. This was a prelude to a wonderful outburst of scholarly activity in the Irish monasteries from the sixth century to about A.D. 800, when it came suddenly to an end.

8 pp. 277 ff.

In the first half of the sixth century there are said to have been three thousand students at a single monastic school at Clonard in Meath north of Dublin. Healy gives detailed descriptions of the life of such students. They lived in little huts of wickerwork wattled with clay or sometimes stone. They raised their own grain, milked their own cattle, kept their own bees, and fished in the streams. One of the most remarkable features of this period is that for a few centuries near the climax of the Dark Ages the Irish led the world in learning and missionary zeal. They wrote hymns and histories as well as laws. Many students came to them from England and the European continent. They sent missionaries to Scotland, England, France, and other countries farther afield.

C. Irish Prosperity and Character

The "cause" of all this may lie in the character of the people, the uplifting force of Christianity, or the powerful stimulus of men like St. Patrick. Two "conditions," without which it could not have occurred, seem to have been agricultural prosperity and freedom from foreign invasion.

One does not have to read much about Ireland to discover that a relatively warm, dry, sunny year is almost sure to be good for agriculture. Nowhere does July in Ireland now average warmer than May in New York or Minneapolis—about 59°. A slight drop in temperature prevents the maturing of grain and even of potatoes. An increase of 4 or 5° would do wonders to improve the crops, even if the average temperature of winter should drop from around 40 to 35°. Something of this sort appears to have happened in the past. The Brehon laws indicate that in Ireland's Golden Age the raising of wheat, as well as of oats and barley, was common. In modern times, however, before there were any governmental incentives, the area devoted to wheat was not one fourth as large as to barley or one twentieth as large as to oats. When agriculture is prosperous the population can increase without lowering the standard of living, and cultural progress is encouraged. Arthur Young says that about 1775, which happened to be a warm period, potato culture was expanding up the hillsides to places never cultivated within living memory, but bearing marks of having been used for grain many centuries earlier. In addition to cereal crops the Irish of the Golden Age seem to have had kitchen gardens, with cabbages, onions, and perhaps carrots or parsnips. Life was quite different from what it was in the cool, wet days when cattle were the chief reliance.

In addition to agricultural prosperity the Golden Age of Ireland was blessed with relative freedom from invasion. Because Ireland lies behind the much larger island of Great Britain it received only the splashings of the migrations which gave England the dominant elements in its present population.[9] The irregularly increasing dryness and summer warmth which helped Ireland made the people of the steppes in Russia and Asia uncomfortable and had much to do with starting migrations. One tribe after another was uprooted until most of Europe north of the Alps was in commotion. Thus when Ireland, relatively speaking, was able to enjoy peace as well as plenty, England was overwhelmed by Jutes, Angles, and Saxons from the continent. They doubtless helped to give England a good endowment biologically, but culturally they were a scourge. From the sixth to the ninth centuries English history is mainly a record of incessant wars between little principalities of these three closely related but highly quarrelsome stocks. The tales of King Arthur give a legendary account of the beginnings of the commotion. There were some intervals of quiet, to be sure. Bede says that in the reign of Edwin, who died in 633, there was such peace in England that a woman with her newborn babe might walk throughout the island without receiving harm. This period appears to have been an especially dry time when the crops were extra good. During the centuries when the climate was most favorable Ireland suffered little from invasions and wars such as hampered progress both in England and on the continent.

Another element may enter into the picture. The Irish climate, as we now know it, does not encourage alertness to so great a degree as do the climates farther east in England and on the continent, as Markham effectively shows. The temperature, to be sure, encourages activity at all seasons, and there is no inertia due to heat, as in the tropics. Nevertheless, there is a psychological difference between Ireland and England somewhat like that between England and the United States. It arises from differences in the degree to which cyclonic storms act as a stimulant. In the northern United States their stimulating effect is often too great. Whether it is sufficiently great in England is open to question. In Ireland it certainly is well below the optimum. The climate there is so oceanic that changes of tem-

---

[9] Huntington, 1924A, pp. 247 ff.

perature are slight even after a severe storm. Moreover, because of the humidity, atmospheric ozone and electricity, with whatever stimulating effect they may have, are reduced to a low level. In the early period of Ireland's Golden Age, the number of storms was probably less than now, but their effect on Ireland was probably more stimulating. The storms presumably followed more northerly paths than now so that dry east winds were common, thus leading to less humidity, more sunshine, and more ozone.

The whole idea of the historic effect of climatic cycles on human alertness is so new that it has not yet been adequately tested, but it deserves careful study. It apparently helps to account for differences in alertness from region to region and time to time both now and in the past. It does not lessen the importance of such factors as poverty or poor political and social conditions, of which absentee landlordism is a good example, but it supplements them in a way that seems illuminating.

Migration must also be considered before we can judge modern Ireland aright. Ireland's cloudiness, dampness, famines, limited trade, and general isolation in spite of physical nearness to centers of activity have constantly tended to drive away many of her most able sons. This has happened not only since migration to America began on a large scale about a century ago but during many previous centuries. The chances for a career have been far greater in England or France than in Ireland. Life in other countries has been pleasanter, and the rewards of good work have been greater. So the young leaders have made the easy journey across the water, while their less alert brothers and cousins have stayed at home. During World War II, as a result of this same type of migration, thousands of Irish worked in England or volunteered for the Allied armies, while their homeland sat passive.

D. Revival of the Human Spirit

The Close of the Middle Ages, The Dawn of a New Era, The Beginnings of Modern Europe—such are the titles of books which deal with the transition from the Middle Ages to the modern era. According to practically all authorities, the period from about 1250 to 1450, especially the fourteenth century, was a time of special alertness, initiative, and originality in most of Europe. Later periods have seen more spectacular achievements, but few, if any, other times, aside from the greatest age of Greece, have seen such a remarkable awakening of the human spirit.

One of the most impressive features of this period is the uniformity with which essentially the same events occurred in many countries from Britain on the west to Poland on the east. As Cheyney [10] puts it, "what happened in one country happened, in a somewhat different form, in others." Throughout western Europe feudalism was dying out. Town life was increasing, and a middle class of merchants and artisans was developing all the way from Spain to Poland and from Italy to Sweden. Capitalism, for the first time, was becoming a powerful agency almost everywhere in Europe. Specialization in industry took great strides. Specialization and progress were peculiarly evident in woolen goods, which were the main article of manufacture until metal products took first place under the impetus of the steam engine. In the period now under consideration banking in almost the modern sense assumed a hitherto unknown importance. An economic system based on money rather than barter began to prevail even among the lower classes.

The gradual fading away of serfdom in France, England, Spain, the Netherlands, and the lands along the Rhine, so hard to trace and so inadequately explained by any sudden or specific provisions of law, was certainly closely connected with the possession of money by the peasantry. Thus money, banking, wealth, trade, and capitalism did their work of attrition upon the agricultural, feudal, custom-controlled middle ages. Agricultural life, feudal institutions, chivalric ideals still subsisted and dominated large regions of Europe and whole classes of society, but alongside of them, interpenetrating them, was the other set of influences, transforming their own age and creating the conditions of further change. [11]

Another outstanding feature of the period from 1250 to 1450 was attempts by the middle class to gain equality with the nobles. In countries as diverse as Spain, France, England, and Germany a wave of middle class activity culminated in meetings of representative parliaments in which the "third estate," the middle class city people, had a share.

The fourteenth century was a period of many assemblages. There was constant traveling and foregathering. The roads were full not only of merchants and pilgrims, but of messengers, clergy and laymen, obeying summons to attend some council, or journey to . . . some place of assembly.

---

[10] p. 328.   [11] Cheyney, p. 62.

Gatherings of all classes except the very lowest were frequent. . . . It was a restless, assembly-loving age.[12]

The word restless is significant. The spirit of the later thirteenth and the fourteenth century in Europe resembled the restless activity of the northern United States today. Although the days of serfdom were not yet ended, even the peasants shared in the mental awakening which was characteristic of this age. Lipson and H. S. Bennett, in their accounts of social and economic life in England, refer specifically to the way in which serfs asserted rights and claimed privileges. Speaking of the Shepherd's Revolt (1251), which spread from France to England, and of the peasant uprising known as the Sicilian Vespers (1282), Cheyney[13] says that "it is the abrupt appearance of the common people on the public scene . . . their unexpected intrusion into the orderly course of events, the unbridled license of their action, and its overwhelming success . . . that attract the attention of the historian. . . . The prevalence of such occurrences is a characteristic of the time that can hardly be disregarded."

In the Netherlands, for example, peasant uprisings occurred in 1255, 1267, 1275, 1280, and other years of that half century. Such insurrections occurred also in the fifteenth century and later, but then they lacked their previous boldness and their tendency to occur in times of prosperity, as well as adversity, simply because the people felt like asserting their rights. A distinctive feature of thirteenth and fourteenth century revolutions was that demands were formulated by the people themselves.

Interest in the Bible, especially in the individual's own interpretation of that book, is a sample of this same sort of mental attitude. By 1380, Wyclif's English Bible was in the hands of the people. The period was one "of insurgency against fixed conditions. Just as the serfs wanted freedom, just as the man of the middle class grasped at the share in the government of town or nation that guaranteed protection to his interests and gave scope to his enterprises, just as the soldier and traveler sought adventure, so the pious soul wanted to seek out its own salvation."[14] All periods, Cheyney continues,[15] are seen to be times of change if observed closely enough, but Wyclif and Hus, the Vision of Piers Plowman, the sermons of John Ball and his ilk, and doctrines of social equality and of the indefensibility of private property are evidence of movements that were especially de-

[12] Cheyney, p. 87.
[13] pp. 16–17.

[14] Cheyney, p. 226.
[15] p. 138.

structive to the relatively calm tempo of the Middle Ages proper. "Instability in institutions and in thought was one of the main characteristics of the fourteenth century." [16]

After the fourteenth century there was a definite change of human attitudes. There was brilliant achievement in art and in many other lines, but it was the ripening of the fruit, not the exuberant swelling of the buds and bursting of the blossoms. Rogers,[17] in preparing his famous *History of Agriculture and Prices in England,* made an exhaustive study of old manuscripts, especially the accounts of monasteries and large estates. From this he draws a most interesting generalization [18] which gives a sort of epitome of the way in which the human spirit went through a psychological cycle within a century or two. Handwriting, says Rogers, changed rapidly and simultaneously all over England, a change which may be related to that which took place in the economy of agriculture. In the days of Henry III (1216–72) "handwriting was delicate and rather cramped"; in those of Edward I (1272–1307) "vigorous and elegant"; in the time of Edward II (1307-27) "bold, coarse letters"; in the early part of Edward III's reign (1327–77) once more vigorous and elegant, but then degenerating into "the clumsy scrawl of the reign of Richard II" (1377–99).

Such differences are commonly ignored, but they may be of deep psychological significance. The characters of the reformer, John Wyclif (1320–84), and of the poet, Chaucer (1300–1400), were formed at a time when handwriting was "vigorous" or "bold." Does this perhaps mean that the kind of vigor and boldness which made people ready to break with precedent was unusually common? Rogers does not mention the nature of the handwriting after 1400, but he emphasizes the change of spirit. Although the fifteenth century as a whole, especially the "mean" reign of Henry Tudor (1485–1509), which was relatively warm and comfortable, was a time of "almost unbroken agricultural prosperity and of great development in manufacturing," there was "no zeal, no learning . . . almost absolute intellectual stagnation."

Cheyney [19] points out that, as the spirit of the fourteenth century faded, the heresy of "Lollardy" was crushed, and the Bible was taken away from the common people. The price of this was "increased dependence of the church on the civil government, the substitution

---

[16] p. 140.   [18] Vol. V, p. 2.
[17] Vol. IV, p. 20.   [19] p. 223.

. . . of cold conformity for warm piety, of a submissive, but stagnant Oxford for one full of life and independent thought." A psychological cycle of this same sort seems to have occurred in almost all phases of life.

E. *Causes of the Revival*

The causes of the accentuated activity of the human spirit at the dawn of the modern era cannot easily be determined. The Black Death, with its enormous mortality in the middle of the fourteenth century, helped the peasants by making labor scarce and land relatively abundant. Widespread famines, the most severe in the history of western Europe, had a similar effect, the worst coming before the Black Death, others afterward. It may also be said that the normal course of social evolution had piled up certain conditions like water behind a dam. When the dam broke, there was necessarily a great surge forward. This, however, does not explain why the dam broke everywhere at practically the same time, although the countries involved were in quite different stages of progress. Copying of one country by another, as Cheyney[20] well says, "is not a satisfactory explanation, since in each country there was a preceding period of embryonic growth which cannot have been imitated. Nor does any testimony to such imitation exist."

The situation becomes clearer when we take account of the physical, as well as the cultural, environment in which this revival of the human spirit took place. We have seen that in our own day prices, business activity, and sales on the stock market vary in harmony with physical cycles which in a broad way belong to the weather. We have seen that library circulation is closely associated with an annual ozone cycle and with the short cycles of a few days which occur in connection with storms. We have likewise seen that in ancient times mental alertness in Egypt, Babylonia, and Greece seems to have varied in essential harmony with the frequency of cyclonic storms. Such storms not only provide rain but are associated with the kind of stimulus that encourages people to take serious books from the library, expand their businesses, and invest in the stock market. In view of all this it seems only reasonable to inquire what kind of weather prevailed from 1250 to 1450 in western Europe.

Figure 79 (page 531) shows that at this period the trees of California made a sudden spurt in growth, with a maximum in the first

[20] p. 329.

half of the fourteenth century. The curve for caravan traffic in Syria and the one for the height of lakes and the spread of human occupancy into dry regions both agree with the tree curve in suggesting humidity in the fourteenth century. Moreover, Macalister's curve of Irish climate, although lower than in the preceding century, indicates that the weather continued to be abnormally cool, wet and stormy until after 1400.

With these conditions in mind let us briefly review the indications as to the climate of the world from about 1250 to 1450, with special attention to the fourteenth century. East of California the next point where we have evidence is Greenland.[21] For three centuries after its discovery by Eric the Red, Greenland was inhabited by Norse Vikings who depended mainly on sheep for a living, although such dependence is now impossible. When Ivar Bardsson went thither, however, on an official mission from Iceland in 1342, he found the place uninhabited, although cattle still wandered in the fields. It is supposed that the Norse were wiped out by an invasion of Eskimos from the north, but what caused the invasion? We suspect that the Eskimos were forced south by a succession of cold years. At any rate, in the thirteenth century the *Kungaspegel,* or *King's Mirror,* warned navigators that the old sailing route around the south end of Greenland must be changed because there was more ice than formerly. Moreover, Norse graves in southern Greenland show a unique feature. After the bodies were buried, trees grew in such a way that their roots were intermixed with the bones. Yet when the graves were opened by modern archaeologists they were in the midst of soil that is permanently frozen, even in summer. The freezing probably dates from the fourteenth century, for that appears to have been the coldest time since A.D. 1000.

In Iceland evidence of increased cold and storminess in the fourteenth century is more abundant than in Greenland.[22] Previously for three centuries crops of grain had been raised, and in some places there had been trees large enough for houses and boats. Now, according to the old chronicles, agriculture practically disappeared. Even the keeping of sheep declined sharply. Wagons, carts, and ploughs went out of use. Their construction became a lost art. Architecture in wood suffered similarly. There was no wood to use, and the fine carved and painted halls of former days gave place to huts of turf half sunk in the earth. Fish became more and more the chief reli-

---

[21] Huntington, 1922, p. 105.   [22] Huntington, 1924A, p. 294.

ance for food. In spite of the consequent increased need for good boats, the large, decked luggers of previous days gave place to small, undecked craft which were not seaworthy. All these developments were just what would be expected when the climate became colder and stormier. The ancient records say that ice began to crowd against the north shore of Iceland so that communication became difficult. After the Black Death (1348) there followed a winter so long and cold that most of Iceland's animals perished. Trade with Europe declined and almost disappeared, partly, at least, because of excessive storminess.

In the British Isles and Europe during the fourteenth century the weather shows greater extremes than at any other recorded period.[23] The Rhine, Danube, Thames, and Po were frozen repeatedly for weeks or months. In no other century are so many cold winters recorded. According to Norlind, the only authentic accounts of the freezing of the Kattegat (the strait between Denmark and Sweden) belong to the years 1296, 1306, 1323, and 1408. In 1323, the coldest year ever recorded, horses and sleighs crossed the Baltic Sea regularly from Sweden to Germany. Cold, snowy winters were often followed by violent spring floods. There were also abundant floods due to rains at other seasons. Floods are recorded in no less than fifty-five summers of the fourteenth century. Hot droughts of unusual severity also prevailed over vast areas. In two different summers the Rhine could be forded at Cologne, and the Danube almost dried up. The "old hot summer" of 1357 was long famous.

Another characteristic feature was great storms which forced the waters of the North Sea far inland, inundating large areas in England, Belgium, and Holland. In 1315 and 1316 cold, rainy summers led to the severest famine ever experienced in England, and the next worst occurred similarly in 1321. In fact, from 1308 to 1322 great scarcity of food prevailed most of the time. Other famines of less severity occurred in 1351 and 1369, and the period from 1346 to 1375 was the longest known period of high prices and relative scarcity of food. Many other facts agree with all these in indicating that from about 1250 onward the amount of storminess and the consequent extremes of weather increased greatly in western Europe. The climax was reached in the first half of the fourteenth century. The unprofitableness of agriculture at this time was apparently one of the chief reasons for the "enclosure" of many fields in Britain and the transi-

23 Norlind, 1914; Petterson, 1912; Huntington and Visher, 1922, pp. 98 ff.

tion from crops to sheep as a main dependence. This change co-operated with at least two other conditions in causing the middle of
the fourteenth century to experience what Rogers calls "a complete
revolution in the social condition of the great mass of the community." The other two causes were, first, the relative abundance
of land and scarcity of labor due to deaths from famine and pestilence, and, second, the spirit of enterprise among people of all
classes, including even the serfs.

Farther east there is also evidence of storminess. In 1306–07 the
Caspian Sea had been rising rapidly for several years and had reached
a height of thirty-seven feet above the present datum level. Whether
it rose higher thereafter we do not know, but we have seen that a
century later it was well above the present level. Farther east the
inland lake of Lop-Nor also rose at about this time, drowning the so-
called Dragon Town on its shores. The reason for this is suggested
when Chinese floods are studied. Yao's list shows that the fourteenth century is the only one with numerous records of floods in
winter as well as summer. They reached a maximum in 1325, the
only year in which a flood somewhere in China is recorded for every
month. Such floods are obviously the result of an unparalleled succession of winter storms. Thus all the way from California across
the Atlantic to Europe and then onward across Asia we have the
same kind of evidence. During the Christian era no other period appears to have rivalled the fourteenth century in the storminess and
unreliability of its weather.

This conclusion seems to be significant in relation to our previous
study of the psychological effect of cycles. Just as a short cycle of
forty-one months is a persistent factor in the fluctuations of pig iron
production and the stock exchange, so a longer cycle of unknown
length seems to be a persistent factor among those which lead to
cycles of history. The climax of general alertness reached in Europe
in the fourteenth century may be associated with the climax of cyclonic storms at that same time. The storms brought with them extremes of cold and heat, drought and flood. They also brought extremes of good years and bad. In some places, such as Ireland, they
wrought economic damage far in excess of any good which they may
have done. In cool, northeastern Germany, too, where the Junkers
were taking root, this seems to have been true. In Italy, on the contrary, especially in the north, which lies in the path of storms, the
favorable effects of increased storminess appear to have much out-
weighed the unfavorable ones. The wealth and grandeur of Venice,

Florence, and Genoa illustrate what happened. In intermediate countries, such as France and England, the increased storminess brought sharply contrasting periods of desirable and undesirable economic conditions.

Even where storms bring famine, they may also bring changes of temperature, waves of ozone, and enhancement of atmospheric electricity, which stimulate people to renewed exertion. Such a psychological effect may have spread over Europe more uniformly than any one kind of economic effect. It may have had much to do with the enterprising spirit of Marco Polo and his fellow citizens and with the revival of learning which brought the old Greek culture to Italy and the West. The same psychological stimulus which made middle class people or even peasants assert their rights in countries as far apart as Spain and Germany may have had a correspondingly energizing effect upon Wyclif and Chaucer in England and upon Dante, Petrarch, and Boccacio in Italy. This psychological awakening based upon the physiological effect of storms may prove to be the missing factor that historians have sought in their attempts to explain the revival of the human spirit which ended the Middle Ages.

F. Heredity, Physical Environment, Culture

The preceding accounts of primitive agriculture, Babylonia, ancient Greece, Ireland, and medieval Europe illustrate the varied character of the many aspects of civilization which can be rightly understood only in the light of the three main principles set forth in this book. The first principle is that civilization is the unfinished, and perhaps never-to-be-finished, product of some great evolutionary force which permeates all nature. Second, the action of this force is swayed by three great factors, namely, biological inheritance, physical environment, and cultural endowment. Third, these three constantly react upon one another, and a knowledge of their combined influence is a prerequisite to a full understanding of history. When all three factors are favorable, civilization makes rapid progress; when all are unfavorable, retrogression is the rule. The cultural results of this mixture of influences are the subject of most books on history and civilization.

In surveying the great evolutionary force which permeates all nature we saw that since the dawn of life living creatures have progressively tended to gain control over more and more complex phases of physical environment. Life apparently began with one-celled creatures, or perhaps viruses, living in a monotonous environment composed solely of seawater. Their successors gradually acquired the power to move of their own volition, utilize the bottom of the sea as well as the water, swim against moving water, and, at last, leave the water and occupy the land. Then land animals acquired the ability to live within the soil, in the air, on the surface, in regions of ice, in grasslands, or in forests. In the forests some took to the trees, acquired new adaptations to a hitherto strange environment, and then brought their new abilities back to the ground with still further adaptations.

Throughout this evolutionary process two basic principles can be seen. First, the great advances are normally associated with one or the other of two kinds of environmental change. First, new forms of life appear to become established mainly when old forms migrate into a new environment, when the environment itself suffers change, or when the population becomes too great for the food supply. Mutations may arise when none of these three conditions prevails, but under such circumstances there is little chance for selection to weed out the less adaptable types and preserve some new species better fitted for the new environment. The second principle is that when a new form of life appears it is never completely new. The greater part of its biological constitution is an inheritance from the past. Hence the adaptation to the new mode of life is not so perfect as it might be if a species had been created solely for one particular environment, one particular density of population, and one particular stage in the evolution of other plants and animals.

The arrival of man upon the earth did not change these fundamental principles. It merely led to their application in new forms. That, in a way, is the chief theme of this book. Something new was assuredly added, just as something new was added when creatures of the ocean first emerged upon the land. That new thing was culture in the form of any and every object or idea of human origin which one generation passes on to another by some means other than biological inheritance. With the advent of civilization human culture expanded so much that many of the best thinkers have now lost sight of the fact that the laws of biological evolution still apply to mankind as forcibly as to amoebas or apes. The addition of cultural conditions assuredly gives us a new type of inheritance, but this does not alter the fact that man, like all other organisms, is physiologically the product of millions of years of biological evolution. Therefore the structure and functions of his body are not primarily fitted for the life he now leads. On the contrary, they may be said to consist of layer after layer of adaptations to first one environmental condition, such as ocean water, and then to another, such as life in trees.

In view of these basic principles Part II of this book is devoted to an attempt to trace some of the ways in which the process of selection now works upon man under the combined effect of physical environment, culture, and density of population. The workings of selection are especially active in migrations, and their results are readily evident when kiths are formed through selective migration followed by isolation, either geographical or social. The selective process can be seen at work in movements of population within the United States as well as elsewhere. Some of its results are visible in kiths such as the Icelanders, Parsis, Jews, Puritans, Chinese Hakkas, and German Junkers. The effect of the selective process upon character is seen, for example, in conquests by nomads who have played a part in history far out of proportion to their numbers. Such selection, however, may be insignificant in comparison with the far-reaching selective process which is now taking place under the influence of modern innovations. World wars are scarcely more than an incident in the profound revolution which has arisen through the recent development of machinery, transportation, medicine, chemistry, and social planning. No one can foretell the exact results of all this, but we may be certain that the same great principles which have governed organic evolution for a billion years or more will still prevail. Selection will assuredly eliminate certain types of people and also certain customs. The present evolutionary stage of civilization may last for centuries, but when it has ended, human beings and customs of certain types will presumably have become scarce or will have disappeared, whereas others which are now scarce will have become common. The change, we believe, will be both genetic and cultural, and no man can now say which will be more important.

In Part III of this book we laid great stress on the physiological adaptations which man has inherited from a vast line of animal ancestors. We began, to be sure, with a study of the geographical distribution of civilization. This led to the conclusion that the main pattern is set by climate but is greatly modified by other conditions, especially migration, diet, and density of population. In studying both climate and diet we found ourselves face to face with man's biological inheritance. We discovered that the human body inherits a hitherto unsuspected sensitivity to atmospheric conditions. Temperature, to be sure, has always been recognized as important, but in such matters as religion we find that it has a pervasive influence which has rarely been fully appreciated. Certain other forms of sensitivity to the air are as yet almost unknown. The resistance of infants, for example, to digestive diseases apparently varies according to their age in a way that suggests an innate adaptation to a particular kind of climate. The peculiar ability of people, especially women, in the reproductive ages of life to resist disease during the late winter suggests the same thing. So does the fact that man still inherits a strong tendency toward a seasonal cycle of reproduction, which appears to be connected with such curious facts as an excess of births of great leaders in the late winter, variations in length of life among people born at different seasons, and outbursts of insanity at the height of the reproductive urge in May or June. Another widely pervasive evidence of sensitivity to the air is seen in the annual cycle of mental activity, which is especially clear in the circulation of serious books by libraries. These many evidences of an innate adaptation to a certain type of climate help to explain why the geographical distribution of civilization is so closely related to that of human vigor.

Diet also plays a vital part in determining human health, thus influencing vigor, character, and the rate of progress. In studying diet as well as climate we are impressed by the importance of the biological inheritance derived from remote ancestors. We also discover that cultural habits and inherited traits often work at cross purposes. Inheritance lays upon mankind the necessity for a varied diet with plenty of vitamins and minerals as well as carbohydrates and proteins. Agriculture and the accompanying increase of population induce many people to rely on a diet which supplies a maximum of carbohydrates and can support the maximum number of people. Hence hundreds of millions of people live at a low level of vigor and competence. Such facts make us realize that, although climate sets the main outlines of the geographical pattern of civilization, great variations are introduced by overpopulation, diet, migration, and other factors.

Another point which deserves emphasis is that cultural habits which do not accord with the geographical environment either cannot establish a footing or else die out. The varied occupations and mores which center around wool, milk, corn, and snow find little place in southern Japan because the physical environment does not favor those particular products. In non-essentials, such as the cut of their coats or beards, men in Trinidad and Stockholm may be alike, but in the vigor of their work they cannot be alike because their degrees of energy are different. On the other hand, in this vital respect Stockholm is bound to resemble Chicago, whereas Trinidad resembles Singapore. Thus in many of their basic qualities the civilizations of regions with a similar type of environment tend to be alike, although in matters which have little relation to physical environment they may differ radically.

Having reached this point in our study, we inquire into the effect of environmental differences from one time to another as well as from place to place. Here we find an almost untilled and very fertile field of study. Our first conclusion is that we live in the midst of an intricate series of cycles, some of which are closely associated with atmospheric differences. Ordinary storms represent one such type of cycle. Perhaps their commonplaceness has actually retarded the scientific study of their remarkable relationships to health, mental activity, psychological attitudes, and practical achievements. Another type of cycle is seen in business of many kinds. Here, for example, we find the 41-month cycle and discover that it is coincident with variations in atmospheric electricity. Examining the animal world, we find another cycle of $9\frac{2}{3}$ years which is similarly coincident with a cycle of atmospheric ozone observed elsewhere. How far atmospheric electricity and ozone are causes or merely concomitants of the cycles in business and in the reproduction of animals we do not know, but clearly the field for further study is wide and alluring.

Long cycles, as well as short cycles, have engaged our attention. During the present century the evidence of cycles with a length of hundreds of years has gradually become clearer. One of their chief characteristics is variations in the number and intensity of ordinary cyclonic storms. This opens the way to a study of specific periods, such as the Golden Age of Greece, the Dark Ages in Ireland, and the Revival of Learning in western Europe. These give an idea of the way in which climatic cycles appear to have influenced the activity of the human mind as well as the vigor of the body, the production of food, and the capacity of a region to support people.

Finally, we have seen that at any particular time civilization makes rapid progress in regions where the physical environment closely fits the needs of the particular cultural stage which has then been attained. Primitive agriculture contributed most to civilization in an environment which included wild wheat, wild but tamable animals, topography which made simple irrigation easy, and a climate warm enough to be comfortable for relatively primitive people in winter and so dry in summer that the heat was not enervating. Such a combination is very different from the optimum for our modern civilization, which needs fuels and minerals, easy communication by water, space for air fields, and a climate which comes as near as possible to the ideal in summer, but can be made comfortable in winter because of our high development of the techniques of clothing, housing, heating, and transportation. Between these two stages there are many others, but all alike conform to the same basic principles. They cannot do otherwise. Whatever the stage of civilization may be, man's rate of progress depends upon the quality of the people as determined by mutations, cross-breeding, and selective processes of the past. The rate of progress also depends upon the degree to which the geographic environment in all its phases is appropriate to the stage of culture previously attained. And, finally, progress and civilization depend upon health and upon the vigor with which people use their innate capacities and cultural advantages.

BIBLIOGRAPHY

AARONSOHN, ALEXANDER. 1913. "Éspeces en voie d'extinction." Pt. II in "Notes on Palestinian Phytogeography." *Bull. société botanique de France.* 60: 585.

ABBOT, C. G. 1931. "Weather Dominated by Solar Changes." *Smiths. Misc. Coll.* Vol. 85, No. 9.

— 1935. "Solar Radiation and Weather Studies." *Smiths. Misc. Coll.* Vol. 94, No. 10.

— 1936. "Cycles in Tree Ring Width." *Smiths. Misc. Coll.* Vol 95, No. 19.

ADAMS, S. W., and NICHOLSON, S. B. 1933. "The Nature of the Solar Cycles." *Proc. Nat'l Acad. Sci.* 19: 371.

ADOLPH, WILLIAM HENRY. Personal communication.

ALBRIGHT, W. D. 1933. "Crop Growth in High Latitudes." *Geog. Rev.* 23: 608–20.

ALLEE, W. C. 1943. "Animal Population Cycles." *Sci. Monthly.* 56: 561–64.

AMERICAN INSTITUTE OF PUBLIC OPINION. 1943. *Report on the Incidence of the Common Cold.* Princeton Univ. Press, Princeton. See also *New York Times.*

American Men of Science. See Cattell.

AMULREE. See Newfoundland Royal Commission.

ANDERSON, C. N. 1939. "A Representation of the Sunspot Cycle." *Bell System Tech. Jour.* 80: 292–99.

ANGOFF, CHARLES, and MENCKEN, H. L. 1931. "The Worst American State." *Amer. Mercury.* XXIV: 1–16, 175–88, 355–71.

ANTEVS, ERNEST. 1925. "The Big Tree as a Climatic Measure." *Quarternary Climates.* Carnegie Inst., Washington.

ARCTOWSKI, HENRYK. 1912. "The Solar Constant and the Variations of Atmospheric Temperature at Arequipa and Some Other Stations." *Bull. Amer. Geog. Soc.* 44: 598–606.

— 1919. "A Study of Changes in the Distribution of Temperature in Europe and North America During the Years 1900 to 1909." *Annals N. Y. Acad. Sci.* 24: 39–113.

BACKHOUSE, E., and BLAND, J. O. P. 1914. *Annals and Memoirs of the Court of Peking.* Houghton Mifflin, New York.

BALFOUR, EDWARD GREEN. 1885. *Cyclopedia of India and of Eastern and Southern Asia.* B. Quaritch, London.

BANKS, CHARLES E. 1930. *The Planters of the Commonwealth.* Houghton Mifflin, Boston.

BANKS, JOSEPH, and Others. 1780. *Letters on Iceland, Containing Observations on the Civil, Literary, Ecclesiastical and Natural History.* 2nd ed. London.

BARZUN, JACQUES. 1937. *Race, a Study of Modern Superstition.* Harcourt, Brace, New York.

BAUER, L. A. 1921. "Measures of Electric and Magnetic Activity of the Sun and the Earth, and Interrelations." *Terrestrial Magnetism and Atmospheric Electricity.* March and June, pp. 33–68.

613

BECK, RICHARD, Ed. 1943. *Icelandic Poems and Stories* (Trans. from *Modern Icelandic Literature*). Princeton Univ. Press.

BECKER, J. E., and McCOLLUM, E. V. *See* McCollum.

BELDING, D. L., and PHELPS, E. B. *See* Phelps.

BENEDICT, F. G., MILES, W. R., ROTH, PAUL, and SMITH, H. M. 1919. *Human Vitality and Efficiency under Prolonged Restricted Diet.* Carnegie Inst., Washington.

BENJAMIN, L. C., YAGLOU, C. P., and CHOATE, S. P. *See* Yaglou.

BENNETT, H. S. 1938. *Life on the English Manor.* Macmillan, New York.

BENNETT, M. K. 1941. "Wheat in National Diets." *Wheat Studies.* XVIII, No. 2.

BERNERT, ELEANOR H. 1944. *Volume and Composition of Net Migration from the Rural-Farm Population, 1930–1940, for the United States, Major Geographic Divisions and States.* U. S. Dep't Agr., Bureau of Agr. Econ., Washington.

BEVERIDGE, SIR WILLIAM H. 1921. "Weather and Harvest Cycles." *Econ. Jour.* 31: 429–52. London.

—— 1922. "Wheat Prices and Rainfall in Western Europe." *Jour. Roy. Astron. Soc.* 85: 412–78. London.

BISHOP, CARL WHITING. 1942. *Origin of the Far Eastern Civilizations: A Brief Handbook.* Smiths. Inst. War Background Studies, No. 1. Washington.

—— *Archaeological Researches in China, 1923–1934.* Unpub. ms.

BISSONNETTE, THOMAS HUME. 1936A. "Early Fertile Eggs from Pheasants." *Bird Banding.* VII, No. 3.

—— 1936B. "Sexual Photoperiodicity." *Jour. Heredity.* XXVII: 171–80.

BLAND, J. O. P., and BACKHOUSE, E. *See* Backhouse.

BOAS, FRANZ. 1911. *Changes in Bodily Form of Descendants of Immigrants.* U. S. Immigration Comm., Gov't Printing Off., Washington.

BOWLES, GORDON TOWNSEND. 1932. *New Types of Old Americans at Harvard and at Eastern Women's Colleges.* Harvard Univ. Press, Cambridge.

BOWMAN, ISAIAH. 1931. *The Pioneer Fringe.* Amer. Geog. Soc. Spec. Pub. No. 13.

BRAND, DONALD, and SAUER, CARL. *See* Sauer.

BRITT, STEUART H., and GRAEBER, ISACQUE. *See* Graeber.

BRITTON, C. E. 1937. *Meteorological Chronology to 1450 A.D.* H. M. Stat. Off., London.

BROOKS, C. E. P. 1919. "The Secular Variation of Rainfall." *Quart. Jour. Roy. Meteor. Soc.* 45: 233–48.

—— 1923. "Variations in the Levels of the Central African Lakes Victoria and Albert." *Geophysical Memoirs.* Air Ministry, Meteor. Off., London.

—— 1926. *Climate Through the Ages.* Ernest Benn, London.

——, and GLASSPOOLE, J. 1928. *British Floods and Droughts.* London.

BRUCKNER, EDUARD. 1891. *Klimaschwankungen seit 1700.* Vienna.

—— 1910. "Klimaschwankungen und Völkerwanderungen im XIX Jahrhundert." *Internationale Wochenschrift für Wissenschaft, Kunst, und Technik.* March 5, Vienna.

BRUNT, DAVID. 1927. "Investigation of Periodicities in Rainfall, Pressure and Temperature at Certain European Stations." *Quart. Jour. Roy. Meteor. Soc.* 53: 1–32. London.

BRYCE, JAMES. 1916. Introduction to *Denmark and Sweden, with Iceland and Finland* by Jon Stefansson. T. F. Unwin, London.

BUCK, JOHN L. 1937. *Land Utilization in China.* Commercial Press, Shanghai.

BUMP, GARDINER. 1939. "Some Characteristics of the Periodic Fluctuations in the Abundance of Ruffed Grouse." *Fourth North American Wildlife Conference Trans.,* pp. 478–84.

BURR, H. S. 1940. "Biologic Organization and the Cancer Problem." *Yale Jour. Biol. and Med.* 12: 277.

BURTON, T. E. 1902. *Financial Crises and Periods of Industrial and Commercial Depressions.* D. Appleton, New York.

BUTLER, H. C. 1920. "Desert Syria, the Land of a Lost Civilization." *Geog. Rev.* Feb., pp. 77–108.

Cambridge Historical Series. Univ. Press, Cambridge, Eng.

CARPENTER, J. RICHARD. 1941. "Insect Outbreaks in Europe." *Jour. Animal Ecology.* Vol. 9.

CARREL, ALEXIS. 1935. *Man the Unknown.* Harper, New York.

CATTELL, J. MCKEEN, and CATTELL, JAQUES, Eds. 1938. *American Men of Science.* 6th ed. The Science Press, New York.

CAUGHEY, J. L., Jr. *See* Draper, 1944.

Census Publication. 1909. *A Century of Population Growth, 1790–1900.* Gov't Printing Off., Washington.

CHAMBERLAIN, HOUSTON S. 1910. *Foundations of the Nineteenth Century.* John Lane Co., New York.

CHAPLINE, W. R., and COOPERRIDER, C. K. 1941. "Climate and Grazing." In *Climate and Man.* U. S. Dep't Agr., Washington.

CHEYNEY, EDWARD P. 1936. *The Dawn of a New Era, 1250–1453.* Harper, New York.

CHOATE, S. P., YAGLOU, C. P., and BENJAMIN, L. C. *See* Yaglou.

CHREE, C. 1925. "The Relation between Sunspots, Terrestrial Magnetism, and Atmospheric Electricity." *Nature.* 115: 982.

CILENTO, R. W. 1930. "Rejoinder to Professor Huntington." *Econ. Record.* 6: 27–132.

CLARK, CARROLL D., and GIST, NOEL P. *See* Gist.

CLARK, CHARLES UPTON. 1942. Trans. of "Compendium and Description of the West Indies," by Antonio Vasquez de Espinosa. *Smiths. Misc. Coll.* Vol. 102. Washington.

CLARK, COLIN. 1940. *The Conditions of Economic Progress.* Macmillan, London.

CLAYTON, H. H. 1902. "Influence of Rainfall on Commerce and Politics." *Pop. Sci. Monthly.* Vol. 60.

—— 1926. "Solar Activity and Weather Changes." *Smiths. Misc. Coll.* Vol. 78, No. 4.

—— 1940. "The 11-Year and 27-Day Solar Periods in Meteorology." *Smiths. Misc. Coll.* Vol. 99, No. 6.

—— 1943. *Solar Relations.* Vols. I and II. Clayton Weather Service, Canton, Mass.

CLIFFORD, M. H., and GODWIN, H. *See* Godwin.

COLBY, C. W. 1907. *Selections from Sources of English History.* London.

COLLINS, HENRY HILL. 1941. *America's Own Refugees: Our 4,000,000 Homeless Migrants.* Princeton Univ. Press, Princeton.

CONYBEARE, C. A. V. 1877. *The Place of Iceland in the History of European Institutions.* James Parker, London.

COOK, CLIFFORD. *See* Furnas.

COOKE, GEORGE ALBERT. 1929A. "Zenobia." *Ency. Brit.* 14th ed.

—— 1929B. "Odaenathus." *Ency. Brit.* 14th ed.

COON, C. S. 1939. *The Races of Europe.* Macmillan, New York.

—— 1942. "Have the Jews a Racial Identity?" In *Jews in a Gentile World,* ed. by Graeber and Britt. Macmillan, New York.

COOPER, CHARLES. 1934. *The English Table in History and Literature.* Sampson, Low, Marston, London.

COOPERRIDER, C. K., and CHAPLINE, W. R. *See* Chapline.

CRIDDLE, NORMAN. 1930. "Some Natural Factors Governing the Fluctuations of Grouse in Manitoba." *Canadian Field Naturalist.* 44: 77–80.

CRIDDLE, STUART. 1938. "A Study of the Snowshoe Rabbit." *Canadian Field Naturalist.* 52: 33–40.

CRILE, GEORGE. 1936. *The Phenomena of Life: A Radio-Electric Interpretation.* W. W. Norton, New York.

DAVENPORT, CHARLES B. 1923. *Body Build and Its Inheritance.* Carnegie Inst. Pub. No. 329, Washington.

DAVIE, MAURICE R. 1923. *A Constructive Immigration Policy.* Yale Univ. Press, New Haven.

DAVIS, WILLIAM M. 1905. "A Journey Across Turkestan." In *Explorations in Turkestan.* Carnegie Inst. Pub. No. 26, Washington.

DECOSSON, ANTHONY. 1935. *Mareotis.* Country Life, Ltd., London.

DEEGAN, WILLIAM. 1941. "A Fifty-nine Year Survey at Yale Reveals Freshmen Are Becoming Younger, Heavier, and Taller." *Research Quarterly.* Vol. 12, No. 4, December.

DEVOTO, BERNARD. 1943. *The Year of Decision: 1846.* Little, Brown, Boston.

DEWEY, EDWARD R. 1940. *Putting Cycles to Work in Science and Industry.* Foundation for the Study of Cycles, New York.

—— 1943A. "Cycles as an Aid to Postwar Planning." *Gen'l Electric Rev.* Vol. 46, May.

—— 1943B. *The Detection and Isolation of Rhythms, an Outline.* Foundation for the Study of Cycles, New York.

—— 1944. Reprint Series. Foundation for the Study of Cycles, New York.

—— *Some Rhythms and/or Periodicities Variously Determined or Alleged.* Unpub. ms.

DEXTER, O. E. 1904. *Weather Influences.* Macmillan, New York.

DORPALEN, ANDREAS. 1942. *The World of General Haushofer.* Farrar and Rinehart, New York.

DOUGHERTY, R. P. 1932. *The Sealand of Ancient Araba.* Yale Univ. Press, New Haven.

DOUGHTY, CHARLES MONTAGU. 1921. *Travels in Arabia Deserta.* Warner and Cape, Boston.

DOUGLASS, A. E. 1919. *Climatic Cycles and Tree Growth.* Carnegie Inst. Pub. No. 289, Washington.

—— 1931. *Tree Rings and Their Relation to Solar Variations and Chronology.* Smiths. Rep., Washington.

DOUGLASS, A. E. 1941. "Dendrochronology and Studies in 'Cyclics.'" In *Conservation of Renewable Natural Resources*. Univ. Penn. Press, Philadelphia.

DRAPER, GEORGE. 1930. *Disease and the Man*. Macmillan, New York.

——, DUPERTIUS, C. W., and CAUGHEY, J. L., JR. 1944. *Human Constitution in Clinical Medicine*. Paul B. Hoeber, New York.

DUERST, J. ULRICH. 1908. "Animal Remains from the Excavations at Anau." *Explorations in Turkestan, Expedition of 1904*. Vol. II, Carnegie Inst., Washington, pp. 341–44.

DÜLL, BERNHARD, and DÜLL, TRAUTE. 1938A. "Kosmisch gelenktes Leben." *Deutschen Rundschau*, January.

——, —— 1938B. "Erd- und Sonnenphysikalische Vorgänge in ihrer Bedeutung für Krankheits- und Todauslösung." *Nosokomeion (Quart. Hospital Rev.)*. Stuttgart.

——, —— 1938C. "Zur Frage solaraktiver Einflüsse auf die Psyche." *Zeitschrift für die gesamte Neurologie und Psychiatrie*. Feb. 8, Berlin.

——, —— 1939A. "Ionosphäre, Troposphäre, Biosphäre." *Die Umschau*. Vol. 26, Frankfurt-M.

——, —— 1939B. "Neuer Beitrag zur Erforschung des Bioklimas." *Die Umschau*. Vol. 31, Frankfurt-M.

——, —— 1939C. "Kosmisch-physikalische Störungen der Ionosphäre, Troposphäre, und Biosphäre." From *Bioklimatische Beiblätter*, 6, No. 2, 65–76, and 6, No. 3, 121–34. Vieweg, Braunschweig.

DUPERTIUS, C. W. *See* Draper, 1944.

DYK, WALTER. "A Study of the Effect of Change of Technique Upon the Warfare of Primitive People." Quoted in Wright's *Study of War*, I: 88. Unpub. ms. at Univ. Chicago.

DZERDZEJEVSKY, B. L. 1943. "On the Question of the Temperature Rise in Arctic Regions (Russian)." *Bull. Acad. Sci., Geog., and Geophys*. No. 2, pp. 60–68. Moscow.

EASTMAN, PARIS R. Personal communication.

ELLIOTT, H. M. B. 1900. *Turkey in Europe*. Edward Arnold, London.

ELLIS, HAVELOCK. 1904, 1927. *Study of British Genius*. London.

ELLIS, HENRY, Ed. 1846. *Polydore Vergil's English History*. Vol. 1. J. B. Nichols and Son, London.

ELTON, CHARLES S. 1929. *The Relation of Animal Numbers to Climate*. Conf. of Empire Meteorologists, Agr. Sect.

—— 1931. "The Study of Epidemic Diseases among Wild Animals." *Jour. Hygiene*. Vol. 31, Oct.

——, and NICHOLSON, MARY. 1942. "The Ten-Year Cycle in Numbers of the Lynx in Canada." *Jour. Animal Ecology*. 11: 215–44.

—— 1942. *Voles, Mice and Lemmings*. The Clarendon Press, Oxford, Eng.

EMERTON, EPHRAIM. 1917. *The Beginnings of Modern Europe*. Ginn, New York.

Encyclopædia Britannica. 1910. 11th ed. Ency. Brit. Inc., New York.

Encyclopædia Britannica. 1929. 14th ed. Ency. Brit. Inc., New York.

EVANS, C. H., and GREEN, R. G. *See* Green.

FAIRCHILD, H. P. 1927. *Immigrant Backgrounds*. John Wiley, New York.

—— 1933. *Immigration, a World Movement and Its American Significance*. Macmillan, New York.

FAY, S. B. 1937. *The Rise of Brandenburg-Prussia to 1786.* Henry Holt, New York.

FLINT, W. P. *See* Shelford.

FOOTT, FRANCES. *See* Lively.

FREEMAN, FRANK N. *See* Newman.

FURNAS, C. C., and COOK, CLIFFORD. 1937. *Man, Bread and Destiny.* Reynal and Hitchcock, New York.

GALE, H. S. 1912. *Notes on the Quaternary Lakes of the Great Basin.* Bull. No. 540, U. S. Geol. Surv.

Gallup Poll. *See* American Institute of Public Opinion.

GANGULEE, N. 1939. *Health and Nutrition in India.* Faber and Faber, London.

GARVIN, J. L. 1929. "English-Speaking World: Origins, Expansion, Relations and Prospect." *Ency. Brit.* 14th ed.

GEIGER, R., and KÖPPEN, W. P. *See* Köppen.

GESSNER, AMY A. 1940. *Selective Factors in Migration from a New York Rural Community.* Cornell Univ. Agr. Exp. Sta., Bull. No. 736. Ithaca.

GIBBON, EDWARD. 1776–87. *History of the Decline and Fall of the Roman Empire.* W. Strahan and T. Cadell, London.

GILFILLAN, S. C. 1920. "The Coldward Course of Progress." *Pol. Sci. Quarterly.* XXXV: No. 3, Sept.

GILKS, J. L., and ORR, J. B. *See* Orr.

GILLETTE, HALBERT P. 1939. "Climatic Cycle of 25,500 Years." *Pan-Amer. Geologist.* LXXI: 107–15, March.

—— 1940A. *Forecasting by Means of Climatic Cycles.* Paper presented before Penn. Water Works Ass'n, Oct.

—— 1940B. "Prospective Dry Years." *Pan-Amer. Geologist.* LXXIV: 165–78, Oct.

—— 1942A. "Menacing Long Series of Droughts." *Pan-Amer. Geologist.* 77: 27.

—— 1942B. "Dating the Ice Age Varves." *Water Works and Sewerage,* Dec.

GINI, C. 1912. "Contributi statistici al problem dell'eugenica." *Estratto dalla rivista Italiana di sociologia.* Anno XVI, Fsc. III–IV.

—— 1934. "Su la portata e gli effetti delle false denuncie di nascita per i nati denunciati al principio dell'anno." *Bull. de l'institut international de statistique.* T. XXVII. La Haye.

GIST, NOEL P., and CLARK, CARROLL D. 1938. "Intelligence as a Selective Factor in Rural-Urban Migration." *Amer. Jour. Soc.* 44: 36–58, July.

——, PIHLBLAD, C. T., and GREGORY, C. L. 1943. *Selective Factors in Migration and Occupation, a Study of Social Selection in Missouri.* Univ. Missouri. Columbia, Mo.

GOBINEAU, JOSEPH A. 1915. (1853–55) *The Inequality of Human Races.* London.

GODWIN, H., and CLIFFORD, M. H. 1938–39. "Studies of the Post-Glacial History of British Vegetation." Pts. 1–4. *Royal Soc. Lon., Philos. Trans.* S. B. No. 562, Vol. 229, pp. 323–406. London.

GRAEBER, ISACQUE, and BRITT, STEUART H., Eds. 1942. *Jews in a Gentile World: The Problem of Anti-Semitism.* Macmillan, New York.

GRANDT, A. D., YAGLOU, C. P., and BENJAMIN, L. C. *See* Yaglou.

GRANT, CHRISTINA PHELPS. 1938. *The Syrian Desert.* Macmillan, New York.

GRAY, CORA E., and ROSE, MARY. *See* Rose.

GREEN, R. G. 1938. "Shock Disease and the Snowshoe Hare Cycle." *Science.* 87: 298–99.

GREEN, R. G., and EVANS, C. A. 1940. "Studies on a Population Cycle of Snowshoe Hares on the Lake Alexander Area." *Jour. Wildlife Management.* Vol. 4.

——, EVANS, C. A., and LARSON, C. L. 1943. "A Ten-Year Population Study of the Rabbit Tick, Haemaphysalis leporis-palustris." *Amer. Jour. Hygiene.* 38: 260–81.

GREENBERG, LEON A., and HAGGARD, HOWARD W. *See* Haggard.

GREGORY, RICHARD. 1930. "Weather Recurrences and Weather Cycles." *Quart. Jour. Roy. Meteor. Soc.* Vol. 56. London.

GRISWOLD, A. WHITNEY. 1943. "The Junkers: Hostages to the Past." *Va. Quart. Rev.* Vol. 19, No. 3.

GROTE, GEORGE. 1847–56. *History of Greece.* London.

GUTHE, K. F., STERNE, THEODORE E., and ROBERTS, W. O. *See* Sterne.

HADDON, A. C. 1924. *The Races of Man and Their Distribution.* Univ. Press, Cambridge, Eng.

HAGGARD, HOWARD W., and GREENBERG, LEON A. 1935. *Diet and Physical Efficiency.* Yale Univ. Press, New Haven.

HALE, GEORGE E. 1920. "Monthly Notices." *Roy. Astr. Soc.* 80: 412.

HALE, GEORGE F. 1937. "The Relation of Maternal Vitamin A Deficiency to Microphthalmia in Pigs." *Texas State Jour. Med.* 33: 228.

HAMILTON, W. J. 1937. "The Biology of Microtine Cycles." *Jour. Agr. Research.* 54: 779–90.

—— 1939. *American Mammals.* McGraw-Hill, New York. Reprint of pp. 261–76 by Foundation for Study of Cycles, New York, 1944.

—— 1941. *Reproduction of the Field Mouse, Microtus Pennsylvanius.* Cornell Univ. Agr. Exp. Sta., Memoir 237, May.

HANKINS, FRANK H. 1931. *The Racial Basis of Civilization: A Critique of the Nordic Doctrine.* Alfred A. Knopf, New York.

HART, B. H. LIDDELL. 1929. "Mongol Campaigns." *Ency. Brit.* 14th ed. 15: 705.

HAUSHOFER, KARL. 1934. *Erdkunde, Geopolitik und Wehrwissenschaft.* Universitätsbuchhandlung, Max Hoeber, Berlin.

HEADLEE, THOMAS J. 1934. *Cycles of Abundance of the Eastern Tent Caterpillar.* N. J. Exp. Sta. Bull. No. 579. (Extended by additional data from author.) New Brunswick, N. J.

HEALY, JOHN. 1908. *Ireland's Ancient Schools and Scholars.* Benziger Bros., New York.

HELLAND-HANSEN, B., and NANSEN, F. *See* Nansen.

HELLMAN, G. 1916. "Über die Ägyptischen Witterungsangaben im Kalendar von Claudius Ptolemaeus." *Sitz.-ber. Preuss. Akad. Wiss.* Vol. 13.

HELLPACH, WILLY. 1911. *Die geopsychischen Erscheinungen des Wetter, Klima, und Landschaft in ihrem Einfluss auf das Seelenleben.* Wilhelm Engelmann, Leipzig.

HENDERSON, LAWRENCE J. 1913. *The Fitness of the Environment.* Macmillan, New York.

HENNIG, R. 1904. *Katalog bemerkenswerter Witterungsereignisse von den ältesten Zeit bis zum Jahre 1800.* Abhandlungen des königlich meteorologischen Instituts, Bd. II, No. 4. A. Asher, Berlin.

HERRINGTON, L. P. 1935. "The Influence of Ionized Air upon Normal Subjects." *Jour. Clinical Investigation.* Vol. 14, No. 1, Jan.

HERRINGTON, L. P. 1938. "The Reaction of Hypersensitive Patients to Atmospheres Containing High Concentrations of Heavy Ions." *Jour. Industrial Hygiene and Toxicology.* Vol. 20, No. 2, Feb.

——, and MORIYAMA, I. M. 1939. "The Relation of Mortality from Certain Metabolic Diseases to Climatic and Socio-Economic Factors." *Amer. Jour. Hygiene.* 28: 396.

HERTZ, FRIEDRICH D. 1928. *Race and Civilization.* Macmillan, New York.

HIGH, S. 1943. "Feudal Hawaii: Paradise, Ltd.; Big Five Corporate Monopolies Collect Their Toll, Going and Coming." *Reader's Digest.* Vol. 42, pp. 19–23.

HINSDALE, GUY. 1936–40. "Climate and Disease, with Special Reference to Heat, Humidity, Sunlight, Heliotherapy, and Seasonal Influence." *Bull. Amer. Meteor. Soc.* Vol. 17, Oct. 1936; Vol. 18, Feb., June–July, Dec. 1937; Vol. 19, Dec. 1938; Vol. 20, Dec. 1939; Vol. 21, Dec. 1940; Vol. 23, Dec. 1942.

HIRSCH, NATHANIEL D. MITTRON. 1926. "A Study of Natio-Racial Differences." *Genetic Psychology Monographs, Child Behavior, Differential and Genetic Psychology,* Vol. I.

HITLER, ADOLF. 1926–27. *Mein Kampf.* F. Eher nachf. München.

HOBBS, ALBERT H. 1942. *Differentials in Internal Migration.* Univ. Penn., Philadelphia.

HOLZINGER, KARL, NEWMAN, HORATIO N., and FREEMAN, FRANK N. *See* Newman.

HOOTON, E. A. 1939. *Crime and the Man.* Harvard Univ. Press, Cambridge.

HOSKINS, CHAPIN. Personal communication.

HOWELL, A. BRAZIER. 1923. "Periodic Fluctuations in the Numbers of Small Mammals." *Jour. Mammalogy.* 4: 149–55.

HOYT, W. G., and LANGBEIN, W. B. 1944. "The Yield of Streams as a Measure of Climatic Fluctuations." *Geog. Rev.* XXXIV: 218–34, April.

HUNTINGTON, ELLSWORTH. 1902. "The Valley of the Upper Euphrates River and Its People." *Bull. Amer. Geog. Soc.* Vol. 34.

—— 1905. "The Mountains and Kibitkas of Tian Shan." *Bull. Amer. Geog. Soc.* 27: 513–50.

—— 1907A. "The Historic Fluctuations of the Caspian Sea." *Bull. Amer. Geog. Soc.* Vol. 39.

—— 1907B. *The Pulse of Asia.* Houghton Mifflin, Boston.

—— 1908. "Description of the Kurgans of the Merv Oasis." In *Explorations in Turkestan.* Vol. II. Carnegie Inst. Pub. No. 73, Washington.

—— 1911. *Palestine and Its Transformation.* Houghton Mifflin, Boston.

—— 1912. "The Peninsula of Yucatan." *Bull. Amer. Geog. Soc.* Vol. XLIV, Nov.

—— 1914A. *The Climatic Factor as Illustrated in Arid America.* Carnegie Inst., Washington.

—— 1914B. "The Solar Hypothesis of Climatic Changes." *Bull. Geol. Soc. Amer.* 25: 477–590.

—— 1915. "A Neglected Factor in Race Development." *Jour. Race Development.* 6: 167–84.

—— 1919. *World Power and Evolution.* Yale Univ. Press, New Haven.

——, and VISHER, STEPHEN S. 1922. *Climatic Changes.* Yale Univ. Press, New Haven.

—— 1923. *Earth and Sun.* Yale Univ. Press, New Haven.

—— 1924A. *The Character of Races.* Chas. Scribner's, New York.

—— 1924B. *Civilization and Climate.* 3rd ed. Yale Univ. Press, New Haven.

HUNTINGTON, ELLSWORTH. 1925A. *Tree Growth and Climatic Interpretations.* Carnegie Inst. Pub. No. 352, Washington.

—— 1925B. *West of the Pacific.* Chas. Scribner's, New York.

——, and WILLIAMS, FRANK E. 1926A. *Business Geography.* 2nd ed. John Wiley, New York.

—— 1926B. *The Pulse of Progress.* Chas. Scribner's, New York.

——, and WHITNEY, LEON F. 1927A. *The Builders of America.* Wm. Morrow, New York.

—— 1927B. *The Human Habitat.* D. Van Nostrand, New York.

—— 1927C. "The Quantitative Phases of Human Geography." *Sci. Monthly.* Vol. 25.

—— 1930. *Weather and Health, a Study of Daily Mortality in New York City.* Bull. Nat'l Research Council, Nat'l Acad. Sci., Washington.

—— 1931. "The Matamek Conference on Biological Cycles." *Science.* 74: 229–35.

—— 1934. *The Selective Action of Migration.* Zbior Prac towarzystwo Geograficzne we Lwowie, Engenjuszowi Romerowi. Lwow.

——, and RAGSDALE, MARTHA. 1935A. *After Three Centuries.* Williams and Wilkins, Baltimore.

—— 1935B. *Climatic Pulsations.* Sven Hedin: Geografiska Annaler, Stockholm.

—— 1938. *Season of Birth.* John Wiley, New York.

—— 1940A. *Principles of Economic Geography.* John Wiley, New York.

—— 1940B. *Principles of Human Geography.* 5th ed. John Wiley, New York.

—— 1941. "Climatic Pulsations and an Ozone Hypothesis of Libraries and History." In *Conservation of Renewable Natural Resources.* Univ. Penn., Philadelphia.

—— 1942A. "The Quality of the People." In *America at War,* ed. by S. van Valkenburg. Prentice-Hall, New York.

—— 1942B. "Solar Disturbances and Interdiurnal Variations of Atmospheric Pressure." *Bull. Amer. Meteor. Soc.* 23: 388–99.

—— 1943. "The Geography of Human Productivity." *Annals, Ass'n Amer. Geographers.* 33: 1–31.

HUNTSMAN, A. G. 1931. *The Maritime Salmon of Canada.* Biol. Bd. of Canada, Bull. No. 21.

HUXLEY, JULIAN S. 1941. *Man Stands Alone.* Harper, New York.

Imperial Gazetteer of India. 1909. Vol. II, Oxford, Eng.

JACOBS, MELVILLE. 1942. "Jewish Blood and Culture." In *Jews in a Gentile World,* ed. by Graeber and Britt. Macmillan, New York.

JAMES, SELWYN. 1943. *South of the Congo.* Random House, New York.

JEVONS, H. S. 1909. "Changes in the Sun's Heat as Causes of Fluctuations of the Activity of Trade and Unemployment." *Contemp. Rev.,* Aug. 1925.

JONES, J. CLAUDE. 1925. "Geologic History of Lake Lahontan." In *Quaternary Climates.* Carnegie Inst., Washington.

JONES, W. H. S. 1907. *Malaria: A Neglected Factor in the History of Greece and Rome.* Bowes and Bowes, Cambridge, Eng.

JUNGER. Referred to in CARPENTER, "Insect Outbreaks in Europe." *See* Carpenter.

KAHLER. *Ergebnisse der meteorologische Beobachtungen in Potsdam in den Jahren 1921, 1922, und 1923.*

KARAKA, DESABHAI FRAMJI. 1884. *History of the Parsis.* Macmillan, London.

KAUTSKY, KARL. 1926. *Are the Jews a Race?* Trans. from 2nd German ed. Internat'l Publishers, New York.

KELLER, ALBERT G., and SUMNER, WILLIAM. *See* Sumner.

KELLER, C. 1913. *The Derivation of the European Domestic Animals.* Annual Report, Smiths. Inst., 1912, pp. 483–91.

KENNEDY, RAYMOND. 1942. *The Ageless Indies.* John Day, New York.

KING, WILFORD I. 1938. *The Causes of Economic Fluctuations.* Ronald Press, New York.

KITCHIN, JOSEPH. 1923. "Cycles and Trends in Economic Factors." *Harvard Rev. Econ. Statistics.* 5: 10–16, Jan.

KLINEBERG, OTTO. 1935. *Race Differences.* Harper, New York.

—— 1938. "The Intelligence of Migrants." *Amer. Sociological Rev.* 3: 218–24, April.

KNITTLE, RHEA M. 1929. "Glass: American." *Ency. Brit.* 14th ed.

KOLLER, A. H. 1937. *The Abbé du Bos—His Advocacy of the Theory of Climate.* Garrard Press, Champaign, Ill.

KOLLMORGEN, WALTER M. 1942. *Culture of a Contemporary Rural Community, Old Order Amish of Pennsylvania.* Rural Life Studies No. 4, Dep't Agr., Sept.

—— 1943. "Agricultural-Cultural Islands in the South." *Econ. Geog.* 19: 109–17, April.

KÖPPEN, W. P. 1914. "Lufttemperaturen, Sonnenflecke und Vulcanausbruche." *Meteorologische Zeitschrift.* 7: 305–28.

——, and GEIGER, R. 1939. *Handbuch der Klimatologie.* Gebrüder Borntraeger, Berlin.

KRETSCHMER, ERNST. 1936. *Körperbau und Charakter (An Investigation of the Nature of Constitution and of the theory of Temperament).* J. Springer, Berlin.

KROPOTKIN, PRINCE. 1904. "The Desiccation of Asia." *Geog. Jour.* Vol. 23.

KRYNINE, D. P. (Research Associate in Soil Mechanics), Yale. Personal communication.

KULLMER, C. J. 1933. "The Latitude Shift of the Storm Track in the 11-Year Solar Period." *Smiths. Misc. Coll.* Vol. 89, No. 2.

—— 1943. "A Remarkable Reversal in the Distribution of Storm Frequency in the United States in Double Hale Solar Cycles, of Interest in Long-Range Forecasting." *Smiths. Misc. Coll.* Vol. 103, No. 10.

KUO, HELENE. 1942. *I've Come a Long Way.* D. Appleton, New York.

LANGBEIN, W. B., and HOYT, W. G. *See* Hoyt.

LAPEYRERE. 1644. "An Account of Iceland," sent to M. de la Mothe de Vayer, Copenhagen, Dec. 18, 1644. In *Collection of Voyages and Travels*, London, 1744. pp. 363–75.

LARSON, C. L., EVANS, C. A., and GREEN, R. G. *See* Green.

LATOURETTE, KENNETH SCOTT. 1934. *The Chinese: Their History and Culture.* I: 328–29, 340, 383. Macmillan, New York.

LATTIMORE, O. 1932. *Manchuria, Cradle of Conflict.* pp. 70–71, 299–300. Macmillan, New York.

LEHMANN and PEDERSEN. 1907. "Das Wetter und unsere Arbeit." *Archiv. ges. Psychol.* Vol. 10, Leipzig.

LEOPOLD, ALDO. 1931. *Report on a Game Survey of the North Central States.* Democrat Pub., Madison.

LIPS, EVA. 1938. *Savage Symphony.* Random House, New York.

LIPSON, E. 1915. *Economic History of England—The Middle Ages.* A. and C. Black, London.

LIVELY, C. E., and FOOTT, FRANCES. 1937. *Population Mobility in Selected Areas of Rural Ohio, 1928–1935.* Ohio Agr. Exp. Sta. Bull. No. 582. Also in Warren S. Thompson, *Research Memorandum on Migration in the Depression.* 1937. Soc. Sci. Research Council Bull. No. 39. New York.

——, and TAEUBER, CONRAD. 1939. *Rural Migration in the United States.* Research Monograph XIX. p. 74. W.P.A., Washington.

LODGE, R. 1901. *The Close of the Middle Ages, 1273–1494.* Macmillan, New York.

LODGE, THOMAS. 1935. "Newfoundland Today." *Internat'l Affairs.* Vol. 14.

LODGE, TOWNSEND. 1938. "Variations in Stanford-Binet I.Q.'s of Pre-School Children According to Month in Which Examinations Were Given." *Jour. Psychol.* 8: 385–95.

LOGAN, RICHARD F. Personal communication.

LOMBROSO, CESARE. 1911. *Crime: Its Causes and Remedies.* Little, Brown, Boston.

LULL, R. S. 1929. "The Pulse of Life." In *Evolution of Earth and Man.* Yale Univ. Press, New Haven.

LUNDBORG, HERMAN BERNHARD. 1926 ed. *The Racial Characters of the Swedish Nation.* Hasse W. Tullberg, Sweden.

MACALISTER, R. A. S. 1935. *Ancient Ireland.* Methuen, London.

MACKAY, ROBERT A. 1934. "Foreign Governments and Politics." *Amer. Pol. Sci. Rev.* 28: 895–900.

MACKENZIE, SIR GEORGE STEUART. 1811. *Travels in the Island of Iceland, 1810.* A. Constable, London.

MACKINDER, HALFORD. 1919. *Democratic Ideals and Reality: A Study in the Politics of Reconstruction.* A. Constable, London.

MACLULICH, D. A. 1935. "Fluctuations in the Numbers of Snowshoe Rabbits." *Forestry Chronicle.* 11: 283.

—— 1936. "Sunspots and Abundance of Animals." *Jour. Roy. Astron. Soc. Canada,* pp. 233–46, August.

MANGELSDORF, P. C., and REEVES, R. G. 1939. *The Origin of Indian Corn and Its Relatives.* Texas Agr. Exp. Sta. Bull. No. 574, May.

MARKHAM, S. F. 1942, 1944. *Climate and the Energy of Nations.* Oxford Univ. Press, New York.

MATTHES, F. E. 1940. *Report of Committee on Glaciers, 1939–1940.* Trans. of 1940; Amer. Geophysical Union.

MATTHEW, W. D. 1915, 1942. *Climate and Evolution.* N. Y. Acad. Sci. New York.

MAULDIN, W. PARKER. 1940. "Selective Migration from Small Towns." *Amer. Soc. Rev.* 5: 748–58, October.

McCARRISON, ROBERT. 1921. "Studies in Deficiency Diseases." *Jour. Roy. Soc. Arts.* Vol. 69.

—— 1928. "Influence of Irrigation on the Nutritive Value of Rice." *Indian Jour. Med. Research.* 15: 915–20.

—— 1936. "Nutrition and National Health." *Jour. Roy. Soc. Arts.* 84: 1047–1107.

McCAY, CAPTAIN D. 1910. *Investigations on Bengal Jail Dietaries.* Scientific Memoirs of Officers of the Med. and Sanitary Dep'ts of the Gov't of India, Calcutta.

McCay, Captain D. 1911. *Investigations into the Jail Dietaries of the United Provinces.* Scientific Memoirs of Officers of the Med. and Sanitary Dep'ts of the Gov't of India, Calcutta.

McCollum, E. V., and Becker, J. Ernestine. 1934. *Food, Nutrition and Health.* 3rd ed. Baltimore.

Means, Philip Ainsworth. 1931. *Ancient Civilizations of the Andes.* Chas. Scribner's, New York.

Mencken, H. L., and Angoff, Charles. *See* Angoff.

Metropolitan Life Insurance Company. 1943. "Summer Babies Are Best." *Stat. Bull.* Vol. 24, June.

Meyer, Eduard. 1929. "Media." *Ency. Brit.* 14th ed.

Miles, W. R., Benedict, F. G., Roth, Paul, and Smith, H. M. *See* Benedict.

Mills, C. A., and Ogle, Cordelia. *See* Ogle.

—— 1939. *Medical Climatology.* Chas. C. Thomas, Springfield, Ill.

—— 1942. *Climate Makes the Man.* Harper, New York.

Mitchell, Wesley. 1927. "Business Cycles, the Problem and Its Setting." pp. 340–41. *Nat'l Bur. Econ. Research,* New York.

Moore, H. L. 1914. *Economic Cycles: Their Law and Cause.* Macmillan, New York.

—— 1923. *Generating Economic Cycles.* Macmillan, New York.

Moreland, W. H. 1920. *India at the Death of Akbar, an Economic Study.* Macmillan, London.

—— 1923. *From Akbar to Aurangzeb—A Study in Indian Economic History.* Macmillan, London.

—— 1925. Trans. of *Jahangirs India,* by Francisco Pelsaert. W. Heffer, Cambridge, Eng.

Moriyama, I. M., and Herrington, L. P. *See* Herrington.

Morton, Henry C. Vollam. 1932. *In Search of Ireland.* Dodd, Mead, New York.

Moseley, E. L. 1938. "What May Be Learned from Stumps." *School Sci. and Math.,* May.

—— 1939. "Long-Time Forecasts of Ohio River Floods." *Ohio Jour. Sci.* 39: 222–31.

Murray, G. W. 1931. "A Small Temple in the Western Desert." *Jour. Egyptian Arch.* Vol. 17.

Nansen, F., and Helland-Hansen, B. 1920. "Temperature Variations in the North Atlantic Ocean and in the Atmosphere." *Smiths. Misc. Coll.* Vol. 70, No. 4.

Nehemiah I: 3–4.

Nesbitt, L. M. 1935. *Hell-Hole of Creation.* Alfred A. Knopf, New York.

Newfoundland Royal Commission. 1933 Report. Parliamentary Reports. Cmd. 4480, Vol. 14. London.

Newman, Horatio, Freeman, Frank N., and Holzinger, Karl. 1937. *Twins: A Study of Heredity and Environment.* Univ. Chicago Press, Chicago.

New York Times. 1894–1941. Misc. items on Indian riots.

—— June 4, 1932. Item on Parsis.

—— April 13, 1941; Jan. 3 and March 2, 1942. Items on colds.

Nicholson, George. 1889. *The Illustrated Dictionary of Gardening.* Amer. Agriculturist, New York.

Nicholson, Mary, and Elton, Charles S. *See* Elton.

NICHOLSON, S. B., and ADAMS, S. W. *See* Adams.

NORLIND, A. 1914. *Einige Bemerkungen über das Klima der historischen Zeit nebst einem Verzeichnis mittelaltlicher Witterungserscheinungen.* Lunds Univ. Arsskrift, N.F., Vol. 10.

ODUM, HOWARD WASHINGTON. 1938. *American Regionalism.* Henry Holt, New York.

OGLE, CORDELIA, and MILLS, C. A. 1933. "Animal Adaptation to Environmental Temperature Conditions." *Amer. Jour. Physiol.* 103: 606–12, March.

—— 1934. "Climatic Influence on the Growth of the Male Albino Mouse." *Amer. Jour. Physiol.* 107: 635.

—— 1936. "Germinal Response (in Male Mice) to Environmental Conditions." *Amer. Jour. Physiol.* 117: 285–91.

OLMSTEAD, A. T. 1912. "Climate and History." *Jour. Geog.* Vol. 10, No. 5, Jan.

ORR, J. B., and GILKS, J. L. 1931. *The Physique and Health of Two African Tribes.* Studies in Nutrition, Med. Research Council.

PEDERSEN and LEHMANN. *See* Lehmann.

PERRINE, J. O. 1944. "Electrical Waves—Long and Short." *Sci. Monthly.* 58: 33–41.

PETERS, C. A. 1939. "Ozone in the 1938 Hurricane." *Science.* 90: 491.

PETERSEŇ, WILLIAM F. 1936. *The Patient and the Weather.* Vols. I–IV. Edwards, Ann Arbor, Michigan.

PETTERSSEN, O. 1912. "The Connection between Hydrographical and Meteorological Phenomena." *Quart. Jour. Roy. Meteor. Soc.* 38: 174–75.

PHELPS, E. B., and BELDING, D. L. 1931. *A Statistical Study of the Records of Salmon Fishing on the Restigouche River.*

PHILBY, HARRY ST. JOHN B. 1920. "Southern Najd." *Geog. Jour.* 55: 15, 23, 66–67.

POOLE, SIDMAN P. 1944. "Geopolitik—Science or Magic." *Jour. Geog.* XLIII: 1–12.

Poor's Register of Directors of the United States and Canada. 1938. Vol. 12.

PORTEUS, S. D. 1931. *The Psychology of a Primitive People.* Longmans, Green, New York.

POWELL, E. A. 1926. *In Barbary: Tunisia, Algeria, Morocco, and the Sahara.* D. Appleton-Century, N. Y.

PREBLE, E. A. 1908. *A Biological Investigation of the Athabaska-Mackenzie Region.* Bureau of Biological Survey, North Amer. Fauna, No. 27.

PRICE, A. GRENFELL. 1939. *White Settlers in the Tropics.* Amer. Geog. Soc. Spec. Pub. No. 23, New York.

PRICE, WESTON A. 1940. *Nutrition and Physical Degeneration.* Paul B. Hoeber, New York.

"Provincial Marketing Surveys of India." 1939. Cited by N. Gangulee in *Health and Nutrition in India.* Faber and Faber, London.

PROWSE, D. W. 1896. *A History of Newfoundland.* Eyre and Spottiswoode. London.

PUMPELLY, RAPHAEL. 1905. "Archaeological and Physico-Geographical Reconnaissance in Turkestan." In *Explorations in Turkestan.* I: 3–19. Carnegie Inst. Pub. No. 26, Washington.

—— 1908. "Ancient Anau and the Oasis-World." In *Explorations in Turkestan.* Vol. II. Carnegie Inst., Washington.

RAGSDALE, MARTHA, and HUNTINGTON, ELLSWORTH. *See* Huntington.

RAWLINSON, H. C. 1866–67. "Note on the Oxus River." *Proc. Roy. Geog. Soc.* Vol. 11.

—— 1879. "The Road to Merv." *Proc. Roy. Geog. Soc.* Vol. 1. N.S.

Reader's Digest. See High.

REEVES, R. G., and MANGELSDORF, P. C. *See* Mangelsdorf.

RENNER, GEORGE THOMAS, and WHITE, CHARLES L. 1936. *Geography.* D. Appleton-Century, New York.

—— 1942. *Conservation of National Resources.* John Wiley, New York.

ROBERTS, W. O., STERNE, THEODORE E., and GUTHE, K. F. *See* Sterne.

ROGERS, THORALD. 1866. *History of Agriculture and Prices in England.* 6 vols. Oxford.

ROSE, HERBERT J. 1925. *Primitive Culture in Greece.* G. H. Doran, New York.

ROSE, MARY S., and GRAY, CORA E. 1930. *The Relation of Diet to Health and Growth of Children in Institutions.* Teachers College, Columbia Univ., New York.

ROSSMAN, J. 1929. "Seasonal Variations in Applying for and Granting Patents." *Jour. Patent Office Soc.* 11: 99–103.

ROSTOVTZEFF, M. 1932. *Caravan Cities.* Oxford Univ. Press, Oxford, Eng.

ROTH, PAUL, BENEDICT, F. G., MILES, W. R., and SMITH, H. M. *See* Benedict.

ROWAN, WILLIAM. 1941. *The Riddle of Migration.* Williams and Wilkins, Baltimore.

SAKURAI, HYOGORO. 1940. "Chinese Are Inferior—Opposes Intermarriage." *China Weekly Rev.* 92: 236–37, April 13.

SANDBURG, CARL. 1926. *Abraham Lincoln: The Prairie Years.* Harcourt, Brace, New York.

SANFORD, GILBERT A. 1940. "Selective Migration in a Rural Alabama County." *Amer. Soc. Rev.* 5: 759–66.

SARGENT, D. A. 1908. "The Physique of Scholars, Athletes and the Average Student." *Pop. Sci. Monthly.* LXXIII: 248–56.

SAUER, CARL, and BRAND, DONALD. 1931–32. "Prehistoric Settlements of Sonora, with Special Reference to Cerros de Trincheras." *Univ. Calif. Pub. in Geog.* 5: 67–124.

SAVAGE, JAMES. 1860–62. *A Genealogical Dictionary of the First Settlers of New England.* Little, Brown, Boston.

SCHELL, IRVING I. 1943. "The Sun's Spottedness as a Possible Factor in Terrestrial Pressure." *Bull. Amer. Meteor. Soc.* 24: 85–93.

—— 1944. Personal communication.

SCHUMPETER, JOSEPH ALOIS. 1939. *Business Cycles: A Theoretical, Historical and Statistical Analysis of the Capitalistic System.* McGraw-Hill, New York.

SEAGRAVE, G. S. 1943. *Burma Surgeon.* Norton Press, New York.

SEMPLE, E. C. 1931. *Geography of the Mediterranean Region.* Henry Holt, New York.

SHAPIRO, H. L. (with the Field Assistance of Frederick S. Hulse). 1939. *Migration and Environment—A Study of the Physical Characteristics of the Japanese Immigrants to Hawaii and the Effects of Environment on Their Descendants.* Oxford Univ. Press, New York.

SHAPLEY, HARLOW. 1929. "Star Clusters." *Ency. Brit.* 14th ed. Vol. 21.

SHELDON, WILLIAM H., STEVENS, S. S., and TUCKER, W. B. 1940. *The Varieties of Human Physique: An Introduction to Constitutional Psychology.* Harper, New York.

—— 1942. *The Varieties of Temperament; a Psychology of Constitutional Differences.* Harper, New York.

SHELFORD, V. E. 1943. "The Abundance of the Collared Lemming in the Churchill Area, 1929 to 1940." *Ecology.* 24: 472–84.

——, and FLINT, W. P. 1943. "Populations of the Chinch Bug in the Upper Mississippi Valley from 1823 to 1940." *Ecology,* 24: 435–55. Also reprinted by Foundation for the Study of Cycles, 1944.

SIMON, ANDRÉ L. 1906. *The History of the Wine Trade in England.* 3 vols. London.

SMITH, E. L. 1939. *Tides in the Affairs of Men.* Macmillan, New York.

SMITH, H. M., BENEDICT, F. G., MILES, W. R., and ROTH, PAUL. *See* Benedict.

SMITH, V. A. 1917. *Akbar, the Great Mogul, 1542–1605.* Clarendon Press, Oxford, Eng.

SOROKIN, P. 1928. *Contemporary Social Theories.* Harper, New York.

—— 1942. *The Crisis of Our Age.* E. P. Dutton, New York.

SPENGLER, OSWALD. 1926–28. *Decline of the West.* Trans. with notes by Charles Francis Atkinson. G. Allen and Unwin, London.

STEFANSSON, JON. 1916. *Denmark and Sweden, with Iceland and Finland.* T. F. Unwin, London.

STEFANSSON, VILHJALMUR. 1922. *The Northward Course of Empire.* Harcourt, Brace, New York.

—— 1939. *Iceland: The First American Republic.* Doubleday-Doran, New York.

STEIN, M. AUREL. 1904. *Sand-Buried Ruins of Khotan.* T. F. Unwin, London.

—— 1938. "Desiccation in Asia: A Geographical Question in the Light of History." *Hungarian Quarterly.* IV, No. 4. Budapest.

STERNE, THEODORE E. 1939. "On Periodicities in Measures of the Solar Constant." *Proc. Nat'l Acad. Sci.* 25: 559–64, Nov.

——, GUTHE, K. F., and ROBERTS, W. O. 1940. "On Possible Changes in the Solar 'Constant.'" *Proc. Nat'l Acad. Sci.* 26: 399–604, June.

STETSON, HARLAN T. 1937. *Sunspots and Their Effects.* McGraw-Hill, New York.

—— 1942. "Solar Radiation and the State of the Atmosphere." *Sci. Monthly,* June, pp. 513–28.

—— 1944. "Cosmic Terrestrial Research." *Sci. Monthly,* March, XVIII: 207–17.

STEVENS, S. S., SHELDON, WILLIAM H., and TUCKER, W. B. *See* Sheldon.

STIEBLING, HAZEL K., and WARE, MEDORA M. 1933. *Diets at Four Levels of Nutritive Content and Cost.* U. S. Dep't Agr. Circular 296, Nov. Washington.

STONE, R. C. 1939. "Comfort Zones and Acclimatization." In Appendix II in *White Settlers in the Tropics,* by A. G. Price. Amer. Geog. Soc.

SUMNER, WILLIAM, and KELLER, ALBERT G. 1927. *The Science of Society.* Yale Univ. Press, New Haven.

SYKES, P. M. 1915. *A History of Persia.* Vol. I. Macmillan, London.

TAEUBER, CONRAD, and LIVELY, C. E. *See* Lively.

TAGORE, RABINDRANATH. 1917. *Nationalism.* Macmillan, New York.

TAIT, R. H. 1939. *Newfoundland, 1497–1933.* Harrington Press, Harrington Park, N. J.

TAYLOR, GRIFFITH. 1919. "Climatic Cycles and Evolution." *Geog. Rev.*, Dec. Vol. 8, pp. 288–328.

—— 1921. "The Evolution and Distribution of Race, Culture and Language." *Geog. Rev.*, Vol. 11, pp. 55–119.

TCHIJEWSKY, A. L. 1934. "Action de l'activité périodique sur les phénomènes sociaux; action de l'ionisation de l'atmosphère et de l'ionisation artificielle de l'air sur les organismes sains et les organismes malades. L'action de l'activité periodique solaire sur les épidemies." In *Traité de climatologie biologique et medicale;* ed. by M. Piery, Masson et als. Paris.

THOMAS, DOROTHY S. 1938. *Research Memorandum on Migration Differentials.* Soc. Sci. Research Council, Bull. No. 43. New York.

THOMSON, ANDREW. 1936. "Sunspots and Weather Forecasting in Canada." *Jour. Roy. Astr. Soc. Canada.* July-Aug., pp. 215–32.

THORNDIKE, EDWARD L. 1939. "American Cities and States: Variation and Correlation in Institutions, Activities, and the Personal Qualities of Residents." *Annals, N. Y. Acad. Sci.* 39: 213–98, Dec. 22

TOLSTOY, LEO NIKOLAYEVICH. 1911. *War and Peace.* E. P. Dutton, New York.

TOYNBEE, ARNOLD J. 1919. *Treatment of Armenians in the Ottoman Empire,* 1915–16. H. M. Stat. Off. Misc. No. 31, London.

—— 1934. *A Study of History.* Vol. III. Oxford Univ. Press, London.

TUCKER, W. B., SHELDON, W. H., and STEVENS, S. S. *See* Sheldon.

VANDERLINDEN, E. 1924. "Chronique des evenements meteorologues en Belgique jusqu'en 1834." *Roy. Acad. Sci., Memoires.* Vol. 6. Brussels.

VAN DOREN, CARL. Personal communication.

VAN PAASSEN, PIERRE. 1922. *That Day Alone.* Dial Press, New York.

VAN VALKENBURG, SAMUEL. 1942 ed. *America at War.* Prentice-Hall, New York.

VISHER, STEPHEN S., and HUNTINGTON, ELLSWORTH. *See* Huntington.

—— 1928. *Geography of American Notables.* Indiana Univ. Studies, No. 79.

—— 1937. "Where Our Notables Came From." *Sci. Monthly*, Aug., Vol. XLV.

Vital Statistics Rates in the United States, 1900 to 1940. 1943. Gov't Printing Off., Washington.

WALLACE, DAVID DUNCAN. 1929. "South Carolina." *Ency. Brit.* 14th ed. Vol. 21.

WARE, MEDORA M., and STIEBLING, HAZEL K. *See* Stiebling.

WEIGERT, HANS W. 1942. *Generals and Geographers: The Twlight of Geopolitics.* Oxford Univ. Press, New York.

WHEELER, RAYMOND H. 1939. "Social Behavior Patterns and Climate." *Soc. Frontier.* 5: 231–37, May.

—— 1940. "The Problem of World Climate." *Bull. Amer. Meteor. Soc.* 21: 46–58.

—— 1943. "The Effect of Climate on Human Behavior and History." *Trans. Kansas Acad. Sci.* 46: 33–51.

—— *Climate and Human Destiny.* Unpub. ms.

WHITE, CHARLES L., and RENNER, GEORGE THOMAS. *See* Renner.

WHITNEY, LEON F., and HUNTINGTON, ELLSWORTH. *See* Huntington.

WHITNEY, PAUL C. 1944. *The Prediction of Tides.* Reprint, Foundation for Study of Cycles, New York.

Who's Who in America. 1937–38. Albert Nelson Marquis, Ed. A. N. Marquis Co., Chicago.

WILDER, GEORGE D. Personal communication.

WILLIAMS, FRANK E., and HUNTINGTON, ELLSWORTH. *See* Huntington.

WOLFE, THOMAS. 1941. *The Hills Beyond.* Ch. 3, pp. 237–39. Harper, New York.

WRIGHT, QUINCY. 1942. *A Study of War.* Univ. Chicago Press, Chicago.

YAGI, T. 1933. *Studies on the Output Curve.* Inst. for Sci. and Labor, Kurasaki.

YAGLOU, C. P., BENJAMIN, L. C., and CHOATE, S. P. 1931. "Changes in Ionic Content of Air in Occupied Rooms Ventilated by Natural and by Mechanical Methods." *Heating, Piping and Air Conditioning.* Oct., pp. 865–69.

——, BENJAMIN, L. C., and GRANDT, A. D. 1933. "Physiologic Changes During Exposure to Ionized Air." *Heating, Piping and Air Conditioning,* June, Aug.

——, and BENJAMIN, L. C. 1934. "Diurnal and Seaonal Variations in the Small-Ion Content of Outdoor and Indoor Air." *Heating, Piping and Air Conditioning.* Jan., pp. 25–32.

YAO, SHAN-YU. 1942. "The Chronological and Seasonal Distribution of Floods and Droughts in Chinese History." *Harvard Jour. Asiatic Studies.* 6: 273–312

YERKES, ROBERT M. 1943. *Chimpanzees: A Laboratory Colony.* Yale Univ. Press New Haven.

YOUNG, ARTHUR. 1892. *Tour in Ireland (1776–1779).* 2nd ed. A. W. Hutton London.

YOUNGHUSBAND, F. E. 1896. *Heart of a Continent.* London.

ZIMMERMAN, C. C. 1927. "The Migration to Towns and Cities." Pt. II. *Amer Jour. Sociology.* 33: 105–09.

INDEX

Aaronsohn, A., 575, 613
Abadite sect, 166
Abbot, C. G., 458, 461, 481, 520, 613
Aboskun, 535
Abraham, 156
Absentee landlordism, 457
Absolute zero, 17
Abul Fazil, 444
Acamas, 585
Accidents, historical, 12
Achaeans, 589
Achievement, measurement of, 104 ff.,
     106*
Activity and weather, 328
Actors, indicators of achievement, 108*;
     in New England, 111*
Adams, a widely used name, 101
Adams, S. W., 517, 613
Adana, 13
Adare, 167
Addis Ababa, 271
Adobe, 295
Adolph, W. H., 451, 613
Adverse selection in famines, 182 ff.
Aegean Sea, 584
Africa, animals, 579 f.; changes in, 6
Age, accuracy of reports, 345, 346*,
     347*; of mothers, 66; relation to
     season of birth, 323
Agricola, Julius, 592
Agricultural productivity, 251*; in Rus-
     sia, 442
Agricultural year of India, 362
Agriculture, cultural stimulant, 307 ff.;
     and diet, 432 ff.; earliest, 307, 573,
     581; relation to selection, 180, 311;
     in South America, 393; and stormi-
     ness, 331 ff.
Air, and evolution, 23 ff.; freshness of,
     358
Air masses, and climatic pulsations, 375;
     and psychological trends, 369
Akbar, 174, 190, 199, 444

Alabama, leaders, 84, 86*, 87*, 89*; mi-
     grations, 78
Albright, W. D., 500, 613
Alcott, A. B., 75
Alertness and climate, 375
Alexandria, climate, 544; Jews in, 161;
     old meteorological record, 543*, 546
Algeria, Abadites in, 166
Alhambra, 196
Alimentary tract, 47
Allahabad, climate, 283, 289
Allee, W. C., 502, 613
Alpaca, 393, 579
Alpines, achievements, 58
Altar River, 555 f.
Altitude of Javanese cities, 265
America, activity, 328 ff.; animals, 579;
     farmers, 75; immigrants, 73; ruins,
     554 ff.; social system, 341 ff.
American Commonwealth, The, 129
American Council of Education, 379
American Institute of Chemical En-
     gineers, 351*
American Institute of Public Opinion,
     238 f., 613
American Men of Science, 81, 86, 613
American Red Cross, 163
American Society of Civil Engineers,
     351*
American Society of Heating and Ven-
     tilating Engineers, 247
Amherst College, stature of students, 55
Ammonites, 29
Amory, Copley, 458
Amulree Report, 131, 134, 613
Anau, bones of animals on, 580
Anazah invasions, 567
Ancestry, 98 ff.; and deficiency, 121 ff.
Anderson, C. N., 479, 613
Andes, civilization, 392; uplift, 558
Angell, a colonial name, 101
Angkor Wat, 396
Angoff, C., 229, 233 f., 613

* Illustrations are indicated by asterisks. All illustrations are indexed under the
     headings "Diagrams" or "Maps." All tables are listed under "Tables."

631